Restructuring for
Caring and Effective Education

This book is printed on recycled paper. ✪

Restructuring for
Caring and Effective Education
Piecing the Puzzle Together

Second Edition

Edited by

Richard A. Villa, Ed.D.
Bayridge Consortium
San Marcos, California

and

Jacqueline S. Thousand, Ph.D.
California State University
San Marcos

·P A U L·H·
BROOKES
PUBLISHING C<u>O</u>

Baltimore • London • Toronto • Sydney

Paul H. Brookes Publishing Co.
Post Office Box 10624
Baltimore, Maryland 21285-0624

www.brookespublishing.com

Typeset by Argosy, West Newton, Massachusetts.
Manufactured in the United States of America by
The Maple Press Company, York, Pennsylvania.

Some of the names and stories of individuals appearing herein are real, some are composites of actual people and events, and others are fictional. In the case of actual people and circumstances, individuals' names and stories have been printed with the individuals' permission. In the case of composite accounts, names and other identifying information have been changed to protect individuals' identities.

The Circle of Courage graphic that appears on pages 62, 129, 242, 389, and 493 was created by George Bluebird and is used with the artist's permission and reprinted with the permission of Reclaiming Youth International. Copyright © 1999 by Reclaiming Youth International.

Permission to reprint the following lyrics and quotation is gratefully acknowledged:

Page 109: "All This Time," written and composed by Sting. Copyright © 1991 G.M. SUMNER. Published by MAGNETIC PUBLISHING LTD. and administered by EMI BLACKWOOD MUSIC INC. in the USA and Canada. All Rights Reserved. International Copyright Secured. Used by Permission.
Pages 161–162: "The Greatest Love of All," by Linda Creed and Michael Masser, copyright © 1977 by EMI Gold Horizon Music Corp. and EMI Golden Torch Music Corp. All rights reserved. Used by permission. WARNER BROS. PUBLICATIONS U.S. INC., Miami, Florida 33014.
Page 328: "The Times They Are A-Changin'," copyright © 1963, 1964 by Warner Bros., Inc. Copyright renewed 1991 by Special Rider Music. All rights reserved. International copyright secured. Reprinted by permission.
Page 394: Quotation from Maya Angelou copyright © 1999. Reprinted by permission of The Helen Brann Agency, Inc.

Library of Congress Cataloging-in-Publication Data

Restructuring for caring and effective education : piecing the puzzle
together / edited by Richard A. Villa and Jacqueline S. Thousand.—2nd ed.
    p. cm.
    Includes bibliographical references and index.
    ISBN 1-55766-386-6
    1. Handicapped children—Education—United States. 2. Mainstreaming in education—United States. 3. Educational change—United States. I. Villa, Richard A., 1952– . II. Thousand, Jacqueline S., 1950– .
LC4031.R399 2000   98-53400
371.9′046′0973—dc21   CIP

British Library Cataloguing in Publication data are available from the British Library.

Contents

About the Editors

Richard A. Villa, Ed.D., President, Bayridge Consortium, 767 Pebble Beach Drive, San Marcos, California 92069. Dr. Villa has worked with thousands of teachers and administrators throughout North America and the rest of the world in developing and implementing instructional support systems for educating all students within general education environments. Dr. Villa has been a classroom teacher, special education coordinator, pupil personnel services director, and director of instructional services. He has authored more than 70 articles and book chapters regarding inclusive education and has co-edited three previous books for teachers, administrators, and parents: *Restructuring for Caring and Effective Education: An Administrative Guide to Creating Heterogeneous Schools* (Paul H. Brookes Publishing Co., 1992), *Creativity and Collaborative Learning: A Practical Guide to Empowering Students and Teachers* (Paul H. Brookes Publishing Co., 1994), and *Creating an Inclusive School* (Association for Supervision and Curriculum Development, 1995). He has presented at numerous national and international conferences and is known for his enthusiastic, humorous style of presenting.

Jacqueline S. Thousand, Ph.D., Professor, College of Education, California State University San Marcos, San Marcos, California 92069. Dr. Thousand has been a teacher educator since 1981 and has more than 20 years of experience in training teachers and providing technical assistance to schools to create inclusive educational experiences for children from preschool through high school. At the University of Vermont, she coordinated an early childhood special education teacher preparation program and one of the first "Inclusion Facilitator" graduate programs (1986–1996) in the United States. As the coordinator of the Vermont Homecoming Project in the early 1980s, she was a pioneer in developing instruction and curriculum modification strategies for including students with moderate and severe disabilities that came to be the "staples" of inclusive practice in the 1990s. With her move in 1996 to California State University San Marcos, she coordinates a teacher credential program that endorses graduates as general and special educators, thus enabling them to advocate for and support students with disabilities as either classroom teachers or special educators. In addition to directing the college's special education credential and master's programs, she continues her commitment to community development by working with leadership and staff of local schools to restructure "special day class" programs and move the teachers and students in these classes into the mainstream. She also works closely with families to make inclusive education communities a reality. She sits on the editorial boards of a number of professional journals and is past co-editor of *Teacher Education and Special Education*. She currently serves on the International Board of TASH (formerly The Association for Persons with Severe Handicaps), an international advocacy association of people with disabilities, their family members, other advocates, and people who work in the disabilities field. Dr. Thousand has authored numerous books, research articles, and book chapters on practical how-to strategies for meeting the needs of all students in general education; adapting curriculum, instruction, and assessment; collaborative teaming; and creative problem solving.

Contributors

María Elena Arguelles, M.Ed.
Senior Research Associate
School of Education
University of Miami
5202 University Drive
Miami, Florida 33146

Jeanne Bauwens, Ed.D.
Professor
College of Education
Boise State University
1910 University Drive
Boise, Idaho 83725

Edvard Befring, Dr
Professor
Department of Special Education
Faculty of Education
University of Oslo
Helga Engs House
Postboks 1140 Blindern
V-0317 Oslo
Norway

Denise Lee Bettenhausen, M.S.
School Principal
Kruse Education Center
7617 Hernlock Drive
Orland Park, Illinois 60462

Mary Blair
Behavioral Support Program
  Specialist
Los Angeles Unified School
  District
Hesby School
Hesby Street
Encino, California 91436

Catherine Bove, M.A.
Support Teacher–Special
  Education
Whittier High School
12417 East Philadelphia Street
Whittier, California 90601

Larry K. Brendtro, Ph.D.
President
Reclaiming Youth International
Post Office Box 57
Lennox, South Dakota 57039

Martin Brokenleg, Ph.D.
Professor of Native American
  Studies
Augustana College
2001 South Summit Avenue
Sioux Falls, South Dakota 57197

Colleen A. Capper, Ed.D.
Associate Professor
University of
  Wisconsin–Madison
1025 West Johnson Street
1186D Education Sciences
  Building
Madison, Wisconsin 53706

James W. Chapple, M.Ed.
Instructional Resource Services
  Coordinator
Northern Ohio Special Education
  Regional Resource Center
1230 Beechview Drive, Suite 100
Vermilion, Ohio 44089

Chigee J. Cloninger, Ph.D.
Associate Professor and Project
    Director
Center on Disability and
    Community Inclusion
University of Vermont
499C Waterman Building
Burlington, Vermont 05405

Jean Collicott, M.Ed.
Principal
Donald Fraser Memorial School
231 Main Street
Plaster Rock
New Brunswick E7G 1W2
Canada

Kim Connor and **Robbie
    Holland**
1900 Bidwell Way
Sacramento, California 95818

Ruth E. Dennis, OTR, Ed.D.
Research Assistant Professor
Department of Education
College of Education and Social
    Services
University of Vermont
499C Waterman Building
Burlington, Vermont 05405

Mary Patricia Dingle, M.A.
Doctoral Student
University of California at Los
    Angeles/California State
    University–Los Angeles
Adjunct Professor
Division of Special Education
Department of Education
California State University–Los
    Angeles
5151 State University Drive
Los Angeles, California 90032

Susan W. Edelman, Ed.D., P.T.
Research Assistant Professor
Center on Disability and
    Community Inclusion
University Affiliated Program of
    Vermont
University of Vermont
499C Waterman Building
Burlington, Vermont 05405

Lori Eshilian, M.A.
Support Teacher–Special
    Education
Whittier High School
12417 East Philadelphia Street
Whittier, California 90601

Mary A. Falvey, Ph.D.
Professor
Division of Special Education
Department of Education
California State University–Los
    Angeles
5151 State University Drive
Los Angeles, California 90032

Mary FitzPatrick
Director of Quality Improvement
Monadnock Developmental
    Services
640 Marlborough Street
Keene, New Hampshire 03431

Mary-Ellen Fortini, Ph.D.
Director of Special Projects
Monadnock Developmental
    Services
640 Marlborough Street
Keene, New Hampshire 03431

Nancy Franklin, M.A.
Inclusion Program Coordinator
Los Angeles Unified School
    District
Hesby School
Hesby Street
Encino, California 91436

Alan Gartner, Ph.D.
Professor and Dean for Research
The Graduate School and
    University Center
The City University of New York
33 West 42nd Street
New York, New York 10036

Michael F. Giangreco, Ph.D.
Research Associate Professor
Center on Disability and
    Community Inclusion
University Affiliated Program of
    Vermont
University of Vermont
499C Waterman Building
Burlington, Vermont 05405

Mary Jane Hibbard, M.A.
Department Chair for Special
    Education Services
Whittier High School
12417 East Philadelphia Street
Whittier, California 90601

Michael L. Hock, M.Ed., CAGS
Assessment Specialist
Special Education Program
College of Education
University of Vermont
451A Waterman Building
Burlington, Vermont 05405

Lisa and **Alan Houghtelin**
2506-A Wanek Road
Escondido, California 92027

Linda Keating, M.Ed.
Content Specialist and Middle-
    Level Educator
Swanton Central School
Swanton, Vermont 05488

Maureen W. Keyes, Ph.D.
Assistant Professor
Department of Exceptional
    Education
University of
    Wisconsin–Milwaukee
7800 West Townsend Street
Milwaukee, Wisconsin 53201

Margaret E. King-Sears, Ph.D.
Associate Professor
Division of Education
School of Continuing Studies
Montgomery County Center
The Johns Hopkins University
9601 Medical Center Drive
Rockville, Maryland 20850

Timothy P. Knoster, Ed.D.
Program Director
Central Susquehanna
    Intermediate Unit
Instructional Support System of
    Pennsylvania
Post Office Box 213
Lewisburg, Pennsylvania 17837

Norman Kunc, M.Sc.
Family Therapist and
    Educational Consultant
Axis Consultation and Training
    Ltd.
340 Machleary Street
Nanaimo
British Columbia V9R 2G9
Canada

Jeffrey Laiblin
Support Teacher–Special
    Education
Whittier High School
12417 East Philadelphia Street
Whittier, California 90601

John Larsen, M.Ed.
Supervisor of Student Services
District 13
566 Riverside Drive
Perth-Andover
New Brunswick E7H 1Z4
Canada

M. Stephen Lilly, Ph.D.
Dean
College of Education
California State University
    San Marcos
San Marcos, California 92069

Dorothy Kerzner Lipsky, Ph.D.,
    M.S.W.
Director
National Center on Educational
    Restructuring and Inclusion
The Graduate School and
    University Center
The City University of New York
33 West 42nd Street
New York, New York 10036

Mary Elizabeth McNeil, Ph.D.
Associate Professor and Director
Center for Professional
    Educational Partnerships
Department of Education
Plymouth State College
University System of New
    Hampshire
17 High Street
MSC #38
Plymouth, New Hampshire
    03264

Connie Miller
Support Teacher–Special
    Education
Whittier High School
12417 East Philadelphia Street
Whittier, California 90601

Patricia H. Mueller, Ed.D.
President
Evergreen Educational
    Consulting
10 Chestnut Lane
Essex Junction, Vermont 05452

Aaron Muravchik, M.A.
Teacher of Writing Skills and
    English as a Second Language
1632 Wellesley Circle #4
Naples, Florida 34116

Ann I. Nevin, Ph.D.
Professor
College of Education
Arizona State University West
4701 West Thunderbird Road
Post Office Box 37100
Phoenix, Arizona 85069

Cecelia Ann Pauley
Good Will Ambassador
8740 Sleepy Hollow Lane
Potomac, Maryland 20854

Joseph F. Pauley
President and Chief Executive
    Officer
Kahler Communications
6701 Democracy Boulevard
Suite 300
Bethesda, Maryland 20817

Judith Ann Pauley, Ph.D.
Chair
Science Department
Connelly School of the Holy
    Child
9029 Bradley Boulevard
Potomac, Maryland 20854

Gordon L. Porter, M.Ed., C.A.S., LL.D.
Supervisor of Student Services
School Districts 10, 12, and 13
138 Chapel Street
Woodstock
New Brunswick E7M 1X9
Canada

Patricia A. Prelock, Ph.D.
Professor
Department of Communication
  Sciences
University of Vermont
407 Pomeroy Hall
Burlington, Vermont 05405

Richard R. Reid, M.Ed., C.A.S.
School Psychologist
South Burlington Supervisory
  Union
South Burlington, Vermont 05401

Richard L. Rosenberg, Ph.D.
Vocational Coordinator
Whittier Union High School
  District
9401 South Painter Avenue
Whittier, California 90605

Richard Schattman, Ed.D.
Principal
Swanton Elementary/Central
  School
24 Fourth Street
Swanton, Vermont 05488

Patrick Schwarz, Ph.D.
Assistant Professor and Chair of
  Special Education
National Louis University
1000 Capital Drive
Wheeling, Illinois 60090

James G. Shriner, Ph.D.
Assistant Professor
Department of Special Education
University of Illinois at Urbana-
  Champaign
Champaign, Illinois 61820

Susan Bray Stainback, Ed.D.
Executive Director
Gulf Coast Consortium for
  Human Empowerment
1600 Gulf Boulevard
Apartment 212
Clearwater, Florida 33767

George T. Theoharis, M.S.
Doctoral Student
University of
  Wisconsin–Madison
1025 West Johnson Street
1186 Education Sciences Building
Madison, Wisconsin 53706

Martha L. Thurlow, Ph.D.
Associate Director
National Center on Educational
  Outcomes
University of Minnesota
350 Elliott Hall
75 East River Road
Minneapolis, Minnesota 55455

Alice Udvari-Solner, Ph.D.
Assistant Professor
University of
  Wisconsin–Madison
225 North Mills Street
Room 224A
Madison, Wisconsin 53706

Steven L. Van Bockern, Ed.D.
Professor
Department of Education
Augustana College
29th and Summit
Sioux Falls, South Dakota 57197

Emma Van der Klift
Consultant
Axis Consultation and Training
  Ltd.
340 Machleary Street
Nanaimo
British Columbia V9R 2G9
Canada

Ro and **Joe Vargo**
Parent Consultants
JOENRO, Inc.
111 Schuler Street
Syracuse, New York 13203

Sharon Vaughn, Ph.D.
Professor
Department of Special Education
College of Education
University of Texas
306 Sanchez Building
Austin, Texas 78731

Prologue

Norris G. Haring

In the summer of 1945, after completing studies in music, I was employed as the music teacher at the Kearney, Nebraska, State Boys Training School. Thirty students from 12 to 17 years of age were enrolled in the band. The boys had been sent to the school because of general delinquency, chronic truancy, shoplifting, and car theft. In addition to delinquent behavior, more than half of the students had cognitive disabilities and exhibited hyperaggressive behavior. All but two of the students were delayed at least 2 years academically.

My teaching strategy was conventional, starting first with ability grouping based on music-reading ability. The group had an extremely wide range of abilities, from the beginners who were becoming familiar with their instruments to those who had good reading ability and technique. I started on scales, chromatics, and sight reading. Following this procedure, after a few weeks, more than half of the students could read simple marches and ballads. As soon as possible, we formed a small ensemble consisting of the boys who could read fairly well. I concentrated on two marches, two waltzes, two ballads, and two Dixieland numbers. The small ensemble, consisting of about 15 students, began to "sound." As a reward for practice and achieving a minimal level of proficiency, I brought them into the big band. This took time because six of the students had minimal pitch discrimination and two had a poor sense of rhythm.

Next, I formed two musical groups. One was a jazz ensemble made up of the most talented band members; the second group included all of the band members, the total class of musicians. The jazz ensemble usually performed two or three selections and played for dances several times a year; however, the total band played only for holidays and selected Sundays in the park. Quite naturally, all of the band members wanted to perform in the jazz ensemble. It was possible for most of the band to advance to the jazz ensemble, but that required a great deal of practice. Another effort designed to improve the band was the tactic known as *challenging for chairs*. About a third of the band members held first and second chairs in each section in the reeds, woodwinds, brass, and rhythm sections. I rewrote the arrangements so that the less talented band members could participate in the less challenging scores.

For the more difficult tunes, certain musicians had only a few bars; on other tunes, they played off the original score. One of the students was unusually skilled at improvising but could not learn to read music well enough. He proved to be valuable in the jazz ensemble, which had 32 bars of ad lib on many selections. (Even good musicians have difficulty in improvising at an early age. Wynton Marsalis could improvise at a young age, but he is an exceptionally gifted musician.) This arrangement proved successful and produced some great sounds; in addition, it involved all 30 students in all performances of the concert band. Looking back on this plan, I realize that I was applying the practice known as the *principle of partial participation*.

The relevance of the previous anecdote is that it highlights the multitude of ways in which teachers can meaningfully include students with a wide range of abilities in learning experiences. Allow me one more example of a historically significant effort toward integrating children with disabilities into general education.

Six years later, while doing research for a dissertation, I conducted studies designed to move students with disabilities from special classes into general education classrooms (Haring, Cruickshank, & Stern, 1958). The first of two studies began by assessing and modifying the attitudes of general educators toward students with disabilities. We provided a series of 10 seminars to increase the educators' familiarity with these students. The seminars included a lecture series by 10 widely known specialists in special education. Immediately after each lecture, the educators met in small groups with group leaders, who were instructed to accept all attitudes and maintain positive discussion.

At the end of the year, the seminars were completed and the knowledge about disabilities and attitudes toward students with disabilities were reassessed. Semidisguised and disguised attitude scales were employed to measure attitudes. General information about the various disabilities was assessed by using a multiple-choice test. Teachers' pre- and posttest performances on the instruments were analyzed through an analysis of variance. We found a highly significant difference in performance for the teachers' pretests versus their posttests, showing that their knowledge had increased. There were no differences, however, in their attitudes toward students with exceptionalities.

The following year, we selectively placed 30 students with moderate to mild disabilities from special classes in 12 general education classrooms. At first, the general education teachers complained, but the complaints decreased when a trained volunteer was assigned to each classroom. By the end of the first quarter, structured plans began to take shape and positive responses were heard frequently in the teachers' classrooms. At the end of the second year of the study, the attitudes of the same teachers were reassessed. In the reassessment, we found highly significant differences in attitudes toward the acceptance of students with disabilities.

From these data, it seemed obvious that attitudes of teachers are difficult to modify in the abstract. Actual experiences with students with disabilities, combined with a 2-week planning period and another trained adult as an assistant, along with a number of refinements and changes, proved to result in a positive, integrated experience.

More than 4 decades have passed since that study was conducted; it was the first effort of its kind involving four school districts and a university in New York state. Even though both the teachers and the administrators considered the experiment with "integration" successful, it was not continued by the administration of the four school districts. Nevertheless, we gained some preliminary information about the process of integration that has been useful since that study. As with the first experience integrating the band with students with disabilities, adapting the curriculum is necessary. Also, providing reinforcement for students with highly varying abilities to work together is a great facilitator. The experiences that we gained from integrating 30 students with disabilities in 12 general classes taught us to maintain natural proportions in the classroom, combine resources and develop cooperative relationships with the people involved, and promote problem-solving attitudes whenever concerns arose.

Permit me to offer one final personal experience to provide a proper perspective on what constitutes progress in taking steps toward inclusion. My first 7 years of schooling took place in a two-room rural school. In my room, there were two students who, if we had had special classes, would have been placed there. One student had Down syndrome; the other had epilepsy and mental retardation requiring intermittent supports. Years after I had left public school, the smaller school districts unified into one large district, and special classes were organized. Students with disabilities like the two who were in my class were pulled out of general education and placed in special classes. Historically, special education was considered an advancement in education. In fact, paradoxically, special education has proved to be a reversal in the trend toward inclusion.

American schools have become increasingly more diverse, a trend that will continue to grow. Fortunately, educators are becoming more successful in including people with disabilities in community environments, schools, and workplaces. Community services are promoting personal autonomy, providing opportunities for social interaction, enhancing quality of life, and facilitating financial independence and personal independence.

DEVELOPMENT OF SERVICES FOR STUDENTS WITH DISABILITIES

Because the most accelerated changes toward the full inclusion of all people in American society have occurred during my professional career (Table 1), I would like to share my perception of these changes with you. Before the 19th century, although I do not remember that far back, there were practically no special services for people with disabilities. If they survived, they remained in their homes and received whatever training there was in the home and the local community.

The so-called age of enlightenment began in 1817, when Gallaudet established a school for deaf people. During the middle of the 19th century, Horace Mann, who was the first to use the term *inclusive schooling*, argued that society has the responsibility for educating all children (Warren, 1995). By the end of the 19th century and the beginning of the 20th century, almost all of the states had formed institutions for deaf and blind people as well as for people with mental retardation and mental illness (White & Haring, 1997). Although this marked the beginning of special services, these services were offered in the most segregated environments.

Special classes for students with blindness, deafness, mental retardation, and physical disabilities began shortly before World War II. By the end of the 1950s, almost all larger school districts had special classes. The smaller districts contracted with the larger districts to provide special services. Special schools and special wings attached to elementary and secondary schools were common because centralizing their resources offered great administrative convenience. This practice became among the strongest and most institutionalized of any in the history of education: Directors of special education established their own empires. So, by the peak of the influence and power of special education, school districts were operating two parallel education systems, with little interaction and communication occurring between them. It became widely known that, once classified as belonging in special education, a student was never again returned to general education.

Table I.   Markers of progress toward full inclusion

1817–1960	States build large state residential institutions for the deaf and the blind, people with mental retardation and people with mental illness, and people who are deemed hyperaggressive/delinquent. (New, elaborate institutions were built well into the 1960s in some states.)
1940–1970	Public school districts establish special classes and special schools. Generally, special education programs are located in central school buildings or centers for special education at the convenience of administrators.
1966–Present	Resource rooms are designated for students with mild disabilities. Students move from special classes to general education for selected activities. Students with behavior disorders spend most of the day in special classes.
1975–Present	Special classes are organized for students with severe disabilities. Classes generally are located in selected elementary and secondary schools under the Education for All Handicapped Children Act of 1975 (PL 94-142).
1980–Present	Regular education initiative (REI) is promoted by Madeleine Will, then head of the Office of Special Education and Rehabilitative Services, U.S. Department of Education. REI formalized the mainstreaming trend. Although the initiative was responsible to the least restrictive environment assurance of PL 94-142, it benefited primarily students with mild disabilities by returning them to general education.
1982–Present	Students with severe disabilities are placed in special classes in their home community schools and selectively placed in general education classrooms for an hour or so per day. The promotion of full inclusion begins.
1988–Present	Lipsky and Gartner (1989), Stainback and Stainback (1988), TASH (formerly The Association for Persons with Severe Handicaps), and Thousand and Villa (1989) promote the full inclusion of all students.
1990–Present	IDEA requires early education for students with disabilities from 2½ years of age.

During the 1960s, a number of demonstration programs were conducted that used the resource room model to provide special services for students with mild disabilities. Students were placed in resource rooms as their homerooms and selectively introduced to general education classes. This model was the first effort to move toward inclusion. The problem was that students with behavior problems spent the major portion of their school day in resource rooms (Haring & Bateman, 1977). The resource room concept began the national trend toward inclusion, which was referred to at the time as *mainstreaming*. This movement preceded the provision of education for students with

severe disabilities. Mainstreaming was a practice that referred specifically to students with mild disabilities.

In 1975, the Education for All Handicapped Children Act (PL 94-
142) was passed. This legislation, requiring that all children of school
age receive a free, appropriate public education (FAPE) in the least
restrictive environment (LRE), caused a critical problem for U.S. public
schools. This legislation included, of course, students with severe disabilities. The law gave the schools 3 years to get ready to include all
children. Never in the history of public education had such an all-
encompassing demand been placed on U.S. schools. Even though
fewer than 1% of the school-age population had severe disabilities, a
large number of teachers with qualifications to teach these children
were required. Practically no research on instruction methods and curricula was available. The situation in the schools was catastrophic.

At about this same time, a small group of educators who saw the
urgency for knowledge and training came together in Kansas City and
established the American Association for the Education of the
Severely/Profoundly Handicapped (AAESPH). This was the beginning of the organization known as TASH.

To complicate the problem further, PL 94-142 provided for an appropriate education in the LRE. This gave rise to a variety of placements that
promoted the setting up of programs in home community schools and
special classes alongside general classes (i.e., side-by-side). In establishing special education, however, wings attached to school buildings were
the most common administrative arrangement. Many larger school districts established elaborate special education centers, and those centers
seemed an obvious placement for students with severe disabilities in
spite of the lack of compliance with the LRE assurance.

REGULAR EDUCATION INITIATIVE

Probably the most significant movement toward integration was the
regular education initiative (REI) because it had the support of
Madeleine Will (1986), the head of the Office of Special Education and
Rehabilitative Services, U.S. Department of Education. At the time, it
was argued that special education classes did not show significant
results compared with results achieved with placement in general education classrooms. Furthermore, special education had the disadvan-
tage of social isolation of students with disabilities.

Although the REI did provide the needed emphasis for instructional and administrative restructuring, the initiative did not address
the critical concern of including students with severe disabilities. This
trend was successful in getting programs for people with mild disabili-

ties to merge resources of special education and general education and began the most important interaction and communication between general and special education teachers (Fuchs & Fuchs, 1994). In a real way, the REI resuscitated conditions as they were before the advent of special classes, albeit with more educational and technological sophistication.

Inclusion Gains Strength

The REI provided the momentum for general education to respond to the more inclusive trend. Inclusion efforts such as the REI were only partially responsive to the LRE requirement because students with severe disabilities continued to be placed separately in most facilities. The terms *integration* and *inclusion* are often used interchangeably. Actually, full inclusion and integration have discriminative features in practice. Integration can be more accurately characterized as follows:

1. Many students who were previously segregated on the basis of their disabilities are brought back into the general classrooms.

2. Various dimensions of integration (physical, temporal, instructional, and social) are considered.

3. Students with mild disabilities are placed in general classrooms on a full-time basis.

4. Students with severe disabilities are served in special education classrooms located in general education schools, with some instruction in environments with peers who are developing typically.

5. Support services follow the students, regardless of environment.

The provisions established by inclusion fulfill the LRE reference to "all students" and are considerably more advanced than those of integration. The characteristics of inclusion (adapted from Gallucci, 1990) are

1. Educating *all children* within schools in their home community and in age-appropriate general education environments

2. Creating school and classroom communities in which *all students* feel that they are accepted, belong, and can achieve their potential

3. Providing instructional and social support and assistance to *all students* who require it within general education and community environments to the greatest degree possible

4. Adjusting, modifying, and eliminating curricula when necessary to meet the needs of *all students* for whom the existing curricula are inappropriate

5. Coordinating the resources of special education, other categorical programs (e.g., English as a Second Language, language assistance programs), and general education to meet the diverse needs of *all students*

6. Restructuring building resources and providing support personnel (General education teachers assume coordinating responsibilities for special education.)

That students with severe disabilities should also be included in general education and that they are entitled to the combined resources of special and general education to achieve a comprehensive, effective educational experience was acknowledged in the literature by the early 1980s (Certo, Haring, & York, 1984; Stainback & Stainback, 1984).

Full Inclusion: The New Age of Enlightenment

My first realization of a major increment of change toward the most radical practice of full inclusion came when I read Susan and William Stainback's (1988) article, "Educating All Students with Severe Disabilities in Regular Classes." They defined *inclusive education* as "providing all students within the mainstream appropriate education programs that are challenging yet geared to their capabilities and needs as well as any support and assistance they and/or their teachers may need to be successful in the mainstream" (p. 16). This definition remains valid at the turn of the 21st century.

Two years later, the Stainbacks (1990) edited their book entitled *Support Networks for Inclusive Schooling: Interdependent Integrated Education.* That book detailed a set of strategies that have served to guide educators throughout the United States who have been promoting full inclusion in their school districts, namely by

- Establishing a school philosophy
- Following the principles of natural proportions
- Including individuals who are directly involved
- Developing networks of support
- Integrating students, personnel, and resources
- Adapting the curriculum
- Maintaining flexibility

Table 2 provides an overview of the various models of special education service delivery.

Table 2. Various models of special education service delivery

Model	Goal	Process	Special services	Focus
Mainstreaming	Return students with disabilities to the general education mainstream as much as possible	Assign students to special education programs, but have them attend general education programs to the extent that they are believed to be capable of benefiting from them.	Special education instruction and related services are provided in special environments (e.g., self-contained classes, resource rooms); few, if any, special services follow the student into the mainstream.	Traditionally considered an option for students with mild disabilities; rarely affected students with severe disabilities
Regular education initiative (REI)	Merge the talents and resources of general and special education to better meet the needs of fast and slow learners alike	Form collaborative working relationships among special and general educators; maintain a continuum of services for the most difficult students.	Most services are provided within the general education classroom; some services are provided in special environments for the students deemed most difficult to teach.	Generally focused on reforming the system for serving students with mild disabilities; maintenance of special classes for serving students with severe disabilities, albeit, perhaps, within general education schools
Integration	Bring students with disabilities into equal membership in the community	Integrate students along four dimensions—physical, temporal, academic/ intstructional, and social.	For students with mild disabilities, mainstreaming to the fullest extent possible; for students with severe disabilities, placement in self-contained classes within general schools, with integration into general, age-appropriate	An attempt is made to meet the needs of students with mild and severe disabilities. In each case, integration into general education environments is attempted to the fullest extent possible; but the expectation is that students with severe

(continued)

Table 2. (continued)

Model	Goal	Process	Special Services	Focus
			classes whenever possible. In both cases, special education services follow the student.	disabilities still need to receive the majority of their services in special education classrooms.
Inclusion	Create school and classroom communities in which all students are accepted, belong, and can achieve their potential.	Place all children in age-appropriate general education classrooms within their neighborhood schools; blend the talents and resources of general education, "at-risk" programs, and special education to meet the needs of all students; adjust or expand the curriculum to meet students' special needs.	Instructional and social support is provided to all students within general education and community environments to the greatest extent possible. Some advocates would maintain a continuum of services to meet extraordinary needs; other advocates would eliminate alternative placement options altogether.	The most vocal initial advocates were those concerned primarily with the education of students with severe disabilities. Many concerned with the education of students with all kinds of learning differences (e.g., students with mild disabilities, second-language learners) see the inclusive education movement as an extension of the REI and part of multicultural education. They believe the concomitant changes in curriculum, assessment, instruction, and staffing patterns that accompany effective inclusion benefit all students.

Full Inclusion Their Way

The first time I met Richard A. Villa and Jacqueline S. Thousand was in Merced, California. Their excellent presentation on the program for the teachers of the Merced Secondary School District made me realize that their kind of enthusiasm and knowledge are exactly what it takes to achieve the goal of inclusive education for all students. It was clear that they understood fully the scope of the task at hand. They described the organizational change required to achieve full inclusion in U.S. schools as a *quantum leap* and the conceptual framework as a *paradigm shift.*[1] It took me a day to catch up with their rapid-fire ideas. Since that meeting in Merced, McGregor and Vogelsberg (1998) have reviewed 214 articles on inclusion that were published since 1994, not including several research articles that I can think of on the subject. The field of inclusion has indeed experienced a quantum leap in the level of activity and concern about inclusive schooling.

This book is a complete revision of *Restructuring for Caring and Effective Education: An Administrative Guide to Creating Heterogeneous Schools* (Villa, Thousand, Stainback, & Stainback, 1992). My preview reading of this revision assured me that it provides the most advanced and comprehensive treatment of its subject available. It truly represents a paradigm shift in the changes facing education. As Villa and Thousand wrote in their letter inviting me to write this Prologue, "One of the things we are attempting to do in this book is to link the inclusion of students eligible for special education with general education school reform initiatives (e.g., democracy in education, authentic assessment, standards, curriculum of caring, leadership, multicultural education). In addition to this linkage, the major focus will be upon creating and maintaining effective inclusive schools and classrooms." So, as the server at your favorite restaurant would say when your dinner arrives, *enjoy!*

REFERENCES

Certo, N., Haring, N., & York, R. (Eds.). (1984). *Public school integration of severely handicapped students.* Baltimore: Paul H. Brookes Publishing Co.

---

[1]Quantum theory proposes a fixed elemental unit of energy that has angular momentum. It assumes that energy is not infinitely divisible and deals with atomic structure and phenomena. *Quantum leap* in physics refers to a sudden alteration in the energy level of all atoms or molecules together with the emulsion or absorption of radiant energy. Also, *quantum leap* is used idiomatically to characterize a great quantity of sudden and extensive change or advance in administrative organization, program, or policy. Similarly, *paradigm shift,* used idiomatically, refers to a major change in the model applied to the thinking and perception about the organization for providing services or doing business.

Education for All Handicapped Children Act of 1975, PL 94-142, 20 U.S.C. §§ 1400 *et seq.*

Fuchs, D., & Fuchs, L.S. (1994). Inclusive schools movement and the radicalization of special education reform. *Exceptional Children, 60*(4), 292–309.

Gallucci, C. (1990). *Project MESH: A summary of current literature on effective school integration.* Unpublished manuscript. (Available from The Office of the Superintendent of Public Instruction Special Education Services, Post Office Box 47200, Olympia, WA 98504-7200)

Haring, N.G., & Bateman, B. (1977). *Teaching the learning disabled child.* Upper Saddle River, NJ: Prentice-Hall.

Haring, N.G., Cruickshank, W., & Stern, G. (1958). *Attitudes of educators toward exceptional children.* Syracuse, NY: Syracuse University Press.

Individuals with Disabilities Education Act (IDEA) of 1990, PL 101-476, 20 U.S.C. §§ 1400 *et seq.*

Lipsky, D.K., & Gartner, A. (Eds.). (1989). *Beyond separate education: Quality education for all.* Baltimore: Paul H. Brookes Publishing Co.

McGregor, G., & Vogelsberg, R.T. (1998). *Inclusive schooling practices: Pedagogical and research foundations.* Pittsburgh, PA: Allegheny University of the Health Sciences.

Stainback, S., & Stainback, W. (1988). Educating all students with severe disabilities in regular classes. *Teaching Exceptional Children, 21,* 16–19.

Stainback, W., & Stainback, S. (1984). A rationale for the merging of special and regular education. *Exceptional Children, 51,* 102–111.

Stainback, W., & Stainback, S. (1990). *Support networks for inclusive schooling: Interdependent integrated education.* Baltimore: Paul H. Brookes Publishing Co.

Thousand, J.S., & Villa, R.A. (1989). Enhancing success in heterogeneous schools. In S.B. Stainback, W.C. Stainback, & M. Forest (Eds.), *Educating all students in the mainstream of regular education* (pp. 89–104). Baltimore: Paul H. Brookes Publishing Co.

Villa, R.A., Thousand, J.S., Stainback, W., & Stainback, S. (Eds.). (1992). *Restructuring for caring and effective education: An administrative guide to creating heterogeneous schools.* Baltimore: Paul H. Brookes Publishing Co.

Warren, D. (1995). Education in the United States. *1995 Grolier multimedia encyclopedia, version 7.0* [CD-ROM]. Danbury, CT: Grolier.

White, O., & Haring, N.G. (1997). *Inclusive education.* Unpublished manuscript. (Available from the Experimental Education Unit, Box 357925, University of Washington, Seattle, WA 98195)

Will, M. (1986). Educating children with learning problems: A shared responsibility. *Exceptional Children, 52,* 411–415.

About Norris G. Haring

Norris G. Haring, Ed.D., Professor Emeritus, University of Washington, Box 357925, Seattle, Washington 98195. Dr. Haring was a pioneer in special education, beginning his career in 1947 teaching adolescents who had been labeled as hyperaggressive and delinquent. He was a school psychologist in the Omaha, Nebraska, public schools. Following 8 years of administration in special education and higher education, he was the founding director of the Experimental Education Unit of the Center for Development and Disabilities at the University of Washington. In 1975, he was among a small group of professionals who founded the American Association for the Education of the Severely/Profoundly Handicapped, now known as TASH, and he was the founding president of the organization. He completed a 5-year study on procedures for training special and general education teachers to organize for full inclusion. In 1993, Dr. Haring was given the Distinguished Graduate Award by the School of Education at Syracuse University. Dr. Haring is Vice President of the Lifetime Advocacy, Guardianship, and Trust Association (LA+) and serves on the Board of Trustees for the Foundation of the University of California at Santa Barbara.

For the Reader

This book is not simply a revision of *Restructuring for Caring and Effective Education: An Administrative Guide to Creating Heterogeneous Schools.* That first edition represented policies, knowledge, beliefs, and practices that were state of the art at the beginning of the 1990s. *Restructuring for Caring and Effective Education: Piecing the Puzzle Together, Second Edition,* offers readers nearly a decade of additional learning with regard to how to make inclusive education work well, a "second generation" of critical questions and answers regarding inclusive practices, and a window on the possible future of inclusive education in the next millennium. This edition pieces together foundational principles in special education (e.g., the principle of social role valorization), guiding principles in the adult disability rights movement (e.g., self-determination, universal design), and critical principles in quality education (e.g., collaboration, creative problem solving, differentiated instruction and assessment) with pragmatic practice through case studies and personal and professional storytelling of how real people can structure and have structured their classrooms, schools, and lives to create caring and effective education communities for everyone.

The book's title retains elements of the first edition's. The book still is about restructuring for caring and effective education. As in the first edition, the editors wanted nothing in the title to refer explicitly to special education or inclusive education: Both editions are intended to raise questions and provide lessons that apply not only to the perceived ability dimension of diversity but also to any dimension of human diversity (e.g., language, culture, gender). The book's cover and the graphic images used to introduce the sections, chapters, and end-of-section reflections were also selected deliberately to represent the book's content. The apple image was selected for the first edition of the book because the "apple for the teacher" image is one long associated with education and good teaching, with awards and other recognition for quality teaching and educational leadership often being symbolized by the actual giving of a "golden apple." The first edition's apple logo was a sliced apple to indicate that the whole of quality education (symbolized by the entire apple) is composed of many different pieces that relate to different aspects of quality, caring, and effectiveness (e.g., organization structure, curricular and instruction practice, professional collaboration).

In this second edition, the book's subtitle is changed to *Piecing the Puzzle Together* because, over and over again, educators and families use puzzle language to describe their questions, concerns, and challenges regarding inclusive education. For example, they might say, "There seem to be so many pieces to the puzzle that have to be pieced together to make it work!" or, "I am still puzzled about [*fill in the blank with questions*]." Thus, the cover image of an apple is continued in this edition, representing, as it did in the first edition, the whole of caring and effective education. The slices of the apple, however, are transformed into puzzle pieces, and each of the five sections of the book and the chapters within those sections carry forward the apple theme, with one puzzle piece added successively at the beginning of each consecutive section.

A second image, a "Circle of Courage" medicine wheel, accompanies the reflections that conclude the book's sections. The Circle of Courage image represents the goals of education from a Native American perspective. This ancient education paradigm has as its overarching outcome the development of courageous youth, which can be accomplished only when the four critical dimensions of courage or goals of education are nurtured. The four dimensions—belonging, mastery, independence, and generosity—that together compose a complete circle, reemerged in the 1990s as the expressed goals of education. We believe that the Circle of Courage should be at the heart of the educational process, as evidenced by the circular puzzle piece in the center of the apple. In this book, the dimensions of the Circle of Courage are discussed in the context of education communities concerned with reclaiming youth at risk of school and societal failure (see Chapters 1 and 3), the effects of exclusion (see Chapter 4), and the state of education curriculum (see Chapter 22). When reading the reflections composed by individuals with disabilities and their family members, however, readers will hear most strongly the call for the Circle of Courage as a fundamental dream and expectation. These people are the ones who have struggled to enable themselves or their children with disabilities to 1) gain access to the *belonging* of the local school communities; 2) experience *mastery* through meaningful and appropriate modifications to curriculum, instruction, and assessment; 3) take risks and take on responsibilities in the real world to develop *independence*; and 4) have the chance to express and experience *generosity* through being givers and receivers of natural peer supports. It is for this reason that the editors thought it fitting that the reflections be introduced by the Circle of Courage image.

To our brothers,
Ernie and Michael,
who were among our first loves.
You were our first playmates, confidantes, and heroes.
Thank you for the continued fun, companionship, and love!

I

Reexamining the
Purposes of Schooling
Working Toward a Common Goal

M. Stephen Lilly

It is entirely fitting that a book focusing on inclusive education for all students should begin with a section on the purposes of schooling. The history of special education in the United States all too often has been based largely on a rejection of the basic values and purposes of general education in favor of alternative aims and means for teaching students identified as having disabilities. True implementation of inclusion principles demands understanding of and commitment to the basic goals and purposes of U.S. public education as well as a determination to achieve those goals for all students.

What, then, are the purposes and goals of public education in the United States? Is there sufficient agreement on these goals to guide such a major social movement as inclusion? Can or should common educational goals be adopted for all students? Or have so many special educators been right all along in arguing for a largely separate system of special education with distinct purposes and goals? These are some of the issues that are discussed in this introduction to the first section of this book.

The education literature is replete with discussions of the purposes of public education, with most entries in the literature consisting of passionate arguments for particular points of view. Goodlad argued that "goals for schooling emerge through a sociopolitical process in which certain sets of interests prevail over others for a period of time" (1994, p. 43). In other words, in addition to being intensely personal, educational goal setting is essentially political. This is to be expected in any service arena that is as publicly owned as public education.

Goodlad (1994) argued that educational goals that have emerged in the United States can be sorted into four basic categories. These categories, with Goodlad's descriptors and some slight embellishments, are

1. *Academic goals,* often referred to as functional literacy and including in 1999 both basic skills and what many have referred to as *cultural literacy* or core knowledge and skills

2. *Vocational goals* to prepare students for productive work, economic responsibility, and career readiness

3. *Social and civic goals* to prepare students to participate in a complex society and especially to ensure the preparation of all young people for maximum effective participation in the civic affairs of American democracy

4. *Personal goals,* or the development of personal fulfillment and love of learning for its own sake

Although public attention to one or another of these goal areas might predominate at different times, the fact is that all are important outcomes of effective education. The standards movement in the United States has brought to the fore the importance of academic goals, and there is increasing pressure across the United States (fueled by language in the Individuals with Disabilities Education Act [IDEA] Amendments of 1997 [PL 105-17]) to apply high standards for educational performance to *all* teachers and their students, including those in special education.

Regarding Goodlad's second category of goals, vocational preparation has long been a mainstay of special education programs, and much of the rationale for traditional special education has been based on the presumption that specialized instruction in separate classrooms results in increased readiness for the workplace for large numbers of students. The problem is that evidence of the effectiveness of separate special education in meeting this goal has been elusive, and actual employment data for graduates of special education programs do not argue for the positive outcomes for which so many have hoped. This is not to say that general education has been stellar in preparing students for the demands of the emerging world of work in the United States; but it can be argued that school-to-career models, which were developed and implemented in general education in the 1990s, hold more promise for effective work-force preparation than most vocational programs that are offered solely or primarily through special education.

Education for civic engagement and effective participation in the democracy are discussed further on in this introduction; the discussion here turns to the fourth goal area that Goodlad cited: personal fulfillment and development of a love for learning for its own sake. This area always has been the favorite of many educators who argue that it is essential that students become lifelong learners and develop a passion for learning. Dewey stated that education "has no end beyond itself" (1916, p. 53), and Goodlad stressed that education is "a process of individual becoming. . . . [T]he essence of the process is the growth taking place in the individual and the meaning of that growth for the individual" (1994, p. 37). I confess to being drawn to this purpose for education like a moth to light; it is in fact hard to argue with its centrality. Although important, it is neither sufficient nor, apparently, a particularly compelling goal for the general public, education policy makers, parents, or even many students. To the four groups just mentioned, love of learning seems an acceptable, even desired, end product of effective education but insufficient in and of itself to ensure quality of life for the next generation and continuation of the U.S. democratic form of government. In other words, educators are free to pursue this goal as long as they simultaneously attend to the other three goals.

This brings us to the third set of educational goals that Goodlad cited: education for civic engagement and citizenship. This goal is saved until last in the discussion because it is, in the view of many, the most comprehensive and engaging purpose of U.S. public education. Tyler wrote that "the American public school was instituted after the War of Independence by political and educational leaders of the time in order to educate the new nation's children to assume the responsibilities of citizenship in a democracy" and that, even though great variability exists in education across the United States, there is a common purpose: "the education of children to become informed, responsible citizens" (1994, p. vii). Goodlad agreed, asking, "Do not schools have a responsibility to balance their contribution to individualism with attention to the understandings and civility that democracy and sense of community require?" (1994, p. x). It is this purpose of education that validates—even requires—attention to important yet often maligned issues such as multicultural education, diversity, and the teaching and modeling of values and moral predispositions. Finally, the citizenship goal is perhaps the most compelling argument for inclusive education for all students because there are minimum levels of knowledge, skill, and competence that all adults must have in order to be effective citizens in a complex and diverse democracy and social community.

Edgar provided an important perspective for special educators on this topic. He wrote of being "disappointed that regardless of how hard I or my colleagues tried we never seemed to find the methods to significantly increase the quality of life for youth with disabilities" (1997, p. 323). Edgar pondered the goals and purposes of education described in the context of education reform and concluded that, for him, the most compelling view of schools is as "centers for the advancement of democracy and the development of citizens who are actively involved in the democratic process" (1997, p. 324). He argued that special educators have been involved insufficiently in the school reform movement and, as a result, have failed in advocacy efforts for students in special education. His vision is of schools "that have as co-priorities individual achievement of market-oriented skills and civic skills and knowledge" and "equal time and resources . . . expended on each of these priorities" (1997, p. 325). In such schools, he pointed out, all students would have a valued place.

I greatly appreciate Edgar's wisdom and courage in arguing that education reform is the best venue for special educators to advocate for children and youth identified as having disabilities. I agree with him that education for citizenship in American democracy must be a primary goal of U.S. schooling while acknowledging the importance of the other three categories of goals cited previously. In my view, until one can say that all four sets of goals are being achieved with all students, public educators have not met our moral and professional obligations. This very imperative—to educate all students more comprehensively and at higher levels of learning while accepting responsibility for achieving assessable outcomes in all four goal areas— defines both the challenge and the promise that educators face in bringing U.S. public education into the next millennium. Our success in meeting this enormous challenge quite literally will determine the future of public education and the quality of life in the United States for future generations.

What does all of this mean for special education? What are the implications of how special educators have approached their work and their efforts on behalf of students? Fundamentally, it means that educators must start over in defining systems that support all students in acquiring advanced skills and knowledge, applying what they learn to the world around them, and achieving lifelong learning skills and predispositions in the process. These educational heights cannot be achieved by using the Balkanized systems that have evolved in special education.

Educators must change the very definitions of fundamental concepts such as learning diversity. The many and competing systems for serving students who are challenged in learning the prescribed curriculum must be forsaken and replaced with a single model for delivering effective instruction in inclusive environments for all students. In the process, certain strongly held beliefs about learning diversity must be abandoned: beliefs that have led educators to build separate and overlapping systems for serving students with disabilities, students who are lagging in particular subject areas, students who are English language learners, students who are from families living in poverty, and all the rest of the students in U.S. public schools. The unnecessary fractionalization of the learning support systems in schools must cease and be replaced by functional systems for providing direct, powerful support for all students who are experiencing difficulty in learning the core curriculum. Educators need to make a pact to abandon service boundaries that require spending large amounts of money on testing and sorting students into learning groups at the expense of direct support of learning activities. Finally, educators must leave their "specialized identities" at the door in setting and agreeing on common expectations for all students served in public education.

Some will argue that this last litany is nothing new but rather a reiteration of arguments made since the 1960s regarding special education labeling, identification, and service systems. I believe, however, that the discussion of inclusive education in fact enters into new territory at this point. When the basic purposes and goals of public education are examined and educators proceed on the assumption that those goals are not only desirable but essential for all students, then the conversation is no longer about special education and general education. Rather, it is about all the ways that have been constructed to separate students from the common goals of schooling and excuse certain groups of educators and parents from active participation in continuously refining those goals and finding more effective methods of achieving them. Inclusion is not about making all education special; it is about creating a single system of education that works for all students. This is, at its essence, a collaborative enterprise, and it starts with common agreement on the purposes of the cherished system of U.S. public education. This is hard work. Let it begin now.

REFERENCES

Dewey, J. (1916). *Democracy and education.* New York: Macmillan.

Edgar, E. (1997). Perspective: School reform, special education, and democracy. *Remedial and Special Education, 18,* 323–325.

Goodlad, J.I. (1994). *What schools are for.* Bloomington, IN: Phi Delta Kappa Educational Foundation.

Individuals with Disabilities Education Act (IDEA) Amendments of 1997, PL 105-17, 20 U.S.C. §§ 1400 *et seq.*

Tyler, R.W. (1994). Foreword: Why do we have public schools in America? In J.I. Goodlad, *What schools are for* (pp. vii–viii). Bloomington, IN: Phi Delta Kappa Educational Foundation.

Chapter 1

Setting the Context
History of and Rationales for Inclusive Schooling

Richard A. Villa and Jacqueline S. Thousand

In the 1980s and 1990s, researchers, policy makers, parents, consumers, and educators discussed changing the predominant pull-out and separate classroom delivery of special education services, using terms such as *mainstreaming, integration, regular education initiative* (REI), *unified systems, heterogeneous schooling,* and *inclusion.* These discussions highlighted some of the perceived requirements for new types of service delivery to be successful, including restructuring, merging general and special education, creating a unified education system, and developing shared responsibility for students (Gartner & Lipsky, 1987; Lipsky & Gartner, 1997; Reynolds, Wang, & Walberg, 1987; Villa, Thousand, Stainback, & Stainback, 1992; Wang, Reynolds, & Walberg, 1987; Will, 1985). This chapter offers a context for inclusive education through a historical perspective and a presentation of multiple rationales that motivate an increasing number of educators, parents, people with disabilities, and policy makers to advocate for the creation of inclusive schooling.

HISTORICAL TREND
TOWARD INCLUSIVE EDUCATION

It is generally acknowledged (Lerner, 1987; Stainback, Stainback, & Bunch, 1989) that the discussion of including students with disabilities in general education was prompted in 1985 by then Assistant Secretary of Education Madeleine Will's Wingspread REI speech and by two subsequent 1986 publications (Will, 1986a, 1986b), even though similar ideas had been published previously (e.g., Stainback & Stainback, 1984). Other authors and their publications became associated with the REI because of similarities in expressed concerns regarding segregated delivery of special education services and proposals for the restructuring or the merger of general and special education (e.g., Gartner & Lipsky, 1987; Lilly, 1986; Reynolds et al., 1987; Stainback & Stainback, 1984; Wang et al., 1987).

Will identified four major negative consequences of the organization and delivery of prevailing separate education services to children with special needs:

1. Eligibility requirements and procedures resulted in many children being denied access to appropriate supports to succeed in the general classroom.

2. Performance expectations of students in separate programs often were lowered on the part of the students themselves, their teachers, and the students' peers.

3. The model of identifying and serving students with learning difficulties tended to be *reactive*, addressing problems after they occurred, rather than *proactive*, attempting to prevent learning difficulties from occurring.

4. "[A] cooperative, supportive partnership" (Will, 1986a, p. 412) among parents, school officials, and teachers did not exist.

Will identified large numbers of children failing to learn in general education, estimating that 20%–30% of school-age children had difficulty learning in school. Given these numbers, Will called for change and advocated for building-level reform. Specifically, "building level administrators must be empowered to assemble appropriate professional and other resources for delivering effective, coordinated, comprehensive services for all students based on educational need rather than eligibility for special programs" (1986a, p. 413).

Will also called for early identification and intervention, curriculum-based assessment, ongoing assessment of student progress and program effectiveness, and stronger parent–professional partnerships. She urged that schools employ principals who could be instructional leaders and general and special educators who could work together as members of an instructional team. Will acknowledged that the success of any reform effort was dependent on the establishment of a climate of trust among educators, parents, and policy makers.

From the start, responses to Will's REI proposal were mixed and emotional. Several authors expressed enthusiastic support and expansion of the REI concepts (Lilly, 1986; Reynolds et al., 1987; Stainback & Stainback, 1985; Wang et al., 1987) and described what the so-called merged education system might be. At a minimum, REI proponents called for the elimination of segregated labels, classrooms, and pull-out programs and services. They expressed optimism about changing what was in the mainstream—general education—by rethinking traditional instructional and curricular approaches. Although the Will proposals referred primarily to children with mild or high-incidence disabilities (i.e., children classified as experiencing mild learning disabilities, mental retardation, and behavior disorders), mention was made of educating a broader range of students full-time in general education.

Others were pessimistic; negative; fearful; and, in some cases, angry (e.g., Duncan, 1987; Lerner, 1987; Lieberman, 1985; McCarthy, 1987; Messinger, 1985). An entire issue (January 1988) of the *Journal of Learning Disabilities* (Wiederholt, 1988) was devoted to issues surrounding the REI. Although the issue was not completely negative, in general the articles in that issue expressed extreme caution and lack of enthusiasm, at least with regard to children with learning disabilities. The journal's editors called for a critical appraisal of assumptions underlying the REI and research in support of the possibility of instructing students with exceptional needs in general education before "wholesale endorsement" (p. 4) occurred.

Expanding the Discussion

Within a short time, the REI debate was broadened to include students with moderate and severe disabilities. Stainback and Stainback were among the first authors to propose the complete merger of general and special education into "one unified system structured to meet the unique needs of all students" (1984, p. 102). Advocacy efforts expanded the REI to enroll all students, including those labeled as having severe and profound disabilities, in the general education classrooms of their local neighborhood schools (Biklen, 1985; Gartner & Lipsky, 1987; Knoblock, 1982). Experimentation began with the actual inclusion and education of students with intense challenges in general classrooms on part-time and full-time bases (Biklen, 1988; Strully & Strully,

1985; Thousand et al., 1986; Villa & Thousand, 1988). Although there appeared to be an emerging recognition of the benefits of local community school placement for students with severe disabilities (Brown et al., 1989; Sailor, 1989), the appropriateness of educating these students in general classrooms was hotly debated. Brown et al. noted that "the major placement issue of the day is whether students with severe intellectual disabilities should be based in regular or special classrooms in home schools" (1989, p. 12). Jenkins, Pious, and Jewell (1990) argued that, even though the REI should apply to most students with disabilities, students with severe disabilities should not be included because their curriculum needs extended beyond those materials classroom teachers were responsible for adapting and delivering to individual learners. Burrello and Tourgee identified students with severe disabilities as the subgroup of students with disabilities for whom "maintaining a self-contained setting in a centrally located place in the building with socialization opportunities was the most realistic program" (1990, p. 33).

Williams, Villa, Thousand, and Fox (1993), however, viewed the discussion of separate class placement for students with severe disabilities as inappropriate for two reasons. First, placement of students with severe disabilities in general classrooms had been occurring for several years in a number of North American schools, and there were documented benefits for students with and without disabilities and their teachers (Nevin, Thousand, Paolucci-Whitcomb, & Villa, 1990; Stainback & Stainback, 1990; Thousand et al., 1986). Second, federal law (i.e., the Individuals with Disabilities Education Act of 1990 [IDEA; PL 101-476]) required placement of students with disabilities to be based on each student's identified needs, not on the categorical label (e.g., severe disabilities) assigned to the student. Raising the question of whether general class placement was appropriate for a category of learners (e.g., students identified as having severe and profound disabilities) "assumes that placement can be made based upon handicapping condition without documentation of an individual student's needs and examination of whether the needs could be met in a regular class based placement" (Williams et al., 1993, p. 333). The central issue was one of appropriate curriculum adaptation to address individual students' needs within general education classroom environments, not whether a category of students should have access to general classes.

Inclusion as Part and Parcel of Educational Reform

In the early 1990s, the REI debate once again expanded. Skrtic described the REI as representing "a number of proposals for achieving the spirit of the EHA [Education for All Handicapped Children Act of 1975 (PL 94-142)] for students with disabilities by extending its rights and resources to *all* students" (1991, p. 149). Thousand and Villa (1991) echoed Skrtic in their suggestion that the focus of the REI debate should be on the future—how to structure education to meet the future needs of all children. Growing public and professional dissatisfaction with the bureaucracy and outcomes of special education (e.g., Wagner, 1989) and recognition of the need for school restructuring for all learners was evidenced in 1992, with an Association for Supervision and Curriculum Development (ASCD) resolution and a report of the National Association of State Boards of Education's (NASBE, 1992) Study Group on Special Education.

The ASCD resolution acknowledged the paradox that federal and state funding of remedial and special education programs is based on assessment and labeling of children, despite increasing empirical evidence that "labeling stigmatizes children and tends to result in segregated services and lower teacher expectations" (ASCD, 1992, p. 2). Thus, one of the organization's six 1992 resolutions was for the full inclusion of special programs through instructional environments that eliminated tracking and segregation, services that focused on the prevention of learning problems rather than on after-the-fact labeling, minimal restrictive regulations, and flexible use of funding to promote success for all children.

The NASBE Study Group on Special Education, after 2 years of study of special education and the general education school reform movement, concluded in its *Winners All: A Call for Inclusive Schools* report that the following five questions must be answered with a resounding *"no"*:

1. Are children currently classified as "special education students" achieving what they are capable of?
2. Are they being prepared for life after school?
3. Are current mainstreaming practices achieving their intended outcomes?
4. Is the separate special education system we have created the best way to educate these students?
5. Has special education been asked to join general education in the reform movement that is now beginning to focus on standards, outcomes, and educating an increasingly diverse student body with individualized instruction? (1992, p. 4)

The NASBE Study Group recommended a major shift in how education services are provided and charged state boards of education to establish goals and policies that supported collaboration between general and special education. The group urged the creation of a unified education system, with major changes in organizational and instructional practices, preservice and in-service personnel preparation, licensure, and funding. The group encouraged teachers to focus on effective instruction rather than on the assessment and labeling of students while ensuring due process, parental involvement, and individualization of services.

Entering the 1990s, the number of schools attempting to actualize the ASCD and NASBE vision of inclusive education grew rapidly. By 1993, almost every state was implementing inclusion at some level (Webb, 1994). The percentage of students with disabilities ages 6–21 served in general education classrooms increased from 32.8% in 1990–1991 to 46% in 1995–1996. Literature also emerged that described some of these inclusive schools (e.g., Villa, Thousand, Paolucci-Whitcomb, & Nevin, 1990; Villa et al., 1992) and the methods that they employed to adapt curriculum and instruction and alter the traditional schooling paradigm (e.g., Falvey, 1995; Neary, Halvorsen, Kronberg, & Kelly, 1992; Stainback & Stainback, 1990, 1992; Stainback, Stainback, & Forest, 1989; Thousand, Villa, & Nevin, 1994; Villa & Thousand, 1995).

Current Situation

Tremendous attention at the federal, state, and local levels remains focused on educational reform.[1] Policy makers are emphasizing the establishment of national and state standards; greater flexibility in the use of funds to support categorical programs; and new, more authentic forms of assessment. Among the most notable comprehensive school reform programs and models that have been developed and disseminated across the United States are the Coalition of Essential Schools (Sizer, 1984), Accelerated Schools (Levin, 1987), Success for All (Slavin, Madden, Dolan, & Wasik, 1993), and the School Development Program (Comer, 1988). Each of these models involves a large network of schools, all of which are attempting to effect comprehensive reform in school organization and instruction. All of these restructuring efforts embrace the values of inclusive education (e.g., valuing of diversity, collaboration, unified services, problem solving, and expanded options in the classroom to support student learning).

---

[1]The remainder of this section on the current situation includes content from a grant proposal submitted to the U.S. Department of Education by Richard A. Villa, Dorothy Kerzner Lipsky, Mary A. Falvey, Alan Gartner, Judy Schrag, Charles Peck, and Mary-Ellen Fortini. The document may be obtained from the Office of Research and University Programs, Graduate School and University Center, The City University of New York.

The Accelerated Schools program is based on three underlying principles: purpose, empowerment with responsibility, and building on the strengths of the entire school community. Accelerated Schools lessons are designed to enrich learning through higher expectations, relevant content, and stimulating instruction (Keller, 1995). The Coalition of Essential Schools comprises secondary schools that emphasize collaborative problem solving and decision making among administration members, teachers, students, and families to create significant long-term reform (O'Neil, 1995). The Success for All program emphasizes the prevention of learning problems and addressing learning challenges through intensive interventions designed to minimally disrupt students' participation and progress in the general education program (Slavin, 1997). Schools that adopt the Comer model establish teams of stakeholders to create a comprehensive plan for the school. The model is based on the belief that the relationship between the school and individual families is at the heart of an impoverished child's success or the lack thereof and includes a comprehensive staff development program (Ramirez-Smith, 1995).

In 1995, the National Center for Educational Restructuring and Inclusion canvassed these and other major nongovernmental reform efforts (e.g., Foxfire, Paideia, National Center for Effective Schools) to determine the extent to which children with disabilities were included in their reform efforts. The results of this canvassing noted increased attention to the inclusion of children with disabilities in these reform efforts but a less-than-coherent plan for supporting students with disabilities in general education environments. Lipsky and Gartner concluded that,

> For the most part, inclusive education activities are initiated at the local school district level rather than through state-level or federal restructuring efforts. In too many school districts, inclusive education remains an isolated activity. Increasingly, however, the placing of special education students into general education classrooms with the necessary supports and aids (i.e., inclusive education) precipitates broader school reform or school restructuring efforts that include both special and general education students. Basically, they become the cause and consequence of each other. (1997, p. 231)

Until the 1990s, the inclusive education movement was viewed as a separate initiative running parallel or even counter to concomitant general education reform efforts (Block & Haring, 1992). In contrast, as Udvari-Solner and Thousand (1995) illustrated, established and emerging general education theories actually emulate the principles and practices underpinning inclusive education. General education school reform initiatives that Udvari-Solner and Thousand identified as offering great promise for facilitating inclusive education included multicultural education; outcome-based education; multiple intelligences theory; interdisciplinary curriculum; constructivist learning; authentic assessment of student learning; multiage groupings; use of technology in the classroom; forms of peer-mediated instruction such as cooperative group learning, teaching responsibility, and peacemaking; and collaborative teaming among adults and students.

In the Goals 2000: Educate America Act of 1994 (PL 103-227), the Clinton administration's education reform legislation, there also was explicit language emphasizing that education goals apply to all students, including those who traditionally have been excluded from educational reforms (e.g., students with disabilities, students with limited English proficiency, students from minority cultures).

The Clinton administration's Assistant Secretary for Special Education and Rehabilitative Services, Judith E. Heumann, in an announcement releasing the Department of Education's Fifteenth Annual Report to Congress, stated,

> Historically, we have had two education systems, one for students with disabilities and one for everyone else. We are working to create one education system that values all students. The regular classroom in the neighborhood school should be the first option for students with disabilities. Administrators and teachers must receive the training and the help they need to make that the best option as well. (U.S. Department of Education, 1997)

With the passage of the IDEA Amendments of 1997 (PL 105-17), the Senate and House Committees reaffirmed the presumption that students with disabilities are to be educated in general education classrooms. In its findings, Congress emphasized the need for high expectations for all students with disabilities, ensuring access to the general education curriculum and coordination of IDEA implementation with other school improvement efforts so that special education can become a service rather than a place where students with disabilities go. The implementation of the IDEA Amendments of 1997 requires significant efforts to ensure access to the general education curriculum and the involvement of general education teachers with individualized education program (IEP) development and implementation for students with disabilities.

At the turn of the 21st century, the inclusion debate clearly has expanded beyond special education and become part of the total school reform movement. The National Education Association, in *The*

Integration of Students with Special Needs into Regular Classrooms: Policies and Practices that Work, noted,

> There is a growing body of . . . evidence that integration can help provide all students with curricular and life skills that expand their opportunities for future success. The current state of knowledge about successful practice makes this an opportune time to reflect on how schools can achieve high quality outcomes in integrated settings for all students. (1997, pp. 4–5)

The National Education Association joined nine other national education associations (the American Association of School Administrators, the American Federation of Teachers, the Council for Exceptional Children, the Council of Great City Schools, the National Association of Elementary School Principals, the National Association of Secondary School Principals, the National Association of State Boards of Education, the National Association of State Directors of Special Education, and the National State Boards Association) in acknowledging the characteristics that enable schools to implement inclusive educational practices fully and successfully:

- Diversity is valued and celebrated.
- The principal plays an active and supportive leadership role.
- All students work toward the same educational outcomes based on high standards.
- There is a sense of community in which everyone belongs, is accepted, and is supported by his or her peers and other members of the school community.
- There is an array of services.
- Flexible groupings, authentic and meaningful learning experiences, and developmentally appropriate curricula are accessible to all students.
- Research-based instructional strategies are used.
- Natural support networks are fostered across students and staff.
- Staff have changed roles to be more collaborative.
- There are new forms of accountability.
- There is access to necessary technology and physical modifications and accommodations.
- Parents are embraced as equal partners. (Council for Exceptional Children, 1995)

RATIONALE FOR INCLUSIVE SCHOOLING

What led people to shift their beliefs, attitudes, values, practices, and policy making toward more inclusive educational opportunities for students with identified learning differences? This section of the chapter suggests various rationales that have been associated with the growing advocacy for inclusive schools in which all students are welcomed, valued, and supported and learn in shared environments.

Goal of Public Education: The Same for All

Since the mid-1980s, the authors have asked tens of thousands of parents, teachers, administrators, students, university professors, and concerned citizens of the United States, Canada, Latin America, Asia, Australia, and Europe to identify the desired goals of education. Regardless of the divergent perspectives, vested interests, or locales of the people queried, their responses were similar and tended to fall into one or more of the four categories shown in Table 1 that are borrowed from Native American culture.

Traditional Native American education was based on the culture's main purpose of existence: the education and empowerment of its children. The central goal was to foster a child's "Circle of Courage" (Brendtro, Brokenleg, & Van Bockern, 1990, p. 34), which was composed of four components of self-esteem—*belonging, mastery, independence,* and *generosity.* (See Chapter 3 for a detailed discussion of the Circle of Courage.) It seems, then, that despite the diversity among the people we have sampled, people still share common beliefs with regard to the desired outcomes for students. Furthermore, the outcomes that people identify for students with educational, physical, social, and emotional challenges are no different from the outcomes that they identify for children who are not labeled as "special" in any way.

Outcomes and Efficacy Data

Historically, much of what has been done in the name of special education has compromised or mitigated against students' opportunity to experience or attain the components of the Circle of Courage. Specifically, in an effort to focus on students' skill development in order to promote their mastery and independence, they were sent to specialized instruction in separate environments. Although it is important for students to develop skills, it is difficult for students to get the message that they *belong* when they are sent down the hall or to a different school to develop those skills. Contemporary motivational theorists (e.g., Brendtro et al., 1990; Glasser, 1998; Maslow, 1987) stress the fulfillment of a child's need to belong as critical if not *prerequisite* to a

Table 1. Frequently identified goals of public education by category

Belonging
Having friends
Ability to form and maintain relationships
Getting along with others, including co-workers
Being part of a community
Being a caring parent and family member

Mastery
Having success and becoming competent in something or some things
Being well rounded
Being a good problem solver
Flexible
Motivated
Literate
Able to use technology
Lifelong learner
Reaching potential in areas of interest

Independence
Having choice in work, recreation, leisure, or continued learning
Confidence to take risks
Being as independent as possible
Assuming personal responsibility
Accountable for actions and decisions
Being able to self-advocate

Generosity
Being a contributing member of society
Valuing diversity
Being empathetic
Offering compassion, caring, and support to others
Being a responsible citizen
Global stewardship

child's motivation to learn. Exclusion of a child from general education, conversely, instructs the child that *belonging* is not forthcoming—that it is not a basic human right but something that must be earned. (See Chapter 4 for an elaboration of this dilemma.)

Research also illuminates the effect of separate education on the attainment of the mastery and independence dimensions of the Circle of Courage. In the late 1980s, research reviews and meta-analyses known as the special education efficacy studies (Lipsky & Gartner, 1989, p. 19) already showed that placement of students outside general education had few or no positive effects for students, regardless of the intensity or type of their disabilities.

Postschool employment data for graduates of separate special education programs suggest high levels of unemployment (more than 50% at 1 year postgraduation) and underemployment (Wagner et al., 1991). In contrast, Ferguson and Ash (1989) found that the more time children with disabilities spent in general classes, the more they achieved as adults in employment and continuing education. This held true regardless of the gender, race, socioeconomic status, or type of disability of the child and regardless of the age at which the child was afforded access to general education. The U.S. Department of Education reported that "across a number of analyses of postschool results, the message was the same: those who spent more time in regular education experienced better results after high school" (1995, p. 87).

In 1990, Vermont's Act 230 declared the state's policy to be that each local school district must collaborate with parents to establish a local comprehensive system of education services to ensure, to the maximum extent possible, that *all* students succeed in general education classrooms. To support implementation of the policy, 1% of the total state special education budget was dedicated to training teachers and administrators in strategies for effectively collaborating to support students in general education and community environments. Each school established a collaborative team of educators (i.e., an instruction support team) to help colleagues avoid special education referrals through the team's provision of advice and additional classroom support. The documented cumulative effects of Act 230 (Vermont State Department of Education, 1993, 1994, 1995) include the following:

- In contrast to the situation in other states, the number of students identified as eligible for special education *decreased* by 18.4% from 1990 to 1995 in Vermont.

- Students' performance, rule-following behavior, and social engagement had not diminished.

- Every school in Vermont has some variation of an instruction support team that, overall, has been judged effective in supporting teachers to avoid special education referrals through the development of the collaborative problem-solving skills of staff.

- Many schools have restructured to integrate special education and other remedial services into the general education classroom. This effort has increased educators' flexibility to collaborate, to use team teaching, cooperative learning, and integrated curriculum approaches. As a consequence, an additional 22,000 students who are at risk of school failure but are not technically eligible for special education have access to special educational supports and expertise.

• Every school has used state funds to expand professional development for all staff in areas such as collaboration, technology, integrated curriculum, discipline systems that teach responsibility, and
crisis prevention and management.

A 1994 review of three meta-analyses of the most effective environments for educating students with special needs concluded that,
regardless of the type of disability or grade level of the student,
"special-needs students educated in regular classes do better academically and socially than comparable students in noninclusive settings"
(Baker, Wang, & Walberg, 1994, p. 34). Hunt, Farron-Davis, Beckstead,
Curtis, and Goetz (1994) found that students with disabilities in inclusive environments had higher-quality IEPs and higher levels of
engaged time than students with disabilities who were educated in
separate classes. In reviewing quasi-experimental studies designed to
compare the academic progress of students without disabilities in
inclusive classrooms with the performance of students who were educated in classrooms without peers with disabilities, Staub and Peck
(1994) found that for children without disabilities in inclusive environments, there was no deceleration of academic behavior. In addition,
Sharpe, York, and Knight (1994) reported the results of a study that
found that there was no decline in the academic and behavioral performance of classmates without disabilities on standardized tests and
report card measures.

With regard to students with severe disabilities, Kelly, Keefe, and
VanEtten (1994) found that they had higher levels of active academic
responding and lower levels of competing behavior in general education environments than they did in segregated classes and schools.
Hollowood, Salisbury, Rainforth, and Palombaro (1995) found the
inclusion of students with severe disabilities not to be detrimental to
classmates. Others found their inclusion to enhance classmates' learning (Costello, 1991; Kaskinen-Chapman, 1992) as well as their own
(e.g., Cole & Meyer, 1991; Hollowood et al., 1995; Staub & Peck, 1994;
Strain, 1983) and to yield social and emotional benefits for all students,
with self-esteem and attendance improving for some students considered at risk for school failure (Kelly, 1992). In summary, for years there
has been evidence that the goals of education (i.e., Circle of Courage
outcomes) are more likely to be achieved when children with and without disabilities are educated together.

A review of the literature conducted by Hocutt (1996) revealed
that there is no compelling evidence demonstrating that placement is
the critical factor in students' social or academic success. The literature

review found that the classroom environment and the quality of instruction have more impact than placement on the success of students with disabilities.

Finally, as Kozol (1991) and others reminded us, there is a gross overrepresentation of minorities in special education and, thus, a racist aspect of continuing separate education programs. For example, African American children are three times more likely than European American children to be placed in special education classes, whereas they are only half as likely to be placed in programs for advanced or gifted students (Scherer, 1992/1993). In summary, Lipsky and Gartner observed,

> The basic premise of special education was that students with deficits will benefit from a unique body of knowledge and from smaller classes staffed by specially trained teachers using special materials. But there is no compelling body of evidence demonstrating that segregated special education programs have significant benefits for students. (1989, p. 19)

Changing Assumptions

Schooling must be based in large part on assumptions about what American society will be like in the *future* and the skills, attitudes, and dispositions necessary for success in such a society. Yet, in many communities, American schools are organized to respond to assumptions about life in the 19th and early 20th centuries. That is, they attempt to educate with excellence the socioeconomic elite, Americanize new immigrant populations, and otherwise track children for stratified work roles in a relatively static factory economy in which questioning, thinking, and creative problem solving are not needed.

Change clearly can be scary and difficult, and maintaining the status quo often wins out over fundamental change. In education, the status quo has been maintained at least in part by sending away every child who fails to learn from or who is not challenged by educational approaches based on the 19th- and 20th-century assumptions just described.

What is exciting in the exploration of mismatches between educational assumptions and practices is that the way in which educators think about children with disabilities *changes*. Educators who understand the curriculum for the 21st century *and* who have risked and succeeded in educating children with disabilities in general education know and will argue that children with disabilities are a gift to educational reform. They are a gift because they force educators to break the paradigm of traditional schooling and try new things so that they are more capable of meeting the unique needs of students with disabilities *and* those of many other students. No longer can teachers "do business as usual." When diverse populations of students are welcomed as members of a school community, standardization, assimilation, and sorting or tracking of students no longer can remain the assumptions or practices that drive or characterize effective education. The changes in curricular, instructional, and organizational practices that are introduced, discovered, rediscovered, and invented (e.g., cooperative group learning, student-directed learning, active participation, detracking, a focus on social skills and communicative competence, community service) benefit many students and accelerate the transformation of curriculum, instruction, assessment, and school organizations to better prepare every student for the future.

Legal Rights and Evolving Case Law

In response to increases in advocacy for the inclusion of children with disabilities in general education at the turn of the 21st century, many ask whether the law regarding the education of children with disabilities has changed. The answer, of course, is "no." Since the Education for All Handicapped Children Act (PL 94-142) was passed in 1975, the law and its subsequent reauthorizations—including the 1990 (PL 101-476) reauthorization and the 1997 IDEA Amendments (PL 105-17)—have reflected Congress' preference for educating students with disabilities in general classrooms with their peers. Specifically, under Section 612,

> To the maximum extent appropriate, children with disabilities, including children in public or private institutions and other care facilities, are educated with children who are not disabled, and special classes, separate schooling, or other removal of children with disabilities from the regular educational environment occurs only when the nature or severity of the disability of the child is such that education in regular classes with the use of supplementary aids and services cannot be achieved satisfactorily. (IDEA, PL 101-476, § 612[a][5])

Since 1975, federal court cases have clarified the intent of the law in favor of the inclusion of students with disabilities in general education. For example, in 1983, the *Roncker v. Walter* case addressed the issue of "bringing educational services to the child" versus "bringing the child to the services." The case was resolved in favor of integrated versus segregated placement and established a *principle of portability*; that is, "if a desirable service currently provided in a segregated setting can feasibly be delivered in an integrated setting, it would be inappropriate under PL 94-142 to provide the service in a segregated environment" (700 F.2d at 1063).

The 1989 U.S. Court of Appeals ruling in favor of Timothy W., a student with severe disabilities whose school district contended that his disabilities were too severe for him to be entitled to an education, clarified school districts' responsibility to educate all children and specified that the term *all* in IDEA meant *all* children with disabilities without exception. In 1993, the U.S. Court of Appeals for the Third Circuit upheld the right of Rafael Oberti, a boy with Down syndrome, to receive his education in his neighborhood school with adequate and necessary supports, placing the burden of proof for compliance with IDEA's inclusion requirements squarely on the school district and the state rather than on the child's family.

In 1994, the U.S. Court of Appeals for the Ninth Circuit upheld the federal district court decision in *Sacramento City Unified School District v. Rachel H.,* in which Judge Levi indicated that, when school districts place students with disabilities, the presumption and starting point is the mainstream. It is noteworthy that the Clinton administration, via the Office of Special Education Programs, filed an *amicus curiae* (i.e., "friend of the court") brief with the Ninth Circuit in support of Rachel's placement in general education classrooms.

Class-action lawsuits also are challenging predominantly segregated special education service delivery systems. For instance, the *Chanda Smith v. Los Angeles Unified School District* (LAUSD) (1993) lawsuit, brought on behalf of more than 65,000 students with disabilities, challenged the special education system of the nation's second-largest school district. A consent decree agreed to by the school district and the plaintiffs is attempting to address the finding that "the district suffers from a pervasive, substantial, and systemic inability to deliver special education services in compliance with special education law" (*Chanda Smith v. LAUSD* Consultant's Report, 1995, p. 3). The consent decree called for compliance with the least restrictive environment (LRE) requirements of the law (e.g., creation of inclusive options, reduction in the number of special day classes serving students with disabilities). It requires extensive and ongoing staff development.

Corey H. v. Chicago Board of Education was a major class-action lawsuit filed in 1992. The lawsuit charged the defendants with systemic failure to educate students with disabilities in the LRE. In deciding the case, Judge Gettleman said, "Chicago Public Schools have languished in an atmosphere of separate and unequal education for children with emotional, mental, and behavioral disabilities" (LRP Publications, 1998, p. 4). In addition, Gettleman stated, "The ISBE [Illinois State Board of Education] continues to this day to deny the seriousness of the [Chicago Board of Education's] noncompliance with the LRE mandate, and continues to deny its own clear statutory obligations to ensure compliance by the city" (LRP Publications, 1998, p. 4). According to the settlement eventually reached in the case, the school district has until 2000 to bring between one third and one half of its 553 schools into LRE compliance, at an approximate cost of $24 million (LRP Publications, 1998, pp. 4–5).

Gaskin v. Commonwealth of Pennsylvania (1995) is a suit of similar breadth brought on behalf of 98% of the 282,340 children enrolled in Pennsylvania's special education programs. This ongoing suit charges local school districts with failure to provide adequate personnel development, supplementary aids, and support services to students placed in general education classes.

A 1999 U.S. Supreme Court decision (*Cedar Rapids Community School District v. Garret F.*) focused on a high school student whose spinal cord was severed at age 4 in a motorcycle accident. The accident left him paralyzed and in need of heath care services, including urinary tract catheterization, tracheostomy, tube sectioning, ambu-bagging during suctioning, and ventilator monitoring. Initially, Garret's family assumed responsibility for his health care needs in school by providing it themselves or by paying others to provide it. In 1993, they requested that the school district pay for the services. The district refused.

The U.S. Supreme Court's decision was clear: School districts are responsible for paying for health care for students who require an appropriate education in the LRE in a manner that ensures their health and safety. If school districts apply the traditional model of cost savings, students with complex health care needs might be placed where the services are (i.e., in schools in which there already are nurses) or clustered together in classes in which health care services could be provided to several students. These service delivery models threaten the mandate of educating students in the LRE.

Proceduralism

It is estimated that, across the United States, from 35% to 50% of special educators' time is devoted to assessment and other documentation related to students' IEPs (Vermont State Department of Education, 1990). Unfortunately, much of the assessment conducted yields little diagnostic information to assist educators in their instruction. Instead, it enables professionals to comply with the legal requirement to categorize students as apples, oranges, or potatoes. Given the widely varying eligibility criteria from one state to the next, particularly in the area of learning disabilities, Ysseldyke (1987) concluded that, on any given day, more than 80% of a school's student body can be classified as having learning disabilities. Even if labels were consistently valid and reliable, there is no evidence suggesting that all children who are given a particular global label (e.g., "autistic," "mentally retarded," "emotional-behavioral disordered," "learning disabled," "severely disabled," "gifted and talented") learn in the same way, are motivated by the same goals or stimuli, or have the same gifts or challenges. As teachers intuitively know, homogeneity among groups of children is a myth.

The proceduralism in special education that mushroomed from the mid-1970s through the 1990s in attempts to implement IDEA clearly focused on the procedures and proxy measures of progress and often unreliable, invalid, instructionally uniform assessment procedures and outcomes. For some parents, special educators, and advocates, procedural issues such as the ones raised here have been enough to fire a call for change in an education system that labels and segregates nearly half of children based on educationally questionable assessment instruments and student-monitoring procedures.

Population Increases

A major concern, particularly for special educators who must assess and then serve those students identified as having disabilities, is the rising number of children who are eligible for special education. For instance, from fiscal year (FY) 1977 to FY 1990, the number of students who were deemed eligible for special education increased by 23% (Fuchs & Fuchs, 1994). In the decade from 1977 to 1987, the number of children labeled as having learning disabilities alone increased by 119% (Lipsky & Gartner, 1989). A portion of these increases can be accounted for by North American educational practices that for far too long provided insufficient or no services for students with even mild disabilities. The staggering and continuing annual rise in numbers is so out of hand, however, that nationally "nearly 50% of our students receive services from or are eligible for a variety of special programs serving students with disabilities, economic or social disadvantages, special talents, etc." (Vermont State Department of Education, 1993, p. 1). Given this fact, educators must stop and ask themselves, Is the disability in the child, or is the disability in the education system we have created?

Disjointed Incrementalism

There has been much discussion about the dual systems of general and special education. In reality, the United States does not have a dual system but a multiple system of education. Aside from general and special education, there is adult education, vocational education, gifted education, rural education, bilingual education, English as a second language education, at-risk education, and more. As pointed out previously, it is increasingly difficult for any child to be eligible solely for general education. Of course, all of these programs, at their inception, are well intended. The problem is that they were launched separately in a disjointed and incremental fashion with their own eligibility criteria, funding formulas, and advocacy groups. That so many "special" programs have been created for so many children suggests that general education, as conceptualized and organized at the turn of the 21st century, is failing an increasing proportion of children.

Funding

Costs associated with the exclusion of children can be significant in terms of dollars as well as in other human terms. For example, for FY 1994, the federal government spent more than $2.5 billion dollars on special education, while local school districts spent $3 billion dollars in addition to general busing costs to transport children with disabilities to special education placements, primarily away from their local schools (Hehir, 1994). The anticipated cost of educating children with disabilities in local school general education was an early 1980s argument for why inclusive education was not possible. Since then, communities across the United States have demonstrated that educating all children in local school general education classrooms does not necessarily cost more. In some cases, the reduction in separate busing costs and the elimination of duplicate services have saved money that then could be used to enrich instructional resources in local general education classrooms, thus benefiting many more children.

Interestingly, some opponents of inclusion have criticized the goal of potential cost savings from returning children to their "home" schools as inappropriate if not unethical. Inclusion should not be promoted for financial reasons alone; educators always must advocate for what is best for children. There is nothing wrong, however, with being fiscally responsible. As already noted, education often has squandered its resources through poor coordination and poor communication among programs, service providers, and advocacy efforts. It is estimated that as much as 55% of all special education funding is used for identification, testing, administration, and other noninstruction services (Rothstein & Miles, 1995).

State formulas for funding special education also have created barriers to progress toward more-inclusive education options. At one time, state funding formulas provided fiscal incentives for serving children with special needs in separate or segregated classrooms and programs. For example, until the mid-1990s, Texas's funding formula for special education paid local school districts 10 times more for instructing students in separate rather than in general classrooms. As a result, Texas had the lowest percentage of students in the United States (5%) receiving an education in general classrooms. In contrast, in 1988, Vermont changed to a fiscally neutral funding formula. The formula offers no incentives or disincentives for placing children with disabilities in general classrooms and allows dollars to follow children rather than be designated for particular programs or places. In 1993, 5 years following Vermont's enactment of Act 230, 90% of Vermont's children who were eligible for special education were educated in general classes. In the 1997 IDEA Amendments, the federal government recognized the need for nationwide reform of state funding formulas and required states that had not already done so to develop placement-neutral funding formulas.

Demonstrations

> More is learned from a single success than from multiple failures. A single success proves it can be done—whatever is, is possible. (Klopf, 1979, p. 40)

Implementation of inclusive schooling practices involves new roles and responsibilities for education personnel and students alike. Klopf's observation highlights the importance of having models to give members of the school community hope for their own success, examples to follow, and veterans to talk with about the implications of change in their lives. The good news is that examples of inclusive education exist in every one of the 50 states (Webb, 1994). Further good news is that general and special education teachers and administrators who have experienced successfully the full inclusion of students with mild, moderate, and severe disabilities (Villa, Thousand, Meyers, & Nevin, 1996) liked it and favored educating students in general education environments through collaborative relationships among all educators. Not surprisingly, administrative support and collaboration were the most powerful predictors of positive attitudes toward inclusion.

Philosophy

A final compelling rationale for education reform is that categorical segregation of any subgroup of people is simply a violation of civil rights and the principle of equal citizenship. Many believe what U.S. Supreme Court Chief Justice Earl Warren wrote in the landmark *Brown v. Board of Education* decision, that separateness in education can

> Generate a feeling of inferiority as to [children's] status in the community that may affect their hearts and minds in a way unlikely ever to be

undone. This sense of inferiority . . . affects the motivation of a child to learn . . . [and] has a tendency to retard . . . educational and mental development. (1954, 347 U.S. at 493)

Many advocates of inclusive education see the parallels with other struggles for human and civil rights and recall images of school administrators of the 1950s and 1960s blocking "white" schoolhouse doors in order to keep out African American children. They are saddened by the fact that, in far too many communities, school officials still block the doors, but this time to keep out children with disabilities. They know that the primary determinant of whether a child with disabilities has access to general education is *where* the child's family happens to live.

Inclusive education also has come to be viewed as part of the reform effort derived from and reviving Dewey's (1916) philosophy and purpose of education in a democratic society. Those involved in the inclusive schooling movement, like those involved in democratic schooling,

> See themselves as participants in communities of learning. By their very nature, these communities are diverse, and that diversity is prized, not viewed as a problem. Such communities include people who reflect differences in age, culture, ethnicity, gender, socioeconomic class, aspirations, and abilities. These differences enrich the community and the range of views it might consider. Separating people of any age on the basis of these differences or using labels to stereotype them simply creates divisions and status systems that detract from the democratic nature of the community and the dignity of the individuals against whom such practices work so harshly.
>
> While the community prizes diversity, it also has a sense of shared purpose. . . . The common good is a central feature of democracy. For this reason, the communities of learners in democratic schools are marked by an emphasis on cooperation and collaboration rather than competition. (Apple & Beane, 1995, p. 10)

CONCLUSIONS

Much has been accomplished and much remains to be done so that all students with disabilities are welcomed, valued, supported, and educated in shared classroom and school environments to attain the desired goals of education (e.g., belonging, mastery, independence, generosity). Despite a steady historical trend toward inclusion facilitated by a growing understanding of compelling rationales such as those presented in this book, the majority of the more than 5.6 million students with identified disabilities in the United States still are educated primarily in places other than general education classrooms (*National*

Study of Inclusive Education, 1995). Why? Because change is a complex process that requires individual change at the most local level. As Furney and colleagues observed,

> Current best practice and research views policy implementation (e.g., LRE implementation in the form of inclusive educational options) not as an event, but as a slow incremental multi-faceted process that must take into account local context and values (Fullan & Stiegelbauer, 1991); encourage the development of local capacity and will (McLaughlin, 1987); and empower local implementers to take ownership for implementing, evaluating, revising, and incorporating changes into daily practice (Fullan & Stiegelbauer, 1991, quoted in Furney, Hasazi, & Destefano, 1997, p. 344)

There is no single, simple method for promoting a complex change such as inclusive education. Ambrose (1987), however, identified five variables (elaborated in Chapter 5) that must receive attention for any change process, including restructuring for inclusive schooling, to be successful. The variables are *vision, skills, incentives, resources,* and *action planning.*

Vision

Clearly, the inclusive education movement has progressed because of educators, parents, policy makers, students, and consumers who have persevered, articulated, and built consensus for their inclusive vision. The result has been schools and school districts across the United States implementing complex systems change initiatives to restructure in ways that welcome, value, and support the diverse learning needs of students with disabilities in general education environments. The Kentucky Education Department concluded, in a follow-up study of 42 schools implementing inclusive education practices, that it did not matter whether the schools began inclusion as a pilot project or adopted it "whole hog." Effective and durable inclusive education programs developed in Kentucky as long as there was a shared vision (i.e., an agenda) with respect to including all students in general education accompanied by responsive professional development activities (National Study of Inclusive Education, 1995).

Skills

Educators' skills also need to develop so that they have both competence and confidence to support inclusive schools and classrooms; they need knowledge about and practice in research-based inclusive practices (Falvey, 1995). Fortunately, at the turn of the 21st century, there are a number of proven organizational, curricular, instructional, and assessment strategies for promoting inclusive education. Co-teaching, collaboration, consultation, creative problem solving, peer-mediated instruction (e.g., cooperative group learning, peer tutoring), mastery teaching, alternate forms of assessment, positive approaches to challenging behavior, reciprocal teaching, social skills training, instructional reinforcement, and educational support teams are but a few of the strategies (Falvey, Grenot-Scheyer, Coots, & Bishop, 1995; Lipsky & Gartner, 1997; Schrag, 1994; Schrag & Burnette, 1993; Thousand et al., 1994; Villa & Thousand, 1995; Villa, Thousand, & Chapple, 1996).

Resources and Incentives

Educators experienced with the inclusion of students with disabilities have identified time, collaboration, administrative support, ongoing training, and technical assistance as some of the resources and incentives for supporting and sustaining school-based inclusion planning and implementation efforts (Villa, Thousand, Meyers, & Nevin, 1996).

Action Planning

Finally, creating inclusive classrooms and schools for students with disabilities requires a creative and collaborative action planning process to 1) challenge and support changes in attitudes and beliefs; 2) construct a new, inclusive culture; and 3) implement new ways of thinking, teaching, assessing, and interacting with colleagues, students, and families. As Curtis and Stollar (1996) observed, action planning through self-analytical and problem-solving methods, combined with sustained effort, brings about system-level improvement. The remaining chapters of this book offer strategies and examples to assist readers to facilitate the creation of inclusive classrooms and schools in their communities.

REFERENCES

Ambrose, D. (1987). *Managing complex change.* Pittsburgh, PA: Enterprise Group.

Apple, M., & Beane, J. (1995). *Democratic schools.* Alexandria, VA: Association for Supervision and Curriculum Development.

Association for Supervision and Curriculum Development (ASCD). (1992). *Resolutions, 1991.* Alexandria, VA: Author.

Baker, E., Wang, M., & Walberg, H. (1994). The effects of inclusion on learning. *Educational Leadership, 52*(4), 33–35.

Biklen, D. (1985). *The complete school: Integrating special and regular education.* New York: Teachers College Press.

Biklen, D. (Producer). (1988). *Regular lives* [Videotape]. Washington, DC: State of the Art.

Block, J.H., & Haring, T.G. (1992). On swamps, bogs, alligators, and special educational reform. In R.A. Villa, J.S. Thousand, W.C. Stainback, & S.B. Stainback (Eds.), *Restructuring for caring and effective education: An administrative guide to creating heterogeneous schools* (1st ed., pp. 7–24). Baltimore: Paul H. Brookes Publishing Co.

Brendtro, L., Brokenleg, M., & Van Bockern, S. (1990). *Reclaiming youth at risk: Our hope for the future.* Bloomington, IN: National Educational Service.

Brown v. Board of Education, 347 U.S. 483 (1954).

Brown, L., Long, E., Udvari-Solner, A., Schwarz, P., VanDeventeer, P., Ahlgren, S., Johnson, F., Grunewald, L., & Jorgensen, J. (1989). Should students with severe intellectual disabilities be based in regular or in special education classrooms in home schools? *Journal of The Association for Persons with Severe Handicaps, 14,* 8–12.

Burrello, L., & Tourgee, B. (Eds.). (1990, June). *Principal letters: Practices for inclusion.* Bloomington: Indiana University, National Academy/Council of Administrators of Special Education.

Cedar Rapids Community School District v. Garret F., No. 96-1793 (U.S. 1999).

Chanda Smith v. Los Angeles Unified School District, No. 93-7044-LEW (GHKX) (C.D. Cal. 1993).

Chanda Smith v. Los Angeles Unified School District Consultant's Report. (1995). (Available from the Chanda Smith Consent Decree Office, LAUSD, 450 North Grand Street, Los Angeles, CA 90012-2100)

Cole, D.A., & Meyer, L.H. (1991). Social integration and severe disabilities: A longitudinal analysis of child outcomes. *Journal of Special Education, 25,* 340–351.

Comer, J. (1988). Educating poor minority children. *Scientific American, 25*(9), 42–48.

Corey H. v. Chicago Board of Education and Illinois State Board of Education, No. 92 C 3409 (N.D. Ill. 1992).

Costello, C. (1991). *A comparison of student cognitive and social achievement for handicapped and regular education students who are educated in integrated versus a substantially separate classroom.* Unpublished doctoral dissertation, University of Massachusetts at Amherst.

Council for Exceptional Children (CEC). (1994). *Creating schools for all our students: What 12 schools have to say: Working Forum on Inclusive Schools.* Reston, VA: Author.

Council for Exceptional Children (CEC). (1995). *Inclusive schools: Lessons from 10 schools.* Reston, VA: Author.

Curtis, M., & Stollar, S. (1996). Best practices in system level consultation and organizational change. In T. Thomas & J. Grimes (Eds.), *Best practices in school psychology* (pp. 11–18). Washington, DC: National Association of School Psychologists.

Dewey, J. (1916). *Democracy and education: An introduction to the philosophy of education.* New York: Macmillan.

Duncan, D.A. (1987, February). *A response to educating students with learning problems: A shared responsibility.* Paper presented at the Annual Meeting of the American Association for Colleges of Teacher Education, Washington, DC.

Education for all Handicapped Children Act of 1975, PL 94-142, 20 U.S.C. §§ 1400 *et seq.*

Falvey, M.A. (Ed.). (1995). *Inclusive and heterogeneous schooling: Assessment, curriculum, and instruction.* Baltimore: Paul H. Brookes Publishing Co.

Falvey, M.A., Grenot-Scheyer, M., Coots, J.J., & Bishop, K.D. (1995). Services for students with disabilities: Past and present. In M.A. Falvey (Ed.), *Inclusive and heterogeneous schooling: Assessment, curriculum, and instruction* (pp. 23–39). Baltimore: Paul H. Brookes Publishing Co.

Ferguson, P., & Ash, A. (1989). Lessons from life: Personal and parental perspectives on school, childhood, and disability. In D. Biklen, D. Ferguson, & A. Ford (Eds.), *Schooling and disability* (pp. 108–140). Chicago: National Society for the Study of Education.

Fuchs, D., & Fuchs, L.S. (1994). Inclusive schools movement and the radicalization of special education reform. *Exceptional Children, 60,* 294–309.

Fullan, M.G., & Stiegelbauer, S.M. (1991). *The new meaning of educational change* (2nd ed.). New York: Teachers College Press.

Furney, K.S., Hasazi, S.B., & Destefano, L. (1997). Transition policies, practices, and promises: Lessons from three states. *Exceptional Children, 63*(3), 343–355.

Gartner, A., & Lipsky, D.K. (1987). Beyond special education: Toward a quality education system for all students. *Harvard Educational Review, 57,* 367–395.

Gaskin v. Commonwealth of Pennsylvania, 23 *Individuals with Disabilities Education Law Report* (IDELR) 61 (Pa. 1995).

Glasser, W. (1998). *Choice theory in the classroom.* New York: HarperPerennial.

Goals 2000: Educate America Act of 1994, PL 103-227, 20 U.S.C. §§ 5801 *et seq.*

Hehir, T. (1994, January). *Toward a better outcome for students with disabilities.* Paper presented at the Texas Council of Administrators of Special Education Mid-Winter Conference, Austin, TX.

Hocutt, A.M. (1996). Effectiveness of special education: Is placement the critical factor? *Special Education for Students with Disabilities, 6*(1), 77–103.

Hollowood, T.M., Salisbury, C.L., Rainforth, B., & Palombaro, M.M. (1995). Use of instructional time in classrooms serving students with and without severe disabilities. *Exceptional Children, 61*(3), 242–253.

Hunt, P., Farron-Davis, F., Beckstead, S., Curtis, D., & Goetz, L. (1994). Evaluating the effects of placement of students with severe disabilities in general education versus special classes. *Journal of The Association for Persons with Severe Handicaps, 19*(3), 200–214.

Individuals with Disabilities Education Act (IDEA) Amendments of 1997, PL 105-17, 20 U.S.C. §§ 1400 *et seq.*

Individuals with Disabilities Education Act (IDEA) of 1990, PL 101-476, 20 U.S.C. §§ 1400 *et seq.*

Jenkins, J., Pious, C., & Jewell, M. (1990). Special education and the regular education initiative: Basic assumptions. *Exceptional Children, 56*, 479–491.

Kaskinen-Chapman, A. (1992). Saline area schools and inclusive community CONCEPTS (Collaborative of Networks: Community, Educators, Parents, The Workplace, and Students). In R.A. Villa, J.S. Thousand, W.C. Stainback, & S.B. Stainback (Eds.), *Restructuring for caring and effective education: An administrative guide to creating heterogeneous schools* (1st ed., pp. 169–185). Baltimore: Paul H. Brookes Publishing Co.

Keller, B. (1995). Accelerated schools: Hands-on learning in a unified community. *Educational Leadership, 52*(5), 10–13.

Kelly, D. (1992). Introduction. In T. Neary, A. Halvorsen, R. Kronberg, & D. Kelly (Eds.), *Curricular adaptations for inclusive classrooms* (pp. 1–6). San Francisco: California Research Institute for the Integration of Students with Severe Disabilities, San Francisco State University.

Kelly, D., Keefe, E., & VanEtten, G. (1994, December). *Academic and social outcomes for students with moderate to profound disabilities in integrated settings.* Paper presented at conference of The Association for Persons with Severe Handicaps, Atlanta.

Klopf, G.J. (1979). *The principal and staff development in the school with a special focus on the role of the principal in mainstreaming.* New York: Bank Street College of Education.

Knoblock, P. (1982). *Teaching and mainstreaming autistic children.* Denver: Love Publishing Co.

Kozol, J. (1991). *Savage inequalities: Children in America's schools.* New York: Crown Publishers.

Lerner, J. (1987). The regular education initiative: Some unanswered questions. *Learning Disabilities Focus, 3*(1), 3–7.

Levin, H. (1987). Accelerated schools for disadvantaged students. *Educational Leadership, 44*(6), 19–21.

Lieberman, L.M. (1985). Special education and regular education: A merger made in heaven? *Exceptional Children, 51,* 513–516.

Lilly, M.S. (1986). The relationship between general and special education: A new face on an old issue. *Counterpoint, 6*(1), 10.

Lipsky, D.K., & Gartner, A. (Eds.). (1989). *Beyond separate education: Quality education for all.* Baltimore: Paul H. Brookes Publishing Co.

Lipsky, D.K., & Gartner, A. (1997). *Inclusion and school reform: Transforming America's classrooms.* Baltimore: Paul H. Brookes Publishing Co.

LRP Publications. (1998). Illinois held liable for Chicago's noncompliance. *Inclusive Education Programs: Advice on Educating Students with Disabilities in Regular Settings, 5*(4), 4–5.

Maslow, A.H. (1987). *Motivation and personality* (3rd ed.). New York: HarperCollins.

McCarthy, J.M. (1987). A response to the regular education/special education initiative. *Learning Disabilities Focus, 1,* 75–77.

McLaughlin, M. (1987). Learning from experience: Lessons from policy implementation. *Educational Evaluation and Policy Analysis, 9*(2), 171–178.

Messinger, J.F. (1985). Commentary on a rationale for the merger of regular and special education, or, Is it now time for the lamb to lie down with the lion? *Exceptional Children, 51,* 510–512.

National Association of State Boards of Education (NASBE), Study Group on Special Education. (1992). *Winners all: A call for inclusive schools.* Alexandria, VA: Author.

National Education Association. (1997). *The integration of students with special needs into regular classrooms: Policies and practices that work.* Washington, DC: Author.

National Study of Inclusive Education. (1995). New York: City Univer-sity of New York, National Center on Educational Restructuring and Inclusion.

Neary, T., Halvorsen, A., Kronberg, R., & Kelly, D. (1992, December). *Curricular adaptations for inclusive classrooms.* San Francisco: California Research Institute for the Integration of Students with Severe Disabilities, San Francisco State University.

Nevin, A.I., Thousand, J.S., Paolucci-Whitcomb, P., & Villa, R.A. (1990). Collaborative consultation: Empowering public school personnel to provide heterogeneous schooling for all, or, Who rang that bell? *Journal of Educational and Psychological Consultation, 1*(1), 41–67.

Oberti v. Board of Education, 995 F.2d 1204 (3rd Cir. 1993).

O'Neil, J. (1995). On lasting school reform: A conversation with Ted Sizer. *Educational Leadership, 52*(5), 14–19.

Ramirez-Smith, C. (1995). Stopping the cycle of failure: The Comer model. *Educational Leadership, 52*(5), 4–9.

Reynolds, J.C., Wang, M.C., & Walberg, H.J. (1987). The necessary restructuring of special and regular education. *Exceptional Children, 53*, 391–398.

Roncker v. Walter, 700 F.2d 1058 (6th Cir. 1983), cert. denied, 464 U.S. 864 (1983).

Rothstein, R., & Miles, K.H. (1995). *Where's the money gone? Changes in the level and composition of educational spending.* Washington, DC: Economic Policy Institute.

Sacramento City Unified School District v. Rachel H., 14 F.3d 1398 (9th Cir. 1994).

Sailor, W. (1989). The educational, social, and vocational integration of students with the most severe disabilities. In D.K. Lipsky & A. Gartner (Eds.), *Beyond separate education: Quality education for all* (pp. 53–75). Baltimore: Paul H. Brookes Publishing Co.

Schrag, J. (1994). *Organizational, instructional, and curricular strategies to facilitate the implementation of inclusive school practices.* Reston, VA: Council for Exceptional Children.

Schrag, J., & Burnette, J. (1993). Inclusive schools. *Research Roundup, 10*(2), 1–5. (Reston, VA: National Association of Elementary School Principals)

Scherer, M. (1992/1993). On savage inequalities: A conversation with Jonathan Kozol. *Educational Leadership, 50*, 4–9.

Sharpe, M.N., York, J.L., & Knight, J. (1994). Effects of inclusion on the academic performance of classmates without disabilities. *Remedial and Special Education, 15*(5), 281–287.

Sizer, T.R. (1984). *Horace's compromise: The dilemma of the American high school.* Boston: Houghton Mifflin.

Skrtic, T. (1991). The special education paradox: Equity as the way to excellence. *Harvard Educational Review, 61*, 148–206.

Slavin, R.E. (1997). Including inclusion is school reform: Success for all and roots and wings. In D.K. Lipsky & A. Gartner (Eds.), *Inclusion and school reform: Transforming America's classrooms* (pp. 375–387). Baltimore: Paul H. Brookes Publishing Co.

Slavin, R.E., Madden, N., Dolan, L., & Wasik, B. (1993). *Success for all in the Baltimore public schools: Year 6 report.* Baltimore: The Johns Hopkins University, Center for Research on Effective Schooling for Disadvantaged Students.

Stainback, S.B., & Stainback, W.C. (1985). *Integration of students with severe handicaps into regular schools.* Reston, VA: Council for Exceptional Children.

Stainback, S.B., & Stainback, W.C. (1990). Inclusive schooling. In W.C. Stainback & S.B. Stainback (Eds.), *Support networks for inclusive school-*

ing: Interdependent integrated education (pp. 25–36). Baltimore: Paul H. Brookes Publishing Co.

Stainback, S.B., & Stainback, W.C. (1992). *Curriculum considerations for inclusive classrooms: Facilitating learning for all students.* Baltimore: Paul H. Brookes Publishing Co.

Stainback, S.B., Stainback, W.C., & Forest, M. (Eds.). (1989). *Educating all students in the mainstream of regular education.* Baltimore: Paul H. Brookes Publishing Co.

Stainback, W.C., & Stainback, S.B. (1984). A rationale for the merger of special and regular education. *Exceptional Children, 51,* 102–111.

Stainback, W.C., Stainback, S.B., & Bunch, G. (1989). Introduction and historical background. In S.B. Stainback, W.C. Stainback, & M. Forest (Eds.), *Educating all students in the mainstream of regular education* (pp. 3–14). Baltimore: Paul H. Brookes Publishing Co.

Staub, D., & Peck, C.A. (1994). What are the outcomes for nondisabled students? *Educational Leadership, 52*(4), 36–40.

Strain, P. (1983). Generalization of autistic children's social behavior change: Effects of developmentally integrated and segregated settings. *Analysis and Intervention in Developmental Disabilities, 3,* 23–34.

Strully, J., & Strully, C. (1985). Teach your children. *Canadian Journal on Mental Retardation, 35*(4), 3–11.

Thousand, J.S., Fox, T., Reid, R., Godek, J., Williams, W., & Fox, W. (1986). *The homecoming model: Educating students who present intensive educational challenges within regular education environments* (Monograph No. 7-1). Burlington: University of Vermont, Center for Developmental Disabilities.

Thousand, J.S., & Villa, R.A. (1991). A futuristic view of the REI: A response to Jenkins, Pious, and Jewell. *Exceptional Children, 57,* 556–562.

Thousand, J.S., Villa, R.A., & Nevin, A.I. (1994). *Creativity and collaborative learning: A practical guide to empowering students and teachers.* Baltimore: Paul H. Brookes Publishing Co.

Timothy W. v. Rochester, New Hampshire, School District, 825 F.2d 954 (1st Cir. 1989).

Udvari-Solner, A., & Thousand, J.S. (1995). Promising practices that foster inclusive education. In R.A. Villa & J.S. Thousand (Eds.), *Creating an inclusive school* (pp. 87–109). Alexandria, VA: Association for Supervision and Curriculum Development.

U.S. Department of Education. (1995). *Sixteenth annual report to Congress on the implementation of the Individuals with Disabilities Education Act.* Washington, DC: Author.

U.S. Department of Education. (1997). *Seventeenth annual report to Congress on the implementation of the Individuals with Disabilities Education Act.* Washington, DC: Author.

Vermont State Department of Education. (1990). *Report of the Special Commission on Special Education, State of Vermont.* Montpelier: Author.

Vermont State Department of Education. (1993). *Vermont's Act 230 three years later: A report on the impact of Act 230.* Montpelier: Author.

Vermont State Department of Education. (1994). *Act 230 evaluation: 1993–1994 preliminary results.* Montpelier: Author.

Vermont State Department of Education. (1995). *Vermont's Act 230 and special education funding and cost study.* Montpelier: Author.

Villa, R.A., & Thousand, J.S. (1988). Enhancing success in heterogeneous classrooms and schools: The powers of partnership. *Teacher Education and Special Education, 11,* 144–154.

Villa, R.A., & Thousand, J.S. (Eds.). (1995). *Creating an inclusive school.* Alexandria, VA: Association for Supervision and Curriculum Development.

Villa, R.A., Thousand, J.S., & Chapple, J. (1996). Preparing teachers to support inclusion: Preservice and inservice programs. *Theory into Practice, 35*(1), 42–50.

Villa, R.A., Thousand, J.S., Meyers, H., & Nevin, A.I. (1996). Teacher and administrator perceptions of heterogeneous education. *Exceptional Children, 63*(1), 29–45.

Villa, R.A., Thousand, J.S., Paolucci-Whitcomb, P., & Nevin, A.I. (1990). In search of new paradigms for collaborative consultation. *Journal of Educational and Psychological Consultation, 1,* 279–292.

Villa, R.A., Thousand, J.S., Stainback, W.C., & Stainback, S.B. (Eds.). (1992). *Restructuring for caring and effective education: An administrative guide to creating heterogeneous schools* (1st ed.). Baltimore: Paul H. Brookes Publishing Co.

Wagner, M. (1989). Youth with disabilities during transition: An overview and description of findings from the National Longitudinal Transition Study. In J.G. Chadsey-Rusch (Ed.), *Transition Institute at Illinois: Project director's report.* Urbana: University of Illinois.

Wagner, M., Newman, L., D'Amico, R., Jay, E.D., Butler-Nalin, P., Marder, C., & Cox, R. (Eds.). (1991). *The National Longitudinal Transition Study of special education students.* Menlo Park, CA: SRI International.

Wang, M.C., Reynolds, M.C., & Walberg, H.J. (Eds.). (1987). *Handbook of special education: Research and practice* (2 vols.). New York: Pergamon Press.

Webb, N. (1994). Special education: With new court decisions behind them, advocates see inclusion as a question of values. *Harvard Educational Letter, 10*(4), 1–3.

Wiederholt, L.J. (Ed.). (1988, January). Special series: The regular education initiative [Entire issue]. *Journal of Learning Disabilities, 21*(1).

Will, M. (1985, December). *Educating children with learning problems: A shared responsibility.* Paper presented at the Wingspread Conference on The Education of Special Needs Students: Research Findings and Implications for Practice, Racine, WI.

Will, M. (1986a). Educating children with learning problems: A shared responsibility. *Exceptional Children, 52,* 411–414.

Will, M. (1986b). *Educating students with learning problems: A shared responsibility.* Washington, DC: U.S. Department of Education, Office of Special Education and Rehabilitative Services.

Williams, W., Villa, R.A., Thousand, J.S., & Fox, W. (1993). Is regular class placement really the issue? A response to Brown, Long, Udvari-Solner, Schwarz, VanDeventeer, Ahlgren, Johnson, Grunewald, & Jorgensen. *Journal of The Association for Persons with Severe Handicaps, 14,* 333–334.

Ysseldyke, J.E. (1987). Classification of handicapped students. In M.C. Wang, M.C. Reynolds, & H.J. Walberg (Eds.), *Handbook of special education: Research and practice: Vol. 1. Learner characteristics and adaptive education* (pp. 253–271). New York: Pergamon Press.

Chapter 2

Inclusion and School Restructuring
A New Synergy

Alan Gartner and Dorothy Kerzner Lipsky

The Individuals with Disabilities Education Act (IDEA) Amendments of 1997 (PL 105-17), which included Congress' reauthorization of the Individuals with Disabilities Education Act (IDEA) of 1990 (PL 101-476), represented the end of a period during which special education was a discrete program activity and provided the basis for inclusive education to become an intrinsic part of broad-scale school restructuring, thereby creating the potential for a new synergy. In the late 1990s, there was a steady if small increase in the number and percentage of students with disabilities who were educated in "regular classes."[1] Federal data from the mid-1990s (for the 1994–1995 school year) showed that 45% of students with disabilities were being served in general education class-

---

[1]In its reports, the U.S. Department of Education classifies students with disabilities as receiving their education in general class environments if they receive no more than 20% of their education in classrooms in other than general education environments (i.e., in resource rooms or in other more restrictive environments).

room environments; this figure is up from 37% in the 1989–1990 school year ("More IDEA students," 1997, p. 3). The bulk of this change represented a shift from students served in resource rooms to those served in general classes. The number of students served in separate classes or more restrictive environments has remained relatively stable.

Although some school districts have made inclusive education a districtwide initiative, more frequently it is a program of an individual school, according to the National Center on Educational Restructuring and Inclusion (NCERI) (1994–1995). Inclusive education, for the most part, is neither systemic nor typical in school districts.

1997 IDEA AMENDMENTS

Despite a drumbeat of attacks on inclusion in the 1990s, Congress, in its deliberations concerning the reauthorization of IDEA, never gave serious attention to weakening the law's requirement that students with disabilities be educated to the maximum extent appropriate alongside children without disabilities. As Laski noted,

> The Senate Committee makes clear that the re-enactment of this federal obligation is purposeful and serious. The Report states, "the Committee supports the long-standing policy that, to the maximum extent appropriate, children with disabilities are [to be] educated with children who are non-disabled." (1997, p. 22)

Indeed, Congress shifted the burden of school districts from specifying the extent to which a child with disabilities would participate with children without disabilities to requiring in the student's individualized education program (IEP) an explanation of the extent to which the child with disabilities will not participate with such children. In effect, Congress was saying that such participation is to be typical and that exclusion must be explained and justified. The basic presumption becomes that children with disabilities are to be educated in general education classrooms with their same-age peers unless there is a compelling educational justification for educating the child with a disability in a noninclusive environment.

Reauthorization Effects on the IEP and the IEP Team

In its description of the 1997 IDEA reauthorization, the Disability Rights Education and Defense Fund (DREDF) pointed out (Lipton, 1997) that the federal courts, in determining whether a general education class with supplementary aids and services is appropriate for a child with a disability, requires that the IEP team address four sets of factors:

1. The educational or academic benefits for the child in the general education class as compared with the benefits of a special education classroom

2. The nonacademic benefits of integration for the child with a disability

3. The effect of the presence of a child with a disability on the teacher and the other children in the general education classroom and whether the use of supplemental aids and services can lessen any negative effects

4. Whether the costs of supplementary aids and services would have a negative effect on the education of the other children in the entire school district[2]

Thus, DREDF concludes,

> When the IEP team makes a determination of whether placement in a regular class is appropriate for a particular child, the full range of supplementary aids and services, such as itinerant teachers, related services, paraprofessionals and assistive technology devices and services must be considered. (Lipton, 1997, p. 16)

The IEP must include the use of such supplementary aids and support services for children and teachers, as well as program modifications in the child's instruction and assessment, to enable the child to 1) attain his or her IEP goals, 2) be involved and participate in the general education curriculum, and 3) be educated with and participate in extracurricular and other nonacademic activities with children without disabilities. These requirements reinforce the language of the Findings section of the 1997 IDEA reauthorization, so that special education can become a service for children with disabilities rather than a place where they are sent. This is further reinforced by the requirement that a general education teacher participate in the IEP process if the child is or may be participating in the general education environment.[3]

---

[2]These four factors were laid out by the Eleventh Circuit in *Greer v. Rome City School District* (1991), one of the four federal appellate-level full inclusion cases (Lipton, 1994).

[3]Because the meeting is a decision-making meeting, it seems inappropriate (if not imprudent) for a school district not to invite a general education teacher to the meeting. Failing to do so would at the least imply a prior decision that services in the general education environment were not appropriate for the child.

Laski (1997) pointed out the importance of defining and requiring supplementary aids and services in the law. Previously, supplementary aids and services were required only in the federal implementing regulations. Declaring that they be provided to enable the child to attain annual goals, be involved and progress in the general education curriculum, participate in extracurricular or nonacademic activities or both, and be educated and participate with children without disabilities prevents parents from having to make the cruel choice of "inclusive placements for socialization versus segregated placements for academic progress. Both progress on IEP goals and progress in the general curriculum are equally important, and the provision of supplementary supports must be directed to the accomplishment of both" (Laski, 1997, p. 23). These changes, as well as those that reinforce and extend parents' rights in the IEP evaluation and placement process, are well-warranted extensions of inclusion at the individual student level.

Reauthorization Effects on the Systemic Level

Other changes provide the basis for viewing the 1997 IDEA reauthorization as taking inclusive education to a new systemic level. Specifically, the Findings section of the law states,

(5) Over 20 years of research and experience has demonstrated that the education of children with disabilities can be made more effective by—

(A) having high expectations for such children and ensuring their access in the general curriculum to the maximum extent possible;

(B) strengthening the role of parents and ensuring that families of such children have meaningful opportunities to participate in the education of their children at school and at home;

(C) coordinating this Act with other local educational service agency, State, and Federal school improvement efforts in order to ensure that such children benefit from such efforts and that special education can become a service for such children rather than a place where they are sent;

(D) providing appropriate special education and related services and aids and supports in the regular classroom to such children, whenever appropriate;

(E) supporting high-quality, intensive professional development for all personnel who work with such children in order to ensure that they have the skills and knowledge necessary to enable them—

(i) to meet developmental goals and, to the maximum extent possible, those challenging expectations that have been established for all children; and

(ii) to be prepared to lead productive, independent, adult lives, to the maximum extent possible;

(F) providing incentives for whole-school approaches and preferral intervention to reduce the need to label children as disabled in order to address their learning needs; and

(G) focusing resources on teaching and learning while reducing paperwork and requirements that do not assist in improving educational results. (§ 101 of the 1997 IDEA Amendments, revising IDEA §§ 601[c][5][A]–601[c][5][G])

In addition to the declarations of the Findings section, the 1997 reauthorization of IDEA promotes inclusive education in several ways:

- IDEA outlaws funding formulas that support students' placement in more rather than less restrictive environments. As studies by the Center on Special Education Finance have abundantly documented (Parrish, 1993; see also ongoing reports by the Center on Special Education Finance), such practices have been typical in most states.

- IDEA authorizes the use of special education funds to support the professional development of all personnel in contact with the child with a disability, including general education classroom teachers and content specialists.

- IDEA states that, in making a determination with regard to a student's eligibility for special education services, lack of instruction in reading or mathematics shall not be a factor; for example, a school cannot accept the inadequacies of instruction in the general education classroom as a basis for declaring that a child has a disability.

- IDEA permits benefits for children without disabilities as a result of the expenditures of special education funds.

- IDEA requires states to establish performance goals for students with disabilities that are consistent with the goals and standards for all children established by the state, to develop indicators to judge these students' progress, and to make public the results of using those indicators. Implementing these provisions will require major changes in practices, perspective, and philosophy.

The 1997 reforms recall the debate of the early 1970s, during the deliberations prior to the 1975 passage of the Education for All Handicapped Children Act (PL 94-142). At that time, there was conflicting testimony among professionals about which students could benefit from education. Finally, tired of the professionals' disputes, Congress, as a matter of belief and ideology more than research-based findings, declared that *all* students were to be served because *all* students could benefit. In the 1997 IDEA Amendments, Congress added an accountability component to service provision and declared that the learning of *all* students must be measured; that it is a matter of public concern; and that the results are to be incorporated in the overall reports for a school, a district, and a state. As noted researcher Ysseldyke observed, "We value only what we measure, and if [students with disabilities] are not in the picture, then people assume that they're not responsible for educating [such students]. Out of sight is out of mind" (quoted in NCERI, 1994–1995, p. 3). Of course, it is equally true that educators measure only what they value.[4]

The changes incorporated in the 1997 reauthorization of IDEA might have allowed Congress to retitle the legislation the *Inclusion Development and Expansion Act*. Without ever using the word *inclusion*, Congress dramatically supported it not only at the level of the individual child with a disability but also as a matter of systemic reform. The new law has the potential to change and to have a positive effect on education for students with disabilities equal to that of its predecessor, PL 94-142. Just as the 1975 law brought students with disabilities (which were called *handicaps* in the mid-1970s) *into* the schoolhouse, the 1997 amendments provide the basis for making them *full members* of the school community. In the years to come, the public is likely to hear less about LRE and more about free, appropriate public education (FAPE). Specifically, in the 21st century, school policies and practices need to focus on and interpret the meaning of appropriateness—in the context of full participation and what is expected of students in general. Curriculum access, outcomes less acceptable than those for other children, and services apart from other children no longer will be accepted as typical. Instead, they will become matters to be explained and justified.

INCLUSIVE EDUCATION IN PRACTICE

What has about a quarter century of the implementation of PL 94-142 (known today as IDEA) taught educators about what facilitates successful inclusive education? Analysis of the reports from some 1,000 school districts on their inclusive education efforts in the National Study of Inclusive Education (NCERI, 1994–1995) identified at least eight factors for success: visionary leadership, collaboration, refocused use of assessment, support for staff and students, funding, effective

---

[4]Nearly 25 years after the passage of PL 94-142 and after the cumulative expenditure of hundreds of billions of dollars, it is disturbing—if not surprising—to read these words of the associate editor of the American School Boards Association: "For the first time, school boards will have tangible evidence of how well their special education programs are teaching their children" (Vail, 1997, p. 17).

parental involvement, and the implementation of effective program models and classroom practices. These eight factors are congruent with the factors identified in a study of 12 inclusive schools conducted by the Working Forum on Inclusive Schools (Council for Exceptional Children, 1994) convened by 10 national organizations.[5]

Visionary Leadership

Villa, Thousand, Meyers, and Nevin (1996), in a study of 32 inclusive school sites in five states and one Canadian province, found the degree of administrative support to be the most powerful predictor of general and special educators' attitudes toward full inclusion. Whereas traditionally leadership is viewed as emanating from the school superintendent, in districts across the United States the initial impetus for inclusive education has come from many sources. These include superintendents; principals; teachers; other school personnel; parents; and, on occasion, a university or state government project. The issue is less the initiator but more a recognition that, for inclusive education to be successful, all stakeholders ultimately must become involved.

Collaboration

Reports from school districts indicate that the achievement of inclusive education presumes that no one teacher can or ought to be expected to have all of the expertise required to meet the educational needs of all the students in the classroom. Rather, individual teachers must have available to them the support systems that provide collaborative assistance and enable them to engage in cooperative problem solving. Building planning teams, scheduling time for teachers to work together, recognizing teachers as problem solvers, conceptualizing teachers as frontline researchers—these means were all reported as necessary for collaboration.

Kentucky, as part of its comprehensive reform of all of its education programs, has implemented extensive programs to serve all students in an inclusive environment through the development of a wide array of program designs for collaboration among the full array of personnel who serve students. Moll (1997), in discussing this reform initiative, pointed out that the development of any collaborative system requires change and growth in every aspect of the education environment (i.e., personnel, curriculum, instruction strategies, school struc-

---

[5]For a fuller description of the implementation of inclusive education, see Lipsky and Gartner (1997), especially Chapters 10–12. From the growing literature on inclusive education, also see Falvey (1995), Stainback and Stainback (1996), and Villa and Thousand (1995).

ture and organization). She cited five elements that characterize a collaborative school:

1. The belief that the quality of education is largely determined by what happens at the school site.
2. The conviction that instruction is most effective in a school environment characterized by norms of collegiality and continuous improvement.
3. The belief that teachers are responsible for the instructional process and accountable for outcomes for all students.
4. The use of a wide range of practices and structures that enable administrators, parents, and teachers to work together on school improvement.
5. The involvement of teachers in decisions about school goals and the means for implementing them. (Moll, 1997, p. 7)

Refocused Use of Assessment

As a screening device for special education determination and classification, numerous studies documented the inadequacy of the system of assessment. According to assessment leader Ysseldyke, given one or another state's definition of *learning disabilities,* a substantial majority of all students would be so classified; indeed, he stated, the determination is little better than a flip of the coin. (For a discussion of these issues, see Lipsky & Gartner, 1997, especially Chapter 3.)

With regard to assessment as a measure of students' progress, inclusive schools and districts are reporting moving toward more authentic assessment designs, including the use of portfolios of students' work and performances and generally working to refocus assessment. As described previously, the 1997 IDEA Amendments established dramatic new standards for assessment of *all* students that require the inclusion of students with significant disabilities.

Support for Students and Staff

From the vantage point of students, support for inclusion often means supplementary aids and support services, which districts report as including assignment of full- or part-time, short- or long-term teacher's aide support; integration of needed therapy services into the general school program; peer supports, such as "buddy systems" or "circles of friends"; and effective use of computer-aided technology and other assistive devices. The character and nature of supports have changed significantly. Differing from the earlier practice of elaborate modification, the newer trends include only as much as needed in order to avoid the provision of "disabling help"; teacher's aides who are assigned to a class rather than "velcroed" to an individual child; the recognition that related services are supposed to entail only what is educationally necessary, not everything that is needed to meet a child's other-than-educational needs; and the integration of computers into the typical work of the classroom rather than their use as a fancy gadget in a special room. Giangreco (1995) and colleagues (Edelman & Giangreco, 1995; Giangreco, Edelman, Luiselli, & MacFarland, 1996, 1997) developed a number of designs that provide the basis for this new approach, especially as it relates to the integration of related services.

Two support factors repeatedly identified as essential for successful inclusive education programs are systematic staff development and flexible planning time for special and general educators and classroom and other personnel to work together.

Funding

Special education funding formulas often have favored restrictive placements for students in special education. The 1997 IDEA Amendments require that states adopt policies that are placement neutral; that is, states must adopt policies that do not contravene IDEA's program mandate regarding LRE placement. Funds must follow the student regardless of placement and must be sufficient to provide the services necessary. Districts report that, in general, inclusive education programs are no more costly than segregated models ("Does inclusion cost more?" 1994; McLaughlin & Warren, 1994; Parrish, 1997). Districts must anticipate one-time "conversion" costs, however, especially for the necessary planning and professional development.

Effective Parental Involvement

Inclusive schools report the importance of parental participation. They encourage parental involvement by providing family support services as well as the development of education programs that engage parents as co-learners with their children. Programs that bring a wide array of services to children in schools report at least two types of benefits— direct benefits to the children and opportunities for parents and other family members to become involved in school-based activities. As the child in an inclusive school becomes a part of the fabric of the school along with his or her peers without disabilities, so, too, the parents of children with disabilities become less isolated. The 1997 IDEA Amendments enhance parents' participation by requiring their participation in all eligibility and placement decisions involving their children and by requiring that they be informed about their children's progress no less frequently than is the district's practice for children without disabilities.

Use of Effective Partnership Program Models

Many partnership and shared responsibility models of inclusion have been successful, including

- A co-teaching model, wherein the special education teacher co-teaches full-time alongside the general education teacher
- A parallel teaching model, wherein the special educator works with a small group of students, both special and general education, in the general education classroom
- A co-teaching consultant model, wherein the special education teacher provides assistance to the general educator, enabling him or her to teach all of the students in the inclusive class
- A team model, wherein the special education teacher joins with one or more general education teachers to form a team to share responsibility for all of the children in the inclusive classroom
- A methods-and-resources teacher model, wherein the special education teacher, whose students have been distributed in general education classes, works with the general education teachers, providing direct instruction, modeling of lessons, and consultation
- A dually licensed teacher model, wherein the teacher holds both general and special education certification and thus is equipped to teach all of the students in an inclusive classroom

Schools have been successful with each of these designs. Factors in adopting a particular model most often depend on local decision making and teachers' preferences.

In Kentucky, a state that (along with Vermont) has the most fully developed restructured and inclusive classrooms, three designs are used:

- Complementary instruction, whereby the general education teacher takes the overall responsibility for the subject matter and the strategic teacher (i.e., special education teacher, a teacher of the gifted, a speech-language pathologist, Chapter 1 teachers, remediation teachers) works with the mastery of specific skills based on the subject matter
- Role reversal teaming (requiring that each teacher have dual certification), whereby both the general education teacher and the strategic teacher are certified in elementary education; here the teachers jointly develop instruction and implement it according to their individual strengths and preferences

- Supportive learning style, whereby both teachers share responsibility for planning; the general education teacher provides basic instruction on the essential content, and the strategic teacher designs and implements supportive and supplementary materials, activities, instruction, and so forth

Basic to each of the previous three designs is a strong professional development component that is incorporated prior to the initiation of the program as well as for ongoing technical assistance.

Use of Effective Classroom Practices

Effective classroom practices, as reported by districts implementing inclusive education, have two overarching characteristics. The first is that the adaptations appropriate for students with disabilities benefit all students. The second is that the instruction strategies used in inclusive classrooms are practices recommended by education reformers and researchers for general education students. Cooperative learning has been identified as the most important instruction strategy supporting inclusive education. Well over half of the districts implementing inclusive education included in the National Study of Inclusive Education (NCERI, 1994–1995) reported using cooperative learning. Additional instruction strategies cited by a quarter or more of the districts include curricular adaptations, students supporting other students, using classroom aides, and using instructional technology.

WHERE WE HAVE BEEN

Just as the 1997 IDEA Amendments provide a framework for the synergy between inclusive education and school restructuring, school practices in the implementation of inclusive education programs are moving to more advanced levels. As school districts across the United States have implemented inclusive education programs, they have moved from first-stage to second-stage inclusion issues. Table 1 presents two columns representing initial or first-stage issues versus more advanced or second-stage issues in implementing inclusive education. Only to some extent are the stages time based; though the second stage represents the cutting edge of current practice, many—perhaps most—inclusive education programs are characterized by first-stage practices and attitudes. Table 1 is meant only to be introductory and preliminary, not final and definitive. Furthermore, it is limited in that it includes neither those issues that came before the first stage (i.e., the largely segregated placements that continued to occur well into the 1980s) nor the second-stage practices that are yet to be implemented in a consistent

Table I. Stages in the implementation of inclusive education

First-stage issues	Second-stage issues
• Should we do inclusive education?	• How do we do inclusive education?
• Inclusive education viewed as only a special education initiative	• Inclusive education viewed as a schoolwide/districtwide issue based on restructuring
• Implementation of inclusion viewed as the responsibility of special education administrators and staff	• Implementation of inclusion viewed as the responsibility of general education administrators and staff, along with special educators
• Inclusive education benefits some special education students	• Inclusive education benefits all students
• Students placed in general education classes must be "ready"	• All students are included, regardless of the intensity of their disability
• Providing elaborate modifications when a student is included	• Providing only those supports and accommodations that are educationally necessary
• Individual paraeducators assigned to students who are included	• Paraeducators assigned to support all students in the inclusive classroom
• Inclusive education seen as parallel to general education reforms	• Inclusive education initiatives are entwined with general education reform
• Students perceived as "belonging" to general or special educators	• Special and general educators assume shared responsibility for all students
• Assessment focused on students' individual progress	• Assessment tied to overall curriculum and instruction
• Outcomes and standards for special education students are viewed as unique to them	• Outcomes and standards for special education students are viewed in the context of those for students in general education
• Teachers who implement inclusive education should be volunteers	• The teaching of students with disabilities is a typical part of all teachers' roles
• Staff development focused on transfer of special education skills to general educators	• Staff development emphasizes development of the discrete and shared knowledge of general and special educators and the development of collaboration between them
• Emphasis is on helping students with special needs adjust to general education	• Emphasis is on empowering all students
• Focus is on inclusive education in the elementary grades	• Focus widens to include middle and high school

(continued)

Table I.   *(continued)*

First-stage issues	Second-stage issues
• Honoring of parents' due process rights	• Movement beyond due process to engagement of parents as partners
• Related services provided outside general classroom	• Related services integrated into the general program activities
• Funding tied to placement	• Funding follows child
• Students remain in inclusive environments for the entire day	• General education classrooms provide a common learning base for all students. Supplemental supports are for the most part provided within the general education classroom environment. However, inclusive education is based on a concept of the delivery of a service, not a location.

Note: Developed in discussions with colleagues Mary A. Falvey, Judith Schrag, and Richard A. Villa.

manner, which will thereby lead to third-stage issues and the necessary synergy between inclusive education and school restructuring.

LOOKING TOWARD THE FUTURE

The future of inclusive education holds potential concerns and opportunities. Perhaps the greatest threat to inclusive education arises when school districts implement it halfheartedly. A school district seeking to implement inclusive education "on the cheap" by not devoting sufficient time and resources to addressing its essential implementation is doing little more than "dumping" children with special needs into general education classrooms. In addition, treating inclusive education as a new program or as an innovation rather than as part of the fabric of school restructuring efforts can significantly decrease the effectiveness of inclusive education programs. School districts implementing successful inclusive education programs have recognized the benefits and consequences of such implementation for all school activities, including curriculum, instruction strategies, assessment, student grouping, personnel utilization and deployment, parental participation, pupil transportation, fiscal affairs, and building and district organization.

Many components of the 1997 IDEA Amendments provide further impetus for the expansion of inclusive education opportunities for all students with disabilities. Illustrative of the potential here is the reissuance by the New York State Commissioner of Education, Richard P.

Mills, of the New York Board of Regents' *Least Restrictive Environment Implementation Policy Paper,* which emphasized the strengthening of the law's LRE requirements.[6] In his transmittal memorandum, Mills stated,

> I am issuing an updated version of this paper to underscore the commitment the Education Department has to implementing our responsibilities in this area and to remind all stakeholders of the importance of these policies. It is essential that school districts review their local policies in preparation for the new IDEA amendments. (1997, pp. 1–2)

Mills directed local districts to examine their policies and practices regarding

- The appropriateness of the general education program
- The provision of supports to enable students to participate in general education services
- Students' attending the school that they would attend if they did not have disabilities, except if otherwise required by their individualized education program (IEP)
- Providing an explanation of why a student with disabilities would not participate with students without disabilities
- Notice to the student's parents about each program and placement option considered for the student and a rationale for rejecting those options
- Documentation of the general education programs and placement options considered in the development of the IEP

The language of IDEA encourages the *relationship of inclusive education to broad school reform.* In some instances, districts implementing inclusive education programs have already recognized the importance of this relationship. The two largest U.S. school systems, the New York City public schools and the Los Angeles Unified School District, are committed to undertake steps that involve both restructuring and inclusion. This commitment is propelled in the New York City school system by a Memorandum of Understanding signed with the Office of

---

[6]New York state's record in this area is particularly woeful; New York ranks among the lowest of the 50 states in the placement of students with disabilities in general education classrooms (U.S. Department of Education, 1996, Table AB1). Nonetheless, the areas identified by the New York State Education Commissioner are appropriate for all 50 states and their school districts.

Civil Rights and in the Los Angeles school system by a consent decree (*Chanda Smith v. Los Angeles Unified School District,* 1993).

Parents' support for inclusive education for their children with disabilities provides a significant opportunity for quality program expansion. Parental support is manifested in numerous ways, including the policy statements of organizations (e.g., The Arc, TASH, and the United Cerebral Palsy Associations), the establishment of organizations that promote inclusion (e.g., the National Parent Network on Disabilities, The PEAK Parent Center, and Schools Are for Everyone [SAFE]), and the initiatives taken by the federally funded Parent Training and Information Centers. Particularly noteworthy here is the work of the Statewide Parent Advocacy Network (SPAN) in New Jersey.

Often, as a last resort, parents use the courts to achieve the inclusive placement that they believe their children need. At the federal appellate level, four full inclusion cases have been decided (*Daniel R.R. v. State Board of Education, Greer v. Rome City School District, Oberti v. Board of Education of the Borough of Clementon School District,* and *Sacramento City Unified School District v. Rachel H.*). In each, the parents' demand for an inclusive placement for their child prevailed over the school districts' refusal to do so (Lipton, 1994). Subsequent cases decided at the federal district court level have generally but not always supported parents' demands for inclusive placements, especially in the cases of younger children. Finally, leaders in the disability rights movement have come to see the importance of their involvement in promoting and implementing inclusion for the sake of the children involved and as part of their larger civil rights agenda. Along with parents, they can become an even more powerful force for change.

CONCLUSIONS

In the restructuring of education to meet the needs of all students, a series of differences are often posed as zero-sum games. For instance,

- Inclusive education versus specialized services
- Classroom activities that support social experiences and friendships versus classroom activities that support acquisition of academic or vocational skills
- Benefits for students with disabilities versus benefits for students without disabilities

O'Brien and O'Brien (1997) asserted that these are false dichotomies and that confronting them is a way both to uncover the feelings that students with substantial disabilities evoke[7] in American society and to use inclusive education as a force for school renewal. More fundamentally, confronting these false dichotomies is a way to address what Minow (1990) called the *dilemma of difference,* or the dilemma of whether differences are viewed as impairments or as a welcomed condition of human diversity. In Sacks's (1995) formulation, the welcoming view of students with disabilities as a condition of human diversity involves recognizing that people with disabilities are *no less human for being different.* For the pedagogue, it involves the Vygotskian observation that "a blind or deaf child achieves the same level of development as a normal [sic] child . . . in another way, by another course, by other means" (cited in Sacks, 1995, p. xvii).

Edmonds said about the education of poor and minority students,

> We can, whenever and wherever we choose, successfully teach all children whose schooling is of interest to us. We already know more than we need in order to do this. [W]hether we do it must finally depend on how we feel about the fact that we haven't done it so far. (1979, p. 29)

Educators know how to implement inclusive education; whether inclusive education strategies and practices are implemented depends only on how they feel about not doing it.

REFERENCES

Chanda Smith v. Los Angeles Unified School District, No. 93-7044-LEW (GHKX) (C.D. Cal. 1993).

Council for Exceptional Children. (1994). *Creating schools for all our students: What 12 schools have to say.* Reston, VA: Author.

Daniel R.R. v. State Board of Education, 874 F.2d 1036 (5th Cir. 1989).

Does inclusion cost more? (1994). *Inclusive Education Programs, 1*(5), 4–5.

Edelman, S.W., & Giangreco, M.F. (1995). VISTA: A process for planning educationally necessary support services. *Language Learning and Education, 2*(2), 17–18.

Edmonds, R. (1979). Some schools work and more can. *Social Policy, 9*(5), 25–29.

Education for All Handicapped Children Act of 1975, PL 94-142, 20 U.S.C. §§ 1400 *et seq.*

Falvey, M.A. (Ed.). (1995). *Inclusive and heterogeneous schooling: Assessment, curriculum, and instruction.* Baltimore: Paul H. Brookes Publishing Co.

---

[7]Hahn (1995) called these feelings *existential* or *aesthetic anxiety.*

Giangreco, M.F. (1995). Related services decision-making: A foundational component of effective education for students with disabilities. *Occupational and Physical Therapy in Educational Environments, 23,* 47–67.

Giangreco, M.F., Edelman, S.W., Luiselli, T.E., & MacFarland, S.Z.C. (1996). Support service decision making for students with multiple service needs: Evaluative data. *Journal of The Association for Persons with Severe Handicaps, 21*(3), 135–144.

Giangreco, M.F., Edelman, S.W., Luiselli, T.E., & MacFarland, S.Z.C. (1997). Helping or hovering? Effects of instructional assistant proximity on students with disabilities. *Exceptional Children, 64*(1), 7–18.

Greer v. Rome City School District, 950 F.2d 688 (11th Cir. 1991).

Hahn, H. (1995). New trends in disability studies: Implications for educational policy. *NCERI Bulletin, 2*(1), 1–6.

Individuals with Disabilities Education Act (IDEA) Amendments of 1997, PL 105-17, 20 U.S.C. §§ 1400 *et seq.*

Individuals with Disabilities Education Act (IDEA) of 1990, PL 101-476, 20 U.S.C. §§ 1400 *et seq.*

Laski, F. (1997). Inclusion and the 1997 IDEA amendments. *TASH Newsletter, 9,* 22–23.

Lipsky, D.K., & Gartner, A. (Eds.). (1997). *Inclusion and school reform: Transforming America's classrooms.* Baltimore: Paul H. Brookes Publishing Co.

Lipton, D.J. (1994). The "full inclusion" court cases: 1989–1994. *NCERI Bulletin, 1*(2), 1–8.

Lipton, D.J. (1997). *Individuals with Disabilities Education Act Amendments of 1997: Summary of changes.* Berkeley, CA: Disability Rights Education and Defense Fund.

McLaughlin, M.J., & Warren, S.H. (1994). *Resources implications of inclusion: Impressions of special educators at selected sites.* Palo Alto, CA: Center for Special Education Finance.

Mills, R.P. (1997). *Least restrictive environment implementation policy paper.* Albany: New York State Education Department.

Minow, M. (1990). *Making all the difference: Inclusion, exclusion, and American law.* Ithaca, NY: Cornell University Press.

Moll, A. (1997). *ASK: HOW can we work collaboratively to ensure success for ALL students: NOT: Do we HAVE to work together to serve students with disabilities?* Paper presented at Summer Institute on Collaboration and Inclusion: Rhetoric to Reality, National Center on Educational Restructuring and Inclusion, The Graduate School and University Center, The City University of New York.

More IDEA students receiving mainstream instruction. (1997, December 23). *Education Daily,* 3.

National Center on Educational Restructuring and Inclusion (NCERI). (1994–1995). *National study of inclusive education.* New York: National Center on Educational Restructuring and Inclusion, The Graduate School and University Center, The City University of New York.

Oberti v. Board of Education of the Borough of Clementon School District, 995 F.2d 1204 (3rd Cir. 1993).

O'Brien, J., & O'Brien, C.L. (1997). Inclusion as a force for school renewal. *TASH Newsletter, 9,* 8–10.

Parrish, T. (1993). *Policy objectives for special education and funding formulas.* Palo Alto, CA: Center for Special Education Finance.

Parrish, T. (1997). Fiscal issues relating to special education inclusion. In D.K. Lipsky & A. Gartner (Eds.), *Inclusion and school reform: Transforming America's classrooms* (pp. 275–298). Baltimore: Paul H. Brookes Publishing Co.

Sacks, O. (1995). *An anthropologist on Mars.* New York: Alfred A. Knopf.

Sacramento City Unified School District v. Rachel H., 14 F. 3rd 1398 (9th Cir. 1994).

Stainback, S.B., & Stainback, W.C. (Eds.). (1996). *Inclusion: A guide for educators.* Baltimore: Paul H. Brookes Publishing Co.

U.S. Department of Education. (1996). *Eighteenth annual report to Congress on the implementation of the Individuals with Disabilities Education Act.* Washington, DC: Author.

Vail, K. (1997). Special pioneers. *American School Board Journal, 32,* 16–18.

Villa, R.A., & Thousand, J.S. (Eds.). (1995). *Creating an inclusive school.* Alexandria, VA: Association for Supervision and Curriculum Development.

Villa, R.A., Thousand, J.S., Meyers, H., & Nevin, A.I. (1996). Teacher and administrator perceptions of heterogeneous education. *Exceptional Children, 63,* 29–45.

Chapter 3

Reclaiming Our Youth

Steven L. Van Bockern,
Larry K. Brendtro, and Martin Brokenleg

Family, school, peers, and community are pivotal in fostering positive development in a child (Bronfenbrenner, 1986). When these worlds of a child are working as they should, childhood becomes a time when the child's fundamental needs are met—a time to love, learn, explore, and give. There is a growing recognition among educators and service providers, however, that these childhood environments are eroding:

> In the absence of good support systems, external stresses have become so great that even strong families are falling apart. The hecticness, instability, and inconsistency of daily family life are rampant in all segments of our society, including the well-educated and well-to-do. . . . We are depriving millions of children of their competence and moral character. (Bronfenbrenner, 1993, as cited in Goleman, 1995, p. 234)

CHILDREN OF DISCOURAGEMENT

Life in technologically rich but spiritually impoverished schools and communities is difficult. The stressors of life in such circumstances

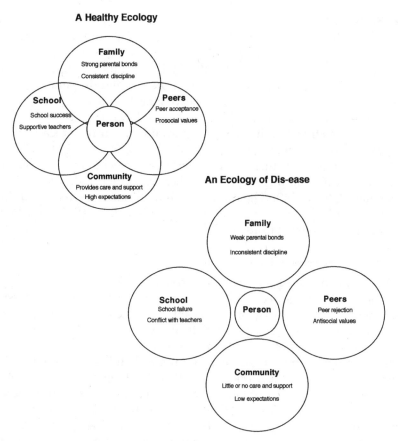

A Healthy Ecology

Family
Strong parental bonds
Consistent discipline

School
School success
Supportive teachers

Peers
Peer acceptance
Prosocial values

Person

Community
Provides care and support
High expectations

An Ecology of Dis-ease

Family
Weak parental bonds
Inconsistent discipline

School
School failure
Conflict with teachers

Person

Peers
Peer rejection
Antisocial values

Community
Little or no care and support
Low expectations

Figure 1.   Child in a healthy ecology and a toxic environment.

create a toxic environment that is spawning a generation of discouraged children who have lost their sense of well-being (Elkind, 1988; Pipher, 1997).

As Figure 1 illustrates, a child in a toxic environment is in an ecology of "dis-ease" rather than a healthy ecology. The child may experience alienation, with inconsistent discipline and weak parental bonds in the family. School becomes a place marked by failure and conflict. Peers either reject the child or promote antisocial values and irresponsibility in false friendships. The community expects little of youth and, in turn, provides little care and support for them. It is in these roots of alienation, failure, irresponsibility, and selfishness that discouraged children are created. A child who is discouraged is in danger of being hurt by and hurting others.

Discouragement in Alienation

The wounds of being an unclaimed or forgotten child are deep and disfiguring. Children with *affect hunger,* a term used by behavioral scientists (Ainsworth, 1989; Bowlby, 1980) who identified a population of children reared in sterile orphanages, strike out and desperately seek ways to fill their need to attach. They connect with gangs and false friends who exploit them. Affect-hungry children become locked in defiant opposition to adults who, if untrained, can reciprocate their anger with counteraggression (Long, Morse, & Newman, 1996). Those who are rejected by their peers have a two to eight times greater chance of dropping out of school (Asher & Gabriel, 1989, as cited in Goleman, 1995, p. 249). The estranged child becomes peer- and adult-wary, often biting the hands that do not feed them (Brendtro, Van Bockern, & Clementson, 1995).

Discouragement in Failure

Schools are powerful cultures that transmit core values to youth. Wozner (1985) suggested that educational environments can be classified as either reclaiming or nonreclaiming. Reclaiming schools are organized to meet the needs of both the young person and society. Nonreclaiming schools operate only to perpetuate a system that values compliance and conformity. The nonreclaiming environment is focused on tending the school rather than teaching students. In nonreclaiming schools, fear of failure becomes a strategy to control youth (Kohn, 1996). It is a place where students feel increasingly less success the more time they spend in school (Currence, 1984; Morse, 1964). Students experience little engagement or opportunity for challenging activities or self-initiative (Goodlad, 1984; Sizer, 1984). White (1959) explained that, deprived of opportunities for success, young people express their frustration through anger or by retreating in helplessness and inferiority. Often it is in school—the very place that is supposed to nurture success—where students experience their greatest failures.

Discouragement in Irresponsibility

Defiant youth may seem to relish freedom from adult control; when their lives are empty of attachment, however, they experience the opposite of true independence. Attachment researchers Bowlby (1980) and Ainsworth (1989) suggested that secure autonomy and responsibility are built on a solid base of ongoing human attachment. Unattached youth may noisily proclaim their pseudo independence ("Nobody tells me what to do!"), but this only masks the reality of what they clearly feel: "Nobody really cares." Fighting this feeling and the resulting sense of powerlessness, some youth assert themselves in rebellious, aggressive, and other antisocial ways. Some become violent. Teenage girls get pregnant (Underwood & Albert, 1989, as cited in Goleman, 1995, p. 237). Still other children, who believe they are too weak or too impotent to manage their own lives, become pawns of others. Lacking a sense of control or autonomy in their lives and with little opportunity to practice responsible independence, youth become discouraged.

Discouragement in Selfishness

Unless the natural desire of children to help and care for others is nourished, they fail to develop a sense of their own value and instead learn to live an empty, self-centered existence in desperate pursuit of empty pleasures in a hedonistic, narcissistic lifestyle. It appears that communities and schools in fact are failing to nourish children's sense of caring, as evidenced by the Search Institute's finding that the spirit of justice and concern for others reaches a peak at fifth grade and then declines (Benson, Williams, & Johnson, 1987). Hedin (1989) further concluded that young people have never been more self-centered or more consumed with money, power, and status than they are at the end of the 20th century. Yet the search for happiness through materialism and selfish pleasure only leads to discouragement for many youth.

Goldstein (1991) noted that much of the psychological literature addresses only the negative side of human behavior. Crime, psychopathology, and aggression are explored in depth. In fact, most of the terms used to describe the emotional and behavioral issues of youth are pejorative and demeaning. Specifically, youth are labeled with "d" words such as disturbed, disordered, deprived, deviant, disadvantaged, disruptive, disrespectful, and disobedient (Brendtro, Brokenleg, & Van Bockern, 1990). Those who work with young people, then, are led to focus on the negative. To further blame dysfunctional parents, delinquent friends, disrespectful schools, or disadvantaged communities—negative labeling itself—does little to solve the problem. Such labeling does not focus on the strengths that can be found in just about every situation and individual, nor does labeling facilitate the building of strengths.

BEYOND DISCOURAGEMENT: THE CIRCLE OF COURAGE

Research (Benard, 1992; Werner & Smith, 1992) suggested that perhaps as many as 70% of children from high-risk environments are resilient and survive in spite of the odds. A resiliency perspective asks why young people stay courageous in the midst of discouragement. This perspective attempts to identify assets and protective factors that ensure a child's well-being. Metaphorically, instead of simply providing an ambulance for those who have driven off the cliff, people who focus on strengthening the child are more interested in setting up roadblocks to prevent the child from going over the edge in the first place.

Researchers have identified some of those roadblocks. In a study of thousands of students in Grades 6–12 in just over 500 communities, Benson (1997) identified internal strengths (e.g., achievement motivation) and external supports (e.g., a mentor) that help protect children in a high-risk community. Benson found that, as the number of assets increased, risk indicators (e.g., alcohol abuse, antisocial behavior, school failure) decreased. He also found that students who did 1 or more hours per week of volunteer community service had reduced risk indicators.

Benard (1992) suggested resilient youth have social competence, problem-solving skills, autonomy, and a sense of purpose and of the future. The community, she argued, can protect its children by providing care and support through affordable housing and employment, by having high expectations of its youth, and by engaging youth in socially and economically useful tasks. Her work suggested that the family needs to express affection, provide order, and set clear expectations. Giving children a sense of their future is yet another protective gift families can provide. Benard affirmed the important role that schools play. When schools foster relationships with teachers and peers, cooperate with the family, ensure success for all, and eliminate negative labels, a child's resiliency is strengthened.

Dropout and alternative education researchers (e.g., Newmann, 1992; Wehlage, Rutter, Smith, Lesko, & Fernandez, 1989) have moved from searching for fixed negative characteristics of students (e.g., poverty, grade retention, family background, truancy, substance abuse) toward a search for school practices that encourage students to persist until graduation. Damico and Roth (1994) synthesized much of this research and concluded that resilient or persistent students had caring teachers who liked them and liked teaching, structured successful learning experiences, conveyed a message that students could learn, used varied instruction strategies, involved students, had small classes, and helped their students become test-smart.

In the book *Reclaiming Youth at Risk: Our Hope for the Future*, Brendtro and colleagues (1990) proposed a strength-based model of youth empowerment. Grounded in contemporary developmental research, the perceptive insight of early youth work pioneers, and

Native American philosophies of child care, these authors suggested that belonging, mastery, independence, and generosity are the core needs of all children. They further argued that these core needs transcend culture and are the birthright of all children. Helping children have these needs met can become the shared vision that drives the work of caring adults.

Adler (1990) suggested that one of the great philosophical mistakes of the late 20th century was to suggest there are no absolute values. All values, he argued, are expressions of either wants or needs. Wants are personal or cultural preferences and are thus relative values; but human needs are universal, and absolute human values are those tied to absolute human needs. Using Adler's reasoning, belonging, mastery, independence, and generosity express absolute values. Children in every culture need to belong. Depriving a child of care is universally evil. Children by their nature are created to strive for mastery; thus, schools that sabotage this motivation for competence are maltreating children. Children from any background have the need for self-determination; to block this development of independence is to commit an injustice. Finally, from the dawn of cooperative civilization, children have sought to give back to others the concern they have been shown by others. If educators fail to provide children with opportunities for caring and generosity, they extinguish their students' human spirit.

Native American philosophies of child care represent what is perhaps one of the most effective systems of child development. These approaches emerged from cultures in which the central purpose of life was the education and empowerment of children. They understood the importance of meeting the needs of belonging, mastery, independence, and generosity. Lakota Sioux artist George Bluebird has portrayed this philosophy of healthy child development as the circular medicine wheel shown in Figure 2. Native Americans see the person as standing in the circle surrounded by the four directions, with the circle being the symbol for life connecting light and dark, good and evil, giving and receiving, and even life and death.

It is notable that contemporary research has validated what Native American cultures intuitively understand. For example, fostering self-esteem is a primary goal in socializing children; without a sense of self-worth, a young person from any cultural or family background is vulnerable to a host of social, psychological, and learning problems (Gilliland, 1988). In his definitive work on self-concept in childhood, Coopersmith (1967) observed that significance, competence, power, and virtue are four basic components of self-esteem. Traditional Native American educational practices addressed each of these four components:

GENEROSITY

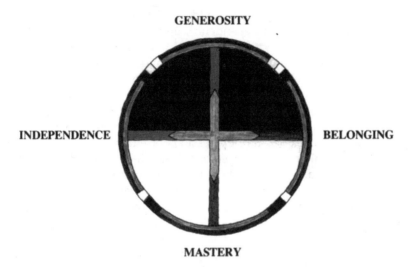

INDEPENDENCE   BELONGING

MASTERY

Figure 2.   The Circle of Courage. (Copyright © 1999 by Reclaiming Youth International; reprinted by permission.)

1) significance was nurtured in a cultural milieu that celebrated the universal need for belonging
2) competence was ensured by guaranteed opportunities for mastery
3) power was fostered by encouraging the expression of independence
4) virtue was reflected in the preeminent value of generosity (Brendtro et al., 1990, p. 35)

Spirit of Belonging

In traditional Native American society, it was the duty of all adults to serve as teachers for younger people. Child rearing was not just the province of biological parents. Children were nurtured within a larger circle of significant others. From the earliest days of life, the child experienced a network of caring adults. Kinship in tribes was not strictly a matter of biological relationships but rather a learned way of viewing those who shared a community of residence. The ultimate test of kinship was behavior, not blood; one belonged if one acted as if one belonged (Walker, 1982).

Marty (1987) observed that contemporary civilization is threatened by a loss of this sense of community that characterizes tribal peoples. Consequently, children at the turn of the 21st century are desperately pursuing artificial belongings (e.g., gangs, cults). For many children who are troubled, healthy belonging is found only in relationships with caring adults who are willing to create a community.

Spirit of Mastery

The goal of Native American education was to develop cognitive, physical, social, and spiritual competence. Among the first lessons that a child learned were self-control and self-restraint in the presence of parents and other adults. Children were taught that wisdom came from listening to and observing their elders. Ceremonies and oral legends transmitted ideals to the younger generation. Stories were used not only to entertain but also to teach models of behavior and ways of perceiving the world. Such lessons became more meaningful with repetition; the more one listened, the more wisdom that was revealed. Stories facilitated remembering information and functioned as a higher-order mental process that made sense of human existence (Reitz, 1988).

Competence or mastery was also cultivated by games and creative play that simulated adult responsibility. Dolls and puppies taught girls nurturing behaviors, and boys were given miniature bows and arrows in preparation for the hunting role. The learning that came from such activities was effortless because the motivation to strive toward competency and group involvement provided powerful intrinsic reinforcement. Play was encouraged but was balanced by an emphasis on work.

Success and mastery produced social recognition as well as inner satisfaction. Native American children were taught to generously acknowledge the achievements of others, but a person who received honor must always accept this honor without arrogance. Someone who was more skilled than oneself was seen as a model, not as a competitor (Standing Bear, 1933/1978).

The simple wisdom of Native American culture was that, because all people need to feel competent, all must be encouraged in their competency. Striving was for the attainment of a personal goal, not to achieve superiority over one's opponent. Just as one felt ownership in the success of others, one also learned to share personal achievements with others. Success became a possession of the many, not the privilege of the few.

Spirit of Independence

Traditional Native American culture placed a high value on individual freedom. Survival outside the camp circle depended on making independent judgments, so training in self-management began in early childhood. Children made decisions, which fostered a sense of responsibility for their failure or success. The individual answered to self-imposed goals and not to demands imposed by others (Bryde, 1971). In contrast to obedience models of discipline, guidance was given without interference. Elders taught values and provided models, but the child was given increasing opportunities to learn to make choices without coercion.

Native American elders believed that, if children were to be taught responsibility, they must be approached with maturity and dignity. In the 19th century, Haines (1888) observed that Indians were fond of their children and treated them with the greatest respect and consideration. The main strategy of behavior control was kindly lecturing that began as soon as the child was able to communicate. Blue Whirlwind (Hassrick, 1964) related that his people never struck their children. Rather, Blue Whirlwind indicated that children were spoken to gently, never harshly, because they were loved. If they were doing something wrong, they were asked to stop. Such gentleness did not imply permissiveness, as a Pegian elder explained: "My parents really pushed and disciplined us as we were growing up. They were very clear as to what our responsibilities were and what they expected from us. If we failed to meet our responsibilities, we were thoroughly lectured on what we were doing wrong" (Graff, 1987, p. 84).

Standing Bear's (1933/1978) approach to rewards and punishments challenges many contemporary theories of child management. Children were never offered prizes or rewards for doing something well. The achievement itself was the appropriate reward, and to put anything above the achievement was to implant unhealthy ideas in the minds of children and make them weak. Likewise, harsh punishment was seen as destructive. In place of rewards and punishments were modeling, group influence, discussion, and positive expectations.

Growth toward independence does not mean that a young person no longer has a need for nurturance. As Maier put it, "Children's ability to separate and manage on their own is anchored in the degree of security of their attachments" (1987, p. 161). Many who work with adolescents confuse those needs by disengaging from dependency relationships while perpetuating behavioral dependence. Native American child care philosophy recognized the necessity of harmonizing apparently conflicting needs by blending autonomy with belonging.

Spirit of Generosity

A recurrent message in Native American culture is that the highest virtue is to be generous and unselfish. Long before he could participate in the hunt, a boy would look forward to that day when he would bring home his first game and give it to people in need (Black Elk, 1932/1993). Training in altruism began in earliest childhood. When a mother would share food with the needy, she would give portions to her children so that they could experience the satisfaction of giving (Standing Bear, 1933/1978). Children were instructed to always share generously without holding back. Eastman (1902/1993) told of his grandmother teaching him to give away what he cherished most, his puppy, so that he would become strong and courageous.

Giving was a part of many ceremonies, such as a marriage or a memorial to a loved one. People engaged in gift giving upon the least provocation: Children brought food to their elders' teepees, and women made useful and artistic presents for orphans and widows. Prestige was accorded to those who gave unreservedly, and those with nothing to give were pitied. To accumulate property for its own sake was disgraceful (Hassrick, 1964).

Unlike communal societies, in which property was owned collectively, individual ownership prevailed in Native American cultures; however, property was not acquired for conspicuous consumption but to be better able to help others. Material possessions were less important than people, and the test of one's right values was to be able to give anything without one's pulse quickening. Those not observing these customs were seen as suspicious characters whose values were based on selfishness. Although generosity served to redistribute wealth, giving had more than an economic rationale. Core values of sharing and community responsibility were deeply ingrained in the community. Giving was not confined to property but rather permeated all aspects of Native American culture.

Native American culture shares with Western democracy the fundamental tenet of responsibility for the welfare of all others in the community. Conrad and Hedin (1987) called for a return to the spirit of service among contemporary youth to counter the attitude of "looking out for number 1" that is rampant in the United States at the end of the 20th century. They noted that nearly all reports on the status of U.S. education recommend more opportunities in the curriculum for students to become involved in community service. Brendtro and Ness (1983) demonstrated that young people who are troubled increase their sense of self-worth as they become committed to the positive value of caring for others. Elkind (1998) suggested that helping others improves young people's self-esteem and that increased self-esteem allows young people to "decenter" and contribute to the well-being of others. Selye (1974), the pioneer of stress psychology, concluded that altruism is the ultimate resource for coping with life's conflicts because, in reaching out to help another, one breaks free from preoccupation with oneself.

BUILDING RECLAIMING
ENVIRONMENTS: MENDING BROKEN CIRCLES

Without belonging, mastery, independence, and generosity, there can be no courage, only discouragement. When the Circle of Courage (see Figure 2) is broken, the lives of children are no longer in what Menninger (1963) called *the vital balance*. This harmony can be created or reclaimed only when the child's environment includes the core values represented in the Circle of Courage. In reclaiming environments, the child's need for belonging is nourished without neglecting the child's corresponding need for autonomy. Youth are taught to make independent decisions as they are taught to respect the wisdom and advice of caring and competent adults. Mastery is ensured in order to empower the child's acts of greater service to others.

Building reclaiming environments is no simple task, although beginning construction can be as simple as changing negative signs that are hung on the walls of the school building, hanging plants in the office, or cleaning dirty walls. Teachers can be trained to encourage greater classroom discussion, and students can be given greater freedom to make choices about assignments and classroom rules. Students might sing at a nursing facility. Although such a start is largely uncoordinated and unorganized, it can lead to more integrative changes that pervade the entire fabric of the learning community. Individuals can initiate construction, but it is best if everyone involved works together to realize the shared goals of belonging, mastery, independence, and generosity. Eventually, a reclaiming philosophy can become internalized in the institutions' norms. At this level, there is a synergy that allows the school community to examine policies, practices, programs, and procedures in light of the developmental needs of young people. The following sections of the chapter highlight ideas that can provide a framework for building reclaiming environments.

Restoring Belonging

Early education pioneers saw positive human attachments as the *sine qua non* of effective teaching. Johann Pestalozzi declared that love, not teaching, was the essence of education. In his classic book, *Wayward Youth*, Aichorn (1935) argued that relationship was at the heart of the reeducation process. His ethic was that affection rather than punishment must be dispensed to youth who exhibit difficult behavior because that is their primary unmet need. Research supports such thinking: Brophy (1986) found that the quality of human relationships in schools and youth service programs may be more influential than any specific techniques or interventions employed.

Teachers with widely divergent instruction styles can be successful if they develop positive classroom climates. Purkey and Novak (1996) offered practical and easily implemented belonging strategies and activities in their book, *Inviting School Success*. Examples include sending postcards to welcome students before classes begin; maintaining "recognition books" that contain articles featuring students; and having each class select an emblem, motto, or class color.

Fahlberg (1991) described three modes of building relationships for preventing and treating attachment problems:

- *Claiming behaviors to foster inclusion:* In any group, there are markers that determine who is an insider and who is an outsider, who is included with the "us" and who is with "them." Addressing people by relationship terms (e.g., friend, son), claiming physical space with possessions and photographs, engaging in ceremonies and songs, engaging in adoption rituals, and adopting clothing styles and insignia shared by group members all serve to include people in the family, the tribe, or the gang if no other alternative is offered. Fahlberg put particular emphasis on claiming activities with children who have been buffeted around in the foster care system.

- *Initiating positive interaction cycles:* This mode includes engaging in pleasurable activities, expressing affection, supporting children in pursuing their outside interests and in achieving goals, and participating in fun and joyful living. Increasing positive social interaction has a reciprocal positive effect: The adult bonds to the child while the young person is emotionally and intellectually stimulated and feels lovable and worthy.

- *Support in periods of high arousal:* These periods might include feelings aroused by a range of crises such as feelings of grief, illness, frustration, or being hurt or injured. Even physical restraint in moments of rage can serve to build positive ties. As the adult walks through these storms of life with the child and alleviates the child's psychological or physical discomfort, bonding and attachment are enhanced. The caregiver develops feelings of efficacy by meeting the child's needs, and the child develops feelings of trust, security, and attachment to the caregiver.

Learning to build relationships with children in crisis can be difficult. People are born with an instinctive urge to fight or flee when threatened, and children in crisis threaten untrained adults. With the understanding that comes with training, however, adults and young people also can learn to be strong and fight these urges to get into conflicts with youth. Building on the work of Redl (1966), Wood and Long (1991), and others, the Life Space Crisis Intervention Institute (Long & Fecser, 1997) developed reclaiming interventions that support youth in periods of turbulence. Instead of walling off the youth in crisis, the goal is to surround the young person by using the crisis as an opportunity to teach and build new skills.

Positive attachments between adults and youth are the foundation of effective education. These individual bonds, however, must be part of a synergistic network of relationships that permeate the school culture. These include positive peer relationships among students, a cooperative teamwork relationship among school staff, and genuine partnerships with parents. The middle school movement, with its emphasis on fostering attachments, does much to foster belonging in schooling. Typically, schedules are designed so that frequent and sustained contact between students and teachers is possible. Often, a team of four or five adults, including teachers, administrators, and counselors, serves a core group of students on a daily basis. Thus, administrators and school board members must see their roles as co-workers in support of their staff, not as superiors trying to dominate. In the final analysis, only adults who are themselves empowered are free to build empowering relationships with youth.

Reconstructing Mastery

Hart (1998), who has summarized brain research related to education, suggested that the brain is designed to detect patterns and works best in nonthreatening, active, and social environments. With increased knowledge of how the human brain functions, schools can be restructured so that they are "brain-friendly."

Traditional educational approaches were developed centuries before humankind had developed any scientific understanding of the human brain. Youth work pioneers such as Montessori (1967), Italy's first female physician, decried the obedience tradition of schooling. She tried to revolutionize learning to be brain-friendly in the belief that curiosity and the desire to learn come naturally to children. Even earlier, Addams (1909/1972), writing in *The Spirit of Youth and the City Streets,* observed that many of the difficulties of youth were related to the reality that they were highly spirited and adventurous and unmotivated by the humdrum routine of most schools. Outdoor education programs build on this spirit of adventure. In some outdoor wilderness programs, the struggle against the elements of nature keeps even the most resistant youth from defying the law of natural consequences

(Bacon & Kimball, 1989). Less risky field trips to rivers, forests, and farms also engage students in ways that sterile, traditional curricula are unable to accomplish. For example, the Illinois River Project (Williams, Bidlack, & Winnett, 1993), which has as its ultimate goal scientific literacy, engages students from more than 150 schools in six states in analyzing water samples from various test sites along rivers. Through an integrated curriculum, students in science, social studies, and English classes examine historical, social, and economic implications of the status of these rivers. A Rivers Project (Williams, 1999) in the areas of chemistry, biology, geology, geography, and language arts can be applied using any river in the world.

Teaching and learning that centers on competition instead of cooperation can be "brain-unfriendly." Teachers eliminate students from practicing and developing skills when they focus on finding, developing, and celebrating the best. Novice ball dribblers and rope skippers, those who need the practice the most, often are the first to sit down when they fail to meet expectations. In *The Second Cooperative Sports and Games Book* (1982), Orlick pointed out that the King of the Mountain–type games that permeate schools keep all but one child from achieving. When the outcome in competition is made to seem important, young people cheat, hurt other children, and engage in deception to get to the top.

Equally unfriendly to the brain are the teacher-dominated instruction techniques of uninspired, lengthy lectures and recitations. In contrast, the whole-language movement recognizes the value of an integrated curriculum that immerses students in authentic projects and social exchange of ideas. Teachers can use stories and Socratic methods (use of questions and teacher–student dialogue) to engage students in important ideas.

As important as academic content is, there is as great a need to ensure that our children develop their emotional intelligence. Yale psychologist Salovey summarized the five main domains of emotional intelligence: knowing one's emotions, being able to manage those emotions, motivating oneself, recognizing emotions in others, and handling relationships (Salovey & Mayor, 1990, as cited in Goleman, 1995, p. 42). Goleman (1995) argued that a person's success in life can be attributed more to his or her emotional intelligence than to his or her cognitive abilities. Findings from the National Center for Clinical Infant Programs support this position. Specifically, the center found that school success is predicted by measures such as being self-assured and interested; knowing what kind of behavior is expected and how to rein in the impulse to misbehave; being able to wait, follow directions, and turn to teachers for help; and expressing needs while getting along with other children (Brazelton, 1992, as cited in Goleman, 1995, p. 193). Information alone does not seem to solve problems. The wars on drugs, teen pregnancy, suicide, alcohol, dropouts, and violence will be lost unless information is combined with attention to young people's longer-term emotional and social development.

Finally, emotional literacy programs do more than increase a student's "emotional IQ." Programs and schools around the United States are finding that academic achievement scores and school performance are improved when the emotional needs of children are strengthened. Such programs include the Child Development Project, the Resolving Conflict Creatively Program, Parents and Teachers Helping Students (PATHS), the Augusta Lewis Troupe Middle School, and the Neva Learning Center (Goleman, 1995).

Recasting Independence

How do people develop responsible independence and self-discipline in youth? Early in the 20th century, educational reformers challenged traditional authoritarian pedagogy and obedience models of developing self-discipline. Montessori (1967), who created schools for disadvantaged children, wrote passionately about the need to build inner discipline. Korczak (1967), a Polish doctor and social pedagogue, proclaimed the child's right to be treated with respect. He created a children's newspaper so that the voices of children might be heard. Dewey (1916/1929), the American pioneer of progressive education, advocated democratic school communities in which students and teachers worked to pose questions and solve problems. All of these youth pioneers shared the understanding that children need to experience power or control in their own lives.

More recently, Glasser (1998) argued strongly for innovations in child management that allow youth to exert power over their lives. His premise is that discipline never really succeeds if it does not recognize the universal need of all people to be free to control themselves and to be able to influence others. Hoffman (1977) cited child development research showing that management by power assertion causes children to perceive moral standards as externally imposed. Often children resist such control or respond to it only when they are under the threat of cultural sanctions. Such studies support an alternative management strategy of inductive discipline, which involves communicating to children the effect of their behavior on others while fostering empathy and responsibility.

To create responsible independence in youth, Kohn (1996) argued that educators need to move from an atmosphere that emphasizes compliance to one that emphasizes community. This approach entails giving children real choices and a say in the classroom, eliminating punitive consequences and rewards, and conducting meaningful class-room meetings. Transferring power to children enables their choosing, trying, and doing—the building blocks of independence. Waiting patiently for a 2-year-old to pour his own milk, allowing a 3-year-old to struggle with her coat, and sending a 6-year-old to the office with a message builds these children's independence.

In summary, obedience models of discipline are based on reactive, arbitrary, and adult-imposed consequences. Control of behavior, the ultimate desired outcome of the obedience model, comes from exter-nal, psychological, and physical threats. In contrast, independence models of discipline are proactive, absent of psychological and physi-cal threat, and dependent on teaching social responsibility. Like the obedience model, control of behavior is the desired outcome. Unlike the obedience model, independence models of discipline seek the child's inner control, a self-efficacy that allows the child to do the right thing when he or she is not under surveillance. Curwin and Mendler (1988), authors of *Discipline with Dignity*, developed a systematic approach to discipline expressly designed to build the child's inner control.

Revitalizing Generosity

Service learning can give meaning to children's lives. Evidence sug-gests that, when youth are involved with helping, positive results occur. Hedin (1989) summarized various research that supports the positive results of volunteer service, including increased responsibility, self-esteem, moral development, and commitment to democratic val-ues. In addition, she cited a series of findings that identify intellectual gains that accrue from helping others.

Maryland was the first state to incorporate volunteerism as part of the curriculum. It produced curricula for high schools, special educa-tion, and middle schools (Ayers & Limages, 1997). Maryland has defined *student service* as caring for others through personal contact, indirect service, or civic action, either in the school or in the communi-ty, that requires preparation and reflection. Stories of service learning success abound in schools all over the state. In Howard County, Maryland, students proposed and worked to pass a bicycle helmet law. The student government organization in Baltimore City opened and continues to run a food pantry in a poor neighborhood. In Allegany County, Maryland, students produced and distributed a booklet about child abuse (Van Bockern, 1993).

Integrating service learning into the curriculum can happen at three levels. First, it can involve extracurricular volunteer work. Students do not receive credit and are not allotted time during school hours to participate. At Chadwick School in Los Angeles, privileged students run a soup kitchen, help individuals with various needs, put on plays, work with children at risk for developmental delays or school failure, and campaign for environmental protection. In Connecticut, students serve as the professional rescue squad for a semirural area. All of these programs value young people's abilities to participate and help in the community (Lewis, 1990).

On another level, a unit may be offered in a general class that complements the traditional course content. In a home economics class, for example, students might sew clothes for homeless families; an English class might publish a newsletter for the local neighborhood watch organization. Teachers might assign independent study work to be done outside class, as did two high school teachers in Sioux Falls, South Dakota: The teachers assigned 81 students in their American studies classes to do volunteer work in the hope that their students would learn the value of giving (Olson, 1990). The assignment was made after the students read Emerson's (1844/1983) essay "Gifts," which states that a gift must be necessary, chosen especially for an individual, and given from the heart. The students were asked to put the words into action. Some worked at a food pantry, and others went caroling at nursing facilities. One group volunteered to help at a shelter for abused women and children. Some offered to volunteer their time at the Humane Society. Four students spent hours at the zoo, feeding penguins or cleaning out the buffalos' pens.

CONCLUSIONS

What children need in order to love, learn, explore, and give—to be whole—is not a mystery. Traditional Native American child-rearing philosophies provide a powerful example of education and youth development at its best. Early European anthropologists described Native American children as radiantly happy, highly respectful, and courageous. Refined over thousands of years, Native Americans' approach to child rearing challenged the narrow perspectives of many latter-day psychological theories and politicians' zero-tolerance, get-tough rhetoric. From Native American cultures, the insight of early youth work pioneers, and contemporary research, one may deduce what can be done to reclaim troubled and troubling youth.

Specifically, families, schools, communities, and caring individuals can work to ensure that children's most basic needs are met. Blaming school systems for allowing children to fall through the cracks frequently misses the mark. Parent (1998) suggested that, too often, children fall through our own fingers. Reclaiming children requires each educator to be courageous and willing to struggle with imperfect systems in order to make sure that belonging, mastery, independence, and generosity are made available for all children.

REFERENCES

Addams, J. (1972). *The spirit of youth and the city streets*. Urbana: University of Illinois Press. (Original work published 1909)

Adler, M.J. (1990). *Truth and religion: The plurality of religions and the unity of truth: An essay in the philosophy of religion*. New York: Macmillan.

Aichorn, A. (1935). *Wayward youth*. New York: Viking Press.

Ainsworth, M. (1989). Attachments beyond infancy. *American Psychologist, 44*(4), 709–716.

Ayers, J., & Limages, A. (1997, December). *Maryland Student Service Alliance*. Available at http://sailor.lib.md.us/mssa/

Bacon, S.B., & Kimball, R. (1989). The wilderness challenge model. In R.D. Lyman, S. Prentice-Dunn, & S. Gabel (Eds.), *Residential and inpatient treatment of children and adolescents* (pp. 115–144). New York: Plenum Press.

Benard, B. (1992). Fostering resiliency in kids: Protective factors in the family, school and community. *Prevention Forum, 12*(3). (Available from the Illinois Prevention Resource Center)

Benson, P.L. (1997). *All kids are our kids: What communities must do to raise caring and responsible children and adolescents*. San Francisco: Jossey-Bass.

Benson, P.L., Williams, D.L., & Johnson, A.L. (1987). *The quicksilver years: The hopes and fears of early adolescence*. San Francisco: HarperCollins.

Black Elk. (1993). *Black Elk speaks: Being the life story of a holy man of the Oglala Sioux* (As told to J.G. Neihardt [Flaming Rainbow]). Alexandria, VA: Time-Life Books. (Original work published 1932)

Bowlby, J. (1980). *Attachment and loss* (3 vols.). New York: BasicBooks.

Brendtro, L., Brokenleg, M., & Van Bockern, S. (1990). *Reclaiming youth at risk: Our hope for the future*. Bloomington, IN: National Educational Services.

Brendtro, L., & Ness, A. (1983). Perspectives on peer group treatment: The use and abuse of guided group interaction/positive peer culture. *Children and Youth Services Review, 4*, 307–324.

Brendtro, L., Van Bockern, S., & Clementson, J. (1985). Adult-wary and angry: Restoring social bonds. *Holistic Education Review, 8*(1), 35–43.

Bronfenbrenner, U. (1986). Alienation and the four worlds of childhood. *Phi Delta Kappan, 67*, 430–436.

74   Van Bockern, Brendtro, and Brokenleg

Brophy, J. (1986). Teacher influences on student achievement. *American Psychologist, 41,* 1069–1077.

Bryde, J.F. (1971). *Indian students and guidance* (Guidance monograph series no. 6: Minority groups and guidance). Boston: Houghton Mifflin.

Conrad, D., & Hedin, D. (1987). *Youth service.* Washington, DC: Independent Sector.

Coopersmith, S. (1967). *The antecedents of self esteem.* San Francisco: W.H. Freeman.

Currence, C. (1984, February 29). School performance tops list of adolescent worries. *Education Week, 3*(8).

Curwin, R.L., & Mendler, A.N. (1988). *Discipline with dignity.* Alexandria, VA: Association for Supervision and Curriculum Development.

Damico, S.B., & Roth, J. (1994). Factors that contribute to students at risk persisting to graduation. *Journal of At-Risk Issues, 1*(1), 30–37.

Dewey, J. (1929). *Democracy and education: An introduction to the philosophy of education.* New York: Macmillan. (Original work published 1916)

Eastman, C.A. (1993). *Indian boyhood* (Native American voices series). Alexandria, VA: Time-Life Books. (Original work published 1902)

Elkind, D. (1988). *The hurried child: Growing up too fast too soon* (Rev. ed.). Reading, MA: Addison Wesley Longman.

Elkind, D. (1998). *All grown up and no place to go: Teenagers in crisis* (Rev. ed.). Reading, MA: Addison Wesley Longman.

Emerson, R.W. (1983). *Essays and lectures of Ralph Waldo Emerson.* New York: Viking Press. (Original work published 1844)

Fahlberg, V.I. (1991). *A child's journey through placement.* Indianapolis, IN: Perspectives Press.

Gilliland, H. (1988). Self concept and the Indian student. In J.A. Reyhner (Ed.), *Teaching the Indian child: A bilingual/multicultural approach* (2nd ed., pp. 57–69). Billings: Eastern Montana College.

Glasser, W. (1998). *Control theory in the classroom* (Rev. ed.). New York: HarperPerennial.

Goldstein, A.P. (1991). *Delinquent gangs: A psychological perspective.* Champaign, IL: Research Press Co.

Goleman, D. (1995). *Emotional intelligence: Why it can matter more than IQ.* New York: Bantam Books.

Goodlad, J.I. (1984). *A place called school: Prospects for the future.* New York: McGraw-Hill.

Graff, J. (Ed.). (1987). Strength within the circle [Special issue]. *Journal of Child Care.*

Haines, E. (1888). *The American Indian*. Chicago: Mas-sin-na-gan Co.

Hassrick, R. (1964). *The Sioux: Life and customs of a warrior society.* Norman: University of Oklahoma Press.

Hart, L.A. (1998). *Human brain and human learning* (Updated ed.). Kent, WA: Books for Educators.

Hedin, D. (1989). The power of community service. *Proceedings of the Academy of Political Science, 37*(2), 201–202.

Hoffman, M. (1977). Moral internalization: Current theory and research. *Advances in Experimental Social Psychology, 10,* 85–133.

Kohn, A. (1996). *Beyond discipline: From compliance to community.* Alexandria, VA: Association for Supervision and Curriculum Development.

Korczak, J. (1967). *Selected works of Janusz Korczak.* Warsaw: Central Institute for Scientific, Technical and Economic Information.

Lewis, A. (1990). In valuing young people. *Phi Delta Kappan, 71,* 420–421.

Long, N.J., & Fecser, F. (1997). *Life Space Crisis Intervention Institute training manual.* Hagerstown, MD: Author.

Long, N.J., Morse, W.C., & Newman, R.G. (Eds.). (1996). *Conflict in the classroom: The education of at-risk and troubled students* (5th ed.). Austin, TX: PRO-ED.

Maier, H.W. (1987). *Developmental group care of children and youth: Concepts and practice.* New York: Haworth Press.

Marty, M.E. (1987). *Religion and republic: The American circumstance.* Boston: Beacon Press.

Menninger, K.A., with Mayman, M., & Pruyser, P. (1963). *The vital balance: The life process in mental health and illness.* New York: Viking Press.

Montessori, M. (1967). *The absorbent mind* (C.A. Claremont, trans.). Austin, TX: Holt, Rinehart & Winston.

Morse, W. (1964). Self-concept in the school setting. *Childhood Education, 41,* 195–198.

Newmann, F.M. (Ed.). (1992). *Student engagement and achievement in American secondary schools.* New York: Teachers College Press.

Olson, C. (1990, December 21). Volunteer work teaches students value of giving. *Argus Leader,* p. A1.

Orlick, T. (1982). *The second cooperative sports & games book.* New York: Pantheon Books.

Parent, M. (1998). *Turning stones: My days and nights with children at risk.* New York: Fawcett Columbine.

Pipher, M.B. (1997). *The shelter of each other: Rebuilding our families.* New York: G.P. Putnam's Sons.

Purkey, W.W., & Novak, J.M. (1996). *Inviting school success: A self-concept approach to teaching, learning, and democratic practice* (3rd ed.). Belmont, CA: Wadsworth.

Redl, F. (1966). *When we deal with children: Selected writings.* New York: Free Press.

Reitz, S. (1988). Preserving Indian culture through oral literature. In J.A. Reyhner (Ed.), *Teaching the Indian child: A bilingual/multicultural approach* (2nd ed., pp. 255–280). Billings: Eastern Montana College.

Selye, H. (1974). *Stress without distress.* Philadelphia: Lippincott Williams & Wilkins.

Sizer, T.R. (1984). *Horace's compromise: The dilemma of the American high school.* Boston: Houghton Mifflin.

Standing Bear, L. (1978). *Land of the spotted eagle.* Lincoln: University of Nebraska Press. (Original work published 1933)

Van Bockern, S. (1993). Profiles of reclaiming schools. *Reclaiming Children and Youth, 1*(4), 12–15.

Walker, J.R. (1982). *Lakota society* (R.J. DeMallie, ed.). Lincoln: University of Nebraska Press.

Wehlage, G.G., Rutter, R., Smith, G., Lesko, N., & Fernandez, R. (1989). *Reducing the risk: Schools as communities of support.* London: Falmer Press.

Werner, E.E., & Smith, R.S. (1992). *Overcoming the odds: High-risk children from birth to adulthood.* Ithaca, NY: Cornell University Press.

White, R. (1959). Motivation reconsidered: The concept of competence. *Psychological Review, 66,* 297–333.

Williams, R. (1999). Rivers project. <http://www.siue.edu/OSME/river>

Williams, R., Bidlack, C., & Winnett, D. (1993, September). At the water's edge: Students study their rivers. *Educational Leadership, 51*(1), 80–83.

Wood, M.M., & Long, N.J. (1991). *Life space intervention: Talking with children and youth in crisis.* Austin, TX: PRO-ED.

Wozner, Y. (1985). Institution as community. *Child and Youth Services, 7,* 71–90.

Chapter 4

Rediscovering the Right to Belong

Norman Kunc

Newtonian principles of physics were regarded as true until Einstein demonstrated that they provided an inadequate explanation of the laws of nature. Similarly, Freudian analysts viewed a woman's admission of being sexually abused by her father as a neurotic fantasy stemming from an Electra complex. Only toward the end of the 20th century did other forms of therapy show that women are accurate in their accounts of being abused. In every field of knowledge, anomalies such as these arise that call into question practices and paradigms (i.e., world views) and necessitate the creation of new paradigms and related practices. It is precisely through this process that a body of knowledge develops. Such a process is taking place in the field of special education. Anomalies have arisen that call into serious question the validity of segregating students with specific physical, intellectual, or emotional needs from students who are developing typically. Moreover, these anomalies demand that new paradigms be created and embraced.

SPECIAL EDUCATION PARADIGM: SKILLS AS A PREREQUISITE TO INCLUSION

In the United States, the Education for All Handicapped Children Act of 1975 (PL 94-142) and the concept of the least restrictive environment (LRE) initially were seen as meaningful steps toward including children with physical, intellectual, and emotional needs within general classrooms. In actuality, however, this legislation and its embedded concept of the LRE still gave credence to segregated, self-contained classrooms for students with disabilities. Although lip service was given to the idea that students would be *included as much as possible,* the underlying paradigm supporting the maintenance of the continuum of services was that students with severe or even moderate disabilities need to learn and demonstrate basic skills (e.g., staying quiet in class, going to the washroom independently) in self-contained classrooms before, if ever, they were to be allowed to enter general classrooms. This educational paradigm can be represented schematically as follows:

STUDENT   →   Skills   →   General classroom

This paradigm has been the basis for the practice of placing students with moderate or severe disabilities in segregated, self-contained classrooms or programs in which the curriculum focus is basic skills instruction. As a result, segregated classrooms generally have been seen as a necessary educational option that must be maintained to meet the needs of only some students.

ANOMALIES IN THE SEGREGATION PARADIGM: LACK OF PROGRESS

The belief in the need for segregation has created a situation in which students with intensive physical, intellectual, or emotional needs enter the school system at the age of 5 or 6 years and are placed in self-contained classrooms or programs in which life skills, age-appropriate behavior, and possibly social interaction with other students are primary goals. These students typically stay in the school system for 15–18 years, and, despite the commitment of hundreds of thousands of dollars, the majority fail to master life skills or appropriate behavior and remain socially isolated throughout their school years. These students have not progressed at a rate that allows for a successful transition into community life (Lipsky & Gartner, 1997;

Villa & Thousand, 1995; Wagner, 1989). Although teachers and teaching assistants may be fully committed to helping students acquire basic skills, many students seem disinterested in, incapable of learning, or unwilling to learn those skills. Moreover, students who do master certain skills often fail to retain the newly acquired skills or cannot replicate them in situations outside the classroom. As a consequence, many graduates of self-contained classrooms enter directly into sheltered workshops or segregated prevocational training programs where they must continue to practice the same basic life skills. The result is that people with disabilities, because they are unable to make the transition into community life, spend years continuously *preparing* for life, a modern version of the experience of Sisyphus.

Often the lack of student progress is blamed on the student. Students are seen as having such severe disabilities that they are incapable of learning appropriate behavior and skills. This answer is losing credibility, however: Research and experience are showing that students in segregated programs *do* imitate and learn but that often what they imitate and learn is the *inappropriate* behavior of their classmates. Furthermore, there is increasing documentation of students who seemed incapable of learning appropriate behavior and skills in segregated classrooms achieving these previously unattainable goals once they are included in general classrooms. It seems, then, that the adherence to paradigms in special education has resulted in the creation and maintenance of an environment in which behavior that arises because of their mental retardation is reinforced rather than modified to prepare them for life outside the classroom.

A far more reasonable explanation for the lack of progress among students with disabilities has to do with the absence of motivation. There are few if any rewards or payoffs for the student for learning new activities in this environment. Students do not *pass* special education classes and thus *graduate* to general education classrooms; they cannot even *fail* special education. In fact, they are sometimes even punished for being successful. For example, I have seen situations in which students have been required to stack blocks in an effort to improve their fine motor control. The students who complete this task successfully are given smaller blocks to stack. Consequently, the task becomes increasingly more difficult, until it is beyond the students' capability to stack the blocks. Educators ask children with disabilities to spend their entire day doing tasks that are meaningless and difficult and then wonder why they learn little in special education classrooms.

MASLOW'S HIERARCHY OF NEEDS AS A PARADIGM FOR MOTIVATED LEARNING

Segregated programs and classrooms have failed to teach students with disabilities appropriate behavior and skills. Environments in which students model, learn, and practice inappropriate or meaningless behaviors have not been successful in preparing individuals for community life. These anomalies challenge the validity of segregation as an educational practice and require that new paradigms—paradigms that incorporate a motivation to learn—be developed.

Educators have a choice. They can either continue to blame the lack of progress in segregated classrooms on the severity of their students' disabilities, or they can have the courage and integrity to question seriously whether there is, in fact, a more effective way to prepare students with disabilities to enter the community after graduation.

In the 1980s, it became apparent that a different paradigm was needed to accomplish the goals set forth for special education. The special education practices prior to the 1980s had been founded on an old paradigm in which skills were seen as a prerequisite to inclusion. An alternate paradigm reverses this order and requires educators to abandon their emphasis on skills temporarily and place the child in the general classroom with appropriate supports. The rationale is that a student's desire to belong, to be "one of the kids," provides him or her with the motivation to learn new skills, a motivation that is noticeably absent in segregated classrooms. This new paradigm is represented schematically as follows:

STUDENT → General classroom → Skills (with support)

This paradigm, with its recognition of the importance of belonging, is not a new concept that was introduced by the inclusive education movement. Maslow (1987), in his discussion of a hierarchy of human needs, pointed out that belonging is an essential and prerequisite human need that must be met before an individual can achieve a sense of self-worth. Maslow posited that the needs of people can be divided and prioritized into five levels. Individuals do not seek the satisfaction of a need at one level until the previous level of need is met. The five levels of need that Maslow identified were physiological, safety/ security, belonging/social affiliation, self-esteem, and self-actualization. They are represented as a pyramid in Figure 1.

Maslow maintained that people's most basic needs are those required for physical survival: shelter, warmth, food, drink, and so forth. Once these needs are met, individuals are then able to address

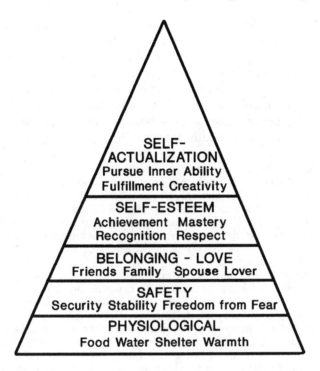

SELF-
ACTUALIZATION
Pursue Inner Ability
Fulfillment Creativity

SELF-ESTEEM
Achievement Mastery
Recognition Respect

BELONGING - LOVE
Friends Family   Spouse Lover

SAFETY
Security Stability Freedom from Fear

PHYSIOLOGICAL
Food Water Shelter Warmth

Figure I.   Maslow's hierarchy of human needs. (From Maslow, A.H. [1970]. *Motivation and personality* [2nd ed., p. 45]. New York: HarperCollins; reprinted by permission of HarperCollins Publishers.)

their needs for safety and security, including freedom from danger. Once the individual's safety is ensured, belonging or love, which is usually found in families, friendships, membership in associations, and communities, then becomes a priority. Maslow stressed that only when people are anchored in a community do they develop self-esteem, the need to assure themselves of their own self-worth. Maslow claimed that the need for self-esteem can be met through mastery or achievement in a given field or through gaining respect or recognition from others. Once the need for self-esteem is largely met, Maslow stated, people develop a new restlessness and the urge to discover and develop their unique gifts or talents. As Maslow stated, "A musician must make music, an artist must paint, a poet must write, if he is to be at ultimate peace with himself. What a man *can* be, he *must* be. He must be true to his own nature" (1970, p. 48). Maslow referred to this final level of need as *self-actualization*.

I believe that the majority of educators would agree that it is tremendously important for a child to develop a sense of self-worth and confidence. However, in our society, especially in the field of education, it has been assumed that a child's sense of self-worth can be developed from a sense of personal achievement that is independent of the child's sense of belonging. If we concur with Maslow, however, we see that self-worth can arise only when an individual is grounded in community. Contained within Maslow's writings is a powerful argument that belonging is one of the central pillars that has been missing from our educational structure for some time. Maslow explained:

> If both the physiological and the safety needs are fairly well gratified, there will emerge the love and affection and belongingness needs. . . . Now the person will feel keenly, as never before, the absence of friends, or a sweetheart, or a wife, or children. He will hunger for affectionate relations with people in general, namely, for a place in his group or family, and he will strive with great intensity to achieve this goal. . . . He will feel sharply the pangs of loneliness, of ostracism, of rejection, of friendlessness, of rootlessness.
>
> We have very little scientific information about the belongingness need, although this is a common theme in novels, autobiographies, poems and plays and also in the newer sociological literature. From these we know in a general way the destructive effects on children of moving too often; of disorientation; of the general over-mobility that is forced by industrialization; of being without roots, or of despising one's roots, one's origins, one's group; of being torn from one's home and family, and friends and neighbors; of being a transient or a newcomer rather than a native. We still underplay the deep importance of the neighborhood, of one's territory, of one's clan, of one's own "kind," one's class, one's gang, one's familiar working colleagues. . . .
>
> I believe that the tremendous and rapid increase in personal growth groups and intentional communities may in part be motivated by this unsatisfied hunger for contact, for intimacy, for belongingness and by the need to overcome the widespread feelings of alienation, aloneness, strangeness, and loneliness, which have been worsened by our mobility, by the breakdown of traditional groupings, the scattering of families, the generation gap, the steady urbanization and disappearance of village face-to-faceness, and the resulting shallowness of American friendship. My strong impression is also that some proportion of youth rebellion groups—I don't know how many or how much—is motivated by the profound hunger for groupiness, for contact, for real togetherness. . . . Any good society must satisfy this need, one way or another, if it is to survive and be healthy. (1987, p. 20)

There is an enormous amount of evidence, surprisingly from the field of corporate management, that providing a person with a sense of belonging is pivotal for that person to excel. Management consultants such as Peters and Waterman (1982) have outlined dozens of strategies for senior managers to use to foster a sense of belonging among staff. Japanese corporations devote huge amounts of energy and money to practices and policies (e.g., mandatory work uniforms, subsidized apartment buildings) that foster belonging among employees.

Belonging—having a social context—is requisite for the development of self-esteem and self-confidence. This is why Maslow positioned self-esteem above belonging in his hierarchy. Without a social context in which to validate a person's perceived worth, self-worth is not internalized. The context can vary from small and concrete, as with babies, to universal and highly abstract, as with artists.

Despite the essential importance of belonging as a precursor to the development of self-esteem and the motivation to pursue education, it is interesting to note that this is the one level of Maslow's hierarchy for which schools provide little nurturance or assistance. Schools have practices and programs to support physiological needs (e.g., subsidized breakfasts, hot lunch programs), safety needs (e.g., traffic, sex, drug, and health education), and specialized learning needs in a vast array of curriculum domains, as well as learning structures to build confidence and esteem (e.g., cooperative group learning, mastery learning models with individualized objectives and performance criteria, esteem-building curriculum units). Yet, creating caring communities was not a mission or a practice in the overly tracked, segregated, excluding schools of the 20th century.

INVERSION OF MASLOW'S HIERARCHY: EARNING THE RIGHT TO BELONG

Despite the wealth of research and personal experience that gives validity to Maslow's position, it is not uncommon for educators to work from the premise that *achievement and mastery rather than belonging are the primary if not the sole precursors for self-esteem.* As Figure 2 illustrates, the education system, in fact, has dissected and inverted Maslow's hierarchy of needs so that belonging has been transformed from an unconditional need and right of all people into something that must be earned, something that can be achieved only by the "best" students. Regardless of the evidence to the contrary (e.g., high incidence of child abuse and neglect), the curricula and the structure of schools are based on the assumption that children who come to school have their physiological and safety needs met at home. Students, on entering school, are immediately expected to learn the curriculum. Successful mastery of schoolwork is expected to foster the children's sense of self-worth, which in turn will enable them to join the community as responsible citizens. Children are required, as it were, to *learn* their right to belong.

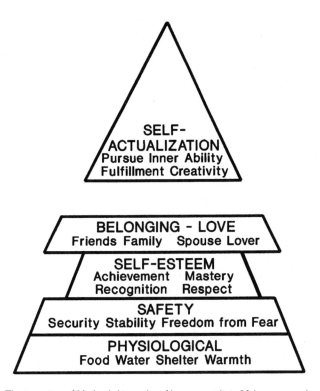

Figure 2.   The inversion of Maslow's hierarchy of human needs in 20th-century education.

I have often heard the claim in the field of education that an effective way to bolster students' self-esteem is to provide students with opportunities to experience a great deal of success. Consequently, efforts are made to ensure that the schoolwork is easy enough so that students have little difficulty in completing the work correctly, thereby fostering trust in their own abilities. As expected, students do begin to develop self-worth. In the process, however, they also learn that their worth as individuals is contingent on their being able to jump through the prescribed academic, physical, or personal hoops.

Maslow's hierarchy of needs not only reminds educators how essential it is for people to live within the context of a community but also shows them that the need for self-actualization necessarily implies that every person has abilities that warrant specific development within themselves. In the education system, however, it is often assumed that only a minority of students are gifted or have an individual calling and are capable of self-actualization. Yet this minority has been created artificially to a large degree by the fact that most schools see only those students with exceptional academic, athletic, and artistic abilities as being deserving of the opportunity to develop their talents. Students with gifts in areas other than these typically are relegated to the world of the typical and the mediocre; their wishes to have special consider-ations so that they may pursue their unique gifts (whether they are automobile repair, the ability to nurture, or a fascination with nature) are seen as self-indulgent fantasies. Consequently, it is only a few priv-ileged students who are granted the luxury to work and concentrate in areas in which they naturally excel. Ironically, because of the prevailing paradigm of the education system, the pursuits of children identified as gifted and talented often occur in segregated programs that can have a negative impact on the children's sense of belonging. Thus, even when educators grant children the opportunity to meet their needs for self-actualization, it is usually done at the expense of their sense of belonging.

CASUALTIES OF THE INVERSION OF MASLOW'S HIERARCHY

The view that personal achievement fosters self-worth is by no means limited to the field of education. The perception that individuals must earn their right to belong permeates society. A central tenet of culture is that uniformity is valued, and conformity is the criterion for belong-ing. Moreover, people are excluded *because* of their diversity. The weight loss craze is a blatant example of the ways in which people feel driven to earn the right to belong. Most dieters engage in a form of self-talk (reinforced by weight loss commercials) that is totally consis-tent with the inverted hierarchy of needs in that they say, "If I lose 50 pounds and go from a size 16 to a size 10 [achievement], then I will feel better about myself [self-esteem], and perhaps then I will be able to regain the lost romance in my marriage [belonging]." Similarly, one can see how the prevalence of workaholism corresponds with the same inversion of needs. The reasoning goes, "If I work 60 hours a week [achievement], then I'll be assured of my own ability in this role [self-esteem], and I will be respected by my colleagues and will not be fired [belonging]." Therefore, society holds belonging as something that is earned through academic or physical achievement, appearance, and a host of other socially valued criteria. Belonging no longer is an inher-ent right of being human. Schools, being a reflection of society, perpet-uate this cultural value.

When a school system makes belonging and acceptance condi-tional on achievement, students are basically left with two options. They can either decide that they are incapable of attaining these expectations and therefore resign themselves to a feeling of personal inadequacy or decide to try to gain acceptance through achievement in a particular area (e.g., sports, academics, appearance). In either case, there are potentially serious negative consequences for students: school dropout, perfectionism and suicide, gangs, and segregated classes.

School Dropout as a Casualty

It is fairly easy to see how students who see themselves as incapable of achieving excellence develop a belief of personal unworthiness as well as a feeling of hopelessness of ever becoming worthy. Our society, including most schools, highly values academic achievement, physical prowess, and attractiveness. Students who do not excel in at least one of these areas are thereby devalued. These are the students who, quite understandably, drop out of school. They remove themselves from the school environment, in which they are devalued, and sometimes enter into other, sometimes dangerous situations in which they are valued.

Perfectionism and Suicide as Casualties

The repercussions of conditional belonging are not limited to those students who fail to excel. There are extremely negative consequences for the achievers as well. When students strive to become shining scholars or all-star centers on basketball teams, they intrinsically learn that their valued membership in the school is dependent on maintaining these standards of achievement. As a result, many students wake up each morning and face a day of ongoing pressure to be "good enough to belong," afraid that, if they blow a test, miss the critical layup shot in the last seconds of the game, or wear the wrong kind of sneakers, their status among their peers and possibly within the school will be sacrificed.

Tragically, a growing number of adolescents find that the endless demand to be "good enough to belong" is beyond them, and they end the struggle by taking their own lives. As one begins to recognize the process of living in a world of conditional belonging, one can better understand why students who commit suicide frequently are those whom we least expect to do so. Although Maslow's hierarchy of needs may not provide a complete framework for understanding and coping with this issue, I believe the absence of belonging in schools is a contributing factor to teenage suicide.

Of course, most student achievers do not take their own lives. The stress that these students feel, however, cannot be minimized. Teachers are well aware of students who are perfectionists, obsessively driven to avoid any slight error despite continual reassurances from family and teachers that such concern is unwarranted. Here again, it is important to step back and see the student within the context of a school and a society that repeatedly send the message that one must earn the right to belong. When community, acceptance, and belonging—some of the most primal needs of being human—are held out as the rewards for achievement, students cannot be expected to believe assurances that they will be accepted as they are. In all likelihood, we do not believe that for ourselves, because everything else in society screams out that belonging is almost totally dependent on perfection. The implicit messages in schools have caused perfection, and, ironically, school personnel perceive this perfectionism as a sign of emotional instability on the part of the student.

Gangs as a Casualty

One environment that seems to offer a sense of belonging to youths is that of gangs. In fact, Maslow's hierarchy of needs seems to provide a plausible rationale for understanding why gangs are popular among youth. Teenage gangs satisfy each level of need in Maslow's hierarchy. When youth join gangs, their physiological needs are met: food; shelter; warmth; and quasi-physiological needs, such as sex, heroin, and crack. Youth are provided with a sense of safety in the knowledge that, if they are ever harmed by another individual or group, the other members of their gang will retaliate viciously against those who caused the harm. Moreover, youth seem to be afforded a strong sense of belonging within the gang, and in this environment the belonging is based not on achievement but instead on simply "wearing one's colors." After passing a one-time initiation ritual, the sense of belonging that gangs provide is extremely close to unconditional. Given this almost unconditional acceptance and inclusion in a gang, members' feelings of self-worth naturally flourish. Anchored in this newly found sense of inclusion and self-worth, many youth begin to focus in those areas in which they excel, such as the criminal code (with all of its technicalities and loopholes), karate, stealing cars, extortion, and so forth.

It should be noted, however, that gangs do not provide youth with a sense of belonging: What they provide is a sense of allegiance. Allegiance differs from belonging in that allegiance relies on a common enemy to provide a sense of fellowship within the group. For example, the sense of cohesion within the Crips comes from the shared hatred of the Bloods and vice versa. Thus, the Crips and the Bloods have a co-dependent relationship wherein their hatred of each other reinforces the cohesion within the group. It matters little whether the rivalry is between the Crips and the Bloods, Harvard and Yale, or Dallas and Miami in the Super Bowl.

It seems that, when a society and culture loses the rituals and practices that provide its members with a sense of belonging, what people settle for is allegiance. Examples of society's increased reliance on allegiance can be found in the almost obsessive interest in professional sports; the unfounded, exaggerated, and usually destructive interest that many people (especially some parents) have in organized minor league and high school sports; and the zealous alliance people forge with a religious, political, or ideological organization or position. As has often been said, "Nothing unites a country like a war." All share the reliance on the creation of a common enemy to bring forth a sense of belonging or community. Perhaps the most central question of inclusive education is, How do we create and maintain a sense of belonging because of our diversity rather than in spite of our diversity?

Segregated Classes as a Casualty: Forcing Children to Earn the Right to Belong

Perhaps the most glaring example of an educational practice that forces students to earn the right to belong is the maintenance of segregated special classrooms and programs. The practice of making segregated classrooms an intermediary and prerequisite step toward inclusion in general classrooms explicitly validates the perception that belonging is something that must be earned rather than an essential human need and a basic human right. Although the intent of segregation is to help students with disabilities learn skills and appropriate behavior, the very act of removing students with disabilities from the presence of students who are developing typically necessarily teaches them that "they are not good enough to belong as others do" and that the privilege of belonging will be given back to them once they have acquired an undefined number of skills. The tragic irony of self-contained classrooms is that, as soon as students' sense of belonging is taken away, their capacity to learn the skills that will enable them to belong is undermined. Herein lies the most painful catch-22 situation that confronts students with disabilities—they cannot belong until they learn, but they cannot learn because they are prevented from belonging. The injustice is compounded by the fact that the lack of progress in a segregated class is seen as further evidence to justify the need for segregation.

It has been argued that segregated classrooms, although possibly inappropriate for students with minor or moderate disabilities, are absolutely necessary for children with severe or multiple disabilities (e.g., Jenkins, Pious, & Jewell, 1990). It is this line of reasoning that has resulted in one of the cruelest and most insidious forms of emotional abuse that ever could be directed at students, let alone students with severe disabilities. The placement of students with severe disabilities into segregated, self-contained classrooms or programs not only excludes them from their peers and the community but also ensures that their isolation is permanent. It is a common practice within segregated classrooms to offer rehabilitative, communication, and life skills programs as necessary requisites for entering the community. This is done in spite of the fact that the specific attributes that have led these students to be segregated, such as physical, mental, sensory, or severe learning disabilities, cannot be reduced to the point at which the student's behavior or skill level approaches what is considered typical. Consequently, the students in segregated classrooms learn not only that they are not good enough to belong but also that *they never will be good enough to belong,* because their disability, and the subsequent reason for their banishment, can never be removed.

PROVIDING BELONGING WITHOUT VALUING DIVERSITY: INAPPROPRIATE USE OF MASLOW'S HIERARCHY TO SUPPORT INCLUSIVE EDUCATION

At this point in this chapter, it is important to issue a caution to those who might be inclined to use Maslow's hierarchy of needs as a rationale for including students with intense educational needs in local school general education programs. If inclusion and belonging are adopted because people see an inclusive educational experience as a more effective way to teach skills and appropriate behavior, then inclusion or belonging opportunities become nothing more than an effective strategy to minimize disabilities. The underlying assumption of this view of inclusion is that children and adults with disabilities should be as typical as possible. When heterogeneous education is viewed in this way, legitimacy is granted to a world in which uniformity and perfection are valued, if not idolized. In this understanding of inclusion, belonging and achievements still are regarded as prerequisite steps to self-worth. The children are placed in environments in which they will feel as if they belong, so that they might learn the prescribed skills to a degree that they might be deemed to really belong in general education. Again, Maslow's concept of belonging becomes misconstrued and inverted in a different but fundamentally inappropriate way, and its effect on children is no less damaging.

All children are children. The perception that some children are typical and others who have disabilities need to be repaired in some way is still a concomitant of a society that values uniformity rather than diversity. The potential of heterogeneous education lies in the possibility of redefining society's concept of what is typical. When children are given the right to belong, they are given a right to their diversity. They are wholly welcomed into neighborhoods as individuals who enrich our lives, without the construction of rehabilitative hoops through which they must jump in order to become "typical enough" to belong.

Moreover, I believe that good educators feel it is their responsibility to help each student discover what his or her individual strengths and capacities are and then facilitate opportunities for him or her to concentrate and excel in those areas. To mold students with disabilities into carbon copies of students who are developing typically so that all have uniform abilities is a betrayal of the awesome wonder of an individual. To attempt to do the same to students without disabilities is no less a travesty.

INCLUSIVE EDUCATION: AN OPPORTUNITY TO ACTUALIZE MASLOW'S HIERARCHY AND REDISCOVER BELONGING AS A HUMAN RIGHT

In the 1980s, my motivation for advocating for the inclusion of students with severe disabilities within general classrooms arose out of a sense of social injustice. I believed that students, by being placed in segregated classrooms or programs, were being denied the opportunities to learn socially appropriate behavior and to develop friendships with their peers. In the intervening time, however, I have become increasingly alarmed at the severity of the social problems in schools. Academic averages at the end of the 20th century were plummeting. The dropout rate was increasing, and teen pregnancy was becoming a major social concern. Teenage suicide was increasing at an exponential rate and was the second leading cause of adolescent death in the United States and Canada (Health and Welfare Canada, 1987; Patterson, Purkey, & Parker, 1986). Extreme violence, drug dependency, gangs, anorexia nervosa, and depression among students rose to the point that these problems were perceived almost as an expected part of high school culture. The job description of teachers vacillates between educator and psychotherapist and at times even becomes that of "benevolent sorcerer." University and corporate establishments also are becoming increasingly vocal about the lack of preparedness of high school graduates. It is little wonder that principals attend high-powered corporate seminars on crisis management rather than the more sedate presentations on curriculum implementation.

What we are witnessing at the turn of the 21st century, I believe, are the symptoms of a society in which self-hatred has become an epidemic. Feelings of personal inadequacy have become so common in schools and culture that we have begun to assume that it is part of human nature. It is certainly questionable whether society will be able to survive if this self-hatred is allowed to flourish.

In attempting to counter this crisis, many supposed pundits of education reform are claiming that we are in desperate need of an immediate return to those values consistent with the words *standards, achievement,* and *curriculum.* Before we run full-speed backward, grasping at these hard words and clutching them close to our bosom, it may be wise to pause, if only for a moment, to consider that these social maladies may stem not from the lack of achievement but from the lack of belonging.

The degree of underachievement and unfulfilled potential in society may not be the result of widespread laziness. It may result from a sense of apathy that so often accompanies the constant demand to be perfect enough to belong. What is needed in society and especially in the education system is not more rigorous demands to achieve and master so that our youth will move closer to ideal perfection. What is needed is a collective effort to search for ways to foster a sense of belonging in schools, not only for students but also for the staff. When we are able to rely on peers' individual strengths rather than expect them to attain complete mastery in all areas, then belonging begins to precede achievement, and we may be welcomed into the community not because of our perfection but because of our inherent natural and individual capacities.

Inclusive education represents a concrete and manageable step that can be taken in school systems to ensure that all students begin to learn that belonging is a right, not a privileged status that is earned. If we are to create schools in which students feel welcomed and part of a community, then we must begin by creating schools that welcome the diversity of all children.

The fundamental principle of inclusive education is the valuing of diversity in the human community. Every person has a contribution to offer to the world. Yet, in society, narrow parameters have been drawn around what is valued and how one makes a contribution. The ways in which people with disabilities can contribute to the world may be less apparent; they often fall outside the goods-and-services-oriented, success-driven society. Consequently, it is concluded that no gift is present, so many educators set about trying to minimize the disability, believing that, by doing so, their students will move closer to becoming contributing members of society.

When inclusive education is fully embraced, we abandon the idea that children have to become typical in order to contribute to the world.

Instead, we search for and nourish the gifts that are inherent in all people. We begin to look beyond typical ways of becoming valued members of the community and, in doing so, begin to realize the achievable goal of providing all children with an authentic sense of belonging.

As a collective commitment to educate *all* children takes hold and typical students realize that "those kids" do belong in their schools and classes, typical students will benefit by learning that their own membership in the class and society is something that has to do with human rights rather than academic or physical ability. In this way, it is conceivable that the students of inclusive schools will be liberated from the tyranny of earning the right to belong. It is ironic that the students who were believed to have the least worth and value may be the only ones who can guide us off the path of social destruction.

REFERENCES

Education for All Handicapped Children Act of 1975, PL 94-142, 20 U.S.C. §§ 1400 *et seq.*

Health and Welfare Canada. (1987). *Suicide in Canada: Report of the national task force on suicide in Canada* (Catalogue No. H39-107/1987E). Ottawa, Ontario, Canada: Statistics Canada.

Jenkins, J., Pious, C., & Jewell, M. (1990). Special education and the regular education initiative. *Exceptional Children, 56,* 479–491.

Lipsky, D.K., & Gartner, A. (1997). *Inclusion and school reform: Transforming America's classrooms.* Baltimore: Paul H. Brookes Publishing Co.

Maslow, A.H. (1970). *Motivation and personality* (2nd ed.). New York: HarperCollins.

Maslow, A.H. (1987). *Motivation and personality* (3rd ed.). New York: HarperCollins.

Patterson, J.L., Purkey, S.C., & Parker, J.V. (1986). *Productive school systems for a nonrational world.* Alexandria, VA: Association for Supervision and Curriculum Development.

Peters, T.J., & Waterman, R.H. (1982). *In search of excellence: Lessons from America's best-run companies.* New York: HarperCollins.

Villa, R.A., & Thousand, J.S. (1995). The rationales for creating inclusive schools. In R.A. Villa & J.S. Thousand (Eds.), *Creating inclusive schools* (pp. 28–44). Alexandria, VA: Association for Supervision and Curriculum Development.

Wagner, M. (1989). Youth with disabilities during transition: An overview and description of findings from the national longitudinal transition study. In J. Chadsey-Rusch (Ed.), *Transition Institute at Illinois: Project director's fourth annual meeting* (pp. 24–52). Champaign: University of Illinois.

Chapter 5

A Framework for
Thinking About Systems Change

Timothy P. Knoster,
Richard A. Villa, and Jacqueline S. Thousand

Why is it that change in schools appears to be so difficult and unwelcome despite general acknowledgment of the need for change? In a general sense, people come to accept the fact that change is inevitable throughout their lives. In light of this truth, why do so many practices in schools appear to be frozen in time like a deer in the headlights of an approaching car? Why is it that teachers often feel confusion and disorientation, anxiety and helplessness, and frustration and despair in their efforts to keep up with the increasing number of recommended practices in education? Furthermore, why is it that changes in belief systems and practices can take root and flourish in some places but the application of similar approaches wither and die on the vine in others?

Questions like these have historically beleaguered educators, politicians, and the general public over the years, at times with a degree of hysteria. Although many factors have contributed to educators' limited success in realizing significant change toward inclusion in the majority of schools in the United States and Canada, one of the primary reasons may have been the predominant focus on the task of operationally defining the form and function of change at the expense of attending to the process and interactive nature of change on a personal level. To paraphrase Wheatley in *Leadership and the New Science: Learning About Organization from an Orderly Universe* (1992), schools cannot be changed by imposing a model developed elsewhere, because there is no objective reality waiting to reveal its secrets to us; there is only what we create through engagement with one another and shared experiences. Exploring this notion further should help to establish a clearer focus for those interested in facilitating change toward inclusive schooling.

Some have argued that the apparent resistance to change in schools is inevitable for individuals who are affected by the changes most directly (e.g., Barker, 1992; Herzberg, 1990; Vaill, 1989). Others have approached the study of change using different paradigms to assess how change is implemented or accommodated by each individual educator, by teams of educators within a given school, by people in the school system (including all buildings within the defined community), or by people affiliated with schools in a general sense within the context of society at large (e.g., Deal, 1987; Parnes, 1988; Scholtes, 1993; Senge, 1990). Although the collective body of information on how change takes place in schools has been helpful in expanding knowledge and has supported an increasing number of schools in their transition toward an inclusive model, widespread and sustained inclusive change across schools has proved elusive to date.

The context for change with which people are confronted in schools is deeply rooted in Western culture's orientation toward understanding the finite details of how things work. Western civilization's energies and attention historically have focused on how to build a better mousetrap. In light of this orientation, one should not be surprised that most approaches to implementing change in school systems represent a natural evolution of the how-to mind-set as many educators seek to find the details or the how-tos, in the form of a recipe for change as if schools were just another version of machinery to be retooled.

In short, the somewhat myopic preoccupation with understanding *how* has in many ways hindered educators in asking questions associated with *why* change occurs. This is not to suggest that gaining an understanding of the finite operating details is not important. Rather, the point is that understanding such detail is not adequate by itself to facilitate durable inclusive change over time within the school community.

The process of change is an intellectual, emotional, and spiritual experience for those whom the change affects directly. In a simplistic sense, the intellectual aspect of change can be framed by addressing the how-to questions associated with inclusive practices (e.g., how to design instruction in heterogeneous classrooms so that all children develop successfully). In a parallel manner, the emotional and spiritual aspects of change can be framed by addressing questions associated with understanding the belief systems of inclusive education (e.g., why all children should learn together in their local neighborhood schools). Facilitating inclusive change requires a comprehensive approach that attends to both the how and the why of the process of change.

FOUNDATIONS FOR
FACILITATING INCLUSIVE SCHOOLING

Writing of school reform efforts of his day, Comenius lamented, "Despite all of the effort [schools] remain the same as they were" (cited in Deal & Peterson, 1990, p. 3). Comenius' observation, made more than 350 years ago, has been echoed by many through the centuries, including Sarason in *The Predictable Failure of Educational Reform: Can We Change Course Before It's Too Late?* (1990). Specifically, Sarason lamented that changing a system is not for the conceptually and interpersonally fainthearted.

Since 1950, divergent approaches to creating improvements in organizations have been articulated, tested, and refined. This rich history of the study of organizational change is timely because the 21st-century society into which our children will venture will be quite different from that of the second half of the 20th century. As many have pointed out (e.g., Benjamin, 1989; Schlechty, 1990; Skrtic, 1991), society in the 21st century will be dominated by a rapidly changing, information-based, communication-dependent, interdependent, worldwide marketplace that will require problem solving, human interaction, self-education, and self-discipline on the part of workers.

The methods or steps that result in fundamental improvements in schooling have been conceptualized and described in different ways. For example, Lewin (1951/1975) conceptualized an effective change process as having three stages: the *unfreezing* of the present level of a group's life or culture, *movement* to a new level, and *refreezing* at the new level. Subsequent authors have described these three phases as *initiation, implementation,* and *institutionalization* (Fullan, 1982; Fullan & Miles, 1992; Fullan & Stiegelbauer, 1991) or *adoption, implementation,* and *continuation* (Eiseman, Fleming, & Roody, 1990b).

Hord, Rutherford, Huling-Austin, and Hall (1987) researched and verified several assumptions about change within schools and concluded first that change is a process that takes time, usually sev-

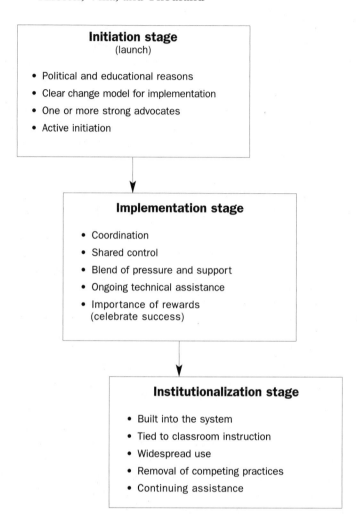

Figure 1.   Adaptation of Fullan's systems change model. (Adapted from Fullan & Stiegelbauer, 1991.)

eral years. They also concluded that change is primarily about individuals and their beliefs and actions rather than about programs,
materials, technology, or equipment. Change is not impersonal;
instead, it is a highly subjective experience. Consequently, change
requires its facilitators to acquire the following dispositions:

1. Be up front.

2. Focus on individuals.

3. Expect the unknown and go with the flow.

Managing Complex Change

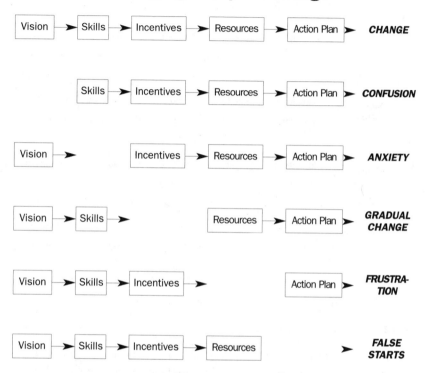

Figure 2. Adaptation of Ambrose's (1987) managing complex change model.

The work of Fullan (1982; Fullan & Stiegelbauer, 1991) has had a great influence on our thinking on change toward inclusive schooling. We were initially impressed with his conceptualization of the phases of change as depicted in our adaptation of his work in Figure 1. In building on this body of work, Villa and Thousand (1992) refined and expanded Fullan's stages to include

1. Visionizing
2. Introducing
3. Expanding
4. Selectively maintaining change and change processes

This expanded framework was based on the belief that effective schools can be built and that they are built by individuals who choose to be stewards of a larger vision.

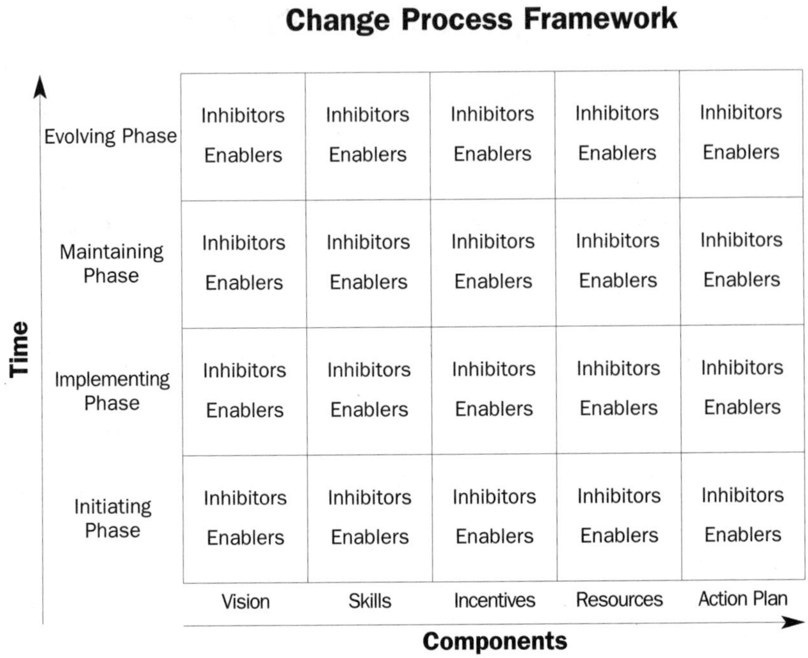

Change Process Framework

	Vision	Skills	Incentives	Resources	Action Plan
Evolving Phase	Inhibitors Enablers	Inhibitors Enablers	Inhibitors Enablers	Inhibitors Enablers	Inhibitors Enablers
Maintaining Phase	Inhibitors Enablers	Inhibitors Enablers	Inhibitors Enablers	Inhibitors Enablers	Inhibitors Enablers
Implementing Phase	Inhibitors Enablers	Inhibitors Enablers	Inhibitors Enablers	Inhibitors Enablers	Inhibitors Enablers
Initiating Phase	Inhibitors Enablers	Inhibitors Enablers	Inhibitors Enablers	Inhibitors Enablers	Inhibitors Enablers

Time (vertical axis) — Components (horizontal axis)

Figure 3. Change Process Framework.

In further building on this logical expansion, we began to look operationally at the necessary component activities associated with each of the four noted phases of change. Figure 2 depicts factors in managing complex change adapted by Knoster (1993) from Ambrose's (1987) framework for managing complex change within organizations that were conducive to our expanded thinking.

Given these foundations for viewing and facilitating inclusive schooling and recognizing the need to further expand a change model so that it would address both the intellectual and emotional aspects of the change process, we formulated the Change Process Framework presented in Figure 3. This framework synthesizes previous conceptualizations of the change process and accommodates the interactive nature of inclusive school reform across the time phases that Fullan and Stiegelbauer (1991) and Villa and Thousand (1992) described, as discussed previously.

INCLUSIVE CHANGE FRAMEWORK

The context of change in schools at the turn of the 21st century is dynamic and complex. In this regard, each school building serves as the unit of analysis in facilitating inclusive change. A building-based approach best accommodates the specific strengths and needs in a site-based manner. Figure 3 depicts a synthesis of five essential components in managing complex change nested within and across four general phases of change at the building level. The Change Process Framework is accommodating to schools wherever they may be in terms of implementing inclusive school reforms. It is our belief that these factors and time phases also can be generalized to the districtwide level to encompass parallel facilitation activities related to inclusive change across multiple buildings with minor adaptation.

Each of the five component factors has an important role across each of the phases of the change process (e.g., vision plays a role in the initiating, implementing, selectively maintaining, and evolving phases). In a like manner, each of the phases comprises relevant activities associated with each of the five factors. For example, throughout the initiation phase, factors associated with vision, skills, incentives, resources, and an action plan are relevant.

Although the framework is presented in a two-dimensional linear format, it is important to understand that dynamic change rarely provides clear onset and offset points. Therefore, a given school is likely to find itself involved concurrently with activities associated with various cells of this framework. This in and of itself should emphasize the importance of action planning across all phases of the change process.

Each of the 20 cells within this framework has a series of relevant questions that need to be addressed. Guiding questions concerning both the why and the how of inclusive schooling are provided across all cells in a phase-by-phase fashion that parallels the theoretical process of change within a given school building. Examples of *hinge points* are given within the context of each guiding question in the form of what have been termed either *inhibitors* or *enablers*. Inhibitors and enablers, for purposes of this chapter, provide illustrations of issues that have been known to either facilitate or impede the process of inclusive school reform. The presence of an inhibitor or an enabler in a given school does not by itself guarantee success or failure. Rather, inhibitors and enablers provide facilitators of change with concrete points of concern for planning supportive activities associated with desired outcomes.

Finally, the descriptions across components within each phase of change as described in the following sections are cumulative in nature. For example, the engagement, or what staff within the building have come to refer to affectionately as *buy-in*, is essential to inclusive school reform. Therefore, different forms of staff engagement are highlighted across all phases of the change process. The greatest degree of detail in all instances is provided under the "Initiating Phase" section, with descriptions in later phases building on the information already described.

INITIATING PHASE

Vision: Part I
Why is inclusive schooling important for *all* stakeholders in the education process? What is in it for each person from his or her mind's eye?

Point 1: Life is full of choices. Exercising our choices calls for judgment. Point 2: Inclusive schools operate on a shared belief system. Beliefs and orientations are personal matters and can therefore be touchy topics to discuss. Point 3: Exercising judgment in how we approach discussing beliefs with regard to inclusive school reform can have a dramatic impact on the realization of durable change. The key to success may lie in finding ways to support others who may appear resistant to seeing the value in change.

Typically, a handful of educators at any given school are interested and in turn willing to consider changing how their school operates and how they interact with their students, based on the belief that the proposed changes will directly benefit children. These inspired educators form a constructive subculture within schools and can serve as great enablers throughout the change process. In order to initiate a sustainable shift in momentum and practice within a given school, however, it is important to nurture a critical mass of educators within the given building to see the advantages of inclusion from possibly a different perspective that better reflects how a significant number of staff feel about their current situation.

For example, one of the typical inhibitors of inclusive change during the initiation phase is the fear of many staff that they will not receive adequate information or support to enable them to be effective in their roles. This fear is often compounded by the fact that there are probably already a few students in each teacher's class who are struggling in the learning process across content areas, and therefore staff may have great difficulty in envisioning how they can be effective with a greater degree of diversity than they may have present already within their classrooms. Contextual factors such as the ones illustrated in this example often define what individual staff members see as their immediate reality and can have a profound impact on their buy-in to the change process. Translating the value of inclusive practice into tangible support structures for staff, along with articulating its value for children, can influence the rate of change positively. Sustainable catalysts of change in the form of committed staff can create the necessary sense of urgency required for change once staff see a value in inclusive reform from their vantage point (e.g., "Integrated and coordinated support will not only help me with this one student, but also with these other students as well").

Vision: Part II

What are the relevant structures and processes for collaboration at the given school to facilitate reaching initial consensus on an inclusive set of beliefs and a mission statement, and what is the plan for social marketing: who, what, when, where, and how?

"One of the greatest barriers to school reform is the lack of a clear and compelling vision" (Schlechty, 1990, p. 137). Unless effort is devoted to building a common vision, confusion for some or many is likely to result.

It is widely accepted that "organizations are governed as much by belief and faith as by rationality and outcome" (Deal, 1990, p. vi) and that any organizational change initiative is guided by belief and faith in a vision. Supporting people to envision a future destination point and building a bridge backward to connect that future point with present realities represents one of the greatest challenges for facilitators of inclusive school reform. The ability to build a bridge backward from a vision has been described euphemistically as the "Merlin factor":

> Legend has it that Merlin the Magician was the great King Arthur's mentor. As depicted in *The Once and Future King* by T.H. White, Merlin had an uncanny ability to know the future. Occasionally he would give others some insight into how he knew what was going to happen before it did. In the book, Merlin and Arthur meet for the first time when young Arthur, while wandering lost, stumbles upon Merlin's forest home. Invited within, Arthur is surprised to find a place already awaiting him at the table:
>   "Ah yes," Merlin said, "How did I know to set breakfast for two? . . . Now ordinary people are born forwards in time, if you understand what I mean, and nearly everything in the world goes forward too. This makes it quite easy for ordinary people to live. . . . But unfortunately I was born at the wrong end of time, and I have to live backwards from in front, while surrounded by a lot of people living forward from behind." (Smith, 1995)

Smith (1995) noted that White's story creates a striking metaphor for the critical factor that characterizes successful leaders of change to imbue their organization with new strategic intent: In short, the Merlin factor is the ability to assess the potential of the present moment from the perspective of a clearly envisioned point of departure in the future.

Leaders in inclusive school reform stress the importance of clarifying for themselves, school personnel, and the community a vision of
success based on the general operating assumptions that 1) all children
are able to learn, 2) all children should be educated together in their
community's schools, and 3) the school system is responsible for
addressing the unique needs of all children. To articulate an inclusive
vision is necessary but not sufficient by itself. People within the school
community need to be actively engaged in the development and adoption of the vision. Again, the ends (i.e., outcomes such as a common
vision) and means (i.e., the process of building consensus in the vision)
must mutually justify one another in order for inclusive reform to
become durable.

Reaching consensus on orientations to practice grounded in
shared beliefs provides a great challenge within our schools. Many of
the traditional structures and hierarchies in schools present formida-
ble inhibitors to the process of having meaningful dialogue among
stakeholders. Sizer (1991) noted three standpoints that would help
change America's schools: focus . . . focus . . . focus. Reaching consensus on a shared focus requires careful attention and activity to
establish two-way lines of communication coupled with open discussion to work through concerns as they arise. Authenticity and integrity in the dialogue and decision-making processes are typically
prerequisites of durable changes in practice. Large-group, small-
group, and paired discussions need to occur in both formally facilitated and extemporaneous formats. The latter occur naturally within
any given school and community and its various subcultures. One
naturally occurring enabler in this regard is that people generally
want to talk with others when faced with important decisions.
Capitalizing on this natural tendency toward dialogue can prove beneficial in many ways. Naturally occurring conversation by itself,
however, is likely to be insufficient to initiate or to maintain a significant change agenda. Therefore, structured dialogue must also be
designed thoughtfully and facilitated over time in order for new orientations and distributed leadership to take root.

The terrain for some of the dialogue, regardless of venue, is likely
to be bumpy. In order for meaningful conversations to occur, participants must be engaged in discussions that are safe and open to reflect
on and question the basic foundations of practice within the given
school. Controversy, properly facilitated, can be a change agent's best
friend in this regard. Significant change is most likely when participants in the collective conversation feel not only safe but also encouraged to raise controversial topics for discussion. Alternatively, to
paraphrase Frederick Douglass, to expect inclusive reform in our

schools without controversy is akin to expecting crops without plowing the ground. Herein lies the implicit importance of attending to the details of the process of change as well as the content of inclusive school reform.

Skills: Part I

Beyond the value to the children at school, why is it important for professional development to occur for *all* staff in a school? On a personal level, what do staff get out of improving their immediate skills in particular practices associated with inclusion?

As a sense of common purpose among staff evolves at a school, natural opportunities for professional development occur. It is not uncommon to find staff at a given school gradually shifting their collective orientation from raising questions such as "Why should our school become more inclusive?" toward questions such as "How can we make our school more inclusive?" Inherent in this shift in attitudes toward inclusion are enabling opportunities to build staff members' skills through focused in-service training.

One of the key inhibitors to address in skill building during the initiation phase is that the change process is a personalized experience for each person involved in the change. Staff at a given school are likely to find themselves at different junctures in the change process, and therefore their relationships with one another are likely to be transformed over time. In light of these contextual factors, it is clear that no one professional development program can move all staff at the same pace of skill development, nor should it. Rather, a healthy professional development program should provide staff who find themselves at different levels of comfort with inclusive reform (i.e., meaningful professional development is individualized or personalized) with meaningful opportunities for self-improvement.

No matter how exciting or promising an innovation, staff need training, guided practice and feedback, and opportunities to solve problems with colleagues to clarify the innovation's nuances (Joyce & Showers, 1995). Furthermore, for the innovation to become the new culture, people must come to understand how the innovation is significant to their personal and professional growth and the growth of their students (Hord et al., 1987). Professional development is a centerpiece in inclusive school reform because it serves as a strategy to reduce anxiety by helping to transform the culture of the school.

In a general sense, staff who acquire a constructive sense of urgency with the reform process are more than likely to view professional development opportunities as means by which to accomplish a shared set of goals. Staff being supported to expand their skills in this sense can actually help themselves to achieve personal goals associated with the common vision in the school. Concomitantly, staff who find themselves in the earlier stages of reorientation toward inclusion may find expanding their skills to be not only a vehicle to become more effective with an increasingly diverse student population but also a vehicle for further connecting with an inclusive vision.

It is impossible to provide all of the training necessary to support inclusive school reform in one common environment or at one time. The reality is that there is truly no ready time for inclusive reform. Therefore, training priorities need to be established by the people most directly affected by the change at the school (i.e., teachers). It is recommended that the selection of initial professional development areas be based on what staff view as their top priority at the onset of the process. For example, one school might begin the process of staff development by prioritizing inclusive practices to support students who present behavior that impedes their learning or the learning of others, whereas another school might start by making accommodations for students with disabilities in the general classroom and using developmentally appropriate practices with these students. The point is that the initial emphasis should be placed on topics and practices that staff view as top priorities. In addition, in-service training should include reflective exercises related to the core beliefs and operating sets of assumptions associated with inclusive school reform. Ultimately, the school community needs to craft and ratify an ongoing comprehensive in-service training agenda that develops "innovation related knowledge, performance skills, and positive attitudes" (Hord et al., 1987, p. 76). Teachers and administrators need to develop inclusive orientations and core competencies such as those described throughout this book.

Whatever the initial focus in content of the training curriculum, it is important to ensure its compatibility with the vision of inclusion. Everyone in the school community should be engaged in various aspects of the in-service training program. Although initial training may be organized and initially delivered to early adopters, engagement by all stakeholders needs to occur over time. No one directly involved with changes in practice should be exempt from participation in the training program if durable long-term change is the goal. Specifically, to excuse those who may be initially reluctant, resistant, or apathetic toward acquiring the disposition and skills to implement inclusive practices can exacerbate divisions among people, promote the development of nonconstructive subcultures and factions, foster resentments, reinforce the mind-set that "this too shall pass," and generally work against the development of an inclusive school culture.

Skills: Part II

How have staff been 1) engaged in dialogue concerning professional development, 2) recruited to actively participate in the design and delivery of the professional development plan, and 3) supported in their endeavors associated with the comprehensive system of personnel development at their school?

Cybernetic systems are self-correcting in nature. Inherently, such systems employ continuous feedback loops from which the organization can learn increasingly effective techniques with which to problem solve. Professional development provides a vehicle by which to help schools become self-correcting in nature by enabling them to become, as Senge (1990) noted, learning organizations. Professional development in the change process must become far more than simply instruction in the basic skills of the educational trade in order for a school to become a dynamic learning environment for all of its members. Staff within the school need to be intimately involved in their own professional development rather than viewed as passive participants in the process. In order for durable change to occur, staff must become intrinsically driven toward their own growth and development through skill development in inclusive practice.

Schools, by their mission, are to facilitate the learning of children. Herein lies an inherent enabler of professional development in that schools exist to foster learning. The way in which learning is defined in some schools, however, also poses an inhibiting factor because children's learning can become distorted into the linear act of imparting knowledge to students, which by its nature implies passive participation by the children. In order for schools to become learning organizations, they must become highly interactive and engaging learning communities for all of their members.

Incentives

How has the relationship between existing priorities and inclusive practices been translated for staff? Has this been done as a forced either-or choice or through a consensus-building approach?

A school system can have a shared vision; personnel can have skills and access to abundant resources; and a plan of action can be set into motion; yet, without incentives that are meaningful to each individual affected by the change, the outcome may be passive or active resistance rather than enthusiastic engagement. (This is one of the primary reasons why many schools appear to provide only "dull" compliance with federal and state laws as well as court orders related to providing education in the least restrictive environment.) Although incentives are important, heavy reliance on what have been termed *extrinsic incentives* (e.g., honors and financial awards) can inhibit durable change. As Sergiovanni explained,

> Traditional management theory is based on the principle "what gets rewarded gets done.". . . [Unfortunately,] when rewards can no longer be provided, the work no longer will be done. Work performance becomes contingent upon a bartering arrangement rather than being self-sustaining because of moral principle or deeper psychological connection. A better strategy upon which to base our efforts is "what is rewarding gets done." When something is rewarding it gets done even when "no one is looking." (1990, p. 22)

This perspective on incentives is further echoed by Kohn:

> We are often encouraged to believe that rewarding people for what they do will cause them to work harder and better. Sometimes we are explicitly schooled in the belief that while punishments and fear are destructive in an organization, rewards and the expectation of recognition are almost, by definition, positive. Research and our long term experiences, if we were attentive to those experiences, suggest exactly the opposite. Rewards and punishments are, in fact, two sides of the same coin . . . and the coin doesn't buy very much. . . . What you are essentially trying to do is control people's behavior. That inevitably backfires because rewards, like punishments, can never buy more than temporary compliance—and they do that at a terrific cost. (1998, p. 7)

Contrastingly, intrinsic motivators for educators typically include recognition of one's own increased effectiveness as evidenced through student growth and development; pride in one's own professional risk taking and growth accompanied by respected colleagues and students; feelings of personal satisfaction; and the experience of *flow*, which is "the state in which people are so involved in an activity that nothing else seems to matter; the experience itself is so enjoyable that people will do it even at great cost, for the sheer sake of doing it" (Csikszentmihalyi, 1990, p. 4).

Inclusive school reform is premised on reaching consensus on a shared set of beliefs and orientations. Thus, one of the greatest enablers (or incentives, in this case) for stakeholders in the process of change can be engagement in the process of articulating one's own beliefs and seeing one's own beliefs reflected in the larger school community's set of priorities. Having direct input into the design and delivery of support structures can also have a positive influence on collaborators in the change process. The bottom line is that staff and families are more likely to invest a higher degree of energy to problem solve the inherent challenges of meeting the needs of all students when they play active roles in program design.

The reality is that, at times, people involved with inclusive school reform are confronted with new and difficult problems that inhibit their collective ability to act spontaneously in an inclusive manner (e.g., a student who presents significant challenging behavior). Such situations are more than likely to try even the strongest team's skills and spirit. Under such circumstances, it is natural for various team members to feel at a loss and therefore to feel compelled to reflect on their beliefs. During such learning stages, comfort can be found in a common sense of purpose with regard to fostering inclusion, coupled with continuous effort and support to learn how to accommodate individuals' needs that were possibly not even present on the radar screen prior to setting the agenda for change. At some point, the ultimate question for all members of the school community becomes, "Do we pull reality toward our vision of inclusion, or do we water down our vision to meet what is considered our current reality?" Genuine and sustainable inclusive change typically depends on people who come to be motivated more by their emotions, values, beliefs, and social bonds with one another than by outside forces or pressure points based on new problems to be solved.

Resources
What is the existing method of resource allocation at the building level? How do we make the best use of limited resources during "ice-breaking activities" associated with inclusive school reform?

Suffice it to say that resources are always tight in school systems. In light of this inhibitor, it is important to plan both short- and long-term funding supports for reform activities in order to make changes accomplished in the initiation phase durable over time.

In instances when inclusive innovation has already been demonstrated repeatedly to be successful across a number of small-scale applications (e.g., 25% of all classrooms), it may be feasible to take an "all at once" approach to reform. Most schools, however, travel the path of incremental steps toward change and therefore require a different approach. The primary resource that drives the change process, regardless of the approach to reform, is time.

Change agents who are contemplating or engaged in change-related activities face a time dilemma resulting from two competing realities. First, it always seems as if there is too little time. Second, change is a process that requires a considerable amount of time and patience.

During the initiation phase, leaders can take a number of enabling steps to accelerate progress. First, it is critical to make an investment in initial training that can evolve into a longitudinal training program.

Second, as vacancies become available (or can be created to support change activities), personnel who share a compatible inclusive vision can be hired. Third, strategically build coalitions and allies among existent groups who are within and outside the school. Networking with external sources who are supportive of the change agenda often results in access to cost-efficient external technical assistance and training resources. Fourth, attempt to redirect existing training resources to jump-start the change initiative through professional development activities (e.g., visitations, conference attendance, on-site professional development through coaching). Fifth, structure increased access to resources through role redefinition.

One potential source of untapped funding that exists in most schools is the redirection of funds away from incompatible practices such as standardized assessments for grouping purposes. Redirecting resources away from such practices and toward activities and practices consistent with the vision is essential. As Sergiovanni pointed out, "A virtuous school gives as much attention to enablement as empowerment; it considers the two to be interdependent parts of the same whole: People should have both the discretion and whatever assistance they need to use it wisely" (1990, p. 117).

We propose that, for educators to readily gain access to the necessary resource of their colleagues' time, change in the structure of time usage and the establishment of new role relationships among staff are required. It is predictable for there initially to be a few professional risk takers who are willing to begin to restructure how they go about their business without extensive supports. Over the course of time, however, even the most enthusiastic educators regress to business as usual if the use of time is not redefined within the school and if resources are not strategically focused on supporting their endeavors. Table 1 provides some concrete examples of strategies related to allotting adequate time to change activities within the initiation phase.

Action Plan
Why do schools engage staff in action planning during initiation and, in turn, set the stage to implement an inclusive school agenda within the strategic planning process of the school district?

Systematic action planning is required to navigate the tumultuous currents of initiating a major change agenda effectively. Individuals within the system may have everything in line in the form of vision, skills, incentives, and resources; but in the absence of an action plan, staff may feel as if they are running on a treadmill endlessly. As the old saying goes, there *is* a difference between working harder and working

Table 1.   Strategies for expanding time for collaborative planning, teaching, and reflection

---

- Ask staff to identify with whom and when they need to collaborate and redesign the master schedule to accommodate these needs.
- Hire "permanent substitutes" to rotate through classrooms to periodically "free up" teachers to attend meetings during the day rather than before or after school.
- Institute a community service component to the curriculum; when students are in the community (e.g., Thursday afternoon), some of the staff meet.
- Schedule "specials" (e.g., art, music), clubs, and tutorials during the same time blocks (e.g., first and second period) so that teachers have 1 or 2 hours per day to collaborate.
- Engage parents and community members to plan and conduct half-day or full-day exploratory, craft, hobby (e.g., gourmet cooking, puppetry, photography), theater, or other experiential programs.
- Partner with colleges and universities; have their faculty teach in the school or offer televised lessons, demonstrations, and on-campus experiences to free up school personnel.
- Rearrange the school day to include 50- to 60-minute blocks of time before or after school for collaborative meeting and planning.
- Lengthen the school day for students by 15–30 minutes per day. The cumulative "extra" student contact hours each month allow for periodic early dismissal of students and time for teachers to meet.
- Earmark some staff development days for collaborative meetings.
- Use faculty meeting time for small-group meetings to solve problems related to issues of immediate and long-range importance.
- Build into the school schedule at least one "collaboration day" per marking period or month.
- Lengthen the school year for staff but not for students, or shorten the school year for students but not for staff.
- Go to year-round schooling with 3-week breaks every quarter; devote 4 or 5 of the 3-week intersession days to teacher collaboration.

---

smarter. Action plans help to guide staff to fit many pieces together into a larger mosaic and, when done well, acquire synergistic qualities. *Action planning* means being thoughtful and communicative about the process of change with regard to how, with whom, and in what sequence of steps or stages change is formulated, communicated, and set into motion. A healthy balance between planning and action must be found in order for change to occur within a reasonable time frame.

As Sting (1991) sang, "People go crazy in congregations, they only get better one by one." It is generally ineffective to plan for change exclusively at a systems level. Change is primarily about individuals and their beliefs and actions rather than about programs and materials. Stated differently, change is lived in the first person (i.e., emotionally) and rationalized in the third person (i.e., intellectually). Change requires its facilitators to focus on the individuals affected by the changes because what matters most in school improvement programs is the people themselves (Clark, Lotto, & Astuto, 1984).

The fact that no two people's histories are exactly alike, coupled with the fact that people react in different ways under stressful conditions, means that no two people's experiences with the change process are exactly alike. Engaging people in the action-planning process, and most specifically in articulating the necessary supports needed to be effective, is essential during the initiation phase. The old saying from the Civil Rights movement, "Nothing about me without me," has particular relevance with regard to recruiting stakeholders to become involved in the action-planning process. As previously noted during the discussion concerning incentives, engaging people in action planning is respectful and encourages personal ownership of change. Formal action planning during initiation serves as the alarm bell tolling that business as usual is about to change.

Action planning is more than likely to occur in stages or phases that parallel the four phases of change outlined in this chapter. Although formal, systematic planning can be an important enabler in the change process, it is important to be cautious about overplanning. To ensure caution about overplanning, action planning should have the vision clearly in sight with identified benchmarks and short-term goals that are within reach. Action planning should not be inhibited through the use of a readiness model, because the reality is that, for some children who are either currently excluded or at great risk of exclusion, there may never be a point in the foreseeable future when everything is in place and everyone is ready. This does not imply that caution should be thrown to the wind; rather, it means that the problem-solving process through collaborative activities needs to carry school staff, students, and their families through uncharted waters from time to time in the process of inclusive school reform.

Action plans can take many forms and require different problem-solving frameworks. In light of this, and having stated the caveats of action planning, Table 2 provides some principles associated with practical strategic planning during the initiation phase.

Senge (1990) emphasized that in healthy organizations, people examine their assumptions about how the organization operates. Change agents therefore are advised to adopt an orientation toward action planning that is based on the following assumptions:

1. No amount of knowledge clarifies which action is the correct action.

2. Each individual's personal version of an action plan is not necessarily the plan that will evolve.

Table 2.   Principles of action planning

Look outside	Throughout the change process, pay close attention to the social, political, cultural, and economic factors affecting your school.
Look inside	Carefully examine internal strengths and limitations of policies, practices, structures, and people.
Walk the talk	Be inclusive through involving stakeholders in the action-planning process from the onset.
Believe in people	Leadership usually exists within the school organization; we need to nurture people to allow their leadership qualities to surface.
Monitor progress	Change is dynamic and requires progress monitoring in much the same way that we, as we should, monitor student attainment of goals and demonstrated outcomes.
Modify plans	Based on progress monitoring, be flexible and adapt action plans as needed, and be committed to the vision and use approaches as the steppingstones.
Revisit vision	Reflection and discussion about the vision should occur not only at the onset of change but should be continuous throughout all phases of change.
Document	Put significant decisions, successes, and failures in writing as systems are often handicapped by their inability to remember their history.

3. Manageability is achieved by thinking big and starting small.

4. Reluctance or lack of participation is not necessarily a rejection of the vision.

5. Facilitating durable change in the culture through engagement and reflection, and not simply installing an innovation, is the agenda.

6. Action plans are to be negotiated and should be based on no less than the operating assumptions in this list (Fullan & Stiegelbauer, 1991).

IMPLEMENTATION PHASE

Vision
Why is it important for staff to celebrate successes throughout implementation, and how do they build in opportunities for teams and individuals to see the relationships among successes and the belief systems associated with inclusive schooling?

Nothing breeds success like success. Capitalizing on social bonds and positive experiences through the development of an *esprit de corps*—a common spirit of inspiring enthusiasm, devotion, and intense regard for the vision and honor of the group—can be powerful throughout the process of change. It is important throughout the implementation phase to facilitate staff in revisiting the vision through the celebration of success.

The celebration of accomplishments can take on many forms and does not need to require additional funding sources. Ideally, structures for celebration can be established within the typical routines of the school year in combination with carefully planned social marketing events by using print materials and various forms of media.

For example, systematically beginning various types of meetings with stories that illustrate achievements can be a powerful and cost-effective strategy. Along with the sharing of stories, it is important to distill the essence of each story into a brief sound bite that highlights the relationship between the story and the vision—the moral of the story, so to speak. Because the devil is typically found in the details of such activities, publicly getting the message out on an ongoing basis in the form of these sound bites is important throughout the implementation phase.

Skills

As experience accrues for staff at the school building, are the mechanisms in place to support staff to continue to upgrade information and skills in effective practice and identify additional skill areas for attention and resources?

Training and support in a learning organization (i.e., in an inclusive school) never ends. Inclusive school reform is about enabling schools to become vibrant environments. Learning in an inclusive school is not limited to only what is taught in the mode of formal curricula, and learners are not narrowly defined as the children who are students. Rather, learning is an endless process involving constant dialogue among all members of the school community.

Within this context of a learning organization, longitudinal professional development activities need to be sustained as implementation occurs. In many ways, the implementation phase provides some of the most fertile learning environments for students and staff.

Professional development needs are likely to change over time as increasing numbers of students gain access to supported educational opportunities at school. During the implementation phase, it is not uncommon to find more than a few child-centered teams struggling with making the necessary accommodations for successful inclusion. In fact, the likelihood of teams' struggling is present over time in relationship to the degree of accommodations needed for particular students and staff.

For example, often a given school launches integrated service delivery models for students who are in pull-out types of programs in their home schools. As success increases for teams working with this initial group of students, members of the school community begin to plan for helping students who have been placed in education programs outside their home school, school district, or both, make the transition back to their home school. Typically, the type and degree of accommodations needed for team success with these particular children stretch the creativity, resources, and spirit of teams. In such instances, it is important that training opportunities continue to be available to staff. In particular, these training experiences need to evolve in a parallel fashion with training needs newly identified by staff, coupled with an ongoing grounding in the vision of the school.

People who are involved with the implementation of change should be involved in longitudinal planning and training in the school. The training program in this phase of the change process needs to address the basic foundations of inclusive schooling (e.g., problem solving through teaming, outcome-based instruction models, child and family centeredness) along with the unique skill development needs of teams working with particular children (e.g., a given team's working with a particular student who is deaf and blind, in addition to foundational needs, also has unique needs that differ from teams supporting children who can see and hear). In order for successful implementation of inclusive school reform to take root and spread within the school, staff need to be a driving force of ongoing training. Adequate fiscal supports for professional development must therefore continue to be provided because there is no point in time when everyone has been retooled.

Incentives

Once the initial pep rallies have subsided, how are staff supported and engaged to maintain their collective sense of urgency with regard to implementing inclusive reform?

Continued investments in staff through professional development, constructive feedback, engagement in decision making, and acknowledgments for successive approximations can serve as powerful incentives throughout implementation. These foundations that are established during the initiation phase need to be carried forward and expanded on during the implementation phase.

In addition to these types of incentives, it is important that the content and process of staff evaluation be relevant to inclusive school reform and tied directly to the professional development program at school. Administrators who oversee this aspect of school operations need to individualize their approaches in a manner that is both consistent and fair to all staff.

Hord and colleagues theorized "seven stages of concern" (1987, p. 30) that individuals involved in change efforts experience. Perhaps the most salient aspect of this theoretical construct is the implicit recognition that it is the *individual* who matters; that each individual needs attention; and that personal attention to matters of concern, coupled with necessary forms of support, can further facilitate internal motivation to support change efforts. As in gardening, inclusive school reform requires constant nurturing and tilling of the soil.

Resources
Are resources dedicated proportionately to support staff-identified priorities?

Because change is typically accomplished in incremental steps, it is important to allocate resources strategically during the implementation phase. Typically, this requires flexibility because unplanned needs are likely to arise as a result of implementing inclusive change activities over the course of the first few years of implementation.

Examples of flexible resource deployment include the ability to alter staffing patterns to meet extraordinary needs for limited periods of time (e.g., schedule additional time for meetings, increase staff presence during particular periods of the day, alter the transportation schedules and arrangements) and the integration of school funds with service delivery dollars from other child-serving systems. In addition to this type of flexibility, it is important to continue to nurture a resource network throughout implementation. Although educators tend to exchange ideas and materials on an informal basis, they rarely think of themselves as integral parts of a resource network (Saxl, Miles, & Lieberman, 1989). A comprehensive resource network is composed of people with diverse perspectives and experience with inclusive school reform. Table 3 depicts constituencies to engage in building a resource network.

Action Plan
Do staff have the opportunity to provide input to and get feedback about the evolving plan of action?

During the implementation phase, a number of factors are likely to emerge that were not present or anticipated prior to change efforts. Predictably, one of the most significant of these may be the degree of diversity of students who are being educated within the ebb and flow

Table 3.   Resource network composition

Current and former colleagues
Family members of children with disabilities in school
Family members of children in school who are not thought to have disabilities
Members of the general community
Children in school with and without disabilities
Adults with disabilities
Publishers and vendors
Professional associations
Local associations
Participants in kindred school improvement movements
Teacher-preparatory entities
External service agencies
External allies in inclusive school reform

of typical school routines. Therefore, it is likely that providing supported education programs for an increasingly diverse student population will result in the need to integrate school services with services from multiple child-serving systems. Action planning during implementation therefore needs to address the questions listed in Table 4.

Often the last group of students to be included in inclusive school reform are children who have histories of impeding behavior. As a school works through the implementation phase, these students, at varying times in the process, begin either the reintegration process or the process of receiving supports in the context of the school prior to placement in external programs. In providing supported programs in such instances, it is not uncommon to need to collaborate with other child-serving systems. To this end, proactive action planning based on the guiding questions listed in Table 4 should prove helpful.

Table 4.   Interagency questions

Are there children who are currently using other services beyond school?
Are there children in our school whom we believe are in need of additional supportive services from other child-serving systems?
How do we best coordinate designing and implementing supportive services among all child-serving systems?
How do we specifically coordinate or integrate various sources of funds to support programming?
How do we establish a constructive, collaborative relationship among agencies within our school's community in a proactive manner?

SELECTIVE MAINTENANCE PHASE

Maintaining momentum for change through implementation requires re-visioning and identifying emerging issues for action. Reflective thinking and conversation serve as primary building blocks in the maintaining phase.

Vision
Have staff been engaged in raising issues of concern and frustration in light of relevant struggles with inclusive practice at the school building within the past few years? What are the structures to facilitate meaningful dialogue on such issues?

A necessary skill in maintaining reform over time is being able to cope with emerging problems as they surface throughout the implementation phase. For example, there is nothing more demoralizing to a team than to be encouraged to identify incompatible practices and then be informed that nothing can be done about those practices.

The open lines for dialogue denoted previously in both the initiation and implementation phases serve as the primary conduit to what Saxl and colleagues referred to as sensing problems in the maintaining phase: "If problems are inevitable, they have to be tracked carefully and looked at for what they are, not treated as occasions for blame, excuses, or defense. That means setting up clear mechanisms for sensing problems" (1989, p. 5-24). There are different forms and types of problems that can emerge logically while maintaining change efforts at both the school building and the school district levels. In order to effectively maintain a commitment to the vision of inclusive school reform, the facilitators of the process need to support local stakeholders in addressing the types of problems that can emerge, as described in Table 5.

Skills
Does inclusive schooling continue to be reflected in the comprehensive system of professional development at the school?

The foundation of effective staff development programs is a clear sense of direction. Just as it can be perilous for people to stand in proximity to the target of an archer who cannot see the bull's-eye clearly, so too can it be hazardous for participants in the inclusive school change process to have fuzzy vision regarding the target of professional development activities. Therefore, it is important to continuously check in with the orientation of activities focused on skill development. To do

Table 5.   Sensing problems

Program factors	Problems that emerge because of the content of practices and/or the processes involved in implementing changes in practice
People factors	Problems that emerge that reflect atrophy of vision, stagnation of personal growth and skill development of participants in the change process, and/or poor group dynamics in decision making
Other contextual factors	Problems that emerge in response to crises, competing priorities from external sources, environmental variables, resource deficiencies, fragmentation or disengagement of resource networks, and refreezing of reflective thought by the stakeholders over time

Adapted from Saxl, Miles, and Lieberman (1989).

this, the benchmarks listed in Table 6 should be used as a common frame of reference against which to assess the relevance of ongoing skill development for all participants in the change process.

As positive outcomes and associated problems with inclusive school reform become realized, participants in the change process increasingly become aware of competencies that need to be further developed. In a parallel manner with the focus of staff development activities in earlier phases of the change process, it is important to have staff in the school maintain ownership of their professional development in order to maintain the momentum of implementation.

Incentives

Have staff in the building contributed to a portfolio concerning their experiences? Is there a conducive climate in place to support staff in taking calculated professional risks in trying out new approaches to accommodate all children in their classrooms?

Beyond the benefits that can be realized as a result of staff owning their personal and professional development, an essential factor in maintaining internal incentives for inclusive practice is how the school as an organization copes with stress and solves problems. As problems related to programs, people, and contexts surface, it is important that the school community address those problems in a manner that is consistent with the vision of inclusive school reform. Table 7 provides an overview of various coping styles to be considered in problem solving during the maintaining phase.

Although the progression of styles described in Table 7 may imply a worst-to-best order, this is not necessarily the case. It is likely that, as

Table 6.   Benchmarks in inclusive school reform

Positive student outcomes as a result of implementation of changes in practice
Built-in program, professional, and student evaluation procedures
Effective social marketing techniques
Good fit with local school and community
Increased commitment and decreased resistance
A collaborative climate within which to raise controversial issues and problem-solve
Continuous feedback loops among all implementers of change
Integration and synthesis with newly emerging technologies and change efforts
Dynamic internal and external networking
Innovative acquisition and use of resources

the many problems typically associated with inclusive school reform emerge, different strategies will be employed at different times based on programs, people, and contextual factors. One of the key considerations in determining which course (or courses) of action to take is how the selected approach will affect staff morale and, as a result, the impact it will have on internal incentives to implement desired change. Just as there is no one formula for inclusive school reform, there is no universal set of right or wrong decisions on which coping strategy to apply under a universal set of circumstances. Rather, decisions need to be reached on a case-by-case basis in light of staff morale and progress toward the vision.

Table 7.   Coping styles

Ignoring	Play ostrich in the hope that it will all blow over
Do nothing	Acknowledge the problem but choose to not address it
Tabling	Acknowledge the problem but decide to defer decision making until a later time
Stonehenging	Address the problem at a snail's pace
Band-Aiding	Look for short-term, quick-fix solution to stop the "bleeding"
Backing off	Slow down rate of implementation of changes
Speeding up	Increase the rate of change to deliberately increase sense of chaos
On-off switching	Increase pace on some activities while slowing rate on others associated with the problem(s)
Reenergizing	Strategically use the team's commitment to the vision to work through it, to "hang in there"
Retooling	Increase specific skill development activities associated with the problem(s)
Redesigning	Step back and relook at action plans and make necessary changes to the overall plan of implementation

Resources
Do staff continue to have access to adequate time for collaboration with colleagues during the ebb and flow of the school routine?

Time continues to be at a premium during the maintaining phase of inclusive school reform. Therefore, it is important to monitor staff perceptions of their use of time and to seek recommendations, on an ongoing basis, about more efficient ways to use time. Although this can be done in many ways, one simple technique is to establish a "parking lot" for ideas on this topic where staff (and students and their families) can make suggestions for consideration throughout the course of the school year.

In addition to monitoring the use of time, it is important to continue looking inside and outside the system for resources to support change. Saxl and colleagues (1989) suggested that there are practical places to discover needed resources. In particular, they categorize the review of internal resources by people, space, equipment, professional materials and supplies, and money.

One of the most readily available yet underused internal resources is the collective knowledge of the people who are members of the school community, including both staff and students. As Glaser and Marks noted,

> It is destructive and wasteful that people should be frustrated and often defeated by difficulties for which somebody else has a remedy. . . . The gap between what we know and what we put to effective use bedevils many fields of human activity—science, teaching, business management, and organizations which provide health and welfare services. (1966, p. 4-21)

It is imperative in the change process that methods are established to harness the resources within the school. The collective knowledge of students and staff represents one important resource in this regard (e.g., engaging students in problem solving with staff). Effectively synthesizing the existing knowledge base in this manner helps to maintain positive changes in practice and problem solve points of concern in the future.

Action Plan
Does inclusive schooling serve as a cornerstone within either the long-range plan or the strategic planning process in place for the building?

Ongoing monitoring of accomplishments as a result of changes in practice is needed during the maintaining phase. Although it is important that schools move from the vision to action, it is also important that ongoing progress-monitoring mechanisms be established to provide information for identifying and solving problems. Senge (1990) noted that one of the primary disabilities that most organizations experience is a lack of institutional memory of their history. Establishing procedures to capture the richness of the change process and monitor progress toward intended outcomes is necessary throughout all phases of the change process.

Monitoring becomes particularly important in the maintaining phase because it serves as a "watchdog" for the vision and all related activities associated with movement toward the realization of the vision. As Baldridge (1983) noted, agents of school change need to make certain that decisions become the platform for actions and that actions help to steer new directions. Monitoring activities therefore need to be dutifully planned and implemented throughout the change process. As information accrues across all components of the action plan, this information must be integrated into the school district's strategic plan of operation. There are two primary advantages to using information derived from progress monitoring in this manner. First, embedding this type of information in the districtwide strategic plan can further ensure central office engagement and ongoing support to maintain accomplishments. Second, use of information in this manner can further facilitate inclusive school reform across all schools in the district.

Acknowledging the importance of progress monitoring as described previously, as well as operational action plans concerning visionizing, skill development, incentives, and resources, should be documented via progress monitored throughout the initiation, implementation, and maintaining phases. This information should be used on an ongoing basis in problem solving and decision making.

EVOLVING PHASE

As the old adage goes, it is important not to mistake the edge of a rut for a horizon. Change is a dynamic process that requires constant vigilance and flexibility toward a common good. It is therefore necessary to provide constant feedback loops for dialogue, problem solving, and the emergence of new ideas and vision.

Vision
To what degree are community priorities in sync with the school's core beliefs and mission statement?

Human services systems are infinitely complex in that, to paraphrase Senge (1990), one can never be fully confident in how one has figured things to be. Establishing the school as a learning organization serves as vital leverage in the change process and can greatly facilitate the evolution of beliefs and practice in a logical manner. Further emphasizing the importance of evolution in change initiatives, Ainsworth-Land, in *Grow or Die: The Unifying Principle of Transformation*, viewed the evolution of thoughts, ideas, and practices as necessary for survival:

> Physical, biological, psychological, and social systems are growth motivated; that is, their behavior acts in the direction of development of higher levels of and more widespread interrelationships. Thus, all systems tend to evolve more organized behavior, becoming integrated through the incorporation of diversity. In the aggregate systems of Nature this is a ubiquitous and irreversible process. (1986, p. 197)

As important as it is to revisit the vision across the initiation, implementation, and maintaining phases of change, it is also important to realize that organizational learning and growth result in the evolving phase. Saxl and colleagues (1989) described the process of refocusing as a natural by-product of collaboration throughout all phases of change. Refocusing of the vision and subsequent practice need to be facilitated on an ongoing basis.

Although commitment to a common vision is a necessary prerequisite to durable change, stifling diversity in perspective and opinion can inhibit evolution of the vision and practice. In the evolving phase, it is important to continue to encourage the sharing of various perspectives and to encourage the discussion of different points of view. There is power in diversity, and it is diversity that serves as a catalyst to evolution toward an emerging synthesis in perspectives on inclusion. The art is in negotiating the delicate balance between a shared common vision and the diversity of perspectives among all stakeholders at school and in the community.

Skills
How are the necessary foundations of inclusive practice being integrated with newly emerging promising practices in the field (e.g., authentic assessment, multiple intelligences)?

Senge (1990) noted that systems-level thinking leads to seeing the interconnectedness of life and viewing issues and situations as a whole rather than as a collection of isolated parts. Whenever problems occur, a systems orientation views these matters as arising from underlying structures that are related to one another rather than seeing them as individual mistakes or ill will. In other words, system problems have causal roots in much the same way as the problem behaviors of individuals. The key is in reaching an understanding of the relationships among all relevant factors.

A systems orientation toward skill development is important during the evolving phase. The active exploration of the interconnectedness among emerging innovative practices can produce synergy through the discovery of new relationships between people and among practices.

Eiseman, Fleming, and Roody, in *Making Sure it Sticks: The School Improvement Leader's Role in Institutionalizing Change,* noted the following:

> Commitment and mastery both lead toward increasing stabilization; the innovation has "settled down" in the system. That stabilization is also aided if administrators decide to mandate the innovation. . . . Where administrators were committed, they also took direct action to bring about organizational change . . . by altering the structure and approach to in service training. (1990a, p. 3.3)

Enhancing structures and approaches to professional development in a manner consistent with nurturing newly emerging perspectives is necessary to best ensure continued growth and development of people and programs or, as some describe, with operating the school through a Kaizen orientation. Simple as well as powerful, *Kaizen* is a term that represents a way of looking at life that can have a profound impact on emerging efforts in school improvement. Simply stated, Kaizen requires that each person do whatever is necessary to improve the situation gradually. Table 8 presents the highlights of the Kaizen orientation, which can have a positive influence on evolving skill development.

Incentives
Are staff being encouraged to take calculated risks? Does a conducive collaborative environment for inclusive schooling continue to be present?

It has commonly been suggested that Albert Einstein noted that the same type of thinking that created today's problems is not adequate to solve those same problems. As was the case during the initiation phase, engaging staff in the process of employing new and creative approaches to problem solving as new conflicts emerge continues to serve as a primary incentive for staff. Facilitating a healthy degree of ownership and commitment to innovation among staff can enable collective increases in innovation over time.

Table 8. Kaizen

A reliance on many people taking lots of little steps in a similar direction to make things better

An emphasis on continual upgrading of skills and innovation

Each person's job is to identify problems and create opportunities to solve them

An understanding that improvement is a day-by-day evolutionary process

---

Leadership in the process of inclusive school reform needs to result in stakeholders in the change process viewing themselves as a significant part of a larger whole—as belonging to something special and unique that is based on relationships. This the process component of the change. By championing inclusive school reform in this manner, leaders can minimize the likelihood of staff mistaking the edge of their current rut for the horizon.

The need to belong is not unique to children in an inclusive school. As Maslow (1987) noted, this is a shared need among all people. As each person acquires a sense of belonging, the stage is further set for maintenance of change through intrinsic motivational systems. This can have a positive effect on not only current change but also continued commitment to further push the envelope. An acquired sense of belonging also increases the likelihood of staff feeling safe enough to take calculated risks toward the expansion of innovative approaches to supporting all children in the school.

It is only through supporting staff to meet their basic needs for safety, security, and belonging that staff can self-actualize their own personal goals for growth and development. Thus, *incentives* and professional development (i.e., skills) are inextricably linked together in the process of change.

Resources
Do resources continue to be directed toward supporting staff in being reflective learners?

A common phenomenon that can occur in schools that have been successful in implementing school reform projects is that, over time, the sense of urgency for change diminishes among the people engaged in the change. When this occurs, it is typically accompanied by diminished resources being devoted to change-related activities. Failure to devote needed resources to inclusive school reform can result in difficulty in maintaining changes achieved and stagnation in people and programs.

The types and forms of resources necessary during the evolving phase of the improvement process parallel resources deployed during earlier phases of change. Vigilance with regard to the removal of incompatible practices is essential. One way to address this issue is through the reduction of resources (e.g., money, time, energy) being dedicated to those practices identified as being incompatible with the vision. Elimination of incompatible practices often results in a more efficient use of scarce resources such as money, time, and energy, which can be redeployed in a manner consistent with desired changes.

As a given school enters the evolving phase of inclusive reform, staff should consider formally exploring additional relationships with other entities that have access to external funds. Exploration along these lines can occur through a variety of means, including writing proposals for various types of grants and partnerships with local industry and civic organizations. Collaboration with other systems that have experienced some degree of success with inclusive school reform or with those interested in inclusive reform who have a history of procuring external resources to support change-related initiatives should become a priority.

In addition, continued collaboration through networks established during the initiation, implementation, and maintaining phases is highly encouraged. Expanding relationships with and among network members can serve as a divining rod of sorts for the location of additional resources to support the evolution of change at schools.

Action Plan
Is there a feedback system in place that facilitates the continued development of useful action plans on a scheduled basis?

The best action plan for the evolving phase of change is to plan for constant change. A significant change effort such as inclusive school reform can serve as a foundation on which to establish a growth-oriented community at school. Each aspect of individuals' lives is interconnected with all other aspects of their lives; action planning across all phases of change mirrors this reality.

Facilitating the further emergence of people and programs requires a commitment to what Ainsworth-Land (1986) referred to as *mutual growth*. In this sense, *mutual growth* means concurrent personal and organizational growth that is constructively codependent in nature—a win–win framework, so to speak.

Although many aspects of action planning are important in the evolving phase, none is more important than that of maintaining and expanding on the infrastructure that facilitates the sharing of information through dialogue and collaborative problem solving. A newly emergent cybernetic system is sought in this phase so that individuals and the organization as a whole continuously learn and reach further than before as a result of the never-ending learning process.

Action planning during the evolving phase of inclusive school reform requires an integration of collective experiences in the context of organizational growth and the subsequent emergence of new future points of destination. Action planning at this stage of inclusive school reform efforts needs to take into account the endless cycles of growth in learning organizations. In essence, each new learning experience serves as a launching platform for the next. As a result, everyone in the school becomes an active learner who continually engages in visionizing, skill building, the creation of sustainable incentives, resource development and deployment, and action planning through continuous feedback and dialogue toward further learning.

CONCLUSIONS

This chapter presents a change framework that synthesizes previous conceptualizations of the change process (Ambrose, 1987; Fullan & Stiegelbauer, 1991; Knoster, 1993; Villa & Thousand, 1992) and accommodates the interactive nature of inclusive school reform. Across the United States and Canada, those who are actively involved in leading changes toward inclusive schooling confirm that the change process takes time and involves not only organizational but also personal, intellectual, and emotional change. The new change framework offered in this chapter not only expands on and integrates previous change models but also addresses the temporal, and intellectual, and emotional aspects of the process of change. It is hoped that this framework assists readers not only to better understand organizational change but also to be equipped to cope more ably with its complexity and personal nature.

Change always results in new roles and responsibilities for everyone involved. Therefore, the process of change must be collaborative in nature and must involve both those individuals who implement the identified changes (e.g., administrators, teachers, other school personnel) and those on whom the change will have an impact (i.e., students, parents, community members) (Villa, Thousand, & Rosenberg, 1995).

Clearly, the monumental and complex nature of reengineering schooling can seem overwhelming. Yet, an increasing number of communities have overcome that overwhelming perceptual barrier and have committed themselves to implementing their vision of inclusive education with integrity. Effective inclusive school organizations can be and are being crafted. Each of these organizations is being crafted by *individuals*—individuals who choose to be courageous and engage what is known about change processes to facilitate the attainment of a vision larger than themselves.

REFERENCES

Ainsworth-Land, G.T. (1986). *Grow or die: The unifying principle of transformation.* New York: John Wiley & Sons.

Ambrose, D. (1987). *Managing complex change.* Pittsburgh, PA: Enterprise Group.

Baldridge, J.V. (1983). Rules for a Machiavellian Change Agent: Transforming the entrenched professional organization. In J.V. Baldridge & T.E. Deal (Eds.), *Dynamics of organizational change in education* (pp. 110–120). Berkeley, CA: McCutchan Publishing Corp.

Barker, J.A. (1992). *Future edge: Discovering the new paradigms of success.* New York: William Morrow.

Benjamin, S. (1989). An ideascape for education: What futurists recommend. *Educational Leadership, 47*(1), 8–14.

Clark, D.L., Lotto, L.S., & Astuto, T.A. (1984). Effective schools and school improvement: A comparative analysis of two lines of inquiry. *Educational Administration Quarterly, 20*(3), 41–68.

Csikszentmihalyi, M. (1990). *Flow: The psychology of optimal experience.* New York: HarperCollins.

Deal, T. (1987). The culture of schools. In L.T. Shieve & M.B. Schoenheit (Eds.), *Leadership: Examining the elusive: 1987 yearbook of the Association for Supervision and Curriculum Development* (pp. 3–15). Alexandria, VA: Association for Supervision and Curriculum Development.

Deal, T. (1990). Foreword. In T.J. Sergiovanni (Ed.), *Value-added leadership: How to get extraordinary performance in schools* (pp. v–ix). San Diego: Harcourt Brace & Co.

Deal, T., & Peterson, K. (1990). *The principal's role in shaping school culture.* Washington, DC: U.S. Government Printing Office.

Eiseman, J., Fleming, D., & Roody, D. (1990a). *Making sure it sticks: The school improvement leader's role in institutionalizing change.* Andover, MA: Regional Lab.

Eiseman, J., Fleming, D., & Roody, D. (1990b). *The school improvement leader: Four perspectives on change in schools.* Andover, MA: Regional Lab.

Fullan, M.G. (1982). *The meaning of educational change.* New York: Teachers College Press.

Fullan, M.G., & Miles, M. (1992). Getting reform right: What works and what doesn't. *Phi Delta Kappan, 73*(10), 745–752.

Fullan, M.G., & Stiegelbauer, S. M. (1991). *The new meaning of educational change* (2nd ed.). New York: Teachers College Press.

Glaser, E.M., & Marks, J.B. (1966). Putting research to work. *Rehabilitation Record, 7*(6), 6–10.

Herzberg, F. (1990). One more time: How do you motivate employees? In President & Fellows of Harvard College (Eds.), *People: Managing your most important asset* (pp. 26–35). Boston: Harvard Business Review.

Hord, S.M., Rutherford, W., Huling-Austin, L., & Hall, G. (1987). *Taking charge of change.* Alexandria, VA: Association for Supervision and Curriculum Development.

Joyce, B.R., & Showers, B. (1995). *Student achievement through staff development: Fundamentals of school renewal* (2nd ed.). Reading, MA: Addison Wesley Longman.

Knoster, T. (1993). *Reflections on inclusion at school and beyond.* Lewisburg, PA: Central Susquehanna Intermediate Unit.

Kohn, A. (1998). How incentives undermine performance. *Journal for Quality and Participation, 22*(2), 7–13.

Lewin, K. (1975). *Field theory in social science: Selected theoretical papers.* Westport, CT: Greenwood Publishing Group. (Original work published 1951)

Maslow, A.H. (1987). *Motivation and personality* (3rd ed.). New York: HarperCollins.

Parnes, S.J. (1988). *Visionizing: State-of-the-art processes for encouraging innovative excellence.* East Aurora, NY: DOK Publishers.

Sarason, S.B. (1990). *The predictable failure of educational reform: Can we change course before it's too late?* San Francisco: Jossey-Bass.

Saxl, E.R., Miles, M.B., & Lieberman, A. (1989). *Assisting Change in Education: A training program for school improvement facilitators.* Alexandria, VA: Association for Supervision and Curriculum Development.

Schlechty, P.C. (1990). *Schools for the 21st century: Leadership imperatives for educational reform.* San Francisco: Jossey-Bass.

Scholtes, P.R. (1993). *The team handbook for educators: How to use teams to improve quality.* Madison, WI: Joiner Associates.

Senge, P.M. (1990). *The fifth discipline: The art and practice of the learning organization.* New York: Doubleday/Currency.

Sergiovanni, T.J. (Ed.). (1990). *Value-added leadership: How to get extraordinary performance in schools.* San Diego: Harcourt Brace & Co.

Sizer, T.R. (1991). No pain, no gain. *Educational Leadership, 48*(8), 32–34.

Skrtic, T.M. (1991). *Behind special education: A critical analysis of professional culture and school organization.* Denver: Love Publishing Co.

Smith, C.E. (1995). *The Merlin factor: Keys to the corporate kingdom.* McLean, VA: Kairos Productions.

Sting [Sumner, G. M.]. (1991). All this time. On *Soul cages* (CD). Los Angeles: A&M Records.

Vaill, P. (1989). *Managing as a performing art.* San Francisco: Jossey-Bass.

Villa, R.A., & Thousand, J.S. (1992). Restructuring public school systems: Strategies for organizational change and progress. In R.A. Villa, J.S. Thousand, W. C. Stainback, & S. B. Stainback (Eds.), *Restructuring for caring and effective education: An administrative guide to creating heterogeneous schools* (1st ed., pp. 109–137). Baltimore: Paul H. Brookes Publishing Co.

Villa, R.A., Thousand, J.S., & Rosenberg, R.A. (1995). Systems change. In M.A. Falvey (Ed.), *Inclusive and heterogeneous schooling: Assessment, curriculum, and instruction* (pp. 395–414). Baltimore: Paul H. Brookes Publishing Co.

Wheatley, M.J. (1992). *Leadership and the new science: Learning about organization from an orderly universe.* San Francisco: Berrett-Koehler Publishers.

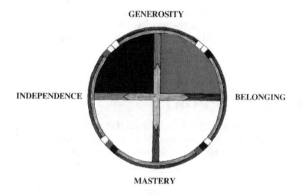

GENEROSITY

INDEPENDENCE

BELONGING

MASTERY

REFLECTION

A Credo for Support

Norman Kunc and Emma Van der Klift

Throughout history,
People with physical and mental disabilities
Have been abandoned at birth,
Banished from society,
Used as court jesters,
Drowned and burned during the Inquisition,
And gassed in Nazi Germany,
And they continue to be segregated, institutionalized,
Tortured in the name of behavior management,
Abused, raped, euthanized, and murdered.
Now, for the first time, people with disabilities are taking
their rightful

"A Credo for Support" is dedicated to the memory of Tracy Latimer.

Place as fully contributing citizens. The danger is that we
will respond with
Remediation and benevolence rather than equity
and respect.
And so we offer you

A CREDO FOR SUPPORT[1]

Do Not see my disability as the problem.
Recognize that my disability is an attribute.
Do Not see my disability as a deficit.
It is you who see me as deviant and helpless.
Do Not try to fix me because I am not broken.
Support me. I can make my contribution to the community
in my way.
Do Not see me as your client. I am your fellow citizen.
See me as your neighbor. Remember, none of us can be
self-sufficient.
Do Not try to modify my behavior.
Be still and listen. What you define as inappropriate
May be my attempt to communicate with you in the only
way I can.
Do Not try to change me; you have no right.
Help me learn what I want to know.
Do Not hide your uncertainty behind "professional"
distance.
Be a person who listens, and does not take my
Struggle away from me by trying to make it all better.
Do Not use theories and strategies on me.
Be with me. And when we struggle
With each other, let that give rise to self-reflection.
Do Not try to control me. I have a right to my power as
a person.
What you call noncompliance or manipulation may
Actually be the only way I can exert some control over
my life.
Do Not teach me to be obedient, submissive, and polite.
I need to feel entitled to say no if I am to protect myself.
Do Not be charitable toward me.
The last thing the world needs is another Jerry Lewis.
Be my ally against those who exploit me for their own
gratification.
Do Not try to be my friend. I deserve more than that.
Get to know me. We may become friends.
Do Not help me, even if it does make you feel good.

---

[1]Copyright © 1995 by Norman Kunc and Emma Van der Klift. Copies of
"A Credo for Support" are available on videotape and in poster format (English
and Spanish versions) from Axis Consultation & Training Ltd., (250) 754-9939.

Ask me if I need your help. Let me show you how you can
best assist me.
Do Not admire me. A desire to live a full life does not
warrant adoration.
Respect me, because respect presumes equity.
Do Not tell, correct, and lead.
Listen, Support, and Follow.
Do Not work on me.
Work with me.

11

Curriculum, Instruction, and Assessment for Inclusive Schooling

A Vision for the Future

Martha L. Thurlow and James G. Shriner

At the core of building a caring and effective education program for any individual is the development of a curriculum, instruction processes, and assessments that support and foster this environment. Several critical assumptions underlie the curriculum, instruction, and assessments that do this. Together, they form our vision of the future of inclusive schooling.

As we look toward the future, we believe that the foundation lies in certain fundamental assumptions about individuals, our expectations for them, and who is responsible for ensuring that high educational standards are met. Specifically, to achieve inclusive schooling that provides youngsters (or adults) with a caring and effective education, we believe that there must be consensus about the following assumptions:

- All individuals can learn.
- Learning is directed toward high standards.
- All educators are responsible for the learning of all students.
- Instruction and assessment are set within the framework of the general curriculum.
- Accommodations are free flowing for all students.
- All students count.

These assumptions drive a vision for the future of inclusive schooling and approaches to curriculum, instruction, and assessment in our schools. Unfortunately, many educators in schools do not embrace these assumptions. Swaying the views of these educators toward a more inclusive position is the challenge for those who want to build and support environments that foster an individual's maximum development.

ALL INDIVIDUALS CAN LEARN

Although we have traditionally spoken of the maxim *All students can learn,* this assumption reflects the broadest view of the concept. We have to presume not only that all students can learn but also that those who educate them and those who administer their programs can learn. This assumption is critical if we are to attain inclusive schooling in which caring and effective education occurs for all. In other words, we must begin with the assumption that those who teach the most challenging students can learn to change their approaches to instruction. Furthermore, this assumption reflects the belief that, rather than the curriculum becoming the driving force, the curriculum is molded to meet the needs of each and every student.

LEARNING IS DIRECTED
TOWARD HIGH STANDARDS

With regard to students with disabilities, the education system has been plagued by low expectations. This restricts instruction approaches and what we believe the curriculum should be for students with disabilities. "High standards" is the call across the United States, and people who are dedicated to improving the education of students with disabilities must join in this call. As of 1999, states have set standards that are to drive curriculum, instruction, and assessments. Yet, we know that there was virtually no involvement of individuals who are knowledgeable about disabilities as these standards were set (Shriner, Ysseldyke, & Thurlow, 1994; Thurlow, Ysseldyke, Gutman, & Geenen, 1997). Until educators recognize the full potential of all students, including students with disabilities, education will be stifled in achieving inclusive schools that truly meet the needs of all students.

ALL EDUCATORS ARE RESPONSIBLE
FOR THE LEARNING OF ALL STUDENTS

Separatism of responsibility for students in schools must become a thing of the past. To attain a caring and effective education for all students requires a recognition that all educators are responsible for the education of all students. When this stance is taken, there is no longer any benefit to be gained by declaring that only special education should be concerned with "those students."

INSTRUCTION AND
ASSESSMENT ARE SET WITHIN THE
FRAMEWORK OF THE GENERAL CURRICULUM

The general education curriculum defines education for nearly all students. In fact, the Individuals with Disabilities Education Act (IDEA) Amendments of 1997 (PL 105-17) require that students with disabilities participate to the maximum extent possible in the general education curriculum.

In the inclusive school of the future, the general education curriculum will guide the goals for the instruction of all students, even those with the most severe needs. It will reflect what we want students to know and be able to do. For some students, this goal will be actualized through the application of bridges between the annual goals set for the student and the general education curriculum. For most students with disabilities, it will be actualized through the general education curriculum itself. Students with disabilities will be provided access to the general curriculum and afforded supplementary aids and services to maximize their participation. Only when a student is likely to gain no benefit from general curriculum participation will curricular goals that are unique to the student be developed and removal from the general curriculum be considered the best option for instruction planning (Rhim & McLaughlin, 1997; Yell & Shriner, 1997).

New assessment provisions in IDEA require that states and districts include students with disabilities in their large-scale assessments and that they report on both the number participating and their performance on the assessments. Crafters of the 1997 IDEA Amendments sought to eliminate the unnecessary exclusion of students with disabilities from assessments because such exclusion may limit an individual's opportunities later in life.

ACCOMMODATIONS ARE
FREE FLOWING FOR ALL STUDENTS

In the future, accommodations will no longer generate the controversy that surrounds them at the turn of the 21st century. Not only will accommodations be included in the instruction provided to students with disabilities and in assessments administered to them, but they also will be deemed appropriate for other students needing them to best benefit from their education. For this to happen, there needs to be much more discussion about the purposes of accommodations in both instruction and assessment. In addition, the findings of research about the extent to which accommodations actually change what is occurring in the classroom and what is being measured in assessments need to be available.

In caring and effective education, we will recognize that the need for accommodations is a continuous variable, not a yes-or-no dichotomy. With this recognition comes the belief that accommodations must be available for all individuals, not just for those with disabilities.

ALL STUDENTS COUNT

In inclusive education, all students must count. They must count not just in philosophical ways but also in evaluation and accountability systems. Across the United States, educators emphasize the importance of accountability for results. In other words, there is a demand for evidence beyond simply showing that students are being educated (i.e., that they are within the education system and are receiving some kind of education). The demand is for evidence related to the results of education, not just for evidence of the education process.

There is evidence that, in many education systems, this is not the case. Even those students who do participate in the general curriculum may be excluded from the accountability system or the assessments that drive it. Even when students do participate in the assessments, their scores may be excluded systematically, again transmitting the message that they do not count, that educators do not have to take responsibility for the scores of these students. In the future, this will not be the case. Students with disabilities will participate in the general assessments, with accommodations as appropriate, and, if participation in these assessments is not feasible, they will participate in an alternate assessment (an assessment designed for a small percentage of students, perhaps 10%–15% of those students receiving special education services).

When all students count, the curriculum, instruction, and assessments will move in directions that promote caring and effective education. In such an education system, *all* students, including those with special learning needs, will thrive. In such an educational environment, those students with disabilities *do* thrive rather than fall by the wayside.

REFERENCES

Individuals with Disabilities Education Act (IDEA) Amendments of 1997, PL 105-17, 20 U.S.C. §§ 1400 *et seq.*

Rhim, L.M., & McLaughlin, M.J. (1997). *State level policies and practices: Where are students with disabilities?* College Park: University of Maryland, Center for Policy Research on the Impact of General and Special Education Reform.

Shriner, J.G., Ysseldyke, J.E., & Thurlow, M.L. (1994). Standards for all American students. *Focus on Exceptional Children, 26*(5), 1–19.

Thurlow, M.L., Ysseldyke, J.E., Gutman, S., & Geenen, K. (1997). *Inclusion of students with disabilities in state standards documents* (Tech. Rep. No. 19). Minneapolis: University of Minnesota, National Center on Educational Outcomes.

Yell, M.L., & Shriner, J.G. (1997). The IDEA Amendments of 1997: Implications for special and general education teachers, administrators, and teacher trainers. *Focus on Exceptional Children, 30*(1), 1–20.

Chapter 6

Achieving Social Justice Through Education for Responsibility

Jacqueline S. Thousand,
Ann I. Nevin, and Mary Elizabeth McNeil

If we are to achieve a richer culture . . . [,] we must weave one in which each diverse human gift will find a fitting place.

Margaret Mead (quoted in Dillon et al., 1993, p. 25)

When asked to articulate their desired goals for public education, educators (i.e., public school teachers, teacher educators) as well as parents and employers are in agreement that youth be prepared to meet the demands of life in the 21st century (Villa & Thousand, 1995). The areas for preparation identified most frequently tend to correspond with the four dimensions of the Circle of Courage described by Brendtro, Brokenleg, and Van Bockern (1990) and Van Bockern, Brendtro, and Brokenleg (Chapter 3). These dimensions—belonging, mastery, independence, and generosity—encompass numerous educational goals or objectives, some of which are presented in Figure 1. Among the most frequently identified desired outcomes are gaining and making sense of new information as lifelong learners; enjoying a life that is balanced between work and recreation;

GENEROSITY
Being a contributing member of society
Valuing diversity
Being empathetic
Offering compassion, caring, support to
others
Global stewardship
Being a responsible citizen

INDEPENDENCE
Having choices in work, recreation,
and leisure
Confidence to take risks
Being as independent as possible
Assuming personal responsibility
Being accountable for actions and
decisions
Being able to self-advocate

BELONGING
Having friends
Forming and maintaining
relationships
Being part of a community
Being a caring parent and
family member

MASTERY
Having success, becoming
competent
Being well rounded
Being a good problem solver
Flexible
Motivated
Literate
Able to use technology
Lifelong learner

Figure 1.   Identified goals of education displayed in accordance with the Native American Circle of Courage education paradigm.

being able to interact meaningfully with people of differing abilities, opinions, ethnicities, and cultural backgrounds; and being responsible. Given these goals, the question that begs an answer is, Does the way in which American and Canadian cultures choose to educate students with disabilities (i.e., inclusive versus segregated education) achieve the articulated goals of education? The education field is in the midst of a still controversial movement to welcome, value, support, and educate the greatest possible number of students with disabilities *within* general education. These efforts to establish inclusive education or inclusion can be advanced by a discussion of social justice issues and social responsibility.

The purpose of this chapter is to focus attention on the responsibility of educators at all levels to achieve social justice through the theoretical, organizational, curricular, instructional, and assessment approaches that they apply. A conceptual model for creating inclusive schools and achieving the Circle of Courage goals of education through teaching responsibility is framed by first considering three definitions of social justice in education. Next, we propose responsibility as a concept that is composed of two aspects: accountability and flexibility (i.e., response-ability) and suggesting ways to alter the roles, rules, and relationships among teacher educators, teachers, pupils, and the community to teach for responsibility, response-ability, and social justice. Implications for teachers and students are illustrated by an example derived from a California high school district.

MEANING OF EQUALITY AS A FORM OF SOCIAL JUSTICE: A CALL FOR DIALOGUE

Equality is a concept that evokes multiple meanings for each individual and perhaps is defined more by its absence than by its presence. How many people have experienced feelings of inequality such as those that might be present between a novice learner and a veteran? How many people have experienced discrimination, or actions associated with unequal treatment, perhaps by being barred from entry into privileged places? How many people have been treated equally in one situation, only to face unequal treatment in another?

Included among these multiple meanings of *equality* is the presence or absence of *educational* equality between people with and without disabilities; between boys and girls; between learners who live in urban and rural environments; and between those of differing races, primary languages, and socioeconomic status. Historically, educators of all nations have struggled with ensuring equality in its various forms. For example, as long ago as the 15th century, Comenius argued that education should be available not just to "one man or a few, or even many men; but to all people together as well as to each separately, young and old, rich and poor, irrespective of birth, men, and women—in short, everyone whose fate it is to have been born a human being" (cited in Kozik, 1980, p. 49). This lofty goal of equal opportunity in education is shared by many educators who advocate for the appropriate education of students with disabilities.

Three Approaches to Distributing Justice

> If you want to be free, there is but one way: It is to guarantee an equally full measure of liberty to all of your neighbors. There is no other.
>
> Carl Schurz (as cited in Dillon et al., 1993, p. 21)

In the interest of developing an understanding of what is meant by *equality*, reflect on the following views of social justice adapted from the discussion by Johnson and Johnson (1987), who interpreted Deutsch's (1975) ideas about equality in the context of how people in a group (e.g., society, community, school) are valued and rewarded. Deutsch contrasted the concept of equality with two alternative concepts of distributing justice—equity and need. His thesis was that the way in which a society or group recognizes its members for their perceived contributions has a marked effect on how members treat one another as well as how effectively the group performs.

Equity   In an *equity* approach of distributed justice, those considered to have made the greatest contributions receive the greatest benefits, recognition, or rewards (e.g., grades, scholarships, admission into advanced placement classes). Inherent in this approach to valuing people are a number of positive and negative outcomes. This approach is highly motivational for those who can achieve the desired goals. People may come to be viewed as valuable only to the extent that they are useful, however. This results in a depersonalization of others and oneself. An attitude that various members have more or less value undermines the basis for self-respect, mutual respect, and responsibility for one another. Second, resultant competition among group members for recognition and valuing can cause morale problems, reduce group cohesiveness, and result in deterioration of communication among members. Third, those who achieve may attribute their success to their worthiness rather than to various other resources at their disposal (e.g., ability, previous experience, training, motivation, personal support). Similarly, those with fewer resources may see themselves or may be seen by others as less worthy, even lazy. Also of concern is the notion of who gets to determine what is of value and a worthy contribution.

Equality   In an *equality* system of distributed justice, all members are recognized equally, regardless of their unique contribution or needs. For example, if a sports team wins a tournament, each member receives an identical trophy or an equal monetary reward. Similarly, if a cooperative learning group completes a task to an excellent standard, all members receive common recognition for excellence. The principle of equality is more congenial than the principle of equity in fostering equal status, fun, positive interpersonal relationships, cooperation, mutual esteem and respect among members, group loyalty, and responsibility. Some people, primarily those who are experienced and successful in an equity system of distributed justice, may feel a sense of decreased motivation in an equality system because the reward is the same regardless of the type of contribution one makes. Others may be too quick to compromise rather than advocate for a particular perspective or outcome, thereby minimizing the quality of the group's achievements. The fear is that individualism is being sacrificed completely for the collective good. Other critics of this approach express a belief that equality is unattainable in that there are always people who cheat to ensure that they gain more than others.

Need   In a *need-based* system of distributive justice, recognition or support is given to the group members who are most in need of recognition or support. To use a schooling example, students with disabilities are given the support, assistance, accommodations, and modifications in instruction and/or curriculum that they need to complete their learning tasks successfully. A natural responsibility of members of a group is to help colleagues who are most in need. The gain of the member helped is seen as far outweighing the possible loss involved in the effort to help. Such a caring-oriented group or society stresses responsibility for each other, permission to ask for and give help, heightened sensitivity to others' needs, and nurturance of one another's genuine needs. Many are supportive of a need system of distributing justice as long as there are unlimited resources (e.g., a well-financed school budget) and thus no competition for distributing the resources. Others fear that some people will feign need and thereby receive needed resources that should be allocated elsewhere.

Comments   All three systems of social justice are present, along with their ethical rationales, in societies. The underlying assumptions of each system are manifested in all aspects of national and local policies and services (e.g., welfare, health care, affirmative action). These three systems of social justice also can be seen in day-to-day educational practices such as inclusive education, discipline systems, and decisions about what to do with students who are different. The *equity* system shows members of a school, business, family, community, or society that excellence is witnessed and celebrated. The *equality* system shows to members that their cooperative efforts are valued. The *need-based* system recognizes each person's unique strengths and challenges, ensuring support when needed.

What Is Social Justice in Education?

Fair is not equal. Fair is everyone getting what they need [to succeed].

From The F.A.T. City Workshop
(Public Broadcasting Service [PBS], 1996)

By examining and contrasting Deutsch's (1975) conceptualizations of equality, equity, and need, we discovered that our own definition of social justice in education is similar to that expressed by Deutsch's need-based approach to justice; that is, social justice in education is achieved by everyone getting what they need to experience success. Our own reflections on the preceding social justice paradigms brought us to this realization. We have found that this approach to social justice in education is imperative to realizing the desired child-centered outcome of educating all children together regardless of disability, gender, race, ethnicity, and socioeconomic status.

If educators are to make a significant impact on their respective public school and university systems, it is critical to create a common conceptual framework for thinking about and addressing issues. To this end, we invite readers to engage in the same reflective process as we did and formulate their own personal definitions of social justice in education. We further invite all readers to share with their colleagues their definitions for the purpose of generating a shared meaning of social justice in education that can guide public school and teacher preparation reform efforts collectively. In education, there are kernels of understanding that all can strive to construct and comprehend in order to develop a shared framework—*social justice* being one and *responsibility* being another. The next section of the chapter proposes an expanded conceptualization of responsibility and suggests roles and responsibilities for teachers and teacher educators in guiding the development of responsible children and youth.

WHAT IS RESPONSIBILITY, AND HOW SHOULD ITS DEVELOPMENT BE GUIDED?

Responsibility is one of the choices that individuals have when facing the consequences of their actions. Instead of accepting responsibility, a person can *lay blame,* such as when a person says, "It's not my fault; she's the one responsible." Another choice is to *play lame,* such as when a person says, "I'm only a learner; I'm not supposed to be able to do this." A third choice is to *show shame* but no changes, such as when a person says, "I'm really ashamed to be so ignorant" but does not do anything about preparing better the next time. Another choice is to *grab the guilt*, such as when a person says, "It's all my fault." This choice prevents others from being responsible.

People's beliefs about responsibility can be revealed by the icons or images that are generated in their minds when the concept of responsibility is suggested to them. Many people view shouldering responsibility in the form of a person lifting a burden to his or her shoulders and carrying it. An image or icon of responsibility as caring is that of a parent cradling a child in his or her arms. Still another image of responsibility shows three or four people linking arms to help one another.

Responsibility can be understood in still another way: by thinking about the global heroes and heroines who represent the best examples of the concept. For instance, Anne Frank, the Dutch teenager who perished in the Holocaust, was able to show responsibility toward others in the midst of her own personal development and in the face of adversity. Mohandas Gandhi of India is an example of a person who took responsible action without resorting to violence.

The enumeration of these people, images, and choices is intended to show the breadth and depth of the meanings associated with responsibility. We also asked an international audience of teacher educators representing 25 different European countries to identify characteristics of responsibility. For the most part, the ideas generated represented the notion of accountability (e.g., acknowledge and be accountable for one's own actions, be aware of the power one has regarding the development of children, know one's own aims or intentions and the consequences of one's own behavior). A few comments, however, went beyond these basic definitions and suggested the need to be able to grow, change, and be a learner—that is, to be flexible.

This chapter hypothesizes that responsibility is composed of two dimensions. The first dimension is *flexibility*—an ability to respond or to exhibit *response-ability*, if you will. The second is *accountability*—a sense of personal ownership or internal self-discipline. It is the professional educator's responsibility to increase children's response-ability or flexibility in order that they might become responsible (i.e., accountable). Similarly, it is a school administrator's responsibility to increase teachers' response-ability or flexibility so that they can empower children to become responsible. It is the responsibility of teacher educators to increase teacher education candidates' competencies in becoming both accountable and response-able or flexible in meeting the educational needs of all of their learners. A major outcome of such an increase in *responsibility* (in this case, in the sense of flexibility with accountability) at all of these levels would be increased social justice (from a needs-based perspective) in education for learners of all abilities and socio-economic classes. In short, all children would be more likely to get what they needed to increase their skills and knowledge in the four goal areas of generosity, mastery, belonging, and independence identified in Figure 1.

TEACHER'S ROLE IN PROMOTING A CURRICULUM OF RESPONSIBILITY

Villa, Udis, and Thousand (1994) pointed out that educators have long recognized that students need continuous and complex instruction throughout their elementary, middle, and high school years to master mathematics, sciences, languages, and so forth. When a child does not learn a concept or a skill, teachers typically respond with a teaching response and reteach the material with additional or different supports or accommodations. Educators have not, however, similarly developed a content area for responsibility. The explicit teaching and modeling of patterns of behavior and habits that represent "responsible" behavior often never occur; instruction is relegated to reactive or quick-fix methods such as seeing a guidance counselor, attending a 6-week social skills group, or writing a behavioral contract. Students who violate rules or otherwise communicate a lack of responsibility provide a prompt to teach. The teaching of responsibility is as demanding as teaching any other curriculum area; it requires careful thought, structured sequencing, and ongoing instruction and reteaching from the day a child enters the school.

Discipline Systems that Are Responsibility Based and that Build Response-Ability

In order for students to learn responsible values, they must perceive that school personnel genuinely care about and for them. Teachers, above all, must demonstrate a needs-based approach to social justice and caring treatment by validating students' efforts and achievements and by creating learning environments that enable students to succeed much more often than they fail. Teachers must also teach responsibility directly by 1) adopting, along with the students, schoolwide discipline plans that promote the learning of responsibility; 2) directly instructing students in prosocial communication skills, anger management, and impulse control techniques; and 3) setting limits to ensure safety.

Models of discipline that are responsibility based (e.g., Brendtro et al., 1990; Curwin & Mendler, 1988; Glasser, 1986; Kohn, 1997) acknowledge conflict as a natural part of life. They transform the educator's role from that of police officer to that of facilitator because student behavior is viewed as contextual. Responses to rule-violating behavior depend on multiple factors (e.g., the time of day, the frequency and intensity of the behavior, the number of other people exhibiting the behavior) and may range from reminders, warnings, redirections, cues, and self-monitoring techniques to behavioral contracts and direct teaching of alternative responses. There are few if–then consequences (e.g., 3 tardies equal a detention; 10 absences result in a grade of F). Instead, teachers provide students with a range of predictable responses to rule violations to reinforce students' choices. Most important is to recognize that the development of student responsibility 1) should be integrated within all of the curriculum areas and considered as important as any other content area, 2) should be concerned with teaching young people how to get their needs met in socially acceptable ways, and 3) should be modeled and coached and reflect ongoing attention from all school personnel (Villa et al., 1994).

Instruction Methodologies that Encourage Response-Able and Responsible Behavior Among Peers

Teachers need to focus on methodologies that allow students to practice being responsible for their own learning. Udvari-Solner and Thousand (1995) synthesized the research and practice related to instruction methodologies and theoretical constructs that promote social justice in education. Table 1 provides brief descriptions of prevalent *theoretical* constructs, *organizational* structures, and *curricular* approaches that are compatible with the tenets of providing inclusive educational opportunities for students with disabilities and that result in increased flexibility (i.e., response-ability) as well as accountability (i.e., responsibility). Teachers and administrators are encouraged to cultivate a renewed interest in learning theories. Teachers are being asked to empower their students to construct a personal understanding of the world through interactions and dialogue with one another and with their teachers. This fundamentally constructivist view of teaching and learning has its origins in the work of Dewey (1933/1998), Piaget (1928/1959), and Vygotsky (1962), which has as its aim and outcome the development of students who are response-able and responsible in their own learning.

Armstrong (1994), Gardner (1983, 1993, 1995, 1997), and Lazear (1994) proposed and articulated procedures for developing children's multiple intelligences (i.e., linguistic, logical-mathematical, musical, spatial, bodily-kinesthetic, interpersonal, intrapersonal, naturalist intelligences). This theoretical perspective of the multiple dimensions

Table 1.   Theories, organizational structures, and curricular approaches that promote social justice in education

Theoretical constructs

Multiple intelligences theory
- Challenges traditional definitions of intelligence as linguistic or logical (see Gardner, 1983; Lazear, 1994).
- Calls into question the practice of labeling—what is a *disability*?
- Promotes valuing of skills other than language and logic.
- Frees educators to see unconventional behaviors by teaching students to express their intelligences productively in other modes.

Constructivist learning theory
- Knowledge is interpreted and developed in a social context.
- Challenges "deficit-driven" approaches to learning.
- Assumes people are always learning (see Poplin, Wiest, & Tarlow, 1996).
- Requires that learner must be met at his or her current level of knowledge (see Stainback, Stainback, & Moravec, 1992).

Organizational structures

Collaborative teaming with adults
- Responsibility in planning for, teaching, and evaluating all children is shared.
- Models cooperative teaching and decision making expected of learners.
- Results in higher teacher–student ratio, allowing for more immediate and individualized instruction for learners who need it.
- Co-teachers acquire one another's skills and methodologies (see Thousand & Villa, 1992).

Multi-age grouping
- Emphasizes a community of learners as heterogeneous.
- Views learning as continuous and dynamic.
- Encourages developmentally appropriate instruction geared for each child's biological or psychological and cognitive developmental time lines.
- Minimizes transitions from year to year or from specialist to teacher (see Udvari-Solner & Thousand, 1995).

Curricular approaches

Multicultural education
- Ideological framework that values 1) fostering human rights and respect for differences, 2) acknowledges the value of diversity, 3) promotes an understanding of alternative life choices, 4) establishes social justice and equal opportunity, and 5) facilitates equitable power distribution among individuals and groups (see Grant & Sleeter, 1989).

(continued)

Table I.   *(continued)*

	• Advocates redesign to make learning environments responsive to specific cultures and learning styles.
Interdisciplinary/thematic instruction	• Uses methods and language from more than one academic discipline to study a central theme, issue, or experience rather than being unidimensional.
	• Minimizes fragmentation of learning for students with disabilities by teaching the curriculum in contextual ways (Udvari-Solner & Thousand, 1995).

of intelligence frees all educators from their responsibility of sorting children into low, medium, and high groups for instruction based on their scores on standardized tests of presumed ability. In combination, constructivist and multiple intelligence theories encourage educators to see and value the differences in learning approaches, rates, and styles of their students and to differentiate curriculum and instruction for all students, thus making the presence of children who are "different" usual and desirable in the *classroom.*

Table 2 explains instruction strategies and *assessment* approaches that promote social justice in education. When teachers use such approaches, students are provided with projects and individually negotiated learning contracts that encourage them to select the topic that they will study, the resources that they will use, and the methods by which they will demonstrate mastery. Learning under such conditions, known as *outcomes-based education,* also yields students who have a greater excitement for and a deeper understanding of the topic that they are studying. McLaughlin and Warren (1992) suggested that even students with intense special needs can be part of an outcomes-based education orientation when the curriculum is defined in broad knowledge and skill areas such as those articulated in the Native American Circle of Courage shown in Figure 1.

Cooperative learning and partner learning are two forms of "peer-mediated" instruction that directly promote social responsibility. Cooperative group learning (e.g., Johnson & Johnson, 1994) provides a set of teaching and learning conditions that allow children to build healthy and productive interpersonal relationships with their peers to yield higher achievement and retention of what they are learning. "Partner learning is an eminent example of individualized instruction in which students work together to achieve educational objectives" (McNeil, 1994, p. 244). McNeil described partner learning or peer-tutoring systems that, when consciously implemented and monitored

Table 2.   Instruction approaches and assessment strategies that promote social justice in education

Instruction approaches

Cooperative learning	• Enables students to learn and work in environments in which their needs are addressed.
	• Transforms classroom into a microcosm of a diverse society similar to the world of work.
	• Students acquire social skills and academic skills (see lesson plans adapted for learners with special needs in Thousand, Villa, & Nevin, 1994).
Peer tutoring/partner learning	• Quality of instruction from peers may be more effective than that from adults because children use language that is more age-appropriate and meaningful and may better understand their peers' potential misconceptions (McNeil, 1994).
	• Students who teach concepts and procedures understand them at a deeper level and thus are engaging in a metacognitive activity.

Assessment strategies

Outcomes-based education	• Curriculum and outcomes are defined in broad, balanced areas of knowledge and skills rather than in narrowly defined academic subjects (e.g., reasoning, communication, problem solving).
	• Premised on the belief that all children can learn and that teachers can structure instruction so that children can succeed (see Spady & Marshall, 1991).
	• Students are expected to demonstrate achievement of outcomes in their own ways.
Authentic assessment	• Closely linked to individualized, performance-based assessment, which has been the preferred mode in special education.
	• Offers a variety of methods by which to assess multiple views of students' productivity.
	• Assessment activities inform and influence day-to-day teaching.

by teachers, encourage children to be responsible for what they know by teaching another learner. Data collected by her student teacher researchers showed that tutors as well as those who were tutored experienced benefits such as increased self-esteem, increased communication skills, and increased achievement.

Teaming and Creative Problem Solving Among Educators

The task of educating an increasingly diverse student population can be overwhelming. No one teacher is capable of successfully meeting this challenge alone. We propose that collaboration among students (through cooperative learning structures) and adults (through cooperative education teams) is a key to meeting the challenge of educating a heterogeneous student population. (Villa & Thousand, 1994, p. 100)

In an effective curriculum of responsibility, it is imperative that children see their educators model responsibility by working together. Most educators, specialists, and professors have a history of working alone and therefore need time and coaching to learn new ways to work together effectively.

Forming and nurturing teaching teams are effective in creating environments that allow children to observe models of teamwork and collaborative decision making in action. Such teaching teams consist of "two or more people in the school and greater community who share cooperative learning planning, instructional, and evaluation responsibilities for the same students on a regular basis during an extended period of time" (Villa & Thousand, 1994, p. 82). Team teaching may take many forms, such as working in a multicultural school district as described in the next section. A special educator and a classroom teacher may join to plan for, instruct, and evaluate the program for a learner with special needs. High school teachers with knowledge in specific content areas (i.e., science, social studies, language arts, mathematics) may form a teaching team with support personnel (e.g., special educator, bilingual educator, speech-language pathologist, psychologist) to plan, instruct, and evaluate the instruction of 100–125 students during an academic year. (For detailed descriptions of how teachers, related services personnel, teacher's aides, and others can collaborate to deliver instruction and develop accommodations for a diverse student population, see Chapters 7, 10, 12, and 13.)

TEACHER EDUCATOR'S ROLE IN PREPARING TEACHERS TO TEACH RESPONSIBILITY AND RESPONSE-ABILITY

Professors who are involved in preparing future teachers can help their students acquire and demonstrate responsibility and response-ability in four ways:

1. Demonstrating and practicing recommended practices
2. Exploring new theories and renewing interest in old theories
3. Collaborating with schoolteachers and children
4. Being a *bold* model

Demonstrating and
Practicing Recommended Practices

As Nevin, Smith, and Udvari-Solner, in a comprehensive discussion of cooperative learning and higher education, pointed out, "Changing college teaching to more active, cooperative learning is not easy. First, faculty must see the need, then they must learn new ways of working with students" (1994, p. 126). Nevertheless, professors must learn, practice, and model the same instruction methodologies that are recommended for public school teachers (e.g., collaboration; creativity; team teaching; cooperative learning; dynamic, interactive hands-on projects) for promoting responsible social behavior. In particular, research (Cooper & Mueck, 1990; Johnson, Johnson, & Smith, 1991; Millis, 1991) suggested that college students' achievement and enjoyment of learning are enhanced when their professors use cooperative learning strategies.

In addition to becoming skilled in the instruction practices described in Tables 1 and 2, professors must develop and model the collaborative and creative problem-solving skills to work as responsible and response-able members of a cooperative teaching community rather than work in isolation. Nevin and Leff (1990), who studied the responses of teachers in training and veteran teachers who participated in creative problem-solving approaches to learning, described an example. They found that many participants were able to improve the results of their problem-solving approaches by taking different perspectives. This metacognitive style of thinking in new ways about often ordinary or troublesome events stimulated a profound shift in their typical ways of experiencing their teaching and learning tasks. "The good news is that there are numerous strategies for enhancing the creative spirit, thinking, and developing actions of an individual or a team so that effective solutions to challenges can be more readily found" (Leff, Thousand, & Nevin, 1994, p. 306).

Exploring New Theories
and Renewing Interest in Old Theories

Teacher education candidates also must be exposed to and comprehend the fundamental theories and practices that are constructivist and responsibility oriented. As discussed previously, such key theorists include Dewey (1933/1998), Gardner (1983, 1997), Piaget (1928/1959, 1930, 1954), and Vygotsky (1962). New theories may need to be developed to help educators at all levels explain and value differences in learning styles and differences based on culture and language. For example, Harris and Nevin (1993) explored how bilingual educators and special educators might collaborate more with one another. They found that ensuring the diversity of the membership of the collaborative team was not enough to ensure equal participation. The teams needed to develop different ways to involve team members, particularly those from the nondominant Anglo culture of the school. In addition, team members who were members of minority cultures needed to learn new ways to negotiate the system. Thus, all members of the collaborative team needed to change their interpersonal interactions to be more sensitive and more effective.

Collaborating with Schoolteachers and Children

Teacher educators can create new partnerships and working relationships with schoolteachers and children to add new knowledge about how teachers and children learn. They can set up collaborative efforts for teachers in training to participate in meaningful internship experiences.

Teacher candidates, like the children they teach, need time and opportunities to apply their instructional and theoretical knowledge in classrooms that nurture responsible and response-able student and teacher behavior through regular reflection on educational practices. Some universities are developing active partnerships with public schools so that professors and school-based faculty co-facilitate the professional development of teacher education candidates. Harris and Cleland (1994) described such a partnership that offered teacher candidates frequent opportunities to 1) observe models of the instruction methods they are acquiring, 2) receive coaching and feedback as they implement their previously acquired theoretical knowledge, and 3) engage in sustained reflection and discourse that research in adult development has found to be so critical in gaining new skills. Participants in this school–university partnership reported that the observation of their professors' responsible teamwork enhanced their enjoyment as well as their success in acquiring new teaching skills.

Paolucci-Whitcomb and Nevin (1985) provided another example of a university–school partnership. They described a graduate-level program that prepared consulting teachers and learning specialists to work collaboratively with classroom teachers. In addition to providing graduate students with a visionary plan for what can be done to adapt instruction so that students with disabilities can be taught with their peers who are developing typically, the partnership provided action research opportunities for the classroom teachers to actualize the vision. Often teachers, along with their consulting teacher research partners and university faculty, published the results of their action research projects subsequently (see, e.g., Wilcox, Sbardellati, & Nevin, 1987).

Being a *Bold* Model

For teacher candidates to be prepared to teach a curriculum for responsibility and response-ability, university faculty must provide bold models, just as teachers must be models for their students and administrators as well as for their faculty. Teacher educators are bold and break significantly from past and current practices in teacher preparation when they focus on instructional and philosophical approaches that value and directly model response-able and responsible teaching behaviors.

Perhaps most important in being a bold model is the concept of walking the walk, not just talking the talk. Teacher educators who demonstrate both flexibility (i.e., a variety of responses) and accountability (i.e., responsibility) help to ensure that future teachers teach both responsibility and response-ability. The overarching goal is to enhance educators' capacities to responsibly communicate, advocate, and negotiate in order to achieve more social justice for their students and themselves. Achieving social justice, again, means that everyone gets what they need to experience success.

A CONTEMPORARY MULTICULTURAL COMMUNITY'S APPROACH TO SOCIAL JUSTICE

> To see what is right, and not do it, is want of courage, or of principle.
>
> Confucius (cited in Thousand & McNeil, 1992, p. 13)

This section describes one community's approach to achieving social justice through education for responsibility, a contemporary multicultural community's approach. The example illustrates the possible changes in roles, rules, and responsibilities of everyone involved in achieving social justice in education.

How might a multicultural community create a mission statement and student profile for its high schools so that it incorporates many of the basic values of social justice and responsibility? Merced, a city of more than 55,000 citizens in California's agricultural San Joaquin Valley, exemplified such an effort. The town and valley experienced a monumental challenge, moving from a rural, agrarian society to a fast-paced society of technology and information while attempting to protect its rich agricultural base. It was within the means of the local agricultural economy to provide all that was needed for local residents to survive. The pace of life was slower and the population was more homogeneous, with little change occurring. During the 1980s and 1990s, the agrarian way of life diminished dramatically. Chronic double-digit unemployment had reached 26% before the closing of the Castle

Air Force Base in 1996, which led to up to 6,000 additional job losses. More than 40% of the population was on public assistance as of 1993 (McNeil & Curtaz, 1994).

Merced has become a multicultural community with one of the largest concentrations of Southeast Asian refugees in the United States and hundreds of immigrant Hispanic worker families joining the community. The academic and other challenges faced by new and low-income students present a serious challenge to the education system at a time when many classroom teachers are confronted with large class sizes, cutbacks in materials and resource personnel, and increasing demands to produce better results. In the attempt to address these issues as well as to welcome and include more fully students from a wide variety of cultural and academic backgrounds, teachers and students with the Merced Union High School district embarked on new endeavors punctuated by opportunities for shared responsibility and increased response-ability.

The Golden Valley High School Experience

In the mid-1990s, more than 2,000 students entered the doors of Golden Valley High School, the first new high school built since the 1960s in this small, formerly agrarian community in central California. Students came from ethnically diverse backgrounds: 33% Hispanic American, 39% European American, 20% Asian American, 7% African American, and 1% Native American/Pacific Islander. In addition, many were from families that faced economic challenges; the poverty rate reached as high as 60% for the Asian American population and 26% for every group other than European Americans. The dropout rate for the entire community remained high, especially for students from ethnically diverse backgrounds (i.e., other than European American) and students who experienced economic challenges. Moreover, the citizens of Merced were concerned that many of these students were not participating in the classes demanding higher-level thinking, the very classes that would prepare them to pursue 21st-century careers and avoid unemployment, underemployment, and welfare.

In response to the grave concern for a large proportion of the student body, the school board, school administration, and community representatives collaborated to create the following mission statement for the new high school, which articulated alternative hopes for its graduates:

> Through a collaborative effort of students, staff, and the community, the mission of Golden Valley High School is to provide academic and real life learning experiences so that its graduates will be creative and innovative;

self aware and self directed; adaptable problem solvers; respectful, friendly and cooperative; technologically adept; successful in career and life
skills; effective communicators; and active contributing members of society. (McNeil & Curtaz, 1994)

The community committee further generated a student profile of the
skills and attributes that they wanted their graduates to possess and
demonstrate, which mirrored the four domains of the Circle of Courage
goals of education (see Chapter 3). The profile includes the following
categories:

Mastery—The ability to communicate effectively in English; the ability
to read, comprehend, critically analyze, and write in an organized
fashion; and competency in the use of research methods and
resources, both traditional and technological

Independence—Knowledge of physical education, exercise, and lifetime
activity or leisure skills; family life and parenting skills; knowledge
of career interest, aptitude, and employment opportunities and skills
(e.g., interviewing, résumés, applications); confidence, punctuality,
and responsibility

Belonging—Appreciation for culture and cultural diversity; the ability
to communicate in a second language; the ability to interact well and
develop skills in conflict resolution; and the ability to solve problems, think creatively, and make decisions

Generosity—Respect for oneself and others, community service, and
extracurricular involvement

To help school personnel achieve these ambitious outcomes, the
school administration collaborated with university and business representatives to create a partnership effort. Federal and local funding
was obtained so that Golden Valley could be not only a high school
but also a fully integrated, seamless Grades 9–14 system of secondary
and postsecondary education for all of its diverse students (McNeil &
Curtaz, 1994). This required collaboration with an existing community coalition of public service agencies, educational institutions, and
private enterprises to address the economic, social, and cultural challenges that faced the Merced community. Important components of
what became known as the *System 9/14 effort* were 1) the inclusion of
students with academic and ethnic diversities, 2) an individualized
career and academic plan for each student, and 3) special support
classes and summer school experiences. To promote students' success, schoolwide instruction practices were studied. Then a staff

development plan was designed to increase the success of students who were deemed to be at risk for school failure. Staff development days for the next 2 years (1995–1996) were devoted to the development of staff knowledge and skills in areas such as thematic instruction, team teaching, interdisciplinary approaches, multiple teaching styles, and cooperative group learning.

As the teaching staff developed these new approaches to teaching and learning, additional strategies were employed to better connect students, teachers, and the community in order to foster student responsibility (i.e., personal accountability), response-ability (i.e., flexibility), and achievement of Circle of Courage goals. Strategies included

- Extending school experiences to include summer leadership training to foster a sense of *belonging* for students from minority cultures (e.g., Southeast Asian Americans, Hispanic Americans, African Americans) who were deemed to be at risk for school failure

- Team teaching among general, special, and guidance personnel to reform classroom teaching and assessment strategies (e.g., cooperative group learning, notetaking with pictographs, homework menu) to improve student *mastery*

- Creating opportunities for students to experience *mastery* in unique situations (e.g., mountain climbing, which involved cooperative team efforts)

- Visits to nearby university campuses to expand students' career expectations to include higher education as a possibility, thereby increasing student *independence*

- Structuring opportunities for civic responsibility and *generosity* (e.g., beautification of the community civic center grounds by student teams)

The strategies showed the teachers and administrators how to became more flexible (i.e., response-able) to actualize their accountability (i.e., responsibility) for this group of students.

Even the first year of implementation witnessed a significant decrease in the dropout rate and a higher attendance rate for the target student group. In addition, a core group of students assumed positive leadership roles within their respective cultures or ethnic groups. They formed a Leadership Club at the high school and recruited new student participants for the second academic year, illustrating the power of positive peer pressure for appropriate participation. After only 3 years of implementation, approximately 400 students (70% of whom were from traditionally underrepresented ethnic groups) had participated in one way or another in System 9/14 activities. Because of their participation in System 9/14 programs, 82 students who otherwise likely would not have graduated did graduate and received their diplomas with the first graduating class of Golden Valley High School.

Transformations in a Multicultural Classroom: The Atwater High School Experience

The following is a classroom-based versus systems-based example from Atwater High School, another school within the Merced high school district. The example shows how a special educator and two classroom teachers shared responsibility (i.e., accountability) by team teaching to increase their response-ability (i.e., flexibility) to achieve more social justice for their learners. In turn, their adaptations (e.g., offering a menu of choices for assignments and new systems of notetaking rather than just one required method) increased their students' responsibility (i.e., accountability). Recognizing that significant gaps existed in grade-point averages between students from low-income and disadvantaged situations and the rest of the student population, three high school teachers (one special education teacher and two history teachers) formed a cooperative teaching team to restructure the curriculum delivery system for a world history course. These teachers understood that many of their students struggled with learning difficulties that stemmed from a variety of sources (e.g., limited English proficiency, diverse ethnic backgrounds). In addition to achievement, self-esteem was an area that teachers wished to promote. The collaborative teaching team decided to focus on eight explicit goals for their work together:

1. To enable 100% of the students to meet minimum criteria, using a revised process of teaching to meet various learning modalities

2. To develop thematic units that connect world history to current events

3. To develop a positive, structured grading system involving portfolios; more flexibility in assignments; immediate feedback; and incentive points for attendance, participation, and outstanding behaviors

4. To promote attendance through follow-up telephone calls to students' homes, buddy systems, and incentive points

5. To increase the number of students eligible for special education completing the world history class successfully, using modified and alternative standards where appropriate

6. To incorporate new curriculum and teaching strategies based on the theory of multiple intelligences

7. To design options to assignments so that students could use preferred learning modalities to acquire and demonstrate knowledge

8. To pre- and posttest students' reading and vocabulary comprehension in order to determine literacy development, assign students to heterogeneous cooperative learning groups, and develop team assignments

Rather than change the *content* of the world history course, the teachers chose to adjust the *delivery system* in order to provide more opportunities for students to be engaged actively with peers and their teachers in the learning process (thus increasing students' flexibility, or response-ability). Table 3 presents a variety of elements that the teachers used to encourage responsibility, educational sociability, and higher achievement.

Outcomes for Students, Teachers, and the Curriculum

The results of the history teachers' creative problem solving were dramatic. They found the homework options or menus and the weekly portfolio to be extremely supportive of students with differing learning styles and preferences. Both the homework menu and the portfolio helped them to monitor and assess student progress and empowered students to track their own progress. Prior to implementing their collaborative teaching model, revised instruction delivery system, and the elements described in Table 3, grades for students in these world history classes told a tale of failure: 49% received a grade of D or F and virtually no students with special needs were enrolled because it was deemed to be so difficult for them to succeed in the class. In contrast, of 270 students who participated in the first year of the new delivery system, only 9% failed to pass. All but 1 of 20 students with special education needs received passing grades. Measures also suggested that the success of the students in this required high school class increased students' confidence in their ability to excel. These data provide an excellent example of an outcome that served as a catalyst for student and teacher self-examination and even more in-depth participation of students and their families in determining and evaluating the types of supports that most effectively and efficiently promote academic success for youth at risk of school failure.

In summary, teachers' strategies of change for responsibility appear to have made a meaningful difference. As students helped and supported one another, attendance, achievement (as reflected in improved grades), and self-esteem increased. Students became more

Table 3.   Elements of responsibility for students

Positive student goals	Outcomes are clearly stated and include goals that go beyond content to focus on students as good citizens and lifelong learners.
Advocate/peer buddy	Students are assigned to an advocate or to a peer buddy system. When a student is absent, the buddy's responsibility to the absent student is to call to share class assignments and homework and to encourage the student to return to class. Grade points are awarded to the caller upon the buddy's return. The peer buddy, *not* the vice principal, provides the contact (hence the contact is one of peer support rather than punishment).
Assignment menu	Teachers create a menu of options from which students choose how they will demonstrate their knowledge.
Weekly portfolio	Students keep a three-ring binder/class notebook for lecture notes, homework, tests, and projects, and they earn grade points on a weekly basis. Students with special needs are provided with modified standards as needed.
Cooperative projects	Students are encouraged to work together on projects and to demonstrate concern and respect for others who are different from themselves and to gain an understanding of ethnic diversity.
New notetaking	Students have the option of drawing pictures to show concepts and to use mind mapping rather than linear outlining systems.
Authentic assessment	Active learning is encouraged through student presentations, group projects, student-generated games and skits, role-playing, videotapes, art projects, and music presentations, as well as through the more traditional term papers, book reports, and written exams.
Bonus points	To stimulate active participation, students earn points toward their final grade by in-class participation in their learning.
Community classroom	Students learn by doing and working as they immediately apply classroom learning to real-world situations whereby they earn credit and learn critical workplace skills with local businesses and agencies.

Designed by J. Jantzen, B. Nagaoka, & S. Wine (1994) for an Atwater High School world history class, Merced, California.

active learners, demonstrated higher levels of learning, and successfully met the challenge to design creative ways of demonstrating what they had learned. Not only did the students experience a transformation in their academics and self-perceptions, but also teachers experienced a transformation in their instruction and assessment procedures so that students were able to *show* their skills.

The success of the collaborative teaching model had a curricular and instructional domino effect. Specifically, additional sections of world history were redesigned to be taught similarly. Teachers of U.S. history classes revised their curriculum to include thematic instruction, portfolio assessment, increased student responsibility, higher expectations, homework options, diverse learning activities, and increased teacher and peer support. Science, mathematics, and language arts teachers followed suit. Not surprisingly, these faculty noticed that *all* students, not just students with identified learning challenges, benefited from the changes. Furthermore, they saw more students expressing confidence in their newly observed abilities by enrolling in increased numbers in advanced placement honors classes than in previous years.

Lifelong Learning for Teachers   To enable Atwater High School faculty to expand their creative endeavors and update their curriculum and instruction approaches, the district arranged release time during the school day for teachers to revise and update their curricula and also allocated a small stipend for teachers to work together over the summer months. In addition, psychologists and special educators were assigned roles that allowed them to be more available to classroom teachers. The special education director often visited schools to encourage new teaching techniques and to ensure that requested materials and journal articles were helping teachers achieve the desired results. In these and many other ways, the administration showed its commitment to a lifelong learning view of becoming more responsible (i.e., accountable) for the response-ability (i.e., flexibility) of the faculty. One of the participating teachers, a veteran of 20 years, expressed appreciation for the support and the changes by describing the experience as the best year of teaching he had ever had.

DISCUSSION

Be responsible for our actions, and take responsible action.

Haki Madhibuti (as cited in Riley, 1993, p. 346)

People in public schools, universities, and communities can rearrange their roles and responsibilities successfully to create learning environments and delivery systems to achieve social justice in the educational arena. To do this, educators at all levels must demonstrate caring and concern by validating students' efforts and achievements and by creating learning experiences that enable students to be response-able (i.e., flexible) and responsible (i.e., accountable) throughout their school careers.

In our own careers, we have observed societies and educators experiencing multiple responses to diversity. Much progress has been made since the 1960s in American society's response to students who learn or behave differently than expected. As Table 4 shows, there are at least four responses to human difference or diversity—*marginalization, reform, tolerance,* and *valuing* (Van der Klift & Kunc, 1994). The first response, *marginalization,* is expressed by avoiding; segregating; and, in some cases, putting an end to people who are different. Our careers began at a time when many of the children with disabilities about whom we were concerned were in segregated classrooms, schools, and even institutions that were more like prisons than classrooms. Society examined such practices in special education and changed or eliminated many of them. Yet other hurdles arose to replace marginalization.

The remedial, therapeutic, and life-skills programs that were developed expressly to help minimize children's disabilities and make them more like children without disabilities led to a second response among educators: that of *reform.* Specifically, educators went from saying "You cannot be with us" to saying "You can be with us, but first you must be like us." In other words, students with learning and other differences needed to be rehabilitated and assimilated before they would be welcomed back into society. The intent was to improve their quality of life through increased functioning and skills development. The promise was future belonging; the real message was "You are not valuable as you are." The reform response to diversity remains in some communities but is being challenged by educators who promote inclusive education (Falvey, 1995; Lipsky & Gartner, 1997; Stainback, Stainback, & Forest, 1989; Thousand et al., 1994).

The third response to student diversity, which at first glance is more appealing than the first two (both of which represent equity approaches to distributing justice), is that of *tolerance.* At the turn of the 21st century, many view intolerance of student and human diversity as morally reprehensible and strive for truly tolerant schools and societies. The intent to create more acceptance of diversity is a worthy goal but one that never will lead to true social justice. In our travels promoting inclusive education, we have learned this through experience. In some schools, when educating children with disabilities in local general education classes is proposed, we hear statements of resignation (e.g., "We will, if we have to"). We hear statements of benevolence or

Table 4.   Responses to diversity

Marginalization	Avoidance, segregation, aggression
Reform	Rehabilitation, assimilation
Tolerance	Resignation, benevolence (false belonging)
Valuing	Diversity is typical, all people have worth and deserve to have a sense of belonging and to share in the benefits of society

false belonging (e.g., "Well, I guess it would be the nice thing to do to help those poor, unfortunate children"). These statements represent tolerance, and simply being tolerated is not the same as being valued. Few have as their life's goal simply being tolerated (N. Kunc, personal communication, April 1997).

To move beyond mere tolerance in education to the fourth and ultimate response of genuine *valuing*, students' diversity must be viewed as being typical. Deutsch's (1975) *needs* approach to social justice must be embraced so that schools can be created in which fair is not necessarily equal; rather, fair is everyone's getting what they need to experience success. This means designing educational experiences that ensure that children experience genuine belonging, mastery, independence, and generosity in the ways Van Bockern, Brendtro, and Brokenleg describe in Chapter 3. This means educating for students' and teachers' responsibility (i.e., accountability) and responsability (i.e., flexibility) through application of the theoretical, organizational, and curricular approaches offered in Table 1 and the exemplary education practices described in Table 2. In the last analysis, to move to genuine valuing means that those who care about children and their education must engage in a self-examination of their own beliefs regarding social justice and their actual education practices in relationship to these beliefs.

Together with students and caring community members, educators collectively have the potential to push society beyond both the blatant and the more subtle forms of marginalization, reform, and tolerance to genuine valuing of the natural diversity that children possess and express. To actualize that potential, however, requires that diversity and differences be acknowledged as part of the natural order of things—they belong to all. To bring this reality into the mind's eye and to close this chapter, invoke pictures of the vast variety of children's faces as you recall Whitney Houston's soaring rendition of "The Greatest Love of All":

> We believe the children are the future.
> Teach them well, but let *them* lead the way.

Show them all the beauty they possess inside.
Give them a sense of pride, make it easier.
Let the children's laughter remind us of who *we* used to be.

(Creed & Masser, 1977)

REFERENCES

Armstrong, T. (1994). *Multiple intelligences in the classroom.* Alexandria, VA: Association for Supervision and Curriculum Development.

Brendtro, L., Brokenleg, M., & Van Bockern, S. (1990). *Reclaiming youth at risk: Our hope for the future.* Bloomington, IN: National Educational Service.

Cooper, J., & Mueck, R. (1990). Student involvement in learning: Cooperative learning and college instruction. *Journal on Excellence in College Teaching, 1,* 68–76.

Creed, L., & Masser, M. (1977). The greatest love of all. On *Whitney Houston* [CD]. New York: EMI/Gold Horizon Music Corp. and EMI/Golden Torch Music Corp.

Curwin, R.L., & Mendler, A.N. (1988). *Discipline with dignity.* Alexandria, VA: Association for Supervision and Curriculum Development.

Deutsch, M. (1975). Equity, equality, and need: What determines which value will be used as the basis of distributive justice? *Journal of Social Issues, 31,* 137–149.

Dewey, J. (1998). *How we think: A restatement of the relation of reflective thinking to the educative process.* Boston: Houghton Mifflin. (Original work published 1933)

Dillon, A., Tashie, C., Schuh, M., Jorgensen, C., Shapiro-Barnard, S., Dixon, B., & Nisbet, J. (1993). *Treasures of celebration of inclusion.* Concord: University of New Hampshire, Statewide Systems Change Project, Institute on Disability/University Affiliated Facility.

Falvey, M.A. (1995). *Inclusive and heterogeneous schooling: Assessment, curriculum, and instruction.* Baltimore: Paul H. Brookes Publishing Co.

Gardner, H. (1983). *Frames of mind: The theory of multiple intelligences.* New York: BasicBooks.

Gardner, H. (1993). *Multiple intelligences: The theory in practice.* New York: Basic Books.

Gardner, H. (1995). Reflections on multiple intelligences: Myths and messages. *Phi Delta Kappan, 77*(3), 202–209.

Gardner, H. (1997). *Extraordinary minds: Portraits of exceptional individuals and an examination of our extraordinariness.* New York: Basic Books.

Glasser, W. (1986). *Control theory in the classroom.* New York: HarperPerennial.

Grant, C., & Sleeter, C. (1989). Race, class, gender, exceptionality, and educational reform. In J.A. Banks & C.A. McGee Banks (Eds.), *Multicultural education: Issues and perspectives* (pp. 46–66). Needham Heights, MA: Allyn & Bacon.

Harris, K., & Cleland, J. (1994, April). *The Quality Undergraduate Education through Site-Based Teacher Education (QUEST) program.* Paper presented at the Annual Conference of the Council for Exceptional Children, San Diego.

Harris, K., & Nevin, A. (1993). Exploring collaboration between bilingual and special educators. *Consulting Edge, 5*(1), 1, 3, 5.

Johnson, D.W., & Johnson, R. (1987). *Creative conflict.* Edina, MN: Interaction Book Co.

Johnson, D.W., Johnson, R.T., & Smith, K.A. (1991). *Active learning: Cooperation in the college classroom.* Edina, MN: Interaction Book Co.

Johnson, R., & Johnson, D. (1994). An overview of cooperative learning. In J.S. Thousand, R.A. Villa, & A.I. Nevin (Eds.), *Creativity and collaborative learning: A practical guide to empowering students and teachers* (pp. 31–44). Baltimore: Paul H. Brookes Publishing Co.

Kohn, A. (1997). *Beyond discipline: From compliance to community.* Alexandria, VA: Association for Supervision and Curriculum Development.

Kozik, F. (1980). *Comenius.* Prague: Orbis Press Agency.

Lazear, D.G. (1994). *Seven pathways of learning: Teaching students and parents about multiple intelligences.* Tucson, AZ: Zephyr Press.

Leff, H. L., Thousand, J.S., & Nevin, A.I. (1994). Awareness plans for facilitating creative thinking. In J.S. Thousand, R. A. Villa, & A.I. Nevin (Eds.), *Creativity and collaborative learning: A practical guide to empowering students and teachers* (pp. 305–319). Baltimore: Paul H. Brookes Publishing Co.

Lipsky, D.K., & Gartner, A. (Eds.). (1997). *Inclusion and school reform: Transforming America's classrooms.* Baltimore: Paul H. Brookes Publishing Co.

McLaughlin, M., & Warren, S. (1992). *Issues and options in restructuring schools and special education programs.* College Park: University of Maryland, The Center for Policy Options in Special Education, and the Institute for the Study of Exceptional Children and Youth.

McNeil, M.E. (1994). Creating powerful partnerships through partner learning. In J.S. Thousand, R.A. Villa, & A.I. Nevin (Eds.), *Creativity and collaborative learning: A practical guide to empowering students and teachers* (pp. 243–260). Baltimore: Paul H. Brookes Publishing Co.

McNeil, M.E., & Curtaz, D. (1994). *System 9/14: School-community-university partnership grant.* Washington, DC: U.S. Department of

Education; Division of Student Services; School, Community, and University Partnership (SCUP) Program.

Millis, B. (1991). Helping faculty build learning communities through cooperative groups. In L. Hilsen (Ed.), *To improve the academy: Resources for student, faculty, and institutional development* (pp. 43–58). Stillwater, OK: New Forums Press/Professional and Organizational Development Network in Higher Education.

Nevin, A.I., & Leff, H. (1990). Is there room for playfulness in teacher education? *Teaching Exceptional Children, 22*(2), 71–73.

Nevin, A.I., Smith, K. A., & Udvari-Solner, A. (1994). Cooperative group learning and higher education. In J.S. Thousand, R.A. Villa, & A.I. Nevin (Eds.), *Creativity and collaborative learning: A practical guide to empowering students and teachers* (pp. 115–127). Baltimore: Paul H. Brookes Publishing Co.

Paolucci-Whitcomb, P., & Nevin, A.I. (1985). Preparing consulting teachers through a collaborative approach between university faculty and field-based consulting teachers. *Teacher Education and Special Education, 8*(3), 132–143.

Piaget, J. (1930). *The child's conception of physical causality* (M. Gabain, trans.). San Diego: Harcourt, Brace & Co.

Piaget, J. (1954). *The construction of reality in the child* (M. Cook, trans.). New York: Basic Books.

Piaget, J. (1959). *Judgment and reasoning in the child* (M. Warden, trans.). Paterson, NJ: Littlefield, Adams. (Original work published 1928)

Poplin, M.S., Wiest, D.J., & Tarlow, M. (1996). Alternative instructional strategies: Constructive, critical, multicultural, and feminine pedagogies. In W. Stainback & S. Stainback (Eds.), *Controversial issues confronting special education: Divergent perspectives* (2nd ed., pp. 153–180). Needham Heights, MA: Allyn & Bacon.

Public Broadcasting Service (PBS). (1996). *Understanding learning disabilities: How difficult can this be? The F.A.T. City Workshop* [Videotape]. Washington, DC: Author.

Riley, D.W. (Ed.). (1993). *My soul looks back, 'less I forget: A collection of quotations by people of color.* New York: HarperCollins.

Spady, W., & Marshall, K. (1991). Beyond traditional outcome-based education. *Educational Leadership, 49*(2), 67–72.

Stainback, S., Stainback, W., & Moravec, J. (1992). Using curriculum to build inclusive classrooms. In S. Stainback & W. Stainback (Eds.), *Curriculum considerations in inclusive classrooms: Facilitating learning for all students* (pp. 3–17). Baltimore: Paul H. Brookes Publishing Co.

Stainback, W., Stainback, S., & Forest, M. (1989). *Educating all students in the mainstream of regular education.* Baltimore: Paul H. Brookes Publishing Co.

Thousand, J.S., & McNeil, M. (1992, March). Preparing school personnel for the 21st century: Issues in teacher preparation and the Responsive Teacher Program. In *Conference Proceedings of Comenius' Heritage and Education of Man for the 21st Century: International Scientific Conference.* Prague: Charles University.

Thousand, J.S., & Villa, R.A. (1992). Collaborative teams: A powerful tool in school restructuring. In R.A. Villa, J.S. Thousand, W. Stainback, & S. Stainback (Eds.), *Restructuring for caring and effective education: An administrative guide to creating heterogeneous schools* (1st ed., pp. 73–106). Baltimore: Paul H. Brookes Publishing Co.

Thousand, J.S., Villa, R.A., & Nevin, A.I. (Eds.). (1994). *Creativity and collaborative learning: A practical guide to empowering students and teachers.* Baltimore: Paul H. Brookes Publishing Co.

Udvari-Solner, A., & Thousand, J.S. (1995). Promising practices that foster inclusive education. In R.A. Villa & J.S. Thousand (Eds.), *Creating an inclusive school* (pp. 87–109). Alexandria, VA: Association for Supervision and Curriculum Development.

Van der Klift, E., & Kunc, N. (1994). Beyond benevolence: Friendship and the politics of help. In J.S. Thousand, R.A. Villa, & A.I. Nevin (Eds.), *Creativity and collaborative learning: A practical guide to empowering students and teachers* (pp. 391–401). Baltimore: Paul H. Brookes Publishing Co.

Villa, R.A., & Thousand, J.S. (1994). One divided by two or more: Redefining the role of a cooperative education team. In J.S. Thousand, R.A. Villa, & A.I. Nevin (Eds.), *Creativity and collaborative learning: A practical guide to empowering students and teachers* (pp. 79–101). Baltimore: Paul H. Brookes Publishing Co.

Villa, R.A., & Thousand, J.S. (Eds.). (1995). *Creating an inclusive school.* Alexandria, VA: Association for Supervision and Curriculum Development.

Villa, R.A., Udis, J., & Thousand, J.S. (1994). Responses for children experiencing behavioral and emotional challenges. In J.S. Thousand, R.A. Villa, & A.I. Nevin (Eds.), *Creativity and collaborative learning: A practical guide to empowering students and teachers* (pp. 369–390). Baltimore: Paul H. Brookes Publishing Co.

Vygotsky, L. (1962). *Thought and language.* Cambridge, MA: MIT Press.

Wilcox, J., Sbardellati, E., & Nevin, A.I. (1987). Cooperative learning aids integration. *Teaching Exceptional Children, 20*(1), 61–63.

Chapter 7

Adaptations in
General Education Classrooms

Sharon Vaughn and María Elena Arguelles

Since the mid-1990s, we have worked in more than 60 elementary, middle, and high schools in which personnel have restructured their programs to meet the needs of all students in their schools. The task has been challenging. For most of these schools, it has required that personnel change roles; curricula be altered; services be adjusted; and interactions with professionals, parents, and students be improved. With few exceptions, the principals, teachers, parents, and students whom we have interviewed have perceived that their hard work has paid off in better services and, in some cases, in documentation of improved outcomes. Mrs. Caballero, an elementary school principal, described it as follows:

> I used to be a special education teacher. I was in a portable out on the other side of the playground with my kids. Yes, and they were always referred to as *my kids*. In fact, if any of my students ever got into trouble during lunch or on the playground, they would get me. They wouldn't follow the

Note: This manuscript benefited from the expert editing of Claire V. Morris, University of Texas.

same procedures as they did for other kids. So, we were always special, and I was always the special teacher. When I became principal I knew that I was going to do everything I could to ensure that all children were participating members of the school community and were involved in general classes as much as possible. (Personal communication, April 1997)

In her school, Mrs. Caballero set a tone whereby all teachers were responsible for all students and then provided intensive, ongoing professional development to ensure that teachers had the necessary skills and confidence to meet the needs of all students appropriately.

Principals and teachers ask several core questions as they consider restructuring their schools to meet the educational and social needs of all students. The first set of questions focuses on how to develop and implement appropriate models. These questions include the following:

- What do successful models look like?
- What are the components of effective models?
- What roles do the teachers play in these models?
- How difficult is it to schedule?
- Do all teachers or only a selected few participate?
- How do principals and teachers promote appropriate interactions among professionals who are collaborating and among teachers and students?

The second set of questions addresses procedures for effectively accommodating students with disabilities in general education classrooms while promoting the education of all students in the classroom. These questions include the following:

- What types of testing and grading accommodations make sense?
- What adaptations can be implemented that will improve outcomes for all students?
- How should the groups in the classroom be organized to enhance students' learning and social acceptance?
- What principles of instruction should be implemented to ensure students' learning?

This chapter is organized around the previous two sets of core questions. The first section of the chapter addresses models of instruction that promote the inclusion of students with disabilities; the second section provides descriptions of accommodations that make a difference for all students.

WORKING TOGETHER TO
ENHANCE OUTCOMES FOR ALL STUDENTS

Structuring the school and classroom environments so that all students recognize their importance and are participating members of the educational community is an essential goal (Falvey & Rosenberg, 1995). Recognizing whether this goal is realized in a classroom or a school is relatively easy. One of the authors of this chapter remembers a colleague telling her that he could spend 30 minutes in a school or classroom and determine whether the environment was conducive to the inclusion of all students. Having visited more than 30 schools within the last 3 years, we agree. The more difficult task is that of assisting educators to modify their environments so that all students are members of the learning community. Jubala, Bishop, and Falvey provided the following suggestions to help educators handle that task: "(1) structuring the classroom environment to provide positive, cooperative relationships; (2) providing a democratic classroom; (3) developing communication and conflict-management skills; (4) encouraging whole-school community building and parent involvement; and (5) enhancing curriculum considerations" (1995, pp. 112–113). Because the needs to belong and to be accepted by others are primary (e.g., Dreikurs, Grunwald, & Pepper, 1982; Maslow, 1987), classrooms that provide the environment just described allow for procedures to resolve conflict and solve problems in ways that enhance outcomes for all students.

Collaborating with Other Professionals

For students with high incidence disabilities to be included in general education environments and curricula, teachers must collaborate. Most teachers, in imagining their professions, do not envision intense collaboration or co-planning and co-teaching with another professional. The following represents a typical teacher reaction:

> I always assumed that I would have my own class with my own students and that it would be a lot like it was when I went through school. My first reaction was not very positive, but now I like it a lot. I guess it's because the person I work with is so terrific. She gives me ideas that help not just with the special students but with all my students.

Most special education teachers also assume that they will have their own students to teach. This notion of sharing responsibilities for the education planning for and the instruction of students with special needs is a difficult adjustment for many general and special education teachers. In fact, simply a change in thinking from "my" students to "our" students represents significant progress for many teachers.

Baker and Zigmond (1995) conducted five case studies in five different states to determine procedures and practices for including students with learning disabilities. Although all five sites differed in many ways, all had in common special and general education teachers who co-taught and co-planned. In fact, all of the special education teachers at these sites had taken on new roles. These findings—that teachers are increasingly co-teaching, co-planning, and accepting new roles—were confirmed through observations of schools that had restructured to meet the needs of students with disabilities better (e.g., Arguelles, Schumm, & Vaughn, 1996; Vaughn, Hughes, Schumm, & Klingner, 1998). How did teachers' roles vary? Baker and Zigmond referred to the role change for special education teachers as a *Jill-of-all-trades* (1995, p. 170). "In addition to teaching students with LD, many of these teachers were now also responsible for teaching students who did not have IEPs, for consulting with teachers in general education, and for participating in teacher assistance teams" (Baker & Zigmond, 1995, p. 170).

Co-teaching: Questions and Answers   Having worked extensively with teachers in co-teaching situations, we have identified some of the questions that teachers frequently ask about how they should handle co-teaching. One of the most important questions is, Who is the "real teacher"? The answer to that question is quite simple and should be demonstrated in all ways in which the teachers interact with each other and the students: When both teachers are in the classroom, both teachers are the "real teacher." This means that the special education teacher cannot always be the teacher who is following up the lesson with support but at least occasionally is the director or lead teacher. This notion of who is the "real teacher" must be communicated to students, not just by the instruction roles that both teachers play but also through other activities. For example, both teachers need to assume responsibility for grading, classroom management, and decision making regarding all relevant academic and behavioral activities. The notion of co-responsibility for the times when teachers are co-teaching is critical; otherwise, many special education teachers become classroom assistants to the general classroom teacher.

Another important aspect of co-teaching is both teachers' use of adequate space, desks, chairs, and keys. One special education teacher explained the problem to me this way: "I feel like the bag lady of the school. I have no place to keep my things. I have no desk, I have no space in any of the teachers' classes in which I work."

A second frequently asked question is, What do we tell the students? What teachers tell students is determined to some extent by the age of the students; however, all students should be informed that they have two teachers, both of whom have the same level of authority when they are in the classroom. It may be effective to introduce the special education teacher as the learning abilities specialist who will work with all of the students from time to time. Klingner, Vaughn, Schumm, Cohen, and Forgan (1998) asked students who had been in a co-teaching classroom what their reactions were to having two teachers. Both the general and special education students agreed that they liked having two teachers. A representative response was, "I like having two teachers because then everyone gets more help."

A third question co-teachers ask is, What do we tell the parents? Many school personnel are concerned that if parents of general education students find out that the second teacher in their child's class is a special education teacher (whether for all or part of the school day), the parents may be concerned that their child's education is being compromised. Several steps can be taken to help alleviate this concern. First, bring parents in early and involve them in the planning for the new program. Bring in guest speakers (e.g., other parents are particularly effective) to present their experiences with similar models. Assure parents that the academic and social progress of all students will be monitored carefully to ensure adequate progress. Invite parents to come to the classrooms and observe the instruction and their child's involvement.

Perhaps the most frequently asked question by co-teachers is, How do we get time for co-planning? In an interview with 40 teachers who had spent a year co-teaching, the most consistent concern is time to co-plan, discuss students' progress, and plan for future instruction units. They simply believed that they spent far too little time co-planning and far too much time winging it. Many teachers described situations in which they did not even share with their co-teacher a lunch period or any breaktime during the entire week. Sometimes they planned while walking down the hall together to the rest room. Most teachers said that their co-planning was "taken out of their hide"; that is, they got together after school hours, in the evenings, and on the weekends. Even for those few teachers who were fortunate enough to have a designated time to co-plan, they reported that this time frequently was usurped by teacher meetings and professional development activities. One suggestion of several of the teachers with whom we worked was to provide a "designated release day" every 6 weeks for teachers who co-teach so that they can monitor students' progress, prepare instruction units, and discuss instruction practices and students' learning. Chapter 10 provides suggestions for assisting school personnel to create time to work together. Effective administrators work cooperatively with teachers to create common planning times.

Co-teaching: Practices and Procedures   Many teachers struggle with defining or understanding their role in a co-teaching situation. Bauwens and Hourcade (1995) provided a list of factors to consider when determining teaching arrangements:

1. For each lesson or unit, what are the skills that each teacher brings to the classroom?

2. What are each teacher's knowledge, background, and comfort level with the content being taught?

3. What instruction procedures are necessary to make the lesson or unit effective? How comfortable is each teacher with implementing these instruction procedures?

4. Have students been taught similar material in the past? Which co-teaching procedures were most effective?

5. Which components of the lesson are most critical? Can the components be divided in a way such that teachers split their responsibilities?

6. How difficult is the material for students to learn? Are there ways to structure the co-teaching best to facilitate learning for all students?

One issue with which many teachers struggle is how to co-teach. In particular, teachers are interested in what the second teacher does when the lead teacher for any given lesson is teaching. In observing more than 70 classrooms in which teachers were co-teaching, we observed a reoccurring theme that we refer to as *grazing* and *tag-team teaching*. *Grazing* refers to occasions when the second teacher moves from student to student to ensure that each student is, for example, on the correct page, completing the assignment, or paying attention during the time when the lead teacher is teaching the entire group. This arrangement often keeps many students attending in class, but it may not be the best use of the second teacher's time. *Tag-team teaching* refers to the process in which two teachers take turns teaching. One teacher teaches the class as a whole, and the second teacher waits his or her turn; then they reverse positions, with the second teacher moving to the front of the room and the previous lead teacher moving to the back. Teachers have commented that they are unsure how to coordinate their teaching in ways that are more effective than grazing and tag-team teaching.

Several alternative practices to grazing and tag-team teaching are available:

- Plan 1, one group: One lead teacher and one teacher teaching on purpose
- Plan 2, two groups: Two teachers teach the same content
- Plan 3, two groups: One teacher reteaches, and one teacher teaches alternative information
- Plan 4, multiple groups: Two teachers monitor or teach, and the content may vary
- Plan 5, one group: Two teachers teach the same content (Vaughn, Schumm, & Arguelles, 1997)

Plans 1 and 5 involve all of the students being taught in a whole-class situation. This is appropriate for many lessons; therefore, prescribing an effective role for the second teacher is important. In Plan 1, the second teacher teaches on purpose. *Teaching on purpose* refers to specific minilessons that are provided by the second teacher for 60 seconds, 2 minutes, or up to 5 minutes to one or two students. The minilessons may serve as a follow-up to previous lessons, an extension of what is presently taught, a check for understanding of key words and concepts, or a strategy by which to facilitate understanding. In Plan 5, the students are also in one group, and the two teachers co-teach the same content simultaneously. Clearly, this requires extensive coordination and is often restricted to experienced co-teachers. One teacher may take the lead in the lesson, and the second teacher may provide mnemonic devices, strategies for learning, examples, and connections to information learned previously. Plans 2 and 3 require that the class be divided into two groups. For Plan 2, the students are divided into two heterogeneous groups, and each teacher instructs one of the two groups. This provides an excellent opportunity for teachers to instruct a smaller group, to allow each student to demonstrate what he or she knows, and to extend information presented previously to the class as a whole. In Plan 3, the students are divided into two groups based on their knowledge of and skills in the designated topic. For example, a small group of students who are having difficulty with a particular lesson or unit can be provided support within the small group, and the second teacher can provide extended information to the students who have mastered the lesson or unit. Plan 4 allows students to be divided into several groups of three to five students per group, depending on the lesson and the students' needs. In this situation, all students can work on the same activity but can work with members of their group, and centers for different activities can be established so that groups can rotate through the different activity centers. Some teachers use small groups as an opportunity to provide small-group instruction in reading and mathematics while the second teacher circulates and provides assistance to other groups. Effective co-teaching involves the application of all of the previous plans.

ACCOMMODATIONS THAT MAKE A DIFFERENCE FOR ALL STUDENTS

Following are several activities that teachers can implement that enhance learning for students with disabilities as well as other students.

Preparing for a Lecture

As more students with diverse needs are included in general education classrooms, teachers are faced with the difficulty of providing instruction to children who have a wide range of ability levels. Pablo, an eighth-grade science teacher who teaches six large classes per day, often asks, How can I provide individual assistance to all these students? It's hard enough trying to cover the required objectives. In addition to careful preplanning, teachers can make several accommodations to facilitate students' learning.

Purpose-Setting Activities   Vaughn, Bos, and Schumm (1997) suggested using purpose-setting activities to provide students with reasons for reading. Reading for a particular purpose enhances the interest of text information (Schraw & Dennison, 1994). These simple activities help guide the lesson and also improve motivation. Purpose-setting activities work best when teachers keep the following points in mind:

- Provide one purpose for reading.
- The purpose should be brief yet meaningful.
- Make setting a purpose part of the teaching routine.
- During and after reading, refer to the purpose of reading the material.
- Place the purpose statement where students can see it (Blanton, Wood, & Moorman, 1990).

Graphic Organizers   Some research evidence indicates that prereading activities used to familiarize students with new material can improve factual recall and comprehension (Glynn & Di Vesta, 1977; Proger, Taylor, Mann, Coulson, & Bayuk, 1970). A prereading activity that can be helpful for all students is the use of graphic organizers. First introduced by Barron and Earle (1973), graphic organizers are used to diagram the lesson's major concepts and supporting ideas to present students with the text's structure before they begin to read. When introducing a topic that is unfamiliar to students, teachers can add pictures and/or photographs to the advance organizers. Adding a pictorial component to the graphic organizers facilitates the comprehension of students whose prior knowledge of the topic is less thorough (Rakes, Rakes, & Smith, 1995; Townsend & Clarihew, 1989). Graphic organizers can be used before, during, or after a lesson. Readence, Bean, and Baldwin (1998) suggested that teachers and students work cooperatively to construct graphic organizers as a class activity. Learning how to construct graphic organizers provides students with a tool that they can use in other classes and other learning situations. The first few times that graphic organizers are used as part of a class activity, teachers should make sure to use think-alouds and to model each step for students. As students practice and become more familiar with graphic organizers, they will be able to construct them with a partner or alone as homework. These activities assist in making the use of graphic organizers an independent process.

Prereading activities aid students in bringing their prior knowledge to the surface and are one of the ways in which teachers can level the playing field as they expose all students to the concepts and the vocabulary to be covered during the lesson. Some students may require assistance during as well as prior to the lesson.

Notetaking

Even though some students may learn how to take helpful notes on their own, many others who find notetaking to be exceedingly difficult may benefit from instruction on how to take notes. Towle (1982) made the following recommendations for teachers who want to assist students in improving notetaking skills:

- Tell students to sit alertly and have on their desks only the materials necessary for taking notes.

- Review vocabulary and concepts related to the topic prior to delivering the lecture. Depending on the students, a list of difficult words may even be posted so that students may refer to them during the lecture.

- Train students to listen for organizational cues or signal words such as *first, next, however, consequently,* and *finally.*

- Teach students to listen for content importance by noticing verbal cues such as a change in the teacher's voice, tone, pitch, or volume, as well as pauses in his or her speaking.

- Elaborate on important points or content.
- Request examples and nonexamples.
- Check for understanding by having students paraphrase certain points.
- Whenever possible, provide students with visual references.

During the first few weeks after teaching students these strategies, it is a good idea to have students share notes with each other and have them compare and discuss differences and similarities.

Textbook Accommodations

Guzzetti, Hynd, Skeels, and Williams (1995) found that between 66% and 76% of secondary students enrolled in science classes reported that they never or rarely used their textbooks beyond completing the assigned questions at the end of the chapter. Findings from a study conducted with students with learning disabilities suggested that these students may be less sensitive to text structure (e.g., description, enumeration, sequence, compare and contrast) than their peers without disabilities (Englert & Thomas, 1987). Teachers may be unaware of how difficult reading some textbooks is for many of their students. Armbruster and Anderson (1984) outlined some of the characteristics teachers should look for when examining textbooks:

- Organization and structure of the textbook
- Whether concepts are addressed one at a time or several are discussed simultaneously
- The clearness and coherence of what is explained
- Whether the text is at the students' instruction level and whether it is appropriate for its purpose
- Whether the text has too many ambiguous or indirect referents
- Whether the text has too many ideas that are not relevant to the topic

FLIP   Another option when trying to determine whether textbooks and other reading materials are appropriate is to have students analyze their own reading materials. FLIP (Friendliness, Language, Interest, Prior knowledge) is a strategy designed to teach students how to decide whether reading materials are suitable for them (Schumm & Mangrum, 1991). This strategy provides teachers with feedback on text difficulty; in addition, once students learn the strategy, they can use it to determine the difficulty of reading materials for their other classes or of any other kind of reading material. FLIP involves a brief overview of a reading assignment during which students examine the introduction, the summary, and the graphic elements of the text in order to determine its friendliness, language, knowledge, and interest:

F Friendliness: How friendly is the reading?

L Language: How difficult is the language?

I Interest: How interesting is the reading?

P Prior knowledge: What do I already know about this topic?

Once teachers determine that textbooks or other reading materials are either too difficult or at an inappropriate reading level, they can make several accommodations, such as study guides, text structures, and selecting important ideas, to assist students.

Study Guides   Large class sizes and the diversity of students make it difficult, if not impossible, for teachers to know whether students are following along, understanding, and engaged while reading. Some students require a gentle hand to guide them during a reading exercise to make sure that they are on task and focused. Instead of having students respond to the questions at the end of a chapter, study guides engage students in activities as they read portions of text. Wood, Lap, and Flood (1992) found study guides to have several advantages: The teacher has control over the questions, students do not have to wait until after they are done reading to find out what they are expected to know, and students must remain engaged and attentive. Depending on the level of students' reading abilities or on the complexity of the reading, teachers may choose to provide students with page numbers or subheadings so that students can follow along in the text and alternate reading with responding.

Text Structures   Although some students pick up text structures over years of reading and schooling, others benefit from direct instruction. Teaching students the structures that underlie expository texts and how they can use this knowledge often enhances their recall and comprehension (Armbruster, Anderson, & Ostertag, 1987; Baumann, 1984). Students with learning difficulties in particular benefit from instruction in text structure because it becomes a useful tool when these students read unfamiliar content (Palincsar & Brown, 1985).

Selecting Important Ideas   Some students have difficulty in deciding which are the main ideas or the important concepts to remember and study in a reading selection or a chapter. Irwin (1991) suggested using a simple activity to teach students how to find the main ideas in what they read. First, the students are divided into small groups or pairs. Then, students read a section of the reading selection or chapter in short segments. Each student writes down the most important idea or concept to remember. Students then compare their topic or concept choices. As a group, they must choose only one. Individual groups' answers can be compared with those of the whole class. Test items can be selected from groups' work. This activity allows students to learn from each other and to engage in a discussion that encourages them to think and to defend their choices.

Testing Accommodations

Ongoing assessment is an integral part of teaching. The results of tests and other types of assessments guide teachers with regard to which concepts should be taught next and which should be taught for a second or third time. However, developing tests that are reliable measures of students' knowledge is not always easy. The next subsection discusses several suggestions that teachers can follow when preparing and administering tests.

It is not uncommon for some students who are attentive during class and put forth effort to do poorly when tested. The use of student-friendly tests (Vaughn, Bos, & Schumm, 1997) is an accurate means of assessing a student's true knowledge on a specific topic, regardless of the student's weaknesses in other areas (e.g., reading, organizational skills). Student-friendly tests have a clear format and include content that has been covered in class. Furthermore, students have been told explicitly what to expect on the test; directions are clear; writing is legible; and sufficient space is provided between items to avoid confusion. Test items are written in the same language and vocabulary that were used during class discussions and lectures. Key vocabulary words may be underlined or written in boldface type to call students' attention to them. Some students may find it helpful to have test items read orally (unless assessing reading achievement); others may require additional time. Providing students with alternative forms of the test (e.g., oral, multiple choice, fill in the blank) or allowing them to take tests on computers are yet other simple testing accommodations that can improve students' performance on tests (Council for Exceptional Children, 1997). Teachers should keep in mind that the goal of assessment is to ascertain what the student has learned and to guide their planning.

Teachers can provide their students with tips on how to become better test takers. In addition to studying, being well rested, and maintaining a positive attitude, students should:

- Look over the whole test before beginning to work
- Be aware of time limits and how much time is spent on each item
- Read directions carefully
- Begin with easier items and leave those that they are unsure of for later
- Review the test before turning it in to the teacher (Rubin, 1991, pp. 399–400)

Although many students learn test-taking skills on their own, many others benefit from direct instruction and practice in test-taking skills and strategies. Giving students the opportunity to discuss, immediately after completing a test, the different techniques they used during the test allows them to learn from each other and to sharpen their metacognitive skills.

Enhancing the Acceptance of Students with Disabilities in the Classroom by their Peers without Disabilities

In addition to academic difficulties, some students with disabilities experience problems with learning some of the subtle social skills that other students pick up automatically as they grow up. Several studies demonstrated that children with learning disabilities and students who are low achievers are rejected more frequently by their peers, identified as being popular less frequently, are not often chosen as playmates, and are not well liked by teachers (Pearl, 1987; Pearl, Donahue, & Bryant, 1986; Vaughn & La Greca, 1988). Teachers can assist all of the students in their classrooms in learning social skills and can provide a classroom environment that enhances their social acceptance among their teachers and peers. Vaughn, Bos, and Schumm outlined the characteristics of a classroom that promotes peer acceptance:

- All members of the class are treated with respect.
- There is a fostering of concern for each other. Students are responsible for themselves and each other.
- If a negative statement is made about a student, the teacher states something positive about that student.
- Teachers serve as advocates for all of the students in the classroom. (1997, pp. 82–83)

Along with creating an accepting classroom environment, several social skills can be taught to students to assist them in monitoring and controlling their own behavior.

FAST   FAST, a social skills mnemonic strategy, consists of four steps that are designed to help students to problem solve:

F Freeze! Don't act too quickly. What's the problem?

A Alternatives! What are the possible solutions?

S Select one! Which is the best solution for the long run?

T Try it! Slowly and carefully—if it doesn't work, what else can I try? (McIntosh, Vaughn, & Bennerson, 1995)

SLAM   SLAM is another social skills mnemonic strategy that McIntosh and colleagues (1995) developed. Students can use this strategy to assimilate negative feedback from and negative remarks made by others:

S Stop whatever you are doing.

L Look the person in the eye.

A Ask the person a question to clarify what he or she means.

M Make an appropriate response to the person.

Principles of Effective Social Skills Training   Like many of the academic skills that students learn, social skills are better assimilated and retained when students are provided with clear and direct instruction, modeling, practice, role-modeling opportunities, and occasions to try new strategies in novel situations. Furthermore, Vaughn and La Greca (1993) made several suggestions for improving the likelihood that students will learn and use social skills strategies:

- Obtain students' commitment to learn the new strategy.
- Assess whether the social skills are appropriate for a specific group of students.
- Identify the steps to be used in implementing the social skill.
- Teach students to monitor the use and progress of strategy implementation.
- Involve peers in social skills training.
- Teach social behaviors that are supported naturally in the learning environment.
- Teach students to adapt the procedures of the social skill taught so that it becomes their own.
- Rehearse skills in a variety of environments.

STUDENTS' PERCEPTIONS OF ACCOMMODATIONS AND INSTRUCTION STRATEGIES

Teachers may be surprised to learn that students have strong and definite opinions about the way in which they are taught. Even those students who often appear shy and withdrawn may share insightful perceptions about their learning when asked. Several research studies have been conducted to learn about students' perceptions regarding various accommodations and instruction strategies for students with diverse needs. This section describes students' perceptions about instruction accommodations, textbook accommodations, and adaptations in test and homework assignments.

Instruction Accommodations

Over all, students prefer general education teachers who attend to individual students' needs, make adaptations in their instruction styles, and are sensitive to students' diverse learning patterns (Vaughn, Schumm, & Kouzekanani, 1993; Vaughn, Schumm, Niarhos, & Daugherty, 1993). Students also appreciate teachers who recognize that some students have difficulties and change the pace of their instruction accordingly (Schumm & Vaughn, 1994).

Textbook Adaptations

Vaughn, Schumm, Klingner, and Saumell (1995) examined middle and high school students' perceptions of adaptations that teachers in the general education classroom made for students with diverse needs. All students who were interviewed (i.e., high, average, and low achievers; students with learning disabilities; students for whom English was a second language) believed that they needed further teacher assistance to learn from their textbooks, and most wanted teacher-directed assistance through prereading and during-reading activities. That study confirmed the findings of Schumm, Vaughn, and Saumell (1992) that students at all levels believed that they needed textbook adaptations that they were not receiving in their classrooms.

Text and Homework Assignments

In their 1994 study, Schumm and Vaughn found that more than half of the secondary students whom they interviewed thought that all students should receive the same homework assignments and tests. Middle school students in particular seemed to favor not being singled out and were concerned with being treated the same as their peers.

The best accommodations, that is, accommodations that are designed to enhance students' learning and to encourage students to work at their full potential, are those that treat students with respect. Accommodations that are provided with the mere purpose of making the assignment easier for the student (and in many cases for the teacher) compromise a student's self-esteem and promote the student's dependence on others. As more and more research in the area of students' perception is being conducted and published, it is becoming clear that students are aware of the intent and the manner in which accommodations are provided. Respectful accommodations are appreciated and perceived as fair and appropriate by all students.

CONCLUSIONS

Assume that Giselle Morales is a social studies teacher at Paul Bell Middle School, a suburban school that has 1) a large special education department and 2) many students who have just arrived from Spanish-speaking countries. She teaches approximately 175 sixth graders in six different classes, 23 of whom have been identified as having learning disabilities, 12 of whom have been labeled as gifted, and 7 of whom have been identified with emotional disabilities. Despite the challenging situation that Ms. Morales faces, a visit to her class makes it obvious that a lot of learning is going on there. Following might be a typical comment of a teacher such as Ms. Morales:

> I truly enjoy my students and being a teacher. I try to make the classes fun and interesting. When I was teaching a lesson on Egypt, we learned about how the Egyptian kings were buried together with their treasures. The students decided what they would like to include in their own treasures and made pyramid models. We played *JEOPARDY!* when it was time to review for the test. I really try to incorporate hands-on and fun activities into my lessons.

Special and general education teachers' ability to collaborate with each other is a vital skill that is increasing in importance as more classrooms include increasingly diverse students. For any co-teaching model to be effective, several criteria must be in place, including:

1. Time to co-plan
2. Knowledge of the procedures involved in the particular model
3. A location where participants can meet

Co-teaching may take many different forms. One common form allows for one teacher to lead and one to teach on purpose.

General education teachers can use prereading activities such as purpose setting and graphic organizers to improve students' comprehension and depth of learning. Many students have difficulty learning in general education classrooms because not all subjects are uniformly interesting or consistent with students' cultural backgrounds and prior knowledge. The pacing and conceptual load of some subjects are unwieldy, and learning tasks such as textbook reading and tests are overwhelming for some students. Teachers can become familiar with the strengths and weaknesses of their textbook by evaluating its subject matter content, structure, readability level, and friendliness level. When developing tests, teachers should consider the clarity of the directions, appropriateness, student-friendliness, and adaptations for administration and scoring.

Some students need assistance in learning social skills that others pick up automatically. Teachers can enhance peer acceptance in the classroom by using instruction programs such as FAST and SLAM. Principles of effectively conducting social skills training include obtaining students' commitment to learn the strategy, involving peers in the training, and teaching for transfer of learning and generalization.

REFERENCES

Arguelles, M.E., Schumm, J.S., & Vaughn, S. (1996). *Executive summaries for ESE/FEFP Pilot Program.* Report submitted to the Florida Department of Education, Tallahassee.

Armbruster, B.B., & Anderson, T.H. (1984). Content area textbooks. In R.C. Anderson, J. Osborn, & R.J. Tierney (Eds.), *Learning to read in American schools: Basal readers and context texts* (pp. 193–226). Mahwah, NJ: Lawrence Erlbaum Associates.

Armbruster, B.B., Anderson, T.H., & Ostertag, J. (1987). Does text structure/summarization instruction facilitate learning from expository text? *Reading Research Quarterly, 21*(3), 331–346.

Baker, J.M., & Zigmond, N. (1995). The meaning and practice of inclusion for students with learning disabilities: Themes and implications from the five cases. *Journal of Special Education, 29*(2), 163–180.

Barron, R.F., & Earle, R.A. (1973). An approach for teaching vocabulary in content subjects. In H.L. Herber & R.F. Barron (Eds.), *Research in reading in the content areas: Second year report* (pp. 84–100). Syracuse, NY: Syracuse University, Reading and Language Arts Center.

Baumann, J.F. (1984). The effectiveness of a direct instruction paradigm for teaching main idea comprehension. *Reading Research Quarterly*, 20(1), 93–115.

Bauwens, J., & Hourcade, J.J. (1995). *Cooperative teaching: Rebuilding the schoolhouse for all students*. Austin, TX: PRO-ED.

Blanton, W.E., Wood, K.D., & Moorman, G.B. (1990). The role of purpose in reading instruction. *Reading Teacher*, 43(7), 486–493.

Council for Exceptional Children (CEC). (1997). Effective accommodations for students with exceptionalities. *CEC Today*, 4(3), 1–15.

Dreikurs, R., Grunwald, B.B., & Pepper, F.C. (1982). *Maintaining sanity in the classroom: Classroom management techniques* (2nd ed.). New York: HarperCollins.

Englert, C.S., & Thomas, C.C. (1987). Sensitivity to text structure in reading and writing: A comparison between learning disabled and non-learning disabled students. *Learning Disabilities Quarterly*, 10, 93–105.

Falvey, M.A., & Rosenberg, R.L. (1995). Developing and fostering friendships. In M.A. Falvey (Ed.), *Inclusive and heterogeneous schooling: Assessment, curriculum, and instruction* (pp. 267–283). Baltimore: Paul H. Brookes Publishing Co.

Glynn, S.M., & Di Vesta, F.J. (1977). Outline and hierarchical organization as aids for study and retrieval. *Journal of Educational Psychology*, 69(2), 89–95.

Guzzetti, B.J., Hynd, C.R., Skeels, S.A., & Williams, W.O. (1995). Improving physics texts: Students speak out. *Journal of Reading*, 38(8), 656–663.

Irwin, J.W. (1991). *Teaching reading comprehension processes* (2nd ed.). Upper Saddle River, NJ: Prentice-Hall.

Jubala, K.A., Bishop, K.D., & Falvey, M.A. (1995). Creating a supportive classroom environment. In M.A. Falvey (Ed.), *Inclusive and heterogeneous schooling: Assessment, curriculum, and instruction* (pp. 111–129). Baltimore: Paul H. Brookes Publishing Co.

Klingner, J.K., Vaughn, S., Schumm, J.S., Cohen, P., & Forgan, J.W. (1998). Inclusion or pull-out: Which do students prefer? *Journal of Learning Disabilities*, 31(2), 148–158.

Maslow, A.H. (1987). *Motivation and personality* (3rd ed.). New York: HarperCollins.

McIntosh, R., Vaughn, S., & Bennerson, D. (1995). FAST social skills with a SLAM and a RAP. *Teaching Exceptional Children*, 28(1), 37–41.

Palincsar, A.S., & Brown, A.L. (1985). Reciprocal teaching activities to promote reading with your mind. In T.L. Harris & E.J. Cooper (Eds.), *Reading, thinking, and concept development: Strategies for the classroom* (pp. 147–159). New York: College Entrance Examination Board.

Pearl, R. (1987). Social-cognitive factors in learning disabilities. In S.J. Ceci (Ed.), *Handbook of cognitive, social, and neuropsychological aspects of learning disabilities* (Vol. II, pp. 273–294). Mahwah, NJ: Lawrence Erlbaum Associates.

Pearl, R., Donahue, M., & Bryant, T. (1986). Social relationships of learning-disabled children. In J.K. Torgesen & B.Y.L. Wong (Eds.), *Psychological and educational perspectives on learning disabilities* (pp. 193–224). San Diego: Academic Press.

Proger, B.B., Taylor, R. G., Mann, L., Coulson, J.M., & Bayuk, R.J. (1970). Conceptual prestructuring for detailed verbal passages. *Journal of Educational Research, 64*, 28–34.

Rakes, G.C., Rakes, T.A., & Smith, L.J. (1995). Using visuals to enhance secondary students' reading comprehension of expository texts. *Journal of Adolescent and Adult Literacy, 39*(1), 46–54.

Readence, J.E., Bean, T.W., & Baldwin, R.S. (1998). *Content area literacy: An integrated approach* (6th ed.). Dubuque, IA: Kendall/Hunt Publishing Co.

Rubin, D. (1991). *Diagnosis and correction in reading instruction* (2nd ed.). Needham Heights, MA: Allyn & Bacon.

Schraw, G., & Dennison, R.S. (1994). The effect of reader purpose on interest and recall. *Journal of Reading Behavior, 26*(1), 1–18.

Schumm, J.S., & Mangrum, C.T. (1991). FLIP: A framework for content area reading. *Journal of Reading, 35*(20), 120–124.

Schumm, J.S., & Vaughn, S. (1994). Students' thinking about teachers' practices. In T.E. Scruggs & M.A. Mastropieri (Eds.), *Advances in learning and behavioral disabilities* (Vol. 8, pp. 105–129). Greenwich, CT: JAI Press.

Schumm, J.S., Vaughn, S., & Saumell, L. (1992). What teachers do when the textbook is tough: Students speak out. *Journal of Reading Behavior, 24*, 481–503.

Towle, M. (1982). Learning how to be a student when you have a learning disability. *Journal of Learning Disabilities, 15*, 90–93.

Townsend, M.A.R., & Clarihew, A. (1989). Facilitating children's comprehension through the use of advance organizers. *Journal of Reading Behavior, 11*(1), 15–35.

Vaughn, S., Bos, C.S., & Schumm, J.S. (1997). *Teaching mainstreamed, diverse, and at-risk students in the general education classroom.* Needham Heights, MA: Allyn & Bacon.

Vaughn, S., Hughes, M.T., Schumm, J.S., & Klingner, J. (1998). A collaborative effort to enhance reading and writing instruction in inclusive classrooms. *Learning Disability Quarterly, 21*(1), 57–74.

Vaughn, S., & La Greca, A.M. (1988). Social interventions for learning disabilities. In K.A. Kavale (Ed.), *Learning disabilities: State of the art and practice* (pp. 123–140). San Diego: College-Hill Press.

Vaughn, S., & La Greca, A.M. (1993). Social skills training: Why, who, what, and how. In W.N. Bender (Ed.), *Learning disabilities: Best practices for professionals* (pp. 251–271). Boston: Andover Medical Publishers.

Vaughn, S., Schumm, J.S., & Arguelles, M.E. (1997). The ABCDEs of co-teaching. *Teaching Exceptional Children, 30,* 4–10.

Vaughn, S., Schumm, J.S., Klingner, J., & Saumell, L. (1995). Students' views of instructional practices: Implications for inclusion. *Learning Disabilities Quarterly, 18,* 236–248.

Vaughn, S., Schumm, J.S., & Kouzekanani, K. (1993). What do students with learning disabilities think when their general education teachers make adaptations? *Journal of Learning Disabilities, 26*(8), 545–555.

Vaughn, S., Schumm, J.S., Niarhos, F.J., & Daugherty, T. (1993). What do students think when teachers make adaptations? *Teaching and Teacher Education, 9*(1), 107–118.

Wood, K.D., Lapp, D., & Flood, J. (1992). *Guiding readers through text: A review of study guides.* Newark, DE: International Reading Association.

Chapter 8

Creating a Community of
Learners with Varied Needs

Mary A. Falvey, Mary Blair,
Mary Patricia Dingle, and Nancy Franklin

It is 8:00 in the morning at Martin Luther King Middle School, a middle school in a large urban school district at which 11- and 12-year-old students in Room 13 are actively engaged in a variety of meaningful learning experiences. This is a humanities class, a combination and integration of English/Language Arts and Social Studies. The students are working in "tribes"—cooperative groups of five students assigned to each group by their teacher (Gibbs, 1994). The students are grouped so that they have complementary strengths, especially across the multiple intelligences abilities.

These sixth graders have been reading, discussing, and reflecting on the life and achievements of the early Egyptians. Today the students, in their tribes, were instructed to create a mural representing the daily life of an adolescent during the early Egyptian period. The students were told to be sure that the mural demonstrated the relationship between facts that they had learned from their textbook about the

Egyptians' lifestyle; classroom discussions; novels and short stories depicting this era that they had read; and resources obtained from the Internet and the library. Students' murals were to be accompanied by a written text reflecting their collective and individual contributions to the mural as well as reflections related to their learning and experiences throughout the unit on early Egypt. To prepare for this activity, Mr. García, the humanities teacher, taught the students to use concept maps or webs in order to organize and connect the facts that they had learned from different sources on this topic.

One of the groups includes a student with special talents in the spatial intelligence area. This student has also been identified as having a specific learning disability. In another group, a student is enormously talented in the linguistic areas of listening, reading, and word processing and has also been labeled as having cerebral palsy and does not use spoken words to communicate. Another group includes a student who is exceptionally talented in the interpersonal area and has a great deal of compassion for others. She also has Down syndrome and low vision. A fourth group includes a student who has a tremendous ability to recall facts and figures because of his logical-mathematical intelligence; he also has the label of autism. The other members of the groups have a range of talents across the multiple intelligences and have not received a disability label. Their teachers assume that all of the students across the groups have enormous gifts and talents. Because these students have intentionally been grouped heterogeneously, they draw on each other's strengths.

Although the students are given 5 days to complete their project, they make significant progress during the period. The bell rings to indicate that the period is over. They pass to second period, which, like first period, lasts for 1 hour, 45 minutes. These students go together to Room 10, where they have their math/science block class. In addition, these students and their core curriculum teachers (humanities and math/science) belong to the same teaching team, which allows them to collaborate, integrate, and coordinate their efforts.

The public education systems in the United States and in other countries are relying less on sorting students by specific labels and abilities; instead, they are grouping students to intentionally create heterogeneous learning experiences, which is reflected in the scenario just described. Sorting students by labels, abilities, or both has done a great deal of damage to students (Oakes, 1985; Sapon-Shevin, 1994). Such sorting has resulted in 1) limited opportunities for students with labels to acquire and obtain the knowledge and information available to students without disability labels; 2) less rigorous educational experiences; and 3) education programs that often focus on students' labels and impairments rather than on their gifts, talents, and uniqueness.

The alternative to sorting or grouping students homogeneously is referred to as *inclusive* or *heterogeneous schooling*. This type of schooling is based on the principle that all students have the right to learn together, regardless of their labels or learning needs. Clearly, in order for inclusive and heterogeneous schooling to be successful, students must receive the necessary services, supports, and resources. Delivering these supports to students with disabilities in general education environments means restructuring the pervasive separate, homogeneous model of special education service delivery that pulls special education personnel and resources as well as the students out of, rather than into, general education.

GENERAL CHARACTERISTICS OF SCHOOLS THAT HAVE BEEN RESTRUCTURED TO ACCOMMODATE STUDENTS' DIVERSITY

If students with disabilities are to be successful learners alongside their peers without disabilities, there is no choice but to dismantle the homogeneous model of special education and replace it with more and closer collaborative teaching arrangements among general and special educators. In addition, it is noteworthy that school communities that are interested in creating access for all students to the learning of meaningful content have not only restructured their model of special education service delivery but also reexamined and retooled their entire approach to assessing, instructing, and partnering with one another and community members (Villa & Thousand, 1995). This section describes six general characteristics of schools that have been restructured successfully to welcome and teach all students (Darling-Hammond, 1997).

Appreciation for Diversity

Schools that have embraced the diverse population of students, whether their diversity is a result of differences in language, culture, religion, lifestyle, or ability, are inclusive. As the population of students becomes more diverse, these schools are more successful at creating schools and programs that reflect the unique needs of students. These schools offer "diverse experiences and perspectives enhances both the power of students' thinking and their range of vision as social members" (Darling-Hammond, 1997, p. 125).

Authentic Performance and Assessment

"Authentic assessments are composed of a variety of performance-based assessment instruments that require students to *generate* a response rather than *choose* a response, and the response that is generated can be demonstrated in a real-life context" (Gage & Falvey, 1995, p. 63; italics in original). Classrooms in which the teachers, students, and parents are genuinely concerned about students' learning emphasize and place tremendous value on students' demonstrating their knowledge and skills in authentic, performance-based ways. These school communities understand that obtaining single or even multiple scores related to students' performance through achievement-type testing does little to inform educators, parents, or students about deep understandings or abilities to apply information in real contexts. Thus, in these schools, there is an increased use of authentic assessment methods, such as portfolios, that consider students' progress over time and across activities. Multiple-choice tests are replaced by rich assessments that are based on multidimensional criteria representing various and applied aspects of an activity or a skill.

Classroom teachers who understand and value authentic assessment are more likely to use assessments to get to know individual students well rather than to use assessments to rank students' performances or to assign a label to their performances. Furthermore, as classroom teachers become more skilled at analyzing how students learn, their ability to support and make accommodations for a more diverse group of learners, including those with disabilities, increases dramatically. It is the presence of children with disabilities that simultaneously causes and enables teachers to become capable of and creative in adapting curriculum and instruction to benefit every child.

Active and Authentic Learning

When students hear something, they often forget it. If students see something, they generally are able to remember it better. If students do something, however, they are more likely to both remember it and understand it. Active and authentic learning experiences are instructional practices that are expressly designed to make learning make sense to students—that is, to make learning meaningful (Good & Brophy, 1997). To facilitate meaningful learning for all students, schools must go beyond the teacher-dominated and didactic approaches that are used in the traditional classroom and give all students the opportunity to learn by doing. Because active and authentic learning experiences help to make instruction make sense to all students, including those with disabilities, such learning experiences diminish the need for excessive adaptations and accommodations for students.

Creating Caring and Democratic Learning Environments

Schools that are built on "authoritarian systems that rely on heavy-handed sanctions ultimately increase the level of student alienation and misbehavior and reduce possibilities for addressing problems constructively" (Darling-Hammond, 1997, p. 138). In contrast, schools that offer students frequent, daily opportunities to practice and learn the rudiments of living within a democratic environment are, in fact, schools that are attempting to develop truly inclusive communities. Schools that intentionally build a sense of trust, caring, and equality among and between students and teachers are more likely to facilitate students' positive relationships and connections. Thus, an essential element of successful schooling is the establishment of relationships and connections by teachers who understand their students' minds and hearts in significant ways (Darling-Hammond, 1997).

No student should go through school as an anonymous and/or unknown participant. Sizer (1992) reminded us that successfully restructured secondary schools have worked creatively and vigorously to ensure that every student has personalized relationships with at least one faculty member. Clearly, schools that overcome large, bureaucratic structures in order to develop educators' personalized relationships with each of their students are most likely to be successful with inclusive schooling.

Collaborative Learning and Teaching

Collaborative learning experiences among students and collaborative teaching activities among faculty are identified repeatedly as essential elements of being able to educate a diverse population of students (Villa, Thousand, Nevin, & Malgeri, 1996). Even in a community in which students share the same cultural and linguistic backgrounds, there is still tremendous diversity in students' strengths and learning styles. Peer support, such as peer teaching, has demonstrable benefits for all learners—those who are doing the teaching as well as those who are being taught (Brown, 1994; Slavin, 1995; Villa, Thousand, Stainback, & Stainback, 1992). Such arrangements and relationships are most successful when teachers carefully assign partnerships and vary students' roles so that everyone has the opportunity to be the teacher and the learner.

In addition to creating a culture of collaboration among students, when faculty create the same culture for themselves and also operate as a team, students' potential for success is enhanced. Collaboration among faculty members enables the assemblage of the collective expertise of each faculty member and allows for the sharing of the work and responsibility (Givner & Haager, 1995; Thousand, Villa, & Nevin, 1994). Schools that embrace the principle of collaboration for students and faculty increase exponentially the resources and expertise to meet the needs of a more diverse student population that includes students with disabilities.

Strong Connections with Families and the Community

A great many students with disabilities, especially those with severe disabilities, are enrolled in inclusive schooling as a result of their parents' advocacy efforts. Those parents have often gone to great lengths and great financial expense to ensure that their children are educated in general education classes with the necessary supports and services. Schools that have a genuine respect for families are more likely to view the advocacy efforts of parents of students with disabilities in a positive light, listen to the students' and the families' dreams and nightmares about the future, and welcome them into their school community. Parents and educators who struggle to work together effectively generally discover that they are able to create learning environments that are welcoming to all students.

Specific Strategies for Promoting Inclusive Schooling

Even in schools in which the restructured characteristics described previously are present, sometimes additional and more specific strategies and supports are needed to facilitate the implementation of inclusive education. The remainder of this chapter examines specific assessment strategies and specific strategies by which to facilitate students' access to learning.

ASSESSMENT STRATEGIES TO SUPPORT INCLUSIVE SCHOOLING

Assessment has received significant attention in the general education school restructuring effort in the contexts of outcomes-based education (Spady & Marshall, 1991), the establishment of national standards (O'Day & Smith, 1993), and performance-based and authentic assessment (Brown, 1994). The majority of the discussions in these areas have not related to students with disabilities specifically, although associated restructuring efforts have had a positive impact on students with disabilities indirectly.

Assessment of students with disabilities has at least three purposes. First, educators must determine students' eligibility for special education services through the individualized education program (IEP) planning process. Second, educators must conduct ongoing assessment in order to determine how students are performing and whether elimination or provision of additional or different supports is needed. Third, educators must evaluate students' performance, whether in relationship to grades, degree of achievement of IEP objectives, or other school or school district measures.

Several critical assumptions must be made when designing assessment procedures and processes. First, all students must be presumed to be competent (Biklen & Cardinal, 1997), even though it sometimes is difficult to determine the specific levels of competence of students with disabilities because of, for example, a student's limited communication abilities. Second, assessment should always yield information about students' strengths, gifts, and talents as well as a delineation of students' needs. Too often prior to the 1990s, the special education assessment process focused primarily on students' impairments and inabilities. Third, assessments should be designed to measure students' skills in a comprehensive manner that capitalizes on the collaboration of a variety of professionals who are involved with the student (e.g., speech-language specialist, general education teacher, adaptive physical education teacher, psychologist). Assessments prior to the advent of inclusive education often resulted in a discipline-specific analysis and a fragmented view of the student, rather than a picture of the student as a complex yet whole person.

Finally, when designing and determining the appropriate assessment procedures to be used, educators should bear in mind that the results should yield sufficient information about students to answer at least the following five questions:

1. How can the learner best demonstrate what he or she knows?

2. How does the learner learn best?

3. What does the learner know?

4. What does the learner need to expand his or her learning?

5. How can educators assist the learner better?

As previously noted, the formal and norm-referenced assessments traditionally used to assess students who qualify for special education services do not address these questions adequately; instead, alternative authentic assessment procedures provide teachers with a broader, deeper understanding of students (Falvey, Givner, & Kimm, 1996).

A Futures-Planning Process for Students

An extremely informative process for learning about students' strengths, needs, and interests is the *futures-planning process* (Falvey, Forest, Pearpoint, & Rosenberg, 1994). Although a variety of different methods have been developed for planning for students' futures, one of the most commonly used processes is Making Action Plans (MAPs) (Falvey et al., 1994; Forest & Lusthaus, 1989, 1990; Lusthaus & Forest, 1987; Pearpoint, Forest, & O'Brien, 1996). This process calls for a friendly atmosphere in which the student and his or her significant others gather to support and generate ideas for building a positive future for the student. In addition to the student, the MAPs futures-planning meeting should include his or her significant others who know the student, such as the student's family (e.g., parents, siblings, aunts, uncles, cousins, grandparents) and friends. The MAPs process might also include those who have specific expertise to teach this student, such as special and general education teachers, related-services personnel (e.g., speech-language therapists, occupational therapists, psychologists).

This gathering occurs in a comfortable environment that is friendly, relaxed, and supportive of the student and the student's family. A facilitator ensures that everyone present participates and that the focus is on building a positive future for the student. A recorder ensures that participants' responses are documented during the meeting. Responses are recorded on large sheets of paper so that everyone has visual access to input as it is generated, respecting those who process visual information more easily than exclusively verbal input.

As discussed by Falvey and her colleagues (1994), the facilitator asks everyone, especially the student, to respond to the following series of questions:

1. What is the student's history?
2. What are your dreams for this student?
3. What are your nightmares for this student?
4. Who is this student?
5. What are the student's strengths, gifts, and abilities?
6. What does the student need in order to reach the dreams and avoid the nightmares?
7. What would the student's ideal day look like, and what must be done to make it happen?

The MAPs futures-planning process provides the student and the other participants a unique opportunity to view the student's past and present as well as a path to the future and provides a major change in the way information about the student's needs are shared.

The MAPs process can be beneficial for any student. Let's take Valerie, for example. Valerie is a student with Down syndrome who, in preparation for her transition from elementary to middle school, invited her favorite classmates, family, and friends to participate in a MAPs meeting. The opportunity for Valerie's peers to participate in the MAPs process was a gift Valerie gave to them that day. Before the meeting, her peers created posters about their own fears about moving to middle school. This information helped to generate dreams and fears about middle school for Valerie and her classmates. The MAPs meeting was important for building a successful middle school experience for not only Valerie but also her peers.

Multiple Intelligences Assessment

In 1983, Gardner, in *Frames of Mind: The Theory of Multiple Intelligences,* challenged traditional beliefs and customs related to the concept of intelligence. His research concluded that intelligence previously had been defined too narrowly and had robbed many children and adults from being afforded experiences to achieve at higher levels. Gardner found intelligence to be multifaceted, requiring educators to broaden their view of who is smart. Traditional views of intelligence largely assess and recognize linguistic and logical-mathematical abilities as indicators of intelligence. Gardner expanded the indicators of intelligence abilities to include visual-spatial; musical; bodily/kinesthetic; interpersonal; intrapersonal; and, most recently (Gardner, 1997), naturalistic abilities. The question that educators and psychologists often struggle with is, How smart is this student? Gardner suggested that this is the wrong question to ask. The question that needs to be addressed is, How is the student smart? This question presumes that all students are smart; they are just smart in different ways.

There are no definitive, scientific ways to assess and measure students' area(s) of intelligence. There are, however, several strategies that educators and psychologists can use to develop a sense of students' strengths across the multiple intelligences areas. First, students can be provided with opportunities to engage in activities that require them to use all eight areas of intelligence. Teachers then can observe and make note of students' preferences and strengths while they are engaged in the different ways of learning. Second, observing students during their free time can provide teachers with critical information about students' areas of intelligence. Generally, students are more likely to initiate and maintain their interest in activities in which they are able to use or show their strengths. Third, observing, recording, and reflecting on the occasions when students behave in ways that are contrary to the classroom rules can also provide critical insight into students' multiple intelligences (Armstrong, 1994). For example, a student who often speaks out of turn may have linguistic intelligence strength, whereas a student who often looks out the window or is "off in space" may be a visual-spatial learner. A student who is constantly in motion may be a bodily/kinesthetic learner. Fourth, interviewing students, their families, and their friends can provide important insights into students' areas of strength. Another way to determine a student's multiple intelligences strengths is to complete a checklist. Checklists (e.g., Armstrong, 1994) can be combined with observations and interviews over time. When using a checklist, educators must be sure that it is not seen as a test that produces absolute, definitive information. Having a variety of methods for obtaining information about students' strengths in multiple intelligences areas is important for tracking students' knowledge and skill acquisition comprehensively as well as helping teachers to design instructional programs for students in ways of knowing that are most meaningful to the students.

Collection of Frequency Data

Collecting frequency data entails recording the number of times that a particular behavior occurs. When collecting frequency data, it is important that the data are collected at the same time each day and that the student has the same opportunity daily to engage in the behavior being observed in order to allow for comparisons to be made across time. Frequency data might involve recording the number of times that a student initiates an interaction with peers or the number of times another student is out of his or her seat. Frequency data can also be used to record progress related to academic goals, such as the number of times that a student is able to read words containing the letters p and b correctly or the number of English and Spanish words that a student who is developing the ability to speak English uses throughout the day. Figure 1 displays sample data collection procedures for each of these examples.

Functional Assessment of Behavior

When students engage in rule-violating behaviors, a functional assessment of the behaviors helps to determine the function or purpose that the behavior serves for the student. For example, observations of a student who pushes other students may reveal that he has few other behaviors in his repertoire to initiate interactions with peers, suggesting

Student: Jamal Davis   Date: April 24, 2000

Frequency of initiations

Arrival	Classroom Discussions	Cooperative Groups	Recess	Lunch	P.E.
√√	√	√√√	√√	√√√√	√

Student: Ivan Petra   Date: May 24, 2000

Frequency of "out of seat," when sitting is expected

Language Arts	Social Studies	Science	Math	Art	Music
√√√√		√√	√√√√√√√		√√

Student: Sara Morales   Date: March 25, 2000

Frequency of correctly reading "p" and "b"

Monday	Tuesday	Wednesday	Thursday	Friday	Total for week
√√√√√	√√	√√√√√√√√√√	√√√√√√√	√√√√	27

Student: Carolina Fajardo   Date: December 1, 1999

Frequency of English and Spanish words used

Arrival	Classroom Discussions	Cooperative Groups	Recess	Lunch	P.E.
Spanish √√	Spanish √	Spanish √√√√√√√√	Spanish √√√√√√√√	Spanish √√√√√√√√	Spanish √√√
English √√√√	English √√√√√√√	English √√√√√√	English	English √√√	English √√√√√√√

Figure 1.   Frequency data collection forms.

that perhaps one function of pushing may be to engage in interaction. Of course, a single observation does not yield adequate information to determine whether this is the function of the pushing. A functional assessment also determines the relationship between the student's behavior and the situations or environments in which the behavior occurs by gathering assessment information across time and environments and from a variety of sources (e.g., student observations, interviews of current and past teachers and parents, student interviews). In the example of the student who was pushing other students, the assessment would include examining when the behavior occurred, who was present, what activities were going on, and what happened following the behavior (i.e., the consequence) (O'Neill, Horner, Albin, Storey, & Sprague, 1997). Given reliable and comprehensive functional assessment information from various sources, it is possible to conduct a functional analysis—that is, the analysis of the probable function, purpose, or communicative intent of the behavior(s)—and develop a positive behavioral support plan for facilitating behavior change and enhancing inclusion in the community (Bishop & Jubala, 1995).

When educators and psychologists recognize that every student behavior has communicative value, they are more inclined to use positive teaching responses rather than negative ones such as punishment or exclusion (Donnellan & Leary, 1995). Research findings (Bishop & Jubala, 1995; Meyer & Evans, 1989; Repp & Singh, 1990) clearly have indicated that the effects of punishment, although immediate, are generally temporary. Therefore, responding to students' rule-violating behaviors with punishment is not an effective long-term teaching method. In addition, excluding students from an environment does not provide them with information on how to behave and respond differently in that environment. Using positive behavioral supports and other proactive strategies that offer students socially acceptable alternatives to rule-violating behaviors is a more effective, respectful, and enduring teaching method.

Curriculum-Based Assessment

Curriculum-based assessment (CBA) is an assessment process often overlooked as a method for obtaining critical information about the strengths and needs of students with disabilities. CBAs are designed to provide individualized, direct, specific information about students' knowledge, understanding, progress, and instructional needs with regard to the core curriculum (Salend, 1998). In addition, CBAs can yield information to help a student's teacher figure out when, where, and which adaptations or accommodations might be needed for a student to participate actively and effectively in the learning process.

Thus, CBAs are useful in determining how students with IEPs can be included in general education activities and curriculum objectives.

Unfortunately, historically, many students with disabilities, particularly those with severe disabilities, had alternative curricula or had limited access to the core general education curriculum and the assessments (CBAs) based on that curriculum. With the Individuals with Disabilities Education Act (IDEA) Amendments of 1997 (PL 105-17), schools are required to include students with disabilities in routine, schoolwide, districtwide, and statewide assessments unless otherwise specified on the IEP. Furthermore, the goals and objectives of a student's IEP are to be related to the general education curriculum. Therefore, it is reasonable to expect many more students to benefit from CBA as an assessment approach.

When conducting a CBA, teachers can offer students a variety of ways to demonstrate their knowledge so that the assessment format or method does not get in the way of students' being able to communicate what they know. Let's examine a science class in which a CBA is used to measure students' knowledge of the human circulatory system through graphic designs that include blanks in which students indicate various parts of the circulatory system. For some students, the teacher could alter the response form and instead request that they complete this task by using verbal responses or by pointing to the correct labels within the graphic representation of the circulatory system. Students with limited literacy skills are thus able to show their knowledge in ways that are not based exclusively on written directions or written responses. Applying multiple intelligences theory to CBA suggests even further ways for students to show their knowledge.

FACILITATING STUDENTS' ACCESS TO LEARNING

Students with disabilities sometimes need adjustments or modifications to the curriculum and/or instructional arrangements in order for learning to be accessible to them. Even if students are unable to achieve independence in certain activities, involving them in the most active way possible is essential. Furthermore, students' participation in general education activities must be facilitated in such a way that it has meaning for them.

A Model for Decision Making to Ensure the Least Intrusive Modifications

A useful decision-making model that Udvari-Solner (1995) designed to assist educators in determining ways in which to meaningfully include

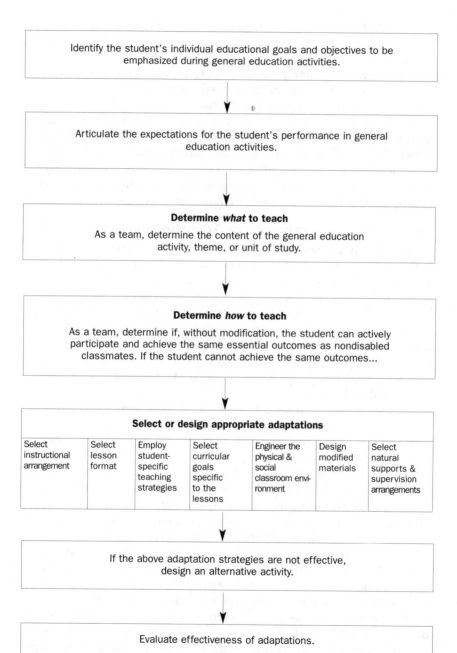

Figure 2. A curricular adaptation and decision-making process. (From Udvari-Solner, A. [1995]. A process for adapting curriculum in inclusive classrooms. In R.A. Villa & J.S. Thousand [Eds.], *Creating an inclusive school* [p. 113]. Alexandria, VA: Association for Supervision and Curriculum Development.)

students with disabilities in the general education curriculum is composed of a series of questions that result in educators making the least intrusive instructional modification possible (see Figure 2). As the model suggests, the first question or consideration for curriculum and instructional strategies in the general education classroom is to determine whether the student can participate without any modifications. Although modifications might assist students' involvement and participation in general education classes, they should be used only when absolutely necessary. It has been demonstrated that, in classrooms in which teachers are using multiple and varied active learning strategies, the need for excessive modifications to the curriculum, instructional strategies, or both is minimized (Udvari-Solner, 1994).

Definition and Examples of Accommodations

Some of the modifications needed for students to participate in meaningful ways are referred to as *accommodations* (Falvey et al., 1996). An accommodation is a support provided to a student that facilitates access to learning and does not alter academic performance standards. For example, a wheelchair (i.e., an accommodation) enables a middle schooler to gain access to the school elevator, allowing him or her to get to fourth-period science class, which is located on the second floor. This accommodation does not alter the performance standards in the student's science class; but without it, the student would not be able to participate in the class.

Let's take a look at another example of a number of accommodations being employed to support a student named Juanita. In a tenth-grade history class, in preparing students for an exam, the history teacher tells the students that they will be tested on their knowledge and skills on the following Friday. The teacher indicates that she will include on the test information from the classroom discussions of the previous 3 weeks and the last three assigned chapters from the English-only textbook. Juanita, a student in the class, does not have the requisite literacy skills to read the text but is able to participate effectively in this class with a variety of accommodations. One of Juanita's peers takes notes in Spanish from the class discussions on carbon paper so that a copy can be given to Juanita. Another student earns extra credit for reading the assigned chapters out loud in Spanish into a tape recorder, giving Juanita a taped version of the assigned chapters. Finally, a student who lives two doors down from Juanita goes to her house after school 3 days per week to study with her. This student reads the notes and turns on the tape recorder to review the chapters with Juanita. Juanita and her neighbor study hard for the test. On Friday, the day of the test, Mr. Gabriel, the special education teacher, and Juanita go to the library so that Juanita can take the test orally without disrupting the other students who are taking the test silently. Mr. Gabriel reads the questions to Juanita, and she dictates her answers to him. Even though Juanita required several modifications, none involved changing the academic outcome standards for her. Thus, these modifications are considered accommodations.

Multilevel Instruction

Accommodations are not always sufficient to facilitate students' meaningful access to the general education class. Some students, especially those who face significant challenges, might require more extensive supports, including supports that alter the academic outcome standards. Such supports, often referred to as *multilevel instruction*, make it possible for students to participate in meaningful ways rather than merely being present in the classroom (Falvey et al., 1996; Udvari-Solner, 1994). Multilevel instruction represents several different approaches. First, a student might be included in the general education curriculum activity but might be subject to a less complex level of expectations than those for his or her peers without disabilities. For example, a fourth-grade student might work on adding two single-digit numbers while the other students work on single-digit multiplication during math class. Second, a student might have a basic functional or direct application to the skill being learned. For example, a seventh-grade student might read a story about present-day events that uses first- and second-grade vocabulary while her peers are reading more-complex stories from ancient Russia. Third, a student might be learning the same content but with a reduction in the performance standards. For example, a third-grade teacher assigns Marcus, a student with significant challenges, only the first 5 words of the weekly 20-word spelling list, which increases in difficulty from the first to the twentieth word. Fourth, a student might be learning the same curriculum but at a slower pace. For example, a kindergarten student might need more time than her kindergarten peers to learn the alphabet and therefore may not learn all 26 letters while in kindergarten. Finally, a student might be expected to learn a substitute or different skill than his or her peers without disabilities are learning. For example, a secondary-age student who is working on increasing his upper trunk and head control might be evaluated on his ability to maintain upper-trunk and head control while his biology class works on specific science abilities.

Grading Students' Performance

When students receive supports, modifications, or both, educators often struggle with ways to grade students' performance fairly. The difficulty that educators encounter with regard to grading is not specific to students with disabilities. There are inherent problems with the traditional grading process instituted in the majority of schools in the United States, especially in secondary schools. Parents, students, teachers, administrators, and eventually employers often interpret grades as objective information about students' actual performance, even though the presumed objectivity of grades is extremely questionable for several reasons. First, there are no agreed-on, specific criteria that are used across teachers and grade levels or within or across schools and school districts. Second, some teachers consider each student's personal progress when assigning grades, whereas others consider only students' performance at the time the grade is assigned. Third, the majority of grading involves the assignment of a single grade, even though it is impossible to use a single grade to evaluate all aspects of students' performance or ability for an entire subject area. These issues, along with the challenges of grading a student who receives supports or modifications, make grading a huge challenge for educators.

Few would disagree that the entire grading structure and the overreliance on a gross letter-grade system need to be examined and modified. Until such examination and modifications to the existing grading structure occur, however, the following grading options should be considered. For students who receive accommodations only, no notation or other modification needs to be made to grades. If a student is receiving multilevel instruction modifications, the grade can be modified by a notation indicating that the student's grade reflects a modified performance standard. When modifying the grading performance standards, rather than relying on a single grade, the teacher can consider using 1) the student's IEP objectives to measure performance rather than grade-level standards, 2) a pass-fail system, 3) a student–teacher-generated contract and evaluation procedures, or 4) a narrative description of the student. For students with disabilities, it is the responsibility of each student's IEP team to discuss the issue of grading and make decisions for grading that make sense for that student and those individuals who will be reviewing the student's grades in the future.

Organizing and Communicating a Student's Individualized Education Program

Every student who qualifies for special education services and supports has an IEP, which, among other things, specifies the objectives that the student will work to accomplish within 1 year. The IEP is an important document for assisting educators to design effective and

Student: Mary Franklin
Date: April 18, 1998
School/Grade: Cooper City Middle School, 6th grade
Case Manager: Nathan Anthony

Related Service/Support Needs:
Communication Specialists, Tuesday & Wednesday, 10 & 12:30
Physical Therapist's Consultation Services 1 time/month
Full-Time Instructional Assistant

Student IEP Goals	Period 1 Science	Period 2 Language Arts	Period 3 Computers	Period 4 Math	Lunch	Period 5 P.E.	Period 6 Social Studies	Hall Passing
Types 3-4 word sentence on computer		3, 4, B	3, 4, B					
Adds single digit addition				3, 4, C	3, C			
Greets others	3, A	3, A	3, A	3, A	3, A	3, A	3, A	3, A
Follows 2-step direction	2, 3, B	2, 3, B	2, B	2, B	3, B	2, 3, B	2, 3, B	2, 3, B
Reads 60 words	3, 4, C	3, 4, C	3, 4, C				3, 4, C	
Holds up head & upper trunk for 2 minutes	3, C	3, C	3, C	3, C	3, C	3, C	3, C	3, C
Eats finger food without assistance					3, 4, C			
Moves wheelchair in desired direction for 10 feet					3, 4, C	3, 4, C		3, 4, C
Develops friendship with at least 2 peers		3, 4, C			3, 4, C	3, 4, C	3, 4, C	3, 4, C

Figure 3. Completed general education matrix for Mary Franklin. (Curriculum and instruction code for supports: 1, no changes; 2, accommodations; 3, multilevel; 4, alternate curriculum. People who provide the supports: A, peers; B, special education teacher; C, paraprofessional.)

needed supports for students. The IEP, however, does not easily and readily communicate where, when, and with whom IEP objectives might be addressed in the school day and week. The IEP–general education matrix (see Figure 3) is a tool that has been helpful in making decisions about, and communicating in a quick and simple way, when and where a student's high-priority objectives might be addressed. The matrix is developed collaboratively by the student's IEP team and additional school and community staff who have direct contact with the student throughout the year. Such a matrix meshes the high-priority IEP objectives with classes, daily routines and classroom activities, and transitions and indicates in which classes or activities priority objectives might be addressed formally or incidentally. One purpose of the matrix is to assist a student's IEP team in choosing when and where learning objectives are addressed in general education activities.

The matrix also may be used to help teams to identify the types of modifications or instructional supports that a student might need to be supported adequately. Codes can be developed and entered on the matrix to represent the kind of adaptations that are expected to be needed to ensure the student's success in each general education activity.

Finally, the matrix can be carried around by the student to show whoever interacts with that student what they are working on throughout the day. In this way, the matrix supports a student's IEP by offering a visual representation of when and where high-priority learning, employment, health, self-care learning, and support concerns can be addressed. It is an easy communication tool that lets anyone who interacts with the student know the program at a glance.

CONCLUSIONS

In our experience of observing and working in schools restructured to implement recommended educational practices in general education and offer IEPs that allow for and encourage active student, parent, and teacher decision making and involvement, such schools are the least challenged by the inclusion of students with disabilities. This chapter described only some of the models and specific strategies to assist schools in implementing inclusive education. Any of these strategies, however, will be effective only if school personnel and school districts stop asking the question, Should we include students with disabilities within the general education program? Instead, they must ask, What are the strategies that need to be created and made available in order for us to effectively implement inclusive education? Successful inclusive educational practices are based as much on beliefs and values as on professional knowledge and skill. Inclusive educational practices both reflect and are dependent on a belief that inclusive education is a moral obligation of a democratic society. To echo the views of Dewey (1933), the great educational philosopher and reformer of the early 20th century, an education in a democracy requires democracy in its education.

REFERENCES

Armstrong, T. (1994). *Multiple intelligences in the classroom.* Alexandria, VA: Association for Supervision and Curriculum Development.

Biklen, D., & Cardinal, D.N. (1997). *Contested words, contested science: Unraveling the facilitated communication controversy.* New York: Teachers College Press.

Bishop, K.D., & Jubala, K.A. (1995). Positive behavior support strategies. In M.A. Falvey (Ed.), *Inclusive and heterogeneous schooling: Assessment, curriculum, and instruction* (pp. 159–186). Baltimore: Paul H. Brookes Publishing Co.

Brown, A.L. (1994). The advancement of learning. *Education Researcher, 23*(8), 4–12.

Darling-Hammond, L. (1997). *The right to learn: A blueprint for creating schools that work.* San Francisco: Jossey-Bass.

Dewey, J. (1933). *How we think: A restatement of the relation of reflective thinking to the education process.* Chicago: Henry Regnery & Co.

Donnellan, A.M., & Leary, M.R. (1995). *Movement differences and diversity in autism/mental retardation: Appreciating and accommodating people with communication and behavior challenges.* Madison, WI: DRI Press.

Falvey, M.A., Forest, M., Pearpoint, J., & Rosenberg, R.L. (1994). Building connections. In J.S. Thousand, R.A. Villa, & A.I. Nevin (Eds.), *Creativity and collaborative learning: A practical guide to empowering students and teachers* (pp. 347–368). Baltimore: Paul H. Brookes Publishing Co.

Falvey, M.A., Givner, C.C., & Kimm, C. (1996). What do I do Monday morning? In S.B. Stainback & W.C. Stainback (Eds.), *Inclusion: A guide for educators* (pp. 117–138). Baltimore: Paul H. Brookes Publishing Co.

Forest, M., & Lusthaus, E. (1989). Promoting educational equality for all students: Circles and MAPS. In S.B. Stainback, W.C. Stainback, & M. Forest (Eds.), *Educating all students in the mainstream of regular education* (pp. 43–57). Baltimore: Paul H. Brookes Publishing Co.

Forest, M., & Lusthaus, E. (1990). Everyone belongs with the MAPs action planning system. *Teaching Exceptional Children, 22*(2), 32–35.

Gage, S.T., & Falvey, M.A. (1995). Assessment strategies to develop appropriate curricula and educational programs. In M.A. Falvey

(Ed.), *Inclusive and heterogeneous schooling: Assessment, curriculum, and instruction* (pp. 59–110). Baltimore: Paul H. Brookes Publishing Co.

Gardner, H. (1983). *Frames of mind: The theory of multiple intelligences.* New York: BasicBooks.

Gardner, H. (1997). Are there additional intelligences? The case of naturalistic, spiritual, and existential intelligences. In J. Kane (Ed.), *Education, information, and transfer motion.* Upper Saddle River, NJ: Prentice-Hall.

Gibbs, J. (1994). *Tribes: A new way of learning together* (4th ed.). Santa Rosa, CA: Center Source Publications.

Givner, C.C., & Haager, D. (1995). Strategies for effective collaboration. In M.A. Falvey (Ed.), *Inclusive and heterogeneous schooling: Assessment, curriculum, and instruction* (pp. 41–57). Baltimore: Paul H. Brookes Publishing Co.

Good, T.L., & Brophy, J.E. (1997). *Looking in classrooms* (7th ed.). Reading, MA: Addison Wesley Longman.

Individuals with Disabilities Education Act (IDEA) Amendments of 1997, PL 105-17, 20 U.S.C. §§ 1400 *et seq.*

Lusthaus, E., & Forest, M. (1987). The kaleidoscope: A challenge to the cascade. In M. Forest (Ed.), *More education integration* (pp. 1–17). Downsview, Ontario, Canada: G. Allan Roeher Institute.

Meyer, L.H., & Evans, I.M. (1989). *Nonaversive interventions for behavior problems.* Baltimore: Paul H. Brookes Publishing Co.

Oakes, J. (1985). *Keeping track: How schools structure inequity.* New Haven, CT: Yale University Press.

O'Day, J.A., & Smith, M.S. (1993). Systemic school reform and educational opportunity. In S.H. Fuhrman (Ed.), *Designing coherent educational policy: Improving the system* (pp. 101–134). San Francisco: Jossey-Bass.

O'Neill, R.E., Horner, R.H., Albin, R.W., Storey, K., & Sprague, J.R. (1997). *Functional assessment and program development for problem behavior: A practical handbook* (2nd ed.). Pacific Grove, CA: Brookes/Cole.

Pearpoint, J., Forest, M., & O'Brien, J. (1996). MAPs, Circles of Friends, and PATH: Powerful tools to help build caring communities. In S.B. Stainback & W.C. Stainback (Eds.), *Inclusion: A guide for educators* (pp. 67–86). Baltimore: Paul H. Brookes Publishing Co.

Repp, A.C., & Singh, N.N. (1990). *Perspectives on the use of nonaversive and aversive interventions for persons with developmental disabilities.* Sycamore, IL: Sycamore Publishing Co.

Salend, S.J. (1998). *Effective mainstreaming: Creating inclusive classrooms* (3rd ed.). Upper Saddle River, NJ: Merrill.

Sapon-Shevin, M. (1994). *Playing favorites: Gifted education and the disruption of community.* Albany: State University of New York Press.

Sizer, T.R. (1992). *Horace's school: Redesigning the American high school.* Boston: Houghton Mifflin.

Slavin, R.E. (1995). *Cooperative learning: Theory, research, and practice* (2nd ed.). Needham Heights, MA: Allyn & Bacon.

Spady, W., & Marshall, K. (1991). Beyond traditional outcome-based education. *Educational Leadership, 49*(2), 67–72.

Thousand, J.E., Villa, R.A., & Nevin, A.I. (Eds.). (1994). *Creativity and collaborative learning: A practical guide to empowering students and teachers.* Baltimore: Paul H. Brookes Publishing Co.

Udvari-Solner, A. (1994). A decision-making model for curricular adaptations in cooperative groups. In J.S. Thousand, R.A. Villa, & A.I. Nevin (Eds.), *Creativity and collaborative learning: A practical guide to empowering students and teachers* (pp. 59–77). Baltimore: Paul H. Brookes Publishing Co.

Udvari-Solner, A. (1995). A process for adapting curriculum in inclusive classrooms. In R.A. Villa & J.S. Thousand (Eds.), *Creating an inclusive school* (pp. 110–124). Alexandria, VA: Association for Supervision and Curriculum Development.

Villa, R.A., & Thousand, J.S. (Eds.). (1995). *Creating an inclusive school.* Alexandria, VA: Association for Supervision and Curriculum Development.

Villa, R.A., Thousand, J.S., Nevin, A.I., & Malgeri, C. (1996). Instilling collaboration for inclusive schooling as a way of doing business in public education. *Remedial and Special Education, 17*(3), 169–181.

Villa, R.A., Thousand, J.S., Stainback, W.C., & Stainback, S.B. (Eds.). (1992). *Restructuring for caring and effective education: An administrative guide to creating heterogeneous schools* (1st ed.). Baltimore: Paul H. Brookes Publishing Co.

Chapter 9

Standards, Assessments, and Individualized Education Programs

Planning for Success in the General Education Curriculum

Michael L. Hock

> Over 20 years of research and experience has demonstrated that the edu-
> cation of children with disabilities can be made more effective by having
> high expectations for such children and ensuring their access in the gen-
> eral curriculum to the maximum extent possible. (Individuals with
> Disabilities Education Act [IDEA] Amendments of 1997 [PL 105-17], §
> 601[c][5][a])

The individualized education program (IEP) is at the heart of special
education. As originally conceptualized by Congress in the Education
for All Handicapped Children Act of 1975 (PL 94-142) and mandated in
the Individuals with Disabilities Education Act (IDEA) of 1990 (PL 101-
476), the term *individualized education program* denotes three interrelated but distinct functions:

1. An IEP is a *program* of specially designed instruction crafted to meet the unique needs of a student with a disability.

2. The IEP is a *process* for planning special education and related services.

3. The IEP is a *legal contract* between education agencies and parents that documents the outcomes and decisions made through collaborative planning.

In theory, the IEP can and should serve multiple functions. It can and should provide lawmakers with a means by which to monitor and enforce special education legislation and should provide education agencies with a means by which to demonstrate legal compliance. The IEP can and should provide teachers with an instructional tool that informs the process of planning, delivering, and evaluating special education services. The IEP can and should give parents a voice in making instruction decisions for their children, provide them with an assurance that special education and related services will be provided, and offer a means of monitoring and evaluating the progress and achievement that result from implementation of the IEP. Most critical of all, the IEP can and should ensure that every child with a disability receives a free appropriate public education in the least restrictive environment.

All of the preceding developments are what Congress intended. Unfortunately, the IEP has generally fallen short of initial expectations for it. To a great extent, IEPs serve only as tools for monitoring compliance with federal legal mandates. It is a form of compliance that often exists only as a paper trail (Morgan & Rhodes, 1983; Stowitschek & Kelso, 1989), in some cases doing little more than creating a false perception of competence and professionalism (Ysseldyke, Algozzine, Richey, & Graden, 1982). In the worst cases, IEPs are a burden for teachers (Dudley-Marling, 1985; Gerardi, Grohe, Benedict, & Coolidge, 1984; McGarry & Finan, 1982) and are of questionable value to parents and students, failing to ensure real and productive educational outcomes (Bateman, 1991; Harry, 1992; Morgan & Rhodes, 1983; Turnbull & Hughes, 1987; Vaughn, 1988). With these unfulfilled promises looming large, it is reasonable to conclude that the heart of special education needs some cardiopulmonary resuscitation.

In the 1990s, schools experienced a flurry of activity focused on rethinking, restructuring, and reforming education. At the center of this activity were standards and assessments. States and local school districts adopted frameworks of educational standards and developed innovative assessment techniques to determine whether students are achieving those standards. Standards and assessments are breathing new life into American education.

The question that this chapter poses is, Might standards and assessments do the same for special education and IEPs that they have done for general education—that is, give special education a strong heart that finally beats steadily? The chapter begins with an overview of the IDEA Amendments of 1997 (PL 105-17), which relate to standards and assessments; provides a model for developing standards-referenced IEPs; and describes performance and portfolio assessments that can be used for monitoring standards-referenced IEPs. It concludes with a discussion of the impact that standards may have on grading and graduation options for students with disabilities.

INDIVIDUALS WITH DISABILITIES EDUCATION ACT (IDEA) AMENDMENTS OF 1997

Was Congress thinking of standards and assessments when it enacted the 1997 Amendments to IDEA? Does the law articulate a role for standards and assessments in special education? Although the term *standards* is rarely used in the 1997 IDEA Amendments, many of the changes in the federal special education legislation spoke directly to a role for standards and assessments in the development and monitoring of IEPs. On a larger scale, the 1997 IDEA Amendments designate standards and assessments as the key indicators for measuring the general health of special education.

The quote that introduces this chapter is from the introductory Findings section of IDEA, in which Congress provided a unifying rationale and philosophy for the entirety of the law. Note the use of the phrases *high expectations* and *access in the general curriculum*. As of mid-1999, 49 of the 50 states had either adopted a framework of educational standards or were in the process of doing so. In those states, high expectations are defined for all students in terms of educational standards. The content, instruction methods, and assessments that compose the general curriculum are to align directly with the standards. For all intents and purposes, standards and the general education curriculum are one and the same. As a result, aligning IEP goals with standards, though not specifically required by law, is a logical means to achieve compliance.

Section 614(d)(1)(a) states that the IEP must indicate "how the child's disability affects involvement in the general curriculum." Section 614(d)(2)(b) requires that special education and related services include those supports necessary for the child "to be involved and progress in the general curriculum." Section 614(b)(2)(1) notes that assessments should include "information related to enabling the child to be involved in and progress in the general curriculum." Section 614(d)(1)(B)(iii) requires that the IEP team include "at least one regular education teacher if [the] child is or might be participating in [the] regular education environment."

Furthermore, Section 612(a)(16) requires state education agencies to establish performance goals and indicators that will aid in monitoring accountability and compliance with IDEA. Performance goals and indicators must be "consistent with other goals and standards for children established by the State," and children with disabilities must be "included in general State and district-wide assessment programs [which typically measure achievement of standards], with appropriate accommodation, where necessary." Alternate assessments must be provided when participation in general assessments, even with accommodations, is not appropriate. How students with disabilities participate in assessments must be articulated in each student's IEP.

If high expectations and the general education curriculum are defined in terms of standards, then standards are for all students, including students with disabilities. An IEP that promotes high expectations and access to the general education curriculum is one that takes its focus from standards and related assessments. Thus, present levels of performance, special education and related services, and objective criteria for monitoring and evaluating IEPs can and should be referenced to standards. State and district accountability for special education also can and should be referenced to standards. Providing a role for standards and assessments in special education, and specifically in IEP development, is a sure way to ensure compliance with the 1997 IDEA Amendments.

A CASE FOR STANDARDS-REFERENCED INDIVIDUALIZED EDUCATION PROGRAMS

Using standards and related assessments in IEP development can satisfy legal requirements. Is it a good idea, however, for students with disabilities? Will the use of standards and assessments actually produce a better IEP? The answer is a resounding "yes," for a number of reasons.

First, the use of standards and related assessments in IEP development promotes inclusion and ensures that inclusion is not tantamount to "watering down" the curriculum. In fact, it does the opposite. A standards framework provides a map for developing IEPs that links IEP goals and objectives to classroom goals and objectives, which are the goals and objectives that are considered important for all students.

It helps the IEP team to establish priorities that are consistently referenced to the skills, knowledge, and behaviors that the student needs to be successful in the general education environment. It also promotes the use of a common language among parents, classroom teachers, and special educators—the language of standards. It gives the IEP a more universal and long-term focus.

Focus is a key benefit of using a broad framework of standards to develop IEPs. Content standards are generally written in terms of the knowledge and skills that an individual needs to become a successful and productive citizen during his or her entire lifetime. Related performance standards provide key developmental indicators that help to determine whether a student, at any point in his or her career as a learner, is mastering content standards at a level sufficient to predict long-term success. For an IEP team, this kind of information can be invaluable, helping to determine a student's present levels of performance in terms of standards-related developmental milestones and charting IEP goals and activities across the years toward a productive transition from school to adult life.

The focus provided by standards also gives IEPs a broad, real-world reference. Of course, there is an intuitive nature to IEP goals and activities. Thus, it makes sense from an independent living perspective for a student with significant cognitive or physical disabilities, or both, to learn how to use a rest room independently, to cross the street, to use public transportation, or to express his or her needs by using a communication board; but when an IEP is referenced to lifelong content standards, the reasons for independent living goals and activities become unified, explicit, and reflective of long-term aspirations for the student. Using *Vermont's Framework of Standards and Learning Opportunities* (Vermont Department of Education, 1996) as an example, independent use of a rest room relates to Personal Development Standards and becomes a matter of making "informed, healthy choices that positively affect the health, safety, and well being of themselves and others" (VT Standard 3.5—Healthy Choices); crossing the street and using public transportation relate to Civic/Social Responsibility Standards, which focus on "taking an active role in the community" (VT Standard 4.1—Service); and using a communication board is evidence that the student is meeting the Vermont Communication Standards, one of which relates to students' proficiency at using "verbal and nonverbal skills to express themselves effectively" (VT Standard 1.15—Speaking). All of these goals and activities relate to the Vermont Workplace Standards that reflect students' "dependability, productivity, and initiative" (VT Standard 3.14—Dependability and Productivity).

Content standards can have broad application across the myriad challenges and needs that the diverse population of students whom we serve in special education programs present. Again using Vermont's standards as an example, for the student with learning disabilities, IEP goals can reflect Worth and Competence Standards, which focus on students' "assess[ing] their own learning by developing rigorous criteria for themselves, and us[ing] these to set goals and produce consistently high-quality work" (VT Standard 3.1—Goal-Setting), and "assess[ing] how they learn best, and us[ing] additional learning strategies to supplement those already used" (VT Standard 3.2—Learning Strategies). For the student with emotional and behavioral disabilities, IEP goals can reflect Relationship Standards, which focus on students' "interact[ing] respectfully with others, including those with whom they have differences" (VT Standard 3.11—Interactions), and "us[ing] systematic and collaborative problem-solving processes, including mediation, to negotiate and resolve conflicts" (VT Standard 3.12—Conflict Resolution). Finally, for older students who are preparing for their transition out of school, Workplace Standards can provide a focus on "develop[ing] a plan for current and continued education and training to meet personal and career goals" (VT Standard 3.16—Transition Planning). These are the standards that are important for all students. The difference for a student with disabilities is not the standards that need to be addressed, but the array of individualized learning opportunities that are provided through an IEP that allows the student to achieve standards.

Some Jargon Busting

The advent of standards in educational reform has certainly created a fair amount of new educational jargon, a lexicon that special educators need to learn if standards are to play a viable role in IEP development. Some jargon busting is in order. First, it is important to understand the difference between planning that is *standards based* and planning that is *standards referenced,* to establish which of these types of planning is preferable in developing an IEP that meets due process requirements and also promotes a student's success in the general education curriculum. The difference relates primarily to the point in planning when standards are put to use. A standards-based approach starts with standards. The priority status of a particular standard is identified first, and appropriate content, instruction, and assessments are developed accordingly. Conversely, in standards referencing, content, instruction, and assessments are developed first or already exist, and the standards to which they relate are identified after the fact.

In *curriculum design*, a standards-based approach has particular merit because it ensures that all instructional activities are aimed specifically toward students' achievement of standards. A standards-based curriculum is direct, purposeful, and efficient. For IEP development, the standards-based approach creates a problem related to individualization. If the IEP team identifies goals and activities initially and exclusively through a review of standards, then there is a risk that priority needs might be overlooked, thus failing to satisfy the mandate for an IEP that is truly individualized and that reflects specially designed instruction. This is not to say that a standards framework cannot play a role in establishing IEP priorities. Because a standards framework tends to be broad and comprehensive, a review of the standards may help parents and teachers to identify priorities for the student that were not readily apparent. The IEP should not be limited by the priorities suggested by standards review, however, nor should a standards framework be the only tool used in establishing IEP priorities, as might be the case in a standards-based approach.

For IEPs, standards referencing is clearly preferable. In a standards-referenced approach, the IEP team begins by identifying a student's unique needs and challenges, using a variety of information sources and then, as a follow-up step, identifies the standards to which the needs and challenges relate. Because most standards frameworks are broad and comprehensive, few if any needs and challenges fail to have a reference in standards. If educators are to ensure that an IEP meets the unique needs of a student with disabilities, then they must keep the standards framework in its proper place. Educators should always start with the child and then move to the standards; that is why standards-referenced IEPs need to be designed.

Nature of Standards-Referenced Individualized Education Programs

What does a standards-referenced IEP look like? Which criteria might be used to judge the quality of standards-referenced IEPs? What kinds of information do they communicate to students, parents, and teachers?

In their basic form, standards-referenced IEPs are as different and unique as the students they are designed to serve. Consistent with past practice, the schools, school districts, and states that use standards in IEP development have continued to put their unique stamp on IEPs. Several key components tend to be present in all standards-referenced IEPs; however, Figure 1 provides a general conceptual model (Hock, 1997).

First, standards are referenced in goals, objectives, and indicators of performance level. Second, standards provide the focus, direction,

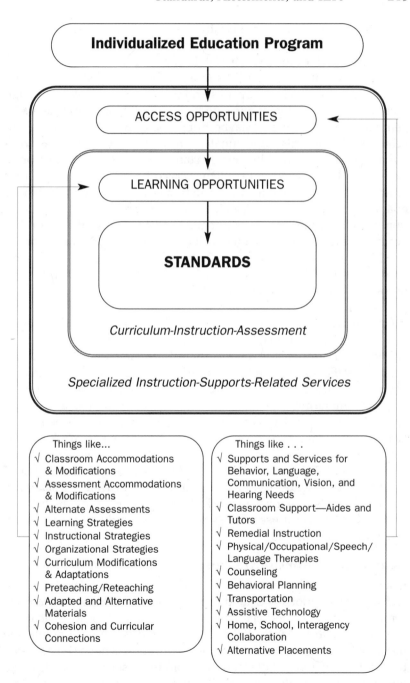

Figure 1.   Key components of a standards-referenced IEP.

and evaluation criteria for specially designed instruction and related services. Finally, standards tell educators whether the IEP is sufficiently comprehensive and whether it is meeting the student's unique needs. Does that mean that IEPs must address every standard that a student is not achieving? Are all standards for all students? Although those questions need to be answered individually for each student, the general answer to both is, "Maybe, but probably not." Ideally, a student achieves all standards. Unfortunately, the reality is that students without disabilities are not achieving all standards, so there is no reason to expect the diverse group of students served by special education programs to be any different. Given that special education regulations guarantee a student with disabilities a free appropriate public education from birth until 21 years of age, an IEP team has that period of years in which to help a student achieve as many standards as possible. The important thing is that IEPs, and the standards that they reference, must be individually designed and selected to meet the unique needs and challenges of the student.

In Colorado, the State Department of Education has suggested that IEP teams use three factors in prioritizing standards for IEP development: relevance, reasonableness, and time. A standard would not be considered a priority if it was clearly outside the parameters of a student's specific special education needs. For example, a foreign language standard may not be relevant for a student with a severe language impairment. For that student, that standard also may not be reasonable if the student is at a transition age and would benefit more from an IEP that focused on community participation skills and employment, nor would it be a good use of the student's remaining time in school. Therefore, relevance and reasonableness can be viewed in terms of a student's overall need and capacity to achieve a standard, the time that a student has to work on the standard, and whether that is the most beneficial use of the student's time and special education programs and supports.

Learning Opportunities and Access Opportunities

In a standards-referenced IEP, specialized instruction, related services, and accommodations and modifications might be treated as *learning opportunities* or as *access opportunities* that ultimately lead to achievement of standards (Hock, 1997). The standard is the focal point—the reason why it is all being done. Special education is not a separate system with a different set of standards from those set for general education students. It is the opportunity that educators provide for some students to meet the standards designated for all students.

What are learning opportunities? In an *education program* that is aligned with standards, learning opportunities are the curriculum, instruction methods, activities, and assessments that enable students to achieve standards. In a *standards-referenced IEP*, learning opportunities are the individualized instruction, classroom supports, related services, and classroom and assessment accommodations and modifications that are provided via the IEP to allow students with disabilities to derive benefit from the learning opportunities provided to all students. They are the "something extra" that defines special education. Thus, through the individualized learning opportunities provided by the IEP, a student with disabilities is able to meet the same standards as his or her classmates. Examples of IEP learning opportunities are listed in Figure 1.

What are access opportunities? *Access opportunities* refer to something fundamental, something that reduces or eliminates the student's ability to benefit from learning opportunities. A particular physical need, counterproductive classroom behaviors, a substance abuse problem, impairments in language skills necessary to comprehend instruction and demonstrate learning, or a lack of requisite skills in reading, writing, and mathematics are examples of students' characteristics that can limit access. To a great extent, challenges of this sort need to be the first order of business for an IEP team; hence the great emphasis on access to the general education curriculum that characterizes much of the 1997 IDEA Amendments.

Access opportunities can be incorporated into IEP goals and activities that reference standards identified specifically and individually to meet the unique challenges presented by a student, standards that, if mastered, will increase the student's potential for success in the general education classroom. Individually selected standards can define the specially designed instruction and related services the student needs. For the student with a physical disability who needs adaptive physical education, a fitness standard such as Vermont's Standard 3.6 ("demonstrating competence in many movement forms and proficiency in a few forms of physical activity") may afford access. For the student who presents significant behavior challenges and needs counseling and a structured behavior plan, a worth and competence standard such as Vermont's Standard 3.1 ("demonstrate respect for themselves and others") may be the key. For the student who abuses substances and needs an interagency wraparound plan to get off drugs, access opportunities might be provided through a personal development standard such as Vermont's Standard 3.5 ("Students make informed, healthy choices that positively affect the health, safety, and well-being of themselves and others"). For the student with academic difficulties who needs a remedial math program in order to succeed in a high school science class, it might be a math and technology standard such as Vermont's Standard 7.6 ("Students understand arithmetic in computation, and select and use, in appropriate situations, mental arithmetic, pencil and paper, calculator, and computer"). For the student with a severe language impairment who needs a speech-language pathologist to preteach words and concepts that are used in classroom instruction, it might be a listening standard such as Vermont's Standard 1.13 ("Students listen actively and respond to communications").

Thus, standards related to access opportunities provide both a rationale and a focus for a variety of special education and related services as well as criteria against which progress can be measured and IEP success can be judged. Access opportunities and the standards to which they relate get students with disabilities into the general education classroom so that they can begin working toward achieving the standards earmarked for all students at their grade level.

Sometimes access opportunities establish a link between the general education curriculum and elements of the IEP that may not have a clear reference in standards (e.g., vision and hearing services, assistive technology, home–school–agency coordination, individual aides and tutors, special transportation services). Although not explicitly standards-referenced, the access opportunities provided through related-services personnel and resources are often the key to inclusion because they provide students with disabilities with an entry to the general education curriculum. Access opportunities like these make it possible for students with disabilities to succeed in the general classroom and in the end to achieve standards. Figure 1 provides examples of access opportunities.

Assessments and the Standards-Referenced Individualized Education Program

Assessments also have a unique function in the standards-referenced IEP. Standards-referenced assessments are designed or selected to communicate to students, parents, and educators in terms of standards. They establish how close the student is to achieving a standard and document the progress the student has made. Standards-referenced IEP assessments work like a "AAA Triptic," those handy travel service maps that use big stars to identify the point of departure and the final destination, and a fat magic-marker line to trace the best possible routes. The metaphor goes something like this:

- *The standard:* "This is where you're going."
- *Standards-referenced assessments that establish status and progress in relation to standards achievement:* "This is where you started and this is where you are now. This is how far you've come, and this is how far you still have to go."
- *Access opportunities:* "Here are the things we [the IEP team] will do to help you get started on the journey."
- *Learning opportunities:* "Here are the things we will do to help you get there and make sure you have a safe and successful trip."

A safe and successful trip, of course, is defined in terms of how well the "IEP Triptic" leads to success in the general education curriculum.

Standards referencing certainly requires some major rethinking of how IEPs should be monitored and evaluated. The concept of objective criteria takes on a whole new meaning. Fortunately, a variety of innovative assessments have emerged from standards-related school reform initiatives, foremost among them being performance assessments and student portfolios.

Performance assessments are built around tasks that are open ended; allow for a variety of methods or approaches toward achieving a correct response; and, depending on the intended use, can reflect a student's unique interests and experiences. To the extent that it is safe and practical, performance tasks are authentic, providing for real-world application of skills and knowledge. Some performance assessments include reflection pieces in which students are encouraged to describe the mental processes or approach used to produce a particular product or response, an extremely valuable diagnostic tool for educators who want to know why a student is not mastering a particular standard. Scoring relies on common language rubrics. Rubrics are analytical scoring guides that describe anticipated performance anecdotally and are often supplemented with benchmark pieces that provide exemplars of specific performance levels.

Generally, a variety of performance assessments are collected for the student in a portfolio. Portfolio selections typically reflect a variety of applications of a particular skill. Vermont's statewide Writing Portfolio Assessment provides a good example of how portfolio assessment works. Across a school year, a student, with assistance from teachers, selects samples of his or her written work to be included in the portfolio. The samples must include an *imaginative piece* (e.g., a short story, a play, a personal narrative); a *personal response* to a book, event, or experience; *writing in a subject area other than language arts,* such as a history or science report; a *best piece* selected by the student with help from the teacher; and a *letter or essay* about the best piece or the whole portfolio. Each piece is first self-scored by the student, then scored by the teacher and, in some cases, by a state-level scorer during an annual random selection of student portfolios. Scoring centers on five dimensions of writing (purpose, organization, detail, tone, and writing conventions) using an analytical scoring guide that describes each dimension of writing in terms of four performance levels. Scoring is qualitative rather than quantitative. No numerical scores are assigned. Instead, scores establish if a particular dimension of writing is *rarely, sometimes, frequently,* or *always* reflected in the piece. The objectivity of this scoring system is enhanced through the use of grade-level benchmark pieces that provide scorers with examples of student writing for each writing dimension at each performance level. Thus, if a scorer is unsure how to rate a portfolio selection, it is possible to locate the benchmark piece that most closely matches the student's work and assign scores accordingly.

Classroom portfolios, or even statewide portfolio assessments such as the one described previously, can easily be adapted for use as IEP assessments. In general, the portfolio assessment model offers a vast improvement over traditional test-based IEP assessments. The value of portfolios becomes apparent at annual IEP reviews. The IEP team looks at the student's work collected across the entire year, not at test scores, which tend to reflect a single snapshot of performance on tasks that rarely reflect authentic applications of skills and knowledge. For some students, videotapes are used instead of pencil-and-paper work samples. The scoring rubrics used to evaluate portfolio entries communicate information in language that most IEP team members can understand, which is of particular benefit for parents, who often find special education jargon and technical language an insurmountable obstacle to full and meaningful participation (Harry, 1992). Students often score their own work and compare results with the teacher's assessments, giving students a meaningful role in the IEP review. As a result, IEP team members are able to judge the efficacy of an IEP in reference to common-language scoring of authentic work samples collected over time with input from the student. The portfolio products are referenced directly to classroom performance and the high expectations articulated in standards.

Performance assessments and portfolios have definitely put a new spin on the concept of objective criteria. The scoring rubric in particular provides a unique and effective tool 1) for measuring a student's progress toward meeting annual goals and short-term objectives and 2) that satisfies regulatory criteria. Objective criteria can mean more than just numbers. Annual goals can be written in forms other than the traditional behavioral objective (e.g., the ever-popular "Jack will identify 200 Dolch Words presented at 2-second intervals with 80% accuracy"). Figure 2(a) shows Jack's IEP, which was prepared using a standards-referenced approach and which employs assessment methods (see Figure 2[b]), including a portfolio assessment, that reflect several approaches to establishing objective criteria. First, note in the column labeled "What do we know about Jack's literacy skills?" that this IEP team clearly employed standards referencing. They started by describing Jack's strengths and challenges in specific terms, including how he's coping emotionally with his reading and writing difficulties. Finally, at the end of the column, they indicate the communication standards that need to be addressed in the IEP, and establish that Jack's learning disability is preventing him from experiencing success in the general education curriculum.

In the third column, the one labeled "How will we know if we are succeeding?" Jack's team used standards to articulate annual goals, and selected or designed a variety of standards-referenced assessments to measure his progress. What follows is a description of four unique methods used to establish objective criteria for monitoring the success of Jack's IEP.

Method 1: Traditional Quantitative Criteria

By October 15, Jack will read at a rate of 60 wpm on Level 1 materials with at least 90% accuracy (using *Project Read* fluency probes).

Because Jack is participating in a classroom-based remedial reading program, his team decided to use the classroom assessments that are part of that program, assessments that are used to determine progress toward achieving standards for all the students in Jack's class. Although the objectives are designed around fairly traditional quantitative criteria, they are clearly referenced to standards and keep Jack's individually designed learning opportunities linked to general education curriculum learning opportunities.

Method 2: Agreement Among Two or More Observers/Scorers Using a Rubric Developed by the Individualized Education Program Team

By October 15, Jack will score in the "I'm getting there" category on at least 3 of 5 criteria (determined by at least 2 scorers).

Student Name: ___Jack Smith___

What do we know about Jack's literacy skills?	What are we going to do to help Jack receive an appropriate education?	How will we know if we are succeeding?
Jack is a fourth grader whose literacy (reading/writing/language arts) has been assessed at the pre-primer–first-grade level. Jack is very interested in mysteries and adventure stories. He really liked *Titanic* and *Pompeii*. However, it was necessary for Jack's teachers to read these books to him. Most of Jack's classmates can read these books independently. Phonological awareness is okay. Jack has adequate decoding strategies and uses picture cues, but he processes very slowly, which is a huge obstacle to comprehension and discourages independent reading. Fluency and automaticity are his biggest problems. Hearing comprehension is excellent.	Jack will receive literacy instruction individually and in small groups using a structured, phonetically based literacy program, 800–1,000 minutes per month (typically 45 minutes per day, 5 days per week) in the fourth-grade classroom provided by the consulting teacher and the reading specialist. Jack will be provided with the following classroom and assessment accommodations: • For classroom activities other than literacy instruction, additional time to process information derived through reading, and additional time to complete writing assignments • For statewide and local large-scale assessments (except when literacy and reading fluency are being assessed), a reader/scribe and extended time limits when necessary	By June 30, Jack will make progress toward meeting VT Communication Standard 1.2—"Students read grade-appropriate material, with 90% accuracy, in a way that makes meaning clear." Reading accuracy will be assessed using Project Read fluency probes. • By October 15, Jack will read at a rate of 60 words per minute on Level 1 materials with at least 90% accuracy. • By January 13, Jack will read at a rate of 60 words per minute on Level 2 materials with at least 90% accuracy. • By April 1, Jack will read at a rate of 60 words per minute on Level 3 materials with at least 90% accuracy. • By June 30, Jack will read at a rate of 60 words per minute on Level 4 materials with at least 90% accuracy.

Figure 2(a).   A standards-referenced IEP that includes several kinds of scoring rubrics that will be used to determine whether the student is meeting IEP goals and objectives.

Figure 2(a). (continued)

Student Name: Jack Smith		
What do we know about Jack's literacy skills?	What are we going to do to help Jack receive an appropriate education?	How will we know if we are succeeding?
Local Project Read fluency standard for Jack's grade level is 60 words per minute. He is currently averaging about 20 words per minute on grade-level materials. Jack is making progress. Over the past 3 months, he has increased from 9 words per minute to 40 words per minute in Level 1 materials. Jack can tell stories with grade-appropriate Purpose, Organization, Details, and Voice/Tone. However, his written versions of these stories don't match grade-level benchmarks. Jack uses a story web when writing, but his portfolio pieces show that he rarely or sometimes uses grade-appropriate Purpose; Organization; Details; Voice/Tone; or Grammar, Usage, and Mechanics (GUM). Pieces rarely exceed three sentences, whereas classmates typically produce pieces of ten or more sentences.	• For content acquisition and written expression in all content areas, readers and/or alternate texts for text materials that exceed Jack's skill level, and scribes for more complex written expression tasks • To encourage continued interest and incentives for learning to read and write, books on tape, particularly books that interest Jack and his classmates, and topics for writing assignments that match Jack's expressed interests and experiences Jack's classroom teacher will be provided with the following supports: • Alternative texts and/or books for "pleasure reading" that match grade-level interests and content but are written at a level that matches Jack's current reading skill level	By June 30, Jack will make progress toward meeting VT Standard 1.3—"Students read for meaning, demonstrating both initial understanding and personal response to what is read." Reading for meaning will be assessed using the attached rubric, which will provide scoring for reading comprehension probes and will be determined by at least two scorers (classroom teacher, consulting teacher, reading specialist, instructional assistant, parents, and/or Jack). • By October 15, Jack will score in the "I'm getting there" category on at least three of five criteria. • By January 13, Jack will score in the "I'm getting there" category on all five criteria. • By April 1, Jack will score in the "Wow, I've got it" category on at least three of five criteria. • By June 30, Jack will score in the "Wow, I've got it" category on all five criteria.

223

Figure 2(a). *(continued)*

Student Name: ___Jack Smith___

What do we know about Jack's literacy skills?	What are we going to do to help Jack receive an appropriate education?	How will we know if we are succeeding?
Jack really wants to read and write by himself. Jack's frustration with literacy has led to resistance and refusal to work on reading activities. He is very afraid his younger sister will learn to read before he does. Despite making progress, Jack is not currently meeting the following Vermont Communication Standards for fourth grade: • Standard 1.2—Read grade-appropriate material with 90%+ accuracy, in a way that makes meaning clear; • Standard 1.3—Read for meaning, demonstrating both initial understanding and personal response to what is read; • Standard 1.5—Draft, revise, edit, and critique written products so that final drafts are appropriate in terms of purpose, organization, details, and voice or tone;	• Books on tape that match grade-level interests and content • Additional personnel support (instructional assistant), with consultation and supervision provided by the special education consulting teacher • Team consultation and support provided by the school psychologist to develop and implement strategies to increase Jack's self-esteem related to literacy The decision to provide the related services listed in the IEP was made based on students' needs in order to benefit from their special education programs.	By June 30, Jack will make progress toward meeting VT Communication Standards 1.5 and 1.6—"Students draft, revise, edit, and critique written products so that final drafts are appropriate in terms of purpose, organization, details, and voice/tone," and "Students demonstrate command of appropriate English conventions, including grammar, usage, and mechanics (GUM)." Writing dimensions and GUM will be assessed using Jack's writing portfolio and will be scored with the Vermont Writing Assessment Analytic Assessment Guide (attached) and grade-level benchmark pieces, as determined by at least two scorers (classroom teacher, consulting teacher, reading specialist, instructional assistant, parents, and/or Jack). • By October 1, Jack will produce writing portfolio pieces of at least five sentences and will score at the "sometimes" level in all writing dimensions. "Sometimes" in GUM will be defined as no more than five errors in a piece.

224

Figure 2(a). (continued)

Student Name: Jack Smith		
What do we know about Jack's literacy skills?	What are we going to do to help Jack receive an appropriate education?	How will we know if we are succeeding?
• Standard 1.6—Demonstrate command of appropriate English conventions, including grammar, usage, and mechanics. Because of Jack's learning disability, he is not achieving in the general curriculum on a level equivalent to his fourth-grade peers in the area of literacy.		• By January 13, Jack will produce writing portfolio pieces of at least seven sentences and will score at the "sometimes" level in all writing dimensions. "Sometimes" in GUM will be defined as no more than five errors in a piece. • By April 1, Jack will produce writing portfolio pieces of at least seven sentences and will score at the "frequently" level in all writing dimensions. "Frequently" in GUM will be defined as no more than two errors in a piece. • By June 30, Jack will produce writing portfolio pieces of at least 10 sentences and will score at the "frequently" level in all writing dimensions. "Frequently" in GUM will be defined as no more than two errors in a piece. Progress reports will be sent to Jack's parents with his classroom report card.
Include present levels of performance, how the student's disability affects the student's involvement and progress in the general curriculum or for preschoolers in appropriate activities, the student's unique characteristics and needs and/or personal educational goals.	Include special education and related services; personnel; frequency; duration; location of service; and, if necessary, accommodations, supplementary aids and services, transition services, extracurricular and other nonacademic activities, or other services.	Include goals and objectives, which include evaluation procedures, objective criteria, and the expected dates for accomplishment. Goals should lead to the student being able to be involved in and progress in the general curriculum.

Vermont Communication Standard 1.3—

Students read for meaning, demonstrating both initial understanding and personal response to what is read

	I'm just learning	I'm getting there	Wow! I've got it!
Retells information from a nonfiction source in his or her own words	With prompts, I can answer specific questions about details.	With prompts, I can answer specific questions about details and tell some information in my own words.	Without any prompts, I can tell about what I've learned in my own words. I can tell at least three pieces of information in the right sequence. I can identify the subject and the main idea.
Retells a story in his own words	With help, I can answer specific questions. Sometimes I put in extra details that weren't really in the story.	With help, I can answer specific questions. I do not add extra details that weren't really in the story.	Without any help, I can tell about the story in my own words. I tell at least three events in the right sequence. I identify the characters and tell at least one detail about each. I can tell the main idea of the story without help. I stay focused on the story without adding extra details.
Locates and uses a variety of sources to gain information	Most of the time, I ask others to find the information for me.	With help, I can find information in the things I read.	I can use a picture dictionary to find a name in the student directory if someone shows me the right page. I can use a CD-ROM reference such as Encarta. With some help, I can find my favorite programs and the times they are on in the TV Guide.
Locates specific information in a reading source: fiction or nonfiction	I have a hard time finding specific information.	If someone shows me the right page, I can find specific information.	I can answer questions by finding the words in reading selections and pointing to them.
Reads and follows written directions	I can read and follow directions that include one direction for the same task.	I can read and follow directions that include two directions for the same task.	I can read and follow directions that include three directions for the same task.

Figure 2(b). Jack's "reading for meaning" rubric.

VERMONT WRITING ASSESSMENT
Analytic Scoring Guide

	Purpose	Organization	Details	Voice or Tone	Grammar/Usage/Mechanics
In assessing, consider	. . . how adequately intent and focus are established and maintained (success in this criterion should not depend on the reader's knowledge of the writing assignment; the writing should stand on its own)	. . . coherence . . . whether ideas or information are in logical sequence or move the piece forward . . . whether sentences and images are clearly related to each other (indenting paragraphs is a matter of grammar/usage/mechanics)	. . . whether details develop ideas or information . . . whether details elaborate or clarify the content of the writing with images, careful explanation, effective dialogue, parenthetical expressions, stage directions, etc.	. . . whether the writing displays a natural style, appropriate to the narrator . . . or whether the tone of the writing is appropriate to its content	. . . the conventions of writing, including: • grammar (e.g., sentence structure, syntax) • usage (e.g., agreement, word choice) • mechanics (e.g., spelling, capitalization, punctuation)
Ask how consistently, relative to length and complexity	. . . intent is established and maintained within a given piece of writing	. . . the writing demonstrates coherence	. . . details contribute to development of ideas and information, evoke images or otherwise elaborate or clarify the content of the writing	. . . an appropriate voice or tone is established and maintained	. . . as appropriate to grade level, command of conventions is evident, through correct English or intentional effective departure from convention

Figure 2(c).   *The Vermont Writing Assessment Analytic Scoring Guide.* (Copyright © 1994 by the Vermont Department of Education; used with permission.)

(continued)

Figure 2(c). (continued)

	Purpose	Organization	Details	Voice or Tone	Grammar/Usage/Mechanics
Extensively	Establishes and maintains a clear purpose and focus	Organized from beginning to end, logical progression of ideas, fluent and coherent	Details are pertinent, vivid, or explicit and provide ideas and information in depth	Distinctive personal expression or distinctive tone enhances the writing	Few or no errors present; or departures from convention appear intentional and are effective
Frequently	Establishes a purpose and focus	Organization moves writing forward with few lapses in unity or coherence	Details develop ideas and information; or details are elaborated	Establishes personal expression or effective tone	Some errors or patterns of errors are present
	Is author's focus clear within the writing? | Yes | | No |	*Does the organization move the writing forward?* | Yes | | No |	*Do details enhance and/or clarify the writing?* | Yes | | No |	*Can you hear the writer? Or, is the tone effective?* | Yes | | No |	*Does the writing show grade-appropriate command of grammar/usage/mechanics?* | Yes | | No |
Sometimes	Attempts to establish a purpose; focus of writing is not fully clear	Lapse(s) in organization affect unity or coherence	Details lack elaboration, are merely listed, or are unnecessarily repetitious	Attempts personal expression or appropriate tone	Numerous errors are apparent and may distract the reader
Rarely	Purpose and focus are not apparent	Serious errors in organization make writing difficult to follow	Details are minimal, inappropriate, or random	Personal expression or appropriate tone are not evident	Errors interfere with understanding

NONSCORABLE
- Is illegible: i.e., includes so many indecipherable words that no sense can be made of the writing, or
- Is incoherent: i.e., words are legible but syntax is so garbled that response makes no sense, or
- Is a blank piece of paper
- For portfolio: does not have required minimum contents

Jack's IEP team designed a special rubric to measure his attainment of reading comprehension standards (see Jack's Reading for Meaning Rubric in Figure 2[b]). It is referenced in the IEP's annual goals and objectives and is paper-clipped to the IEP. Along the lefthand side of the rubric, the IEP team has listed several short-term objectives, mastery of which will lead to mastery of the annual goal. The rubric refines the assessment one step further, essentially establishing interim short-term objectives for each of the short-term objectives. Performance levels were written in the first person (e.g., "I'm just learning," "I'm getting there," and "Wow! I've got it") to help Jack become a key participant in monitoring his own progress toward achieving designated standards.

To increase the objectivity of this assessment, the IEP team has indicated that progress will be determined by at least two observers or scorers. No numbers are employed, but the assessment's reliance on interobserver agreement makes it objective. Notice that Jack and his parents are listed as potential observers. The rubric was designed to serve as a self-assessment tool for Jack and thus expresses performance levels in self-assessment terms. Because Jack does not read well, his special educator added photos to the rubric that feature a range of Jack's facial expressions—how he looks when he's just learning (somewhat pensive, with a crooked finger at his lips), when he's "getting there" (a slightly reserved smile), and when he finally experiences a "Wow! I've got it" (big smile and two thumbs up).

Method 3: Portfolio Pieces, a Calibrated Rubric, and Grade-Level Benchmarks

Writing dimensions . . . will be assessed using Jack's writing portfolio and will be scored with the *Vermont Writing Assessment Analytic Scoring Guide* and grade-level benchmark pieces.

Jack and all of his classmates have a writing portfolio. These portfolios contain students' self-selected best pieces and represent a range of written expression applications, from letters to works of fiction that use dialogue. Portfolio pieces are scored using the *Vermont Writing Assessment Analytic Scoring Guide* (Vermont Department of Education, 1994), which is referenced in Jack's individual goals and objectives, and paper-clipped to his IEP (see Figure 2[c]). The guide is a calibrated rubric, which means that the rubric was field tested with hundreds of scorers, and its criteria and performance levels were refined and redefined until scorers could consistently agree on how a piece of writing should be scored. Calibration activities continue on a yearly basis to ensure that scorers can use the rubric objectively.

The *Vermont Writing Assessment Analytic Scoring Guide* also relies on benchmark pieces to increase interscorer reliability. In a standards-aligned curriculum, benchmarks are milestones on the standards map—indicators of where a student should be at any particular point in his or her career as a learner. Benchmark pieces are actual samples of student writing that match each performance level on the rubric and reflect the level of writing that might be expected from a student at the grade level at which assessment occurs. Benchmark pieces increase a scorer's objectivity because scorers have at their disposal clear exemplars of the range of proficiency represented by the rubric.

Because Vermont's statewide writing portfolio assessment is based on a cross-sectional model that focuses on three specific grade levels, benchmark pieces are available for only the fifth, eighth, and tenth grades. Jack is a fourth grader. Fortunately, the teachers in his school have identified benchmarks for every grade level. Even if they had not, however, Jack's classroom teacher could supply samples of classmates' work that could serve as benchmarks to determine Jack's level of performance in relationship to IEP goals.

Benchmark pieces are terrific IEP tools. In addition to their role in establishing objective criteria, benchmarks can help the IEP team form realistic goals and objectives that are based on real samples of student performance. They also enhance communication among parents and educators because progress is referenced to clear exemplars rather than to test scores or to words such as *improving* or *not doing so hot*. Finally, benchmark pieces are effective instruction tools. Jack's teachers can show him rather than tell him what good writing looks like. Because benchmarks represent a range of performance, however, teachers can expose Jack to one level at a time so that he does not become frustrated by expectations that look unattainable.

Method 4: Additional Quantifying of Performance Levels on a Calibrated Rubric

"Sometimes" in GUM will be defined as no more than five errors in a piece (of at least five sentences).

Jack really has trouble with English language writing conventions such as grammar, usage, and mechanics (GUM). His IEP team anticipated relatively slow progress on mastering GUM and wanted their IEP assessments to demonstrate increments of progress that were more discreet than what could be measured with the state's analytic scoring guide and benchmarks. Therefore, the IEP team decided to define one element of the rubric in terms specific to Jack's expected progress (i.e., no more than five errors in a piece of at least five sentences). In this way, Jack's IEP team expanded the objectivity of the rubric and grade-level benchmarks to create objective criteria that are specific to Jack's unique needs.

Measuring Behavioral Goals

Fortunately, Jack does not have any real behavior problems in the classroom, but many other students served by special education do. How can IEP teams establish objective criteria to determine whether students with emotional and behavioral challenges are attaining standards-referenced IEP goals and objectives? Again, rubrics employed by multiple observers seem to be the answer.

The personal development standards rubric shown in Figure 3 was designed for a student who has been identified as having an emotional and behavioral disability. This rubric has a number of unique features. First, it encompasses specific standards that put the student's behavior challenges in a positive context. Rather than simply eliminate undesirable behaviors such as calling out in class, refusing to follow directions, and getting involved in verbal and physical altercations with classmates, the selection of personal development standards focuses the IEP on positive and productive alternatives. The student learns to demonstrate respect for him- or herself and others, dependability and productivity, and respectful interactions with others, including those with whom he or she has differences. The positive direction of this IEP ensures that the student receives specially designed instruction to help him or her develop adaptive communication strategies, productive work habits, and conflict resolution skills that will ultimately improve his or her chances of leading a successful adult life.

The personal development standards rubric is both an IEP assessment and an instruction tool. Initially, it was used in every class that the student attended. Results were discussed with the student, and, when he scored in the "Not Evident" category, his teachers helped him plan alternative strategies he could use the next time he encountered a particular conflict or difficult situation. Points were calculated, and improvements earned rewards. Periodically, the student rated his own performance, using the rubric as a self-monitoring device. His parents used the rubric at home. Eventually, the observations were faded to once a day, then to once a week, and finally to intervals predetermined by the IEP team when multiple observers, including the parents, used the rubric to determine the efficacy of IEP services.

Personal Development Standards Rubric

Date: _____   Class: _____

Student will demonstrate respect for himself and others (VT Standard 3.3)	1 Not Evident	2 Partially Evident	3 Evident	4 Evident with Independence
Student will raise hand to speak and allow teacher to acknowledge him.	1 Spoke out	2 Raised hand but didn't wait for teacher's attention	3 Raised hand and waited but with verbal or physical prompts	4 Raised hand and waited for teacher's attention without prompts
Notes:				
Student will follow principal's, teacher's, or assistant's directions.	1 Did not follow directions	2 Attempted to follow directions but not fully	3 Followed directions but with prompts	4 Followed directions without prompts
Notes:				
Student will interact respectfully with others, including those with whom he has differences. (VT Standard 3.11)	1 Not Evident	2 Partially Evident	3 Evident	4 Evident with Independence
Student will demonstrate appropriate verbal interactions	1 Verbal aggression	2 Began verbal aggression but stopped after prompts	3 Appropriate verbal interactions but with prompts	4 Appropriate verbal interactions without prompts
Notes:				
Student will demonstrate appropriate physical interactions	1 Physical aggression	2 Began physical aggression but stopped after prompts	3 Appropriate physical interactions but with prompts	4 Appropriate physical interactions without prompts
Notes:				

Figure 3.   An IEP assessment that is referenced to personal development standards targeted for a student with an emotional and behavioral disability.

Figure 3.   (*continued*)

Student will demonstrate dependability, productivity and initiative (VT Standard 3.14)	1 Not Evident	2 Partially Evident	3 Evident	4 Evident with Independence
Student will complete assignments	1 Neither completed satisfactorily nor submitted on time	2 Completed assignment but not satisfactorily	3 Completed assignment satisfactorily with prompts	4 Completed assignment satisfactorily, on time, and without prompts
Notes:				
Student will demonstrate neatness and organization in work completed	1 Frequent smudges, erasures, crumpled or torn	2 Some attention to neatness and organization	3 Much attention to neatness and organization, but with assistance	4 Neat and organized work without assistance
Notes:				
Student will address daily needs (cafeteria, rest room, nurse visitation) by conducting himself in an appropriate manner while going to and coming from destination (transition time)	1 Inappropriate behavior in transitions	2 Began inappropriate behavior but stopped after prompts	3 Appropriate behavior in transition but with prompts	4 Appropriate behavior in transition without prompts
Notes:				
		TOTAL POINTS EARNED: _____		

RETHINKING TRADITIONAL
SPECIAL EDUCATION ASSESSMENTS

With the advent of standards-referenced IEPs, what is the appropriate role for traditional standardized norm-referenced assessments? What will become of the psychoeducational batteries and individual achievement tests that line the shelves of special educators' offices everywhere? Because eligibility determination in most states still requires the use of psychometric measures, it is likely that these tests will be around for a while. However, special educators may need to rethink how they use standardized tests in the development of standards-referenced IEPs. Here is why. Most of the standardized tests used in special education were developed in the late 1970s and early 1980s in response to PL 94-142. Thus, they were developed about a decade before anyone gave any serious consideration to standards-based school reform, and nearly 2 decades before the 1997 IDEA Amendments. Although the tests have been revised and renormed, they tend to reflect content and consensus curricula that were contemporary at the time the tests were developed. The tests were not designed to measure students' attainment of standards, so they do not.

In one study (Hock & Thousand, 1997), 40 teachers in training at a large California university and 20 Vermont special educators were asked to conduct a content analysis of five standardized tests commonly used in special education. Content was assessed against the respective states' mathematics standards, which in both cases mirror standards recommended by the National Council of Teachers of Mathematics. The purpose of the study was to determine whether the tests measure the skills and knowledge taught in standards-based mathematics programs. Results were consistent across raters. All of the tests addressed arithmetic and computation standards, skills and knowledge that accounted for as much as 90% of a test's mathematics content. Some, but not all of the tests, addressed functions, algebra, statistics, and probability standards. None addressed reasoning and problem-solving standards. For the most part, test content that was labeled *problem solving* was actually arithmetic embedded in word problems. These results confirm earlier studies (McDonnell, 1997; Taylor, 1994) that suggested that traditional multiple-choice tests alone are inadequate to measure students' proficiency against content standards.

Should special educators start leaving standardized norm-referenced tests on the shelf? Probably not. As noted previously, special education eligibility still tends to be determined through norm-referenced comparisons, particularly in the severe discrepancy calculations that define learning disabilities in most states. In addition, many special educators have developed a comfort level with particular assessments and have learned to employ them with some utility for diagnostic purposes. However, IEP teams need to be aware that the content of traditional standardized norm-referenced tests probably does not match the content of the general education curriculum. Therefore, development of IEP present levels of performance statements, as well as eligibility decisions, could be suspect unless test-based information is supported by data that are specific to classroom progress and performance. In order to develop IEPs that ensure a student's success in the general education curriculum, IEP teams need to develop and use assessments that are referenced specifically to the standards to which that curriculum is aligned.

GRADES, GRADUATION, AND THE STANDARDS-REFERENCED INDIVIDUALIZED EDUCATION PROGRAM

Even before standards-based school reform, grades and graduation were a conundrum, and not just for students with disabilities. What does an "A" really mean? Does it mean that the student worked hard or has made a lot of progress? Does it mean that the student mastered the course content, or does it mean that the student completed a checklist of projects and assignments without really learning much? Does it mean that the student displayed lots of teacher-pleasing behaviors or maybe was offered grade amnesty (e.g., "If you turn in all your homework, I'll give you an "A" even though you didn't really earn it")? For the student with a disability, does an "A" mean any or all of the preceding things, or does it mean the student achieved IEP goals? What happens when it is time to translate grades into graduation? Should seat time count? Should a student who passed all required courses with a "D" average graduate, even though few basic competencies were mastered? What about the student with a disability who spent the bulk of time in school working on individualized goals? Should that student graduate with age-peers or stay in school until the special education entitlement runs out?

As part of standards-based school reform, many states and school districts have moved to grading systems and graduation criteria that are linked to standards. Although standards-based grading and graduation have clarified these issues for most students, they have intensified the issues for IEP teams. To a great extent, having high expectations for students with disabilities and ensuring their success in the general education curriculum mean that the IEP team must consider classroom grades and graduation requirements when developing the IEP. To do otherwise complicates many important decisions, often with great legal risk to schools, and personal risk to the student. How should grades and graduation be addressed in the standards-referenced IEP? Some thoughts follow.

IEP teams should define the specific criteria that are used to determine a grade and determine what grades mean in terms of promotion and graduation. The team may also want to discuss grade-linked special recognition such as honor role and honors groups. To a great extent, grades can be defined by using the same criteria used to define assessment accommodations and alternate assessments. An "A" for a student who receives classroom accommodations should mean the same thing as the "A" received by a student who did not receive accommodations. In a standards-aligned curriculum, the "A" means that the student receiving accommodations and modifications mastered the same standards as any other student who earned an "A." Both students earn credit toward graduation. For students participating in an individualized alternate curriculum, even when delivered in the general education classroom, the meaning of grades needs to be clarified so that no one is misled. Often grades from an alternate curriculum do not mean that the student has mastered the same standards or content, or that the student earned credit toward the standard diploma. Instead, the grade may mean that the student has mastered individual IEP standards and is working toward alternate graduation requirements. This is true even when the classroom teacher enters the grade on a typical report card, a source of confusion for some parents and students. Again, the IEP needs to be clear about what a grade means.

The risks associated with not defining grading criteria are many. A student, for example, may receive a stellar report card; but, at the end of the year, the teacher argues that the student should not be promoted because of insufficient progress toward mastering grade-level skills. During many years of stellar report cards, the student has never been selected for the honor role. At graduation time, the student and parent assume that sufficient credits have been earned for a standard diploma; but the diploma is denied, or an IEP diploma is substituted for the standard diploma. In each of these cases, arguments can be offered to support the decisions, some good and some not so good. The important point is that none of these occurrences should have been a surprise. All of these decisions should have been discussed and made within the context of the IEP.

When schools use standards-based grading systems and standards-referenced IEPs, no surprises are necessary. Standards-referenced IEPs make it clear whether the student is working on classroom standards or individualized access standards. The related assessments, often classroom assessments, define what kind of progress has been made and whether progress and performance are related to classroom performance standards or individualized performance standards. When general education curriculum and IEPs are aligned to a standards framework, and grading criteria are clearly defined, graduation requirements and decisions are relatively easy to address in the IEP—that is, unless the state or school district uses minimum competency testing to determine who should or should not graduate (see Thurlow, Ysseldyke, & Anderson, 1995, for a thorough treatment of this subject).

Legal precedence on minimum competency testing was established in a landmark case involving a student who argued that she had failed a Florida graduation test because she had not been taught the content that was tested (*Debra P. v. Turlington*, 1983). Although Debra was not a student with a disability, the decisions in her case still have important implications for IEP teams. First, diplomas were established as a right of property under the U.S. Constitution. As result, tests used to determine whether students should receive a diploma must be valid and reliable, and test content and school curriculum must match. In addition, students and parents must receive sufficient notice of what must be learned to pass the graduation test. Finally, if any of these requirements is not met, the entity giving the test is liable for any hardships experienced by the student.

This decision, and others that have followed, do not require schools to modify the content or standards assessed by minimum competency tests, or change other graduation requirements for that matter. The courts have consistently held, however, that students with disabilities must be allowed to participate in graduation testing and that testing must produce results that are valid for the student (*Board of Education of Northport–East Northport Union Free School District v. Ambach*, 1983; *Brookhart v. Illinois State Board of Education*, 1983).

These decisions make it clear that IEP teams must plan accommodations so that students with disabilities can participate in minimum competency testing. They must provide alternate assessment methods when a student cannot participate even with accommodations. It is also important that students and parents are given advance notice of graduation requirements, at age 14 or in the ninth grade, so that decisions can be made about appropriate programs and services and, ultimately, whether the student works toward the standard diploma or some alternative. When curriculum and standards are aligned with the assessment, and standards are referenced in IEPs, these decisions are less complicated. When that is not the case, the correct course often is not readily apparent.

CONCLUSIONS: BREATHING NEW LIFE INTO SPECIAL EDUCATION

In concluding this chapter, let us return to the basic question that starts it: Will standards and assessments serve special education in the same way they have served general education—to breathe in some new life? Noting that special education and standards-based reform are potentially compatible, McDonnell, McLaughlin, and Morison (1997) pointed to two major barriers that may stand in the way of melding standards into effective special education practice: First, standards-based reform expectations exceed the limits of professional practices and expertise; second, adding special education, with its rules and entitlements, into standards-based reform efforts compounds the professional and technical problems that already exist. Although there does not seem to be much room for argument with these concerns, the inevitable follow-up questions have to be, "Should that stop us?" and, in light of the 1997 IDEA Amendments, "Do we really have any choice?"

Certainly, the ability of special education to inculcate standards-based reform into its methods and practices is limited by the efforts and progress of general education to achieve standards alignment. An IEP referenced to standards works best when the general education curriculum, instruction, and assessments are also referenced to standards. Nonetheless, special education cannot play wait and see. Special education needs to be a major partner in standards-based reform efforts, at the least, in the ways described in the following subsections.

Systemwide Involvement

Special education teachers and administrators, as well as parents and consumers, always need to be involved when any reform effort is planned and discussed in order to advocate for students with disabilities and to determine how special education fits in. For special education, standards-based school reform presents not only some unique challenges but also some viable opportunities. Plans need to be made to ensure that special education is reformed in ways that are consistent and compatible with changes in general education to make the best use of the opportunities provided by standards and assessments.

Professional Development

Special education also needs to be a part of professional development opportunities that support standards-based reform. Standards-referenced IEPs can bring special education closer to general education than it ever has been. To make it work, special educators need to develop a more comprehensive understanding of general education curriculum, instruction, and assessment, and they need to master the new methods and concepts that are defining standards alignment. Special educators and general educators need to start attending the same workshops, seminars, and courses. Those workshops, seminars, and courses need to address the implications of standards alignment for all students.

Research

Special education also needs to fill some of the knowledge gaps that standards-based school reform has created. Research opportunities abound, particularly with regard to assessment participation. Educators need to know the effects of assessment accommodations and modifications on score comparability. They need to know whether some tests are more equitable than others in terms of students' participation and the accuracy of the results. Educators need to learn how standards can be incorporated into IEPs and how performance assessments and portfolios can enhance IEP development and monitoring. Above all, educators need to know whether standards-referenced IEPs are actually an improvement.

Renewed Commitment to Inclusive Education

Standards-based school reform creates a new frame for viewing inclusive education. In an education system aligned with standards, students with disabilities are truly included only if they are working toward the same standards as students who do not have disabilities, and only if they are valued participants in standards-based accountability assessments. Standards-referenced IEPs that include assessment accommodations help ensure that inclusion does not move backward by standing still.

Standards and assessments are, in fact, the tools that have been needed to make inclusive education work for all students. Standards provide clarity to expectations for all students; they define general education, making it possible to design IEPs that are linked directly to the general education curriculum. The new assessments that have followed standards alignment provide a more authentic means by which to determine success for all students, making it possible to evaluate the efficacy of IEPs by using the same criteria that are applied to general education.

One thing has not changed: The IEP is still the heart of special education. With some effort and a renewed commitment to inclusive education, standards and assessments can be the lifeblood coursing through its veins.

REFERENCES

Bateman, B. (1991). *Better IEPs: Doing it the right way.* Unpublished manuscript, University of Washington at Seattle.

Board of Education of Northport–East Northport Union Free School District v. Ambach, 469 N.Y.S.2d 669, 457 N.E.2d 775, 60 N.Y.2d 758 (N.Y. Ct. App. 1983).

Brookhart v. Illinois State Board of Education, 697 F.2d 179 (7th Cir. 1983).

Debra P. v. Turlington, 564 F. Supp. 177 (M.D. Fla. 1983).

Dudley-Marling, C. (1985). Perceptions of the usefulness of the IEP by teachers of learning disabled and emotionally disturbed children. *Psychology in the Schools, 22,* 65–67.

Education for All Handicapped Children Act of 1975, PL 94-142, 20 U.S.C. §§ 1400 *et seq.*

Gerardi, R.J., Grohe, B., Benedict, G.C., & Coolidge, P.G. (1984). More paperwork and wasted time. *Contemporary Education, 56*(1), 39–42.

Harry, B. (1992). An ethnographic study of cross-cultural communication with Puerto Rican American families in the special education system. *American Educational Research Journal, 29,* 471–494.

Hock, M.L. (1997). *Access to learning opportunities: Planning for students with standards challenges.* Burlington: University of Vermont.

Hock, M.L., & Thousand, J.S. (1997). *[Standards related content analysis of traditional standardized tests used in special education].* Unpublished raw data.

Individuals with Disabilities Education Act (IDEA) Amendments of 1997, PL 105-17, 42 U.S.C. §§ 1400 *et seq.*

Individuals with Disabilities Education Act (IDEA) of 1990, PL 101-476, 20 U.S.C. §§ 1400 *et seq.*

McDonnell, L.M. (1997). *The politics of state testing: Implementing new student assessments.* Los Angeles: National Center for Research on Evaluation, Standards, and Student Testing, University of California at Los Angeles.

McDonnell, L.M., McLaughlin, M.J., & Morison, P. (Eds.). (1997). *Educating one and all: Students with disabilities and standards-based reform.* Washington, DC: National Academy Press.

McGarry, J., & Finan, P.L. (1982). *Implementing Massachusetts' special education law: A statewide assessment* (Final report). Boston: Massachusetts State Department of Education. (ERIC Document Reproduction Service No. ED 226 542)

Morgan, E.L., & Rhodes, G. (1983). Teachers' attitudes toward IEPs: A two year follow-up. *Exceptional Children, 50,* 64–67.

Stowitschek, J.J., & Kelso, C.A. (1989). Are we in danger of making the same mistakes with ITPs as were made with IEPs? *Career Development for Exceptional Individuals, 12*(2), 140–151.

Taylor, C. (1994). Assessment for measurement of standards: The peril and promise of large-scale assessment reform. *American Educational Research Journal, 31*(2), 231–262.

Thurlow, M.L., Ysseldyke, J.E., & Anderson, C.L. (1995). *High school graduation requirements: What's happening for students with disabilities* (Synthesis Report 20). Minneapolis: National Center on Educational Outcomes, University of Minnesota at Minneapolis.

Turnbull, K.K., & Hughes, D.L. (1987). A pragmatic analysis of speech and language IEP conferences. *Language, Speech, and Hearing Services in the Schools, 18,* 275–286.

Vaughn, S. (1988). Parent participation in the initial placement/IEP conference ten years after mandated involvement. *Journal of Learning Disabilities, 21*(2), 82–89.

Vermont Department of Education. (1994). *Vermont Writing Assessment Analytic Assessment Guide.* Montpelier: Author.

Vermont Department of Education. (1996). *Vermont's framework of standards and learning opportunities.* Montpelier: Author.

Ysseldyke, J.E., Algozzine, B., Richey, L., & Graden, J. (1982). Declaring students eligible for learning disability services: Why bother with the data? *Learning Disability Quarterly, 5*(1), 37–44.

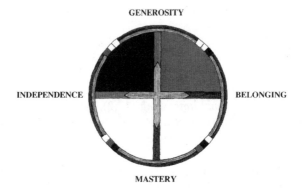

GENEROSITY

INDEPENDENCE

BELONGING

MASTERY

REFLECTION

In the Mainstream
A Confirmation Experience

Ro and Joe Vargo

What is amazing to us is the awesome responsibility of being the parents of a daughter with a disability. We work and pray to learn to accept this challenge and opportunity that is this beautiful child. We adjust to the differences that she presents and, after a time, learn to see those differences as a gift. Our vision for Rosalind was and is quite simple. We want her to be a full and valued member of her school, her neighborhood, and her faith community, as she is in our family. If there

This reflection is based on an article by Rosalind Vargo published in the January 1998 (Vol. 31, No. 4) issue of *Catechist*, the official magazine of the National Catholic Catechist Society.

was any one thing that inspired us, it was our vision—no, our passion—to afford her every opportunity to be included.

Our journey has taught us that we cannot work in isolation to accomplish Rosalind's inclusion. Rather, we must collaborate with others to make it work. It does not matter whether it is as simple as a discussion on the telephone about how to adapt arrangements for Rosalind to participate in a field trip (curriculum modifications) or convincing church officials to include her in a sacramental rite (intervention strategies) or as complex as advocating for more inclusive schools (e.g., collaboration, teamwork, normalizing environments). With little or no training, we still get the job done every day with the support of others.

ACCEPTING THE CHALLENGE

Confirmation preparation is a 2-year process for everyone in our Catholic diocese. Our family took the opportunity because it was a vehicle not only to teach students about the gospel message through the Confirmation curriculum but also to model the message. Our daughter's Confirmation class was composed of 12 students, including Ro and one other youth with a significant disability.

Confirmation preparation did not begin as an educational model for us. Rather, it was a life experience that 9 years before had involved us in preparing our daughter Ro for her First Communion. Although most Catholics have come to see First Communion as a developmental milestone in the life of a young Catholic, our family initially saw it as an insurmountable obstacle because of Ro's having Rett syndrome (for a brief description of Rett syndrome, please see page 248 at the end of this reflection), a rare neurological disorder that has left her with physical and mental challenges.

When we embarked on First Communion all those years ago, Ro was still in an autistic-like stage typical of most girls with Rett syndrome. (This disease occurs exclusively in girls.) Her behavior was turbulent and unpredictable. She was nonverbal and communicated through gestures and eye reactions to words we spoke and the pictures we showed her. Yet, our desire that Ro should celebrate First Communion like the rest of her parish friends was unrelenting. In the end, our feelings mirrored those of any Catholic parent. We realized that all we needed to do was to invite Ro to the table of the Lord. Today, we are still in awe of that First Communion experience; it left us with a profound sense of the workings of the Holy Spirit in our lives.

Each Sunday, Ro attends mass with her family. We sit close to the folk group because Ro finds music soothing and comforting. She is still nonverbal, and we continue to communicate with her through the use of gestures and pictures. We ask Ro, through the use of a single picture of a child receiving communion, if she "would like to receive Jesus," and, consistently, she nods, "Yes." Just after the consecration, she begins smiling, eagerly awaiting our asking of the question.

Ro continues her education in the Syracuse public school system, where she attends general education classes with appropriate support personnel and curriculum modifications. This inclusion of Ro in her neighborhood school community strengthened our resolve to have her included in her church community as well. So, for years, she had been active in church special functions such as family nights, potluck suppers, Lenten prayer groups, and youth group activities. Our parish family was eager to include her as before, without a clear sense of how she might fit in. Again, we relied heavily on the guidance of the Holy Spirit. Never were the gifts of knowledge, wisdom, and courage needed more.

TEACHER, FAMILY, AND PEER SUPPORTS

Ro formally enrolled in our parish's Confirmation program, and, to facilitate her involvement, I (Ro's mother) volunteered to co-teach the class. It was important to me to be involved actively as the teacher to emphasize that Ro was not merely bringing her mother to class as her support but that I was co-teaching the whole group. In taking on this role, I employed the methods that work well with all children, not just those with disabilities. Specifically, I used music, lights, small-group activities, hands-on experiences, and American Sign Language (ASL). For example, at prayer time, I would turn off the lights in our gathering room, leaving a single candle burning. The prayer was usually short and read by a student. Ro was interested and watched her peers intently. When we taught the gifts of the Holy Spirit, we laid seven gift-wrapped packages on the prayer table. These were tangible items to associate with the word *gift*. ASL was incorporated subtly, with two new signs introduced in each class. ASL is so beautiful that all of the young people loved learning some of it. Instruction was almost always done in small groups. Lecture was found to be less successful in keeping Ro's or anyone else's attention, and it was limited to 15 minutes per session.

Our daughter did need refocusing and support throughout class time. Although we made some classroom adaptations in the first year, more were necessary in the second year because she had to adjust to a different teacher and different support people. On the advice of the Director of Religious Education, we invited a Confirmation graduate to be a support person for Ro. So as not to single out or draw attention to Ro, this person also acted as a resource for the whole class. On days on which the support person was unable to attend, Ro's sister Josie provided support during class. This worked well because Josie was just a year and a half younger than Ro and her classmates and fit nicely into the peer group without looking too obvious.

Many of the other *Confirmandi* (i.e., members of the Confirmation class) knew Ro, either through church experiences or from having made their First Communion with Ro. Others attended the same public school, so it was natural for them to have Ro in their class. They were patient with her silliness, polite about her falling asleep, and gentle in their interactions with her. Some kids were comfortable sharing a book with her or including her in their small-group discussions. A 15-minute, structured down time at the beginning of class spent coloring, playing cards, and working on puzzles helped immensely to facilitate interactions.

SERVICE PROJECTS

Developing the concept of shared community with Ro was remarkably easy. For example, she participated in the local CROP walk to raise money to fight hunger. Although she was unable to complete the 6-mile challenge, she managed to walk a mile and a half and collected more than $30 in pledges. For Ro, this was a huge physical accomplishment, and it was important for the other kids to see her participating as much as she could.

Ro also joined her classmates in visiting and planning activities at a neighborhood adult residential facility. There, she moved from person to person, engaging them in smiles and hugs, happy to be a part of the activity and the fun. In fact, she did this better than most of her classmates because it is very easy for her to be social and friendly. It is, in fact, one of her best assets.

ASSESSMENT

Because Ro is nonverbal and has significant physical limitations, it was clear to us that we needed to find other ways to develop her learning and comprehension. As we had done during her First Communion catechesis, we looked for subtle signs in her behavior and demeanor as well as her yes-or-no nodding to indicate understanding. Ro's smiles, body movements, and attentiveness clearly showed her eagerness, happiness, and spirit, and her persistence was indeed remarkable. Each week she climbed steps, 55 in all, to come to class. Yes, we counted them!

SPONSOR

The process of helping Ro choose a sponsor and a Confirmation name revealed a great deal about her readiness for Confirmation. Her choices were inspired and faith-filled. For months, we had been talking to Ro about who her sponsor might be by naming possible candidates for her either orally or on paper. Her sisters—Josie, age 13, and Mary, age 10—helped in the discussions. Mary commented, "You know, Mom, I think it is important that Ro pick someone she likes and looks up to; but, more importantly, I think it should be someone who really *loves* Ro and feels comfortable with who she is!"

Using photographs and printed names, we asked Ro to show us in some way whom she preferred as her sponsor. For 2 months, she consistently said "Yes" to everybody! She just could not make a choice. We were getting frustrated, and I said to my husband, Joe, "As much as I hate the idea, I think we are going to have to make the decision for Ro. It is getting pretty late." Still, we held off for some sign.

On Christmas Eve, as our family knelt in prayer before the manger scene that Ro loves to look at, Jennifer, a family baby sitter and friend, came over to kiss Ro and wish us all a Merry Christmas. Jennifer was one of the remaining choices for Ro's Confirmation sponsor! In a lull during the conversation, Ro looked at me with those telling, piercing, and direct eyes, and her head nodded, "Yes." In the confusion of the moment, I almost missed her message for me. Her gaze was relentless, however. When I realized what Ro was communicating, I whispered in her ear, "Ro, do you want Jen to be your sponsor?" Her gaze remained intense, and she smiled and nodded "Yes."

Ro sent Jennifer a bunch of balloons the next day with a simple card requesting that Jennifer be her sponsor. Jennifer came to our house in person an hour after she received the balloons to tell Ro that she would love to be her sponsor! Ro loves Jen, and they have a very special relationship. Jennifer has been comfortable in providing for Ro's personal hygiene and feeding needs over the years, and she has always treated Ro as a "real person," a teenager!

On that Christmas Eve before our celebration of the newborn King, Ro had shown us—not only we as her parents but I as her teacher—that she understood the importance and the role of a Confirmation sponsor by choosing a faith-filled person who loved her. I guess I needed to learn the lesson again about patience and waiting. Ro understood what she needed to do. She just wanted some extra time for this special task. I thanked the Holy Spirit for not letting me overlook it!

NAMESAKE

The circumstances leading up to the choice of Ro's namesake were just as inspiring as making the choice itself. After many verbal choices, Ro nodded emphatically to the name Teresa. We first thought she might have made this choice because a former teaching assistant she had been fond of was named Teresa. Again, we had so much to learn. We believe she chose the name Teresa after the Little Flower of Jesus, Theresa of Lisieux. We presented Ro with picture books and information on the Little Flower. It was inspiring to find some incredible similarities. St. Theresa was 15 years old, the same age as Ro, when she entered the convent. She was a child who believed not in great deeds but in great love. She trusted God implicitly, and her childlike love, trust, and faith were what endeared her to God and others. She was chronically ill for much of her young life. She sounded so much like Ro!

CEREMONIAL CONSIDERATIONS

Several questions still remained. How was Ro going to write her letter to the bishop? How was she going to go to the altar rail alone? How was she going to communicate with the bishop about her namesake? Again, as in her First Communion preparation, I heard these words in my nightly prayers: "Trust me." One by one, the answers came to us.

Ro's letter to the bishop was accomplished by compiling about 20 sentences and asking her questions one by one, such as, "Do you want this sentence in your letter to the bishop?" One by one, she responded to each question. Before we typed the letter, we asked Ro if she wanted to tell the bishop of her disability. She emphatically nodded, "Yes."

CONFIRMATION DAY

When the big day came, we were nervous and apprehensive—both of us as parents and I as her teacher. We watched in utter amazement, not only at Ro's behavior but also at that of another student, Chris, who has autism. We all witnessed the courage of Chris and Ro that day and their ability to "hold it together" throughout the ceremony. They were alert and attentive. Ro's eyes closed with the calling of the Holy Spirit on the group and opened to the words, "It's time." With 10 other friends, Ro and Chris received the gifts of the Holy Spirit. The liturgy culminated with their receiving the Eucharist from the bishop as he called them each by their chosen Confirmation name: "Teresa, the Body of Christ"; "Joseph, the Body of Christ."

The end of the liturgy left us limp and weepy. We had again witnessed the gifts of the Holy Spirit unfold through this faith experience with Ro. Also, we remembered the words of our pastor, who had said some 9 years earlier, in anticipation of Rosalind's First Communion, "I am excited about the idea of Rosalind receiving First Communion, but I am even more excited about the effect her receiving communion will have on others."

CONCLUSIONS

The inclusion of Catholic youth with disabilities in celebrating the sacraments of the faith is not only a God-given right that must be nurtured by parishes and dioceses but also a *necessity*. This cannot be overemphasized. Confirmation is the sacrament that expects adult action based on faith-filled understanding, knowledge, piety, counsel, courage, wonder, and awe. These attributes can be fulfilled only through real-life experiences.

What if Ro and Chris had not shared the same classroom with the other *Confirmandi*? What would we have learned? What would they have learned if they had been prepared separately from the group? This would have been a message contrary to the very core of their Church. Instead, the experience was perfect. All Confirmation candidates learned and grew in the notion of a "Church community" because it was open and accessible to all. All of the teachers learned and grew in the notion that serving all members of their church can be difficult and different but always rewarding. Parishioners learned and grew in the idea that people with disabilities can be included in the mainstream of sacramental life. These were outcomes that a teacher can be proud of—outcomes that a parent can be proud of!

ABOUT RETT SYNDROME

A period of stagnation or regression follows a typical birth, during which period the child loses purposeful use of the hands, replacing it with repetitive hand movements that become almost constant while awake. For the first time in history, some of the most respected medical researchers in the field have agreed that the most fundamental disability in Rett syndrome is not intellectual but physical. There is no known cause or cure for Rett syndrome. For more information, call the International Rett Syndrome Association at 1-800-818-RETT [7388].

III

Emerging Collaborative and Creative Roles and Processes in Inclusive Schools
Collaborating to Connect the Inclusion Puzzle

Ann I. Nevin

As a teacher educator in the area of special education, I have both witnessed and participated in the dramatic shifts in policies and practices that have occurred on behalf of children and youth with identified disabilities. In 1969, I taught students with disabilities in segregated classrooms using behavior modification procedures. Gradually, I learned to incorporate principles of reinforcement and applied behavior analysis in my interactions with fellow teachers and eventually with principals and administrators. Today, I find myself embracing pedagogical constructs and practices such as metacognitive, constructivist, and multiple intelligences theories and employing instruction practices, such as cooperative group learning, that are based on principles of social psychology and group dynamics. These changes in theories and practices have been accompanied by changes in the roles that I have assumed. At one time, I was the expert consultant in the Triadic Model of Consultation, passing on knowledge and expertise to a mediator who then applied the new knowledge and skills in interactions with children and youth. Then I moved into the role of a collaborative consultant, in which there were more equal two-way interactions. My collaborative teaming experiences rely on more dynamic interactive and mutually constructive processes. It is clear that new collaborative roles have been and will continue to be required in order to meet the challenges of providing caring and effective education for all students.

When considering "new" collaborative roles in education, it may be easy to overlook the underlying assumption that is operating as we discuss these roles. The underlying assumption is that it is possible to create a collaborative ethic as a way of doing business in public education. However, the difficult truth is that a collaborative ethic does not yet prevail in most U.S. public schools. Sarason, a cogent researcher and writer in the area of school reform, stated, "Schools have been intractable to change and the attainment of goals set by reformers. A major failure has been the inability of reformers to confront this intractability" (1990, p. xiii). Unless those who want to reform schools toward the practice of a collaborative ethic face this intractability, new collaborative roles are likely to meet the same demise as other reform efforts, even those that are legally mandated.

What has happened since 1990, when Sarason made those comments about school reform, that might provide hope for those of us who want to experience a collaborative ethic in our schools? First, there exists a growing body of research that provides compelling evidence that collaboration is effective in achieving the outcomes mandated by the Individuals with Disabilities Education Act (IDEA) of 1990 (PL 101-476). Collaboration has been applied systematically to various school-based student service configurations (e.g., multidisciplinary child study team, co-teaching teams) and school-based development practices (e.g., staff development, curriculum planning). Research has indicated improved functioning and effectiveness of school-based teams, such as teacher assistance, instructional support, and teaching teams from preschool through elementary and middle school to secondary school, as well as adult collaboration at the district-, city-, and statewide systems levels (for an extensive review of this literature, see Villa,

Thousand, Nevin, & Malgeri, 1996). In fact, this evidence influenced the Individuals with Disabilities Education Act (IDEA) Amendments of 1997 (PL 105-17), resulting in stronger requirements for collaboration among educators, parents, and students.

Yet there remains the question of what are "new" collaborative roles? At the turn of the 21st century, there might be at least three "arenas" in which new, perhaps as-yet-unnamed, roles might emerge:

1. Searching for and inventing new paradigms for collaboration

2. Actualizing mandated roles ("IDEAlizing" the spirit of the law)

3. Changing roles demanded by global communication systems

SEARCHING FOR AND INVENTING NEW PARADIGMS FOR COLLABORATION

Villa, Thousand, Paolucci-Whitcomb, and Nevin (1990) argued that the very process of engaging in collaborative teamwork can facilitate the invention of a new paradigm of collaboration. The process of collaboration requires a continuous adaptation in order to make room for multiple perspectives. New paradigms, by definition, require collaborators to set aside their current collaborative practices in order to experiment with the new ones. What might such new paradigms yield in terms of new collaborative roles?

It might be instructive to extrapolate from the changes in roles that occur when a school district begins to shift from a past practice of segregating students for special instruction to a practice of including students with special needs. When considering the topic of accountability in this shift, people must move away from a past perspective that specific groups of school personnel (e.g., principals, department chairs, special education coordinators) must supervise to ensure accountability. Within the new practices of inclusive schooling, accountability is seen as a collaborative responsibility wherein collaborators "document how they hold one another accountable for learner outcomes, the processes they use to achieve outcomes, and the relationship between their beliefs and actions" (Villa et al., 1990, p. 288).

New collaborative roles may be needed in the decision-making process for selecting a research methodology to evaluate the impact of inclusive schooling. People must move away from a past perspective (or paradigm) that certain roles are the purview of specially trained people (e.g., university-based teacher educators and researchers, consultants from think tanks) who have the purported expertise to decide which theories, skills, and measures are best. What is needed is an agenda for research, evaluation, and training that is collaboratively developed by university and school personnel and their co-equal participants (the students, parents, and citizens of the school system). Such a new paradigm would require new roles for all involved: professors, researchers, school personnel, citizens, parents, and students.

ACTUALIZING MANDATED ROLES ("IDEAlizing" THE SPIRIT OF THE LAW)

Several roles that are mandated by IDEA and its 1997 reauthorization include parent collaboration, interagency collaboration, teacher collaboration, and university collaboration. It is difficult to admit that some school personnel continue to avoid, resist, and sabotage the actualization of real partnerships with parents, teachers, university teacher educators, and personnel from other agencies. The chapters in this section provide specific processes that can help us all learn new ways to actualize real partnerships.

The role of *parents* as genuine partners *with* school personnel and auxiliary service providers would mean that their expertise would be sought after and respected as much as the expertise of the so-called professionals. Sadly, the existing research indicates that, too often, parents continue to be treated as less than equal partners (see Thousand, Villa, & Nevin, 1997, for a review). In Chapter 11, Giangreco, Cloninger, Dennis, and Edelman describe the role of creative problem solvers and delineate procedures that can result in benefiting from the expertise of parents.

New roles for *teachers* might mean that all educators (special educators and classroom teachers) would be hired and assigned to teaching teams instead of exemplifying the "lone arranger" model of teaching, wherein one person is given the sole responsibility for a group of learners, working as the lone arranger of instruction. In Chapter 10, Thousand and Villa delineate some of these new roles for educators who participate in collaborative planning and teaching teams. Bauwens and Mueller provide new ways of thinking about "software, hardware, and mindware" in Chapter 12. They suggest new roles for aides, classroom teachers, and special educators as they work collaboratively with students and parents.

New roles for *university teacher educators* might require crossing the disciplinary boundaries between colleges of education, colleges of arts and sciences, and colleges of social work in order to model for future professionals in various agencies (e.g., schools, social services, welfare) the collaborative skills that they will be required to have in order to practice. Chapter 13, by Giangreco,

Prelock, Reid, Dennis, and Edelman, suggests more generic roles for related-services personnel (in contrast to discipline-specific roles) that might provide important guidelines for educators of the next generation of teachers and related-services personnel.

CHANGING ROLES DEMANDED BY GLOBAL COMMUNICATION SYSTEMS

Consider the impact of new technologies such as video teleconferencing, "live" Internet chat rooms, electronic mail, and classroom sites on the World Wide Web, where students self-construct portfolios of their progress as home pages. Some data suggest that the Internet and electronic mail provide more reciprocity and parity in that the contributions of any one correspondent may be received without the stereotypes associated with identifying the "parent," the "teacher," the "specialist," or the "client," which can happen subconsciously in face-to-face meetings. What might collaboration look like, feel like, and sound like if it were conducted via the World Wide Web?

In summary, the chapters in this section contain a wealth of information from researchers and practitioners alike. The future of U.S. public schools as places where a collaborative ethic prevails has never looked brighter.

REFERENCES

Individuals with Disabilities Education Act (IDEA) Amendments of 1997, PL 105-17, 20 U.S.C. §§ 1400 *et seq.*

Individuals with Disabilities Education Act (IDEA) of 1990, PL 101-476, 20 U.S.C. §§ 1400 *et seq.*

Sarason, S.B. (1990). *The predictable failure of educational reform: Can we change course before it's too late?* San Francisco: Jossey-Bass.

Thousand, J.S., Villa, R.A., & Nevin, A.I. (1997). Including all the experts: Effective collaborations for student success. *Reaching Today's Youth: The Community Circle of Caring Journal, 1*(3), 13–17.

Villa, R.A., Thousand, J.S., Nevin, A.I., & Malgeri, C. (1996). Instilling collaboration for inclusive schooling as a way of doing business in public education. *Remedial and Special Education, 17*(3), 169–181.

Villa, R.A., Thousand, J.S., Paolucci-Whitcomb, P., & Nevin, A.I. (1990). In search of new paradigms. *Journal of Educational and Psychological Consultation, 1*(4), 279–292.

Chapter 10

Collaborative Teaming
A Powerful Tool in School Restructuring

Jacqueline S. Thousand and Richard A. Villa

In schools that have restructured successfully to meet the needs of all students, personnel consistently identify collaborative teams and the "collaborative teaming" (Thousand et al., 1986, p. 36) group decision-making process that they employ as keystones to their success (Stainback & Stainback, 1990; Thousand, 1990). In the mid-1980s, Patterson, Purkey, and Parker (1986) argued that every school needs *many* collaborative teams to invent meaningful learning opportunities for an increasingly diverse student population and to explore the problems that traditional school structures, through the end of the 1990s, failed to conceptualize or to address adequately. Similar themes were reflected in Senge's (1990) claim that collaborative teaming is necessary for individual insights and decisions to be translated into action and for individual skill development to propagate to other individuals and other teams. Collaborative accomplishments set a tone and standard for working and learning together throughout the larger organization, whether the organization is a business, a government entity, a school, a family, or a community.

In this chapter, the rationale for and a definition of a *collaborative team* are followed by a detailed discussion of the elements of the *collaborative teaming process*. Throughout, specific administrative actions for fostering collaborative teams and encouraging collaborative teaming processes within the school community are suggested.

RATIONALE FOR
COLLABORATIVE TEAMS WITHIN SCHOOLS

Although collaboration is not yet the norm in many North American schools, calls for collaboration have been made repeatedly for decades by numerous educational groups with diverse interests (see National Study on Inclusive Education, 1994, 1995). In the early 1970s, collaboration was advanced by legislated school improvement reforms. At the turn of the 21st century, the effectiveness of collaborative activities is supported by a strong database from both research and practice, and the emerging evidence has been documented for preschool through high school levels and adult as well as systems levels (Idol, Nevin, & Paolucci-Whitcomb, 1993, 1999; Villa, Thousand, Nevin, & Malgeri, 1996). At least two conclusions can be drawn about effective collaboration and the achievement of outcomes for children with disabilities. First, learners with special education needs can be served effectively in *inclusive* environments when educators, support personnel, and families collaborate. Second, effective collaborators can expect *improvements* in the academic and social skills of children and youth with special needs. As for the benefits to adults, positive outcomes can be experienced in at least three domains: school restructuring, teacher empowerment, and basic need satisfaction.

Collaboration and School Restructuring

Within the school restructuring movement, collaborative teams and teaming processes have come to be viewed as vehicles for inventing the solutions that traditional bureaucratic school structures have failed to conceptualize. Various collaborative structures—site-based decision-making teams (Glickman, Gordon, & Ross-Gordon, 1998), ad hoc problem-solving teams (Patterson et al., 1986; Skrtic, 1987), teacher assistance teams (Chalfant, Pysh, & Moultrie, 1979), collaborative planning and teaching teams (Thousand & Villa, 1990a, 1990b)—have been recommended and described. Team structures bring together people of diverse backgrounds and interests so that they may share knowledge and skills to generate new and novel methods for individualizing learning, without the need for dual systems of general and special education (Nevin, Thousand, Paolucci-Whitcomb, & Villa, 1990; Skrtic, 1987).

Collaborative teams not only assist adults with their work but also offer students a model of the type of work structure they can expect to encounter as citizens of a highly complex and interdependent 21st-century global community. Communication and collaboration skills are among the core skills identified as essential for survival in the 21st-century work world. Educational futurists (Benjamin, 1989; Wiggins, 1989) therefore recommend that schools structure multiple opportunities for students to see these skills modeled and valued by their teachers as they operate in collaborative teams. They also recommend that students be invited to join adults as active members of the various instruction and decision-making teams of the school (Villa & Thousand, 1996).

Collaboration and Teacher Empowerment

The initiative to empower teachers offers another rationale for collaborative teaming within schools. Schlechty argued that teacher empowerment, through participatory decision making,

> Promises to yield better decisions and results. That such a promise is not hollow is attested to by the fact that some of the greatest recoveries in American business (Xerox and Ford, for example) have been based in large part on restructuring aimed at empowering and developing all employees—from the lowest in the hierarchy to the highest. (1990, p. 52)

Evidence is mounting to suggest that teacher empowerment through collaborative decision making will result in desired outcomes of school restructuring—shared ownership of problem definitions and solutions (Duke, Showers, & Imber, 1980; Fullan & Pomfret, 1977); the exchange of skills (Thousand et al., 1986); the use of higher-level thinking processes and the generation of more novel solutions (Thousand, Villa, Paolucci-Whitcomb, & Nevin, 1992); and attendance and participation at meetings, persistence in working on difficult tasks, and attainment of the group's goal (Johnson & Johnson, 1997; Rosenholtz, Bassler, & Hoover-Dempsey, 1985).

Collaboration and Basic Need Satisfaction

Glasser's (1985, 1986) control theory offers a final compelling rationale for collaboration and teaming among school personnel. *Control theory* proposes that people choose to do what they do because it satisfies one or more of five basic human needs: survival, power or control in one's life, freedom or choice, a sense of belonging, and fun. Based on interviews of members of 30 teams that regularly collaborate to plan for, evaluate, and teach heterogeneous groups of students, we concluded that collaborative team arrangements do help educators to meet these five basic needs (Thousand & Villa, 1990a). Specifically, collaborative teams enhance teachers' potential for *survival* and *power* in educating a diverse student body by creating opportunities for 1) the regular exchange of needed resources, expertise, and technical assistance and 2) professional growth through reciprocal peer coaching. In collaborative teams, members experience a *sense of belonging* and *freedom* from isolation by having others with whom to share the responsibility for accomplishing difficult tasks. Finally, it is *fun* to problem solve creatively and to engage in stimulating adult dialogue and social interactions.

DEFINITION OF A COLLABORATIVE TEAM

Simply recognizing the need for collaborative teams within schools does not tell us how teams should operate—which critical elements are needed for a team to be optimally effective. We offer a definition of a *collaborative team* that represents an integration of 1) our firsthand experiences with school-based teams that actively support students in heterogeneous learning environments (Thousand et al., 1986; Thousand & Villa, 1990a; Villa & Thousand, 1995); and 2) our reading of the literature regarding cooperative group learning (e.g., Johnson & Johnson, 1999), collaboration and consultation (e.g., Fishbaugh, 1997; Friend & Cook, 1996; Idol et al., 1993; Pugach & Johnson, 1995; Thomas, Correa, & Morsink, 1995), adult cooperation (e.g., Brandt, 1987; DeBevoise, 1986; Hord, 1986; Johnson & Johnson, 1987; Lieberman, 1986; Quick, 1992), and group theory (e.g., Johnson & Johnson, 1997). A *collaborative team* may be defined as a group of people who agree to

1. Coordinate their work to achieve at least one *common, publicly agreed-on goal* (Appley & Winder, 1977)

2. Hold a *belief system* that all members of the team have unique and needed expertise (Vandercook & York, 1990)

3. Demonstrate *parity,* the equal valuation of each member's input (Falck, 1977), by alternately engaging in the dual roles of teacher and learner, expert and recipient, consultant and consultee (Villa, Thousand, Paolucci-Whitcomb, & Nevin, 1990)

4. Use a *distributed functions theory* of leadership in which the task and relationship functions of the traditional lone leader are distributed among all members of the group (Johnson & Johnson, 1997, 1999)

5. Employ a *collaborative teaming process* that involves face-to-face interaction; positive interdependence; the performance, monitoring

and processing of interpersonal skills; and individual accountability (Johnson & Johnson, 1997, 1999)

Although all five of these components are considered critical to the success of a collaborative team, the last element—the collaborative teaming process—is the focus of the remainder of this chapter. When the collaborative teaming process is operating, the other four components automatically are attended to and practiced.

ELEMENTS OF AN
EFFECTIVE COLLABORATIVE TEAMING PROCESS

An effective collaborative team, in large part, is the adult analogue of an effective student cooperative learning group (Johnson & Johnson, 1999). For both adults and children, groups perform best when five elements that define the *collaborative teaming process* are in place:

1. Face-to-face interaction among team members on a frequent basis
2. A mutual "we are all in this together" feeling of positive interdependence
3. A focus on the development of small-group interpersonal skills in trust building, communication, leadership, creative problem solving, decision making, and conflict management
4. Regular assessment and discussion of the team's functioning and the setting of goals for improving relationships and more effectively accomplishing tasks
5. Methods for holding one another accountable for agreed-on responsibilities and commitments (Johnson & Johnson, 1997; Thousand & Villa, 1990b)

In observing and working with school-based teams across North America, the authors have discovered and experimented with a variety of strategies for ensuring that teams experience or practice each of the five preceding elements. The strategies discussed in this section represent just some of the tools for promoting these five elements. In no way are they meant to be an exhaustive prescription of "how-tos" in collaborative teaming. As more teams learn and practice collaborative teaming principles, new strategies surely will be invented.

Frequent Face-to-Face Interaction

It is the regular face-to-face verbal interchanges among members of a team that enable them to problem solve creatively. During face-to-face exchanges, team members "piggyback" on the ideas of others with divergent viewpoints, knowledge bases, training, and work and life experiences. In this way, teams generate novel solutions that go beyond the usual and obvious first and second solutions that may or may not have worked in the past (Parnes, 1981, 1988). The outcomes of face-to-face interaction are different from those that a single team member would produce alone; that is to say, "Two heads are better than one."

Those of us who have served on teams, committees, and councils have experienced the challenges that occur when regular face-to-face interaction is disrupted. There are times when groups are so large that there is too little opportunity during a limited meeting time for any one person to express his or her ideas or feelings. There is the problem of scheduling a common meeting time among people whose calendars are booked 1 or 2 months in advance. There are the late-comers, the early departers, and those members who attend meetings only sporadically. There is the challenge of communicating team decisions and homework assignments to absent members efficiently. There are physical arrangements that make it difficult to see and communicate with other team members and environments that are just plain unpleasant.

What follows are strategies for dealing with the issues that arise in structuring face-to-face interactions within teams. Many of these strategies also reinforce the collaborative team norm of "parity" (i.e., the equal valuation of each person's input).

Team Membership: Who Should Be on a Team?   In our view, only three questions need to be answered in order to determine who should be on any collaborative team:

1. Who has the expertise that the team needs to make the best decision?
2. Who is affected by the decision?
3. Who has an interest in participating?

The rationale for asking the first question has to do with effectiveness —for teams to make informed decisions, they need to engage as members the people with the greatest available knowledge or expertise regarding the issue or the child of concern. Of course, who may be considered necessary as a team participant changes based on the issue or the child. This is why, in many schools, a differentiation is made between a *core* team—a small group of people who are most immediately and directly involved with a specific learner or task—and an *expanded team*—a larger team comprising the core team plus the various other experts who are called in, as needed, based on the specific topics included in the team's meeting agenda.

The rationale for the second question ("Who is affected by the decision?") has to do with democratic processes and fairness. According to Schlechty, "There is, at present, considerable discussion of work place democracy, shared decision making, and participatory leadership. Behind these discussions lies the assumption that those who are affected by decisions should be involved in them" (1990, p. 51). We find it ironic that, in the past, planning teams for students eligible for special education did not routinely include the people most affected by their decisions—the students themselves. By the end of the 1990s, a number of schools routinely invited students to participate on their own planning teams (Thousand & Villa, 1990b; Villa & Thousand, 1996). We also find it disturbing that some teams consider it inappropriate for teaching assistants, who provide direct support to challenged students, to participate as decision makers on students' planning teams, even though many of the team's decisions determine the daily activities and responsibilities of teaching assistants.

The rationale for the third question ("Who is interested?") has to do with appreciating enthusiasm and thinking beyond the obvious. Often, within the school or the greater community, there are people who are excited about the focus of a particular team. For example, suppose the planning team for a new first-grade student with multiple disabilities is challenged with developing a computer-based communication system for the student. Further suppose that a high school advanced mathematics teacher has expertise and an interest in any type of new application of computer technology. If given the opportunity, this teacher might bring great energy, creativity, and excitement to the first-grade team, even though he or she might not be the obvious first choice as a team member.

Team Size and Communication Systems   Collaborative teams can get big at times. For example, it is not uncommon for a student with severe disabilities to have an individual program planning team with more than 20 members (e.g., the student, parents, teachers, human services and employment agency personnel, special support staff, a physician, occupational and physical therapists, administrators, peer advocates). Curriculum planning teams that involve all interested parties may include an entire school's teaching staff. Evidence regarding group size for student learning groups suggests an optimal size of four to six members (Johnson & Johnson, 1999). A group of four to six members is large enough to ensure variety in resources and viewpoints and small enough for each person's resources to be used and for each person to have an opportunity to speak and have his or her contributions appreciated. A group of this size requires a minimum of energy to be devoted to coordinating and ensuring equity in participation.

Hare (1994) stated that teams of up to 10 members can function with all members participating actively. The reported experiences of effective school-based collaborative teams and our own experiences suggest that, under certain conditions—when team members have a unified vision, highly developed interpersonal skills and relationships, and time (i.e., more than the usual 60-minute maximum meeting time)—it may be possible for school-based teams of up to 10 members to function effectively. Our recommended ideal number for school-based team membership, however, remains no more than six or seven members. Given that many school-based teams exceed this ideal number, which strategies to reduce group size and maintain communication among absent members should be employed?

Methods for Reducing Group Size   One method for reducing size is to use *core teams* that can be expanded to include other members as needed. When creating the agenda for subsequent meetings, members of the core team first identify and sequence the anticipated topics and then determine which members of the *extended team* are needed to address each of the issues adequately. These extended team members are invited for all of the meeting or at least that part of the meeting in which their expertise and interest will be of help. A second method is to elect representatives to a representative committee. The responsibility of each of these members is to solicit input, share products, and seek endorsement for decisions from their respective stakeholder groups (e.g., grade-level teachers, aides, administrators). Glickman and colleagues (1998) offered procedures for involving members of large groups through various combinations of subgroups, representative committees, and entire faculty meetings.

Communication and Proxy Systems   There are always times when core or extended-team members must miss a meeting. When this occurs, the need arises for an agreed-on system for absent members to offer input into and receive information regarding outcomes of team meetings. A system for prompt production and delivery of meeting minutes to all team members, including absent members and others who have a "need to know" (e.g., the principal, a physician, the special education administrator), is a simple but critical communication strategy. Meeting minutes, however, often do not give the reader an idea of how and why a team made the decisions reflected in the minutes. Having a "buddy" who gathers information prior to the meeting, represents the absent person's information and perspective during the meeting, and has contact (by telephone or in person) following the meeting to explain the meeting's minutes adds a personal touch and reduces the likelihood of misunderstanding. It also invokes the absent member's presence through a *proxy*. Another method for invoking an absent member's presence is to place an empty chair in the meeting circle as a physical reminder to respect, consider, and discuss the absent member's likely viewpoint when making decisions..

How to Get People to Attend   Getting certain participants of a team to come to team meetings, arrive on time, and stay until the end are some of the most frequently stated challenges to face-to-face interactions. A simple strategy for promoting attendance is for team members to agree on a regular meeting time (e.g., every Tuesday from 2:30 P.M. until 3:15 P.M., the third period of every first and third Thursday) that is held "sacred." A responsibility of school administrators is to work with teachers to first identify the various team arrangements that exist or are needed within the school (e.g., in-service planning team, school restructuring committee, building-based instruction support team, curriculum-planning team, individual student planning teams) and then modify the school's master schedule to enable staff to meet. A variety of strategies have been employed to increase collaboration time (Thousand & Villa, 1995; Villa & Thousand, 1990). For example, the school day may be altered to allow teachers time together without students (e.g., lengthen the school day by 15 minutes so that students may be released a half-day early every other Thursday afternoon; shift the students' school hours so that the 20 minutes of "free" teacher time before and after school are consolidated into a 40-minute morning time block designated for collaboration). Administrators may release classroom teachers for meetings by substituting on a regular basis or teaching one period per day. Volunteers, student teachers, or a permanent substitute also may release and provide coverage for instruction staff.

One of the most effective methods for increased meeting attendance is for team members to discuss and agree on group norms regarding attendance, such as the following:

"Other activities (e.g., dental appointments, other meetings) will not preempt team meeting times."

"Meetings will start and end on time."

"Late arrivals and early exits will be frowned on."

To deal with latecomers, it may be important to establish a norm that meetings will not be interrupted to update tardy members. Instead, tardy members will be briefed on what they missed during a planned break or at some time following the meeting. A record in the minutes of participants' arrival and departure times also may be employed as a motivator and as a method of accountability for timely attendance. To highlight the importance of attendance, minutes of meetings should identify, in separate columns, the names of those who attended and those who were absent from part or all of the meeting.

The work of collaborative teams typically is distributed between maintenance activities (e.g., updates and sharing of data, reviewing the agenda, creating the agenda for the next meeting, assigning tasks to be completed before the next meeting) and problem solving. Creative problem solving among team members requires tremendous cognitive energy and can be sustained for no more than 20 or 30 minutes before productivity begins to wane (Parnes, 1989). Although both maintenance and problem-solving activities take time, limiting the duration of meetings (e.g., to a maximum of 60 minutes) can make future attendance more attractive in at least three ways. First, time limits acknowledge that each team member has other commitments and responsibilities outside the meeting. Time limits also communicate predictability (i.e., "We *will* finish within an hour!"). Finally, limiting the duration of a meeting respects team members' need for a break from high-energy cognitive work.

Considerations for Frequency of Meetings   When deciding how often a team should assemble face to face, team members must balance three realities:

1. Teams can address only so many agenda items in a 50- or 60-minute time period.

2. Teams must be timely in their responses. They must meet frequently enough that they can respond quickly to serious issues (e.g., a teacher goes on emergency medical leave and a long-term replacement must be found, a student suddenly begins to demonstrate aggressive and dangerous behaviors).

3. Teams need time to focus on the positive, to meet for reasons other than in response to problems or crises. Taking time to celebrate positive outcomes and to engage in proactive rather than reactive decision making both energizes and helps to build relationships among team members.

Newly formed teams often report that, in their first few meetings, they overestimate the amount of work or number of agenda items that they can manage collaboratively in a limited time frame. They also report, however, that as they continue to meet and develop their own work styles and problem-solving approaches, they become increasingly more efficient, thus making it possible to meet less often or for shorter periods of time.

Physical Environment   The arrangement of a team's physical environment symbolically communicates the team's values, the way in which people are expected to behave, and how much team members value themselves and the group's mission (Johnson, 1979). Arranging for face-to-face orientation of team members, privacy, and comfort enhances the potential for effective collaborative interaction.

Create a Circle   Effective collaborative teams arrange themselves in a circle, so that all team members can "see the whites of one another's eyes" and readily interact face to face. One common mistake in arranging a meeting space is to assemble team members at a long, rectangular table. This arrangement has a number of inherent problems. First, it suggests that some team members (e.g., those seated at the head of the table) may have more power than others and, in this way, fails to promote a value system in which all members' contributions are valued equally. Second, team members can see and interact easily with only the one or two people seated directly across from them. Finally, given that approximately two-thirds of human communication is expressed nonverbally through facial expression, hand gestures, and other body language (Hamachek, 1981), the rectangular arrangement seriously impedes members' ability to give or receive complete messages and increases the likelihood of miscommunication. If a circular table cannot be found or is so large that it interferes with the sharing of materials, we recommend that chairs be arranged in a circle with no table at all. In this arrangement, materials can be displayed easily or passed to any group member, with an easel and a large newsprint pad used for public recording of the agenda, members' contributions, and outcome minutes. Some collaborative teams find it comfortable to work in a circle on the floor, particularly when they need to huddle over a common set of task materials.

Arrange for Privacy   Generally, teams are most productive in workplaces that are as free as possible from distractions and interruptions. Privacy—being out of earshot of adults and students who are not members of the team—is essential when confidentiality is an issue.

Arrange for Comfort and Satisfaction of Human Needs   It is important to remember that people are not able to function optimally unless certain basic needs are met. Meeting spaces, then, should be neither too hot nor too cold. Nourishment may be needed, particularly for early morning or late afternoon meetings. Several school teams have responded to this need for food and drink by creating the role of and rotating the responsibility for being the group's snack provider. Having a clean room with windows, comfortable chairs of adult size, good acoustics, and background music are but a few of the many physical conditions that may not only enhance a group's performance but also highlight that this collection of people and their goal are worthy. In comfortable and nurturing environments, group morale and feelings of well-being and enjoyment are more likely to occur (Johnson, 1979).

Positive Interdependence

> *Positive interdependence* is the perception that one is linked with others in a way so that one cannot succeed unless they do (and vice versa), and that their work benefits you and your work benefits them. It is the belief that "you sink or swim together." Positive interdependence is the essence of small groups, organizations, families, communities, and societies. It promotes working together to maximize joint benefits, sharing resources, providing mutual support, and celebrating joint success. (Johnson & Johnson, 1997, p. 399)

Positive interdependence is the second critical element of the collaborative teaming process. There are many paths to creating positive interdependence, and we recommend structuring as many as possible. The more paths there are, the clearer the "all for one, one for all" message will be among team members. The following subsections discuss strategies for fostering feelings of positive interdependence by 1) publicly stating group and individual goals, 2) distributing leadership functions among team members, and 3) creating common rewards and responsibilities.

Publicly Stating Group and Individual Goals *Group goals* are critical to team functioning. They guide the team's actions and serve as criteria for resolving conflict and judging the group's effectiveness. They also create the tension or achievement motivation necessary to get people to coordinate their work. Group goals, however, are not the only goals that influence team members' behavior. It is important to acknowledge that all team members join teams with certain individual goals or agendas.

Suppose, for example, that a new school restructuring committee is formed. One teacher may join the committee because she finds the prospect of change exciting. Another may join in order to minimize the feared personal impact of change. Yet another may join with the objective of decreasing the amount of time for which students are pulled out of the classroom for remedial and special education services. These committee members have quite diverse personal and professional goals, yet all have a common requirement for team participation—that is, faith that each individual's goals will be considered when team decisions are made. For this faith to be fostered, teams must spend time exploring the relevance of group goals to each member's individual goals. This, of course, requires that individual goals become public statements so that *hidden agendas*—personal goals that are inconsistent with group goals and that are not revealed to other group members— are not suspected. Hidden agendas thwart team effectiveness by creating mistrust and suspicion among team members who do not understand why a particular team member seems to be acting at cross-purposes with the dominant goals of the group.

When teams first come together, then, a critical first step is to discuss group and individual goals publicly. We recommend a procedure that begins with each team member's perceptions of the group goals being stated and recorded. With this information, common goal statements then are debated, settled on, and publicly posted. Given these agreed-on group goal statements, the next step is for team members to reveal their individual personal goals—what it is they want or need from the group in order to work toward the common goal. For team members to honestly engage in this second activity, there must be some level of trust among all group members. The authors acknowledge that such trust may not exist in some groups, such as those in which members differ significantly in their viewpoints, have dysfunctional team histories, or are strangers to one another. In these groups, some members may be reluctant to reveal hidden agendas. For these groups, however, the public discussion of goals is even more important, for it models a teaming process that presumes honesty, trust (i.e., openness, sharing), and trustworthy (i.e., acceptance, support) behaviors as norms governing future behavior of team members.

As a final step in this process, team members must be encouraged to take a win-win position, to agree to both forward the group's goals and ask for what they need to achieve their own personal objectives, recognizing that, at times, personal and group goals may seem to be in conflict. Although the entire process may take some time, particularly for diverse teams, it goes a long way toward creating a sense of positive interdependence and ownership for a team's purpose. Many teams that have engaged in this process report their surprise at how discrepant members' perceptions are initially and how motivated and respected they feel at the end. The process of goal discovery is one that should be repeated periodically with longstanding teams for at least two reasons. First, a team easily can get caught up in the day-to-day details of its work and lose sight of its vision. A review of goals can energize and set a team on course. Second, group and individual goals are likely to and should change over time; time for discovery of these changes needs to be built into a long-term collaborative teaming process.

Distributing Leadership Functions Among Team Members   In accordance with the distributed functions theory of leadership prescribed for collaborative teams, each member of a team takes on some of the job functions of the traditional single group leader and has a responsibility to promote both goal achievement and interpersonal relationships. The power of this interpretation of leadership is that, when practiced, it creates positive interdependence in the form of *resource, role,* and *task* interdependence. The role of administrators who are interested in promoting effective collaborative teaming is to model this definition of leadership in team meetings. Administrators in schools that are new to this type of equitable group structure find that team members often become confused about the administrator's role on the team and try to impose familiar structures in which the administrator is looked to for major or controversial decision making, the arranging of meetings, recording and disseminating the minutes, and so forth. Administrators introducing collaborative teaming processes must be careful to demonstrate their belief in the collaborative process through their behaviors; that is, they must model and expect others to demonstrate equity and parity when engaging in the collaborative teaming act. This does not mean that other, more hierarchical relationships (e.g., supervisor–supervisee) outside the team structure will disappear or change. It is imperative, then, that the situations in which distributed leadership and collaborative teaming processes are to be practiced are distinguished from those in which they are not.

Positive Resource Interdependence   Positive resource interdependence exists when team members have differing knowledge, skills, and material resources that they share with one another to help get a job done. A distributed functions definition of leadership inherently recognizes that schools and, therefore, collaborative teams that operate within them are a natural and rich source of human resources and resource interdependence. Each individual in a school has unique talents, interests, training, and work and life experiences to bring to a team. "When group members *perceive* their potential contributions to the group as being unique, they increase their efforts" (Johnson & Johnson, 1997, p. 140; emphasis added).

Positive Role Interdependence   Another type of resource interdependence is created through a division of labor *during* team meetings. From one meeting to the next, team members rotate different leadership responsibilities or roles that promote either task completion or the maintenance of relationships among members. Within this structure, the team has as many leaders as members, and the message is communicated that no one person alone has the expertise, authority, or material or information resources needed to accomplish the team's goals.

Numerous task roles (e.g., timekeeper, recorder) and relationship roles (e.g., observer, encourager) have been prescribed and defined by various authors (Glickman et al., 1998; Quick, 1992; Thousand & Villa, 1992). Exactly which roles are employed during a team meeting depends on the nature of the work and the level of interpersonal skill development of group members. For example, when conflict and controversy are expected, there may be a need for a conflict recognizer to identify emerging conflicts and signal the group to stop and assess whether the steps of conflict resolution should be initiated. A harmonizer role also may be needed to help conciliate differences by looking for ways to reduce tension through humor and nonjudgmental explanations. A praiser role would be important for groups in which the contributions of members are rarely affirmed or accepted. When team discussions become dominated by a handful of participants, the equalizer role can be activated. The equalizer encourages participation of quiet members and regulates the flow of communication by seeing that all members have equal access to "air time."

Any task or relationship social skill may be transformed into a role to be practiced by and rotated among team members. Two roles that Vermont school-based collaborative teams use are the "but watcher" and "jargon buster" roles. The job of the but watcher is to help team members defer judgment during creative problem-solving processes by monitoring and signaling members' use of blocking, oppositional, or judgmental language such as, "Yes, but. . . ." A jargon buster has the job of signaling (often with a loud noisemaker) whenever a specialized term that might not be understood by a team member is used. The jargon user must then define the term or use an analogous lay term. This is an important role for teams that include professionals who use specific technical language to describe their work and their ideas. The jargon buster role prevents people who are unfamiliar with particular jargon terms from feeling intimidated or that they are less-than-equal team members. Its also establishes a norm that it is all right not to know what something means. Once team members are familiar with the meaning of jargon terms, the group may use the terms to enhance group efficiency and promote group interdependence. Having a common language builds a sense of team identity and spirit.

Positive Task Interdependence   Distributed leadership requires that the teaming process ensure an equitable division of labor for the completion of the various homework assignments that need to be finished before the next meeting. Collaborative teams may promote equity in homework distribution by periodically reviewing the published record of work assignments, which appear as Action Items in the meeting minutes. If such monitoring reveals that one or two team members regularly assume the majority of the homework tasks, at least one of three problems with positive interdependence exists: 1) team members may be "freeloading" (i.e., taking advantage of the group's size to avoid work); 2) members' ownership of the group goal may be waning; or 3) those doing most of the homework may not trust that work that was primarily their responsibility in the past can be managed as effectively by others. Inequity in the division of labor diminishes a group's sense of cohesion and requires the team to explore the causes and possible actions for reestablishing balance (e.g., setting a norm that each team member must take on at least one homework item each meeting, limiting the number of homework items for which a single person may volunteer).

Creating Common Rewards and Responsibilities A final way in which positive interdependence may be promoted within collaborative teams is by structuring *reward interdependence*—common rewards for group members' collective work. Reward interdependence ensures that the recognition of one member's contributions does not overshadow the equally important but not as visible contributions of another. A norm within collaborative teams is that successes are celebrated collectively—no one person receives special recognition. As a result, when goals are achieved, all members may share in the gratification of having contributed to their achievement. A responsibility of administrators and teaching staff is to jointly explore and identify what team members view as a reward or incentive for collaboration. At a minimum, teams should structure celebration time into every meeting's agenda. During this time, each member shares at least one positive statement or piece of good news regarding students, goal-related activities, or professional accomplishments. Villa and Thousand (1990) identified a broad range of incentives for collaboration, including "*team* of the year" rather than "*teacher* of the year" awards, off-campus teamwork retreats, and the trading of "comp time" (earned by attending meetings outside school hours) for released time from in-service or planning days.

With joint rewards comes joint responsibility. There are times when a team's goals are not achieved and plans do not work out as hoped (e.g., the grant is not funded, the curriculum is not adopted by the school community, the reading program for a learner fails). Teams that swim together also must *sink* together. When a team faces disappointment or failure, it is the collective *we* and not a single individual who accepts responsibility.

Interpersonal Skills for Collaboration

It is not enough to create collaborative teams. For collaborative teams to function effectively, members must have knowledge of and use the small-group interpersonal skills needed for collaboration. Of course, people are not born with group interaction skills, nor do these skills magically appear when needed. In addition, few adults have had the opportunity to receive the kind of instruction and practice in small-group interpersonal skills that many children and young adults do in schools and colleges in which cooperative group learning and partner learning structures are employed routinely (Villa & Thousand, 1996). As a consequence, many newly formed school-based collaborative teams include individuals who have never been required to work as part of a team, and therefore such individuals lack the collaborative skills to do so.

The good news is that collaborative skills can be learned and that learning how to collaborate is no different from learning how to play a game or ride a bicycle built for two. It requires the team to create opportunities for members to 1) see the need for the skill, 2) learn how and when the skill should be used, 3) practice the use of the skill, and 4) discuss (i.e., receive feedback about) how well they are using the skill (Johnson, Johnson, & Holubec, 1993, 1994).

LEARNING ABOUT SOCIAL SKILLS BY ESTABLISHING GROUP NORMS

> The norms of a group are the group's common beliefs regarding appropriate behavior for members; they tell, in other words, how members are expected to behave. . . . All groups have norms, set either formally or informally. (Johnson & Johnson, 1997, p. 424)

In effective teams, members talk about and understand their norms. They structure time to agree on a written list of group norms or rules and discuss how, when, and why the norms and rules should be applied. During the discussion, the team should not only identify desired behaviors but also define and offer examples of the behaviors and share the reasons why these behaviors are so important to their group's functioning. Norms are important to groups because they help to equalize the level of influence of group members. Both timid and powerful members gain from setting mutually agreed-on norms because norms bring regularity and control into the group without any one person having to apply personal power to direct interpersonal interactions. The following might be some typical collaborative team norms:

Everyone on the team should participate.

We should start and end meetings on time.

We should use first names when addressing one another.

We should not use foul language.

Structuring the Practice of Collaborative Skills and Norms

Knowing what demonstration of a particular collaborative skill looks and sounds like in practice and why it is important in no way guarantees that members will choose to practice and subsequently master the skill. Three assumptions relate to the practice of interpersonal skills within teams. The first assumption is that other team members are critical to skill development. Their support and feedback determine whether skills are practiced correctly and often enough to be performed naturally and automatically. The second assumption is that peer pressure from team members and administrators to practice collaborative skills must be balanced with support for actually doing so. When unskilled team members (e.g., a dominant person, a person afraid of speaking, a person who fails to carry out homework assignments, a person who fails to understand ideas) are present, other team members are responsible for sending these team members two messages: 1) "We want you to practice this specific collaborative skill," and 2) "How can we help you?" Conversely, each team member must learn how to identify and ask for support in practicing collaborative skills. A final assumption is that there is a direct relationship between the frequency of collaborative interactions and the number of team members with highly developed interpersonal competence and that the more skilled the team members, the more productive and fun team meetings will be.

There are several ways in which team members and administrators can encourage the practicing of interpersonal behaviors or norms. First, all members can and should try to model desired social skills. Second, any team member may stop the group at any time to describe a needed behavior and ask the team members to perform it. For example, a member might say, "There seems to be a lot of interrupting. I think we need to slow down and listen more closely to what each of us has to say. How about if we observe a new norm—after someone finishes talking, we all count off 2 seconds in our heads and speak only after that amount of time has passed?" Another method is to establish group norms that are examined regularly and modified to meet the group's changing interpersonal dynamics. Among these norms should be a "policing" norm that sets an expectation that members will enforce all other norms immediately after a violation. Teams may wish to create and assign a specific role of "norm enforcer" to legitimize and guarantee attention to norm violations. Enforcement needs to become as consistent as possible and may require outside intervention, such as coaching by a supervisor, the arrangement of formal training in collaborative skills for all team members, or the establishment of collaboration as an *expected* and *inspected* job function. Perhaps the most effective way of encouraging practice is to target two or three specific collaborative skills for practice during each team meeting and to discuss at the meeting's end how often and how well members demonstrated the skills.

What Collaborative Skills Are Needed?

Interpersonal skills in trust building, communication, leadership, creative problem solving, decision making, and conflict management have been identified as important to the success of collaborative team efforts. Johnson and colleagues (1993, 1994) identified four levels of social skills that team members use at various stages of group development:

1. *Forming:* Initial trust-building skills needed to establish a collaborative team

2. *Functioning:* The communication and leadership skills that help manage and organize team activities so that tasks are completed and relationships are maintained

3. *Formulating:* Skills needed to stimulate creative problem solving and decision making and create deeper comprehension of unfamiliar information

4. *Fermenting:* Skills needed to manage controversy and conflicting opinions, search for more information (e.g., obtain technical assistance), and stimulate revision and refinement of solutions

Specific skills in each of these four categories are identified in Figure 1 and represent a composite of skill lists generated by members of collaborative teams across Vermont. This skill list is not meant to be exhaustive; it is meant to exemplify norms and social skills teachers have identified as important to group functioning. The list is presented as an assessment tool to assist teams in targeting skills for more intensive discussion, training, and practice. The instrument is constructed so that individual or team functioning may be rated by individual members or by the team as a whole.

Individuals on a collaborative team are at a variety of levels in their collaborative skills. It can be expected, however, that, in the beginning, newly established teams should focus on the *forming* skills, which 1) build trust and facilitate members' willingness to share their ideas, resources, and feelings; and 2) ensure that team members are present

Name: _____   Team name: _____

Directions for Individual Assessment

Reflect on your behavior while working as a member of your team. On a five-point scale (1 = I never do; 5 = I always do), rate yourself on the following skills. Select and place a star next to the two to four skills that you wish to improve.

Directions for Group Assessment

Reflect on your team's functioning. On a five-point scale (1 = We never do; 5 = We always do), rate your entire team on the following skills. Compare your ratings with those of your teammates and jointly select two to four skills to improve. Place an arrow next to the skills that your team has selected.

Forming Skills
(Trust building)

Self   Group

_____ I/We arrive at meetings on time.   _____
_____ I/We stay for the duration of the meeting.   _____
_____ I/We participate(d) in the establishment of the   _____
          group's goal.
_____ I/We share individual personal goals.   _____
_____ I/We encourage everyone to participate.   _____
_____ I/We use members' names.   _____
_____ I/We look at the speaker.   _____
_____ I/We do not use put-downs.   _____
_____ I/We use an appropriate voice volume and tone.   _____

Functioning Skills
(Communication and distributed leadership)

Self   Group

_____ I/We share ideas.   _____
_____ I/We share feelings when appropriate.   _____
_____ I/We share materials or resources.   _____
_____ I/We volunteer for roles that help the group   _____
          accomplish the task (e.g., timekeeper).
_____ I/We volunteer for roles that help to maintain a   _____
          harmonious working group (e.g., encourage
          everyone to participate).
_____ I/We clarify the purpose of the meeting.   _____
_____ I/We set or call attention to time limits.   _____

Figure I.   Individual and group assessment of collaboration skills.

(continued)

Figure 1.   *(continued)*

Functioning Skills *(continued)*
(Communication and distributed leadership)

Self   Group

_____ I/We offer suggestions on how to accomplish the   _____
task effectively.

_____ I/We ask for help, clarification, or technical assistance   _____
when needed.

_____ I/We praise team members' contributions.   _____

_____ I/We ask team members' opinions.   _____

_____ I/We use head nods, smiles, and other facial   _____
expressions to show interest and/or approval.

_____ I/We offer to explain or to clarify.   _____

_____ I/We paraphrase other team members' contributions.   _____

_____ I/We energize the group with humor, ideas, or   _____
enthusiasm when motivation is low.

_____ I/We relieve tension with humor.   _____

_____ I/We check for others' understanding of the concepts   _____
discussed.

_____ I/We summarize outcomes before moving to the next   _____
agenda item.

Formulating Skills
(Decision making and creative problem solving)

Self   Group

_____ I/We seek accuracy of information by adding to or   _____
questioning summaries.

_____ I/we seek elaboration by relating to familiar events   _____
or by asking how material is understood by others.

_____ I/We ask for additional information or the underlying   _____
rationale.

_____ I/We seek clever ways of remembering ideas and   _____
facts (e.g., posters, visual aids, notes, mnemonics,
public agendas)

_____ I/We ask other members why and how they are   _____
reasoning.

_____ I/We encourage the assigning of specific roles to   _____
facilitate better group functioning (e.g., process
observer).

_____ I/We ask for feedback in a nonconfrontational way.   _____

_____ I/We help to decide the next steps for the group.   _____

Figure I.   *(continued)*

Formulating Skills *(continued)*
(Decision making and creative problem solving)

Self   Group

_____   I/We diagnose group difficulties regarding tasks.   _____

_____   I/We diagnose group difficulties regarding   _____
         interpersonal problems.

_____   I/We encourage the generation and exploration of   _____
         multiple solutions to problems through the use of
         creative problem-solving strategies.

Fermenting Skills
(Conflict management)

Self   Group

_____   I/We communicate the rationale for ideas or   _____
         conclusions.

_____   I/We ask for justification of others' conclusions or ideas.   _____

_____   I/We extend or build on other members' ideas or   _____
         conclusions.

_____   I/We generate additional solutions or strategies.   _____

_____   I/We test the "reality" of solutions by planning and   _____
         by assessing the feasibility of their implementation.

_____   I/We see ideas from other people's perspectives.   _____

_____   I/We criticize ideas without criticizing people.   _____

_____   I/We distinguish differences of opinion when there is a   _____
         disagreement.

---

and oriented toward working together. As the team continues to meet, members need to practice their *functioning* skills. The most effective communication and leadership behaviors at this juncture are those that help team members send and receive information, stay on task, discover efficient work procedures, create a pleasant and friendly work atmosphere, and encourage team members to assume individual responsibility for effective teamwork rather than expect someone else (e.g., the principal, the specialist) to do it. The *formulating* skills allow for high-quality products and productivity. Teams will want to explore and receive training in specific models or methods of decision making and problem solving (Schein, 1987, 1999), such as brainstorming (Osborn, 1963) and Parnes's (1981, 1985, 1988) creative problem-solving (CPS) process. Performance of *fermenting* skills is evidence that collaborative team members have succeeded in recognizing controversy and conflict as opportunities to uncover divergent perspectives for the purpose of creating new and novel solutions. Individual team members' competence and confidence in handling conflicts increase as a function of a positive attitude toward and an appreciation for differences of opinion within the team.

What Do You Do with Dysfunctional Behaviors?

Few of us are ideal team members all of the time. Consequently, many people ask, "What do we do with disruptive or dysfunctional team members?" As a rule, dysfunctional behaviors that occur infrequently or in isolated situations may be ignored. Humor also may be used to lightly call attention to the behavior (e.g., "Rich, I guess you are really excited about this topic. Let's check in with other team members to find out what they think about it"). Finally, attention may be called to alternative desired behaviors. For example, Jackie frequently interrupts. Consequently, during processing time, Lu notes how Phyllis's and Andy's careful attention to others' statements allows them to elaborate or "piggyback" on ideas, which results in even better ideas.

When a team member's behavior becomes incessant and distracting to the group, direct confrontation should be initiated. Confrontation often is uncomfortable for both the confronter and the confrontee; yet, at times, it is needed. If it is judged that the individual who is going to receive the negative feedback will respond positively to the enforcement of group norms, any team member may initiate the feedback process. If it is judged that the individual will be embarrassed or angered or that the public feedback will escalate the individual's behavior, a supervisor or one of the team members who has a positive relationship with the individual should offer the feedback in private.

Corey and Corey (1997) and Kemp (1970) prescribed a five-step procedure for confronting a team member with regard to dysfunctional behavior:

1. Observe the team member's and others' responses.
2. Try to understand why the team member may be persisting in the behavior.
3. Describe to the team member the behavior and its impact on the team, using nonjudgmental language.
4. Establish some rules for minimizing future disruptions.
5. Turn the unfavorable behavior into a favorable one (e.g., assign an "aggressor" the role of devil's advocate for certain issues, have the "joker" open each meeting with a funny story, assign a "dominator" the role of "encourager" or "equalizer," have the person who often wanders off the topic signal whenever anyone gets off track).

Monitoring and Processing Group Functioning

The first assumption concerning the practice of interpersonal skills is that feedback from other team members is required for a person to learn a skill correctly. The designation of a specific time during team meetings to assess and discuss how well members are interacting is an important aspect of ensuring that the collaborative skills necessary for teams to cooperate are acknowledged, reinforced, and mastered by team members. One of the goals of a collaborative team is to help members become consciously aware of their behaviors in the team. It is not uncommon for team members to be unconscious or haphazard in their use of social skills. Processing heightens the awareness of effective behaviors and is intended to increase the number of times that team members perform these effective behaviors. It helps to ensure that the behaviors are engaged in consciously and deliberately.

Processing time is also needed for team members to assess and discuss other aspects of collaborative teaming—for example, to what extent goals or tasks were accomplished, how well members performed their designated roles, which actions of team members were helpful and which were unhelpful, and which actions need to continue or to change. Processing allows teams an opportunity to set goals for improving relationships and accomplishing tasks more effectively. It can be the most difficult component to incorporate into a team's regularly scheduled activities, however. This is particularly true for newly formed teams, which tend to be more task oriented than relationship oriented and which often actively resist giving up 5 or 10 minutes of meeting time to focus on maintaining relationships. Administrators can prompt and reinforce team processing by 1) modeling processing procedures at all collaborative team meetings that they attend; 2) establishing and clearly communicating a processing norm—that is, an expectation that teams include processing time in all meeting agendas; and 3) policing the norm by periodically dropping into team meetings or reading the meeting minutes.

Processing involves three main elements: 1) methods for observing and monitoring team members' behavior, 2) time to process, and 3) procedures for processing group functioning.

Methods for Observing and Monitoring Team Members' Behavior For team members to understand their effectiveness as a team, they need information about their own behaviors. Process observations are aimed at recording and describing members' behaviors as they occur during team activities. From the observed behavior of team members, an observer can make inferences about how the team members are relating to each other. One method for gathering observational data is to assign an observer role that rotates among team members from one meeting to the next. The observer may observe all or part of the meeting. The role of observer is difficult because it requires attention to both the tasks at hand and other members' interactions. It is vital, however, in achieving the goal of making all collaborative team members skillful participant observers who are capable at all times of simultaneously engaging in team activities and noticing how well members are interacting, even when they are not assigned the specific observer role.

Another way to gather information is to have an outside observer with monitoring and processing skills (e.g., an administrator, a member of the guidance staff, an educator skilled in cooperative group learning procedures) observe, record, and later provide feedback regarding targeted interpersonal skills or overall team functioning. A third way is to use both outside and inside observers. The following steps (Johnson & Johnson, 1999) are usually involved in process observations:

1. The team selects the collaborative skills (usually no more than two or three) to be observed.

2. The observer checks for understanding of the skills to be observed.

3. An observation form is prepared (see, e.g., Figure 2). The form specifies the skills to be observed and the name of each team member.

4. As the meeting progresses, the observer records on the observation form how frequently each team member performs the specified skills. The observer also keeps an anecdotal record of good examples of skill performance and other events that take place that should be shared with the team but do not fit into the categories being observed.

5. The observer summarizes the observations in writing.

Time to Process   Processing should occur at every team meeting. Five to ten minutes usually is a sufficient time period to conduct processing. Although processing usually occurs at the ends of meetings, we recommend also structuring a brief period halfway through a meeting to 1) cope with interpersonal problems that interfere with the group's functioning or 2) alter the agenda so that more time may be devoted to items that emerge as most important. An agenda should never be cast in stone. It is much better for team members to agree to focus on only one or two of the original agenda items than to come to a meeting's end and feel unsuccessful because they have failed to cover all of the agenda.

Collaborative skills	Names of team members					

Figure 2.   A generic observation form to be used by process observers during team meetings.

Procedures for Processing Group Functioning   When observers describe their observations, they are giving *feedback*. At least six steps (Johnson & Johnson, 1999) are involved in providing feedback:

1. The observer begins by asking team members how well they think they used collaborative skills.

2. The observer shows the observation sheet to team members.

3. The observer asks members to draw conclusions about what the observation data mean.

4. Team members present their own interpretations of their observed behaviors. The observer presents his or her summary of the observation information. Each member receives feedback.

5. The observer acknowledges members who used collaborative skills frequently and effectively by relating specific incidents such as, "Did you notice how often Julie summarized our discussions for us?" or "I heard members praising one another by saying things like. . . ." The observer also encourages other team members to make similar acknowledgments.

6. Team members make inferences from the observations about how well the group functions and publicly set individual and group goals for improving social skills and task performance at the next meeting.

In providing feedback, a number of rules regarding constructive criticism apply: 1) use team members' names and make eye contact with them; 2) avoid judgmental words such as *excellent* or *poor*; 3) use descriptive personal statements such as "I observed . . . ," or "I heard . . ."; and 4) be genuine—avoid giving false compliments or being unrealistically positive. Processing needs to be taken as seriously as accomplishing the team's tasks because the two are very much related. Processing also should be done in a variety of ways. Varying processing procedures keeps the activity vital and interesting to team members. Several processing methods are identified and described in Table 1.

Individual Accountability

Individual accountability exists when the performance of each group member is assessed individually to

1. Inform the group which members need more assistance or encouragement in completing their work

Table 1.   A sampling of processing procedures

Procedure	Definition	Examples
My accomplishment	An individual volunteers or is selected to state verbally what he or she did to help the team.	"I shared my opinions." "I told you how I felt."
Turn to your neighbor	In a round-robin, each member takes a turn complimenting the person to his or her left regarding a task or relationship-building behavior used in the group.	"You were an excellent timekeeper." "I appreciated your humor when things were getting tense."
Group share	As a whole group, team members discuss what they did well during their team meeting.	"We remembered to process midway through the meeting." "We all took turns speaking."
Communications work	Each member of the team quickly reports what he or she contributed to the group's work.	"I contacted the Chamber of Commerce and brought important information to the meeting."
Strength bombardment (oral)	One member of the team is selected and each member of the team tells that individual how he or she helped the team that day.	"You helped to generate multiple alternative solutions to our problem."
Strength bombardment (written)	Each member of the group writes his or her name on an index card. The cards are passed around and everyone comments in writing on one another's cards. Each card eventually returns to the person whose name appears on the card.	"John was early to the meeting." "John brought great refreshments." "John suggested ideas we really could use."
Checklists	Individuals score and share items on a checklist of 5–10 items. The items address behaviors the team has identified as important to their functioning.	1. I acknowledged others' ideas. 2. I used humor to relieve tension. 3. I helped clarify statements. 4. I encouraged others to speak.

(continued)

Table 1. *(continued)*

Procedure	Definition	Examples
Continua	Individuals react to a continuum for a series of statements and then share their perceptions.	1. I felt supported by the group. No Somewhat Yes 2. More than one person directed the group's work. No Somewhat Yes
Incomplete statements	Team members are given a sheet of paper that contains incomplete statements. The team members describe their performance by completing each statement.	"We could improve our team functioning by ..." "We are really good at ..."
Audio- or videotaping	The team meeting is audio- or videotaped. A single member, a subgroup, or the entire team views the tape. Instances and noninstances of selected behaviors are discussed.	"Watch this segment. You will see an example of body language that shows interest and support."
Role evaluation	Individuals and teammates describe how well each team member completed his or her assigned role.	"I used my noisemaker whenever I heard a jargon term." "You noted whenever someone made a 'yes, but' type of statement."
Outside observer	A person who is not a regular member of the team observes and shares observations with the team or individual team members.	"Mary checked to be sure everyone agreed before she recorded decisions." "During the first 15 minutes, Rich was silent."
Goal setting	Individuals or teams set goals for future behavior.	"I am going to praise others' contributions more." "We need to structure into our agenda time to celebrate."

2. Increase members' perceptions that their contributions to the group effort are identifiable and that they must fulfill their responsibilities in order for the group (and themselves) to be successful. (Johnson & Johnson, 1997, p. 400)

Methods of holding one another accountable are necessary to clarify each member's responsibilities, minimize freeloading or social loafing (Johnson & Johnson, 1997), and help members feel as if their efforts are valued. Regular monitoring and processing of collaborative skills ensure individuals' accountability for their interpersonal behaviors. The Collaborative Team Meeting Worksheet, displayed in Figure 3, has proved to be an effective tool for promoting individual accountability for meeting attendance and equitable distribution of work during and after meetings. The worksheet also ensures attention to the other elements of the collaborative teaming process (i.e., face-to-face interaction, positive interdependence, collaborative skill performance, processing).

A copy of this worksheet should be used by the team's recorder at each team meeting. In order to emphasize individual accountability for meeting attendance and *face-to-face interaction*, names of present, late, and absent members are recorded on the worksheet. Others who are not expected at the meeting but need to be informed of team outcomes (e.g., extended-team members, administrators) also are noted so that minutes may be forwarded to them. Accountability for *distributed leadership* and *positive role interdependence* is structured by having a place to assign roles. Roles may be task related (e.g., timekeeper, recorder), relationship oriented (e.g., encourager, observer), or roles that reinforce a team ethic of *parity* (e.g., equalizer, jargon buster). As indicated in the worksheet, roles are assigned in advance of the next meeting. This ensures that timekeepers, recorders, jargon busters, and others who need certain materials to carry out their roles are prepared for the next meeting. Advance role assignments also prompt team members to rotate roles from one meeting to the next.

Notice that the team is prompted to create the agenda for the next meeting before they disband. This ensures accountability for attendance because all members are alerted (at the meeting and through the minutes) to the date, location, purpose, and time of the next meeting. It also promotes *positive goal interdependence*. People take an interest in events and objectives that they themselves have helped to formulate; the process of jointly constructing a future meeting agenda therefore motivates people to participate in the next meeting.

Examination of the "Agenda" section of the worksheet in Figure 3 reveals that the following elements are incorporated into all meetings:

1. Time limits for every agenda item
2. A time to celebrate (the practice of positive reward interdependence)

Team Meeting Worksheet

People present: **Absentees:**   **Others who need to know:**
[*Note late arrivals*]

Roles: **This meeting:**   **Next meeting:**
  Timekeeper
  Recorder
  Equalizer
  Other: _____

Agenda

Items   Time limit
1. Positive comments   5 minutes
2.
3. Processing (task and relationship)   5 minutes
4.
5. Processing (task and relationship)   5 minutes

Minutes of Outcomes

Action items   Person(s) responsible: By when?
1. The way in which we
   will communicate
   outcomes to absent
   members and others
   who need to know is

   _____

2.
3.

Agenda Building for Next Meeting

Date: _____   Time: _____   Location: _____

Expected agenda items:
  1.
  2.
  3.
  4.
  5.

Figure 3.   Effective collaborative team meeting worksheet.

3. A time, at the midpoint and the end of the meeting, to process members' progress toward goal achievement and members' use of collaborative skills

The empty numbered spaces listed in the Agenda section of the worksheet (see Figure 3) represent the actual content of each meeting—the subtasks that contribute to the group's achievement of its overall goals. Although the agenda proposed at the end of a meeting guides the construction of the actual agenda, many events can occur between meetings. Consequently, the actual agenda items can and should be modified at the beginning of each meeting to reflect such intervening events. Furthermore, the agenda should be constructed and recorded publicly (rather than on the worksheet) in order to promote a feeling of positive goal interdependence among team members.

Some teams choose to keep process minutes—minutes that record the actual discussion that occurs during a meeting. All teams need to keep outcome minutes that specify homework assignments in the form of action items for individual team members. The Minutes of Outcomes section of the worksheet (see Figure 3) is intended to prompt equitable distribution of the work following a meeting and, in this way, promote *positive task interdependence.* One leadership function that concerns homework involves checking to be sure that everyone understands and agrees to perform their respective homework and action items. This leadership function may be performed by the recorder, or another team member may be assigned this role of checker. As indicated on the worksheet in Figure 3, one action item that must be attended to following all meetings is the communication of meeting events and outcomes to those who need to know but were not present. The team needs to decide how these communications will be delivered and who will deliver them.

The collaborative teaming meeting worksheet (see Figure 4) blends the meeting formats of several effective school-based collaborative teams in Vermont. We encourage readers to experiment with the worksheet and to modify and personalize it. Before making a change, however, readers should consider and discuss how the change might diminish or enhance the likelihood that team members will feel compelled to practice the critical elements of the collaborative teaming process.

CONCLUSIONS

This chapter first defines an effective collaborative team and then discusses a variety of strategies for promoting the five elements of a collab-

---

The "Are We Really a Team?" Worksheet

Directions: Circle the points to the right of each question only if *all* group members answer "yes" to the question. Tally the total number of points circled. The maximum score is 100 points.

	Points
1. Do we meet in a comfortable environment?	4
2. When we meet, do we arrange ourselves so that we can see each other's faces?	4
3. Is the size of our group manageable (e.g., 7 or fewer members)?	4
4. Do we have regularly scheduled meetings that are held at times and locations agreed on in advance by teammates?	3
5. Do needed members:	
a. Receive an invitation? (*Note:* Needed members may change from meeting to meeting based on the agenda items.)	2
b. Attend?	2
c. Arrive on time?	2
d. Stay until the end of the meeting?	2
6. Do we start our meetings on time?	3
7. Do we end our meetings on time?	3
8. Do we update tardy members at a break or following the meeting rather than stopping the meeting in midstream?	3
9. Do we have a communication system for:	
a. Absent members?	2
b. People who need to know about our decisions but who are not regular members of the team?	2
10. Have we publicly discussed the group's overall purpose?	3
11. Have we each stated what we need from the group to be able to work toward the group's goals?	3
12. Do we distribute leadership responsibility by rotating roles (e.g., recorder, timekeeper, encourager, facilitator)?	3
13. Have we established norms for behavior during meetings (e.g., all members participate, no "scapegoating")?	3
14. Do we explain the group's ground rules to new members?	3
15. Do we feel safe to express our genuine feelings (negative and positive) and to acknowledge conflict during meetings?	3
16. Do we consciously attempt to improve our communication skills (e.g., giving and receiving criticism, perspective taking, creative problem solving, conflict resolution) by	
a. Setting aside time to discuss our interactions and feelings	3
b. Developing a plan to improve our interactions next time we meet?	3
c. Arranging for training to improve our skills?	3

Figure 4.   A collaborative team meeting worksheet to be used during team meetings.

(continued)

Figure 4. *(continued)*

	Points
17. Do we use a structured agenda format that prescribes that we	
a. Have identified agenda items for a meeting at the prior meeting?	2
b. Set time limits for each agenda item?	2
c. Rotate leadership roles?	2
d. Devote time for positive comments and celebration?	2
e. Have public minutes?	2
f. Discuss group effectiveness in accomplishing tasks, communicating, abiding by ground rules, and coordinating actions?	2
18. Do we consciously identify the decision-making process (e.g., majority vote, consensus, unanimous decision) that we will use for making a particular decision?	3
19. Do we summarize the discussion of each topic before moving on to the next agenda item?	3
20. Do we refocus attention when the discussion strays from the agenda?	3
21. Do we generally accomplish the tasks on our agenda?	4
22. Do we distribute among ourselves the homework/action items?	4
23. Have we identified ways for "creating" time for meetings?	4
24. Do we have fun at our meetings?	4

Our score = _____   Total possible points = <u>100</u>

orative teaming process that personal experience and literature on school reform, collaborative consultation, group theory, and cooperative group learning suggest enhance team cohesion and productivity. Our hope is that the administrators, teachers, parents, and students who read this chapter will experiment with some of the strategies that are recommended here. To assist readers in getting started, we have constructed the questionnaire that appears in Figure 4. In recognition of the fact that simply calling a group a collaborative team in no way ensures that it in fact functions as one, the questionnaire is labeled the "Are We Really a Team?" worksheet. The questionnaire is intended to serve as both a review of the team-building strategies that this chapter presents and a tool for assessing a team's health. For team members to practice all of the items on the questionnaire simultaneously would be overwhelming. Therefore, we recommend that, after administering the questionnaire, team members select a few items on which to focus. We further advise teams to readminister the worksheet (see Figure 4) periodically so that they may celebrate their growth and target new collaborative processes for future growth.

What can administrators do to facilitate healthy collaborative teams? To answer this question, the readers are reminded of our description of a collaborative team as the adult analogue of a cooperative learning group. When teachers who use cooperative learning structures find that things are not working as they should, they take one or both of two courses of action. In all cases, they observe their groups, analyze the groups' functioning in relation to the critical elements of an effective cooperative group, and adjust to ensure that the desired elements are in place. Frequently, they also use the student groups to generate the solutions to their perceived problems. Administrators would do well to follow these teachers' lead—to remember that the trick in establishing and maintaining the health of school-based collaborative teams is to pay careful attention to the critical elements of an effective team and to trust the collective wisdom and creativity of team members.

REFERENCES

Appley, D.G., & Winder, A.E. (1977). An evolving definition of collaboration and some implications for the world of work. *Journal of Applied Behavioral Science, 13,* 279–291.

Benjamin, S. (1989). An ideascape for education: What futurists recommend. *Educational Leadership, 47*(1), 8–14.

Brandt, R. (1987). On cooperation in schools: A conversation with David and Roger Johnson. *Educational Leadership, 45*(3), 14–19.

Chalfant, J., Pysh, M., & Moultrie, R. (1979). Teacher assistance teams: A model for within building problem solving. *Learning Disability Quarterly, 2,* 85–96.

Corey, M.S., & Corey, G. (1997). *Groups: Process and practice* (5th ed.). Pacific Grove, CA: Brookes/Cole.

DeBevoise, W. (1986). Collaboration: Some principles of bridgework. *Educational Leadership, 43*(5), 14–19.

Duke, D., Showers, B., & Imber, M. (1980). Teachers and shared decision-making: The costs and benefits of involvement. *Educational Administration Quarterly, 16,* 93–106.

Falck, H. (1977). Interdisciplinary education and implications for social work practice. *Journal of Education for Social Work, 13*(2), 30–47.

Fishbaugh, M.S.E. (1997). *Models of collaboration.* Needham Heights, MA: Allyn & Bacon.

Friend, M.P., & Cook, L. (1996). *Interactions: Collaboration skills for school professionals* (2nd ed.). White Plains, NY: Addison Wesley Longman.

Fullan, M., & Pomfret, A. (1977). Research on curriculum and instruction implementation. *Review of Educational Research, 47,* 335–397.

Glasser, W. (1985). *Control theory.* New York: HarperCollins.

Glasser, W. (1986). *Control theory in the classroom.* New York: HarperCollins.

Glickman, C.D., Gordon, S.P., & Ross-Gordon, J.M. (1998). *Supervision of instruction: A developmental approach* (4th ed.). Needham Heights, MA: Allyn & Bacon.

Hamachek, D. (Speaker). (1981). *Self-concept dynamics and interpersonal processes* (Cassette Recording No. 5). Tulsa, OK: Affective House.

Hare, A.P. (1994). *Small group research: A handbook.* Greenwich, CT: Ablex Publishing Corp.

Hord, S.M. (1986). A synthesis of research on organizational collaboration. *Educational Leadership, 43*(5), 22–26.

Idol, L., Nevin, A.I., & Paolucci-Whitcomb, P. (1993). *Collaborative consultation* (2nd ed.). Austin, TX: PRO-ED.

Idol, L., Nevin, A.I., & Paolucci-Whitcomb, P. (1999). *Collaborative consultation* (3rd ed.). Austin, TX: PRO-ED.

Johnson, D.W. (1979). *Educational psychology.* Upper Saddle River, NJ: Prentice-Hall.

Johnson, D.W., & Johnson, F.P. (1997). *Joining together: Group theory and skills* (6th ed.). Needham Heights, MA: Allyn & Bacon.

Johnson, D.W., & Johnson, R.T. (1987). Research shows the benefit of adult cooperation. *Educational Leadership, 45*(3), 27–30.

Johnson, D.W., & Johnson, R.T. (1999). *Learning together and alone: Cooperative, competitive, and individualistic learning* (5th ed.). Needham Heights, MA: Allyn & Bacon.

Johnson, D.W., Johnson, R.T., & Holubec, E.J. (1993). *Circles of learning: Cooperation in the classroom* (4th ed.). Edina, MN: Interaction Book Co.

Johnson, D.W., Johnson, R.T., & Holubec, E.J. (1994). *The new circles of learning: Cooperation in the classroom and school.* Alexandria, VA: Association for Supervision and Curriculum Development.

Kemp, C.G. (1970). *Perspectives on the group process: A foundation for counseling with groups* (2nd ed.). Boston: Houghton Mifflin.

Lieberman, A. (1986). Collaborative work. *Educational Leadership, 45*(3), 4–8.

National Study on Inclusive Education. (1994). New York: City University of New York, National Center on Educational Restructuring and Inclusion.

National Study on Inclusive Education. (1995). New York: City University of New York, National Center on Educational Restructuring and Inclusion.

Nevin, A.I., Thousand, J.S., Paolucci-Whitcomb, P., & Villa, R.A. (1990). Collaborative consultation: Empowering public school personnel to provide heterogeneous schooling for all. *Journal of Educational and Psychological Consultation, 1*(1), 41–67.

Osborn, A.F. (1963). *Applied imagination: Principles and procedures of creative problem-solving* (3rd rev. ed.). New York: Scribner.

Parnes, S.J. (1981). *The magic of your mind.* Buffalo, NY: Creative Education Foundation/Bearly Limited.

Parnes, S.J. (1985). *A facilitating style of leadership.* Buffalo, NY: Creative Education Foundation.

Parnes, S.J. (1988). *Visionizing: State-of-the-art processes for encouraging innovative excellence.* East Aurora, NY: D.O.K. Publishers.

Parnes, S.J. (Speaker). (1989). *Creative problem-solving workshop with Sid Parnes* [Videotape]. Burlington: University of Vermont, Center for Developmental Disabilities.

Patterson, J.L., Purkey, S.C., & Parker, J.V. (1986). *Productive school systems for a nonrational world.* Alexandria, VA: Association for Supervision and Curriculum Development.

Pugach, M.C., & Johnson, L.J. (1995). *Collaborative practitioners, collaborative schools.* Denver: Love Publishing Co.

Quick, T.L. (1992). *Successful team building.* New York: AMACOM Books.

Rosenholtz, S., Bassler, O., & Hoover-Dempsey, C. (1985). *Organizational conditions of teacher learning* (NIE-G-83-0041). Urbana: University of Illinois.

Schein, E.H. (1987) *Process consultation: Vol. 1. Its role in organizational development.* Reading, MA: Addison Wesley Longman.

Schein, E.H. (1999). *Process consultation revisited: Building the helping relationship.* Reading, MA: Addison Wesley Longman.

Schlechty, P.C. (1990). *Schools for the 21st century: Leadership imperatives for educational reform.* San Francisco: Jossey-Bass.

Senge, P.M. (1990). *The fifth discipline: The art and practice of the learning organization.* New York: Doubleday/Currency.

Skrtic, T. (1987). The national inquiry into the future of education for students with special needs. *Counterpoint, 4*(7), 6.

Stainback, W.C., & Stainback, S.B. (Eds.).(1990). *Support networks for inclusive schooling: Interdependent integrated education.* Baltimore: Paul H. Brookes Publishing Co.

Thomas, C.C., Correa, V.I., & Morsink, C.V. (1995). *Interactive teaming: Consultation and collaboration in special programs* (2nd ed.). Upper Saddle River, NJ: Merrill.

Thousand, J.S. (1990). Organizational perspectives on teacher education and renewal: A conversation with Tom Skrtic. *Teacher Education and Special Education, 13,* 30–35.

Thousand, J.S., Fox, T., Reid, R., Godek, J., Williams, W., & Fox, W. (1986). *The homecoming model: Educating students who present intensive educational challenges within regular education environments* (Monograph No. 7-1). Burlington: University of Vermont, Center for Developmental Disabilities.

Thousand, J.S., & Villa, R.A. (1990a). Sharing expertise and responsibilities through teaching teams. In W.C. Stainback & S.B. Stainback (Eds.), *Support networks for inclusive schooling: Interdependent integrated education* (pp. 151–166). Baltimore: Paul H. Brookes Publishing Co.

Thousand, J.S., & Villa, R.A. (1990b). Strategies for educating learners with severe handicaps within their local home schools and communities. *Focus on Exceptional Children, 23*(3), 1–25.

Thousand, J.S., & Villa, R.A. (1992). Sharing expertise and responsibilities through teaching teams. In W.C. Stainback & S.B. Stainback (Eds.), *Support networks for inclusive schooling: Interdependent integrated education* (pp. 151–166). Baltimore: Paul H. Brookes Publishing Co.

Thousand, J.S., & Villa, R.A. (1995). Managing complex change toward inclusive schooling. In R.A. Villa & J.S. Thousand (Eds.), *Creating an inclusive school* (pp. 51–79). Alexandria, VA: Association for Supervision and Curriculum Development.

Thousand, J.S., Villa, R.A., Paolucci-Whitcomb, P., & Nevin, A.I. (1992). A rationale for collaborative consultation. In S.B. Stainback & W.C. Stainback (Eds.), *Controversial issues in special education: Divergent perspectives* (pp. 223–232). Needham Heights, MA: Allyn & Bacon.

Vandercook, T., & York, J. (1990). A team approach to program development and support. In W.C. Stainback & S.B. Stainback (Eds.), *Support networks for inclusive schooling: Integrated and interdependent education* (pp. 95–122). Baltimore: Paul H. Brookes Publishing Co.

Villa, R.A., & Thousand, J.S. (1990). Administrative supports to promote inclusive schooling. In W.C. Stainback & S.B. Stainback (Eds.), *Support networks for inclusive schooling: Integrated interdependent education* (pp. 201–218). Baltimore: Paul H. Brookes Publishing Co.

Villa, R.A., & Thousand, J.S. (Eds.). (1995). *Creating an inclusive school.* Alexandria, VA: Association for Supervision and Curriculum Development.

Villa, R.A., & Thousand, J.S. (1996). Student collaboration: An essential for curriculum delivery in the 21st century. In S.B. Stainback & W.C. Stainback (Eds.), *Inclusion: A guide for educators* (pp. 171–191). Baltimore: Paul H. Brookes Publishing Co.

Villa, R.A., Thousand, J.S., Nevin, A.I., & Malgeri, C. (1996). Instilling collaboration for inclusive schooling as a way of doing business in public education. *Remedial and Special Education, 17*(3), 169–181.

Villa, R.A., Thousand, J.S., Paolucci-Whitcomb, P., & Nevin, A.I. (1990). In search of a new paradigm for collaborative consultation. *Journal of Educational and Psychological Consultation, 1*(4), 279–292.

Wiggins, G.P. (1989). The futility of trying to teach everything of importance. *Educational Leadership, 47*(3), 44–59.

Chapter 11

Problem-Solving Methods to Facilitate Inclusive Education

Michael F. Giangreco, Chigee J. Cloninger, Ruth E. Dennis, and Susan W. Edelman

Inclusive education practices require people to work together to invent opportunities and solutions that maximize the learning experiences of all children. This chapter presents ways of planning, adapting, and implementing inclusive educational experiences for students of varying abilities. It is a how-to chapter that is based on the assumption that inclusive educational experiences are desirable for children with and without disabilities. As Giangreco and Putnam (1991) pointed out, when people use terms such as *inclusion*, they may mean different things. To assist readers to understand what we mean by *inclusive education* in this chapter, a five-point definition is presented in Table 1.

This chapter is adapted from Giangreco, M.F., Cloninger, C.J., Dennis, R.E., & Edelman, S.W. (1994). Problem-solving methods to facilitate inclusive education. In J.S. Thousand, R.A. Villa, & A.I. Nevin (Eds.), *Creativity and collaborative learning: A practical guide to empowering students and teachers* (pp. 321–346). Baltimore: Paul H. Brookes Publishing Co.; adapted by permission.

Table I.   Basic components of inclusive education

Inclusive education is in place when each of these five features occurs on an ongoing, daily basis.

1. *Heterogeneous Grouping*   All students are educated *together* in groups where the number of those with and without disabilities approximates the *natural proportion*. The premise is that "students develop most when in the physical, social, emotional, and intellectual presence of nonhandicapped persons in reasonable approximations to the natural proportions" (Brown et al., 1983, p. 17). Thus, in a class of 25 students, perhaps there is one student with significant disabilities, a couple of others with less significant disabilities, and many students without identified disabilities working at various levels.

2. *A Sense of Belonging to a Group*   All students are considered members of the class rather than visitors, guests, or outsiders. Within these groups, students who have disabilities are welcomed, as are students without disabilities.

3. *Shared Activities with Individualized Outcomes*   Students share educational experiences (e.g., lessons, labs, field studies, group learning) at the same time (Schnorr, 1990). Even though students are involved in the same activities, their learning objectives are individualized and, therefore, may be different. Students may have different objectives in the same curriculum area (e.g., language arts) during a shared activity. This is referred to as *multilevel instruction* (Campbell, Campbell, Collicott, Perner, & Stone, 1988; Collicott, 1991; Giangreco & Meyer, 1988; Giangreco & Putnam, 1991). Within a shared activity, a student also may have individualized objectives from a curriculum area (e.g., social skills) other than that on which other students are focused (e.g., science). This practice is referred to as *curriculum overlapping* (Giangreco & Meyer, 1988; Giangreco & Putnam, 1991).

4. *Use of Environments Frequented by Persons without Disabilities*   Shared educational experiences take place in environments predominantly frequented by people without disabilities (e.g., general education classroom, community worksites).

5. *A Balanced Educational Experience*   Inclusive education seeks an individualized balance between the academic/functional and social/personal aspects of schooling (Giangreco, 1992). For example, teachers in inclusion-oriented schools would be as concerned about students' self-image and social network as they would be about developing literacy competencies or learning vocational skills.

Inclusive education is in place only when all five features occur on an ongoing, daily basis.

An inclusive school, therefore, is "a place where everyone belongs, is accepted, supports, and is supported by his or her peers and other members of the school community in the course of having his or her educational needs met" (Stainback & Stainback, 1990, p. 3). It is designed to benefit everyone—students with varying characteristics (including those with disabilities) as well as teachers and other school personnel. Readers who are interested in the philosophical rationale for inclusive education are referred to the wide variety of resources available (e.g., Bauer & Shea, 1999; Hunt & Goetz, 1997; Lipsky & Gartner, 1997; McGregor & Vogelsberg, 1998; Stainback & Stainback, 1996; Villa & Thousand, 1995).

The remainder of this chapter is divided into six sections. The first section presents contextual information regarding the challenges associated with educating a diverse group of students in general education environments and activities. The second describes characteristics of effective problem solvers as well as the Osborn–Parnes Creative Problem-Solving (CPS) process. The third section delineates three variations of the CPS process that utilize the creative powers of children and adults to generate options for the inclusion of classmates with diverse needs. The fourth section offers suggestions for evaluating the impact of CPS strategies on the educational experiences of students, and the fifth and sixth sections discuss implications of using CPS in education.

CHALLENGE OF EDUCATING DIVERSE GROUPS IN HETEROGENEOUS GENERAL EDUCATION ENVIRONMENTS AND ACTIVITIES

> We can, whenever and wherever we choose, successfully teach all children whose schooling is of interest to us. We already know more than we need in order to do this. Whether we do it must finally depend on how we feel about the fact that we haven't done it so far. (Edmonds, 1979, p. 29)

Edmonds's (1979) comment reflects a vision of U.S. education that remains unfulfilled and acknowledges the challenges that schools face in realizing this vision. Table 2 contrasts major distinctions between traditional approaches of coping with students' diversity and more contemporary, inclusion-oriented approaches. These distinctions are presented in order to set a context—to highlight the assumptions and approaches that enable educators to meet the challenge of educating diverse groups of students in heterogeneous general education environments and activities more effectively.

It should be noted that even if educators embrace the inclusion-oriented educational tenets presented in Table 2, they still should and do have legitimate questions about *how* educational alternatives work and what the impact of these practices will be. Their questions include the following:

- How can I, as a teacher, accommodate such a wide array of student needs without sacrificing quality?

- Is it not a lot of pressure on one person—the teacher—to generate all of the accommodations that need to be made?

- How will the inclusion of students with diverse needs affect the social and academic outcomes of the other students?

Table 2. Approaches to educating students with diverse characteristics

Traditional approaches	Inclusion-oriented alternatives
The teacher is the instructional leader.	Collaborative teams share leadership.
Students learn from teachers, and teachers solve the problems.	Students and teachers learn from each other and solve problems together.
Students are purposely grouped by similar ability.	Students are purposely grouped by differing abilities.
Instruction is geared toward middle-achieving students.	Instruction is geared to match students at all levels of achievement.
Grade-level placement is considered synonymous with curricular content.	Grade-level placement and individual curricular content are independent of each other.
Instruction is often passive, competitve, didactic, and/or teacher-directed.	Instruction is active, creative, and collaborative among members of the classroom community.
People who provide instructional supports are located, or come *primarily* from, sources external to the classroom.	People who provide instructional supports are located, or come *primarily* from, sources internal to the classroom.
Some students do not "fit" in general education classes.	All students "fit" in general education classes.
Students who do not "fit in" are excluded from general classes and/or activities.	All students are included in general class activities.
The classroom teacher and general education team assume ownership for the education of general education students, and special education staff assume ownership for the education of students with special needs.	The classroom teacher and general education team (including special educators, related services staff, and families) assume ownership for educating all students attending the school.
Students are evaluated by common standards.	Students are evaluated by individually appropriate standards.
Students' success is achieved by meeting common standards.	The system of education is considered successful when it strives to meet each student's needs.

- How will the inclusion of students with diverse needs affect my capacity to provide a quality education to all of my students?

Research in North American schools has yielded sufficient evidence to convince us that the answers to these questions are positive, although much remains to be done. Specifically, our conclusions include the following:

- Diverse student *needs can be accommodated* within general class activities while a high-quality education is maintained for all students.

- The responsibility for developing accommodations can and should be *shared* among many members of the classroom community, including not only the adults within the school but also the students.

- Well-planned inclusion can have *positive* social and academic outcomes for students with and without disabilities.

- Teachers who choose to meet the challenge of educating diverse groups of students *improve* their teaching for the entire class (Hunt & Goetz, 1997; McGregor & Vogelsberg, 1998).

OSBORN–PARNES CREATIVE PROBLEM SOLVING AS A METHOD FOR INCLUDING STUDENTS WITH DIVERSE NEEDS IN THE CLASSROOM

The CPS process (Parnes, 1985, 1988, 1992, 1997) is one method for empowering teams of teachers and students to work together to meet the challenges of educating a heterogeneous school population. CPS is a generic strategy designed for addressing a variety of challenges and opportunities. The process was articulated first in 1953 by Osborn (1953/1993), the person who coined the term *brainstorming*. CPS was further developed by Osborn's protegé and colleague, Parnes, who promoted the use of CPS in many fields—advertising, product development, business, and education. Clearly, creativity is recognized as a valuable process and outcome in education and a necessary skill for professionals who must restructure schools to meet the changing needs of society. Within education, CPS historically was associated with the education of children labeled as gifted. Only since the late 1980s has CPS been applied to inclusion-oriented education issues. As a consequence, in the late 1990s people increasingly began recognizing that approaches to teaching students at opposite ends of the academic achievement continuum hold benefits for the multitude of children in between. What follows are some basic tenets of the Osborn–Parnes CPS process represented as characteristics of effective problem solvers.

Characteristics of Problem Solvers

To be optimally successful in using the CPS process, participants must exhibit certain behaviors and dispositions identified as characteristic of effective problem solvers. Six of these characteristics are described in this section:

1. Problem solvers believe everyone is creative and has the capacity to solve problems.
2. Problem solvers are optimistic.

3. Problem solvers alternate between divergent and convergent thinking.

4. Problem solvers actively defer and engage their judgment.

5. Problem solvers encourage "freewheeling" and fun.

6. Problem solvers take action.

Problem Solvers Believe Everyone Is Creative and Has the Capacity to Solve Problems   Everyone has heard statements such as "I'm not creative" or "I could never come up with those kinds of ideas." Many people limit the many useful ideas that they are capable of generating by minimizing their personal creative potential. The fact is that people use their creative problem-solving abilities constantly in daily life without even noticing it. Creative abilities are being used every time a person rearranges the furniture, makes a substitution in a recipe, improvises by using an object in place of an absent tool, adapts a game to play with a child, or plans a schedule.

In education, as in many other fields, people have been encouraged to believe that certain experts hold the key to special knowledge or creative solutions. As a result, there is a tendency to become unnecessarily dependent on outside consultants to solve problems while becoming increasingly less confident in one's own abilities in deference to others'. In contrast, this chapter's authors believe any group of people has the ability to solve the many challenges of inclusion-oriented schooling through the use of CPS. By working together, teams of people can identify solutions and take actions that no individual could accomplish alone. The practice of using CPS strategies within teams can enhance individual team members' personal growth and creative capacity in a broad range of situations.

The steps of CPS take advantage of the abilities that people already have and encourage people to emphasize and deliberately use their existing abilities to solve problems. Learning the basics of CPS is easy. People already know how to do most or all of what is needed, and they have been doing it naturally for all of their lives. The new learning comes in practicing the use of these existing skills in new and deliberate ways.

Problem Solvers Are Optimistic   CPS, or any other problem-solving method, is based on optimism. Problem solvers enter the process with the knowledge that every challenge they face *can* be solved, usually in more than one way.

Problem Solvers Alternate Between Divergent and Convergent Thinking   A central concept embedded in the Osborn–Parnes CPS process is that of actively alternating between divergent and convergent thinking. This means that at each stage of the

CPS process, there is a time to consider the challenge in broad, divergent ways and to be open to many possibilities. Then, within the same stage, the problem solver is encouraged to think convergently—to narrow the focus and make a choice from among the many possibilities, allowing the process to continue.

Problem Solvers Actively Defer and Engage Their Judgment   People frequently inhibit their creative abilities by prematurely engaging their judgment; in essence, they are generating ideas and attempting to evaluate them at the same time. Firestien (1989) likened this to driving a car with your feet on the brake and the gas pedal at the same time. Firestien's analogy points out that such an approach is unlikely to get anyone far. Effective problem solvers refrain from this practice and identify times to actively defer judgment and times to engage judgment purposefully. These times correspond with divergent and convergent thinking. In a divergent phase, judgment is actively deferred. In a convergent phase, judgment is purposefully engaged.

Problem Solvers Encourage Freewheeling and Fun   Having fun and being playful with ideas is crucial to effective problem solving. We might think of humor and playfulness as the oil that keeps the creativity engine lubricated and running smoothly. Creative insights as well as humor can be facilitated by bringing together elements that seem incongruent. Gary Larson's *The Far Side* cartoons are prime examples of incongruency that are both creative and humorous.

Sometimes it may be difficult for people to be playful when the challenges they face are serious; yet, playfulness is essential. During training workshops, we have observed teachers practicing the use of CPS in noneducation situations and doing an excellent job of being playful and having fun with their ideas. When the same teachers were asked to apply CPS skills to educational challenges, however, many reverted to old "school meeting behaviors" that were anything but fun and seriously interfered with their capacity to problem solve creatively. It is easy for people to fall back into familiar patterns and traditional group interactions. Therefore, when using CPS, it is critical to be mindful of this hazard and guard against it with collective playfulness. If people do not enjoy using CPS strategies, they are less likely to use them in the future.

Problem Solvers Take Action   Problem solvers extend the power of their optimism by acting on their ideas. Ideas that are generated do not have to be earth shattering or world changing. Some people do not use the ideas that they generate because they judge their ideas not good enough. Yet, as Osborn observed, "A fair idea put to use is better than a good idea kept on the polishing wheel" (cited in Parnes,

1988, p. 37). As people start to use CPS and get into new habits that accentuate their creative problem-solving abilities, they find themselves generating more and better ideas. The key is to act, not to wait for the perfect solution before taking action. Better ideas always may be implemented later if and when they are discovered.

STAGES OF THE OSBORN–PARNES CREATIVE PROBLEM-SOLVING PROCESS

The information regarding the six stages of the Osborn–Parnes CPS process presented in Table 3 and described on the following pages is based on descriptions of the process outlined by Osborn (1953/1993) and Parnes (1985, 1988, 1992, 1997) and insights gained from the authors' use of the process (Giangreco, 1993).

Developing creativity capabilities is a lifelong undertaking (Parnes, 1985, 1988) that should be thought of more as the development of a *creative attitude* than as the learning and application of specific steps and procedures. Thus, the Osborn–Parnes CPS process should be used as a springboard for inventing or personalizing CPS models and techniques. Some of the variations that we have developed to help with the challenges of school and community inclusion are highlighted in the next section. Cycling and recycling through the CPS process and its variations internalize the creative attitude and make creative problem solving a part of one's daily routine rather than an isolated tool used only in certain contexts (e.g., school versus home or family) or with certain problems (e.g., student versus systems change issues in education reform).

Stage I: Visionizing or Objective-Finding   Have you driven down the same road many times and later realized that there was something on that road you had not noticed before? The first stage of CPS helps one become increasingly aware of challenges and opportunities by *sharpening the powers of observation*. It prepares people to use all of their senses and perceptions to explore new possibilities and search for opportunities. The following rules or dispositions will help a problem solver at this stage:

- Think of objective-finding as a starting point or a general challenge.

- Think *divergently* by considering a variety of potential problems to solve. Remember to *defer judgment* and have fun.

- Expand possibilities and free yourself from real or perceived boundaries by imagining, wishing, dreaming, and fantasizing.

- Think *convergently* by focusing on one challenge that you really want to solve.

Table 3. Stages of the Osborn–Parnes Creative Problem-Solving process

Stage 1: Visionizing or Objective-Finding At this initial stage, the problem solvers heighten their awareness through imagining potential challenges. First, they are divergent, considering a variety of possible challenges. Then, they converge by selecting one to begin solving.

Stage 2: Fact-Finding Problem solvers gather as much information as possible about the selected challenge by using all of their perceptions and senses. By asking "who, what, where, when, why, and how" questions, problem solvers are divergent in considering multiple perspectives regarding the challenge. They finish this stage by identifying facts they believe to be most relevant to the challenge.

Stage 3: Problem-Finding The purpose of this stage is to clarify the challenge or problem by redefining it in new and different ways; by rephrasing the challenge as a question, "In what ways might I/we ... ?"; and by asking the question "Why?" or "What do I/we really want to accomplish?" This process is repeated until the problem solvers restate the problem in a way that makes the most sense and is most appealing to them.

Stage 4: Idea-Finding At this stage, the objective is to defer judgment while generating as many ideas as possible to potentially solve the challenge. Playfulness and wild ideas are encouraged. To come up with ideas beyond the obvious, problem solvers attempt to make new connections between ideas through analogies, manipulation of ideas (e.g., magnifying, minifying, reversing, eliminating), and hitchhiking (i.e., making new associations by building on someone else's idea).

Stage 5: Solution-Finding At this stage of the process, a variety of criteria are considered and ultimately selected for evaluating the merit of ideas. Problem solvers use the criteria to assist in selecting the best solution.

Stage 6: Acceptance-Finding The problem solvers refine the solutions to make them more workable. The objective is to turn ideas into action through the development and implementation of an action plan. Regular evaluation of the solution helps problem solvers discover new challenges and ways of addressing them as the action plan is carried out.

Based on Osborn (1953/1993) and Parnes (1985, 1988, 1992).

- Remember that challenges come in different sizes. Pick one that is small enough to be solved in the time available. By starting with manageable challenges, teams and individuals are more likely to experience success, develop a creative attitude, and practice and improve their creativity skills.

Stage 2: Fact-Finding The purpose of fact-finding is to identify and list as many facts about the challenge as team members can think of. There is an important relationship between facts and potential solutions. From obvious facts come obvious ideas; from less obvious facts come less obvious and possibly more inventive solutions. To start fact finding, set a relatively short time limit, such as 5–8 minutes. Fact-finding is a quick-paced, rapid-fire listing of what people believe to be true about the challenge situation. The facts should be presented briefly and *without* explanation, judgment, or discussion. In other words, use the approach of the fictional Joe Friday (the character from the famed television series *Dragnet* [Webb, 1952–1959/1967–1971]) and solicit "just the facts, ma'am, just the facts." Always record and save the list of facts for use later during the CPS process (e.g., during idea-finding). The following are tips for increasing the likelihood that all of the relevant facts emerge:

- Use all of your senses and perceptions to describe what you know about the challenge. Remember, facts can be feelings, so they may be listed also.

- Ask who, what, where, when, why, and how questions about what is and is not true of the challenge situation.

- Think divergently and defer judgment to generate a large quantity and variety of facts. If someone states an opinion with which you do not agree, do not dispute it; rather, accept it as that person's opinion (e.g., "Larry believes that students act out because they simply are bored during class").

- Stretch beyond the obvious facts.

- Ask yourself, "What does the challenge or the facts about the challenge remind me of?"

- Think convergently by selecting a subset of relevant facts to assist during problem finding in the next stage.

- Record and save the list of facts. These will be used again later in the process, especially during idea-finding.

Stage 3: Problem-Finding   Sometimes the initial selection of a challenge is right on target; at other times, the initial selection is just a starting point. The purpose of problem-finding is to clarify the challenge or the problem by considering different ways of viewing it. When rephrasing the challenge at this stage, it is helpful to state the challenge in positive terms by using the starter phrase, "In what ways might we . . . ?" and repeating the question until the team feels comfortable that it has teased out the real issues.

Next, be convergent and select one of the new challenge statements that the team agrees it wants to solve. Consensus may be prompted by asking team members a question such as, "Which of these challenges do we most desperately want to accomplish or solve?" Problem-finding is an important stage of CPS because, as John Dewey observed, "A problem well defined is half solved" (cited in Parnes, 1988, p. 72).

Stage 4: Idea-Finding   Ideas are potential solutions to the challenge statement selected at Stage 3. Where do these ideas come from? Central to idea-finding is *brainstorming* (Osborn, 1953/1993). Brainstorming is a divergent idea-generating process in which judgment or even praise is deferred in order to help problem solvers stretch beyond the obvious. Quantity is the key, because it is likely that the first ideas generated will be the same old ideas. It is important to keep the ideas flowing as quickly as possible and to limit sessions to 5–10 minutes. Good brainstorming sessions do not look anything like a typical group meeting; in brainstorming sessions, there is little quiet time and people speak in single words or short phrases rather than in sentences. Other important techniques to jar ideas loose are *forced relationships* (Parnes, 1988, p. 158), *synectics,* and *incubation.* These techniques are described briefly in the paragraphs that follow.

Forced relationships are achieved when two objects, ideas, or concepts that appear to have little or no relationship to each other are combined or rearranged in some way to generate a new idea to solve a problem. These new connections between apparently unlike entities are made by looking for similarities, analogies, metaphors, or other comparisons between characteristics of the two objects or ideas.

With regard to *synectics,* Gordon and Poze (1979) explained that learning occurs when people *make the strange familiar.* Creativity and invention, however, are facilitated when people *make the familiar strange.* Among the ways of making the familiar strange is to search for new ways of seeing the challenge and facts by *identifying new relationships* through paradoxes, analogies, metaphors, associations, and connections. (For more information, see Gordon [1987] and Gordon and Poze [1979].)

Incubation involves moving away from the challenge for a time to engage in different activities and returning to the challenge later.

As mentioned earlier, ideas also may emanate from facts. Thus, it is important to use facts from Stage 2 in conjunction with *idea joggers* by combining or manipulating facts or their dimensions. Idea joggers include questions such as, What would the situation look like if something (e.g., a fact about the situation) were 1) minified/made smaller, 2) magnified/made bigger, 3) rearranged, 4) eliminated, 5) reversed, or 6) turned upside down or inside out?

Idea joggers may involve *manipulating* dimensions of a fact; for example, if part of a problem situation is *visual* (e.g., In what ways might the school building or the classroom be improved in appearance?), applying idea joggers to visual dimensions such as color, shade, brightness, design, or contrast can generate ideas. Although facts can lead directly to ideas, theoretically the more idea joggers applied and combined, the more ideas that are likely to be generated.

Some ideas that are generated may be wild and unusable. These ideas have tremendous potential value, however, because other ideas may be spurred by them in a *hitchhiking* effect. For example, a class of first graders was presented with the forced relationship of a magazine photograph of a tropical beach scene and the challenge, "In what ways might we help our new classmate, Amy, feel welcome?" One student enthusiastically blurted out, "Let's take her to Bermuda!" The next student said, "I could play with her in the sandbox during recess." This student apparently hitchhiked on the previous idea by identifying similarities between the beach in Bermuda and facts she knew about the schoolyard (e.g., both have sand used for play) (Giangreco, 1993). Idea-finding concludes by focusing on promising ideas.

Stage 5: Solution-Finding   Solution-finding involves evaluating and selecting from the ideas generated in Stage 4. It begins divergently, with an individual or group considering a wide variety of potential criteria that might be used to evaluate the ideas. For example, ideas about potential accommodations for an individual student might be judged by the following criteria, framed as questions:

1. Is the accommodation feasible?

2. Is the accommodation time efficient for the teacher?

3. Does the student like the idea?

4. Will the accommodation likely enhance the image of the student among peers?

5. Is it consistent with the team's philosophical orientation or shared values?

6. Will the accommodation promote independence and responsibility rather than dependence and helplessness?

Next, the individual or team needs to converge on a subset of criteria and use them to evaluate the ideas. Selecting solutions can be facilitated by cross-referencing ideas and criteria arranged in a matrix. Ideas are listed along the side, and criteria are listed across the top. The matrix offers space to rate each idea based on each criterion. Rating may be as simple as a plus versus minus scoring system or as complex as a scale that weighs criteria differently. Remember, whichever scoring method is used, it is *not* intended to be a formula that removes decision-making power. Rather, the criteria and rating method are intended to provide a rational framework for considering the merits of each idea. Fundamentally, solution-finding is a convergent stage of the CPS process in which judgment is engaged to select or combine ideas for which a plan of action is then devised and implemented.

Stage 6: Acceptance-Finding   In acceptance-finding, the problem-solving task is to first think divergently by asking and answering who, what, where, when, why, and how questions in order to explore a variety of ways to make the selected solution(s) more workable and effective. The team then acts convergently, developing a step-by-step plan of action. The entire process ends with the problem solvers taking action and regularly evaluating the effectiveness of the selected solution(s). New challenges that arise during implementation may be viewed as *opportunities*—opportunities to cycle through the CPS process again, to invent yet more new solutions, to continue to develop a creative attitude and disposition, and to hone creativity skills.

VARIATIONS OF THE OSBORN–PARNES CREATIVE PROBLEM-SOLVING PROCESS THAT TAP STUDENTS' NATURAL CREATIVITY

This section describes three variations of the CPS process that have been field tested in some Vermont classrooms. The variations are dedicated specifically to developing ways of enhancing meaningful participation for class members when the group includes students with a wide range of abilities and characteristics. The variations focus on the challenge of including an individual student. Although this approach was successful as a starting point, users of the variations are encouraged to consider the challenge as the meaningful inclusion of all class members in the classroom community.

The variations described in this section tap the innate creative abilities of students. Although it may be preferable to teach children a complete problem-solving process (e.g., Eberle & Stanish, 1985), less complete variations have proved to be effective for on-the-fly classroom use. CPS variations work so well because people are by their nature creative; the variations simply "fill in the blanks" for steps missing from the creative processes each teacher develops on his or her own. It should be emphasized that CPS and its variations are generic tools for students to use to address—individually or in groups—a range of academic, social, or personal challenges other than those described in this chapter.

Heterogeneous Grouping and Inclusion-Oriented Education: A Prime Opportunity to Engage Creative Processes

Before detailing each of the three CPS variations, we would like to return to an examination of the context in which the variations are useful. We all know educators who look at students who have widely differing educational needs and use that observation to justify ability grouping within a classroom or the exclusion of some students from typical classes rather than determine in which ways students' uniqueness can be appreciated and supported. For problem solvers with an inclusive education orientation, placement in the classroom of students with widely differing educational needs is a naturally occurring incongruity or "forced relationship." Therefore, heterogeneous, inclusive classrooms offer a prime opportunity for many creative ideas and solutions to be developed and tried. Inclusive education and creative problem solving therefore are positively interdependent characteristics of effective schooling.

CPS and its variations work best if a *creative attitude, atmosphere, and culture* exist within the classroom and school community. An additional issue, therefore, in using CPS with and for children in schools is how to promote a culture of creativity so that students eventually identify and engage in creative problem-solving strategies even when they are not asked to do so. The following are some strategies that classroom teachers and administrators have used to establish more creative school cultures:

Establish and use a collaborative team approach in which members of the classroom and school community work together toward common goals (Thousand & Villa, 1992)

Be sure that adults model collaborative, open, creative, and problem-solving behaviors (e.g., deferring judgment) for students

Involve students in making important instructional decisions

Give students ongoing opportunities to solve important problems in an atmosphere in which their ideas are welcomed and acted on

Create opportunities for students to see that there can be more than one right answer to any problem or question

Create ongoing opportunities for learning to be active and fun

As adults, be ready, willing, and able to learn from students as well as from each other

Issues in Peer-Supported Problem Solving

Because the problem-solving strategies described in this chapter engage children in problem solving for a peer, concerns arise with regard to whether having classmates focus on a particular student unnecessarily draws negative attention to the student or otherwise infringes on the privacy and rights of that individual. Such concerns should always be considered seriously. Peer-supported problem solving can be a powerful and effective strategy if precautions designed to protect students' rights and dignity are observed. Specifically, educators should be sure to

Obtain *parental consent* and permission

Obtain *student consent* (Discuss in private the possibility of peer-supported problem solving with the student who will be the focus of discussion and seek feedback and approval before proceeding. For students with communication challenges, explore various observational strategies and augmentative approaches to determine their interest in involving peers in planning processes.)

Respect students' *privacy and confidentiality* needs (For some students, the type of personal information that may be revealed and used in problem solving with classmates may be nonthreatening; for other students, the same information may be considered extremely sensitive and private.)

Use CPS variations respectfully with *other* class members, regardless of whether they have a disability. This establishes the process as a *general* classroom tool for addressing daily challenges and building class community.

CPS Variation 1:
"One-Minute Idea-Finding," or "Ask the Kids"

The simplest and quickest variation used in inclusive classrooms is to have the teacher ask the students for their ideas, using the steps presented in Table 4. It is remarkable how many excellent ideas students generate when they simply are presented with information, a challenge, and a request for their ideas.

To illustrate the "Ask the Kids" variation, consider the experience of a class of third graders who are preparing a mural as a culminating activity of their social studies unit on cities:

> The teacher divided the class into four heterogeneous groups of five students each. One group included Betty, a girl with intensive educational needs. The teacher assigned each group a part of the city to paint or draw (e.g., downtown business area, residential neighborhoods, waterfront, industrial sites). Using cooperative group skills (Johnson, Johnson, & Holubec, 1993) that the class had practiced throughout the year, each group was asked to reach consensus about what would be included in their part and decide who would be responsible for each part. Each group

Table 4.   Steps in the "One-Minute Idea-Finding" or "Ask the Kids" strategy

Step 1.	*The teacher presents introductory lesson content or activity directions to the class.* This provides the students with some information about the challenge (i.e., fact-finding). They already know other general information about themselves and the classroom.
Step 2.	*The teacher presents a selected challenge to the class.* For example, a teacher might say, "We are going to be conducting a science experiment in small groups. In what ways can we make sure Molly (a student with educational challenges) is included in the activity?" This step combines objective-finding (CPS Stage 1) and problem-finding (Stage 3). An alternative phrasing that might be more inclusive and respectful would be to ask, "We are going to be conducting a science experiment in small groups. In what ways can we make sure that everyone in each group is included in the activity?"
Step 3.	*The teacher asks the students to offer their suggestions for 1 minute in an atmosphere of deferred judgment.* This is the idea-finding stage of the CPS process. The ideas may be recorded on the chalkboard or elsewhere.
Step 4.	*The class selects from the ideas generated the ones they wish to use.* This is the solution-finding stage of CPS.
Step 5.	*The students participate in the class activity and use their ideas.* This last step represents the acceptance-finding stage of CPS.

also had to coordinate with every other group so that, when finished, the four pieces could be joined to make a single large mural of a city to be displayed in the hallway. The teacher told the students that they should be prepared to explain what they did within and between groups and why.

The teacher then asked the class, "How can we make sure that Betty has ways to participate in this activity?" Mark said, "She's up there in her wheelchair, and we're here on the floor with this big paper. We could get her out of her chair and bring her down here with us." Karen suggested, "It's good for Betty to have her arms moved, and I know blue is her favorite color. I could help her hold and move the paint brush to paint the sky and water." Janet thought, "Betty could help carry our group's list of ideas to the other group so we can see how our parts will fit together." "Hey! That makes me think—maybe we could have Betty run the tape recorder so we can tape our list rather than writing it!" said Joe. (Giangreco, 1993, p. 122)

The key is to *ask* students for *their* ideas. So often we do not do so. This CPS variation is quick, easy, and effective but is limited for two reasons. First, students may come up short on ideas or, after using this strategy repeatedly, give "standard" answers rather than develop new, creative alternatives. Second, although student ideas may lead to meaningful inclusion of the classmate with disabilities, their suggestions may or may not address the individualized learning needs of the student. This represents a common problem in inclusion-oriented classrooms. A student may be welcomed and included, but individual learning objectives may not be adequately or deliberately addressed through participation in class activities. Despite its limitations, this

Table 5. Fact-finding backup procedure to Step 3 of "One-Minute Idea-Finding"

Step 3: The teacher asks the students to offer their suggestions for 1 minute in an atmosphere of deferred judgment (idea-finding). The ideas may be recorded on the chalkboard or elsewhere.

Fact-Finding Backup Procedures

3a.	If students do not answer, offer a very limited number of ideas or offer standard ideas—the teacher stops and has the students list facts about the activity and class.
3b.	The teacher encourages the students to search for ideas that may be spurred by looking at the facts.
3c.	If an insufficient number of ideas are generated by looking at direct relationships between the facts and ideas, idea-joggers can be applied to the facts to generate additional ideas.

simple variation is consistent with the notion of developing natural supports internal to a classroom and simultaneously facilitating inclusion and a culture of creativity.

CPS Variation 2:
"One-Minute Idea-Finding with a Fact-Finding Backup"

The "One-Minute Idea-Finding with Fact-Finding Backup" variation addresses the problem of students' getting stuck for ideas or giving standard solutions. The variation takes advantage of the relationship between facts and ideas. As previously noted, ideas can come directly from facts or "idea joggers" used to consider facts from new perspectives.

The steps of this variation parallel those of the first "One-Minute Idea-Finding" variation (see Table 4). The backup process occurs at Step 3, as outlined in Table 5. Using the previous example about Betty's participation in the social studies mural activity, Giangreco offered the following example of how a teacher might assist students to break through to new ideas:

> The teacher could say, "Okay, what do we know about this activity?" As the students use their powers of observation to fact-find, ideas might be spurred. The teacher could continue to facilitate idea-finding by asking probing, idea-jogging questions, such as, "What would happen if we took that fact and reversed it, cut it in half, or made it bigger?" Perhaps the teacher then would present an object as a *forced relationship* to stimulate the students to look for similarities, connections, analogies, or metaphors between the object and the challenge that might help solve the problem. Using these procedures, Andrea realized, "We need to get paper and paints from the supply room [fact-finding]; Betty could go to the supply room with us and help carry back the stuff we need and give it to the other kids" [idea-finding]. Marc added, "We'll be painting with a lot of different colors [fact-finding]. Hey, maybe Betty could use her switch to turn on

a fan. Then the paint would dry faster and we could do more painting" [idea-finding]. (1993, p. 123)

This variation is quick and addresses the issue of what to do if students get stuck for ideas. It does not, however, address the problem of inclusion-oriented classrooms mentioned previously—that is, a student being welcomed and included but individual learning objectives not being adequately or deliberately addressed.

CPS Variation 3:
"Get Some Help from SAM—A Good Friend"

The third variation was once called the "short-focused option" (Giangreco, 1993, p. 123) because the variation, being less extensive than the full CPS process, can be completed in a *short* period of time (i.e., less than 10 minutes) while *deliberately focusing on the individualized learning objectives* of a student. The deliberate attention on learning objectives distinguishes this third variation from the two described previously. The short-focused option, however, is not a friendly name; one colleague jokingly suggested renaming the variation "John." Another hitchhiked, saying, "Why not just a name?" Using the forced relationship technique in combination with metaphors and connections between a person's name and the short-focused option were explored. The name Sam came to mind because of a good friend named Sam. The short-focused option also could be considered a good friend in helping us to pursue quality, inclusive education. Thus, this variation was fondly renamed SAM. SAM is not an acronym for anything, although it could be (e.g., Short Accommodation Method, Super Adaptation Method, Sane Approach Method, Subversive Accommodation Mishaps, Sequential Adaptation Map, Supersonic Activity Maker, Sure-Fire Analog Miracle, Stimulating Amplification Method).

When to Call on SAM for Assistance   SAM may be called on prior to a lesson as a preplanning activity by the teacher or by a team (e.g., teacher and classroom assistant together, teacher and special educator together). When done in advance, the classroom teacher must have an idea of how the lesson or activity will be presented because SAM can assist in adapting the original plans to address a mismatch between the planned lesson and the needs of one or more students.

Certain types of activities (e.g., large-group discussions, small-group tasks, independent work, quizzes, labs) may be a consistent part of a classroom scene. If the activities are recurring formats, with variations in content, facts generated by observations of these activities may be useful in generating adaptation ideas for a *series* of similar situations. This avoids continually having to reinvent the wheel. For example, a series of options may be developed for each time a quiz is given, a lab experiment is planned, or a large-group lesson is implemented.

Examples: The Double-Edged Sword   Although examples are desirable because they can illustrate a process, they are included here with some hesitation. Any time an example is used, there always is the danger that it will become a standard response. The caution, therefore, is to remember that the examples offered here are not the *only* solutions. They may prompt piggybacking or hitchhiking ideas onto them, but clearly they are not the only usable ideas.

The examples embedded within the following steps are based on the student description presented next. As discussed previously, approaches that focus on the inclusionary challenges of an entire class rather than an individual student may be beneficial. In such instances, knowing the learning objectives for other students is necessary to use the SAM variation effectively.

Molly is 11 years old and attends fifth grade at Mountainview Middle School. Molly lives at home with her mom, dad, and younger brother. She is known for her lovely smile and her pleasant personality and is sought after for friendship by her classmates and the children who live in her neighborhood. Molly is considered stubborn and noncompliant by some people, but those who know her best view her simply as strong-willed. Molly enjoys using headphones to listen to many kinds of music. She likes going on almost any kind of outing with family or friends, especially shopping trips with her parents. Her favorite activities include playing on playground equipment, going swimming, playing with her dog, and sledding in the winter.

Molly seems to enjoy being around other people but does not always react as if she knows others are present. This may be due, in part, to the fact that Molly has some hearing and vision loss. Molly has some physical disabilities as well and no formal mode of communication. Thus, it is difficult to determine her sensory abilities precisely. Although Molly has been labeled as having intellectual delays, those who know her have been unwilling to accept any label that limits expectations of her abilities. As her dad pointed out, "We just can't be sure how much she understands or what her potential is, so let's proceed as if she understands everything!"

Currently, Molly communicates primarily through facial expressions (e.g., smiling, frowning). She makes some sounds that family members understand to represent pleasure or discomfort. Her parents have pointed out that they would expect few other people to understand the meaning of these vocalizations unless their meaning had been explained previously. People communicate with Molly by speaking (to take advantage of her residual hearing), using gestures, and showing her objects and pictures (to accommodate for her visual impairments).

Molly gets from place to place by having others push her wheelchair. Molly has limited use of her arms and needs at least partial assistance with most daily activities. Her favorite foods are tacos, fruit, and pizza; she needs to have these and other foods cut into small pieces and fed to her. Molly, her teacher, the classroom assistant who supports her, classmates, and family members receive the support of an integration specialist (special educator), occupational therapist, physical therapist, speech-language pathologist, and deafblindness specialist.

Steps in Using SAM   Before getting assistance from SAM, it is important to become familiar enough with the basic principles of CPS (e.g., alternating between divergent and convergent thinking, deferring judgment, using idea joggers) and characteristics of problem solvers previously discussed in this chapter to apply them throughout the SAM process. The steps of SAM presented here parallel the six stages of the generic CPS process.

Step 1: Identify the Challenge and Develop a Challenge Statement: SAM starts by identifying a class, activity, or situation in which the needs of a particular student differ significantly from the range of educational needs of other students. For example, Molly, described earlier, attends a fifth-grade science class in which much of the curricular content appears not to match her individual educational needs. Yet, there are many opportunities for Molly's educational needs to be met through existing class activities if the activities are adapted slightly or if new science activities are invented.

Next, a challenge statement is developed. Figure 1 offers a worksheet format for getting assistance from SAM. As Figure 2 illustrates, with the SAM variation of CPS, objective-finding and problem-finding have been combined into a single challenge statement. The challenge statement, "In what ways might we address the educational needs of [*insert student name*] in [*insert name of class or activity*] class or activity?" is applied to the student and the situation to become, for example, "In which ways might we address the educational needs of Molly in science class?"

Step 2: Identify the Facts About the Student's Educational Needs and the Class or Activity: The lefthand column of Figure 1 is used to list facts about the student's program and educational needs. Student facts include a brief description of priority individualized education program (IEP) goals, desired learning outcomes beyond IEP priorities, and the general supports necessary to successfully participate in the educational program. As the lefthand column of Figure 2 shows, the following are Molly's priority learning outcomes:

Make choices when presented with options.

Greet others.

Follow instructions.

React to people by displaying an observable change in behavior.

OBJECTIVE-FINDING
AND PROBLEM-FINDING: In what ways might we address the educational needs of _____ in _____ ?
(student's name)   (class/activity)

FACT-FINDING		IDEA-FINDING	
Facts about student's needs 1	Facts about class/activity 2	Direct ideas 3	Indirect ideas 4

Figure I. SAM creative problem-solving worksheet. (Based on Osborn–Parnes Creative Problem-Solving process [Parnes, 1985, 1988, 1992, 1997].)

313

Figure I. *(continued)*

SOLUTION-FINDING

Potential Ideas	Criteria				
	Addresses student need	Neutral or positive for students without disabilities	Likely to support valued life outcomes	Perceived as usable by users (e.g., teacher)	Other: ___ ___ ___
1.					
2.					
3.					
4.					
5.					
6.					
7.					
8.					
9.					
10.					
11.					
12.					

ACCEPTANCE-FINDING

What needs to be done?

Who is going to do it?

When is it going to be done?

Where will it be done?

How can the ideas be improved?

Offer assistance to others.

Engage in active leisure with others (e.g., play group games).

Use adapted microswitch to activate battery-operated devices.

Do a classroom job with peer(s).

This is only a *partial* listing of all of the learning outcomes generated by Molly's support team, which includes her parents.

In the second column of the SAM worksheet (Figures 1 and 2), observations about the class or activity may be listed. These facts should include what the teacher and students actually do (e.g., teacher shows a videotape, class plays an educational game, students draw diagrams, groups of students build a model). To gain accurate information about a class may require one or more members of a student's support team to observe in the classroom. In Molly's situation, it is more crucial to identify what the teacher and students *do* than to identify the curricular content of the general education lesson. Thus, no observed event is insignificant, because any activity may prove to be useful in either prompting or being an idea for adapting a lesson. For example, which adaptations or accommodations for Molly do the facts about science class (see Figure 2) bring to mind?[1]

Before the bell rings, the teacher and students *greet* each other and talk informally.

Students hand in their homework by leaving it in a box on the teacher's desk.

A *student turns off the lights* before a film is shown.

The *teacher* passes out the quiz.

Remember, when facing curriculum overlapping challenges, the nature of activity in a classroom is more important to developing adaptations than the actual lesson content is. When classroom approaches are primarily passive and teacher directed, opportunities for meaningful

---

[1]The SAM worksheet presented in Figure 1 is meant to offer a format to facilitate systematic exploration of possibilities at each step of the SAM process. The authors acknowledge that the SAM form has limited space and likely will be insufficient for all of the ideas that will be generated. It may be easier, therefore, to simply have the form available as a reminder of the SAM process and to write ideas as lists on blank sheets of paper. SAM users also are encouraged to modify or develop their own SAM worksheet formats and share them with the authors.

OBJECTIVE-FINDING
AND PROBLEM-FINDING:

In what ways might we address the educational needs of ___Molly___ in ___Science___ ?

(student's name) (class/activity)

FACT-FINDING		IDEA-FINDING	
Facts about student's needs 1	Facts about class/activity (partial listing)	Direct Ideas (partial³ listing)	Indirect Ideas (partial⁴ listing)
1. Makes choices	1. Students greet each other and teacher before class bell rings.	Teach/practice greeting before bell rings.	Student chooses which game to play.
2. Greets others	2. Students hand in homework to box on teacher's desk.	Work on active leisure (game skills) during educational games and instruction following.	Student gets opportunity to react to classmates by having "homework box" on her desk.
3. Follows instructions	3. Teacher tells students agenda for class.		
4. Reacts to people	4. Teacher turns off lights and shows short video.	Caring for class pets with a peer may be a class-room job.	Student offers assistance to others and gets opportunities to react by handing out quizzes.
5. Offers assistance	5. Teacher assigns small groups to play educational games to reinforce video.		
6. Engages in active leisure	6. Teacher passes out quiz.		Student uses switch to activate TV/VCR and listen to music when adapted quiz is completed.
7. Uses "switch"	7. Some students who finish early feed class fish and gerbils.		
8. Does classroom job with peer(s)			

Figure 2. SAM creative problem-solving worksheets completed for Molly.

Figure 2. *(continued)*

SOLUTION-FINDING *(partial listing)* Potential Ideas	Criteria				
	Addresses student need	Neutral or positive for students without disabilities	Likely to support valued life outcomes	Perceived as usable by users (e.g., teacher)	Other: ___ ___ ___
1. Student chooses game	+	+	+	+	
2. Homework box on desk	+	+	+	+	
3. Hand out quizzes	+	+	+	+	
4. Switch for lights	+	+	+	—	
5. Switch for TV/VCR	+	+	+	—	
6. Switch for tape player	+	+	+	+	
7. Greeting before class	+	+	+	+	
8. Cares for class pets	+	+	+	+	
9. Plays educational games	+	+	+	+	
10. Grades quizzes with key	+	—	—	—	
11. Record and play tape of class agenda	+	+	+	—	
12.					

ACCEPTANCE-FINDING

What needs to be done?

Who is going to do it?

When is it going to be done?

Where will it be done?

How can the ideas be improved?

participation for curriculum overlapping are more limited. When classroom approaches are active and participatory, opportunities for meaningful participation expand. A goal of creative problem solving, therefore, is to increase teachers' use of more active and participatory instruction approaches.[2]

Step 3: Generate Direct and Indirect Ideas: A first level of idea-finding involves a systematic comparison of each fact about the student (see the first column in Figure 2) with each fact about the class or activity (see the second column in Figure 2) to look for direct, obvious relationships. Any direct ideas that arise through this comparison are recorded in the third column of Figure 2, labeled Direct Ideas. Given 8–10 facts in each of the two fact columns, the comparison process should take no more than a few minutes.

Let us compare the facts about Molly and her class listed in Figure 2. It is immediately apparent that there is a direct relationship between the second fact in Column 1 (i.e., greets others) and the first fact in Column 2 (i.e., students greet each other and the teacher before the bell rings). This class appears to offer a natural time to teach and practice greetings. Notice also that Molly's goal of participating in active leisure with peers relates directly to the teacher's planned activity for students to play educational games. Their activity is a natural opportunity for Molly to follow instruction related to game playing (e.g., rolling dice, picking up cards, moving a marker). Another direct relationship exists between Molly's need for doing a classroom job and the activity of feeding and caring for the classroom fish and gerbils. Clearly, caring for the classroom animals could be a class job done with a classmate.

Systematically comparing facts about a student's needs and classroom routines may reveal that naturally occurring opportunities for meaningful inclusion already exist, without the need for significant changes in routine. The number of such opportunities, however, may be insufficient for an educational experience of adequate quality; there-

---

[2]Information about the student may come from any of several sources. If using COACH (Giangreco, Cloninger, & Iverson, 1998), this information may come from one of three sources: 1) the Program-at-a-Glance, 2) the Scheduling Matrix, or 3) the student's schedule. A Program-at-a-Glance lists a full set of facts regarding the content of the student's educational program. A Scheduling Matrix provides a set of facts as they relate to particular classes or major class activities. Both identify priority objectives for a student, other anticipated learning outcomes, and general supports the child's team has decided are needed for student participation in classes. SAM has been pilot tested in environments where COACH was used to generate information about the focus student. Of course, information about a student may be generated or collected in many other ways, directly (e.g., direct observation) and indirectly (e.g., record review and interviews with the student, family members, friends, school personnel).

fore, it may be necessary to invent adaptations to existing routines or invent completely new experiences.[3]

After identifying direct ideas, it may be necessary to look for *indirect ideas* by applying idea joggers to facts. Following the same pattern used to find direct ideas, facts about the student and facts about the class or activity are compared while applying an idea jogger (e.g., ask, "What would happen if we eliminated this fact or made it bigger or smaller?"). At this point, it is critical to defer judgment about the quality, usefulness, or feasibility of the ideas that result. For example, suppose the idea jogger of *reversing* were applied to the facts in Figure 2. The teacher intends to assign small groups to play educational games to reinforce content presented in the videotape. By reversing who chooses the game from teacher to student, an idea is generated for Molly to work on choice making, a priority goal for her (see Column 4 of Figure 2).

Suppose the idea jogger of *rearranging* were applied to Molly's goal of reacting to the presence of other people and the fact that, in this science class, students hand in homework by placing it in a box on the teacher's desk. Rearranging the place where homework is turned in so that the homework box is on Molly's desk would create as many opportunities for interaction as there are students in the class.

Combining *rearranging* with the idea jogger of *minifying/making smaller* and applying them to the fact that the science teacher passes out quizzes and Molly needs practice in reacting to and offering assistance to others could lead to the indirect idea of having Molly and a classmate, rather than the teacher, pass out quizzes. To keep the pace of classroom activities typical, the task could be made smaller so that Molly hands out 5 quizzes in the same time that her partner hands out 20. Although all of the ideas just described may seem small, they do match the student's identified needs.

Step 4: Evaluate Ideas and Choose Solutions: Step 4 involves solution-finding and convergent thinking. In this step, direct and indirect ideas are evaluated based on a set of criteria. The four criteria on the SAM worksheet (see Figures 1 and 2) are offered as starting points for evaluating ideas. Ideas are listed in abbreviated form in the lefthand column of the SAM worksheet (see Figures 1 and 2), then each idea is judged according to the selected criteria. Using the four criteria included on the worksheet, one may ask:

---

[3]Although the two fact-finding and idea-finding steps are presented here in a linear, sequential fashion, we have found shifting attention back and forth between the two sets of facts to be a powerful technique for prompting ideas for adaptations. For example, once educational needs are listed, each new class/activity fact can be compared with the needs to see if an idea is immediately spurred. These ideas should be recorded as they are generated.

Does this idea address an identified student need?

Is the idea positive or at least neutral in terms of its likely impact on students without disabilities?

Is the idea likely to yield valued life outcomes (e.g., friendships and affiliations; access to meaningful places and activities; choice and control that match a person's age, health, and safety)?

Is the idea perceived as feasible and meaningful by the user (e.g., the teacher)?

As already noted, the process of applying criteria to potential ideas is intended to assist with decision making. Criteria therefore must match the situation and be adjusted, replaced, eliminated, or otherwise changed to match the unique characteristics of a situation. Items may be rated by using whichever method is preferred and makes sense, as long as preferred solutions have been selected by the end of this step.

Step 5: Refine Ideas to Develop and Carry Out an Action Plan: Once solutions have been selected, they must be refined. Idea joggers continue to be helpful in accomplishing this end. For example, suppose that a direct idea is generated about playing an educational game as an accommodation for Molly. When looking carefully at the nature of the game, Molly's physical characteristics likely would prompt the question, "What if the game parts were bigger?" This type of simple adaptation might allow Molly to participate, at least partially, with game materials. The "who, what, where, when, why, and how" questions facilitate the development and delivery of a CPS action plan. As ideas are implemented, CPS users must remember to be alert to new facts and new ways to make the familiar strange. Also, it should be noted how repeatedly cycling through the SAM and other CPS variations develops a creative attitude and competence.

EVALUATING THE IMPACT OF USING OSBORN–PARNES CREATIVE PROBLEM-SOLVING PROCESS WITH REGARD TO STUDENTS' EDUCATIONAL EXPERIENCES

For any educational innovation, it is crucial to evaluate the innovation to determine whether it is achieving its intended outcomes. The use of CPS is intended, at a minimum, to 1) increase the frequency and quality of instructional involvement within heterogeneous groups, 2) meet the educational needs of the student with disabilities, 3) meet the educational needs of students without disabilities, and 4) provide support mechanisms and teaching adaptations for the teacher and other mem-

Evaluation of Intervention Impact on Inclusion: ____ PRE or ____ POST

Student name _____ Grade/placement _____

Lesson/activity _____

Lesson/activity time of day _____ Length of lesson/activity _____

Observation dates: from _____ to _____ Number of observations _____

Teacher(s) of the lesson/activity _____

Name of respondent _____
Describe the extent of involvement (e.g., how, what) for the student with special needs

in the lesson/activity: _____

_____

_____

Average number of minutes of participation: ____ min out of a total of ____ possible
  minutes
Average number of opportunities/turns for participation per lesson: _____
Compared to classmates, the time and opportunities for participation by this student
  typically are:

___ significantly less   ___ slightly less   ___ about the same   ___ more

Based on your observations of the lesson/activity prior to _____ (list
  intervention):
1. How involved was the student in the lesson/activity?
   Not involved   Very involved
     1   2   3   4   5   6   7   8   9   10
   Comments:

2. How much did the student benefit educationally (based on his/her individual
   educational program) from participation in the lesson/activity?
   Not at all   Very much
     1   2   3   4   5   6   7   8   9   10
   Comments:

3. Did you have a clear idea which of the student's individual goals and objectives
   could be addressed during this lesson/activity?
   Not at all clear   Very clear
     1   2   3   4   5   6   7   8   9   10
   Comments:

4. Did you have enough usable instructional ideas to include the student with special
   needs in meaningful ways during this lesson/activity?
   Insufficient number   More than sufficient number
     1   2   3   4   5   6   7   8   9   10
   Comments: _____

(continued)

Figure 3.   CPS Impact Evaluation. (From Giangreco, M.F. [1993]. Using creative problem-solving methods to include students with severe disabilities in general education classroom activities. *Journal of Educational and Psychological Consultation, 4*, 131–132; reprinted by permission of Lawrence Erlbaum Associates.)

Figure 3. *(continued)*

5. Did you use an identifiable method to develop ways of including the student with special educational needs in this lesson/activity?

No identifiable method   Clearly identifiable method

 1   2   3   4   5   6   7   8   9   10

Comments:

6. What impact did the methods used to include the student with special needs (not the presence of the student) in this lesson/activity have on the educational growth (academic/social) of other students?

Negative impact   Positive impact

 1   2   3   4   5   6   7   8   9   10

Comments:

7. How confident are you that the methods used to include the student with special needs in this lesson/activity can be generalized to other lessons in the same content area and/or other content areas to more fully include this student?

Not confident   Very confident

 1   2   3   4   5   6   7   8   9   10

Comments:

8. To what extent did the methods used to include the student with special needs lead to improved valued life outcomes (VLO) for the student (e.g., affected relationships with others; expanded access to settings and activities; improved health/safety; offered choice or control)?

Did not improve VLO at all   Improved VLO significantly

 1   2   3   4   5   6   7   8   9   10

Comments:

9. Overall, how satisfied are you with the current extent and quality of involvement of this student in the lesson/activity?

Not satisfied   Very satisfied

 1   2   3   4   5   6   7   8   9   10

Comments:

---

bers of the classroom community. Measurement techniques, such as frequency counts, time samples, and item-by-item ratings of specific target behaviors, may answer certain evaluation questions. Teachers, however, may find more user-friendly (Meyer & Janney, 1989, p. 263) forms of measurement useful to augment more-traditional approaches, such as the CPS Impact Evaluation offered in Figure 3.

A teacher may complete the CPS Impact Evaluation form before and after using CPS and its variations in a classroom. Direct observations of a student in the class, combined with the preintervention use of the evaluation, give a quick overview of the situation without interfering with instruction or taking an inordinate amount of time. Once CPS strategies have been applied for a sufficient amount of time, the teacher may again use the CPS Impact Evaluation form as a postintervention measure. Comparison of pre–post responses offers a relatively simple and quick assessment of the perceived impact of the use of CPS.

Clearly, this type of evaluation may not yield reliable responses across team members (e.g., teacher, parents, students, special educator, principal). When team members who have independently completed the evaluation form disagree on pre- or postassessments, the tool serves another function—it prompts team members to engage in a dialogue, which should facilitate a collective understanding of educational programs, a shared framework for adjusting instruction, and improved teamwork.

EDUCATIONAL IMPLICATIONS OF USING THE OSBORN–PARNES CREATIVE PROBLEM-SOLVING PROCESS

This chapter opens with the proposition that inclusive education arrangements are desired alternatives to more exclusionary traditional approaches. The Osborn–Parnes CPS process and its variations are offered as a set of procedures for empowering teams to meet the challenge of meaningfully instructing heterogeneous groups of learners.

There are many implications of mastering and using CPS and its variations, particularly in the education of students who otherwise might be excluded from general education opportunities. Table 6 offers anticipated benefits for students with disabilities and their peers without disabilities; Table 7 suggests positive outcomes that educators should expect when they use the problem-solving methods described in this chapter.

Table 6.   Implications of using CPS for students with and without disabilities

CPS engages students in the solution of real-life problems and challenges, which are an essential characteristic of effective education (Dewey, 1938/1998).

CPS encourages students to believe they can solve problems, either independently or with the support of others in the class.

CPS offers students at all levels of academic achievement the opportunity to assist in solving relevant challenges faced by them or their classmates and establishes all students as valued contributors.

CPS offers opportunities for students to be included in general class activities in ways that meet their individualized educational needs.

CPS offers opportunities for students to learn and practice problem-solving skills on an ongoing basis to address relevant challenges.

The collaborative, nonjudgmental, and action-oriented aspects of CPS encourage a sense of community building among classmates when the process is used to address challenges that are of concern to the group.

CPS can encourage and reinforce many desirable academic and affective skills (e.g., observation, analysis, evaluation, perspective taking, building on another's ideas, synthesizing ideas).

Table 7.   Implications for professionals working with students in heterogeneous groups

CPS encourages teachers to be open to the possibility that there is more than one "right" answer.

CPS encourages teachers to provide the kinds of active, problem-solving learning experiences that educational leaders have advised us are essential now and will be increasingly vital as we enter the 21st century.

CPS encourages teachers to be ongoing learners and especially to open themselves to learn from the children in their classes.

CPS provides a method for distributing the pressures of instructional accommodations in inclusive classrooms across a wider group of problem solvers.

CPS used by teachers can enhance their capacity to teach all children by recognizing existing options for teaching heterogeneous groups, adapting other existing options, and inventing new options.

CPS encourages teachers to design interesting, active approaches to education that account for student input and result in motivating learning experiences.

Taking action is the first, middle, and culminating step for any problem solver, including those of us who are interested in excellence, excitement, and equity in education. We would do well, therefore, to follow the advice of Kettering to "keep on going and chances are you will stumble on something, perhaps when you least expect it. I have never heard of anyone stumbling on something sitting down" (cited in Parnes, 1988, p. 89). The CPS strategies offered in this chapter should help us to keep on going, for, as Cheyette noted, "creativity is converting wishful thinking into willful doing" (cited in Parnes, 1988, p. 105).

REFERENCES

Bauer, A.M., & Shea, T.M. (1999). *Inclusion 101: How to teach all learners.* Baltimore: Paul H. Brookes Publishing Co.

Brown, L., Ford, A., Nisbet, J.A., Sweet, M., Donnellan, A., & Gruenewald, L. (1983). Opportunities available when severely handicapped students attend chronological age appropriate regular schools. *Journal of The Association for Persons with Severe Handicaps, 8,* 16–24.

Campbell, C., Campbell, S., Collicott, J., Perner, D., & Stone, J. (1988). Individualized instruction. *Education New Brunswick, 3,* 17–20.

Collicott, J. (1991). Implementing multi-level instruction: Strategies for classroom teachers. In G. Porter & D. Richler (Eds.), *Changing Canadian schools: Perspectives on disability and inclusion* (pp. 191–218). Downsview, Ontario, Canada: G. Allan Roeher Institute.

Dewey, J. (1998). *Experience and education.* West Lafayette, IN: Kappa Delta Pi. (Original work published 1938)

Eberle, B., & Stanish, B. (1985). *CPS for kids: A resource book for teaching creative problem-solving to children.* East Aurora, NY: D.O.K. Publishing.

Edmonds, R. (1979). Some schools work and more can. *Social Policy, 9*(5), 25–29.

Firestien, R. (1989). *Why didn't I think of that? A personal and professional guide to better ideas and decision-making.* East Aurora, NY: D.O.K. Publishing.

Giangreco, M.F. (1992). Curriculum in inclusion-oriented schools: Trends, issues, challenges, and potential solutions. In S.B. Stainback & W.C. Stainback (Eds.), *Curriculum considerations in inclusive classrooms: Facilitating learning for all students* (pp. 239–263). Baltimore: Paul H. Brookes Publishing Co.

Giangreco, M.F. (1993). Using creative problem solving methods to include students with severe disabilities in general education classroom activities. *Journal of Educational and Psychological Consultation, 4,* 113–135.

Giangreco, M.F., Cloninger, C.J., & Iverson, V.S. (1998). *Choosing outcomes and accommodations for children (COACH): A guide to educational planning for students with disabilities* (2nd ed.). Baltimore: Paul H. Brookes Publishing Co.

Giangreco, M.F., Dennis, R., & Edelman, S. (1991). Common professional practices that interfere with the integrated delivery of related services. *Remedial and Special Education, 12*(2), 16–24.

Giangreco, M.F., Edelman, S., Cloninger, C., & Dennis, R. (1993). My child has a classmate with severe disabilities: What parents of nondisabled children think about full inclusion. *Developmental Disabilities Bulletin, 21*(1), 77–91.

Giangreco, M.F., & Meyer, L.H. (1988). Expanding service delivery options in regular schools and classrooms for students with severe disabilities. In J.L. Graden, J.E. Zins, & M.J. Curtis (Eds.), *Alternative educational delivery systems: Enhancing instructional options for all students* (pp. 241–267). Washington, DC: National Association of School Psychologists.

Giangreco, M.F., & Putnam, J.W. (1991). Supporting the education of students with severe disabilities in regular education environments. In L.H. Meyer, C.A. Peck, & L. Brown (Eds.), *Critical issues in the lives of people with severe disabilities* (pp. 245–270). Baltimore: Paul H. Brookes Publishing Co.

Gordon, W.J.J. (1987). *The new art of the possible: The basic course in synectics.* Cambridge, MA: Porpoise Books.

Gordon, W.J.J., & Poze, T. (1979). *The metaphorical way of learning and knowing.* Cambridge, MA: SES Associates.

Helmstetter, E., Peck, C., & Giangreco, M. (1994). Outcomes of interactions with peers with moderate or severe disabilities: A statewide survey of high school students. *Journal of The Association for Persons with Severe Handicaps, 19*(4), 263–276.

Hunt, P., & Goetz, L. (1997). Research on inclusive educational programs, practices, and outcomes for students with severe disabilities. *Journal of Special Education, 31*(1), 3–29.

Johnson, D.W., Johnson, R.T., & Holubec, E.J. (1993). *Circles of learning: Cooperation in the classroom* (4th ed.). Edina, MN: Interaction Book Co.

Lipsky, D.K., & Gartner, A. (Eds.). (1997). *Inclusion and school reform: Transforming America's schools.* Baltimore: Paul H. Brookes Publishing Co.

McGregor, G., & Vogelsberg, R.T. (1998). *Inclusive schooling practices: Pedagogical and research foundations: A synthesis of the literature that informs best practices about inclusive schooling.* Baltimore: Paul H. Brookes Publishing Co.

Meyer, L.H., & Janney, R. (1989). User-friendly measures of meaningful outcomes: Evaluating behavioral interventions. *Journal of The Association for Persons with Severe Handicaps, 14,* 263–270.

Osborn, A.F. (1993). *Applied imagination: Principles and procedures of creative problem-solving* (3rd rev. ed.). Buffalo, NY: Creative Education Foundation Press. (Original work published 1953)

Parnes, S.J. (1985). *A facilitating style of leadership.* Buffalo, NY: Bearly Limited in association with the Creative Education Foundation.

Parnes, S.J. (1988). *Visionizing: State-of-the-art processes for encouraging innovative excellence.* East Aurora, NY: D.O.K. Publishing.

Parnes, S.J. (Ed.). (1992). *Source book for creative problem-solving: A fifty year digest of proven innovation processes.* Buffalo, NY: Creative Education Foundation Press.

Parnes, S.J. (1997). *Optimize the magic of your mind.* Buffalo, NY: Creative Education Foundation Press.

Schnorr, R. (1990). "Peter? He comes and he goes . . .": First-graders' perspectives on a part-time mainstream student. *Journal of The Association for Persons with Severe Handicaps, 15,* 231–240.

Stainback, S.B., & Stainback, W.C. (1996). *Inclusion: A guide for educators.* Baltimore: Paul H. Brookes Publishing Co.

Stainback, S.B., & Stainback, W.C. (1990). Inclusive schooling. In W.C. Stainback & S.B. Stainback (Eds.), *Support networks for inclusive schooling: Interdependent integrated education* (pp. 3–23). Baltimore: Paul H. Brookes Publishing Co.

Thousand, J.S., & Villa, R.A. (1990). Strategies for educating learners with severe disabilities within their local home schools and communities. *Focus on Exceptional Children, 23*(3), 1–24.

Thousand, J.S., & Villa, R.A. (1992). Collaborative teams: A powerful tool in school restructuring. In R.A. Villa, J.S. Thousand, W. Stainback, & S. Stainback (Eds.), *Restructuring for caring and effective education: An administrative guide to creating heterogeneous schools* (1st ed., pp. 73–108). Baltimore: Paul H. Brookes Publishing Co.

Villa, R.A., & Thousand, J.S. (Eds.). (1995). *Creating an inclusive school.* Alexandria, VA: Association for Supervision and Curriculum Development.

Webb, J. [Producer and Director]. (1952–1959/1967–1971). *Dragnet* [Television series]. Los Angeles: Mark VII.m

Chapter 12

Maximizing the
Mindware of Human Resources

Jeanne Bauwens and Patricia H. Mueller

Come gather 'round people wherever you roam,
And admit that the waters around you have grown,
And accept it that soon you'll be drenched to the bone.
If your time to you is worth savin',
Then you better start swimming or you'll sink like a stone.
Oh, the times they are a-changin'.

From "The Times They Are A-Changin'," Bob Dylan (1967)

Who would have thought the lyrics from Bob Dylan's 1960s ballad would be used as an introduction to a chapter about inclusionary practices? It may seem far-fetched but actually is quite fitting. This stanza speaks as a subtle reminder of where we are and what we need to do with regard to educating all students; that is, "The times they are a-changin'." In schools at the turn of the 21st century, for example, there is a fast-emerging consensus about the relative proportion of students from diverse backgrounds who represent significant differences in ability levels, cultural backgrounds, and/or linguistic backgrounds.

Researchers in the 1980s projected from immigration and birth rates that, by 2000, the majority of the school-age population in 50 or more major U.S. cities would be from language minority backgrounds (Tucker, 1990). Students with disabilities are being included at accelerating rates as a result of federal reauthorization efforts that explicitly clarify the intent of earlier federal legislation that students be served in the context of an age-appropriate general education curriculum as the first phase of their individualized education program (IEP). Accompanying these two changes, general educators are required under Section 504 of the Rehabilitation Act of 1973 (PL 93-112) to alter the curriculum and instruction procedures for numerous students who are not eligible for special education services. Some states (e.g., Vermont Act 230, 1990) have legislated that a comprehensive instruction support system be developed so that students who are at risk (or "at promise") receive the additional boost that they may need to succeed in school.

Instead of describing students as at risk, we believe that, based on demographic shifts, many general and special educators are at risk because of their inability to educate this ever-expanding, diverse clientele effectively. In fact, the pressure on teachers to educate all students effectively is so great that a few teachers have reported being exposed to shouting matches at faculty meetings because of frustration, and thus they feel as if they are "sinking like a stone."

COPING WITH CHANGING TIMES

The question paramount in teachers' minds is how to cope (i.e., "swim") with the rapidly changing community of learners within contemporary American school systems. An abundance of literature clearly articulates numerous strategies for accommodating this ever-shifting population. One consistent finding is the need for the human resources to work more closely in tandem with one another. In her 1986 report, Madeleine Will, then an assistant secretary of the U.S. Department of Education, stated that the education system was fundamentally flawed and that educating students with learning problems must be a shared responsibility. In addition, as a result of its Working Forum on Inclusive Schools, the Council for Exceptional Children (1994) identified 12 overriding features characterizing inclusive schools, one of which was collaboration and cooperation. Zemelman, Daniels, and Hyde (1998) suggested that, based on national curriculum reports, there should be more delivery of special help to students within the general classroom and more varied and cooperative roles of teachers as well. The common element, then, of people working together is a life-preserving device to save ourselves from "sinking like a stone."

Collaboration (co-laboring) is certainly not a new concept. In fact, it is the way of the world. World peace clearly depends on our ability to work together, as do the personal relationships we craft. Collaboration is not just a professional skill but a critical life skill that all must possess.

In all education arenas, adults must model for students how to work in harmony with one another more than ever before. What educators clearly recognize is that they have the hardware, the software, and the *mindware*—that is, the human resources—to serve all students. What educators must do, however, is connect mindware in new and unique ways to cope with the ever-changing composition of students in their classrooms.

One highly effective way of using mindware is through *cooperative teaching*, a term that was coined by Bauwens, Hourcade, and Friend in 1989 and that has since been refined and elaborated in a book entitled, *Cooperative Teaching: Rebuilding the Schoolhouse for All Students* (Bauwens & Hourcade, 1995). Bauwens and Hourcade defined *cooperative teaching* as

> A restructuring of teaching procedures in which two or more educators with distinct sets of skills work in a coactive and coordinated fashion to jointly teach academically and behaviorally heterogeneous groups of students in educationally integrated settings, that is, in general classrooms. (1997, p. 43)

The preceding definition has been refined further since 1997, but a critical feature remains that two or more adults agree to be present simultaneously in the general education classroom to educate a diverse group of students. The sole intention of cooperative teaching is to exchange mindware in order to create a teaching and learning environment that accommodates all students. The philosophy undergirding two or more adults working in this collaborative teaching approach is that *all* educators are responsible for educating *all* students.

CONCERNS ABOUT COOPERATIVE TEACHING

Not everyone is sold on swapping their mindware in this way. For instance, many special educators and related services providers are frightened about job security and are concerned about the welfare of their students when these students with disabilities are fully included in the general education classroom. General educators are often angry about their newly acquired teaching role; previously, they often shifted the responsibility for educating students with diverse needs to someone else or to a different classroom. In effect, many educators may feel as though they are "sinking like a stone" because they do not agree with the changes that are being suggested for educating all students in their classrooms.

Why do educators feel this way? There are three underlying issues inherent in attempting to unite mindware within schools. First, many educators do not know how two or more adults can share the classroom, the teaching load, or both effectively and efficiently. After all, most of these adults have solo teaching histories as both learners and educators. Second, resistance to change permeates many education environments, especially at the secondary level. For instance, a study (Oakes & Wells, 1997) of secondary schools concluded that people know how to provide all students with rich opportunities to learn; but the culture of the schools seriously limits this effort. This difficulty is clearly evidenced when educators state that certain students "don't fit in" in their classrooms. In essence, educators continue to try to "place a round peg in a square hole" rather than envision a learning environment that celebrates diversity and provides *multiple pathways* for all students to learn. This dilemma may stem from educators' deep-seated beliefs about which students public education should serve and where students who "don't fit in" should be served. That is, to what extent should students with disabilities be included with or excluded from being educated with their peers? Third, there are gaps in educators' knowledge about research-based strategies and/or skills in implementing recommended practices so that all students can and do learn. This disparity exists for those preparing future educators as well. In fact, members of the National Commission on Teaching and America's Future (1996) stated that some school administrators directly attribute first-year teachers' lack of knowhow to college and university teacher preparation programs.

The crux of this chapter is to provide a kaleidoscope of ways in which two or more adults can connect their mindware effectively by using cooperative teaching efforts in the context of the general education classroom. Without a clear "mind movie" of possibilities, educators will be in the same room but not on the same page. We have chosen to create a mind movie by grouping pictures into three distinct categories based on which adults are teaching together cooperatively (see the appendix at the end of this chapter). The first set of graphic illustrations (Figures 1–8) depicts a general educator and paraeducator working collaboratively; the second set (Figures 9–16) portrays ways in which a general and special educator might cooperate; and the final set

(Figures 17–24) shows the general, special, and paraeducator teaching together. In addition to these role groupings, examples at the elementary and secondary levels are provided in the discussion that follows. Note that the roles delineated can be interchanged in any of these figures; alterations for students with more intensive needs also may be necessary.

GENERAL EDUCATOR AND PARAEDUCATOR TEACHING COOPERATIVELY

Often in a general education classroom in which a paraeducator has been assigned, the paraeducator performs one of two major tasks: clerical duties or working one-to-one with the same student for an entire class period or sometimes, unfortunately, for an entire school day (Mueller, 1997). This section portrays a significantly different and elevated role for the paraeducator assigned to work with a general education class. Students need to view *all* adults as being responsible for the learning of *all* students, not just for a selected few. With more than one adult in the classroom, the teaching and learning environment should be distinct from the typical, one-teacher general education classroom (Garnett, 1996).

Figures 1–8 illustrate how the general educator and the paraeducator can teach cooperatively in either an elementary or a secondary classroom. In all of these figures, the mindware of both adults is maximized, not minimized. The figures illustrate teachers sharing their actual teaching responsibilities rather than the paraeducator being relegated to aide-type tasks (e.g., duplicating materials, checking workbook pages, obtaining materials). Thus, students are exposed to true collaboration in a natural classroom environment.

General Educators and Paraeducators at the Elementary Level

Initial Instruction   Figure 1 portrays the initial phase of the instruction process, wherein the general educator introduces a story by showing students the cover of a trade book while the paraeducator makes her thinking conspicuous by "talking out loud" about the potential content of the book. Then both adults take turns reading the story to the students. Throughout this storytelling activity, one adult interjects questions related to the story's content. After completion of the story, the adults in the classroom use direct instruction to present a minilesson on giving feedback, using a T-chart format. For example, the lefthand column of the chart would have the heading "Looks like," and the righthand column heading would be "Sounds like." Students then would be asked to elicit the actual behaviors they might hear or see when the targeted behavior is being displayed appropriately.

Guided Practice   In the second phase (Figure 2), students are assigned to work as partners during guided practice; students who need additional support are grouped into threes. Each dyad or triad is given a bag containing five different books with vivid illustrations on the covers. In turn-taking fashion, each student selects a book, reads the title, makes a prediction about the contents of the book based on the title and the illustration on the cover, and then receives immediate feedback from his or her partner(s). Students then confirm their responses by reading the story together and then reviewing the answer written on an index card in the back of the book. The general educator and paraeducator closely monitor the dyads to confirm that they are making appropriate predictions as well as giving the appropriate type of feedback. On occasion, one of the two adults may spend a considerably greater amount of time with a particular group of students.

Independent Practice   During the next segment of the storytelling minilesson, independent practice (Figure 3), the adults redistribute the books to each student. The students are asked to practice making predictions on their own while the two adults monitor and coach them by asking varied questions targeted at their particular level of functioning. Students then self-select one of the books and compare their prediction with the actual story line. If a student needs assistance in reading the book, one adult may work one-to-one with him or her while the other adult monitors the entire group. In addition, there may be some books on tape for particular students to listen to and confirm their initial response.

Evaluation   As one means of evaluating a student's skill in making predictions, the general educator and the paraeducator in the Figure 4 example have designed a computer-assisted evaluation instrument by scanning in various book covers and developing a multiple-choice format using varied levels of question prompts. The general educator calls four students to the back of the room for their individual evaluations (Figure 4) while the paraeducator monitors the remaining students as they read their self-selected trade books. For the next activity, students go to the library and review trade books to make a prediction and select ones to read. A final activity is to go to a local bookstore to review the trade books there.

General Educators and
Paraeducators at the Secondary Level

Initial Instruction   During the initial stage of instruction (Figure 5), the general educator introduces the main topic (the "big idea") of the unit as the paraeducator interjects additional information while displaying visual representations of the information so that the idea being introduced is conceptualized as clearly as possible. Then the paraeducator elicits input from students by asking them to write down what they want to learn more about on separate Post-It notes. Students then place the Post-It notes on the board at the back of the classroom. While the paraeducator remains at the board at the back of the room (categorizing the students' interests), the general educator visually maps out the major topics, tasks, and activities. The general educator then asks students to transfer key tasks and due dates to their personal calendars. Prior to the end of the day's session, both adults view the planning board to reconfirm the next day's lesson.

Guided Practice   While the general educator takes roll, the paraeducator provides an overview of the guided practice activity (Figure 6) by describing the jigsawed cooperative learning task and then assigns students to heterogeneous groups of five or six. The general educator displays a listing of the differentiated reading tasks to be completed by members of each group, using a current magazine article. Both adults monitor students reading their assigned sections of the magazine. The paraeducator then posts charts in distinct areas of the room and instructs students to move into their focus groups to answer specific questions posted on the charts that are related to their section of the readings. Both adults monitor the group discussion to make sure that all questions are answered correctly. The general educator then directs students back to their heterogeneous groups to reteach their assigned sections to their peers. Both adults monitor this peer-tutoring effort. At some point during the small-group activity, the paraeducator and the general educator meet at the planning area to fine-tune the next day's lesson.

Independent Practice   In the independent practice session (Figure 7), the general educator reviews a question-writing strategy with the students and then assigns them to write independently several questions about each section of the magazine article discussed during the previous class session. During the independent task, the paraeducator takes roll while monitoring as the general educator completes additional paperwork tasks. Both adults closely monitor and give the students immediate feedback on their questions. After the question-writing task, students form dyads to answer the questions collaboratively. Prior to the end of this class session, the adults debrief each other and identify students who had difficulty with writing questions and develop a plan for a brief peer tutoring and reteaching opportunity during the next class session.

Evaluation   After a brief reteach and review session, students are given a list of questions at varied levels of difficulty that focus on applying the content discussed in the magazine article. Students are then asked to select one question and respond to it independently (Figure 8). Once this task is completed, each student proceeds to one of two checkpoints, one at which the paraeducator evaluates their written response for mechanics and another at which the general educator evaluates both the breadth and the depth of their responses. In this arrangement, students are given quick feedback so that rewriting can occur immediately.

GENERAL EDUCATOR AND
SPECIAL EDUCATOR TEACHING COOPERATIVELY

Only in the 1990s did special educators begin to actually work for extended periods of time in general education classrooms. Prior to this time, special educators often assigned a paraeducator to monitor students on their caseload in the general education classroom. Although this is not an inappropriate use of the paraeducator's time, the special educator must become more visibly involved in the general education classroom.

Unfortunately, when special educators join the general education classroom, a prevailing teaching strategy is to get the student through the task rather than to actually differentiate instruction by altering or designing lessons that have *multiple pathways* so that all students can succeed. Garnett argued, "General educators continue to hold on to the belief that treating students differently is somehow detrimental—either bad for the individual, not good for the group, or both—voiced with particular concern for 'fairness'" (1996, p. 9). The special educator frequently waits until the general educator assigns the task and then relentlessly assists students who have been targeted or labeled in completing that particular task, regardless of its suitability, utility, and/or relevance for students with identified/special needs. All too often, the task is either inappropriate (i.e., instruction in nontransferable content that in most instances is passively and privately done) or not at the students' level of functioning. In either case, the teaching arrangement does not take advantage of the expertise of the adults in the classroom. Transforming the curriculum to portray research-based recommended practices (Zemelman, Daniels, & Hyde, 1998) needs to become the object of collaborative teaching efforts. The figures in this section illustrate the potential of cooperative teaching between general and special educators. Examples at both the elementary and secondary levels show a variety of ways in which both adults can extend their expertise in a co-active and coordinated fashion to teach all students effectively and efficiently.

General Educators and
Special Educators at the Elementary Level

Initial Instruction and Guided Practice   In this first session, the general and special educators begin by introducing the big idea during a lesson about fractions. They break the class into heterogeneous halves and start their initial instruction with both adults presenting the same content but to two smaller groups of students (Figure 9). They debrief at the end of the session while each student meets with a counterpart from the other group to paraphrase what he or she has learned. During the next session, the special educator begins the lesson by introducing the task (what and why) while the general educator describes how the students will work together (pairs share) and in which physical formation (shoulder-to-shoulder). Using cognitive manipulatives (e.g., kinesthetic tasks that require students to think out loud while moving objects and discussing the task), they take turns showing and telling about fractional parts (Figure 10). Pairs then merge and begin discussing how fractions might be used in various situations (e.g., cooking, cleaning, eating). This brief application activity allows time for the educators to plan collaboratively for the next cooperative teaching session.

Independent Practice and Evaluation   Cooperative teaching allows for three levels of independent practice of the same task to occur simultaneously. For example, one group may be supervised closely (Figure 11, top right). In another group, students check in with peers if they need additional support, and the remaining students (Figure 11, left and bottom) work independently. This time, the general educator works with four students who need the most support or frequent monitoring/coaching (Figure 11, top right) while the special educator monitors the other 21 students. Immediate regrouping occurs when the special and general educators notice that students need either more or less support (see arrow in Figure 11 indicating one partner shifting from group to independent work).

In the final independent practice phase of this lesson (Figure 12), students are individually checked on their knowledge about fractional parts using a simulated pizza picture. The general and special educators have developed in this example a number of cognitive tasks that allow all students to show what they know about fractions. They each meet privately with a preassigned number of students for the short evaluation check. While some students are being evaluated, others are completing an art activity applying fractional parts. On completion of the student evaluation, all students have a pizza party while the educators meet and debrief about the results and plan for the reteaching extension lesson.

General and Special Educators at the Secondary Level

Initial Instruction and Guided Practice   In the social studies class, students are introduced to a new country that they will study via a dialogue about the unit between the general and special educator at their planning area of the classroom. Students are then asked to count off by twos (i.e., 1–2, 1–2). All of the "1s" move to an area of the room where they identify what they know about the identified country, and the "2s" move to the what do we want to know area to generate questions about the identified country (Figure 13). Students then rotate to the other area, and the adults repeat the task with each new group. Once each group has completed the task, the general educator reviews the information and questions that were developed with one group of students and then categorizes these data. The special educator does the same with the other group. The students in each group then share these data with the other group.

While the general educator groups students according to interests, the special educator introduces the students to an instruction strategy called *coop-coop* (Kagan, 1996). This is a cooperative learning structure wherein students work cooperatively in small groups to complete a project and then each group cooperatively shares its unique topical information with the entire class (thus the name *coop-coop*). The general educator then displays the groupings to the students. The lesson closes with the students participating in a group-building activity while the general and special educator debrief and prepare for the next lesson.

The next session begins with the students moving into six deep-study groups based on their assigned area of interest (Figure 14). The general educator briefly reviews the schedule of events and encourages students to note the critical dates in their agenda books (i.e., calendars) while the special educator monitors completion of the task. Then the special educator conducts a minilesson about how to retrieve information while the general educator interjects thought-provoking "What if" tidbits.

Next, the general educator explains a contract that delineates for groups their specific research tasks while the special educator distributes the actual form. Both adults assist groups in completing the contract collaboratively. Students are encouraged to swap telephone numbers with other members of their group. Some students go to the library with the special educator while the general educator remains in the classroom to assist some groups that are still differentiating roles, tasks, or both on their contracts.

Independent Practice and Evaluation   The independent practice session (Figure 15) begins with students reviewing their research contracts. Both educators monitor groups and pose questions related to where students might locate additional information. Students then have additional time for research before they return to their group and share their findings in a round-robin fashion. The general and special educators then role-play how to present their lesson collaboratively rather than in a turn-taking fashion. Students have a few minutes to brainstorm ways to present their lesson while the adults debrief and discuss plans for the next lesson.

After several in-class days for independent research and group planning and preparation, students are ready to share information collaboratively with their classmates (Figure 16). The general educator begins by reviewing with the first team of presenters, whose topic is a particular country's modes of transportation, the specified time frame and ways for students to monitor their time. Simultaneously, the special educator describes to the student audience how to complete the peer evaluation. Once the presentations begin, both adults observe the presentation and complete their evaluations along with the audience. It is important to note that Sam, a student with severe cognitive delays, is a member of the first group of presenters. His teammates designed their presentation collaboratively so that Sam is actively involved as the conductor of the train that they crafted to present their transportation topic.

GENERAL EDUCATOR, PARAEDUCATOR, AND SPECIAL EDUCATOR TEACHING COOPERATIVELY

More often than not in the 21st century, students with mild disabilities will receive special education services in the general education classroom, thus bringing special educators and other related-services providers (e.g., Title I teachers, speech-language pathologists) into the classroom. Simultaneously, in many schools, students with significant disabilities are being included in these classroom environments. Frequently, these students bring with them a paraeducator. We are not suggesting that every classroom have three adults in a classroom, but we do believe that it is important to utilize all adults in the classroom efficiently and effectively. Imagine the teaching and learning possibilities if there were three adults working in harmony in the same classroom environment; there are tantalizing possibilities here. Unfortunately, all too often, when we visit classrooms with several adults, we hear the general educator transmitting information in one, lone voice while the other adult(s) listen passively. It calls to mind the stereotype of highway road crews—one person does most of the work while the rest "hang out." After the lecture, the other adults often converge on a few targeted students and remain with them for the entire instruction time. Figures 17–20 show a variety of ways in which three adults can truly provide differentiated instruction co-actively for the students.

General Educators, Paraeducators, and Special Educators or Specialists at the Elementary Level

Initial Instruction   Figure 17 depicts a primary classroom in which three language development skills groups are taught simultaneously for approximately 20 minutes, three times per week. Each instruction group uses the same curriculum materials; but the emphasis varies, depending on the students' skill levels, thus enabling students to progress at their own pace. Flexible grouping occurs through weekly evaluations and planned face-to-face debriefing sessions. Regrouping of students is based on both skill growth and need, not on labels (e.g., gifted, learning disabled). In addition, the three adults rotate skill group assignments twice each month so that they become familiar with more than one group of students. The remaining 10 minutes of this 30-minute block are devoted to the adults' debriefing and troubleshooting. This occurs while the students participate in various open-ended language interaction activities monitored by students from the nearby university, parent volunteers, or both. (In this example, the speech-language pathologist might replace the special educator as the third adult teaming with the general educator and the paraeducator.)

Guided Practice   During the guided practice session (Figure 18), the special educator describes the task while the general educator displays the heterogeneous group assignment sheet and the paraeducator distributes an envelope of pictures. In round-robin fashion, students select a picture, think about what the picture illustrates, and then tell a story about it to their peers. Each of the three adults closely monitors certain targeted students within various groups for application and generalization of skills previously taught.

Independent Practice   In the independent practice session (Figure 19), students are seated in back-to-back partner formation and given a bag that has a number of miscellaneous objects. One student picks out an object and describes it to his or her partner. The partner listens to the five clues and tries to guess what the object might be. While this activity is occurring, all three adults are conducting informal contextual (i.e., ecological) language evaluations of students within their dyads or triads. It is important to note that students who experience learning or language difficulties are distributed across all three groups so that all adults have an opportunity to observe these students applying their language skills.

Evaluation   The three adults assess specific language skills (i.e., asking questions, initiating conversations) (Figure 20). As students participate in a language-oriented application game within triads, the adults conduct a brief language sample with members of each group. On completion, the adults immediately share these data to determine new skill groups.

General Educators, Paraeducators, and Special Educators at the Secondary Level

Initial Instruction   Figures 21–24 depict a unit in which the concept of work ethics is played out in functional ways. The general educator introduces the big idea of work ethics by providing students with a brief definition (Figure 21). The paraeducator and special educator interject ideas and paint a vivid picture by dialoguing and creating a T-chart of what work ethics look and sound like. The general educator also interjects by asking a series of "what if" questions to which the paraeducator and special educator each respond by giving their personal opinions.

Guided Practice   The next session begins with the paraeducator welcoming the students back and setting the stage for the day's session while the general educator unobtrusively takes roll and distributes coded 3-by-5 cards on the floor in strategic locations. The special educator then facilitates the first activity: a quick review about what they know about work ethics. Students are asked to write three things: two truths and one lie. As they write, the three adults monitor and coach students to respond. The paraeducator then explains how to play "Guess the Fib." After 5 minutes, the general educator regains students' attention and asks them to identify the letter they have on their 3-by-5 card (P, M, or I). Once detected, students move to the area where an adult is holding up a placard that matches the letter on their card (Figure 22).

Then students brainstorm the pluses (P), minuses (M), and interesting things (I) that they know about work ethics. Students rotate through these three stations at approximately 2- to 3-minute intervals. After the station work, the educators invite students to face the center of the room, where the paraeducator has on a business suit and the general and special educator are prepping for an interview. One depicts a polished, confident interviewee; the other, an awkward, inept interviewee. The paraeducator says, "First impressions . . . hmm," and then an interview ensues. Next, the students are asked to form groups of three and role-play good and bad first impressions from the shake of a hand to the final words. This guided practice session concludes with a minilesson on giving feedback, and then students practice this skill collaboratively.

Independent Practice and Evaluation   The independent practice session (Figure 23) commences with the adults taking turns introducing the day's lesson (e.g., special educator, "What?"; general educator, "Why?"; paraeducator, "How?"). Using a structured notetaking format that has been created specifically to match the content of the videotape information, the students are asked to critique three videotape clips of people applying for a job.

While students watch the videotape, the three adults debrief each other at the back of the classroom. After the videotape ends, the general educator asks the students to form groups of three while the special educator rewinds the videotape and takes the lead on further analysis of the first videotape clip. The general educator and paraeducator simultaneously monitor the students' discussions. The educators rotate to discuss the remaining portions of the videotape, taking the lead and monitoring in turn. The lesson wraps up with a brief overview of the next session (i.e., businesspeople visiting and discussing with students their impressions of work ethics behaviors).

Additional Applications   In preparation for the practice conversations with businesspeople, the educators each invite three to four visitors to class. When students arrive, the stations are set up with the visitors seated (Figure 24). The general educator introduces the session while the paraeducator displays the form that each student will give to the visitor as the special educator distributes them on the floor near each student. Then the special educator displays and discusses the observation forms while the general educator distributes two forms to each student. As the visitors begin their conversations, the three adults monitor to make sure that the observers are watching and writing on the feedback sheets. In closing, each student is given his or her set of completed evaluations and is assigned to write a self-analysis as the out-of-class activity.

During the next session, the general educator and paraeducator each take a group of students out to observe work ethic behaviors on the job while the special educator remains in the classroom helping students who have not yet completed their written self-analyses. When the students who were out observing return, they are assigned to write a descriptive analysis of what they saw. The paraeducator monitors this activity while the general educator takes another small group to another local business. As the students who are working on their initial analyses finish, the special educator regroups students to compare and contrast appropriate work behaviors at several different businesses.

CONCLUSIONS

From where we sit in our respective roles as a university professor in education (Jeanne Bauwens) and former state coordinator of paraeducator training and current special education administrator (Patricia H. Mueller), we acknowledge that the linking of mindware via cooperative teaching is not always easy. In fact, educators should expect discomfort as new roles change and are refined. With discomfort, however, comes the possibility of significantly altering the educational outcomes for all students and adults in a diverse classroom environment. For paraeducators and special educators, working with students who are developing typically can reduce burnout and provide them with learning benchmarks, skills typically mastered by age-peers. For paraeducators, cooperative teaching reduces the "Velcro effect," or the feeling of being stuck to one student day in and day out. For the student, it reduces the likelihood of developing a dependency on one person. For the general educator, cooperative teaching provides an opportunity to try out one's water wings with regard to innovations with the support of someone in close proximity in case he or she is needed.

For cooperative teaching to be most successful, we recommend that, at a minimum, school personnel, with assistance from institutions of higher education, agree to and act on the following:

- Provide relevant, ongoing staff development for all parties involved in cooperative teaching partnerships, focusing on cooperative teaching approaches and effective instruction strategies. Specifically for general and special educators, provide in-service and preservice training on how to work effectively with paraeducators. For paraeducators, require preservice training and provide orientation to the school, staff, and students prior to the first day of school.

- Develop comprehensive written job descriptions that articulate the collaborative role expectations of all adults, to include general educators, special educators, paraeducators, related-services providers (e.g., Title I teachers, speech-language pathologists, occupational therapists, physical therapists), and administrators. Components of such job descriptions include job qualifications, specific roles and responsibilities, orientation and training to perform the job, and supervision and evaluation guidelines.

- Establish consistent, face-to-face interaction with all members of the cooperative teaching team (including paraeducators) to promote successful working relationships. Use effective collaborative teaming techniques (e.g., distributed role leadership, written agendas with time limits, conflict resolution strategies) to solve problems creatively, constructively, and harmoniously. Manipulate work schedules so that planning efforts can occur during the work day or create new scheduling systems to find the time to collaborate (Raywid, 1993).

- Develop an action-planning process to initiate, implement, and evaluate the cooperative teaching approach, once selected.

- Disseminate information about cooperative teaching to your local school board(s) and community members so that they gain an understanding of the new model and can provide their support. In the wider context, share information on the Internet, write a news release or an article, present papers at conferences, and/or encourage visitors to observe the program.

Cooperative teaching, as we have described it, provides all of us—educators and students—with greater opportunities to reach our full potential. It allows educators to share their strengths and talents to enhance the learning of all students in a creative and nurturing environment, founded on mutual respect for what each member brings to the team. It allows students to interact with a variety of adults who bring differing styles, personalities, and characteristics to the learning environment. When cooperative teaching is really working, educators and students share successes of their learning through the stories they share and celebrate. Here is one such story as retold by Crystal Marble, a Vermont paraeducator working in a high school, who described building a collaborative IEP:

> As I began the year, I knew my work would be cut out for me because inclusion was a fairly new concept in the school. The teacher was clear about his fears in making the process work. He believed strongly that I had all the expertise with the students on IEPs and that he had none. Whenever one of our students had a positive experience, he made sure to tell me it was a result of my efforts, not his. One day after class, I said, "My IEP for you is that by the end of the year, you recognize it was not Me but We creating student success."
> From that day on, I made daily efforts to be involved with the whole class. Not only did this effort free up the teacher to work with the students needing special assistance, but it sent a clear message to the students that everyone had needs and that, together, the teacher and I were meeting those needs. The students with IEPs were no longer being singled out because they were involved with all class activities and because we were working with everyone.
> By Spring of that school year, the teacher and I had developed a strong personal and working relationship. We had become partners in education, truly reaping the benefits of our students' successes. The payoff for me was that the teacher's actions really were transformed into We, not just Me! This experience is proof positive that when collaboration

becomes the natural way we carry out our day to day activities, everyone wins! (Marble, 1994)

REFERENCES

Bauwens, J., & Hourcade, J.J. (1995). *Cooperative teaching: Rebuilding the schoolhouse for all students.* Austin, TX: PRO-ED.

Bauwens, J., & Hourcade, J.J. (1997). Cooperative teaching: Picture the possibilities. *Intervention in School and Clinic.*

Bauwens, J., Hourcade, J.J., & Friend, M. (1989). Cooperative teaching: A model for general and special education integration. *Remedial and Special Education, 35*(4), 19–24.

Council for Exceptional Children. (1994). *Creating schools for all our students: What twelve schools have to say.* Washington, DC: National Education Association.

Dylan, B. (1967). The times they are a-changin'. On *Bob Dylan's greatest hits* [CD]. Los Angeles: Columbia Records.

Garnett, K. (1996). *Thinking about inclusion and learning disabilities: A teacher's guide.* Reston, VA: Council for Exceptional Children.

Kagan, S. (1996). *Cooperative learning.* San Juan Capistrano, CA: Resources for Teachers.

Marble, C.S. (1994, November). A collaborative IEP: From me to we. *The Paraeducator Newsletter.* (Available from University Affiliated Program of Vermont, University of Vermont, Burlington, VT 05401)

Mueller, P.H. (1997). *A study of the roles, training needs, and support needs of Vermont's paraeducators.* Unpublished doctoral dissertation, University of Vermont, Burlington.

National Commission on Teaching and America's Future. (1996). *What matters most: Teaching for America's future.* New York: Author.

Oakes, J., & Wells, A. (1997). Enabling all students to learn. *Phi Delta Kappan, 6,* 735–736.

Raywid, M. (1993). Finding time for collaboration. *Educational Leadership, 51*(1), 31–43.

Rehabilitation Act of 1973, PL 93-112, 29 U.S.C. §§ 701 *et seq.*

Tucker, G.R. (1990). Cognitive and social correlates of additive bilinguality. In J.E. Alatis (Ed.), *Georgetown University Roundtable on Languages and Linguistics* (pp. 90–101). Washington, DC: Georgetown University Press.

Will, M. (1986). *Educating children with learning problems: A shared responsibility.* Washington, DC: U.S. Department of Education, Office of Special Education.

Zemelman, S., Daniels, H., & Hyde, A.A. (1998). *Best practice: New standards for teaching and learning in America's schools* (2nd ed.). Portsmouth, NH: Heinemann.

Appendix: Figure Gallery

GENERAL EDUCATOR AND PARAEDUCATOR WORKING COLLABORATIVELY (FIGURES 1–8)

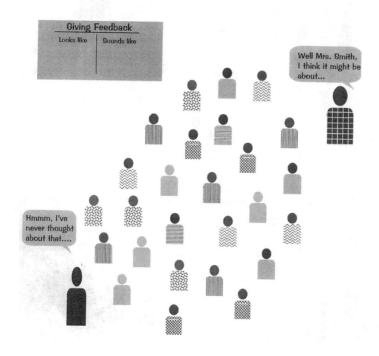

Figure 1. Cooperative Teaching between the general and paraeducator at the elementary level during initial instruction.

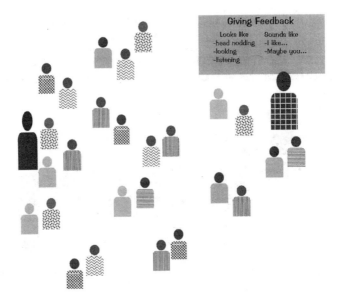

Figure 2. Cooperative Teaching between the general and paraeducator at the elementary level during guided practice.

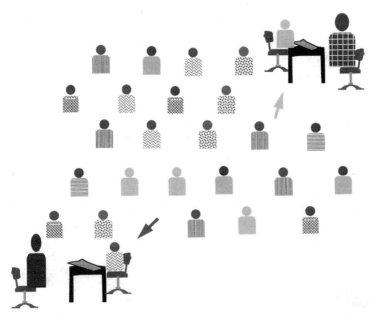

Figure 3. Cooperative Teaching between the general and paraeducator at the elementary level during independent practice.

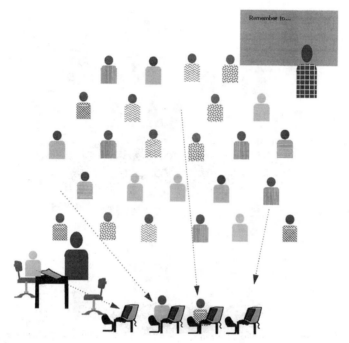

Figure 4. Cooperative Teaching between the general and paraeducator at the elementary level during individual accountability.

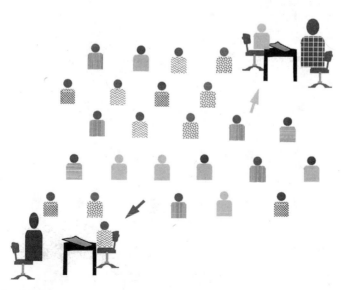

Figure 5. Cooperative Teaching between the general and paraeducator at the secondary level during initial instruction.

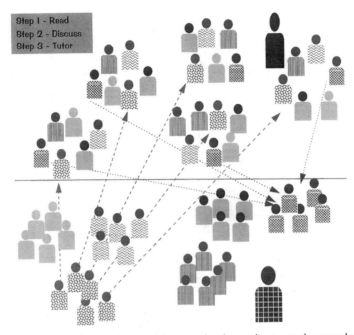

Figure 6.   Cooperative Teaching between the general and paraeducator at the secondary level during guided practice.

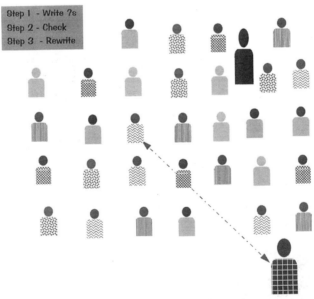

Figure 7.   Cooperative Teaching between the general and paraeducator at the secondary level during independent practice.

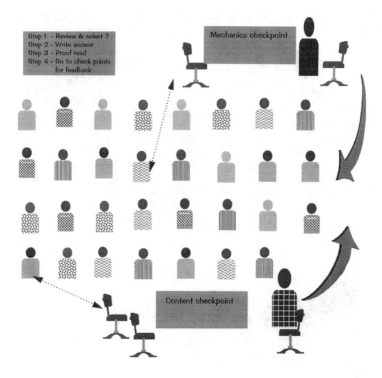

Figure 8. Cooperative Teaching between the general and paraeducator at the secondary level during individual accountability.

WAYS IN WHICH A GENERAL EDUCATOR AND A SPECIAL EDUCATOR MIGHT COOPERATE (FIGURES 9–16)

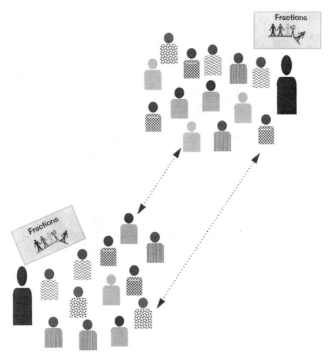

Figure 9.   Cooperative Teaching between the general and special educator at the elementary level during initial instruction.

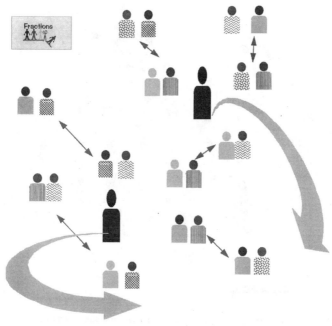

Figure 10. Cooperative Teaching between the general and special educator at the elementary level during guided practice.

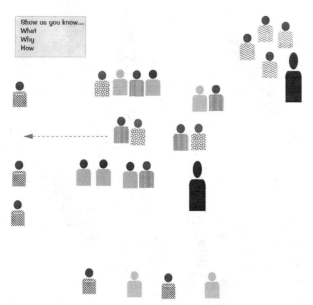

Figure 11. Cooperative Teaching between the general and special educator at the elementary level during independent practice.

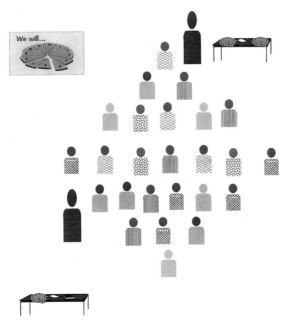

Figure 12.   Cooperative Teaching between the general and special educator at the elementary level during individual accountability.

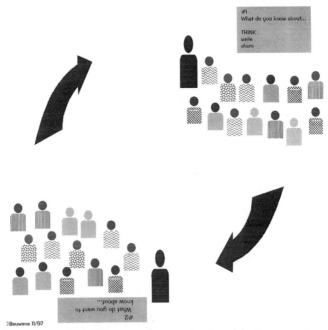

Figure 13.   Cooperative Teaching between the general and special educator at the secondary level during initial instruction.

Figure 14. Cooperative Teaching between the general and special educator at the secondary level during guided practice.

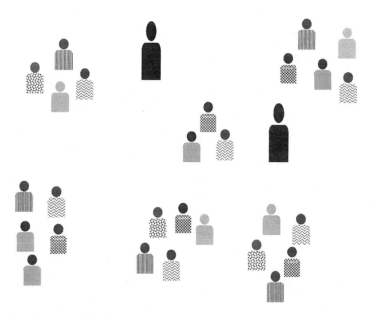

Figure 15. Cooperative Teaching between the general and special educator at the secondary level during independent practice.

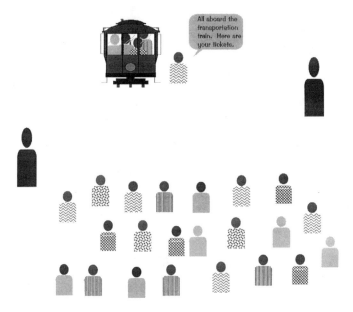

Figure 16.   Cooperative Teaching between the general and special educator at the secondary level during individual accountability.

GENERAL, SPECIAL, AND PARAEDUCATOR TEACHING TOGETHER (FIGURES 17–24)

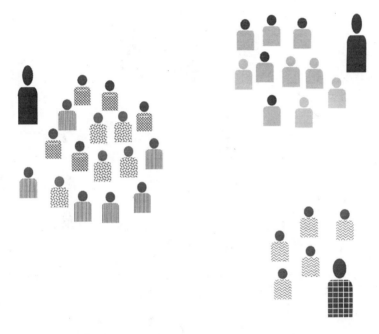

Figure 17.   Cooperative Teaching between the general, special, and paraeducator at the elementary level during initial instruction.

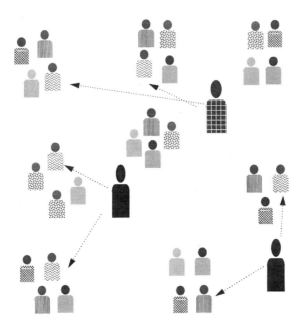

Figure 18. Cooperative Teaching between the general, special, and paraeducator at the elementary level during guided practice.

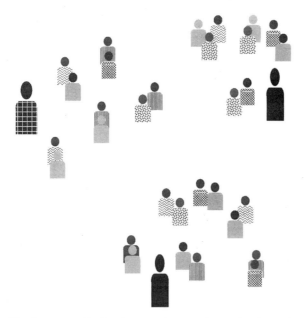

Figure 19. Cooperative Teaching between the general, special, and paraeducator at the elementary level during independent practice.

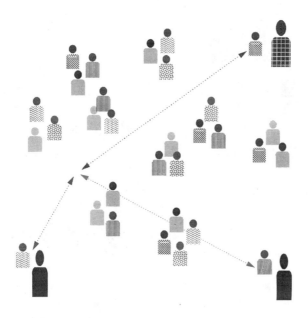

Figure 20.   Cooperative Teaching between the general, special, and paraeducator at the elementary level during individual accountability.

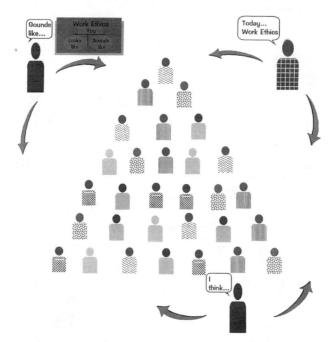

Figure 21.   Cooperative Teaching between the general, special, and paraeducator at the secondary level during initial instruction.

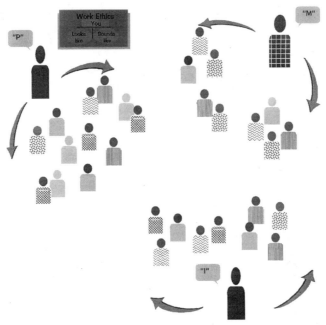

Figure 22.   Cooperative Teaching between the general, special, and paraeducator at the secondary level during guided practice.

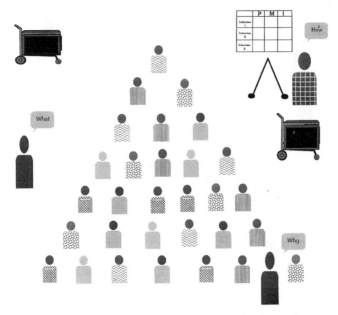

Figure 23.   Cooperative Teaching between the general, special, and paraeducator at the secondary level during independent practice.

Figure 24. Cooperative Teaching between the general, special, and paraeducator at the secondary level during individual accountability.

Chapter 13

Roles of Related Services
Personnel in Inclusive Schools

Michael F. Giangreco, Patricia A. Prelock,
Richard R. Reid, Ruth E. Dennis, and Susan W. Edelman

Related services providers such as speech-language pathologists, school psychologists, physical therapists, and occupational therapists serve vital roles in supporting the education of many students with disabilities in general education environments. Related services personnel can provide students with disabilities *access* to an appropriate education and facilitate students' pursuit of important *learning outcomes* through the application of the specific skills associated with their

Partial support for the preparation of this manuscript was provided by the U.S. Department of Education, Office of Special Education and Rehabilitative Services under the funding category, Research Validation and Implementation Projects for Children who are Deaf-Blind, CFDA 84.025S (H025S40003-97), awarded to The University Affiliated Program of Vermont at the University of Vermont. The contents of this paper reflect the ideas and positions of the authors and do not necessarily reflect the ideas or positions of the U.S. Department of Education; therefore no official endorsement should be inferred.

respective disciplines and the collaborative skills required to work effectively with others in the context of a family-centered approach in general education classrooms and other inclusive environments (Rainforth & York-Barr, 1997).

It is important to note here that much of the knowledge and many of the skills that related services personnel possess are not exclusive or unique to any particular discipline and may or may not be possessed by all those of a particular profession. The fact that someone has a related services title (e.g., physical therapist, speech-language pathologist) in no way guarantees that he or she has had training or experience to provide inclusive school-based services for children with a wide range of developmental disabilities. Furthermore, every discipline that serves students with disabilities overlaps with other disciplines to varying degrees, sometimes substantially so. This is one reason why it is important to consider the potentially overlapping roles that general and special educators, family members, and related services personnel share. In inclusive education models, team members must communicate with each other to identify the potential interrelationships among their disciplines and to avoid unnecessary gaps, overlaps, and contradictions among their recommendations and activities. This communication is essential to ensure that individually determined student supports are provided in ways that 1) effectively achieve specified outcomes, 2) use resources in a responsible manner, 3) are status enhancing or status neutral for the student, and 4) are "only as special as necessary" (Giangreco, 1996).

From the initial passage of the Education for All Handicapped Children Act of 1975 (PL 94-142) through the Individuals with Disabilities Education Act (IDEA) Amendments of 1997 (PL 105-17), there has been confusion about what *related services* are and how they should be provided. By federal definition, a *related service* is any "developmental, corrective, or other supportive service" that is "required to assist a child with a disability to benefit from special education" (Individuals with Disabilities Education Act [IDEA] Amendments of 1997, PL 105-17, 34 C.F.R. § 300.24). Some children with disabilities may benefit from specialized services during non–school hours that are not educationally necessary. Making the distinction between what is educationally necessary and what is medically or otherwise necessary has been and continues to be one of the most contentious issues pertaining to school-based related services. Criteria that must be met to establish educational necessity are addressed under the heading "Educational Necessity" in this chapter.

Although there are numerous examples of related services providers offering excellent support services to students with disabilities, related services have been provided since the mid-1970s in ways that too often 1) do not match the IDEA definition of *related services;* 2) do not abide by court rulings pertaining to related services (e.g., *Board of Education of the Hendrick Hudson Central School District v. Rowley,* 1982; *Irving Independent School District v. Tatro,* 1984); 3) do not coincide with exemplary practices for educating students with disabilities (Fox & Williams, 1991; Meyer & Eichinger, 1994); and 4) do not adequately support students with disabilities in general education classes. Some of these historically common yet interfering practices are listed in Table 1 (Giangreco, Edelman, & Dennis, 1991; Giangreco, Edelman, Luiselli, & MacFarland, 1996; Giangreco, Edelman, Luiselli, & MacFarland, 1998; Giangreco, Edelman, & Nelson, 1998).

Simply stated, appropriately provided related services are too important for students, families, and school personnel to be provided in ways that interfere with the education of students with disabilities. Therefore, the remainder of this chapter is designed to encourage quality provision of educationally necessary related services. First, seven generic roles of related services providers are offered as constructive alternatives to many of the historically interfering practices discussed. These are also listed in Table 1. Next, four brief case studies pertaining to school psychology, speech-language pathology, occupational therapy, and physical therapy are presented and discussed. Each of these case studies provides 1) a description of a child, 2) examples of indi-

Table 1. Historically common practices that interfere with the provision of educationally necessary related services

1. Families and school personnel interact with related-services personnel as "experts" rather than collaborative team members.
2. Families and general educators have insufficient involvement in related-services decision making.
3. Groups of individuals serving the same student do not always function as a team.
4. Typically, no process is used to assist in making related-services decisions.
5. Autocratic decisions about support services are made by related-services providers in isolation without consideration of the interrelationships among the services provided by team members.
6. Each discipline develops separate goals based on discipline-specific assessments.
7. Related-services planning, implementation, and evaluation often are unrelated to the educational program.
8. Pull-out approaches that do not match the intended educational functions of related services are used.
9. Students are placed in special education schools or classes so they can receive related services rather than being provided services that support them in general education programs and placements that are less restrictive.
10. Group members often defer to one another rather than risk the potential conflicts associated with openly addressing support services decisions.

vidualized education program (IEP) goals or accommodations for which the team agrees the related service was necessary, 3) an example of a commonly applied support for which the team decides that the provision of the related service was not necessary, and 4) examples of how the related services personnel provided support in ways that were consistent with their generic roles as described in this chapter. The chapter ends with implications for facilitating an increasing quality of related services that are educationally necessary and effective in assisting children with disabilities.

GENERIC ROLES OF RELATED SERVICES PROVIDERS

Based on our observations, interactions, and research with related services providers, several roles that cross disciplinary boundaries have emerged. Recognition of these generic roles reinforces the need to examine critical approaches to service delivery by support service personnel. Each of these generic roles is described in the following sections.

Establish a Shared Framework

All decision making about the education of children is based on beliefs, values, and assumptions. A shared framework consists of a team's common set of beliefs, values, or assumptions about education, children, families, and professionals that they negotiate through active participation and contribution. As professionals, educators and related services personnel may have been socialized to serve and protect their own disciplines. When teams develop a shared framework, each member's existing beliefs about his or her own profession may be challenged. This can be threatening for some professionals who fear a potential loss of their traditional role and believe that their professional skills will be devalued. In reality, when professionals open themselves to new ways of thinking, acknowledge the limitations of their own knowledge, and seek out shared paths with other team members, their value in the eyes of other team members, including families, is often raised. Table 2 offers examples of beliefs, values, and assumptions that guide the authors of this chapter when educating children. Readers are invited to consider the ways they might reword these statements to reflect their teams' evolving shared frameworks. In their study of attitudes regarding education and related services provision for students with multiple disabilities, Giangreco, Edelman, MacFarland, and Luiselli (1997) suggested that teams can explore the extent of their members' agreement about important foundational beliefs by asking each team member to rate his or her beliefs or practices on a scale from 1 to 10 (e.g., 1 = Strongly dis-

Table 2. Examples of shared framework statements

Education:
- Is a reciprocal process of learning and mutual support between students and teachers (used here in the broadest sense)
- Should have an important mission (e.g., education should result in positive changes in individually determined valued life outcomes for students such as personal health, social relationships, and access to meaningful places and activities)
- Should result in outcomes that provide students with opportunities to contribute to their own support as well as contribute to a larger community of people (e.g., family, classroom, workplace, neighborhood, town, country)

Children (with and without disability labels):
- Are all entitled to the supports they need in order to receive an appropriate education (e.g., human supports, technology)
- Are all worthy of our time, energy, and resources regardless of the type or extent of their individual characteristics (e.g., disability, gender, cultural heritage, economic status)
- Should be given equal access to the same places and opportunities

Families:
- All have important knowledge, insights, and/or skills to contribute to their child's education
- Should be treated with respect and in culturally sensitive ways
- Must be included in decisions that will affect them

Professionals:
- Should be committed to lifelong learning for themselves as well as their students
- Should continually strive to interact with students, families, and each other in ways that are respectful and constructive
- Should collaboratively clarify their roles and responsibilities so that they are working in concert toward common goals

Excerpted from Giangreco, M.F. (1996). *Vermont independent services team approach: A guide to coordinating educational support services* (pp. 4–5). Baltimore: Paul H. Brookes Publishing Co.

agree; 10 = Strongly agree). This can be done anonymously so that team members feel free to be honest about their perspectives. Then the team can review the members' responses to identify their similarities and differences as well as clarify their interpretation of the rated items. In this way, team members can actively participate in developing a shared framework that evolves over time.

Establish Common Goals and Avoid the "Expert Trap"

Collaborative teamwork is a term that frequently is misused. Many groups formed to serve the educational needs of a student with disabilities have been labeled inaccurately as a team. Although such groups may demonstrate several characteristics of teamwork as described in the literature (e.g., involving people affected by team decisions, sharing resources, having regular meetings with an agenda, rotating roles, reaching consensus) (Thousand & Villa, 1992; see also

Chapter 10), they fail to engage in arguably the most defining and foundational characteristic of a team—the pursuit of shared goals. Teamwork does *not* mean agreeing to have *different* goals for each discipline that subsequently are stapled together and inaccurately labeled a "team IEP." This common and problematic practice of having separate goals stems at least in part from our professional socialization as specialists or experts. Traditionally, we think of people from specialized disciplines such as psychology or occupational therapy as specialists or experts in their field. In reality, an individual's level of skillfulness within a discipline can range from novice to expert. Furthermore, parents, teachers, and special educators often are not considered specialists or experts. Parents, however, are experts regarding their child. Similarly, general and special education teachers have skills and knowledge that differ from those of other team members.

Through teaming, people learn new skills that they need to implement specific strategies or programs and can gain access to training, technical assistance, or consultation from teammates with specialized skills. If related services personnel are viewed as experts and parents and teachers are not, an unproductive hierarchy is inadvertently established within a team, unrealistic expectations among team members are created, and genuine collaboration is disrupted. The expert trap can and must be avoided by encouraging people to value the contributions of each team member and practice principles of role release and support (Rainforth & York-Barr, 1997).

Help Parents and Teachers to Become Better Consumers

Having parents and teachers become increasingly knowledgeable consumers of support services makes sense. Parents are the only adults likely to be involved with a student throughout the student's school career. Teachers typically are the professional staff who spend the most time with a student in school. Conversely, most related services providers interact with the students whom they serve much less frequently.

A first step in becoming a better consumer is to become more knowledgeable about which support services personnel have to offer. Perhaps more important is to find out the specific skills and knowledge of the personnel who are or will be working with a student. For example, although it is important for a teacher or a parent to know that speech-language pathology is a discipline that includes a subspecialization in augmentative and alternative communication (AAC), it is more important to know whether the speech-language pathologist assigned to a student who needs such supports in fact has those skills. If not, team members are poised to select alternatives to meet the student's needs, such as 1) having the speech-language pathologist learn new skills, 2) identifying another speech-language pathologist who has the needed skills, or 3) identifying a person from another discipline who has the needed skills (e.g., special educator, occupational therapist, assistive technology specialist). Feedback from parents of children with disabilities has indicated that related services personnel are perceived more favorably by families when they acknowledge the limitations of their own skills, express a willingness to work together to solve identified problems, and act on those concerns (Giangreco, Cloninger, Mueller, Yuan, & Ashworth, 1991). These parents also expressed appreciation when services were well coordinated.

Ensure the Educational Relevance and Necessity of Support Services

The professional literature is replete with criteria for making related services decisions for students with disabilities. Some criteria may be situationally useful (e.g., age, history) and others highly suspect (e.g., level of parental involvement, geographic location of the student, student abilities or willingness to follow instructions). Two criteria, however, appear to be essential across all situations: educational relevance and educational necessity.

Educational Relevance   First, teams should always consider whether a proposed support service is educationally relevant based on the student's IEP. For example, if an occupational therapist suggests that her service is intended to assist the student in handwriting *and* handwriting is an identified component of the IEP, then relevance is established. Conversely, if handwriting is not part of the IEP, then relevance is not established. In other words, there is not a match between the content of the IEP and the proposed service. Identifying this kind of mismatch may be a sign that 1) team members have separate agendas specific to their professional disciplines, 2) related services recommendations are being made inappropriately prior to knowing the student's IEP's content, or 3) the group has not established common goals. Alternatively, it may be a sign that the content of the IEP needs to be adjusted.

Educational Necessity   If a proposed support service is established to be educationally relevant, then the team must consider the second essential criterion of educational necessity. It is conceivable that a service may be educationally relevant but not educationally necessary. There are at least six basic ways to judge the educational necessity of proposed services:

1. Absence of service interferes with education
2. Consider gaps, overlaps, and contradictions

3. Check with the sender and receiver

4. Generalization across environments

5. Only as special as necessary?

6. Provided appropriately during non–school hours

First, we can ask, "Will the absence of the proposed service interfere with the student's access to or participation in his or her education program?" If the answer is yes, then the service is necessary.

Second, if the service passes the initial considerations for relevance and necessity, then the team must consider potential gaps, overlaps, and contradictions among the related services. For example, appropriate therapeutic positioning may be suggested by *both* the occupational therapist and the physical therapist. If the therapists' skills overlap in this area, the team needs to decide whether the overlap is necessary and desirable. A gap could occur if each therapist assumes that the other is handling the therapeutic positioning issue, only to find out later that neither was doing so. Contradictions also occur when support services providers make conflicting recommendations based on their disciplinary perspectives. For example, a physical therapist may recommend that a child's head be positioned at midline during instruction, whereas the vision specialist may recommend nonmidline head positioning to account for maximum use of residual vision. This example illustrates the importance of support services providers' communicating with each other on an ongoing basis, expanding their own breadth of knowledge, and working collaboratively with each other to design learning experiences that make the most sense for the student.

A third way to explore the potential necessity of support services is to check with both the sender and the receiver of the service. For example, an occupational therapist (sender) may say that she needs to serve the function of transferring specialized information and skills regarding eating and drinking to the classroom assistant (receiver) who works with the student at lunchtime. Although serving this function may meet the previous test for necessity, the team may agree that the classroom assistant is sufficiently experienced and skilled with this particular student that such support is not necessary. Alternatively, the potential receiver of a service can make it known that he or she needs a certain type of support. A newly hired classroom assistant (receiver) may have no experience in assisting a child with oral-motor difficulties to eat and therefore may require transfer of information and skills from the occupational therapist (sender). When possible and age appropriate, it is always desirable to check directly with the student (receiver) to gain his or her perspective on the need for a proposed service. This can provide not only essential information but also experience in self-advocacy.

A fourth test for necessity is to consider whether a service provided in one context can be adequately generalized to other environments without the direct involvement of the specialist. For example, in one situation, a school psychologist assisted a student's core team members by sharing specialized information and skills pertaining to positive behavioral supports in the general education classroom. The team needs to determine whether the psychologist needs to transfer directly the same information and skills across all environments in which this support is needed (e.g., gymnasium, cafeteria, playground, library, cocurricular activities) or whether the information and skills can be transferred adequately by the core team classroom staff to other places and people, possibly with the psychologist monitoring to ensure quality and accountability.

As a fifth test of necessity, the team should consider whether the proposed services are "only as special as necessary" (Giangreco, 1996, p. 35). This consideration is intended to avoid the drawbacks inherent in providing well-intended but potentially harmful "overservice." Team members can ask whether the proposed related services can be provided appropriately in more typical ways through the use of natural supports (e.g., existing school staff, classmates) and more typical materials and activities. In part, this concept 1) has its historic roots in the special education literature (Reynolds, 1962) and 2) is supported by the U.S. Supreme Court case of *Board of Education of Hendrick Hudson Central School District v. Rowley* (1982), in which the provision of a sign language interpreter as a related service for a student with a hearing impairment was denied because the court found evidence that the student was and had been benefiting adequately from instruction without a sign language interpreter.

A sixth and final test asks the team to consider whether the proposed service can be provided appropriately during *non*–school hours. If it can be, then it need not be provided as a school-based related service. This criterion was established in the Supreme Court's ruling in *Irving Independent School District v. Tatro* (1984), a case pertaining to clean intermittent catheterization (CIC) as a related service. The court ruled that the school in that case had to provide CIC because the student needed to receive this intervention a few times during the school day; therefore, this case represented an important example of allowing a student *access* to education. If, however, a health procedure needed to be done for a student once a day and the time of day was not a critical factor (e.g., the procedure could be provided at 6:00 A.M., noon, or 6:00 P.M.), then the school would not be responsible for providing that service, because it could be delivered appropriately during non–school hours. Application of this standard, established in the *Tatro* case, should be considered carefully. The Code of Federal Regulations has established that certain supports that are related to school but occur during non–school hours indeed are appropriately provided related services. Support for students with disabilities to participate in co-curricular activities, community-based training, and parent training are examples of such supports.

Working in the Context of the General Education Program and Environment

As related services providers spend more time supporting students with disabilities in general education classes, they are faced with a markedly different context than they may have experienced when working in special education classes, schools, or clinics. Specifically, general education teachers have indicated that they most appreciate specialists who 1) function as collaborative team members rather than in isolation as experts; 2) help teachers and parents work on the child's education goals rather than impose separate therapy goals; 3) provide assistance at times and in ways that consider the operation of the classroom in order to avoid disruption; and 4) use approaches that are not overly technical or specialized, so that the student may avoid being unnecessarily stigmatized (Giangreco, Dennis, Cloninger, Edelman, & Schattman, 1993). Related services personnel are perceived to be more effective when they attend to these contextual differences that are important to teachers. (See Chapter 7 for extended discussion of the general education context.)

Engaging in a Variety of Functions

In a study by Giangreco (1990), 318 special educators, related services providers, and parents of students with severe disabilities rated a set of support services functions commonly cited in the professional literature. These respondents indicated that the four most important functions for serving students with severe disabilities were 1) developing adaptations, equipment, or both to allow for active participation or to prevent negative outcomes (e.g., regression, deformity, discomfort, pain); 2) transferring information and skills to others (e.g., related services providers, educators, parents); 3) serving as a resource, support, or both to the family; and 4) applying discipline-specific methods or techniques to promote active participation, to prevent negative outcomes, or both. These essential functions may be augmented by discretionary functions (e.g., promoting typical developmental sequences, being a liaison between the school and medical service providers) that are individually and situationally appropriate. It is essential for team members to have a shared understanding of which functions each person serves and how they are interrelated to support the components of a student's education program. Furthermore, all individually selected functions should be pursued within the context of collaborative and ongoing assessment, planning, implementation, and evaluation.

Traditionally, related services support to students often decreases with students' chronological age. We suggest that age should be considered in a different light. Specifically, as a student grows older, he or she may be presented with new environments and opportunities that call for different types of supports and potential increases in services. This can occur at times of major transitions (e.g., from preschool to school services, from middle school to high school); during participation in community-based experiences; or during transitions to adult services and employment situations (Sowers, Hall, & Rainforth, 1992). Clarifying the functions served by each team member and their interrelatedness helps to further develop the team's shared framework and allows members to purposely explore service functions for potential gaps, overlaps, and contradictions.

Evaluating the Impact of Related Services

Once the team has begun to implement a related service, the question becomes whether the provision of the support service has been effective. Outcome measures for related services for students with disabilities are not always easy to determine, because more traditional standardized assessments of skill development are often inappropriate. Thus, many teams have neglected to assess the impact of support services interventions as vital components of their service provision. Meaningful assessment of related services outcomes for students with disabilities is critical.

The first step in evaluating the impact of a support service is to recall which components of the education program the service was intended to support. Knowing this, the team can ask individually appropriate questions such as, "Has the service provided access to or allowed for participation in the educational program?" or "Has the service facilitated improvement in identified learning outcomes that would probably not occur in the absence of the service?"

A larger question the team should ask is, "Does the student experience positive changes in his or her life as a result of the service?" In other words, is the student's life better in ways that are valued by the student and his or her family, and, if so, how? Furthermore, is the student's life better because he or she received this service? Thinking about these kinds of quality-of-life issues is complex and highly individualized (Dennis, Williams, Giangreco, & Cloninger, 1993). However,

Step 10.1
Evaluation of Impact Process
for Learning Outcomes

Directions: Answer the following questions to discuss student progress toward IEP Annual Goals or Additional Learning Outcomes categories.

Student name: _Keisha_ _____ Date of team meeting: _11-8-97_ _____

Team members participating in discussion: ___ _D.L., V.R., W.B., J.S., R.A._ _____

---

1. **Annual Goal** or **Additional Learning Outcome(s)** being discussed: _____
   Comment, describe events, objects, feelings with signs, symbols, speech _____

2. **Valued Life Outcome(s)** being facilitated through the learning outcome(s): _____
   Choice & Control _____

---

3. When was the last time this learning outcome was discussed by the team?
   Date: _10-8-97_ _____

4. What has been done to teach the student this learning outcome since it was last discussed? _Lots of conversation with adults, peers. Uses computer_ _____
   programs. _____

5. What progress has the student made on the learning outcome? _Little speech:_ _____
   uses 40 signs: 1, 2 & 3 signs together. Understands at least 60 _____
   signs. Uses 20 symbols spontaneously. Understands at least 30 _____
   symbols. _____

6. What changes, if any, has the student experienced on the corresponding Valued Life Outcome(s)? _Chooses computer programs, free time activities; asks to go_ _____
   places, uses items. _____

7. What changes, if any, need to be made in the educational program to enhance progress or facilitate the corresponding Valued Life Outcome(s)? _Move_ _____
   instructional assistant out of peer interactions; teach more students _____
   and adults more signs _____

(continued)

Figure 1.   Evaluation of impact process for learning outcomes, step 10.1. (From Giangreco, M.F., Cloninger, C.J., & Iverson, V.S. [1998]. *Choosing outcomes and accommodations for children: A guide to educational planning for students with disabilities* [2nd ed., p. 262]. Baltimore: Paul H. Brookes Publishing Co.; reprinted by permission.)

parents of children with disabilities have identified several high-priority valued life outcomes: 1) being safe and healthy, 2) having networks of personally meaningful relationships, 3) having choice and control that

Figure I.   *(continued)*

Step 10.1
Evaluation of Impact Process
for Learning Outcomes

Directions: Answer the following questions to discuss student progress toward IEP Annual Goals or Additional Learning Outcomes categories.

Student name: ___Keisha___ Date of team meeting: ___11-8-97___
Team members participating in discussion: ___D.L., V.R., W.B., J.S., R.A.___

---

1. **Annual Goal** or **Additional Learning Outcome(s)** being discussed: _____
   Shares with others

2. **Valued Life Outcome(s)** being facilitated through the learning outcome(s):_____
   Meaningful relationships
   Meaningful activities in various places

---

3. When was the last time this learning outcome was discussed by the team?
   Date: ___10-8-97___

4. What has been done to teach the student this learning outcome since it was last
   discussed? _Modeling by adults and peers, using "give and get"_

5. What progress has the student made on the learning outcome? _About 90% for any_
   items with adults; 90% for low preference with peers; 50% for high
   preference. Says "No." Only 1 time grabbed child

6. What changes, if any, has the student experienced on the corresponding Valued Life
   Outcome(s)? _Children ask her to play more. She is welcome in groups more._
   Can go to office & cafeteria to deliver items.

7. What changes, if any, need to be made in the educational program to enhance
   progress or facilitate the corresponding Valued Life Outcome(s)? ___More on___
   giving and responding with signs for high-preference items ("No." "Not
   now." "5 minutes." etc.).

Choosing Outcomes and Accommodations for Children   •   © 1998 by Michael F. Giangreco   •
Baltimore: Paul H. Brookes Publishing Co.

matches one's age and cultural context, 4) having a variety of interesting places to go and meaningful activities to do, 5) having a home to live in, now and in the future, 6) engaging in personal growth and lifelong learning, and 7) contributing to one's community (Giangreco, Cloninger, et al., 1991; Giangreco, Cloninger, & Iverson, 1998). A simple evaluation process has been developed as part of COACH (*Choosing*

Step 10.2
Evaluation of Impact Process
for General Supports

Directions: Answer the following questions to discuss the student's status regarding the identified General Supports category; use one page for each area.

Student name: _Keisha_ Date of team meeting: _11-8-97_
Team members participating in discussion: _DL, VR, WB, IS, RA_

---

1. **General Supports** category being discussed: _Teaching others_
   Items: _Others learning signs_

2. **Valued Life Outcome(s)** being facilitated through these general supports: _____
   Meaningful relationships, meaningful activities/places

---

3. When was the last time these general supports were discussed by the team?
   Date: _10-8-97_

4. What has been done since then related to these general supports? _Val and Willa_ _sign for all class activities. Two "formal" sign classes for children every_ _day (5 minutes)._

5. What is the current status of these general supports? _Ongoing implementation_

6. What changes, if any, has the student experienced on the corresponding Valued Life Outcome(s) as a result of having these general supports provided? _Signs more_ _with peers and Val both receptively and expressively._

7. What changes, if any, need to be made in the educational program regarding these general supports to facilitate the corresponding Valued Life Outcome(s)? _Others in_ _school need more instruction. Short lessons "on-the-fly" and at faculty_ _meetings. Teach in other classes, especially of same grade._

Choosing Outcomes and Accommodations for Children • © 1998 by Michael F. Giangreco •
Baltimore: Paul H. Brookes Publishing Co.

(continued)

Figure 2. Evaluation of impact process for learning outcomes, step 10.2. (From Giangreco, M.F., Cloninger, C.J., & Iverson, V.S. [1998]. *Choosing outcomes and accommodations for children: A guide to educational planning for students with disabilities* [2nd ed., p. 270]. Baltimore: Paul H. Brookes Publishing Co.; reprinted by permission.)

Outcomes and Accommodations for Children: A Guide to Educational Planning for Students with Disabilities, Second Edition; Giangreco et al., 1998) to address students' learning outcomes (see Figure 1) and general supports provided to students (see Figure 2). These approaches focus

Figure 2. *(continued)*

Step 10.2
Evaluation of Impact Process
for General Supports

Directions: Answer the following questions to discuss the student's status regarding the identified General Supports category; use one page for each area.

Student name: *Keisha*   Date of team meeting: *11-8-97*

Team members participating in discussion: *Debbie, Val, Jane, Willa, Robert*

---

1. **General Supports** category being discussed: *Materials preparation*
   Items: *Advance preparation*

2. **Valued Life Outcome(s)** being facilitated through these general supports: _____
   Choice & Control, Meaningful activities

---

3. When was the last time these general supports were discussed by the team?
   Date: *10-8-97*

4. What has been done since then related to these general supports? *Regularly used materials have been duplicated, some laminated.*

5. What is the current status of these general supports? *ongoing*

6. What changes, if any, has the student experienced on the corresponding Valued Life Outcome(s) as a result of having these general supports provided? *Meaningful participation occurs in most lessons, activities. She has more choices of materials to use during center time.*

7. What changes, if any, need to be made in the educational program regarding these general supports to facilitate the corresponding Valued Life Outcome(s)? *When need adjustments on unplanned activities, need access to materials. Keep box of "stuff" handy. Research software for upcoming units.*

on their impact on students but can be a helpful adjunct to evaluate the impact of the service provision.

CASE STUDIES

In this section, the generic principles of providing the educationally relevant and necessary related services discussed thus far in the chapter
are illustrated through four related services (i.e., school psychology,
speech-language pathology, occupational therapy, physical therapy).
Each case example describes a student with disabilities and explains
how a related service was needed or not needed for the student to
receive an appropriate education.

School Psychology

Historically, the practice of school psychology as a related service has
been severely limited by the way in which the psychologist's role has
been defined. An overwhelming amount of most school psychologists'
time is spent in assessment activities related to the determination of
special education eligibility of a student (Levinson, 1990). This leaves
little time for the psychologist to offer other types of services that fall
within the purview of school psychology. Although assessment and
evaluation remain important aspects of the school psychologist's role,
in inclusive schools, the emphasis shifts to the program development,
monitoring, and support necessary for the success of the student.

Elliot

Elliot was diagnosed as having attention-deficit/hyperactivity disorder
(ADHD), combined type, and was making the transition from his
local elementary school to middle school. The psychologist, having
worked with Elliot during his elementary school years, was invited to
a transition meeting at the middle school in the spring of Elliot's last
year in elementary school, Grade 6. Others in attendance included
Elliot's mother; the sixth-grade teacher; his special education support
teacher; the school nurse; three middle school teachers who would
have Elliot as a student in the coming year; the middle school special
educator; and, of course, Elliot.

   In years past, the middle school staff might have looked to the
school psychologist for "expert" opinions on Elliot's disability, questions about his behavior, and suggestions regarding how he should be
taught. This day, the meeting took a different course as Elliot's current classroom teacher and special educator outlined Elliot's learning strengths as well as areas that challenged him. His mother shared
her feelings regarding Elliot's prior school experiences and described
some of the challenges that she faced in the home. Most important,
Elliot described learning situations and activities that he enjoyed and

those that were difficult for him. This fact-finding was used as part of a broad set of information to help the team identify learning priorities for Elliot that could be translated into his annual IEP goals. The team also clarified expectations for his participation within the general education curriculum and general support needs.

Once these foundational decisions were made, the team asked the question, "What kind of supports will Elliot need to be successful at the middle school and to pursue his IEP?" It was at this point that the many and varied skills of the school psychologist were considered in concert with those of other disciplines to address Elliot's educational needs. The team decided that Elliot and the school psychologist together would provide staff with general information regarding ADHD.

Elliot's mother informed the team that she and Elliot's physician decided to try medication to see whether it would help counter the effects of ADHD. The team agreed that the school psychologist would develop a behavioral data collection system for use by Elliot's teachers and parents. These data would allow the physician to make informed decisions regarding dosage adjustments for optimal effect. In addition, the psychologist would interview Elliot at regular intervals in order to obtain Elliot's insights into his own academic and social functioning.

Elliot's mother and his sixth-grade teacher both raised concerns regarding his peer relationships. His mother believed that he had trouble making friends, and his teacher had observed that his relationships with his classmates were characterized by frequent conflicts. The team agreed that the school psychologist and the middle school teachers would work together to develop a schoolwide process for resolving conflicts (Johnson & Johnson, 1991). This process would be team-taught to all students by teachers and the school psychologist. They also would instruct Elliot and his classmates in these and other social skills in the contexts in which they would need to be demonstrated, such as the classroom, the lunchroom, the schoolyard, the hallways, and the school bus (Goldstein, 1988; Goldstein & McGinnis, 1997). Aware of community resources, the school psychologist recommended that Elliot participate in a week-long outdoor adventure learning program jointly offered during the summer vacation months by a community recreation program and a local social services agency. This summer program would be attended by many of Elliot's future middle school classmates from neighboring communities. This experience was aimed at enhancing important social skills such as teamwork, communication, problem solving, and trust building. The psychologist would facilitate interagency support for Elliot through a referral to the sponsoring agencies.

Elliot's scenario highlights how a psychologist's time, skills, and efforts can be focused to provide critical support to a student with a special educational need. As Levinson, Fetchkan, and Hohenshil (1988) pointed out, school psychologists can experience greater job satisfaction when they are able to expand their work efforts beyond traditional role boundaries.

Speech-Language Pathology

The case of Stephen illustrates a collaborative team's implementation of a speech-language intervention.

Stephen

Stephen was a 14-year-old high school freshman who had a fluency disorder that was complicated by a written language challenge. As a young child, Stephen had been a late talker and first received speech-language intervention in preschool. He responded well to intervention, and, by the end of kindergarten, he no longer required direct services from a speech-language pathologist. At the beginning of second grade, Stephen was referred again to the speech-language pathologist, this time for a fluency problem (stuttering). He continued to experience fluency problems throughout grade school. During sixth grade, it was also noted that Stephen had difficulty with formulating ideas to develop written narratives. He required support to brainstorm potential topics, outline key ideas, sequence his ideas, and monitor his written language structure. The speech-language pathologist provided both direct and in-classroom intervention to facilitate Stephen's fluent speech and his written language.

As Stephen's team met to discuss his goals for the upcoming year, they considered the educational relevance and necessity of direct speech-language intervention. His IEP included two major priorities: 1) to increase successful participation in class discussions by creating a "fluency-friendly environment" and 2) to expand his written language skills in a variety of genres (e.g., narrative, descriptive, expository, persuasive).

Up to this point in Stephen's school career, his team members had clearly identified the relevance of related services support. However, high school presented some new challenges in terms of Stephen's schedule, his adjustment to multiple teachers and academic subjects, and his increased responsibility for independent writing assignments. Furthermore, Stephen expressed interest in being a self-advocate to support his own needs. Teachers who knew of Stephen's fluency disorder shared their concerns regarding strategies that should be used to support him. They also worried about the level of support he might require for completing his written language assignments across subject areas.

An action plan was developed with input from Stephen, his parents, a speech-language pathologist, a classroom teacher whom Stephen identified as particularly helpful during his eighth-grade experience, and the guidance counselor of his high school. Based on team discussions, it became apparent that the role of the speech-language pathologist should shift from a direct services provider to a consultant who would support Steven's general education teachers. The following steps were agreed on to begin to create a fluency-friendly environment:

1. Stephen, the speech-language pathologist, and the guidance counselor would plan a meeting with all of Stephen's Grade 9 teachers. Stephen decided that he would demonstrate his stuttering behavior at that meeting because his stuttering was not always obvious to the naive listener.

2. In collaboration with the speech-language pathologist, Stephen would work with his teachers to help them understand which level of support would help to ensure his comfort in participating in class discussions. Stephen might ask for teachers to adapt the strategies they used to call on him. Supports might also include Stephen's cueing the teachers when he was ready to give a book report or scheduling a time before class to prepare or to practice oral presentations with the teacher.

3. As Stephen begins to develop a relationship with a particular teacher, that teacher and the guidance counselor (rather than the speech-language pathologist, who is in the building for only 2 days per week) would become mentors in the academic environment with whom Stephen can check in on a regular as-needed basis. Stephen could also use these individuals to practice his slow speech or to warm up before giving an oral presentation in class.

4. Stephen and the speech-language pathologist would continue to communicate with the guidance counselor to ensure that both Stephen's teachers and Stephen were comfortable with the intervention plan for managing his fluency challenges.

5. Stephen determined that it would be helpful to talk about his stuttering, particularly with his science and history classmates because these classes required a significant amount of discussion and lab work with a partner.

As a support for Stephen's written language impairments, the freshman English teacher offers writing practice opportunities to all interested students twice a week after school. Peers also were identified who could help any students requiring assistance with editing and reflection on the content of their written language. Stephen indicated that he would feel comfortable with access to these resources to support his written language problems.

It was clear to the team that Stephen needed and wanted to generalize his skills and strategies in this high school environment. The speech-language pathologist trusted that Stephen's primary goals would be supported by his general education environment with the addition of teachers and peers he identified as confidants. The speech-language pathologist would remain a support person for brainstorming new ideas on a quarterly basis.

Occupational Therapy

Pediatric occupational therapists are trained to promote the development of motor, play, social, adaptive, and perceptual abilities of children who experience a wide range of developmental challenges. As a related services provider in special education programs, an occupational therapist can support a child's ability to function as independently as possible and to benefit from his or her education program. The following case study illustrates this type of support.

Lazaro

Lazaro, a lively 3-year-old boy, had been determined eligible for special education because of delays in development associated with his diagnosis of Down syndrome. Using a family-centered education-planning process, the IEP team, which included Lazaro's parents, the preschool general education teacher, and the early childhood special educator, began the process of IEP development. The occupational therapist was asked to provide information about Lazaro's present level of functioning to help the team make decisions. Unlike past practice, the assessment information was not used to determine separate goals for occupational therapy but rather to help determine which services might be needed and how services would fit together to support Lazaro's development.

The information provided by the occupational therapist was based on multiple sources, including formal and informal assessments, observations, interviews, and record reviews. She noted that Lazaro had strengths in social skills and motor imitation, a persistent approach to activities, and an interest in other children and play materials. Generalized low muscle tone had an impact on his development of balance and equilibrium in standing and walking, postural stability in sitting, grasp strength, dexterity, and oral-motor control. Lazaro could walk but did not run. He had difficulty with going down steps. He had the ability to grasp and release self-care items, toys, and writing materials but lacked dexterity and strength to pull on clothing or use fasteners in dressing. He made marks with a crayon but did not hold a crayon in his fingers or imitate lines or shapes. He also had difficulty with matching shapes, assembling simple puzzles, and organizing the front and back of his clothing.

Lazaro's parents were worried that Lazaro often choked on pieces of solid food. He had difficulty with biting through some foods, chewing adequately, and drinking without spilling. He occasionally drooled. He was communicative, using facial expressions and hand gestures as well as vocalizations. Lazaro used a number of single words, but these words were not easily intelligible by those who were not familiar with his communication style.

Using information from the occupational therapist and others, the team identified six educational priorities that would be translated into IEP goals for Lazaro: 1) sustaining social interactions with peers; 2) making requests (e.g., for food, toys, activities, people); 3) safe eating and drinking; 4) independent dressing skills; 5) functional use of objects (e.g., toys, crayons, other classroom materials); and 6) increased balance in walking and descending stairs. The team also agreed that Lazaro would benefit from exposure to all aspects of a typical preschool curriculum, with the understanding that initially partial participation in some activities might be expected. Next the team determined needed general supports and accommodations, which included teaching others, including staff and classmates, about textures and foods that were safe for Lazaro to eat at snacktime and exercising precautions to prevent Lazaro from choking. The team agreed that the least restrictive place for Lazaro to pursue his education program was in a typical preschool environment because that environment provided him the opportunity to access materials, activities, and models he needed to address his priority learning outcomes and to benefit from exposure to a range of typical preschool activities.

Determining which, if any, support services Lazaro needed to benefit from his education program was a team decision. To make informed decisions, each team member reviewed information gathered during assessments conducted by the IEP team. The occupational therapist focused her attention on the information from parents, teachers, and other specialists, including the physical therapist and speech-language pathologist, related to the family-selected educational priorities and preschool curriculum. Although the occupational therapist had skills related to much of Lazaro's education program, the team decided that occupational therapy involvement was needed to address only some of Lazaro's educational needs because other team members could provide needed supports more appropriately in a way that was only as special as necessary. For those priorities with which the occupational therapist was to be involved, she would continue to collaborate with other team members to identify long- and short-term IEP objectives and strategies to support and assess the objectives. In Lazaro's case, the following decisions were made:

1. The occupational therapist did not need to be involved in the listed IEP priority of sustaining social interactions with peers. The team agreed that the preschool teacher and the parents, working together, could address this goal adequately by creating social experiences and providing Lazaro with instruction and support.

2. The team agreed that the occupational therapist did not need to be involved in the listed IEP priority of making requests, because her proposed input substantially overlapped that of both the speech-language pathologist and the special educator. Recognizing the potential future need for occupational therapy involvement related to communication, the team agreed that their decision should be revisited in 2 months.

3. Team members agreed that the occupational therapist did need to address the safe eating and drinking IEP priority. Although there were identified overlaps in this area with the speech-language pathologist, the team decided that the overlaps were necessary. The occupational therapist would serve Lazaro indirectly through the speech-language pathologist and teacher. The occupational therapist would play a major role in suggesting increasingly challenging food textures, types, and sizes for home and school snacks. She also would select or construct adaptive eating materials such as an adapted cup with a straw. In addition, the occupational therapist would serve as a liaison among the family, medical service providers, and the education team.

4. The team agreed that the occupational therapist needed to support dressing skills by sharing knowledge and resources with other team members. She would consult with the teachers and the parents regarding accommodations and strategies for putting on and taking off clothing. The teachers were to take responsibility for practicing dressing at appropriate times throughout the school day. The occupational therapist also was to assist the family in selecting shoes, boots, and clothing fasteners that were most appropriate for Lazaro. The team discussed the probability that, once the parents learned the principles behind the selection of appropriate clothing, this aspect of occupational therapy involvement could be reduced or eliminated.

5. The team agreed that the occupational therapist did not need to be involved in the listed IEP priority of imitating skills of daily life by using objects for intended purposes, because the teacher was skilled in this area and it was an integral part of her typical program. The occupational therapist would remain available on a consulting basis for times when the team members required her specialized knowledge and skills.

6. The team agreed that the physical therapist could provide consultation to the teacher and physical education program at the preschool, suggest activities and games for the group, and monitor Lazaro's progress and needs in order to address the listed IEP priority of increased balance in walking and on stairs. Occupational therapy involvement in this priority was not needed.

Physical Therapy

The following case study illustrates an education team's incorporation of physical therapy intervention for Tina.

Tina

Tina loves school! She has many friends, two of whom are in her third-grade general education class. Tina has some unique needs in school because she has cerebral palsy (severe spastic quadriplegia). Her needs for physical assistance and therapeutic movement and positioning are everpresent, given her tightly flexed arm postures and strong patterns of extension in her trunk, neck, and hips. She wears a wrist splint on one hand and molded ankle–foot orthoses (i.e., braces) on her feet. Her wheelchair has a custom seat design that promotes a stable, upright posture. Tina does not use speech but has learned to use a chin switch mounted upon her wheelchair to operate a variety of toys, musical devices, and a simple scanning device. This year Tina's team included her classroom teacher, classroom instruction assistant, speech-language pathologist, occupational therapist, physical therapist, and mother.

Using COACH (Giangreco et al., 1998), a family-friendly process, Tina's mother selected a set of five discipline-free priorities to be restated as annual goals on her IEP. Tina's priorities were 1) making choices; 2) engaging in individual leisure activities; 3) completing tasks independently; 4) identifying objects, pictures, and symbols; and 5) initiating and sustaining social interactions. Several additional learning outcomes, beyond the IEP priorities, were identified together by the team based on Tina's individual needs and on the general education curriculum for her school. Some of these additional learning outcomes included responding to yes-or-no questions, expressing "more," learning to complete a classroom assignment, using the computer, and achieving selected language and math outcomes using a multilevel curriculum approach.

General supports also were identified by the team. The team recognized that the success of Tina's school experience would depend in part on providing her with necessary supports as well as on providing supports to those who worked with her. In addition, there were a number of tasks that needed to be done for Tina by others, with regard to which skill acquisition by Tina was not expected. For example, feeding, dressing, and personal hygiene were tasks that the team had decided would be done for Tina. There was no expectation that she would learn the physical aspects of these skills, although she was encouraged to learn about related communication and social skills (e.g., making choices, expressing "more," expressing refusal, cooperation) that built on her strengths. In addition, Tina needed to be moved from place to place in her wheelchair and in and out of her chair using specialized positioning and movement techniques and equipment that kept her positioned comfortably. Staff needed to use good body mechanics to avoid injury (e.g., lower-back strain). Physical environments throughout the building and on school grounds needed to be assessed to determine the need for accessibility adaptations. Equipment management was also needed for seating, computer access adaptations, switches, the scanning device, and a prone stander that allowed Tina to be upright during activities when other students were standing. Classmates and school staff needed to be taught about Tina's communication and interaction strategies and her movement and safety needs, including the equipment she used. Finally, instruction accommodations had to be made each week for language arts; math; and specials such as music, art, and library time.

Table 3. Tina's physical therapy service plan

Identified outcome or support	Specific need	Function to be served	Collaborate with…
Specialized positioning and movement techniques	• Recommended positions to match classroom activities and Tina's needs	Developing adaptations	Classroom teacher
	• Select and assist in procurement of positioning equipment	Developing adaptations	Classroom teacher and administrator
	• Teach staff safe and effective movement and positioning assistance techniques	Teaching others	Team
	• Teach staff safe body mechanics for transferring and lifting Tina	Teaching others	Team
	• Ongoing evaluation and monitoring of use of techniques taught	Teaching others	Team
	• Documentation on videotape and in notebook of photographs for descriptions and examples of appropriate use of techniques	Teaching others	Team
Accessible activities and environments	• Evaluate the need for increased accessibility in physical education, art room, and for field trips, and plan accordingly	Teaching others, making adaptations	Physical education and art teachers, classroom teacher
Manage equipment	• Monitor fit and condition of wheelchair, prone stander, and adapted seat	Adaptations	
	• Document person to call for repairs of equipment		
Instructional accommodation	• Develop instructional accommodations for physical education class	Adaptations	Physical education teacher
Develop emergency evacuation procedures	• Determine appropriate evacuation route and procedures from various positions and locations around school	Adaptations	Classroom teacher, building principal

Tina's team considered the needs for service support using a collaborative process intended to ensure that services would be both educationally relevant and educationally necessary. For the physical therapist, this meant participating with the team to determine support needs. They determined that the physical therapy service plan would include 5 hours per month of indirect physical therapy support with a potential for decreasing to 2 hours per month once certain supports were in place. Table 3 outlines the resulting physical therapy service plan for Tina.

There were no IEP goals or additional learning outcomes for which the team determined the need for physical therapy support. Initially, both physical therapy and occupational therapy support were considered potentially necessary for Tina to learn a classroom job (e.g., making deliveries, caring for classroom plants and animals). Both types of therapists had experience and skills 1) collaborating with teachers on selecting an appropriate job, 2) analyzing motor performance on selected tasks, and 3) determining adaptations. In Tina's case, the team decided that the overlap between these two services was not a desirable overlap and that the occupational therapist, who had a background in working in supported employment, would be responsible for that area of support. Tina's plan illustrates a situation in which the therapeutic involvement of a related service exclusively related to *general supports* rather than to any direct learning outcomes.

IMPLICATIONS FOR PRACTICE

This chapter describes the generic roles that related services providers can play to support the education of children with disabilities and provides several applications of those roles in inclusive preschool through high school education environments. The chapter also offers criteria for teams to use in making decisions about related services provision. These criteria, framed as questions, include the following:

1. Are proposed related services educationally relevant?
2. Are proposed related services educationally necessary?
3. Are proposed related services only as special as necessary?

Given this backdrop, we see several implications for practicing related services providers. First, related services providers are encouraged to reexamine their models of service provision so that they can increase their constructive involvement on teams, decrease the fragmentation and isolation often associated with itinerancy, and ask how their services will improve a student's learning and success in his or her education environment. Second, to be better prepared as collaborative decision makers, service providers need to participate in cross-disciplinary training. Through this exchange of discipline-specific information, they will be better prepared to plan, implement, and evaluate a student's education program in a nonduplicative and coordinated fashion. Third, providers must trust that their collaborators can adequately take on a role they traditionally have viewed as their own. This trust can be built through initial and ongoing communication among team members that is reciprocal in nature. Cross-disciplinary and discipline-specific training can further build team capacity and trust. Fourth, related services providers must strive for accountability in the efforts of those individuals delivering cross-disciplinary activities that are agreed on by the team. Finally, team members should create a process for evaluating what they are doing and demonstrating the relationship of what is being done with regard to the valued life outcomes identified for and by the students being served.

The phrase *valued life outcomes* refers to what has commonly been called *quality of life* in the literature. By pursuing quality of life as an outcome of education, we hope that the lives of *all* our students are better as a result of having attended our schools and receiving the support services that are provided. This is no less true of and no less important for students with disabilities. Noted educator Burton Blatt emphasized the temporal, relative, and individual nature and importance of quality of life for people with disabilities when he so eloquently stated,

> There will be necessarily empty places, as it is equally certain that there will be times when there seems to be too much. . . . The brimming cup has little to do with the size of the cup or the temporary nature of its contents. . . . It is all in the mind and, for sure in the soul. (1987, p. 358)

REFERENCES

Blatt, B. (1987). *The conquest of mental retardation.* Austin, TX: PRO-ED.

Board of Education of the Hendrick Hudson Central School District v. Rowley, 102 S. Ct. 3034 (1982).

Dennis, R.E., Williams, W.W., Giangreco, M.F., & Cloninger, C.J. (1993). Quality of life as a context for planning and evaluation of services for people with disabilities: A review of the literature. *Exceptional Children, 59,* 499–512.

Education for All Handicapped Children Act of 1975, PL 94-142, 20 U.S.C. §§ 1400 *et seq.*

Fox, T., & Williams, W. (1991). *Best practice guidelines for meeting the needs of all students in local schools.* Burlington: University of Vermont, University Affiliated Program of Vermont.

Giangreco, M.F. (1990). Making related service decisions for students with severe disabilities: Roles, criteria, and authority. *Journal of The Association for Persons with Severe Handicaps, 15,* 22–31.

Giangreco, M.F. (1996). *Vermont interdependent services team approach: A guide to coordinating educational support services.* Baltimore: Paul H. Brookes Publishing Co.

Giangreco, M.F., Cloninger, C.J., & Iverson, V.S. (1998). *Choosing outcomes and accommodations for children: A guide to educational planning for students with disabilities* (2nd ed.). Baltimore: Paul H. Brookes Publishing Co.

Giangreco, M.F., Cloninger, C.J., Mueller, P., Yuan, S., & Ashworth, S. (1991). Perspectives of parents whose children have dual sensory impairments. *Journal of The Association for Persons with Severe Handicaps, 16,* 14–24.

Giangreco, M.F., Dennis, R.E., Cloninger, C.J., Edelman, S.W., & Schattman, R. (1993). "I've counted Jon": Transformational experiences of teachers educating students with disabilities. *Exceptional Children, 59,* 359–372.

Giangreco, M.F., Edelman, S.W., & Dennis, R.E. (1991). Common professional practices that interfere with the integrated delivery of related services. *Remedial and Special Education, 12,* 16–24.

Giangreco, M.F., Edelman, S.W., Luiselli, T.E., & MacFarland, S.Z. (1996). Support service decision-making for students with multiple service needs: Evaluation data. *Journal of The Association for Persons with Severe Handicaps, 21,* 135–144.

Giangreco, M.F., Edelman, S.W., Luiselli, T.E., & MacFarland, S.Z. (1998). Reaching consensus about educationally necessary support services: A qualitative evaluation of VISTA. *Special Services in the Schools, 13*(1–2), 1–32.

Giangreco, M.F., Edelman, S.W., MacFarland, S.Z., & Luiselli, T.E. (1997). Attitudes about educational and related services for students with deaf-blindness and multiple disabilities. *Exceptional Children, 63,* 329–342.

Giangreco, M.F., Edelman, S.W., & Nelson, C. (1998). Impact of planning support services on students who are deaf-blind. *Journal of Visual Impairment and Blindness, 92*(1), 18–29.

Goldstein, A.P. (1988). *The Prepare Curriculum: Teaching prosocial competencies.* Champaign, IL: Research Press Co.

Goldstein, A.P., & McGinnis, E. (1997). *Skill-streaming the adolescent: New strategies and perspectives for teaching prosocial skills* (Rev. ed.). Champaign, IL: Research Press Co.

Individuals with Disabilities Education Act (IDEA) Amendments of 1997, PL 105-17, 20 U.S.C. §§ 1400 *et seq.*

Irving Independent School District v. Tatro, 104 S. Ct. 3371 (1984).

Johnson, D.W., & Johnson, R.T. (1991). *Teaching students to be peacemakers.* Edina, MN: Interaction Book Co.

Levinson, M.E. (1990). Actual/desired role functioning, perceived control over role functioning, and job satisfaction among school psychologists. *Psychology in the Schools, 27,* 64–74.

Levinson, M.E., Fetchkan, R., & Hohenshil, T.H. (1988). Job satisfaction among practicing school psychologists revisited. *School Psychology Review, 17,* 102.

Meyer, L.H., & Eichinger, J. (1994). *Program quality indicators (PQI): A checklist of most promising practices in educational programs for students with disabilities* (3rd ed.). Syracuse, NY: Syracuse University School of Education.

Rainforth, B., & York-Barr, J. (1997). *Collaborative teams for students with severe disabilities: Integrating therapy and educational services* (2nd ed.). Baltimore: Paul H. Brookes Publishing Co.

Reynolds, M. (1962). A framework for considering some issues in special education. *Exceptional Children, 28,* 367–370.

Sowers, J., Hall, S., & Rainforth, B. (1992). Related service personnel in supported employment: Roles and training needs. *Rehabilitation Education, 4,* 319–331.

Thousand, J.S., & Villa, R.A. (1992). Collaborative teams: A powerful tool in school restructuring. In R.A. Villa, J.S. Thousand, W.C. Stainback, & S.B. Stainback (Eds.), *Restructuring for caring and effective education: An administrative guide to creating heterogeneous schools* (1st ed., pp. 73–108). Baltimore: Paul H. Brookes Publishing Co.

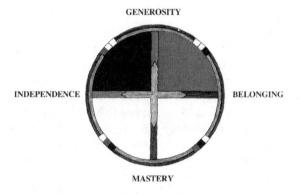

GENEROSITY

INDEPENDENCE

BELONGING

MASTERY

REFLECTION

Collaboration for "Regular" Lives
An Invitation to Our Children's Teachers

Lisa and Alan Houghtelin

Jamie Houghtelin (left) with co-editor Jacqueline S. Thousand (right).

THE NATURE OF DREAMS

Jamie is our daughter. We love her. We have dreams for her. Our dreams are essentially the same as any parent's. We want our daughter to be happy—to have friends, to have opportunities to explore the world every day, to discover her own interests and strengths, and to learn who she is. We want her to feel good about herself and her work. We want her to have choices. We want her to have the basic necessities of life and a little bit extra, just for fun. We want her to experience joy and to have the self-confidence and resilience she will need to learn from pain and disappointment. We want her to be the most competent and contributing member of society that she can be.

More important, our daughter has her own dreams. We, as parents, must be the advocates of our daughter's right to dream and have the confidence in her ability to realize her dreams. We must create opportunities and possibilities until she can create them for herself.

In order for any dream to come true, a person must first believe that it is possible. Because our daughter experiences significant academic, social, and physical challenges, some people say that parents such as we are in denial. They say that our child's challenges make the realization of her and our dreams an impossibility. This has not been our experience.

Jamie is 13 years old now. She is a real teenager, as she likes to remind us numerous times each day. She loves dancing and turning up her music too loud. Her room is a mess, and lately her parents are a major pain to her most of the time. Throughout her school years, Jamie has attended public school in general education classrooms with all of the other kids—kids with and without labels, each with his or her own special characteristics. When Jamie was very young, we gambled that, rather than be protected and isolated in separate special classrooms, she would want to be right in the middle of life, grappling with the messiness, the unpredictability, the fun, and sometimes the heartbreak of being part of a community.

The community is where Jamie always has been, and, because of that, as we write this, she is at a meeting of her church youth group with a friend she's had since second grade. Tomorrow she goes to her middle school, which is deep into the process of restructuring to include all students in general education classes, making it possible for Jamie to continue to be with her friends from elementary school.

We must say that Jamie's life is not perfect. Her disabilities and people's reactions to them create some constant barriers. Jamie does not have as many opportunities to go off independently with her friends as she would like. There are days when the telephone does not ring for her. Yet, Jamie has a relatively rich life. She loves learning about sea mammals, cats, and babies. She has friends of every age, of different cultures, and with and without disabilities. There are three young men who think she is pretty special. Jamie has friends with whom she makes up plays, cooks, looks up Hanson's web site, and does art projects. She has friends who are on her swim team and in her ballet class. She has her own dreams to be a teacher, a veterinarian, an artist, an actress, and a doctor; to work with kids; and to have a great wedding.

IMPORTANCE OF TRUE COLLABORATIVE TEAMING

For our family, the process of keeping Jamie included in school and in community programs has not been easy or even nice at times. However, it has absolutely been worth it. Key to getting Jamie where she is today is collaboration: the hard work and dedication of many people who have come together to create and implement the supports that Jamie needs to experience success. To clarify what we mean by *collaboration*, we restate the definition of effective collaborative teams articulated in Chapter 10 of this book (pages 257–258): A *collaborative team* may be defined as a group of people who agree to

1. Coordinate their work to achieve at least one *common, publicly agreed-on goal* (Appley & Winder, 1977)

2. Hold a *belief system* that all members of the team have unique and needed expertise (Vandercook & York, 1990)

3. Demonstrate *parity*, the equal valuation of each member's input (Falck, 1977), by alternately engaging in the dual roles of teacher and learner, expert and recipient, consultant and consultee (Villa, Thousand, Paolucci-Whitcomb, & Nevin, 1990)

4. Use a *distributed functions theory* of leadership in which the task and relationship functions of the traditional lone leader are distributed among all members of the group (Johnson & Johnson, 1999; Johnson, Johnson, & Holubec, 1993, 1994)

5. Employ a *collaborative teaming process* that involves face-to-face interaction; positive interdependence; the performance, monitoring, and processing of interpersonal skills; and individual accountability (Johnson & Johnson, 1999; Johnson, Johnson, & Holubec, 1993, 1994)

We know that collaboration, as defined in the previous list, does exist because we have read the literature on inclusive education and talked to people and visited places where effective teaming happens. Sadly, we cannot write about our own experience with truly effective collaborative teams, because we never really have been part of one. Clearly, Jamie has had *enough* support in general education to experience real benefits from her schooling. However, these benefits have come at a tremendous cost to us in time and emotional and psychic energy. Why, despite our best efforts and the involvement of many competent and caring teachers, has it been so hard for us?

In our family's case, Jamie's support teams seem to have gotten stuck at the first step of the collaborative teaming process, coming to a common and publicly agreed-on goal. Without members of an education team agreeing that general education classrooms with needed supports are the best place for all children, the exciting and rewarding work illustrated in the previous chapters on collaboration is made most difficult. When a team is stuck at the first step, parents who have inclusive education as the goal for their children are compelled to make unwelcome requests of teachers to quickly change the nature and activities of their professional lives. When the goal of inclusive education is not shared, parents often find themselves to be the sole enforcers of the remaining elements of an effective collaborative team. Namely, parents end up

- Requesting or demanding frequent face-to-face interactions
- Convincing others that children and their friends as well as family members have unique and needed expertise that is of true value to the process
- Demonstrating leadership skills to promote the process of creative problem solving
- Holding others accountable for providing negotiated services
- Attempting to maintain good interpersonal relationships with the other members of the team throughout the collaborative process

Doing all of this is exhausting and seemingly never ending.

AN INVITATION TO DREAM TOGETHER

Despite the less-than-perfect experiences that we have had with collaboration, we are totally committed to modeling, encouraging, and acknowledging collaborative teaming throughout Jamie's years in school and beyond. The very good news is that with the emerging research studies and personal stories highlighting the benefits of collaboration for inclusive education, more and more education professionals are coming to understand, agree with, and commit to the goal of supporting all children to experience "regular" lives.

Parents know that educators come to the profession of teaching to make a difference in the lives of children. Parents also *want* teachers to make that positive difference for their children. With this as a common goal, parents and teachers become natural allies.

Teachers, please consider this reflection an invitation to dream with parents and children. Please consider it an invitation to collaborate with us to make a huge difference, to make the "impossible" dreams a reality. We cannot make it happen without you.

$$* \quad * \quad *$$

1999 UPDATE

We are pleased to report that, thanks to the vision, commitment, and hard work of the principal and staff at Rincon Middle School, collaborative teaming for the purpose of educating students with and without disabilities together is a reality at Jamie's school. Jamie is a self-confident and well-supported seventh grader and is excited by all that she is learning. Our dreams continue to come true!

REFERENCES

Appley, D.G., & Winder, A.E. (1977). An evolving definition of collaboration and some implications for the world of work. *Journal of Applied Behavioral Science, 13,* 279–291.

Falck, H. (1977). Interdisciplinary education and implications for social work practice. *Journal of Education for Social Work, 13*(2), 30–47.

Johnson, D.W., & Johnson, R.T. (1999). *Learning together and alone: Cooperative, competitive, and individualistic learning* (5th ed.). Needham Heights, MA: Allyn & Bacon.

Johnson, D.W., Johnson, R.T., & Holubec, E.J. (1993). *Circles of learning: Cooperation in the classroom* (4th ed.). Edina, MN: Interaction Book Co.

Johnson, D.W., Johnson, R.T., & Holubec, E.J. (1994). *The new circles of learning: Cooperation in the classroom and school.* Alexandria, VA: Association for Supervision and Curriculum Development.

Vandercook, T., & York, J. (1990). A team approach to program development and support. In W.C. Stainback & S.B. Stainback (Eds.), *Support networks for inclusive schooling: Integrated interdependent education* (pp. 95–122). Baltimore: Paul H. Brookes Publishing Co.

Villa, R.A., Thousand, J.S., Paolucci-Whitcomb, P., & Nevin, A.I. (1990). In search of a new paradigm for collaborative consultation. *Journal of Educational and Psychological Consultation, 1*(4), 279–292.

IV

Examples of
Inclusive Schooling in Action
CREATE Inclusive Schools

Margaret E. King-Sears

We do the best we can with what we know; when we know better, we do better.
—Maya Angelou

Maya Angelou's wise words relate to many aspects of life, including education. Educators and parents across the United States are seeking to do better now that we know better about how to educate students with disabilities in their neighborhood schools alongside their peers without disabilities. The authors in this section of the book paint vivid pictures of how they did better once they knew better, and they also are clear that the learning process is unending. Their picture is constantly evolving as they embrace new students and dismantle old systems. Unlike artists, who begin with a blank canvas, educators and parents begin with a canvas that already contains the old picture: pictures of students with disabilities segregated in different schools and different classrooms, pictures of teachers who are long accustomed and fervently attached to old ways of separating students with disabilities in special education classrooms, and pictures that seemed right for many years because they were the best educators knew how to do at that time.

Now we know better. Now we know that the long-term outcomes for students with disabilities after their school years are less fulfilling and less productive when, all of a sudden, peers without disabilities and students with disabilities are expected to live, work, and play together when the school system has separated them during their formative years. It no longer makes sense to fragment services and isolate peers from each other when we now know ways to provide richer and more relevant services for peers with and without disabilities learning alongside each other. We also know that changing the existing picture is not easy. Deciding where to place the initial brush strokes must be determined by teams of parents and school personnel, and selecting the colors for new practices, although exciting and energizing, is always effortful.

Creating the portrait of inclusive school services for students with a range of disabilities—and their peers without disabilities—may initially seem to be an overwhelming process. Frequently asked questions include the following:

Where do we start?

What model should we use?

What kind of training do we need?

Valid questions such as these and corresponding ideas from others who are creating their portraits are eloquently captured by the authors of the following chapters in this section. Single, right, and one-size-fits-all answers to these questions, however, do not exist. What are available, fortunately, are multiple ways for teams to develop collaboratively inclusive systems that work well for their students in their schools, for members of their school and community staff, and for their parents. Several common elements are evident in each of the students' and schools' stories presented in this section:

- Everyone found somewhere to start, but each school began at a different place.
- Foundational starting places must begin with knowing the students.
- All journeys toward more inclusive schools are marked by ups and downs, trial-and-error, and learning curves.
- A flexible plan, a shared vision, and a monitoring process keeps people moving, accountable, and progressive.

As I read through the chapters in this section, I am struck by how many different people came together in so many different ways to do so many different things to create inclusion within their classrooms. Variations in resources, personalities, students' needs, school structures, and expertise preclude a "paint by numbers" formula that works well for everyone. Five themes are evident throughout this section and are described next for others who, as Maya Angelou would say, now know better and are eager to create inclusive experiences for their schools.

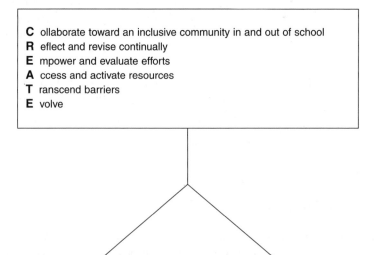

CREATE Your Inclusive Portrait

C ollaborate toward an inclusive community in and out of school
R eflect and revise continually
E mpower and evaluate efforts
A ccess and activate resources
T ranscend barriers
E volve

COLLABORATE TOWARD AN INCLUSIVE COMMUNITY IN AND OUT OF SCHOOL

People who make inclusive schools work do not just coordinate and cooperate; they collaborate in ways that challenge and transform traditional boundaries and practices into shared responsibilities for meaningful academic and social education. People who used to pull students out of general education classes for services do not just deliver those services in general education environments, they collaborate with school staff, parents, and students in ways that escalate the relevance of services and promote sharing of techniques. Students with disabilities who formerly left classrooms for specialized instruction or attended special schools receive enriched education alongside their peers without disabilities. Students without disabilities who never got to know their peers with disabilities are getting to know them not only during school hours but also during after-school extracurricular opportunities. Parents who in the past typically deferred to school professionals' decisions realize that they are experts about their youngster's characteristics—critical knowledge that is valued and used by school personnel in effective, inclusive schools.

As vividly described in each chapter of this section, teachers, administrators, students, and parents create new portraits of their schools as they collaborate to make inclusion work. For no one was it easy; for no one was it a clear path; and for no one was it always successful. As you read individuals' stories, however, also note how their beliefs that inclusion is ethically and educationally the right path influenced their actions, how they persisted to overcome challenges and barriers in their way, and how they found along the way that individuals grew beyond the point that they had envisioned initially. Furthermore, the individuals who grew were not just the students with disabilities: Their peers without disabilities, their teachers, and their families realized benefits that promoted their responsibilities as citizens.

REFLECT AND REVISE CONTINUALLY

Considerable reflection occurs among people working in inclusive schools. Prioritizing students' learning outcomes precedes decisions about how to include students in general education instruction experiences. Determinations of how to include students effectively were made creatively and systematically so that the relevance of the experiences was clear, methodologies were varied, and responsibilities were shared. People reflected individually and collectively and considered several key concerns frequently voiced about inclusion:

- How are students with disabilities progressing?
- What is the impact of inclusion on students without disabilities?
- Who else can benefit from the specialized techniques that traditionally were reserved for students with labels?

- How well are parents' voices being heard?
- What are students saying about how well inclusion is going?
- What should be done differently the next time to enhance inclusion efforts?

EMPOWER AND EVALUATE EFFORTS

People must be empowered to make decisions and choices when inclusive schools are created. Adults involved in the experience include all of the adults in the school and the community. Students involved in the experience include peers without disabilities and the student with a disability label him- or herself. *Empowerment* means relinquishing total control and sharing responsibility. Note, for example, how administrators described in the following chapters highlight how leadership was shared versus mandates being imposed, how educators and students were involved in choices about how inclusion would occur, and how parents were considered significant team members. Also note that people did not just physically place students in inclusive environments without concurrent evaluation of the effects of the inclusion efforts. When changes needed to occur based on the results of their efforts, the team discussed such changes and decided collaboratively on their next steps. Benefits for students with and without disabilities were evaluated, which enabled parents and teachers to be satisfied that efforts were advancing, not hindering, educational outcomes for all students.

ACCESS AND ACTIVATE RESOURCES

Two hallmarks of effective inclusive programs are how existing resources are used in new ways and how additional resources are accrued. For some programs, inventorying existing resources indicates that staff can be used in new ways to provide accommodations and assistance for students and teachers. For example, instruction assistants who formerly were relegated to handling clerical tasks can assist more with instruction activities. Administrators in some inclusive schools have provided release time for general and special educators to collaborate by initiating weekly student activities that others can oversee, providing a floating substitute teacher who manages multiple classes during a school day, or inviting guests from the community to visit classrooms throughout the school on a predictable schedule (e.g., a half day set aside as career day every other week).

Key questions to ask are whether existing resources are being used in effective and efficient ways and whether students' learning experiences can be embedded within activities that are already occurring at the school. For example, in one school, a special educator gained access to the middle school teachers' clerical tasks (e.g., photocopying, sorting, stapling, stacking) as an opportunity to have students with moderate cognitive disabilities learn vocational tasks. Mutual benefits occurred—the general educators became more receptive to including the students in their classrooms and differentiating curriculum expectations; the special educator acquired authentic vocational tasks for the students to complete; and, for one period per day, the students were able to learn functional curriculum by performing tasks that already existed at the school. The students also developed valuable relationships with those teachers and their peers when they were effectively included in middle school content areas where differentiated learning outcomes were available.

In other situations, peers without disabilities are prepared to be peer buddies for their classmates with disabilities in ways that promote understanding and valuing of differences, learning opportunities, and friendships—for students with disabilities and their peers without disabilities. In still other inclusive environments, cooperative learning experiences show yet another way that students are being used as resources for each other while the students' educational experiences are enhanced.

People from universities, businesses, and community agencies are being activated as resources. Extending such partnerships beyond the schoolhouse door enables access to monetary, resource, service, and other types of supports that enhance inclusion efforts within schools and their communities.

TRANSCEND BARRIERS

Many parents and professionals who are dedicated to inclusion have been pioneers in creating such opportunities for youngsters with disabilities. Initial efforts within classrooms, schools, and school systems have not been easy. Yet, even with paths being paved before them, people still encounter barriers along the way. Consequently, people who are working to create effective inclusive classroom environments are resilient and persistent in finding ways to overcome, bypass, or remove barriers in their way. People who are initially learning about inclusion need the time, opportunity, training, and support to change old ways of thinking about and implementing education programs into new ways that transform learning environments into learning communities that promote heterogeneous educational experiences. Sometimes what may be perceived as a barrier (e.g., a teacher who is resistant to including a student) is really a request (e.g., he or she needs training and support). It is important when initiating efforts toward inclusion that parents, professionals, and school staff have a voice in creating their portrait of inclusion; otherwise, barriers of resistance may develop in the form of people perceiving that mandates are being imposed instead of their voices being heard and listened to.

Providing information to people, having them visit successful inclusive environments, and setting up conversations with other educators who have experienced the same trepidation when venturing into the new territory of inclusion are essential to transcend barriers. Some additional tips for transcending barriers follow:

- Listen to people, and hear beyond the words they are saying to what their needs are. For example, some teachers (both general and special educators) fear inclusion because they are not sure what to do and how to do it. Validate such fears, and provide training and support as they learn about and practice new techniques.

- Involve everyone in the planning and implementation processes. People who have inclusion mandated and imposed on them without any, or without sufficient, training and support have been set up for unpleasant experiences.

- Recruit supporters who share some part of the vision of inclusion. In one school, both the principal and assistant principal, realizing that some of their teachers would react negatively to controversy associated with the term *inclusion*, talked with staff about the principles embodied by the term. Educators at their school could believe that every student who lived in their neighborhood had a right to be educated at their school, and sharing that vision was a key to the eventual development and implementation of inclusion.

- Expect challenges, but do not perceive them as setbacks. People who view challenges as learning opportunities are more likely to develop creative and effective solutions.

- Take risks and be creative. Speculate about what might work, and try it!

EVOLVE

What do inclusive portraits look like? Each looks different because each portrait is painted with different brush strokes on a canvas that began as a unique picture. The brush strokes may begin tenuously, or they may begin boldly. The colors and shapes vary, just as the individuals involved in inclusion are distinct. How long does it take to complete the portrait? Completion is never achieved, because evolution occurs constantly. What worked well last year for those teachers, students, and parents changes for next year's population. Returning to a paraphrase of Maya Angelou's words, today we do the best we can with what we know, and tomorrow—when we find out more effective, creative, and authentic ways to ensure that more youngsters with disabilities have more opportunities to learn alongside their peers without disabilities—we will do those things. We can anticipate viewing future portraits created by today's students—with and without disabilities—who are experiencing inclusive education that evolve from those portraits created today. We can learn from the authors in the following chapters, who have learned from their students and their experiences, what their inclusive portraits look like and how their evolution is transforming, challenging, and exciting. Perhaps they will inspire readers to use a few new brush strokes to "CREATE" inclusive portraits now that they "know better about how to do better."

Chapter 14

Restructuring to Create a High School Community of Learners

Lori Eshilian, Mary A. Falvey,
Catherine Bove, Mary Jane Hibbard,
Jeffrey Laiblin, Connie Miller, and Richard L. Rosenberg

With increasing numbers of elementary schools moving toward inclusive educational practices, there remain amazingly few examples of systemic inclusion at the high school level. Whittier High School (WHS), located in Whittier, California, is one exception. WHS is a large urban school serving a diverse community of students representing different ethnic, cultural, and religious groups; varying abilities; and a wide range of socioeconomic levels. Until several years ago, it was a traditional high school. It maintained separate special education programs for its students with mild, moderate, and severe disabilities, following the national move over the past decades from a separate developmen-

Some of this chapter originally appeared in Falvey, M.A., Eshilian, L., Miller, C., Zimmerman, F., Russell, R., & Rosenberg, R. (1997). Developing a community of learners at Whittier High School. In D. Sage (Ed.), *Models and strategies for inclusive education at the secondary level*. Syracuse, NY: National Professional Resources Publishing; reprinted with permission.

tal model, to a functional skills community-based focus, to social mainstreaming. What makes this latest system change effort toward full inclusion unique and central to its success is that the initiative did not come from special education. Instead, it was a schoolwide initiative to restructure to improve the curriculum, instructional strategies, organizational practices, and support services that would benefit *all* students.

WHS began this restructuring effort in 1992. Although strong district and school-based administrative leadership influenced the restructuring efforts, it was a group of teachers, parents, and students who met weekly for a year who ensured that a "restructured" high school would be realized. WHS's restructuring process was closely linked with the Coalition of Essential Schools movement (Sizer, 1992); WHS officially became a member of the Coalition of Essential Schools in 1994. The Coalition of Essential Schools are schools devoted to the principle that all students can learn and that the educational community must develop personalized and meaningful learning experiences so that all students can succeed. The Coalition is committed to placing students at the center of the learning activities, where they are the workers and the teacher is the facilitator. In addition, rather than teaching students to memorize a large number of unrelated facts, the Coalition is committed to the idea that students need to learn more about how they learn and how to conduct research to gain information. Authentic teaching and assessment are also critical elements of the Coalition.

Restructuring first occurred in the lower grades, with ninth- and tenth-grade teachers and students reconstituting themselves into smaller teams. The Coalition's Nine Common Principles were adopted as guiding principles for encouraging academic achievement for *all* students in the teams. For juniors and seniors, attention also was directed toward career paths (e.g., establishing a computer academy) to assist students in identifying career opportunities; make connections between work, their community, and the curriculum; set educational and career goals for themselves; and internalize the need for achievement in high school.

As an integral part of this restructuring movement, special educators at WHS became active members of all committees. For example, they participated on interdisciplinary curricula writing teams that were developing curriculum standards, so as to facilitate access to the curriculum for *all* students, including those with disabilities. In committees, the concept of including students with disabilities was not discussed as a separate issue; rather, discussion focused on effective education for all students. Special education staff continuously participated in all restructuring discussions, assisting the staff to draw connections between the goals of inclusive education and the goals of restructuring. Participation of special educators on committees enabled them to become familiar with the curriculum in general education classes, to plan team teaching arrangements with general education teachers, and to begin to develop adapted materials and modify assignments that would support students to fully participate and find success in classes.

The outcome of a year of planning, writing, and development was a committed staff dedicated to ensuring that educational practices matched the "all means all" principles of the Coalition of Essential Schools (Sizer, 1992). When school opened in the fall of 1993, every freshman eligible for special education was fully included in core curricular and elective courses alongside his or her classmates without disabilities. This was in contrast to the approximations of inclusive education that had been achieved in previous years. Although the special education faculty had successfully "mainstreamed" most students with disabilities into various general education classes, inclusive education was not a school norm and was not associated with other core curriculum and instructional initiatives. Students with disabilities often were placed in general education classes based on which teachers were willing to have students with disabilities in their classroom rather than students' interests and needs. Efforts were made to place students with the "best" teachers who employed active learning strategies, causing their classrooms often to be overcrowded. Through the restructuring planning process, more teachers became knowledgeable and successful in implementing active learning and other inclusive practices, which empowered and opened them up to welcoming students with disabilities into typical high school classes alongside their peers.

SPECIFIC SYSTEMS CHANGE EFFORTS RESULTING IN INCLUSION

Among the strategies that contributed to WHS's successful restructuring were the following:

1. Adoption of a set of guiding principles (i.e., Essential Schools Principles)
2. The development of a shared mission statement based on these principles
3. Administrative leadership to maintain a focus on this vision
4. Collaborative teaming processes
5. Total staff development efforts directed toward learning new methods of curriculum development, active learning practices,

instructional strategies that support diverse learners, and authentic assessment

6. The allotment of time for staff to plan together for the present instructional situation and students' needs in the future

All of these variables have repeatedly been identified as critical to any successful school restructuring endeavor (e.g., Villa & Thousand, 1995; see also Chapter 10). In the context of a high school, it further is necessary to break away from practices and organizational structures that compartmentalize and divide faculty and students. To accomplish this, WHS divided the school into smaller units, established block scheduling, emphasized active learning and authentic assessment strategies, and made special efforts to develop a community of learners. The following sections detail how WHS went about accomplishing these dramatic changes in school culture.

Dividing the School into Smaller Units

In the fall of 1993, the ninth grade was reorganized so students were clustered into one of three smaller teams. In the following year, similar clustering was extended to the tenth grade; in 1997, it was further extended to one eleventh-grade history/English team. The teams are intended to facilitate students' academic success through more personalized and longer-term relationships with teachers and one another. Students and teachers generally remain in their same teams for their first 2 years of high school.

The "schools within a school" teams at WHS are composed of core curriculum teachers, two "support teachers" (formerly called "special education teachers"), an administrator, a school counselor, and one or two paraprofessionals supported by special education resources. Teachers use an interdisciplinary approach to delivering the core curriculum in the areas of humanities (combining of English and social studies), M.A.S.S. (combining of math and science studies), and U.S. studies (combining of history and American literature).

The elimination of the "special education teacher" label was considered critical to changing the perception that only "specialists" can work with students with disabilities. Thus, WHS selected the term *support teacher* to identify staff who, in collaboration with general education teachers, supported (and coordinated services for) students eligible for special education. Support teachers take on a variety of collaborative roles with the general education teachers. They co-teach or team teach with content area teachers within heterogeneous classrooms and function as a support to all students, not just those who qualify for special education services.

To enable members of the team to work more effectively together, the administration scheduled a common preparation period and located classrooms in close proximity to one another. Teachers may be more responsive to and assume greater responsibility for students experiencing some difficulties because they have more time and opportunity to meet regularly to share information about students' progress and challenges.

Subsequent to the restructuring efforts, students' poor attendance was a significant contributor to poor grades and general school failure. Advisement activities were developed to help each student clarify individual goals and develop a greater commitment to participating in school programs and activities. These activities, together with greater personalization provided through the team approach, have yielded significant improvement in student attendance. Because California funds schools on the basis of attendance, such improvements also have resulted in an increase in fiscal resources available to the school district.

The restructuring at WHS has resulted in teachers becoming coaches and facilitators of learning rather than "experts" in specific subject matter. Special and general educators work together to blend their expertise in order to become generalists rather than specialists. This is a major change in the traditional way high school teachers have typically identified and described themselves.

At WHS each professional is viewed as having unique contributions that are needed by their colleagues. For example, support teachers have experience and training in modifying instruction for students who learn at different rates and in different ways; they also provide input into effective teaching strategies in specific curricular areas (e.g., reading). General education team members have extensive knowledge of the curriculum and strategies for teaching the curriculum to groups of diverse learners. Together, teammates are better able to respond effectively to the educational needs of students with labels (special education, limited English speaking, gifted). Support teachers also report that working as a member of a team not only has enhanced their own knowledge of the core curriculum but also created a sense of membership and belonging within the greater school community.

At WHS, the individualized education program (IEP) and individualized transition plan (ITP) processes have become very dynamic and student empowering. WHS has merged the IEP and ITP processes and engaged students and their parents (as well as general education counselors, administrators, teachers, support teachers, and vocational coordinators) as active participants in planning not only for a student's school life, but life beyond school. Preparation for postgraduation life is a focus of every student's IEP/ITP meeting.

Block Scheduling

WHS teams have also divided their daily schedules into blocks of time. Instead of teachers teaching five periods each day, they teach two blocked periods per term plus one class outside of their team. By block scheduling integrated subject matter, the teacher/student ratio is reduced from approximately 180 to 90 students per teacher. Block scheduling has dramatically increased the opportunity for more personalized teacher–student time (Thousand, Rosenberg, Bishop, & Villa, 1997).

The fact that block scheduling affords more time to concentrate on a particular subject, topic, or activity does not mean that instruction actually changes to accomplish this end. Teachers have needed to adapt their teaching styles and strategies to accommodate the increased time block (i.e., 1 hour and 53 minutes). Teachers arrange a variety of activities throughout the block, ranging from cooperative groups to individual practice, group instruction, and group projects.

The benefits of block scheduling are many. Because the curriculum is also taught in an integrated approach, students have the opportunity to explore and better understand the interrelationship of subject matter. There is time to put together the ideas they learn, conduct in-depth analysis, and apply critical thinking and problem-solving skills required in the "real world." There is time to see that a subject may have many different facets. For instance, in ninth-grade world geography, students' study goes beyond knowledge about locations and land forms. Students are introduced to the history of a country and its culture by studying literature, music, media, art, architecture, foods, customs, and traditions and are encouraged to express their knowledge through a variety of written, auditory, and visual formats. Furthermore, a connection is made to math and science as students learn about mathematical and science beliefs and discoveries associated with the country.

With block scheduling and team clusters, when academic problems do arise, early support from the close-knit team of teachers can help a student avoid failure and turn the problems into solutions. Block schedule classes are where students receive recognition as individuals with unique talents, learning styles, and needs. The structure and pace of these classes provide a more comfortable, supportive learning environment, allowing more time for students to learn and practice skills together. The teachers get to know each student better, and students receive more personal attention, advisement, and support.

Heterogeneous Grouping of Students and Faculty

Heterogeneous Student Grouping   The "all-too-frequent" method of organizing students in secondary programs referred to as *tracking* has been intentionally decreased at WHS by eliminating what was previously called the "basic" track, the track identified for the students who were the least successful. All students, including those with disabilities, now are required to enroll, participate, and learn in core college preparatory courses throughout their 4 years of high school. This encourages students to focus on higher academic goals and to be prepared for postsecondary educational opportunities and offers all students a solid and comprehensive curriculum consistent with the Individuals with Disabilities Education Act (IDEA) Amendments of 1997 (PL 105-17).

The benefits of homogeneously grouping students for the purposes of instruction have not been substantiated in research studies. In fact, many students have suffered negative effects when grouped homogeneously (Allan, 1991; Oakes, 1985; Sapon-Shevin, 1994). In order to create a community of learners that reflects the characteristics of the larger community in which the students live, they need to be taught in groups of students reflecting the range of characteristics, abilities, and ethnicities within the entire community. In addition, homogeneous grouping of students has been based on a traditional view of intelligence, that is, a view in which intelligence is linear and on a continuum from bright to not so smart. This view of intelligence is narrow and does not reflect newer perspectives of intelligence, including the concept of multiple intelligences (Gardner, 1983), which is discussed in more detail in the next section of this chapter. In addition, rather than grouping students so they experience learning only with others who learn at the same pace and in the same way, grouping so students learn to work within a diverse learning community undoubtedly better prepares them for the heterogeneous "real world." The more diverse the learners, the broader and more applicable the learning experience can be.

Heterogeneous grouping of students at WHS was and continues to be a highly valued guiding principle. However, complete restructuring for heterogeneity has not yet been fully realized. WHS continues to find itself affected by political factors that demand "honors courses" (for those with high academic skills) and separate course standards for students who qualify for English as a second language (ESL). However, these classes (i.e., honors, ESL) do not exclude students with disability labels. Placement of students with disability labels into honors courses has been less frequent but continues to be an option for students with disabilities. Many teachers at WHS are committed to working to eradicate the political forces that insist on grouping students by such categories.

Heterogeneous Faculty Grouping Not only the students, but the faculty of WHS work in more heterogeneous groupings. Unlike traditional high school settings in which only those teachers in the same "department" or discipline work together, the math/science, social studies, English/humanities, and support teachers of each cluster team work together to write curricula, plan lessons, and develop and deliver educational programs to meet the needs of students assigned to their team. These new groupings offer faculty opportunities to go beyond their initial area of expertise or certification and engage in "role release," the "giving away" of one another's specialty knowledge and skills so that all may become "generalists" more capable of teaching adolescents and young adults.

In the past, students with IEPs were matched to special education teachers based on their categorical label (e.g., students with learning disabilities were assigned to teachers labeled "resource" teachers, students with low incidence labels were assigned to special education teachers and classrooms). As a result, teachers might have two or three special educators interacting with them to support students with various labels in their class. This was an inefficient and confusing use of the special educators' time and expertise. Therefore, WHS moved to a non-categorical system of support for students in which each support teacher is assigned to a team of classroom teachers and provides whatever is needed for the students to be successful in those teachers' core curriculum classes. Each support teacher now works with a heterogeneous caseload of students who qualify for Severely Handicapped (SH), Learning Handicapped (LH), or Resource (Related Services Personnel; RSP) services. (These categories are based on California's categorical funding labels; they are not characteristic of students' needs.)

Because all students are now enrolled in core curriculum classes, this is where the support is needed and provided. The additional support benefits not only those students identified as needing specialized services, but many other students who do not qualify for specialized services but who, nevertheless, experience their own unique challenges in learning. The amount and type of consultation and in-class support provided to classroom teachers is determined by the faculty team, based on students' individual learning needs. Table 1 identifies levels of student support available to students at WHS.

The numbers of students entering ninth grade and qualifying for special education services has steadily increased over the years. In the 1997–1998 school year, 183 students qualified for specialized services.

Table I. Levels of support

Total staff support: Support staff remain seated in close proximity to student(s) and bring materials/supplies for them. Staff also assume responsibility for developing or acquiring support strategies and materials that will increase student success.

Classroom companion (peer support): Students who take Student Service class for credit or fellow classmates who agree to assist other student(s) in academic or elective classes. These students may assist in mobility to and from class, carrying or remembering materials, taking notes, accomplishing assignments, facilitated communication, and acting as role models for social/friendship interactions. These students may also participate in development of support strategies.

Daily in-class staff support: Support staff assist many students by moving around the room and providing support as needed. Staff act as role models for cooperation, collaboration, acceptance, and respect for all skill levels. Staff also assume responsibility for developing or acquiring support strategies and materials that will increase student success. Staff may supervise or teach small groups within the class.

Team teaching: Support staff assume half of the responsibility for teaching the curriculum, as prearranged by both the classroom and support teachers. Both teachers assume responsibility for the development of multilevel curriculum, appropriate teaching strategies, grading, the learning environment, and student arrangements that allow for a high level of success for all students.

Part-time daily support: Support staff provide support to student(s) at a predetermined time or on a rotating basis. Staff should maintain awareness of curriculum and assignments to encourage student productivity, successful completion of assignments, and tutorial or organizational support. Support staff may also bring supplemental materials for classroom use. Support teachers may also suggest cooperative learning group combinations between students who may work well together in other classes.

Stop-in support (one to three times per week): Support staff observe students to determine possible need for increased support. They assist the classroom teacher in setting up peer support for recording assignments or notes. They maintain open communication and accessibility to the classroom teacher and to the student.

Consultation: Support staff meet regularly with the classroom teacher to keep track of student progress, assess need for supplemental materials, problem solve, and maintain positive and open communication.

Nine credentialed support teachers were available, so each teacher coordinated services for approximately 21 students, representing a balanced proportion of students with mild to severe disabilities. By consulting, collaborating, and sharing materials and strategies among one another, the support teachers are better able to serve the range of students whose services they coordinate and avoid clustering service coordination by students' disability category (i.e., mild versus severe disability).

Communication among the entire teaching faculty is important and always a challenge. The benefits of discussing individual students' learning styles, methods for applying certain teaching strategies across

---

Student Information

Student's name _____ Age _____ Grade _____

Support teacher _____

Conference period _____ Extension _____

Parent/guardian _____

Home telephone _____

School schedule/teacher

	Subject	Rm. #	Support staff
Period 1	_____	_____	_____
Period 2	_____	_____	_____
Period 3	_____	_____	_____
Period 4	_____	_____	_____
Period 5	_____	_____	_____
Period 6	_____	_____	_____

Functional grade levels   Reading _____ Writing _____ Math _____ Social _____

Student requires accommodations in:

Health _____
Vision _____
Hearing _____
Mobility _____
Behavior _____
Attending _____
Other _____

Areas of student strength _____
_____
_____

Level of support needed

__ Total staff support   __ Part-time daily support
__ Daily in-class support   __ Stop-in weekly support
__ Classroom peer support   __ Consultation

Student's communication style   Student's communication difficulties

__ Verbal   __ Word-finding problems
__ Limited verbal/gestural   __ Problems with drawing conclusions
__ Facilitated communication   __ Sequencing difficulties
__ American Sign Language   __ Limited short-term memory
__ Communication   __ Understanding abstract thoughts
   board/pictures   __ Articulation problems

Individualized education program (IEP) goals/objectives:

_____
_____
_____
_____
_____

Figure I.   Student information form.

(continued)

Figure 1. (*continued*)

Student's work habits in the classroom		
Works independently	Yes	No
Is motivated to work	Yes	No
Follows directions easily, self-initiates assignments	Yes	No
Does homework, completes work independently	Yes	No
Brings materials to class	Yes	No
Is usually on time	Yes	No
Is organized, remembers assignments	Yes	No
Is able to do independent written work	Yes	No

Type of assistance needed to learn

__ Prompt to get started
__ Directions: Repeated, restated, simplified, written, drawn
__ Materials read out loud or books on tape
__ Take oral exams
__ Support for organizing notebook, materials, assignments
__ Extra time to finish work
__ Reduce length of assignments
__ Alternative or modified assignments
__ Alternative assessment
__ Move around occasionally
__ Daily/weekly work and/or attendance contract
__ Other _____

Recommended grading options

__ Letter grade diploma track, with appropriate accommodations
__ Letter grade diploma track, with appropriate accommodations and modifications to curriculum
__ Pass/fail, diploma or nondiploma track, with modifications to curriculum
__ Pass/fail, nondiploma-track based on individualized goals and objectives

curriculum areas, and so forth are clear. Yet, time is always short for such communications to occur. Consequently, WHS faculty devised and use the communication form shown in Figure 1 to facilitate the passing of important student information between support teachers and general educators. Note that, among other things, the form examines how that student best learns, what support strategies have been successful, and the level of support the student might need.

Active Learning Strategies

As a component of the restructuring effort, WHS faculty and staff have been involved in various in-service training experiences to develop their use of active learning strategies. There has been extensive training in cooperative group learning strategies, the development of units that focus on interdisciplinary instruction, and specially designed academic instruction in English (SADIE) training. Many staff also received training to design curriculum and lessons based on critical thinking, problem-solving, and researching skills (versus the memorization of basic facts). In addition, several faculty attended in-depth training on the use of multiple intelligences instruction in the classroom.

It is the faculty's philosophy that active teaching strategies increase and improve student engagement in learning, encourage greater student contributions, and enable students to use higher order thinking skills and to choose among a variety of ways to demonstrate their knowledge and skills. The use of these strategies also encourages more teacher collaboration and team teaching, as professionals share units and lessons developed under these models.

Cooperative Group Learning   One of the greatest changes in the instruction at WHS is the increased use of cooperative learning groups for purposes of teaching, demonstrating knowledge, and problem solving. Research has demonstrated that cooperative groups promote high academic achievement, improve self-esteem, promote active learning, enhance social skill development, and influence peer acceptance and friendships (see Jubala, Bishop, & Falvey, 1995, and Putnam, 1998, for additional research in these areas). Although the benefits of cooperative group learning have received substantial documentation in the literature, much of the emphasis and use has been with elementary-age students. Clearly, the benefits for older students are no less than for younger students, particularly because cooperative learning experiences are designed to teach students the skills to collaborate with others and reach common goals, skills identified by employers as critical for success in the interdependent employment fields of the 21st century.

At WHS, the teachers use several strategies to facilitate students' participation in cooperative groups. First, the students' desks are physically arranged in such a way that they encourage interactions among students. Second, students are intentionally grouped heterogeneously so that group interdependence is fostered. Third, the teacher provides students with materials and resources that promote sharing in order to participate and work toward the assigned common goal. Each group also is required to conduct further research and seek out additional resources in order to fulfill their assignment. Today, cooperative learning can be observed in nearly every class and is used frequently in most.

Teaching and Assessing from a Multiple Intelligences Framework   In addition to implementing cooperative groups, teachers have adopted a new view on intelligence that has assisted them to personalize instruction and assessment so that it is meaningful to all students. In 1983, Howard Gardner challenged the traditional view of intelligence with his pivotal book *Frames of Mind: The Theory of Multiple Intelligences*. In this book and the subsequent work of others (e.g., Armstrong, 1987, 1994; Lazear, 1994), it is pointed out that standardized methods of measuring students' abilities often only identify a limited portion of their talents, focusing primarily on linguistic and logical/mathematical areas of intelligence and ignoring musical, bodily/kinesthetic, visual/spatial, interpersonal, and intrapersonal intelligences as well as the most recently identified naturalistic intelligence. By recognizing students' strengths (or intelligences), it is much easier to develop a personalized instructional plan that capitalizes on those strengths to facilitate learning and simultaneously offer instructional opportunities in nonstrength areas of intelligence.

Multilevel Instruction and Integrated, Thematic Instruction   As teachers became more comfortable using a variety of active learning strategies, they also became more comfortable with students working on different levels, which is referred to as multilevel instruction. The concept is based on the premise that students do not learn the same way, at the same time, using the same materials (Falvey, 1995). Once teachers accepted this concept, strategies for responding to the multiple skill levels of students could be brainstormed and implemented. Table 2 offers a few examples of supports for facilitating students' learning at multiple levels.

Table 2.   Examples of support strategies

Arrangements

Cooperative learning groups	Specific seating arrangements
Paired reading/writing	Specific behavior plan/clues
Study carrels	Active learning strategies
Reduce seat time in class	

Material equipment

Books on tape	Computers and software
Videotapes	Calculators
Tape recorders	NCR/carbon paper
Communication aids	

Communication aids

Study guides	Learning logs
Vocabulary lists	Organizational aids
Main idea summaries	Skeletal outlines
Writing process aids	Highlight reading material
Prewritten notes	Preformatted material

Individualized support

Facilitation (e.g., communication, movement, thinking)
Shortened/modified/eliminated assignments
Oral tests
Open-note/open-book tests
Reword, rephrase instructions, questions
Picture cues
Cut-and-paste work

At WHS, core curriculum teachers and support teachers also work together to develop integrated thematic curriculum units. The teachers have used a format developed by Roger Taylor (1994) for writing integrated curriculum units that emphasize active learning instruction, multilevel instruction, and opportunities for students to use and develop their multiple intelligences.

Authentic Assessment

A critical issue related to the inclusion of students with diverse learning needs and ability levels is that of assessment and grading. Just as traditional didactic teaching strategies fail to meet the needs of many learners, so do traditional assessment strategies. Because teachers at WHS work so closely together with the students on their teams, they develop a more in-depth and comprehensive knowledge of students' strengths, learning styles, and needs. Because of this increased familiarity with students, they are less inclined to use formalized methods to assess student performance and, instead, prefer to assess students' skills in more meaningful ways. The point of assessment is not to teach students how to take a test for the purposes of passing but rather to determine students' growth in knowledge, understanding, and application of identified educational goals.

Performance Standards and Authentic Assessment

Performance standards and authentic assessment are gaining popularity and acceptance nationwide and among educators, parents, and students of WHS. Performance standards known as *expected schoolwide learning results (ESLRs)* currently are under development by the WHS staff. ESLRs are the skills and behaviors that a school expects of all students. Table 3 offers examples of ESLRs in seven areas. WHS is using ESLRs to directly influence the learning activities and assessment within the core curricular courses. Specifically, classroom activities and lessons are geared around achieving the ESLRs, and teachers are supported to develop authentic, performance-based assessments that are closely connected to ESLRs. WHS teachers are developing rubrics in order to assess group and individual progress related to the ESLRs.

Rubrics
Rubrics may be used by teachers not only to assess and give students feedback on their performance, but also to communicate in advance to students the critical elements of assignments. Figure 2 presents a sample mathematics rubric used by a WHS math educator that assesses the ESLR of an "effective communicator" while demonstrating knowledge of basic graphing skills. A rubric also may be developed for the content of an entire course. Figure 3 presents a fourth-quarter rubric for a WHS integrated math and science studies (MASS) course. On this rubric, "2" indicates that a student needs more practice

Table 3.   Expected schoolwide learning results (ESLRs)

Our high school will prepare its graduates to be:

Collaborative workers who

Use effective leadership and group skills
Manage interpersonal relationships within culturally diverse settings
Teach other significant competencies
Contribute and function in various group roles

Effective communicators who

Convey significant messages
Receive, interpret, and use the messages of others
Read, write, speak, and/or listen reflectively and critically

Healthy individuals who

Demonstrate knowledge of diverse cultures that fosters tolerance for individual
    differences
Establish, practice, and support appropriate hygiene, nutrition, and physical fitness
Exhibit self-discipline and responsibility
Use time effectively
Create and adapt to change
Demonstrate skills in resolving conflicts through positive, nonviolent alternative
    actions

Self-directed learners who

Plan for the future by setting goals
Use self-evaluation while implementing ideas
Develop, monitor, improve, and use effective learning strategies
Establish and adhere to standards of behavior
Overcome obstacles by effective application of skills or strategies

Complex thinkers who

Identify, assess, analyze, integrate, and use available resources and information
Use logical and effective decision-making processes
Develop solutions to problems based on justifiable rationales

Community participants who

Contribute time, energy, and talents to improve their school, community, state,
    nation, or world
Demonstrate positive and productive citizenship

Quality producers who

Develop, create, and support intellectual, artistic, practical, and physical works
Establish and use quality standards
Implement and use advanced technology
Organize, analyze, combine, and assess essential data in order to create and
    construct models

Rubric for presentations

For a "4" a student will:

— Explain all aspects of the problem and solution correctly
— Ask questions of the audience throughout presentation
— Use correct and clear audiovisual aid(s)
— Speak loudly for all to hear
— Maintain eye contact with entire audience

For a "3" a student will:

— Explain most aspects of the problem
— Ask questions of the audience
— Use correct audiovisual aid(s)
— Speak loudly for all the hear
— Maintain eye contact with audience

For a "2" a student will:

— Explain some aspects of the problem
— Use audiovisual aid(s)
— Speak clearly

Rubric for graphing

For a "4" a student will

— Write neatly
— Draw a line or curve accurately
— Extend the line or curve as far as possible on the graph
— Label the line or curve with a rule
— Label x and y axes and table
— Draw arrows on lines and graphs
— Plot all points correctly
— Make a table with appropriate number of positive and negative x values
— Label the x and y axes with accurate and appropriate scales
— Use graph paper, straight edge, and pencil

For a "3" a student will

— Write legibly
— Plot all points correctly
— Make an accurate table with appropriate number of positive and negative x values
— Label the x and y axes with accurate and appropriate scales
— Use graph paper, straight edge, and pencil

For a "2" a student will

— Plot some points correctly
— Develop a table
— Draw x and y axes
— Use a pencil

Figure 2.   Math course I evaluation.

MASS Evaluation Sheet   Name _____
Quarter Four

Equations	4	3	2
Two- and three-step			
Multistep			
Fraction, decimal			
Two-variable			
Quadratic			

Science	4	3	2
Periodic table			
Significant figures			
Scientific notations			
Unit analysis			
Project			

Graphing	4	3	2
Lines			
Curves			
Finding rule			
Slope, intercept			
Midpoint, distance			
Interpretation			

Guess and check tables	4	3	2
Set up table			
Three guesses			
Write equation			
Use equation			

Concepts	4	3	2
Area perimeter			
Calculators			
Factoring			
Foiling			
Measurement			
Orders of operation			
Percents			
Polynomials			
Pythagorean			
Statistic, probability			
Systems			

Week #	Q3	1	2	3	4	5	6	7	8	9	Total	Average
End date		4/23	4/30	5/7	5/14	5/21	5/28	6/5	6/12	6/19		
Attendance												
Assignment												
Participation												
Organization												
Labs												
Project												

Notes:

Figure 3.   Rubric for an integrated math and science study (MASS) course.

Table 4.   Independent research projects

1.   **Paradoxes:** The South African government officially ended its apartheid policy in 1991. Research which laws were repealed and assess to what extent Black citizens are equal to whites.

2.   **Attributes:** Research the life of Nelson Mandela before his imprisonment in 1964 and after his release in 1989. Create a product that shows his qualities as a leader in South Africa.

3.   **Analogies:** Compare the effects of the independence movement of the British Colonies in North America in the late 1700s with the independence of the British Colonies in South Africa in the early 1900s. Prepare an oral report or find clips from films that demonstrate their similarities and differences.

4.   **Discrepancies:** Because many families must exist by primitive farming methods and subsistence farming quickly depletes the soil of necessary nutrients, our rainforests are rapidly vanishing. Contributing to the problem are companies that log and strip mine the land without replanting the trees. Research what is happening to the plant and animal life in the rainforests. Show what species may be extinct if the problem is not solved. Graph the statistics and show how life in Los Angeles affects life in the rainforests and what we can do to reverse or halt the damage already done. How might our lives change if the rainforests, animals, and plants were replaced?

5.   **Provocative questions:** If you were a child from a different cultural background (e.g., Masai, Bedouin, Egyptian, Afrikaaner), how would you preserve your heritage in modern America? Develop a collage that shows all aspects of your life in Whittier—for example, school, home, family, religion, dress, music, friends.

6.   **Examples of change:** Through a puppet show, role playing, or a photo essay, show past, present, and future American views of Africa. You may want to get an idea of how our views of Blacks have changed over the years by viewing movie clips of *The Gods Must Be Crazy, Zulu, Mandela,* and *Tarzan, the Ape Man.*

7.   **Examples of habit:** In support of human rights in South Africa, create a museum exhibit that shows the detrimental effects of apartheid.

8.   **Organized random search:** Use any biography about a political or civil rights leader and write a diary of that leader covering 7 days of an important incident in that individual's life.

9.   **Skills of search:** Research traditional African meals and create a menu. Don't forget to put prices on the menu.

10.   **Tolerance for ambiguity:** In certain parts of Africa and Australia some people have built their homes under the earth's surface, in order to combat the oppressive heat conditions. Create a pamphlet that could be used by Amnesty International that shows some of the oppressive conditions that some people have been forced to live in because of apartheid.

11.   **Intuitive expression:** Create a 10-minute video clip showing the differences between Black children and white children in South Africa. Pay close attention to, for example, their clothing, games, music, and dance.

12.   **Adjustment to development:** With the abolishment of apartheid, many South Africans will have to make adjustments in their living conditions. Make a bulletin board advertising the types of jobs that will be available because of this change in living styles.

(continued)

Table 4. (*continued*)

13. **Study creative people and the creative process:** Research the life of one of the following: Nelson Mandela, Oliver Tambo, Archbishop Desmond Tutu, or Piet Willem Botha. Make a collage showing examples of their creativity.
14. **Evaluate situations:** In the novel *Cry, the Beloved Country*, identify and describe at least three situations that illustrate how ways of life for whites and Blacks in South Africa were changed by the apartheid policy. Prepare a radio news commentary explaining your analyses.
15. **Creative reading skill:** Using Kohlberg's Theory of Moral Development, determine the probable stages of Absalom, Stephen Kumalo, his brother John, Arthur Jarvis, and James Jarvis in the novel *Cry, the Beloved Country*.
16. **Creative listening skill:** Choose a favorite song and change the lyrics to reflect some aspect of African culture (e.g., food, dress, religious beliefs, spiritual values).
17. **Creative writing skill:** Write an epitaph for three of the following characters from the novel *Cry, the Beloved Country*: Stephen Kumalo, Mrs. Kumalo, Gertrude, Absalom, Arthur Jarvis, Mrs. Jarvis, or James Jarvis.
18. **Visualization skill:** After reading Maya Angelou's poem "Africa," create a graphic that translates Angelou's words about Africa into symbolic pictures.

and instruction with a particular concept. A "3" indicates that the student understands enough to go on to the next level of instruction, and a "4" reflects mastery of and superior performance on a particular concept. Students can chart their progress from Level 1 through Level 4 for each critical element of the course. Such a rubric-based approach versus a grade-based approach emphasized for students the importance of mastering the content versus simply making the grade. Students can tell at a glance in what areas they have achieved adequate or masterful performance and in what areas they need continued work.

Project Work   Project work is another performance-based means of allowing for authentic assessment. WHS ninth-grade humanities faculty require each student in the course to complete one project each quarter. Table 4 lists possible projects among which students can choose to demonstrate their understanding of a unit on Africa. As a culminating event, each student displays or demonstrates his or her project to classmates, further extending individual learning to all students. Rather than dictating a single way of demonstrating knowing, these projects allow students to select an area of special interest and to use a variety of intelligences to demonstrate their acquired knowledge of the subject matter. Table 5 lists the variety of ways in which students can choose to demonstrate and exhibit their knowledge and skills in all areas of the curriculum. Teachers develop strategies to encourage students to select different products for each assignment and to stretch themselves beyond their current levels for academic skill development as well as higher-order thinking.

Table 5. Products/exhibitions to demonstrate knowledge

Advertisement	Map with legend
Ammonia imprint	Mazes
Animated movie	Movie critic
Annotated bibliography	Mural
Art gallery	Museum exhibit
Block picture story	Musical performance
Bulletin board	Musical instruments
Cartoon	Needlework
Chart	New law
Children's book	Newspaper article
Choral reading	Oral defense
Clay sculpture	Oral report
Collage	Painting
Collection	Pamphlet
Comic strip	Papier maché
Computer program	Petition
Costumes	Photographic essay
Critic	Photographic display
Crossword puzzle	Pictures
Database	Picture story
Debate	Plaster model
Demonstration	Play
Detailed illustration	Poetry
Diary	Pop-up book
Diorama	Press conference
Display	Project cube
Drama	Prototype
Edibles	Puppet show
Etching	Puzzle
Experiment	Radio program
Fact tile	Rebus story
Fairy tale	Riddle
Family tree	Role-play
Film	Science fiction story
Filmstrip	Sculpture
Flip book	Skit
Game	Slide show
Graph	Slogan
Hidden picture	Song
Illustrated story	Survey
Interview	Tapes
Journal	Television program
Labeled diagram	Time line
Large-scale drawing	Transparencies
Learning center	Travel booth
Lesson	Travel brochure
Letter	Vacation plan
License plate	Videotape
Magazine	

Adapted from Taylor (1994).

Issues in Grading with Authentic Assessment Approaches

WHS teachers continue to struggle with the translation of authentic assessments into grades for report cards. Grades always have been subjective indicators of student progress and achievement. However, in high schools, passing grades translate into accumulated units needed for a graduation diploma that is critical for the job market. Grades and grade point averages become critical indicators for entrance into postsecondary education. Grading of students with disabilities often has been a "stumbling block" in providing inclusive educational services. In inclusive schools, a variety of strategies must be developed to communicate in meaningful ways the progress of students eligible for special education in core curriculum general education classes. These strategies must value a variety of participation levels on the part of students, as WHS has done with its grading procedures. (See Chapter 9 for an in-depth discussion of assessment and grading issues.)

Specifically, a student who follows the course sequence utilizing the same curricular materials, with accommodations made for his or her specific disability (e.g., uses calculators or spelling aids, completes reduced amount of work, uses books on tape, or uses alternative modes to exhibit content mastery rather than a written product) is graded with the same A–F system used throughout the school district. A student who requires adaptation of materials or assignments and who may have some portions of the curriculum modified will receive a comment on the report card and transcripts that indicates that the grade reflects the use of these adaptations and modifications. The student may receive an A–F grade or a P (i.e., passing) grade depending on what the student's team determines best communicates his or her participation and achievement in the specific course. Some students who receive significant adaptation and modification and who do not necessarily follow the typical scope and sequence of study in a particular course also may receive an A–F or a P grade. However, the course number on their transcript will be a specialized code number that indicates that a significant level or number of modifications or adaptations were used. Other students whose curriculum is modified, adapted, and who may have alternative goals and objectives often receive a NG, which indicates a nongraded status.

Summary

WHS staff are continually attempting to develop and improve on grading rubrics and other authentic assessment procedures across all integrated curricular areas and grade levels in order to allow students with different learning styles and varying abilities to be more accurately and objectively evaluated for their individual progress. Of course, for all students with disabilities, the curricular focus and the grading methods are individualized and based on the IEP, which specifies individual performance objectives and standards.

Developing a Community of Learners

It is important to note that the elementary and middle schools that are the "feeder" schools to WHS are a separate school district and have only recently begun exploring inclusive education options for students with disabilities. Thus, prior to coming to WHS, the majority of students with mild to severe disabilities experienced segregated schooling, in which they were placed full- or part-time in self-contained classes. This means, then, that students with and without disabilities who enter WHS do not have a longitudinal history of interacting with one another, nor have students with disabilities had adequate exposure to the core curriculum within general education classes.

Given this context, it may seem remarkable that one of the most observable qualities of WHS is the positive reciprocal relationships among students with and without disabilities. This is true because, over the years, very deliberate actions have been taken to foster positive interactions through such activities as ability awareness in-services for all freshmen, development of peer tutoring arrangements, sponsoring of Circle of Friends support groups, and other unique arrangements designed to facilitate friendship development. Since WHS began its restructuring efforts in 1992, a guiding principle and, thus, the emergent climate of the school has been the acceptance of diversity and belonging and membership within classroom communities. All students' names appear on roll sheets and all students are in attendance in classrooms from the first day. Artificial arrangements for students to gain access to core curriculum or elective classes no longer are necessary.

WHS has a school service program in which students may enroll to earn credit for providing more formalized support to classmates who need assistance to fully participate in academic or elective classes. However, students also naturally and automatically extend support to classmates with special needs through cooperative learning activities, paired partnerships for individual activities, and spontaneous assistance, as a need arises. It is usual to observe students offering to tie an untied sneaker, assisting in carrying a classmate's lunch from the cafeteria, taking turns pushing a wheelchair, and supporting a classmate with motoric challenges to move from class to class. As one student stated when referring to her experiences as a peer support, "US and THEM is a problem . . . we don't want us and them. We need to look beyond the disabilities and understand . . . show people respect and see the inside. . . . We are the same. . . . All of us have the same heart." She continued, "The best way to teach new peers is to take them into classes where the students are and share a means to support the students."

Two significant results of the WHS restructuring movement have been 1) the development of a true community of learners in which all students give and receive support and 2) the recognition on the part of faculty, administration, and parents that the inclusion of students with disabilities is a natural component of a school striving to be excellent for all students. The following scenario illustrates how the valuing of all members of a classroom community can be and was developed.

Mr. Kole's classroom is one in which students are extremely active and involved in the daily activities of the class. Mr. Kole is a math/science teacher on one of the ninth-grade teams. There are 32 students in the class with varying abilities and challenges, including students identified as gifted as well as students with severe, multiple medical needs. Because Mr. Kole teaches the same students for two periods in a row as a result of block scheduling, he is able to use art, music, drama, and history to convey the math and science core curriculum. Each year the students are involved in research projects, simulated courtroom situations, and other activities. Mr. Kole uses a wipe board to delineate the weekly schedule of goals, objectives, daily assignments, and nightly homework.

Mr. Kole works closely with the support teacher, Ms. Garcia, to design collaboratively lessons that they hope will meet all students' needs. When necessary, they develop adaptations for select students; the students who need adaptations are not always students with disabilities. Many benefit from this more individualized approach to teaching. Some adaptations often used in Mr. Kole's class are templates for math computation, readily available manipulatives allowing for students to share their results visually and verbally rather than solely in written work.

José, a student with severe multiple disabilities, uses a wheelchair and is wheeled into class by a different classmate each week. A group of students developed on their own a volunteer rotation to support José's mobility. Ms. Garcia modifies José's math materials to address his IEP objectives and math proficiency. While José works on number recognition, most of the other students are working on simple, and eventually, multistep algebraic equations. Another one of the students, Jerome, who has autism, is working toward academic credits while being supported through facilitated communication (see Biklen & Cardinal, 1997, for further information about facilitated communication). Three of his classmates have been trained to "facilitate" with Jerome so that he can communicate.

Another student in Mr. Kole's class has Down syndrome, while three other students have learning disabilities. In their teaming arrangement, Ms. Garcia and Mr. Kole strive continually to verify that all students are involved and engaged in learning in meaningful ways. Students with identified disabilities are integrated into different cooperative learning groups within Mr. Kole's class. Ms. Garcia is available to assist any student. As a result, she functions as a second classroom teacher who co-teaches and co-plans instruction with Mr. Kole and assists students who need support, when they need it.

On the Monday morning of the twelfth week of the first semester, the topic is solving algebraic equations. Mr. Kole, after reviewing the weekly schedule with the students, announces that he would like the students to convey in whatever form they would like the solution and the method for solving the following algebraic problem: $2x + 1 = 10$. He tells the students to be creative and use any method that makes the most sense to them. He tells them they can use their "multiple intelligences" and write a poem, draw a picture, tell a story, use objects to represent the algebraic problem, and so on. He also asks the students to imagine a situation in which they might need to be able to use such a problem in their lives now or in the future.

José participates with two of his peers to write out and use objects to represent the algebraic problem. José has the poster they created attached to his wheelchair, and he takes on his lap tray all of the other materials to the front of the class for the demonstration. José also chose the colored markers and poster paper used to share their answers. Jerome, through facilitation by a classmate, is able to provide a verbal explanation of the problem and when he might use it. All of the students, including those with disabilities, use a variety of response modalities and are successful at demonstrating knowledge related to the algebraic problem or at least participating in a meaningful way. Not only do students enjoy presenting their methods of representing the algebraic problem, they are fascinated and impressed by their peers' multifaceted presentations of the problem.

Following class, during their common planning time, Mr. Kole and Ms. Garcia debrief and assess the outcomes of the day's class. Mr. Kole comments that, for him, one of the great benefits of the school's restructuring is that students without disabilities get so many more opportunities to naturally develop their creative problem-solving skills and enhance their own capacity for creativity by facilitating the involvement of their classmates with disabilities. Ms. Garcia agrees that the students were enormously inventive and wonders if they feel the personal empowerment they show as they work and include all members of their groups. They both agree that a real sense of community seems to have developed in the class over the past 11 weeks.

When educators try to measure successes, often the information is reduced to numbers, formulas, and percentages and generally does not

426 Eshilian et al.

take into account the personal growth that students and school personnel make. This scenario offers a more authentic method for assessing 1) individual student growth and 2) a school community's growth
in teaching in meaningful ways and valuing and respecting student
diversity.

CONCLUSIONS

Although it has been challenging at times to create the changes at
WHS, overall the majority of the faculty, students, administration, and
parents are enthusiastic about these changes. Everyone has grown as a
result of the dedication of WHS staff to restructure for heterogeneity.
There always will be room for continued development on the part of
students, families, and staff; specifically, there are unresolved issues
and a need for action, especially in the areas of authentic assessment,
grading, and graduation diploma requirements; the use of educational
strategies that respect and encourage the development of all types of
intelligences; and making technology available and accessible to all
students.

Certainly one of the most significant changes that needs to take
place at the state (and federal) level is the unification of general and
special education systems. The separation of the two systems has hindered progress towards providing appropriate special education services within general education classrooms. One general education
teacher at WHS reflected on the irony that most civil rights movements
have historically struggled to bring about fair and just laws, while the
civil rights movement for inclusive education is struggling to make
schools comply with the laws that have been in effect for over 20 years.
To change schools, particularly secondary schools, to better meet the
needs of all students requires more than changes in paradigms and
practices; it requires a great deal of courage, conviction, and commitment on the part of everyone—families, school administrators, teachers, teacher trainers, government officials, and students themselves.
The good news is that there now are examples across North America
such as Whittier High School for people to look to for inspiration to
take on the challenge to go beyond compliance with the law to the
crafting of schools that model the democratic society we attest to be.

REFERENCES

Allan, S.M. (1991). Ability-grouping research reviews: What do they
say about grouping and the gifted? *Educational Leadership, 48*(6),
60–65.

Armstrong, T. (1987). *In their own way: Discovering and encouraging your child's personal learning style.* Los Angeles: Jeremy P. Tarcher.

Armstrong, T. (1994). *Multiple intelligences in the classroom.* Alexandria, VA: Association for Supervision and Curriculum Development.

Biklen, D., & Cardinal, D.N. (1997). *Contested words, contested science: Unraveling the facilitated communication controversy.* New York: Teachers College Press.

Falvey, M.A. (Ed.). (1995). *Inclusive and heterogeneous schooling: Assessment, curriculum, and instruction.* Baltimore: Paul H. Brookes Publishing Co.

Gardner, H. (1983). *Frames of mind: The theory of multiple intelligences.* New York: Basic Books.

Individuals with Disabilities Education Act (IDEA) Amendments of 1997, PL 105-17, 20 U.S.C. §§ 1400 *et seq.*

Jubala, K.A., Bishop, K.D., & Falvey, M.A. (1995). Creating a supportive classroom environment. In M.A. Falvey (Ed.), *Inclusive and heterogeneous schooling: Assessment, curriculum, and instruction* (pp. 111–130). Baltimore: Paul H. Brookes Publishing Co.

Lazear, D. (1994). *Seven pathways of learning: Teaching students and parents about multiple intelligences.* Tucson, AZ: Zephyr Press.

Oakes, J. (1985). *Keeping track: How schools structure inequality.* New Haven, CT: Yale University Press.

Putnam, J.W. (Ed.). (1998). *Cooperative learning and strategies for inclusion: Celebrating diversity in the classroom* (2nd ed.). Baltimore: Paul H. Brookes Publishing Co.

Sapon-Shevin, M. (1994). *Playing favorites: Gifted education and the disruption of community.* Albany: State University of New York Press.

Sizer, T. (1992). *Horace's school: Redesigning the American high school.* Boston: Houghton Mifflin.

Taylor, R. (1994). *Reshaping the curriculum: Using an integrated, interdisciplinary approach.* Oakbrook, IL: Curriculum Design for Excellence.

Thousand, J., Rosenberg, R., Bishop, K.D., & Villa, R.A. (1997). The evolution of secondary inclusion. *Remedial and Special Education, 18*(5), 270–284.

Villa, R.A. & Thousand, J.S. (Eds.). (1995). *Creating an inclusive school.* Alexandria, VA: Association for Supervision and Curriculum Development.

Chapter 15

Chronicles of Administrative Leadership Toward Inclusive Reform

"We're on the train and we've left the station, but we haven't gotten to the next stop"

Alice Udvari-Solner and Maureen W. Keyes

Effective leadership is a critical component in the development and nurturance of successful inclusive school communities (Keyes, 1996; MacKinnon & Brown, 1994; Rossman, 1992; Servatius, Fellows, & Kelly, 1992; Stainback & Stainback, 1991; Villa & Thousand, 1990; Villa, Thousand, Meyers, & Nevin, 1996). Exhortatory lists containing directives for administrators are plentiful. Examples of these inventories have been shared, suggesting the need for more demonstrative evidence from principals working to eventuate inclusive schools. However, the case studies and practical examples of effective leadership are sparse.

Contributors' note: We invite you to share your stories of effective leadership for inclusive education via e-mail by sending them to Maureen W. Keyes at <mkeyes@uwm.edu> or to Alice Udvari-Solner at <Alice@soemadison.wisc.edu>.

Morgan and Demchak (1996) and Schaffner and Buswell (1996) defined critical elements for successful inclusive programming, offering lists that contain key recommendations, many of which implicate the prerequisites of solid and committed administrative leadership. Their endorsements included strong leadership, knowledge of the change process, respect for and acknowledgment of success and challenge, and the need for a common articulated philosophy and strategic plans to implement inclusive practices that include staff development opportunities and considerations for creative configurations of resources. Shinsky (1992) and Whitaker (1997) offered recommendations that echo this advice, along with the added dimensions of administrators who model behaviors of caring, service, and acceptance of others.

Lists such as these offer many worthwhile directives and serve as skeletal templates for administrators to measure their efforts. Yet, inventories of recommendations without examples of situations or real-life challenges to demonstrate administrators' commitment to reform status quo practices fall short of providing direction and support for those in the throes of the systems change.

Perhaps more exhaustive illustrations of effective leadership could provide better direction to one middle school administration that Fox and Ysseldyke (1997) described. The results of their case study, entitled in part "Lessons from a negative example," summarized the critical component of effective school change—active support of the

Our heartfelt appreciation is expressed to the following administrators who shared their expertise and thoughts with us during this project. Their collective spirit to champion quality education for all children was truly inspiring: Sue Abplanalp, Winnie Aitch, Jennifer Allen, Jane Belmore, Libby Burmaster, Adell Fair, Julie Frentz, Barbara Goss, Steve Hartley, Mary Hyde, Kery Kafka, Kathyrn LaFond, Tom McGinnity, Mary Beth Minkley, Mary Ramberg, Estell Sprewer, Carolyn Strutz, Linda Sweeney, and Martha Wheeler-Fair.

We want to thank Darcy Holmes, Sonja Rode, and Theresa Grueneberg for their skill and patience in transcribing the interview data that resulted from this project. We are grateful for the assistance of Mary Ann Fitzgerald, Jan Glodowski, Peg Keeler, Nancy Caldwell-Korpela, Paula Kluth, and Catherine Witty in carrying out the interviews.

The retreats were funded in part by The Wisconsin School Inclusion Project and The Wisconsin Department of Public Instruction Discretionary Grant: Accommodating Diverse Learners Through Collaborative Curriculum Planning–Madison Metropolitan School District.

This chapter is dedicated to Haven Ilona Udvari-Solner. Born during the completion of the chapter, she has been my ever-present companion and my constant reminder why we must work together to make schools just, humane, and accommodating.

principal—with this observation: "The principal provided support but did not actively lead the process. He said he had other priorities" (1997, p. 91). In summarizing lessons learned, Fox and Ysseldyke included this recommendation: "Provide the staff with active leadership from people who believe in or, at least, are really open to inclusion" (1997, p. 95). In addition, in describing the need for effective staff development, Fox and Ysseldyke recommended involvement by building principals. Underlining these results, Trump and Hange (1996) interviewed 48 teachers about their impressions of inclusive education efforts. The results of these interviews indicated that administrative leadership was considered either the greatest support or the greatest obstacle to the institution and spread of inclusive schooling efforts.

With staff continually citing administrative support as pivotal in terms of inclusive schooling reform, it is paramount that effective administrators share their efforts with those in similar situations. This chapter offers selected stories shared by building principals and central office staff as they began to chronicle their personal and professional journeys toward inclusive schools for children. Analysis and distillation of interview data provide a glimpse into 17 schools. The manner in which these administrators were chosen and the data were collected is described, followed by examples of effective administrative behaviors to promote the development and ongoing support for inclusive schools. In concluding, the challenges still facing these administrators are examined briefly and successful administrators are invited to share their stories.

PROCESS OF CHRONICLING INCLUSIVE ADMINISTRATIVE LEADERSHIP

The authors of this chapter initially were enlisted to compose a comprehensive case study of a school and its leadership that exemplified the critical tenets of inclusive education. As we began discussions about the selection of such a site, we realized that each of our candidate schools had unique conditions worthy of examination. Furthermore, we were cognizant of the fact that no school, to our knowledge, had reached the so-called pinnacle of inclusive practice. Instead, there were many schools that were engaged in dramatic evolutionary change guided by effective and committed administrators. The administrators who participated in this project also were well aware of this evolution, as is illustrated in the quote selected as the subtitle of this chapter: "We're on the train and we've left the station, but we haven't gotten to the next stop." The responses from administrators verified that good inclusive practice is still a work in progress in most schools.

As we worked within these schools, observed instruction practices, and spoke with teachers and families throughout the districts, interesting exemplars emerged of specific actions or approaches employed by the administrator that prompted or moved forward efforts to effectively include all students. The focus of this chapter quickly took shape as we realized that a collection of these individual stories may have universal applications and associations to other schools engaged in inclusive reform.

Selection of Participants and Data Collection

The development of this chapter became a collaborative endeavor between the authors and a number of administrators in Madison Metropolitan School District and the Milwaukee public school system. The process of gathering the contributions and perspectives of the principals and central office staff resulted in a rare opportunity to engage in reflection, celebration, community building, and coalescing as transformative action began for both the authors and the participants.

Twenty participants were asked to take part in this project. The group was composed of 17 principals and 3 central office staff, including an assistant deputy superintendent, a director of special services, and a director of teaching and learning. Principals constituted the majority of participants, with 5 high school, 2 middle school, and 10 elementary school administrators represented. Their selection was made through peer and teacher nominations. Based on our work in the Madison and Milwaukee school districts and our ongoing communication with university personnel, parents, teachers, and administrators, we asked the simple question, "Can an administrator who has been instrumental in shaping inclusive practice be identified?" The names of those participants selected for the project were offered repeatedly by constituents and peers. By soliciting nominations from both the Madison (estimated population 250,000) and Milwaukee (estimated population 1 million) area school districts, we intended to capture realistic representations of the challenges facing administrators from both a metropolitan and a large urban school district.

The data for this project were collected through in-depth interviews using an open-ended protocol. The participants were invited to either a one-half-day or one-evening retreat in their respective communities. The retreats were designed not only to gain insight into the participants' expertise but also were conducted to acknowledge and honor their contributions toward systemic change. The forum of the meetings included the following data collection strategies:

1. Reflection and writing time were arranged for participants to organize their thoughts in response to the questions that guided interviews and discussions. Some individuals jotted handwritten notes, and others responded using laptop computers. These narrative responses served to clarify, expand, and corroborate information gathered from interviews.

2. Small-group and individual interviews were conducted by the authors, doctoral students, or project facilitators, all of whom were familiar with methods of qualitative data collection. Each interview was audiotaped, and in some cases a second interviewer was involved to monitor the recording and to take a written record of the dialogue.

3. Focus group discussions with multiple participants culminated the gatherings. These group discussions allowed for elaboration of concepts, identification of common themes, and networking regarding specific issues and challenges among the administrators.

Table 1 represents the primary questions used to guide the interviews. Despite this list of questions, interviewers were encouraged to use the protocol loosely so that administrators could lead or pursue personally important elements of their experiences. It was acceptable if some responses strayed from the original question(s) because our goal was to capture their accounts in a manner that was meaningful to them.

Data Analysis

The audiotapes of the small-group, individual, and focus-group interviews were transcribed verbatim for review and analysis. The handwritten notes and typed responses of participants were matched with corresponding interview transcripts for a supportive record. We both reviewed all of the transcriptions and coded them individually. The first round of coding was employed to identify themes and examples that corresponded with essential leadership behavior and theoretical orientations represented in the research literature. In addition, transcripts were reviewed for unique representations of practice not typically depicted in the literature base. We then compared and negotiated identified codes. Narratives that particularly exemplified key themes were selected as archetypes for inclusion in the manuscript.

To ensure validity and trustworthiness, member checks of the transcripts and information included in the manuscript were conducted by asking the various interviewers and a sampling of interviewees to read the documents. The interviewers and participants were asked to verify that the content represented the interaction and dialogue that

Table 1. Semistructured interview protocol

1. What led you to become an advocate for inclusive schooling practices?

2. How have you demonstrated the commitment to inclusive practices to your staff, students, parents, community, and your administrators? Can you think of strategies or practices that you purposely employed in order to advance your vision for inclusive schooling?

3. How have you supported inclusive practices on a more indirect level? For example, have you made changes or decisions that influenced a caring school community/climate, shared decision making, and empowering of staff and students to make choices?

4. Describe an example of support for inclusive practices beyond your school building. What have you done in your community, with families, or through policy development to promote the inclusion of all students?

5. What type(s) of instructional or curricular practices do you promote and/or find teachers using in successful inclusive classrooms?

6. Do you consider spirituality (not necessarily in terms of organized religion) as a component of your leadership? If so, what comes to mind when you think of translating your spiritual values about diversity and/or students with disabilities into practice?

7. Describe an experience that "shook" your commitment to inclusive practices. Or, describe an incident in which you met obstacles and/or challenges to your commitment to inclusive practices. What was your response?

8. What do you need personally to continue your efforts at inclusive schooling?

9. What do you think is needed on a larger scale (beyond your own school) to advance this agenda?

10. If you could give advice to a principal or an administrator initiating inclusive practices, what would it be?

had taken place during the interview. Specific participants who were represented through quotes or depicted in narratives were asked to review transcripts and our interpretations for correctness and responsible portrayals. Once this chapter was written, representative administrators from both geographic areas were given an opportunity to read it and offer feedback.

STORIES FROM THE FIELD: PROMOTING INCLUSIVE PRACTICES

The premise for this project and the development of the questions that guided dialogue with administrators was based on the theoretical framework entitled, "A Developmental Taxonomy of Empowering Principal Behavior" (see Reitzug, 1994). In this section, Reitzug's theoretical framework is presented, and its relationship to the various themes and stories that emerged from the data, including quotes or narratives from specific participants, is established.

Reitzug's developmental taxonomy of empowering principal behavior includes three specific types of administrative traits that engender leadership toward school reform. Empowerment is the overarching attribute of effective administrative leadership behavior in this theoretical model. *Empowerment* in this context refers to releasing the power of staff, students, and parents to create and shape their own futures (Sage & Burrello, 1994). Reitzug's research identified support, facilitation, and possibility as vehicles by which leaders promote empowerment.

The first element of the framework, *support*, is defined as the way that the principal "creat[es] a supportive environment for critique" (Reitzug, 1994, p. 291). The second element, *facilitation*, refers to the ways that administrators stimulate teachers' thinking to reconsider their ideas or their pat responses to problems from a different perspective. The final element is *possibility*, which Reitzug defined as "giving voice by actualizing products of critique" (1994, p. 291). Reitzug listed the examples of tangible resources such as money and equipment and intangible resources such as time and opportunity that provide the means by which to bring about change. Each element and its defining characteristics are identified in Table 2. In the following sections, chronicles from various administrators are shared to exemplify effective attributes of leadership reflected in Reitzug's model. The interview excerpts and narrative anecdotes may help nudge others on similar journeys to the next stop.

Support: Creating a Supportive Environment for Critique

Creating schools that are inclusive often requires administrators to engender an environment in which members begin to question the status quo. Administration and faculty must critically examine the ways in which certain groups of students are either excluded or included in the learning community. To begin this process of critical analysis, members engaged in and affected by the reform must feel a sense of support for their actions (Sergiovanni, 1994). Creating such an environment entails providing the conditions that enable teachers and students to feel psychologically and emotionally safe to express themselves. Establishing trust, promoting a schoolwide philosophy of acceptance, encouraging risk taking, and fostering confirmation of self were recurring themes expressed by these administrators that helped to establish supportive environments.

Building Capacity for Trust   Estell Sprewer, director of Milwaukee Public Schools, Division of Special Services, described her years as building principal of an elementary school that had segregated

Table 2.   A developmental taxonomy of empowering principal behavior

Types of empowering behavior	Descriptors and behaviors

Support **Creating a supportive environment for critique**
Providing teachers greater control and autonomy
Providing autonomy with responsibility for supporting practice
Shifting problem-solving responsibility
Encouraging giving voice
Communicating trust
Encouraging risk taking
Encouraging the confirmation of self
Honoring teachers' opinions
Providing opportunities for conversations with others
Developing teams
Developing inquiry-oriented dispositions in order to test knowledge claims
Modeling inquiry

Facilitation **Stimulating critique**
Stimulating teachers to view theory as a starting point subject to testing and revision
Asking questions
Requiring justification of practice based on personal practical knowledge
Directing attention to unnoticed aspects of the environment
Critique by wandering around
Providing alternative frameworks for thinking about teaching and learning
Providing staff development (e.g., opportunities, readings, ideas)
Focusing attention on unequal power relationships

Possibility **Making it possible to give voice by actualizing products of critique**
Developing commitment to self as professional (providing resources to be used on students' behalf)
Providing tangible resources (e.g., money, equipment, materials)
Providing intangible resources (e.g., time, opportunity)
Encouraging activity on behalf of acquiring resources and advancing client interest
Encouraging grant writing
Soliciting donations of funds and materials

From Reitzug, U.C. (1994). A case study of empowering principal behavior. *American Educational Research Journal, 31*(2), 291; reprinted by permission. Copyright © 1994 by the American Educational Research Association.

Roman typeface = descriptors compiled from Prawat (1991). Italics = empowering behaviors from Reitzug's study data.

programs for children with disabilities and for students who had been labeled as gifted and talented. She described how she built a level of trust with parents, teachers, and children as she worked to both dismantle the segregated programs and develop an inclusive model:

> I started talking to parents who were then just absolutely adamant about not having their child [with a label of gifted and talented] mixed in with anybody else. I kept saying, "I guarantee you that your child will not lose anything, and if we can't keep that promise to you, then you can certainly remove your child and take your child out." I will never forget this one little boy [one who had been enrolled in the self-contained special education program for children with emotional disturbance] who had been the worst in terms of behavior and noncompliance. When he received Mrs. Waterly [as his instructor]—she was one of the intermediate PAT (Program for the Academically Talented) people and an excellent teacher—he said, "Wow, well, finally I'm going to learn something." We went through a lot of redefining. I had consulting teachers come in, and we had a lot of in-services. We talked about expectations that the PAT teachers had. [We talked about] the strategies that they used and how to use some of those strategies or break those same strategies down so that they applied to a whole class. I had a staff that trusted me in a sense, [one] that followed me. I worked as hard as they did, and we got in there and we said, "This is what you need and we're going to try to do this." And it worked—it *worked*! It was a difficult year. It was a difficult year for parents. It was a difficult year for the staff. And it was a difficult year for me. But after that first year, I think that people will tell you now they would never go back to the way it was.

The preceding story emphasizes the commitment made by the administrator to preserve the elements of programming that parents found valuable or believed were at risk when a change was imminent. Trust was established in part because the concerns of the parents were solicited and acknowledged. In this instance, trust was maintained with teachers because the principal provided the resources and strategies necessary to initiate the change in practice.

As a newly hired principal in the Madison school district, Sue Abplanalp organized new social events and maintained customs unique to her school's culture, thereby contributing to an atmosphere of trust:

> Providing teachers with [social] opportunities to get together was essential. We started Wednesday morning breakfasts at [our school], and it has been well attended since the first week of school. Carrying out all of the "traditions" of [the school] was something I held dear to my heart. [The staff] used to have rooftop barbecues and secret outings, which I continue to support. I think keeping the rituals assures comfort that many need and helps to establish the trust needed to create change.

Promoting a Schoolwide Philosophy and Climate of Acceptance among Staff and Students The mission statement of Malcolm Shabazz High School in Madison, Wisconsin, reads:

> The mission . . . is to create a harassment-free learning environment where all people, regardless of previous academic performance, family background, socioeconomic status, beliefs, abilities, appearance, gender, or sexual orientation are respected. It is a school where all students are encouraged to take academic and social risks. . . . Curriculum and personalized instruction are multicultural as well as challenging. A strong sense of community exists in which students are asked to participate in school decision making. Fundamental to the school's philosophy are viewing the student as a whole person and strengthening the connection between the student, family, and community.

Steve Hartley is principal of this alternative high school, which serves approximately 140 students. All of the students, many of whom would be considered nontraditional learners or among those who have felt marginalized and alienated in other city high schools, attend Shabazz by choice. An atmosphere of acceptance is fostered by explicit attention in policy and practice to the learning environment. Hartley says the school was founded on the belief that the atmosphere in which you learn is as important as what you learn. As steward of this philosophy, Hartley says students can leave their labels at the door:

> We don't recognize the label or use the label. We treat the kid as a whole while recognizing learning style differences. These personal differences are respected, whether these differences are cross-dressing [or] purple hair; you can't write and need to dictate to others, or you have depression issues.

A nonharassment policy that incorporates this language of respect for individual differences is formally taught as part of the required high school curriculum and is enforced by administration, staff, and students. In Shabazz I, a class in which all students must enroll, scenarios involving responses to multicultural, gay, lesbian, bisexual, and disability issues are brought to the forefront. Conflict resolution is presented in tandem with these issues. Regular school meetings and half-day workshops on topics such as homophobia, unlearning racism, and respect are jointly planned and facilitated by staff and students.

Hartley believes that everyone must be visible in the daily life of the school and that their rights and needs must be reflected in the school's policies and improvement plans. The tenets of acceptance and respect are further reinforced in Hartley's suggestions for interactions between teachers and students:

> The first thing I tell substitutes who enter this building is, "Don't tell any-body to do anything. . . . But if you ask a kid at Shabazz, they will bend over backwards to help you out." Personal relationships are incredibly important. [Students] will do things based on a relationship [with] a teacher, not based on an assignment. Unless the students are actively involved [in the relationship], they will not respond.

At the elementary level, Julie Frentz has employed a simple but powerful strategy to change the climate in her school. Frentz is the principal of Emerson Elementary School, which serves as the primary base within the district for those students who are homeless or live in shelters. Students often enroll at the school with little or no notice; some remain for a day, and others remain for months. The dynamic nature of these families' living arrangements challenges both students and staff to develop meaningful connections with these children. Frentz tries to guard against students' feeling excluded by using formal strategies to welcome any new student:

> We started a [custom] called First Friends. Fourth graders are [taught how to be] tour guides and buddies to new students as they come into the building. The new students are interviewed and given a tour of the building from the perspective of a schoolmate. Their pictures and the personal information they would like to share are posted on a hallway bulletin board. [During their first week,] they receive a coupon to have lunch with the principal and be read to by the librarian. Each classroom teacher has been encouraged to develop welcoming activities that include assigning a classmate who has the express responsibility to help the new student learn the ropes.

Exiting or leaving the school community also is viewed as an important event at Emerson. When departures can be predicted, Frentz believes time must be allowed to engage students in the process of say-ing goodbye. Students who are leaving are given the opportunity to visit various teachers of their choice to promote a sense of academic, emotional, and social closure. When students depart unexpectedly with unknown destinations, teachers often ask students in their class-room to write farewell letters to send off their classmate.

Encouraging Risk Taking   Two elementary school principals from Milwaukee—Martha Wheeler-Fair of Starms Early Learning Center and Mary Beth Minkley of Congress Year-Round School—described the importance of modeling risk taking in their own actions.

These administrators conveyed a message to work toward a goal that may entail mistakes and difficult problem solving, risks from which many educators shy away:

> They watch us take a lot of risks. They watch us as we model it. And articulate it. I have three paras [i.e., former education assistants] who are now my teachers. And I say to them, "If you're here to collect a paycheck, forget it. We have to work and keep abreast of the best practices. I expect you to go to conferences. I encourage you. I want you to have discussions on it."
>
> The people on our staff realize that the operative word is work. You're always in the process. You're always trying to get to a place [that] you will never get to. If we're trying to have schools for the 21st century, then we've got to be ready. Sometimes we win, and sometimes we lose and go back to the drawing board and say, "OK, let's rethink this." This is what we thought parents wanted, this is what we thought would work, and it's not really doing that. What do we need to do next? So, the whole group sort of problem-solves around those kind of issues together. We really try to figure out where we need to go next. So it's a process, and it will always be a process.

Fostering Confirmation of Self Administrators talked about the challenges of supporting inclusive reform and inserted the critical role that recognition of both student and staff effort plays in its success. Leaders praised, formally acknowledged contributions, shared authority, and promoted responsibility in decision making. These public and private confirmations of ability and worth appeared to promote cohesive actions toward inclusive ends. Support for the personal growth and contribution by teaching assistants or paraprofessionals (referred to hereinafter as *paras*) was discussed by Martha Wheeler-Fair and Mary Beth Minkley at length in terms of explaining effective inclusive programming for students: •

> In our building, paras are [treated as] teachers. They are not there to run off copies, they are not secretaries, they are not peons, they are not there to do outside duties. They have lots of skills. As a matter of fact, in the 7 years since these programs have been opened, we have had 10 paras who [have become] teachers. We were able to hire them when we opened up the new program. They went back to school, and now they are on staff with us. So these are folks who have a real knowledge base about what this program really looks like. . . . But one of the other things they also do is that they really help us with our parent involvement because they are part of the teams that do home visits, and they are good home visitors. They do the whole works.

A sense of empowerment for students is promoted at Malcolm Shabazz High School in Madison, Wisconsin, through instruction and dialogue about personal learning styles. Steve Hartley provided this account:

> The notion is that every kid understands himself as a learner. So, they know, "I need information presented this way, not that way. . . . I am a physical learner." You hear them talking about themselves in that [manner]. You hear them use the language. They become proactive in their own [education]. They put pressure on teachers [to respond when they say], "I need information presented this way, you can't just tell me. . . . I need to see it."

Facilitation: Stimulating Critique

Once a school community develops a supportive atmosphere conducive to critique, it becomes necessary to encourage educators to scrutinize their own actions and the dynamics within their own learning organization. It is important to understand the ways in which leaders encourage others to review, critique, and question the context and culture of their schools. The manner by which administrators facilitated the growth of inclusive practices included expressing personal values, using reflective dialogue and critical questioning, creating constancy of purpose, promoting specific curricular and instruction approaches, and revealing incongruities in practice and philosophy.

Expressing and Extending Personal Values   Blase and Kirby suggested that expectations for changes in attitudes and behavior are "largely derived from [the administrator's] personal values regarding appropriate human interaction and school purposes" (1992, p. 24). These administrators did not just parrot district initiatives and goals; they disclosed their own personal visions, belief systems, and basic assumptions about living. In doing so, moral purposes and alternative frameworks for thinking about teaching and learning were extended to the teaching staff.

Mary Ramberg, a former principal of Cherokee Middle School and the director of teaching and learning in the Madison school district, articulated the importance of an administrator expressing values and providing critical resources to actualize practice:

> Purposeful inclusion was the expectation, and I think that this was made explicit in a variety of ways. Elimination of tracking was one way. Emphasizing that one of our responsibilities was to challenge all of our students in heterogeneously grouped classrooms was another way. This was a clear value that was frequently communicated. We talked specifically about inclusion in faculty meetings and elicited from staff ideas that were boiled down into a one-pager that remained in the teacher handbook for many years [and was] entitled, "What Does an Inclusive Classroom Look Like? and How Do You Get There?" This was also a value around

which we made decisions. I decided that the most significant things that I could do administratively were to maintain the smallest classes possible, deal administratively with student behaviors that negatively [affected] learning, and cheerlead. It is difficult to assess how and to what extent the philosophy and values of an administrator permeate a school's culture. Sometimes, if there are positive relationships with staff who hold similar values, a reality can be created.

In our interviews, we were struck by the pervasive appearance of these values and belief statements when no direct interview questions on the topic had been posed. The following quotations are representative of the value statements that made their way into our conversations:

When I think of inclusive education, I think of effective, seamless practices for all children (e.g., exceptional educational needs, English as a second language, whichever other labels there are out there). My question to my staff and to myself is always, "Is this how I would want my own child to be educated? Is this the kind of school I would want my own child to attend?" I continually have a sense of urgency for all the children at Midvale, an urgency to provide the best possible instruction that will allow them to be readers, writers, and mathematicians. I feel it [is] a social responsibility we have undertaken. (Jennie Allen, principal of Midvale Elementary School)

Whatever the problem is that comes to me—I do not just respond to resolve the issue. Instead, I try to figure out, How can we solve this problem, keeping in mind that this may be an opportunity to expand the way we think about serving kids? (Jane Belmore, principal of Elvehjem Elementary School)

I have come to understand the importance of the learning cycle rather than the teaching cycle. The idea is that you assess, then plan, then evaluate what you have planned based upon what you see children have learned—and then you do it all over again. The reason [why] you do all of this is for learning, not for teaching. . . . The teacher is not the center of this; it's the child. (Mary Hyde, principal of Glendale Elementary School)

[As] a core belief, I think that it is only in an inclusive environment, where there are multiple perspectives, that human dignity and human creativity flourish. (Libby Burmaster, principal of West High School)

I have not yet encountered anything that has made my commitment to inclusive practices falter. And often it is that commitment that resonates in the core of my being and allows me not to give in to staff demands or influences. It encourages me to stand fast and strong when resources are tight and pressure is fierce. Often that commitment is brought forth when staff indicate that a student "really doesn't belong" in a classroom. I feel outraged because that feels like exclusion. Any sort of exclusion causes me to remain steadfast in my goal to include all people in all ways. The obstacles I frequently meet are based, in my opinion, upon a person's skill level. I am challenged by knowing that I need to meet a person "where they are" and bring them from that place forward—even though [that place] may be far away from where I want them to be. (Julie Frentz, principal of Emerson Elementary School)

I guess the most important thing I can do is be an advocate by voicing my opinion, modeling and letting teachers know about best practices, and [by continuing to ask] myself the same question when I am not sure about what to do: Is this in the best interest of the child? . . . I have a desire to be an advocate for equality, regardless of age, disability, race, religion, sexual orientation, ability, gender, and anything else I forgot. It's part of my vision for justice. (Sue Abplanalp, principal of Lowell Elementary School)

Sue Abplanalp tells how these values are extended to others in informal interactions:

I had a conversation with a new [staff member] at our school. She said she did not believe in inclusion because it doesn't work for everyone. Some kids are too distracted, some are too noisy, some are too disruptive. I think she was missing the point of inclusion. To have inclusion, the community must be built first. The classroom needs to become a family, and, as in any healthy family setting, nobody gets excluded because they don't fit in correctly. If families across the country live with these children in their homes, then why should they be excluded in the classroom?

Using Reflective Dialogue and Critical Questioning
One of the most important ways that a principal can engender an atmosphere for empowering school reform is by stimulating inquiry for him- or herself and among teachers and students. Questioning to promote reflection has been identified as a critical feature of administrative and teacher practice to frame problems and determine alternative courses of action (Liston & Zeichner; 1986, 1991; Schön, 1983, 1987; Udvari-Solner, 1996). Jennie Allen, principal of Midvale Elementary School, described her practices:

My job is to look at individual children, look at the service delivery system in my school, and then ask the tough questions that will promote questioning and discussion: What are we doing as a school to meet the needs of all children, whatever their strengths and needs? Are our practices, in other words, what we teach and how we teach, effective for our children? Are we using our resources in the most effective way possible for children? What kinds of paradigm shifts do we need to make to meet the needs of our children? These are the tough questions that I know are hard to answer. [These are the questions] that people may have to take a leap to answer and may not be able to answer. It's my job to ask the questions, whatever the answers may be. I may not always like the answers, and sometimes I anticipate the answers to be very different. [However,] I want to plant the seeds of doubt. I want people to begin to think about things differently. That is how I see change coming about. It allows change to come about in a more natural fashion rather than mandating it and dictating it and saying, "This is the way it is going to be."

This critical questioning was instrumental in beginning a shift from a segregated early childhood program to inclusive service delivery for students with disabilities. Allen recalled:

Midvale had an early childhood program that ran as a separate entity. Now, think about this—we had eight kindergartens, and then we had a separate early childhood kindergarten program with 10 or so 5-year-olds. . . . I kept asking the early childhood kindergarten teacher, "Why are the children educated separately? We are a primary center, and if we think of ourselves as a primary center, why do we have children who are educated outside of the eight kindergartens that we have at our school?" I remember the early childhood teacher looking at me and saying, "Well, I don't know, and I don't like it." I said, "Well, then, we have to do something about it." Out of that conversation, after a year of conversation, we now have a team-taught kindergarten [that includes students with disabilities] and no longer have a separate early childhood program.

Allen's approach of posing the tough questions also was used in preparation for educators who had committed to team teaching:

Before team-taught classrooms came about we had some very lengthy discussions. [Discussions] about simple things like, How do you feel about having a roommate? Essentially, you are getting a roommate. So, how do you feel about sharing a room, having somebody else's desk in that room, and their stuff, and their mess? What are you going to do the first time there is a behavior problem in the classroom? Who is going to do the disciplining? Who is going to make the telephone call home? How are you going to decide that? During planning time, do you co-plan? How many weekdays a week are you going to co-plan? How many days are you going to go separately and plan? Who will teach which learning groups? Those are the kinds of discussions that need to take place. The message [behind those questions] was that I was not going to allow [one person] to act as an educational assistant in this classroom and the other person as the teacher.

Creating Constancy of Purpose: Linking the Tenets of Inclusive Education to Other Schoolwide Reforms and Priorities Based on assessments of students, building practices, and self-evaluations, Mary Hyde, principal of Glendale Elementary School, began extensive schoolwide restructuring by engaging her staff

in goal setting. The result was the following building priorities that centered broadly around learning and increasing achievement:

1. Raising the achievement levels of all students in reading and writing
2. Coordinating the curriculum to ensure sensible learning progressions in sequence, content, and processes within and between grade levels and to bring teachers into similar instructional orientations
3. Building a sense of community by promoting safety and peace
4. Fostering partnerships with parents
5. Attending to the number and types of transitions that interfered with or facilitated learning for students

Hyde believed that developing consensus in setting these priorities was a necessary precursor to guide decision making about change in practice. These shared goals also gave direction with regard to how she and her staff spent their time and money. She emphasized that these collective priorities are aligned with and promote inclusive principles. Hyde underscored the important role of the principal to help make explicit these connections for people—that is, how implementing national reforms or district initiatives advances a building priority or how building priorities inherently interact with and influence one another. For example, establishing methods in her school for positive conduct and safety clearly influenced the climate that would promote all children's learning to read. When examining the priority that targeted learning transitions, Hyde recalled:

> We looked at the number of transitions that students and staff were making, and we realized the people who were least able to make transitions smoothly were the people who were making the most transitions. The number of transitions also caused us to have less profitable learning time. This realization prompted discussion and action regarding how and when students identified with disabilities received specialized assistance. The overarching goal to reduce unnecessary transitions for all students bolstered the rationale and practice of maintaining instruction in general education settings for students with disabilities. Maybe the single biggest contribution I made is constancy of purpose . . . continuing to hold up the priorities that we established as the direction we are going [and] then asking how what we are trying to do relates to what we said we are all about.

Kery Kafka discussed the importance of clear direction, too:

> Well, I think one major thing to me is to always pay attention to the system and the structure that you are dealing with. Don't worry about indi-

vidual people or their beliefs. Don't focus on trying to have all of the right people in the right places, because you won't make it. There are too many variables you can't control. So, if you develop a structure in the building that promotes what you are looking for with such things as having time for people to meet with each other, having collaboration, having learning teams of teachers across all disciplines including the special education teachers on those learning teams, [then] you will see change. You have to just pay constant attention to the system to see where and how that system can be set up to get people collaborating, talking with each other, sharing ideas, focusing on student growth, [and] developing alternative assessments.

Promoting Specific Curricular and Instruction Approaches Administrators described the importance of new ways to teach that are extended to all children as essential in developing successful inclusive outcomes. An emphasis on literacy education, cooperative and partner learning, multiage grouping, service learning, peer mediation and schoolwide responses to conflict resolution were approaches that were repeatedly endorsed by the participants.

Carolyn Strutz, the principal at Fairview Elementary School in Milwaukee, described the implementation of a schoolwide social skills program as a critical component to successful inclusive programming for children with behavior challenges. She explained how the Stop and Think program teaches children how to assess conflicts by considering one of three options: ignoring, talking it over with the person, or enlisting the help of another adult. Strutz described the way in which special education staff brought their expertise to general educators in helping to develop a schoolwide program to promote positive behavior:

> We [attended] an in-service called Second Step. We carried over [special education strategies] to our [general] education program, and we saw tremendous difference in the social behaviors of [all of] our children. [Second Step is a program designed to provide prosocial skill instruction to an entire school body.] We started our own program, which [we] called Stop and Think. That was tremendously successful on the playground, in the hallway, and in the classrooms. [As a staff, we began] talking about dealing with crisis, anger management, and problem solving [in consistent ways].

Martha Wheeler-Fair and Mary Beth Minkley described the use of looping, in which teachers keep the same students in their classrooms for two or three academic years in order to develop continuity in programming. In addition to looping, Minkley's school is open year-round, another solution developed jointly by staff and administrators to solve many of the problems encountered when developing inclusive education programming that is responsive to unique learning challenges.

Revealing Incongruities in Practice and Philosophy

Administrators talked about the importance of confronting staff and asking for clarification when practices and philosophies do not mesh. In effect, administrators used their actions and questions as a "springboard for the analysis" (Reitzug, 1994, p. 299) of the relationship between actions and beliefs, as expressed in the cliché *walk the talk*.

Kery Kafka described a problem-solving session with a group of students and their teacher. Kery uses much of the total quality management (TQM) and continuous improvement philosophies in her work. Her administrative style asserts the critical role of beliefs and actions. In the following dialogue, Kery shared an example of how she extended this work into the classroom:

> I'm working with this one math class right now that had a 40% failure rate, and it is a mixed bag of kids, a mixture of special ed, [general] ed—you know, a medium-level math class—and we tried a different approach. [I] went in and said, "There's a 40% failure rate in this class, and this doesn't make any sense." I used the story about how people don't wake up and come to school wanting to fail. Teachers don't get up and decide to come and do the worst job possible. It doesn't make any sense for me to spend time yelling at the teacher and saying that [the person] must be a lousy teacher or yelling at kids and telling them they must be stupid kids. Let's figure out what we can do about this failure rate. Does anyone want to do this? So, students agreed and set a failure rate target in the second quarter at 10%. Then we worked with our quality tools, from TQM and continuous improvement methods, to develop solutions. I did a check with them this morning [halfway through the quarter], and they're at [a] 15% failure rate right now. [They reported] that they were being held accountable during the school day, during that class, to demonstrate that they knew something, so they [had] better listen, they [had] better take notes, [and] they [had] better pass these tests.

Julie Frentz describes her philosophy on developing solutions to challenges as she attempts to provide a springboard for alternative resolutions to issues:

> I personally grappled with whole school management issues [during my first year] and found that teachers expected the principal to do much of the [behavior] management. So, when management issues presented themselves, I tried to ask teachers, "Whose job is it really?" When a teacher complained to me that she didn't like the way a fifth-grade student was running in the hall, I said, "Whose job is it to stop him from running?" The response to this question was, "It's mine if I saw him." The teacher acknowledged that it was difficult and scary to do. [My feeling is] that's okay, let it be hard and scary to do; but I need to know that you know it's your responsibility. [I have tried] to instill that it's everyone's responsibility for management; it's everyone's responsibility for how people behave in our general environments, hallways, lunch rooms, bath-

rooms, at recess, and in the library. If we believe that everyone belongs to the school and we are all part of the school, then we are all responsible for managing the school. [This has] caused me to change my practice. . . . I do not want teachers to think that sending the student to me is an adequate solution. I want teachers to see themselves as part of the problem-solving process and part of the [process of] providing the consequences.

Possibility: Actualization and Products of Critique

The final aspect of Reitzug's (1994) framework of empowering leadership behavior is possibility—that is, ways in which administrators actualize a school environment that supports the tenets of inclusive education for staff and students. The decision to act on one's commitment to inclusive programming was described as pivotal by all interviewees. Examples from the featured research include translating belief into practice by engaging parents and teachers in developing responsive activities, developing creative financial resources, and keeping friends in high places.

Translating Belief into Practice Moving from an expressed philosophy to daily practice requires administrators to make definitive and practical decisions regarding instructional organization. Mary Ramberg related an instance that required significant changes in class configurations and equitable school offerings to rectify tracking practices that unintentionally had excluded groups of students:

At each grade level, the school had "regular" math and "enriched" math. I believed that this was substantively, practically, and symbolically wrong. Substantively, tracking students in mathematics (and thus often skewing the other classes into tracked classes as well) made no sense if we believed that all students could learn (i.e., no one had a "math gene") and wanted all students to eventually be able to do the same things—e.g., take algebra by tenth grade. If that was the belief and the goal, we needed to offer all students access to the same educational opportunities. Practically, when we tracked, classes became racially and socioeconomically identifiable, and lower-track classes often became more difficult to manage. Symbolically, who would want "regular" [math] if "enriched" [math] were available. So, at the beginning of my third year at the school, we eliminated "regular" mathematics. This was another "top down" decision, though it was widely anticipated. Teachers had over a semester of "warning" and were given release time to prepare. In addition, they adopted a new textbook to support the heterogeneously grouped instruction. During the first year of implementation, teams of teachers had additional release time to develop materials to support differentiation as well as cooperative, open-ended, and investigative activities in mathematics. At this same time, teachers were very engaged in infusing the NCTM [National Council of Teachers of Mathematics] standards [i.e., national math standards] into their classroom mathematics instruction. This significantly supported inclusion because students were expected to be engaged in complex mathematical thinking. Being good at computation was not a prerequisite.

Martha Wheeler-Fair described a creative method that she and her staff developed to help ensure more appropriate education planning and programming for students:

> We've started a process in our school called the descriptive review. We do it for [all children, those with special education labels and those without], based on teachers' having difficulty figuring out what to do about any youngster's academic progress or . . . behavioral progress in a classroom. [We call] folks to, what we call, a descriptive review. They bring background information about the [student], and they talk about what they would like to have the youngster do. [Staff are encouraged to formulate a proactive statement.] It's like, "I would like Jane to sit in her seat for 20 minutes to work with us in a cooperative group." And if that's the challenge, then everyone [shares] their perspective; everybody has a voice. [In addition,] there is [an]other group of us [who] sit in on the meeting. Then we offer suggestions and recommendations [about] what they might try. . . . So, [there is] a lot of teaming, a lot of collaboration, trying to really figure out what to do. . . . Parents are involved, too.

Another way that administrators actualized their inclusive school environments was by promoting regular home visits for all children. Mary Beth Minkley and Martha Wheeler-Fair described this aspect of their program:

> Home visits, [they are] so important. I had a couple [of teachers who] did their first home visits this year, and they came back high as a kite. They were so [grateful that they said,] "Thank you." At first, they were very hesitant; but once they get out there and really get involved with those families and see the difference that home visits make, they really are enthusiastic. My parent coordinator is even making up little gifts so [that] when they go, if they have a little child, one person can be playing with the child and the other can be talking with the parent. We have this flexible menu [as to how home visits can be carried out]. We have had teachers who have met parents and sat down for a cup of coffee. They have gone to jobs and met them for lunch, or they go after school. . . . Because my teachers were beginning to feel they were not getting in enough home visits, we took one of our days that we might have spent for an in-service, and we used it as a home visitation day. So, teachers and their families could home visit on a Saturday. That was great. We did one in November, and we're doing another one in March just because we want to make sure that beyond parent–teacher conferences, we get another chance to talk with parents. That really was exciting to them. We also have teachers who do things like [having] an ice cream social at Bayshore [a local mall]. She had 34 families come in out of the 50 students, 35 adults.

Developing Creative Finances   Principals were creative in the way that they sought out additional monies, reallocated existing funds, and generally found ways to meet the needs of their schools. Martha Wheeler-Fair described a creative allocation of monies:

> One of the things that my staff has agreed to is [for] resources to be spent on human power, so we don't purchase textbooks. That's why we are ungraded; we have no textbooks. Because we don't buy textbooks, we're able to afford to have an educational assistant assigned to every one of the teachers in our building. We are allowed to make some decisions that really support our [ability] to do full inclusion; [we] have ungraded and multiage [classrooms]. We have used our money differently [from] many others. In addition, we have spent a lot of money on staff development. There is much money spent on making sure that staff members get the information they need to develop the skills and the expertise to work in teams. We've done a lot with team building. We have done a lot with curriculum because that is also a piece that's important for us.

Other examples of seeking alternative financial support were grant writing and donations by various community agencies. In addition to actual financial products, other resources were considered. Creative utilization of human resources was cited by all administrators. The primary reference in terms of staff distribution was the use of cross-categorical programming whereby students with special education labels could be supported by a team of teachers, one of whom may or may not have the particular certification program or background to match the child's labeled disability.

Keeping Friends in High Places   Participants discussed the necessity of involving central office administrators in building-level decisions. One administrator, Barbara Goss, described the way that she tried to enlist more cooperation:

> I think we became a real bug for central office. We were on the telephone daily with central office because of the numbers [of students with support needs in our building]. We were disproportionately high [compared] with the rest of the system. What was it, 12%–14% systemwide and we had 22% [of our population with identified special needs]. And so, we were calling central office every day, every day.

CONCLUSIONS

In summary, principals supported, facilitated, and actualized inclusive environments for students in a multitude of creative ways. Positive forms of influence that involved clarifying, coordinating, and communicating a unified purpose (Blase & Kirby, 1992; Heck, Larson, & Marcoulides, 1990) were more evident than displays of formal authority to promote change.

Courage was a recurring theme for these administrators—the courage to relentlessly pose the difficult, the contrary, the controversial, and the seemingly unanswerable questions. Tom McGinnity, Deputy Superintendent of the Milwaukee Public Schools, reminded us of the definitive question that administrators must have the fortitude to continually propose: "Who has the right to exclude somebody?"

The challenge that administrators face in this time of change is a difficult one. Fullan (1993) stated that we cannot make a difference in the lives of students by playing it safe. Skilled change agents with a moral purpose are needed. Most of those with whom we spoke had a clear vision of what could or should be, but in terms of providing assistance along the way, inclusive school change remains daunting. As Julie Frentz said, "It is still murky territory between empowerment, decision making, and choice."

Administrators spoke of their need for support and power to open the windows of opportunity to refashion their schools and reallocate both human and financial resources as collectively deemed fitting because, as we know, change comes from within. In an effort to continue compiling examples to help those experiencing the various growing pains, triumphs, and challenges on the road toward inclusive education, we invite administrators, teachers, parents, and students to share with us their chronicles. In retelling your stories, we may collectively find ourselves at the proverbial "next stop."

REFERENCES

Blase, J., & Kirby, P.C. (1992). *Bringing out the best in teachers: What effective principals do.* Thousand Oaks, CA: Corwin Press.

Fox, N.E., & Ysseldyke, J.E. (1997). Implementing inclusion at the middle school level: Lessons from a negative example. *Exceptional Children, 64*(1), 81–98.

Fullan, M.G. (1993). *Change forces: Probing the depth of educational reform.* New York: Falmer Press.

Heck, R.H., Larson, T.J., & Marcoulides, G.A. (1990). Instructional leadership and school achievement: Validation of a causal model. *Educational Administration Quarterly, 26*(2), 94–125.

Keyes, M.W. (1996). *Intersections of vision and practice in an inclusive elementary school: An ethnography of a principal.* Unpublished doctoral dissertation, University of Wisconsin–Madison.

Liston, D., & Zeichner, K. (1986). Reflective teaching and action research in preservice teacher education. *Journal of Education for Teaching, 16,* 213–238.

Liston, D.P., & Zeichner, K.M. (1991). *Teacher education and the social conditions of schooling.* New York: Routledge.

MacKinnon, J.D., & Brown, M.E. (1994). Inclusion in secondary school: An analysis of school structure based on teachers' image of change. *Educational Administration Quarterly, 30*(2), 126–152.

Morgan, C.R., & Demchak, M. (1996). *Addressing administrative needs for successful inclusion of students with disabilities in Rural Goals 2000: Building programs that work.* (ERIC Document Reproduction Service No. ED 394 767)

Prawat, R.S. (1991). Conversations with self and setting: A framework for thinking about teacher empowerment. *American Educational Research Association, 28,* 737–757.

Reitzug, U.C. (1994). A case study of empowering principal behavior. *American Educational Research Journal, 31*(2), 283–307.

Rossman, G.B. (1992). *State policy for integrating all students.* Thousand Oaks, CA: Corwin Press.

Sage, D.D., & Burrello, L.C. (1994). The principal as leader. In D.D. Sage & L.C. Burrello, *Leadership in educational reform* (pp. 223–248). Baltimore: Paul H. Brookes Publishing Co.

Schaffner, C.B., & Buswell, B.E. (1996). Ten critical elements for creating inclusive and effective school communities. In S.B. Stainback & W. C. Stainback (Eds.), *Inclusion: A guide for educators* (pp. 49–65). Baltimore: Paul H. Brookes Publishing Co.

Schön, D.A. (1983). *The reflective practitioner: How professionals think in action.* New York: BasicBooks.

Schön, D.A. (1987). *Educating the reflective practitioner: Toward a new design for teaching and learning in the professions.* San Francisco: Jossey-Bass.

Sergiovanni, T.J. (1994). Organizations or communities? Changing the metaphor changes the theory. *Educational Administration Quarterly, 30*(2), 214–226.

Servatius, J.D., Fellows, M., & Kelly, D. (1992). Preparing leaders for inclusive schools. In R.A. Villa, J.S. Thousand, W. Stainback, & S. Stainback (Eds.), *Restructuring for caring and effective education: An administrative guide to creating heterogeneous schools* (1st ed., pp. 267–284). Baltimore: Paul H. Brookes Publishing Co.

Shinsky, J.E. (1992). *Techniques for including students with disabilities: A step-by-step practical guide for school principals* (2nd ed.). Lansing, MI: Leadership Support Series.

Stainback, W., & Stainback, S. (1991). Promoting inclusive education:

What happened in one school. *Quality Outcomes-Driven Education,* *1*(3), 15–25.

Trump, G., & Hange, J. (1996). *Concerns about and effective strategies for inclusion: Focus group interview findings from West Virginia teachers.* Charleston, WV: Appalachia Educational Lab. (ERIC Document Reproduction Service No. ED 397 578)

Udvari-Solner, A. (1996). Examining teacher thinking: Constructing a process to design curricular adaptations. *Remedial and Special Education, 17*(4), 245–254.

Villa, R.A., & Thousand, J.S. (1990). Administrative supports to promote inclusive schooling. In W.C. Stainback & S.B. Stainback (Eds.), *Support networks for inclusive schooling: Interdependent integrated education* (pp. 210–218). Baltimore: Paul H. Brookes Publishing Co.

Villa, R.A., Thousand, J.S., Meyers, H., & Nevin, A. (1996). Teacher and administrator perceptions of heterogeneous education. *Exceptional Children, 63*(1), 29–45.

Whitaker, C.E. (1997). *Managing inclusion: A study of principal leadership in inclusion* (Doctoral dissertation, Virginia Polytechnic Institute and State University, 1997). *Dissertation Abstracts International, 57/09,* 3777.

Chapter 16

The Swanton School District (Franklin Northwest Supervisory Union)

A Second Look at an Inclusive School

Richard Schattman and Linda Keating

The Franklin Northwest Supervisory Union (FNWSU) is a collection of five independent school districts in rural northwestern Vermont. The union's evolution from a dual system of categorical and segregated special and general education services to a single full-inclusion model was not an isolated change originated, directed, or orchestrated from within special education. Rather, it was a gradual cultural evolution of related community, school, and personal attitudes that took on a life of its own.

In Escher's (1996) pen-and-ink sketch of "Metamorphosis," the beginning and end of the picture appears well defined, whereas the process of transformation is somewhat elusive. This chapter chronicles a school system's transformation—or metamorphosis—to an inclusive education system, one in which all students benefit from full-time general education classroom placement. Clearly, any retrospective account of a system's change process makes the process appear far more planned and deliberate and less elusive than it actually was. This update of our account of the FNWSU in the first edition of this book (Schattman, 1992) focuses on the Swanton Elementary School District, the largest elementary district in the FNWSU. We present a historical analysis that reviews our school's strategic planning process and changes in organizational practices, focusing on an emergent approach to shared leadership and new models for configuring classrooms. In addition, more contemporary contextual factors such as the influence of national and state standards, including Vermont's Framework of Standards and Learning Opportunities (Vermont Department of Education, 1996) and Vermont's Equal Educational Opportunity Act of 1997 (Act 60, Vt. Stat. Ann. tit. 16, §§ 4000–4029 [1998]), are discussed as elements of an emerging context for the implementation of inclusive education (Roach, 1995).

What continues to be so interesting about the FNWSU and the Swanton School District? There are many fine examples of inclusive school communities in which all or most students with individualized education programs (IEPs) are educated in age-appropriate general classes in their neighborhood schools (Hasazi, Johnson, Liggett, & Schattman, 1992). At the turn of the 21st century, federal and state policies are in greater alignment with inclusive practices than at any time in U.S. history. Interestingly, the Swanton School's metamorphosis in the early 1980s occurred at a time when there were few examples or models of inclusion and the literature and research were only beginning to focus on practices of full inclusion (Lipsky & Gartner, 1989; Stainback & Stainback, 1990; Will, 1986).

The FNWSU is composed of five separate and independent school systems, four elementary districts, and one unified high school district. The student population of the FNWSU is approximately 3,000, with the Swanton School District accounting for 670 students. In the Swanton School District, approximately 9% of the student population is identified as eligible for special education services, and 40% of the students are eligible for free or reduced-cost lunches. Of the students attending schools in the Swanton School District, 20% are Native Americans.

In 1980, the schools of FNWSU, including the Swanton School District, provided special education services in a manner similar to most other Vermont districts. Students with mild learning challenges were educated in general education classes of their local schools, with consulting teacher and resource room support. Students identified as having more significant learning difficulties for the most part were segregated from their community school general classes and sent to out-of-district regional special education programs, referred to as *area programs.* Area programs included classes for students who had been labeled educable mentally retarded (EMR), trainable mentally retarded (TMR), and multihandicapped (MH). Each class was staffed with a special education teacher and special education paraprofessionals and received consultation from related-services personnel (e.g., speech-language therapy, occupational and physical therapy).

The practice of educating children with more significant learning impairments in segregated area programs was premised on a number of assumptions:

- Homogeneous grouping enabled an intensification of services that would enhance students' achievement, including the provision of related services.

- Special education teachers were the only trained staff with the skills and ability to educate children with significant special education needs.

- Congregating children with like needs was economically justifiable.

- Segregated placements along a continuum of restrictiveness (Reynolds, 1962) reflected the intent of the Education for All Handicapped Children Act of 1975 (PL 94-142).

- Students with special needs should be protected from the unfair competition and social ridicule that might occur if they had to be educated with students in general education classes.

Since 1986, there have been no self-contained special education classes or resource rooms in the Swanton School District; children are supported through a noncategorical continuum of services in general education classes and in the community. These special education support services include supplemental professional and paraprofessional instruction and related services (e.g., speech-language, psychological, occupational, physical therapy) provided via consultation and direct instruction of students in the general education environment. Although a fully inclusive approach was implemented by 1986, it continues to evolve to meet the diverse and changing needs of our learning community.

BEGINNING THE JOURNEY AND THE EMERGENCE OF A STRATEGIC PLAN

In the early days of the journey in the FNWSU, the Swanton School District played a leadership role. There is little doubt that the traditions of segregated special education area programs would have persisted had Swanton School personnel not decided to consider the notion of outcomes-based instruction (Bloom, 1984; Guskey, 1997). Although the tenets of outcomes-based instruction (OBI) models address the needs of students with varying abilities within general education classes, the literature of outcomes-based instruction (and many other classroom-based instruction strategies) in general did *not* address the needs of students served in isolated special education classrooms. Although it is clear that most classroom-based instruction strategies appropriate for students without disabilities also are appropriate for students eligible for special education, such a strong connection had not been made in the literature of the early to mid-1980s (Bikel & Bikel, 1986; Skrtic, 1991). Consequently, in 1982, when the Swanton School District first considered the adoption of an outcomes-based approach, they did not consider its application to students with disabilities.

In 1982, FNWSU schools began to explore the possibility of embracing an outcomes-based approach to the provision of instruction. It was the belief of the FNWSU's central office administrators that, in order for teachers to embrace OBI, they needed to participate in multiple forums in which they could receive information about and debate the merits of OBI. Consequently, teachers and administrators participated in workshops, attended conferences, and read the professional literature to become knowledgeable about and familiar with outcomes-based models. Formal and informal discussion groups were organized to examine both issues related to OBI and the community's goals for its schools. More formal meetings occurred during school hours, on professional development days; informal meetings tended to be get-togethers at individuals' homes and often included community and school board members.

Such meetings continued for more than 1 year and proved to be invaluable for two reasons. First, they helped people formulate and define a school philosophy and mission and desired student outcomes that reflected hopes for all children and specified what each child should learn as a result of participating in our schools. Second, by engaging a broad range of concerned individuals who eventually would be affected by a shift in the union's mission and practices, the discussions enhanced the likelihood that individuals would feel that they had "ownership" of the emerging ideals.

After a year and a half of community conversations, a vision and a mission emerged. The Swanton School Vision remained substantially the same for most of the last 2 decades of the 20th century. It states, "The Swanton School is a caring, responsible, respectful, community of learners. Our work is supported by inquiry and reflection and promotes personal integrity, citizenship, and lifelong learning." This vision has provided the Swanton School with a map for its journey. Staff, parents, and other community members use the vision as a compass for conversations about what they are doing, how effective the school's practices are, and which direction they might take next. Ideas consistent with the tenets of the vision are given serious consideration, and conflicting ideas are soon abandoned. The vision has provided the school with a sense of continuity and direction. Although the vision was evident in our daily lives at school, greater detail was needed to guide discrete decisions (Noddings, 1995). The school's mission and beliefs, presented in Figure 1, provide a framework for more discrete and programmatic decision making. Together the vision, mission, and beliefs have guided our changes in practice at both the classroom and systems level. The Swanton School Mission states,

> The Swanton School Community believes that given enough time and appropriate instruction students will achieve what is considered necessary to learn. We recognize that students arrive at school with differing backgrounds, influences and needs. We are committed to the concepts of fairness and justice which reflect a concern for each individual's development, dignity, and growth potential. Approaches to discipline and social responsibility in our school will promote behavioral changes that empower students to understand their obligations to others as members of a democratic society.

By 1983, the FNWSU mission was understood by most teachers and administrators, and the administration began to use the mission statement and its indicators as a framework for examining and discussing instruction, staff development, discipline, community relationships, and the school's climate. As these discussions continued, the relationship between these seemingly disparate activities became clear. No longer did staff development seem unrelated to instruction, instruction unrelated to discipline, or community relationships unrelated to the school's climate. As Figure 1 illustrates, all of the varied facets were viewed as related to one another, and the glue holding it all together was a commitment to a common vision and mission.

Incongruities between the vision, mission, and practice emerged; many of our practices were challenged, including ability tracking at the primary and secondary levels and readiness classrooms. The most striking incongruity was the practice of segregating students based on the type and severity of their disabilities or educational challenges. If we truly believed in our mission statement—that all children could learn, given appropriate time and resources—how could we justify sorting out some students and sending them away to segregated area programs rather than educating them in age-appropriate classes of their neighborhood schools?

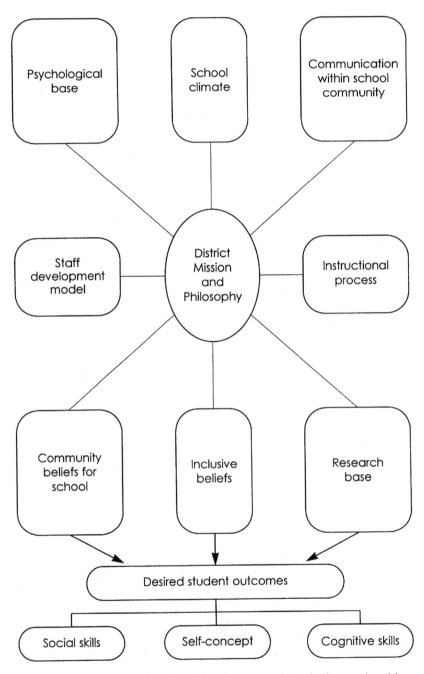

Figure 1.   Franklin Northwest Supervisory Union's outcomes-driven developmental model.

Initially, the discussions regarding our segregation practices were somewhat academic and abstract. However, the discussions became concrete as we began to examine the effects of segregation with regard to the attainment of our stated desired student outcomes for all children, which appear in Table 1. Through our self-examination, we discovered a number of disturbing things. First, we saw the children who attended the area programs climb into the *same* school bus as their neighborhood peers and brothers and sisters each morning, disembark at the neighborhood school, and wait in a special section of the playground until the special bus took them away to their out-of-district program. Once on the special bus, they traveled up to 45 minutes with other children deemed appropriate for segregation to a school for the children of a community other than their own. We decided to ask children attending area programs and their siblings how they felt about this routine. Consistently, they responded that it was diminishing, humiliating, and embarrassing. Clearly, this practice violated our first student outcome that schools should enhance children's feelings of self-worth.

A more in-depth look into the area classes revealed that some inclusion opportunities were provided for the students attending the area classes. However, they were minimal, and they were not with siblings and peers from the students' home school and community. Consequently, the primary models of age-appropriate social skills for students in the area classes were the adult special education staff and other children with disabilities in the room. Thus, Swanton's segregation of students with disabilities effectively denied them opportunities to achieve our second desired student outcome of social skills development.

Finally, our practice of segregation was viewed in relationship to our third stated desired outcome of developing students' higher-level cognitive skills. Special classes had the capacity to employ special techniques to teach specific skills. Unfortunately, our review of the literature

Table 1.   Desired outcomes for all students attending the Swanton School

---

Outcome 1: Development of a good self-concept
. . . feel competent and positive about themselves as learners; the process of education should enhance, not diminish, one's feeling of self-worth

Outcome 2: Development of appropriate social skills
. . . develop the necessary social skills that will enable them to participate fully in school, work, and home life

Outcome 3: Development of higher-level cognitive skills
. . . learn well, progress in the curriculum to the greatest extent possible and learn to be an independent, self-directed learner

---

led us to believe that the specialized capacity of segregated programs, in fact, had negative effects on students (Lipsky & Gartner, 1989). Specifically, the teacher-directed instruction methods commonly employed in special classes encouraged students' dependence on others (i.e., teachers, paraprofessionals) rather than the development of self-directed, independent learning and higher-level reasoning and problem-solving skills. This issue became alarming when we began to consider how the dependent relationship fostered in a segregated model might contribute to a lifelong pattern of dependence.

This self-examination process caused the Swanton community to conclude that, for a group of children with disabilities, the practices we employed clearly violated our stated mission. We were faced with three options: 1) We could modify our philosophy and mission so that it did not address *all* children, 2) we could learn to live with and ignore the discrepancy between our values and practices, or 3) we could change our practices. The majority of teachers, administrators, and community members who pondered this dilemma decided to initiate a planning process that they hoped would facilitate a change in practices so that students who were segregated could be educated in a manner consistent with our stated mission and philosophy.

CHANGES IN ORGANIZATIONAL PRACTICES

It is one thing to know that change is needed or to know which specific practices need to change. It is quite another thing to know how to implement needed changes so that they become a meaningful and integrated part of the school culture. Swanton teachers, administrators, and parents joined forces to draw a map for the organizational change needed to align the school's practices with its vision, mission, and beliefs. Two areas that emerged as essential for planning and change were, first, modifying the leadership structure to be more responsive and collaborative and, second, creating new and more flexible classroom configurations to accommodate a broader range of abilities.

Shared Leadership

When the mission of the school was defined in terms of the educational needs of all children, the system became more complex. Quickly we realized that traditional hierarchical models of school leadership could no longer manage the complexities of systemic change. Shared leadership at the Swanton School meant that teachers, administrators, students, parents, and other community members had formal and informal opportunities to influence changes made in the school.

Swanton's shared leadership model includes three broad components: the administration, the design team, and the task forces.

Swanton's shared leadership structure is a collaborative model wherein the administration provides leadership and enables others to assume leadership responsibilities. Leadership is multifaceted and includes visionary, reflective, strategic, historical, and celebratory aspects. It was the responsibility of the administrative team to ensure a role for all stakeholders involved with the change process. By subscribing to a model of shared leadership, the potential for broad-based and creative approaches to planning and problem solving was achieved. The design team was a group composed of community members and included the school's co-principals, teachers, the assistant superintendent, a student, a board member, and a parent. The design team's activities ensured that schoolwide decisions were consistent with the Swanton vision and mission. In addition to the administrative team and design team, task forces were an essential part of Swanton's shared leadership model. Task forces involved staff, students, and the community in developing goals consistent with the school's vision and mission, identifying targets that are measurable in terms of student outcomes, developing action plans, and assessing progress. Task forces have focused on middle-level education, literacy, technology, early education, social responsibility, and community collaboration. Figure 2 describes the relationship between the various aspects of Swanton's shared leadership model. In Swanton's shared leadership model, every voice may not be heard on every issue, and every decision may not be made at a committee, building, or task force level; but collaborative approaches to decision making may be used when the complexity or nature of an issue so warrants.

Classroom Configurations

Full inclusion expands the range of abilities in general education classes. To respond to this reality, Swanton teachers examined a range of classroom configurations and placement options. Traditional class configurations wherein one teacher taught one class worked for some of our students but not all of them. By exploring other ways to configure classes, teachers, and resources, we were able to create a myriad of options that better accommodated a broad range of needs in our student population.

Many teachers saw a need to create a sense of a small community or family within the school system as inclusive restructuring efforts changed the dynamics of the classroom. Looking beyond the scope of traditional resources and support for the classroom teacher yielded a

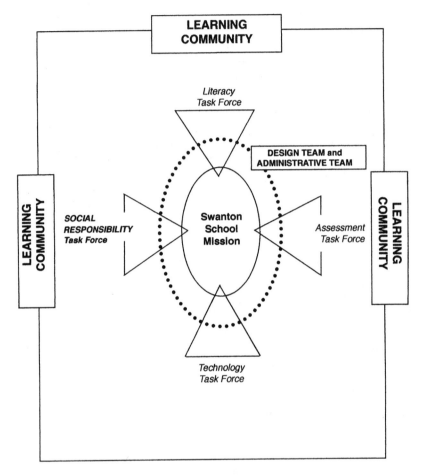

Figure 2. Swanton School District leadership model.

new vision of teacher collaboration (Sarason, 1995). Most teachers sought a collaborative partner in teaching. These teaching teams yielded a variety of classroom structures: single-grade, multiage classrooms; multiyear programs in which two teachers alternated grade levels so that they could team teach and keep a class for 2 years (looping); single-grade two-teacher teams; and multigrade two-teacher teams as well as some more traditional arrangements. Special educators became members of teams as consultants, teachers, and collaborative planners. Block scheduling provided the flexibility to schedule mutual planning times for teachers who chose to collaborate. In fact, teachers designed and set the master schedule for the school. If our efforts to support students' education were to effect systemic change, we learned that a tacit respect for the complexity of the system needed to be upheld. As we continue to challenge ourselves as a learning organization (Senge, 1990), we must continue to look at the evolving context in which we exist.

STANDARDS AND THE EVOLVING CONTEXT FOR INCLUSIVE EDUCATION: TRANSFORMING SCHOOLS AND STUDENTS' PERFORMANCE

Arguably, the most defining characteristic of change in education is the presence of national and state standards. If we are to continue to develop our ability to address the educational needs of *all* children in integrated classroom environments, we must understand the emerging framework that standards define.

In his foreword to the first edition of this book, Wiggins (Villa, Thousand, Stainback, & Stainback, 1992) noted that the text's core thesis is that "all students would learn if schools were well run and focused on student performance" (1992, p. xi). In 1992, this concept was presented as a radical one. Ironically, at the turn of the 21st century as this second edition is published, we are at just such a juncture in public education in Vermont. Vermont's Act 60 (Equal Educational Opportunity Act, 1998) and *Vermont's Framework of Standards and Learning Opportunities* (Vermont Department of Education, 1996) have the potential to serve as dual catalysts for providing the kind of opportunity that Wiggins suggested is necessary to effect a commitment to "public, measurable, and self-obligated results" (1992, xii). The ground could not be more fertile for sowing the seeds necessary to transform the schools of Vermont and elsewhere into learning organizations willing to accept the diversity of their students and to ensure, as Wiggins stated, "that all students get their entitlement" (1992, p. xv).

Of course, Vermont is not unique in its focus on and interest in standards. What may be unique is the particular attention that both of these documents pay to the application of standard setting for *all* schools and *all* children. In the state of Vermont, implementation of school and curricular standards and the expectation of achievement are meant to be fully inclusive. Quite early in the drafting and development of a set of common expectations and learning outcomes, there was an emphasis on including all of Vermont's children. Quite clearly, the preliminary plan was to set clear expectations for *all* students and schools, provide instruction and a school environment that are aligned with these expectations, measure performance in relation to those expectations, and create opportunities for professional development that enable educators to accomplish this goal.

As noted previously, some of these expectations are firmly established in Vermont state law. Vermont Act 60, also known as the Equal Educational Opportunity Act of 1998, requires schools to "implement and continually update standards for student performance . . . standards that are rigorous, challenging, and designed to prepare students to participate in and contribute to the democratic process and to compete in the global marketplace" (Vt. Act 60, 16 Vt. Stat. Ann. § 164). At the local level, it is expected that each school will implement a standards-based articulated curriculum and support needed implementation of standards (Petit, 1997). A wide variety of resources have been targeted for this purpose, including resources associated with the State Department of Education's special education budget.

In addition, Act 60 states that all schools "shall assess student performance under this plan using methods of assessment developed by the State Board of Education" (Vt. Act 60, 16 Vt. Stat. Ann. § 165). For the first time in Vermont's history, *all* students will participate in these standards-based assessments. In the rare situations in which this kind of testing is inappropriate to assess learning, a modification plan incorporating necessary accommodations within a framework of guiding stipulations is required. This necessary shift in expectations for all students is embedded in raised expectations for all schools in the state (Harris & Carr, 1996). All Vermont schools will be held to quality standards.

The Vermont Framework of Standards and Learning Opportunities has already begun to change the way in which children with disabilities are educated in the Swanton School. The Framework of Standards and Learning Opportunities has created a guide for the Swanton School's next generation of change to support the educational needs of all of its children. The framework has encouraged us to raise expectations and improve learning for all students. It has made explicit our goals for what students should know and be able to do.

Swanton is no longer implementing a fully inclusive model in a quasi-supportive policy environment. The Vermont Framework is explicit with regard to its expectations and defines *all* students as

- Students who have been denied access in any way to educational opportunities, as well as those who have not
- Students who are female as well as those who are male
- Students who are African American, Hispanic, Asian, American Indian, or members of other minorities as well as those who are part of the racial or ethnic majority
- Students who are socioeconomically disadvantaged as well as those who are more advantaged

- Students who have not been successful in school as well as those who have been successful (p. A.3)

The intention is not to exclude any student from the expectations embodied in the framework and to provide the necessary accommodations for these students and specifically delineate them in the IEP.

LESSONS LEARNED

With both Act 60's emphasis on equal education for all and the Vermont Framework of Standards and Learning Opportunities' explicit definition of *all students,* conditions in Vermont seem optimal for improving the performance of all students. However, frameworks of standards and even the guidelines of state law do not guarantee high performance outcomes or inclusive practices. The critical interpretation of these quality, content, and performance standards rests at the classroom level. Standards must translate into standards-based instruction and standards-based assessment in each and every classroom and for each and every student.

In order to meet the standards, students need *access* to the rigorous content, to instructors who are knowledgeable about pedagogy, to equitable resources, to the time necessary to learn, and to a safe and healthy learning environment. Students need *instruction* that provides experience that builds on their prior knowledge and facilitates the acquisition of new knowledge and skills. They need teachers who use a variety of teaching strategies, and they need to participate in a variety of roles as learners. They need a plethora of learning experiences that enable them to apply their knowledge and skills as well as reflect on their learning. Critical to fully inclusive education, they need learning environments that can be adapted to their learning needs. Students need *assessment and reporting* of learning results that reflect a variety of assessment strategies, often involving them in the development of the assessment. They need clearly established performance criteria before they are assessed, and they need information reported to them about their learning that enables them to take steps to improve their own learning. Students also need to be able to see the *connections* between and among their learning experiences so that their learning is relevant. They need to know that an entire community supports their learning in order for that relevance to resonate. Finally, students need instruction that reflects the *recommended practices* in teaching discrete fields of knowledge.

Interestingly, these conditions necessary for changing and improving education for all children have been the backbone of the special education paradigm since the inception of the Education for All Handicapped Children Act of 1975. A standards-based pedagogy contributes to an educational context that supports an inclusive approach to both special and general education. In Swanton, knowledge of the Vermont Framework of Standards and Learning Opportunities has created a common language enabling *all* teachers to discuss the conditions necessary for *all* students to meet the standards. In the past, the IEP was a means for a select group of students to acquire special accommodations, individualized programs, and the allocation of unique resources. With the shift to standards-based education, all children are eligible for this type of individualized consideration. As the context of special education and general education have merged, classroom and special education teachers have embraced new strategies for working together. Classroom and special education teachers frequently plan activities together and team teach. Special educators and general education teachers develop rubrics together to assess students' performance relative to standards addressed in both the IEP and the general curriculum. No longer is the special education teacher relegated to working only with children eligible for special education. Resources are shared to the benefit of *all* children.

CONCLUSIONS

North American schools are being challenged to improve and become more effective (Hilliard, 1991). For some, *effective* means preparing graduates to be competitive in the world economy; for others, *effective* means higher overall scores on standardized tests of achievement. People of the FNWSU and Swanton school system chose to interpret *effective* in terms of social justice; that is, they saw that a community could consider its schools effective only if the schools tried to be effective for everyone, including students with the most challenging needs. The very act of culling out some students (e.g., those with disabilities and labels; those who may adversely affect aggregate achievement scores) precludes a school from being eligible for consideration as effective.

The commitment of the FNWSU and the Swanton School District to restructure to address the diverse needs of learners emanated from the belief that the needs of each child justify the allocation of additional resources, the restructuring of programs, and the provision of a genuinely individualized education program. Certainly, the schools of FNWSU still are far from perfect. They continue to have a distance to go to meet the needs of all children as well as they would like, but they are committed to that end.

As the Swanton School continues to evolve in its ability to meet the diverse needs of *all* of its students, a common ground for improving the performance of all students continues to expand. The historical tenets that are reflected in a fundamental commitment to an inclusive local philosophy are joined with a statewide emphasis on standards-based achievement for all students. The interaction of planning, collaboration, leadership, and standards provides schools with the necessary elements to respond to the educational needs of *all* children. The success or failure of our efforts is most likely to be determined by our willingness to grow as learning organizations, reflecting and changing with our eyes always focused on our vision, mission, and beliefs.

REFERENCES

Bikel, W.E., & Bikel, D.P. (1986). Effective schools, classrooms, and instruction: Implications for special education. *Exceptional Children, 52*(6), 489–500.

Bloom, B.S. (1984). The search for methods of group instruction as effective as one to one tutoring. *Educational Leadership, 41*(8), 4–17.

Education for All Handicapped Children Act of 1975, PL 94-142, 20 U.S.C. §§ 1400 *et seq.*

Equal Education Opportunity Act (Vermont Act 60), Vt. Stat. Ann. tit. 16, §§ 4000–4029 (1998).

Escher, M.C. (1996). *The graphic work of M.C. Escher* (Rev. ed.; J.E. Brigham, trans.). New York: Wings Books.

Guskey, T.R. (1997). *Implementing mastery learning* (2nd ed.). Belmont, CA: Wadsworth.

Harris, D.E., & Carr, J.F. (1996). *How to use standards in the classroom.* Alexandria, VA: Association for Supervision and Curriculum Development.

Hasazi, S.B. , Johnson, A.P., Liggett, A., & Schattman, R. (1992). *National study of the implementation of LRE policy: Final report and findings* (Federal grant project). Washington, DC: U.S. Office of Special Education and Rehabilitative Services, Office of Special Education Programs.

Hilliard, A. (1991). Do we have the will to educate all children? *Educational Leadership, 9,* 31–35.

Lipsky, D.K., & Gartner, A. (1989). *Beyond separate education: Quality education for all.* Baltimore: Paul H. Brookes Publishing Co.

Noddings, N. (1995). A moral defensible mission for schools in the 21st century. *Phi Delta Kappan, 76*(5), 365–368.

Petit, M. (1997). *Wrapping policy around good practice.* Montpelier: Vermont State Department of Education.

Reynolds, M. (1962). A framework for considering some issues in special education. *Exceptional Children, 28,* 367–370.

Roach, V. (1995). Supporting inclusion: Beyond the rhetoric. *Phi Delta Kappan, 77*(4), 295–299.

Sarason, S.B. (1995). *Parental involvement and the political principle: Why the existing governance structure of schools should be abolished.* San Francisco: Jossey-Bass.

Schattman, R. (1992). The Franklin Northwest Supervisory Union: A case study of an inclusive school system. In R.A. Villa, J.S. Thousand, W.C. Stainback, & S.B. Stainback (Eds.), *Restructuring for caring and effective education: An administrative guide to creating heterogeneous schools* (1st ed., pp. 143–159). Baltimore: Paul H. Brookes Publishing Co.

Senge, P.M. (1990). *The fifth discipline: The art and practice of the learning organization.* New York: Doubleday/Currency.

Skrtic, T.M. (1991). The special education paradox: Equity as the way to excellence. *Harvard Educational Review, 61*(2), 148–206.

Stainback, W.C., & Stainback, S.B. (Eds.). (1990). *Support networks for inclusive schooling: Interdependent integrated education.* Baltimore: Paul H. Brookes Publishing Co.

Vermont Department of Education. (1996). *Vermont's Framework of Standards and Learning Opportunities.* Montpelier: Author.

Villa, R.A., Thousand, J.S., Stainback, W.C., & Stainback S.B. (Eds.). (1992). *Restructuring for caring and effective education: An administrative guide to creating heterogeneous schools* (1st ed.). Baltimore: Paul H. Brookes Publishing Co.

Will, M. (1986). *Educating students with learning problems, a shared responsibility: A report to the Secretary.* Washington, DC: U.S. Department of Education, Office of Special Education and Rehabilitative Services.

Wiggins, G.P. (1992). Foreword. In R.A. Villa, J.S. Thousand, W.C. Stainback, & S.B. Stainback (Eds.), *Restructuring for caring and effective education: An administrative guide to creating heterogeneous schools* (pp. xi–xvi). Baltimore: Paul H. Brookes Publishing Co.

Chapter 17

You *Can* Teach
an Old Dog New Tricks

Patrick Schwarz and Denise Lee Bettenhausen

The purpose of this chapter is to describe the stages of evolution in education practice that supported education teams to change from old thinking to new thinking during an 8-year period in a suburban central Illinois public elementary school district that became inclusive in its practices. To become a community that values diversity, acceptance, and collaboration, dramatic restructuring took place during this 8-year period. During these 8 years, practices that promoted segregation, isolation, and dependence had to be eliminated. A belief that all children, including children with disabilities, have the right to be educated, to belong, to grow, and to develop friendships in the natural classroom environments of their neighborhood school needed to be instilled and

The authors wish to thank Richard A. Villa for his idea of the title of this chapter, which came up during an informal, humorous telephone discussion. The reference to an "old dog" in the title has nothing to do with the age or tenure of a teacher; rather, it refers to old thinking about learning, teaming, and teaching practices.

installed as an ethic and a schoolwide and districtwide vision. During the first 4 of these years, self-contained special classrooms needed to be eliminated within this school and the school district. In this chapter, the philosophy and practices that made this change possible are outlined for each year of the 8-year period.

YEAR I

The primary reason for entertaining the idea of inclusive schools in this district was that students with challenges in the special education program were being isolated from the context of their neighborhood schools, peers, neighbors, and the best learning models available. Students without disabilities in general education classrooms were not learning about the diversity in their own community; rather, they were being sheltered from the talents, abilities, and gifts that students with diverse needs bring to classrooms.

The first year of the district's journey toward inclusive education was the 1990–1991 school year. That first year was characterized by awareness and information gathering related to the topic of inclusive education. The education of administrators about inclusive philosophy and practices was a major focus. The year began with a summer retreat for teachers, families, community members, and administrators at which the topic of inclusive education was introduced by the specialized services director and the principals of Kruse Elementary and Fulton Elementary schools. These three individuals were invested in taking a risk to improve the special education services being provided in the district, which were far from effective. Following the retreat, a subcommittee was formed to focus on inclusive practices. The subcommittee of eight individuals was composed of two family or community members, four teachers, and two administrators. One of the charges of this subcommittee was to study materials related to inclusion, disseminate this information, and make a recommendation to district personnel regarding future actions toward more inclusive options for students with disabilities. The subcommittee studied inclusive practices being implemented across the United States, school law, interpretation of law by the courts, and how inclusion fit with the philosophy and direction of the district.

Concurrently with the subcommittee's study, one of the members, the principal of Fulton Elementary School, started a small inclusive education pilot project. Fulton Elementary School was one of six schools in the Tinley Park/Orland Park community, with 450 students in kindergarten through fourth-grade classrooms. With the support of Project Choices, a state-funded project that granted incentive money and provided technical assistance for districts wishing to move to more inclusionary practices, the pilot began. It involved two students, one with moderate and one with severe cognitive learning challenges; previously, these students had been educated in a self-contained classroom, so they were returning to and being supported by special education staff in a general education classroom environment.

During the pilot experience, staff were asked to provide feedback about the impact of inclusion that was taking place. Although the educators were positive about the practices that supported students with challenges in the general education classroom, they had concerns about certain students for whom this school was not their home, their neighborhood school. Although peer relationships developed for all of the newly transitioned students in the school environment, these students who were not within their home school did not have the social benefits after school and on weekends that the students for whom this was their home school had. The principal of the pilot school decided to discuss these concerns with the principal of these students' actual home school, who was surprised that she was unaware there were students in her school who had siblings who were sent to the other school because of past practices of self-contained special education service delivery. Because of the fact that these students had never attended a music program, fun fair, or social event in their neighborhood school, this principal was prompted to join in inclusive pilot efforts for her school during the next school year.

At midyear, the subcommittee formed at the summer retreat issued a report that set forth the following core values, principles, and premises regarding the value of the pilot efforts:

1. The social, emotional, and psychological benefits of receiving an appropriate education in one's home school are of value to all students.

2. Learning occurs best in home schools, in which students with various needs have the opportunity to learn, grow, and interact with and model each other.

3. Home school education affords all students with and without disabilities an opportunity to develop positive relationships.

4. As students interact as classmates and friends in their home school, it helps to develop a society that accepts and values the inclusion of all people in every aspect of community life.

The purpose of the report recommendations was to encourage the study of inclusive practices among administration and staff of other schools, with the ultimate goal of installing inclusive practices across the school district. Administrative support grew as the following statement of support illustrates: "If you put everything aside that we have to deal with on a daily basis, I would want this for my child" (R. Gardner, personal communication, January 1991).

Several school administrators decided to end the school year by attending a weeklong summer Inclusion Institute in Chicago sponsored by McGill University (Montreal, Quebec, Canada), where they developed action plans for the following school year. Also during the summer, three new special education professionals who had training and experiences in delivering inclusive education were hired as inclusion facilitators to promote further efforts.

YEAR 2

Year 2 was marked by continued implementation of the inclusive practices initiated at the two schools that had begun the pilot efforts during the first year. A collaborative teaming process among general and special educators and weekly team meetings were established to provide students' support teams with a systematic vehicle for planning and problem solving on a regular, face-to-face basis. Initially, this collaborative teaming structure supported only students with identified disabilities; quickly, people saw the benefits of regular team meetings, and the structure and process were expanded to address issues of students with any type of individual need. Teacher responsibilities were discussed and identified on weekly action plans, as were needed supports and accommodations in curriculum and instruction for individual students. Technical assistance delivered by the district program supervisor was critical in training and modeling for involved personnel the innovative teaming, teaching, and adaptive processes needed to make inclusive education work.

Dissemination of outcomes of the pilot project was important in the second year. Information about pilot successes was shared in monthly school staff meetings. Every teacher in the school district was invited to visit the pilot inclusive education classrooms before the end of the second school year. Any teacher who was targeted to receive a new student in Year 3 from a self-contained classroom visited that classroom as part of the transition planning for Year 3.

Also during the second year, the school board adopted a philosophy or mission statement that mandated a home or neighborhood school model for the entire school district. The philosophy or mission statement read as follows:

> We believe that our primary goal is to help all students to become contributing members of society, working and interacting together in an inclusionary process. To this end, it shall be a matter of district policy, to

the fullest extent possible, to enroll all students in their home school. This position statement is the first step in a logical progression toward the establishment of the concept of full inclusion, over a period of time, as a basic tenet of our school district.

Following the retreat of June 1991, three subcommittees were formed to study the implications of the tentative goals established by the retreat group. One of those subcommittees was assigned the study of the concept of a home school. The concept relates to the school assignment for the instruction of students with disabilities. A report of that group was presented on February 14, 1991. The previous statement grows out of the subcommittee report and of out of our consideration of work done in the school district during the 1990–1991 and 1991–1992 school years.

Home school refers to the delivery of appropriate education and related services in the school to which a student with a disability would be assigned if he or she did not have disabilities. Services would be provided in age-appropriate classes to the fullest extent possible with support from a variety of teachers and support staff. *Full inclusion,* the next logical step beyond the home school, refers to the assignment of each student to the age-appropriate class to which he or she would have been assigned if the student did not have disabilities.

During the 1990–1991 school year, one elementary school participated in the Illinois State Board of Education–supported Project Choices Program. During that school year, the program was extended to another elementary school. Although not part of Project Choices, our middle school has also included seven students with multiple needs in the general school community. In all, 15 students with significant challenges have been involved in the inclusion program. All of the students who have been part of Project Choices will continue to be included next year and each year following. Having started the process for these young people, there was no turning back. In order to accommodate this process, it was essential that we move to the home school concept in September 1992.

As a result of the experiences of the previous $1\frac{1}{2}$ years, we were convinced of the benefits derived from the inclusion model and of the inevitability of its place in the education process. The Illinois State Board of Education, through its regular education initiative (REI), had made the inclusionary model a goal for Illinois. It was anticipated that it would be mandated for all schools in the following few years. We did not feel it was right to wait for the mandate.

Year 2 ended with a week of formal training for all school district professionals on the topic of inclusive education. The whys and hows of heterogeneous, collaborative schooling and school restructuring strategies were the focus of the first day of training (Thousand & Villa, 1992). The pilot model demonstration teams presented the successes and growth of their pilots on the second day. Students with disabilities, together with their friends, families, and supporting professionals, explained and demonstrated Making Action Plans (MAPs) (Pearpoint, Forest, & O'Brien, 1996), individualized education programs (IEPs), Personal Futures Planning (Mount & Zwernik, 1988), and the Circles of Friends friendship-building process (Forest, 1987) to the trainees. Curricular planning, the development of adaptations, and instruction strategies for heterogeneous groups were the topics of the fourth day. On Day 5, attending professionals developed action plans for each school in the district. This "Inclusion Week" was a powerful mechanism of paving of the way for the third year of school district change.

YEAR 3

The third year was characterized by greater movement toward full implementation of a "zero-reject model" (Brown et al., 1983, p. 74), with the home school notion being initiated for every child. All students made the transition to their neighborhood school. A major thrust of the third year also was to secure formal planning and team meeting opportunities for more teachers in the school district. During planning meetings, general educators shared their lesson plans for the upcoming week, and team members undertook a decision-making process to determine whether activities could be delivered without adaptations or whether alternate presentation of the material (e.g., cooperative learning) was favorable for the student and the entire class. General education classroom coverage needed to be addressed so that planning meetings could occur. Release time for teachers was accomplished through a floating substitute, team teaching, and creative scheduling for teacher arrangements.

Another important area addressed during this year was the changing of report card formats to accommodate a wider range of student performance. IEP goals and objectives were infused into general education curriculum area progress on the new report card. Staff development continued. Roles of staff in general and special education evolved so that both were more engaged in individualizing education for all students. Special educators took on new "ownership" of students with general education needs, and general educators had great input into the education of students with unique needs, whether those needs included a cognitive or a physical challenge, a learning disability, interfering behaviors, or English as a second language.

YEAR 4

In the fourth year, the district finally achieved the start of a full inclusion approach by eliminating all self-contained classrooms. Whichever supports a student needed were identified, designed, and delivered by grade-level teams of special and general education teachers. The skills and expertise of teachers were combined to carefully structure the level of support identified for each student. The aim in Year 4 was to fully restructure the manner that related services were provided in order to support the goals, objectives, and skill development of students in general education environments. Related services were provided in general education settings. Pull-out services occurred only to assess needs of the student, and this information then was shared in planning meetings to determine how to support each student best in general education classroom environments. The purpose of related services was viewed as a support to enable a student to gain access to the school's education program rather than as a separate program in and of itself.

One of the more notable changes in this district's first 4 years of its journey toward the full "citizenship" of its students was a change in the attitude of the general educators. When asked to observe special education classrooms during the second year of the project, many general educators reacted with anxiety about the changes that they were going to face in their classrooms. The same educators reported that the inclusive education model, though not easier, was much better than the previous self-contained, segregated options. They saw positive changes in students' behaviors, including behaviors that presented "big-time challenges." Their observed enhancement of age-appropriate learning outcomes and significant gains in students' meeting their IEP goals also contributed to their positive attitude changes. They acknowledged that this would not have been possible when students were limited to education and relationships only with other students who exhibited challenging behaviors or other significant disabilities.

Upon reflection, it seems that a critical ingredient that contributed to success during the first 4 years of the change process was restructuring services so that the individualized support needed by students was delivered to them and the classroom teachers. Without access to a full array of education services and assistive devices individually designed and made available to support the student in the classroom, this model clearly would have failed.

Consideration of the thoughts and fears of parents of both children with disabilities and children who were developing typically was also vitally important to the initial success of these efforts. A districtwide parent group was developed for all parents who wished to attend.

Here, families expressed concerns. There were families who had concerns that students without disabilities would make fun of the students with disabilities. This did not prove true, owing to the diversity awareness work that was done with all students. Some parents worried that their sons and daughters with disabilities would lose therapy time. Again, this did not occur; the nature and purpose of therapies changed to support these students' access to the curriculum. At these parent forums, family members also got to describe the positive impact of inclusion on their lives. Families of children with disabilities reported that their sons and daughters were being asked to play, to go to parties, and to be a friend. Parents of children with disabilities began to participate in Parent Teacher Association meetings and became involved with the general workings of their neighborhood schools.

During the following 4 years, the inclusive education model in the district evolved, meshed with, and supported all of the other recommended practice initiatives (e.g., authentic assessment, whole language, active learning) that were being promoted. Inclusion had a great and positive effect on the other innovations being fostered and shaped (e.g., collaborative teaming, multilevel instruction, cooperative learning groups, hands-on activities, experientially based instruction, computerized instruction, use of assistive technology, use of learning centers).

YEARS 5 AND 6

As inclusion became a value in the school system, more and more staff were hired by the district rather than by the local special education cooperative. This meant that by the sixth year, all former special education cooperative staff were school district employees. Local control of staff was seen as critical to maintaining and advancing the inclusive education vision. Staff development opportunities continued based on staff-identified needs. Courses were offered in 1) methods for working with students with autism, 2) methods for working with students who had attention-deficit/hyperactivity disorder (ADHD), and 3) assistive technology. Consistent training of teacher assistants became the responsibility of school and district staff development committees, which further promoted the quality of inclusive practices in the school system. Teachers began expressing needs for staff development (e.g., block scheduling, creating support plans for students of diversity) that were different from those that had been articulated 5 years earlier (e.g., mainstreaming strategies, conducting range-of-motion exercises).

Planning continued to be refined and systematized. Often strategies that were discussed for particular students were found to be helpful for many other students as well. By that time, all teachers were requesting planning time with special services support. The special education staff were gaining knowledge in general education curriculum and classroom instruction, and general educators were learning more about strategies to meet individual students' needs. Former barriers between general and special education were dissolving, and joint planning, implementation, and assessment were becoming the norm. General and special educators began developing units of study together and assessing all students together. Classroom teachers felt supported by their teams and thus were willing to test new ideas and strategies. Coping with change and struggling with implementation of new concepts became a team effort.

Other district and school programs were also affected by inclusive philosophies and procedures. The English as a second language program began using the planning model and inclusive services delivery strategies used in inclusive programs. The Title I support program in reading became a classroom-based service delivery model instead of a pull-out model, reflecting the inclusive vision of the district. The separate program for students who had been labeled as gifted or talented was revised to reflect similar in-class service delivery models that inclusive practices and philosophies promoted. Students with emotional and behavioral challenges provided the most significant issues to staff members. Additional creative program options (e.g., service learning, investigative projects) and additional teacher assistants were brought in on a case-by-case basis.

Another challenge for the school was to integrate new staff members into the changed philosophical and service delivery model. Most special education staff had backgrounds and experiences with traditional pull-out models of service delivery. The philosophical or recommended practices statement shown in Table 1 was crafted and provided to new staff members to help them understand the profound changes taking place within the education system (Schwarz, Bettenhausen, & Kruse Education Center staff, 1994). Developing these statements was a focusing event for the staff involved. The statements continue to provide guidance and a backbone for inclusion. In addition to the sharing of the statements in Tables 1 and 2, several district schools provided new teachers with specific training. Because of the changes in the school system, support for new staff became the norm.

During the fifth and sixth years of the inclusive school change efforts, calls to visit the school and district poured in. To allow visita-

Table 1.   Philosophy and recommended practice statement for new staff

WE BELIEVE:

That students of diverse abilities and educational background need to learn from one another.

Our purpose is to find the "best way" of making education work well for students with individual differences.

We can meet the needs of all students with diverse needs by individualizing the curriculum for the range of students' abilities.

Modeling for students from one another is essential in learning.

Support means more than just supervision: It means preplanning to make informed, educational decisions for all students.

We own all students: Boundaries are minimized in our model.

Most school- and community-based objectives for students with disabilities in primary and intermediate grades can be met in the settings of same age peers without disabilities.

We need to empower students to be in general education settings whenever possible based on their individual needs and the degree they can tolerate the expectations or adapted expectations in the classroom.

The focus of related service support is to provide expertise within their area to successfully integrate and enhance the general education curriculum.

Every student is an "individual." Individual goals and objectives come first.

The focus of learning is to make students more independent and empower everyone to be an effective learner and citizen.

Source: Schwarz, Bettenhausen, and Kruse Education Center staff. (1994).

tion without compromising instruction during these 2 years, a visitation system was developed, and 52 groups visited the district's schools. Many staff received calls to present at state, national, and local district conferences. This public recognition helped to solidify the profound changes in their school system as well as their beliefs in inclusive education.

YEARS 7 AND 8

An inclusive education philosophy became completely ingrained in the school system's practices in the seventh and eighth years of the district's inclusion efforts. Joint "ownership" of students with special needs is a common school practice. In Year 8, the program for students who had been labeled as gifted adopted a model that developed individual plans for students from an inclusive model philosophy. Site-based decision making decentralized special education and made it a local school responsibility. Joint planning and collaborative practices shifted teachers' focus to individual students' needs and growth. These changes affected the general student population in that when teachers

Table 2.   Recommended practices in inclusive education

Rule of thumb: Can a special educational need be met in the places where everybody else is being served educationally?

We should be able to answer a "why" question that relates to our philosophy of normalization for all educational decisions made.

We're asking everyone to take ownership of all students:
general educators = students with a disability
special educators = general population

All curriculum for students with a special educational need should be individually challenging. Adaptations should relate to the curriculum and individual need whenever possible ... parallel curriculum as a last resort.

Decisions are made on a team basis. Because of the collaborative model everyone is expected to contribute about all children during the team meeting.

All planning has the purpose of informing the team of what is going on in the respective classroom beforehand so decisions can be made to teach as is, adapt, change the presentation of the lesson, look at grouping, or seek a different activity.

Relationships with parents are professionally oriented at all times and must uphold the school philosophy.

Assistive technology and adaptation decisions are made by the entire team for each individual student.

If a team makes decisions about a strategy to utilize with a student, all team members must promote and utilize the strategy.

Pull-out and parallel curriculum are to be utilized only with a strong rationale from the team and primarily for assessment purposes. Everything needs to be verified in the general education classroom.

Preteam planning is the focus of students' programs to promote peer involvement and uphold inclusion in activities.

Goals and objectives for all educational and related areas are to be written by the team in an integrated, embedded IEP process, rather than separate goals from various related service areas that may overlap.

Everyone's ideas in the team meeting are valued. Participation and commitment to the team process come before other daily responsibilities at the time the team meetings are taking place. This will make or break student success so all members must give the team their full undivided attention and participation.

Developing these statements was a focusing purpose articulating event for the staff involved.

The statements continued to provide guidance and a backbone, even today. In addition to the belief statements, many schools provide training or support for new teachers and because of the changes in this school system, support for staff new to the school became the norm.

observed any child not showing educational growth, individualized strategies were brought to bear on that child. No longer did students need to be labeled to be provided with education strategies that supported their learning styles and needs.

In the eighth year of implementation, it was decided that it was time to once again examine the special education services in the district through a district program committee composed of parents, teachers, administrators, and community members. The committee's task was to examine the district's programs systematically and make recommendations to the school board for further improvement and change. One of the committee's specific charges was to complete an analysis of special service programs, related services, practices, and structures to determine 1) whether they adhered to the district's philosophy, mission, policy, and professional roles and practices; 2) whether they should be modified to reflect better the district's policies, philosophy, mission, and professional roles and practices; and 3) if modifications were recommended, what the specific benefits to children might be. In examining the special education programs, their findings included those presented in Table 3.

These recommendations clearly reflect how the inclusive philosophy permeated the district's practices and beliefs, as did testimonials from members of the education community. For example, in Pointer's study, one board member said,

> The whole organization has been impacted in a positive way by inclusion—teaming, planning, and collaboration. Teachers really work together, and there is a strong emphasis on making the kids learn. It doesn't matter who does what—special education or not. It's a team effort. (1997, p. 112)

In the same study, a central office administrator commented,

> When the board saw how money being spent on special education benefited all students and they couldn't tell if the teacher teaching was a special education teacher or a general education teacher, and when they saw the children in the classroom and couldn't tell the students who were special education or not; this had a major impact on their thinking. (1997, p. 115)

Pointer also recorded the observation of a parent of a child with autism, who said, "I think it is a philosophy and an attitude that all kids belong together" (1997, p. 111).

Probably the strongest statement supporting the transformation of this school district is the change of thinking of the longtime faculty. Many of these people watched, waited, and absorbed what happened.

Table 3.   Recommendations for future actions regarding special education

---

FACILITIES:

A thorough investigation of facilities in the district must take place to add spaces or redesign spaces to accommodate teachers working together.

PROFESSIONAL DEVELOPMENT:

Continue professional development by offering presentations or refresher topics related to progressive practices in education.

Develop a computerized resource site so that personnel can effectively share district expertise.

In this way the school community will continue to support and increase the comfort of all staff and include new staff who are working with students with challenges.

PARENTAL INVOLVEMENT:

Develop a plan with the family at the earliest school entry level so they are encouraged to take an active role in their child's progress in a clearly defined way.

Develop a column in the district newsletter designated for discussion of some aspect of new, innovative practices being introduced to the school.

Work to increase comfort of parents by encouraging them to bring a friend or other support system to scheduled meetings.

PROGRAM/PRACTICES:

Provide more planning time for general and special educators to meet and plan.

Provide more in-service and support for students with behavioral challenges.

Reexamine service delivery for students with English as a second language.

Reexamine early childhood programming to increase interaction with general education.

PRACTICES TO CONTINUE:

General and special education teachers working together to plan for students to increase instructional skills.

Planning time for teams.

Related support that does not change a student's placement once identified in need of special education services.

Provisions for various learning needs.

Providing services that address a wide range of learning needs.

Inclusion of students with special educational needs in the general education classroom.

Providing positive role models for inclusion students in a variety of disability areas through inclusive practices.

Several of these staff members requested students with challenges to be in their classrooms. The assurance of a student support team and a problem-solving approach provided the security that these members needed to take on a new challenge and improve the quality of education for all at the school.

CONCLUSIONS:
REFLECTING ON 8 YEARS OF CHANGE

This chapter offers a case study of a suburban midwestern school district that underwent significant change in education practices as a result of its commitment to *inclusive education,* defined as welcoming all learners in general education environments in the school. This process comprised an 8-year evolution, which was based on the "start small but think big" principle. A single inclusive education pilot project helped eventually to change an entire education system for the better.

The case study this chapter examines nicely illustrates the progression of a system through the four phases of change described in Chapter 5. Years 1 and 2 represented the initiating phase. Years 3 and 4 represented the implementing phase. The fifth and sixth years represented the maintaining phase, and the final 2 years represented the evolving phase. Also seen throughout the case study are examples of each of the five essential components of managing complex change—namely, vision, skills, incentives, resources, and action planning (see also Chapter 5). The success of School District 146 of Tinley Park and Orland Park may be attributed to the district's attention to developing vision, skills, resources, incentives, and action plans at appropriate times and in appropriate ways.

Many exciting things happened and continue to happen for individual children as a result of welcoming all learners into the general education classroom. For instance, Brian, a fifth-grade student with significant challenges resulting from cerebral palsy, became secretary of his school's student council. As we all remember from our own school days, student council elections can be quite competitive. Brian's edge, interestingly enough, came directly from his disability. Brian speaks by using assistive technology—a computer with a voice output device. When it was Brian's turn to deliver his speech to the student body, the principal held the microphone in front of the computer's speaker. The students went wild. According to them, this way of delivering a speech was "cool." Brian won the election with more votes than all of the other candidates combined. Every student in the school learned something positive about individuals' differences from Brian. Brian's confidence and preparedness to make a contribution and lead a productive, fulfilling life could be nothing but enhanced by this and other, similar experiences.

Brian had opened doors for his friends as well by his inclusion. For example, Matthew, one of Brian's friends, helped Brian with putting on and taking off his coat daily. Being an enterprising 12-year-old, Matthew decided that there had to be an easier way for Brian to put on his coat. So, Matthew researched clothing design at the Chicago Public Library and came up with a coat design that was adapted perfectly to Brian's physical challenges. A zipper was placed along the entire length of the top of Brian's sleeve to allow Brian to work around his physical challenge more easily. This design ultimately won acclaim for Matthew as a state "Invent America" winner. Both boys benefited from this experience in ways that would have been denied them in a segregated school system. Matthew's creativity was activated, recognized, and celebrated. Brian's daily life was made a bit easier.

For Brian and Matthew, inclusion was a good thing. Many new stories of how inclusion affected students' lives positively continue to unfold in the school district. We took the trip toward inclusion along with Brian and Matthew, and we hope that their remembrances of the school district's journey help readers to see the hows of getting to inclusion as well as the whys of continuing forward.

REFERENCES

Brown, L., Nisbet, J.A., Ford, A., Sweet, M., Shiraga, B., York, J., & Loomis, R. (1983). The critical need for nonschool instruction in educational programs for severely handicapped students. *Journal of The Association for the Severely Handicapped, 8,* 71–77.

Forest, M. (1987). *More education integration: A further collection of readings on the integration of children with mental handicaps into regular school systems.* Downsview, Ontario, Canada: G. Allan Roeher Institute.

Mount, B., & Zwernik, K. (1988). *It's never too early, it's never too late: A booklet about Personal Futures Planning* (Pub. No. 421-88-109). St. Paul, MN: Governor's Planning Council on Developmental Disabilities.

Pearpoint, J., Forest, M., & O'Brien, J. (1996). MAPs, Circles of Friends, and PATH: Powerful tools to help build caring communities. In S.B. Stainback & W.C. Stainback (Eds.), *Inclusion: A guide for educators* (pp. 67–86). Baltimore: Paul H. Brookes Publishing Co.

Pointer, B. (1997). *One school district's transformation of special education practices: Adopting inclusion. A case study.* Unpublished manuscript, Teachers College, Columbia University, New York City.

Schwarz, P., Bettenhausen, D.L., & Kruse Education Center staff. (1994). *Philosophy and recommended practice statement.* Orland Park, IL: Kruse Education Center.

Thousand, J.S., & Villa, R.A. (1992). Collaborative teams: A powerful tool in school restructuring. In R.A. Villa, J.S. Thousand, W.C. Stainback, & S.B. Stainback (Eds.), *Restructuring for caring and effective education: An administrative guide to creating heterogeneous schools* (1st ed., pp. 73–108). Baltimore: Paul H. Brookes Publishing Co.

Chapter 18

New Brunswick
School Districts 10, 12, and 13
The Story Continued . . .

Gordon L. Porter, Jean Collicott, and John Larsen

We are pleased to update our chapter from the first edition of *Restructuring for Caring and Effective Education: An Administrative Guide to Creating Heterogeneous Schools* (Porter & Collicott, 1992) (hereinafter referred to as "Part I"). Since the publication of the original chapter in 1992, inclusive education has continued to be a key feature of public education in the Canadian Province of New Brunswick in general and specifically in the communities that were part of New Brunswick School Districts 28 and 29. There have been many organizational and program changes since 1992, but commitment to the inclusion of all students in heterogeneous classrooms has remained strong. Some developments of the 1990s even strengthened the inclusion mandate and led to an extension of practices over a wider area.

Following is a report on the legislative and organizational changes, followed by details of the evolution of the program and support systems that make inclusion work. The chapter concludes with a descripton of areas that need further development as New Brunswick's schools move forward.

CHANGES IN MANDATE

The New Brunswick provincial government provides the basic mandate for the inclusion of students with special needs into general classrooms in their neighborhood schools. In 1996, a new Education Act was passed in the Province of New Brunswick, and the mandate for inclusion was maintained despite minor changes in definitions and matters of process. The act also confirmed in legislation the reorganization of school districts and school administration in New Brunswick. A more modest move in 1992 saw a number of school districts merged and their administrative structures consolidated. This change led to Districts 28 and 29 becoming District 12. The subsequent 1996 reorganization took this change a step further, with District 12 placed in the same administrative jurisdiction as District 10 and District 13, the school regions to the south and north, respectively, of District 12. The new "zone" or "superintendency" is made up of Districts 10, 12, and 13 and is administered by a single superintendent, with a "director of education" for each of the districts. Supervisory and administrative staff work cooperatively in this framework to deliver support to students, teachers, and schools.

The result of this organizational change is an increased emphasis on identifying and sharing recommended practices between three school districts. This sharing has been particularly strong in student services and is reflected in the extension of a number of the practices described in Part I. This process was mandated by the superintendent and actively encouraged and welcomed by the directors of education. Cooperative sharing of effective and recommended practices was embraced, and it was agreed that the approach that had evolved in District 12 would be the basis for moving forward. The result was a thorough integration of the student services staff in Districts 12 and 13. Although a cooperative relationship was also established with District 10, geography has tended to limit the number of joint policy and training initiatives.

There was a definite advantage to spreading our collective efforts over a wider range of schools and communities. The Director of Education in District 13 was particularly anxious to see the inclusion initiatives from District 12 extended to her area. As a former principal in several schools, she observed that "I initially worked without a school-based team and then worked with the school-based student services team model which I decidedly favor" (C. Spragg, personal communication, February 1998). The mandate of district student services staff was to implement the following initiatives in District 13:

- Establish school-based student services teams in each school
- Move toward the collaborative consulting teacher model or "method and resource teacher model" (see description in Part I)
- Assist teachers in the use of multilevel instruction (see description in Part I)
- Carry out in-services in the areas named in the previous three bulleted items

In this update, we describe only the first initiative; the others are addressed in Part I.

SCHOOL-BASED STUDENT SERVICES TEAMS: SUPPORT AND COLLABORATION

Collaboration in schools requires a flexible, problem-solving approach that is often characterized by role release. This is a process in which people do not adhere closely to the work defined in profession-specific job descriptions but instead use a collaborative process to break down barriers that inhibit good communication and effective problem solving. Without some structure, collaboration does not occur, because professionals are unsure when, where, and with whom they should discuss specific issues. The school-based student services team provides a context for effective collaboration. Membership of this team usually includes the principal, vice-principal, methods and resource staff, guidance counselors, and teacher assistants. This group works to provide assistance to classroom teachers, students, and students' families. They also cope with a range of school or classroom issues from behavior problems to a lack of appropriate academic progress.

How the Teams Work

In traditional school practice, it is often the principal who is responsible for establishing and maintaining a school's culture and general administration. The principal also is charged with the supervision of staff, managing student behavior, and ensuring that the curriculum is delivered appropriately. A school that accepts the challenge of including each student, however, cannot be successful if all of these responsibilities are the mandate of just one person. Successful inclusion requires teamwork and collaboration.

The single factor that has emerged as most critical to schools' success with inclusion, since Part I was written, is the school-based student services team. In 1992, we were much more focused on the new role of the special educator, who we referred to as the *method and resource teacher*. As time passed, we continued to see the method and resource role of the special educator as important; but we came to understand that the teamwork and joint accountability that are generated through the school-based student services team are the most powerful innovations. In a well-managed inclusive school, providing for students' needs and adequate levels of instructional coaching and support becomes the responsibility of the full school staff. The efforts of the method and resource teachers, guidance counselors, principals, and vice-principals in supporting teachers overlap as they work together as a team.

In Districts 12 and 13, the team meets weekly to discuss any issues that arise related to students, teachers, or the school as a whole. The weekly meeting provides a forum for the team to share their current work and discuss emerging situations. It allows for direction to be set and responsibility assigned for coordination of activities. Agenda items might include specific students' problems, teachers' concerns, project management, school reentry for an individual student, and school environment issues with regard to service needs and opportunities and issues involving educational change. The team monitors staff stress and the school's ability to meet students' needs. They look for opportunities to intervene to ensure that learning opportunities are not being missed. Team members are expected to act as student advocates, but they are also expected to be supportive of teachers. Discussion and planning at team meetings can help avoid duplication of effort and can result in more effective plans for students and teachers. They can also help avoid conflict between staff members and formal or informal factions within the school. The meetings help create conditions for clear communication and establish consistent intervention strategies. The team process encourages appropriate resolution of problems at the school and can assist the administration with innovative approaches to resolving problems.

Team meetings can cover any number of topics, but they are typically not the appropriate forum for case conferences, parent meetings, or other regular problem-solving sessions. Rather, the meetings help assess which problems are most pressing and which should be a priority for staff action. The team may recommend or plan an interagency case conference, a problem-solving meeting, or a meeting with parents and student. The team decides whether sufficient work has been done at the school level and reviews programs and supports. The range of perspectives of team members can generate new ideas for consideration. Follow-up is the responsibility of individual team members and takes place at a different time or involves a referral to the district team for additional consultation.

The success of the school-based student services team model in supporting inclusion in Districts 12 and 13 schools was confirmed by both informal and formal surveys. Of 13 principals in District 12, 11 identified the school-based team as the single most important factor in supporting school success and effective efforts at instruction improvement. The other two principals rated the school-based team as the second most critical factor.

Fifty-five members of school teams in eighteen schools in District 13 completed a survey in June 1998. Three questions on the role of school teams produced the following results: All of the respondents either agreed (39%) or strongly agreed (61%) with the following statement: "The student services team in my school meets regularly and positively contributes to school climate and student success in learning." Almost every respondent either agreed (55%) or strongly agreed (43%) with this statement: "The student services team in our school successfully focuses on problem solving and strategy development." Only one respondent (2%) disagreed with this statement.

One of the commitments of District 12 (described in Part I), and more recently of District 13, is to the ongoing professional development of staff members. This commitment takes the form of monthly in-service sessions for method and resource teachers and for guidance counselors. These sessions are usually separate; but several times each year, the two groups do meet together. In addition, we have found it helpful to hold "school level meetings" that involve separate gatherings for elementary schools, middle schools, and high schools. Included in these level meetings are method and resource teachers and guidance staff, along with principals and vice-principals. Student services issues are also discussed at training sessions for administrators and classroom teachers.

The success that we have had with the school-based student services team model is encouraging. The team model provides a focus for staff members in a position to deliver critical support to classroom teachers and improves the overall effort toward meeting students' needs. It is an approach that we plan to continue and enhance.

Meeting the Challenge of Students' Behavior

School administrators, teachers, parents, and students in Districts 10, 12, and 13 have been providing broadly based support for inclusion. There is no focused lobby to turn back the clock and return to segregated

Table I. Behavior Protocol of Districts 10, 12, and 13

A first goal for all school staff is to establish an environment in which distractions that interfere with daily learning and teaching are kept to a minimum. Teachers can do this by facilitating an understanding of appropriate behaviour and adjusting school and classroom dynamics. Comprehensive organization and planning to avoid discipline related problems is referred to as "preventive discipline."

- Have a complete discipline plan of action
- Adopt a teamwork approach
- Teach self-management and self-discipline
- Invite good discipline
- Focus on student success and self-esteem
- Implement firm, fair, and calm enforcement
- Plan lessons thoroughly
- Continuously monitor classroom environment
- Minimize problems early

---

programs to serve students with special needs. The success of the late 1980s and the 1990s moved our attention to new issues and new problems. Of these, the quest for strategies that help us teach students with challenging behavior is the most critical.

Districts 12 and 13 recognized that teachers were being asked to teach all students in the general classroom and needed support to work with those students who exhibited oppositional and defiant behaviors. A training program called *nonviolent crisis intervention* was introduced, and all teachers, teacher assistants, administrators, school secretaries, bus drivers, and interested parents in the district were shown ways to recognize escalating behaviors and successfully defuse situations that arise because of those behaviors. They were also taught how to cope with out-of-control behavior without harming a student or themselves in the process. Each year, refresher courses are provided to those participants who feel they need to upgrade and reinforce their skills in these areas.

In addition to the training provided, District 12 also drafted a set of behavior protocols that were distributed to each teacher in the district. The protocols were reviewed and revised in 1998 for use in Districts 10, 12, and 13. This document provides a step-by-step guide for those coping with students with challenging behaviors and lists what the classroom teacher can do and what the school team is expected to do before a student is referred to outside services or suspended from school. The protocols have helped teachers feel more in control of behavior in the classroom and have worked to diminish the feeling that time-outs, straps, and expulsions are the only way to cope with students' oppositional behavior.

A behavior support team was also set up in Districts 12 and 13. The team is composed of district student services administrators, a psychologist, and several school social workers. The team accepts referrals from schools, parents, or community agencies and provides teachers with support in coping with the individual situations that teachers present. The team is also the liaison to the several external programs and agencies that assist the school system with difficult cases. The team is the means by which extra planning time might be granted to a school and/or a teacher and also is the means by which the school may receive additional paraprofessional support from a teacher assistant, mentor, or tutor. A summary of the approach taken in the behavior protocol is provided in Table 1.

EXPERTISE WITHOUT THE EXPERT MODEL

One of the challenges of creating an inclusive model is to build confidence and competency among general school staff while maintaining the specialized knowledge and skill that specialists or experts bring to the needs of students with special needs.

Expert Model

Traditionally, the development of school supports has involved medical and pathological explanations of problems followed by professional intervention. Development of professional interventions has been premised on the professional's having special knowledge to apply to the problem. The model was to have the expert assess, identify the problem, and prescribe treatment to be carried out by the school or by a professional outside the education system. This seemed acceptable when schools employed a narrow range of strategies to meet students' needs. It enabled them to transfer the problem to someone else and cast blame if the interventions proved unsuccessful. In many cases, this model also resulted in a dynamic that linked diagnosis (i.e., labeling) with intervention funding.

Forces for Change

With the move to inclusive education there also came a systems perspective—a sense that the environment could have a significant impact on how a child performed in school. There was increasing sensitivity to the needs of all students and greater acceptance of the responsibility to educate them in a way that met the needs of all students. Teachers retain ownership of student problems but seek help when their strategies are not successful. Previously, there was frustration with the process of referral and treatment. Typically, it took a long time to complete assessments, and the recommendations frequently failed. Concrete actions and strategies to improve the classroom environment were nowhere to be found.

New Framework

Support is provided by experts—people who have had considerable professional education and experience in a particular field of practice and who work from a problem-solving perspective. This is important because their knowledge and experience are used to identify and develop the best approach for solving the problem, an approach that usually seeks to provide some choice for the student, the teacher, the school, and the student's family. The use of expert knowledge tends not to be student focused. It is directed at supporting the school with ideas and strategies that will lessen problems and increase learning through changing teachers' practices, the school's procedures, peer support systems, family involvement, and student interventions.

When teachers need assistance with specific student needs, the school-based student services team is the first recourse for support. The resulting professional interventions have become solution focused, systemic, and educational rather than problem focused, pathological, and student centered. This team looks at school practices and how they meet students' needs and seeks to create an environment that is conducive to all students' learning. The district staff exist to support the school teams. Membership on the school-based student services team includes education consultants, school psychologist, social workers, and speech-language pathologists. Support is provided by working with the school staff and integrating additional strategies as part of school team interventions. This allows professionals to use their expertise within a process that treats participants as equals and focuses on managing the problems in the school or in the classroom. District team members participate in problem solving, attend school team meetings as needed, conduct in-service to schools, and provide coaching to school staff on an individual basis. If needed, they provide direct intervention for students. In this way, their interventions are timely, relevant, and tailored to the needs of the students.

CONCLUSIONS

Yesterday's solutions can become today's problems. The move away from an expert model can create problems if not managed well. If the support system is not responsive and the process by which to gain access to support is not clear, teachers may struggle without effective assistance. In this environment, the need for formal expert assessment may still be required; but there is a danger that some problems may go unrecognized and that time may be wasted with general and ineffective interventions. Districts 12 and 13 continue to struggle with pressure from parents and the medical community, as well as from some teachers, to always use a clinical or a medical model to explain the learning difficulties of students. We need to work more thoroughly with our community to provide education and training in this area. There is a danger in using generic explanations for all problems, so we need to ensure that we cultivate our expert knowledge to identify unique problems requiring novel approaches. Only with a commitment to inclusion as a social and community value and by a continuing search for recommended practices throughout the student services program can we maintain high expectations for the future.

REFERENCES

Education Act of 1996, Province of New Brunswick, Canada.

Porter, G.L., & Collicott, C. (1992). New Brunswick School Districts 28 and 29: Mandates and strategies that promote inclusive schooling. In R.A. Villa, J.S. Thousand, W.C. Stainback, & S.B. Stainback (Eds.), *Restructuring for caring and effective education: An administrative guide to creating heterogeneous schools* (pp. 187–200). Baltimore: Paul H. Brookes Publishing Co.

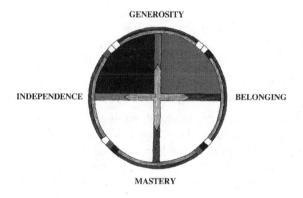

GENEROSITY

INDEPENDENCE

BELONGING

MASTERY

REFLECTION

A Conversation with Rachel Holland's Parents

Richard A. Villa with Robbie Holland and Kim Connor

R.A.V.: Without a doubt the *Holland* decision [*Sacramento City Unified School District v. Rachel H.*, 1994] is one of the landmark inclusion court cases in the United States. You fought for more than 5 years to have your daughter, Rachel, included. Despite winning at a due process hearing, you had to continue to fight because the Sacramento School District kept appealing the decisions. You won at the district court and federal appeals court levels. The U.S. Supreme Court refused to hear the case and let the lower-court ruling stand. As you know, Jacque and I are editing a new book. We plan to end each section of the book with a reflection. We thought it would be an excellent idea to include an interview with you as the reflection to the case study section of the text. Your experiences with and perspectives on inclusion will be invaluable to those who work in inclusive environments and those parents and educators who are struggling to create inclusive classrooms and schools. Thank you for agreeing to be interviewed.

How did you first learn about this thing called *inclusive education* and know that it was what you wanted for your daughter, Rachel?

K.C.: When Rachel was in preschool, there was a get-together at a Unitarian church. Michael Rosenberg, from our Local Area Board on Developmental Disabilities, had invited us to attend. We heard another parent, Jeff Strully, speak about his daughter Chantelle's inclusion. She was included as a full member of a general education classroom.

R.H.: I remember thinking, *What a wild idea, maybe for someone else.*

K.C.: And yet, a lot of what he said resonated within us.

R.H.: At that time, Rachel was placed in an inclusive summer camp. She was there because we had no other choices. When we spoke with the camp staff about our concerns, the camp director, Evelyn, asked us, "Why don't you just go home and leave her here with us?" They began to tell us about her progress, about all the things that she could do, and about all the fun she was having.

K.C.: We actually hid in the bushes and watched. We had been told that she had limited language ability. Watching from the bushes, we saw her doing what the camp staff said she could do. We saw it. She had friends. She was acquiring more language because she had 20-some kids speaking with her daily.

R.H.: One day, a little boy from the camp came up to me, not knowing that I was Rachel's father, and said, "Rachel Holland, she used to be retarded." When he didn't know her, he considered her to be retarded. When he got to know her, she was just Rachel.

K.C.: I'd say the paths that led to inclusion started when we first heard our child had a disability and felt as if we didn't know a thing. You kind of accept what you are told. You don't know what to expect. There are no milestones or standards, but then you hear a message that says that the world could be different. Then we started looking at our child differently. You move away from the total acceptance of the experts' advice, the turning over of the decision making to other people. You start to watch your child and see what her needs are. We began to regain confidence about our ability to parent. We saw what motivated Rachel, what excited her, and how she learned. We were looking for successes, any successes. The successes were happening, but not in a special day class. The progress was made at the integrat-ed summer camp. Rachel provided the proof. If you wanted to know what worked, you needed to watch her. It was right in front of us.

R.H.: It became logical that we would want Rachel to continue to be included.

R.A.V.: What other events or experiences bolstered your views on inclusion?

K.C.: We started to experience resistance about what we had come to know and experience as being best for Rachel. This led us on a search for recommended practices. We knew nothing about our rights.

R.H.: We started to learn all the jargon and terms, including *least restric-tive environment [LRE], SELPA [special education local program area],* and *local area plan.*

K.C.: We met some folks such as Tom Neary at California State University–Sacramento. We made friends in Davis, where there was a lab school. They worked with parents and included their children in preschool so that by the time their children went to their local schools, the children had already experienced inclusion. Those folks really helped us! They came to our first individualized education program (IEP) meeting.

R.H.: Meeting Marsha Forest helped us as well. She gave us some great ideas on how to facilitate friendships, ideas that we used for several years. Seeing videotapes from some inclusive schools in Ontario, Canada, helped, too.

K.C.: Going to the Supported Life Conference here in Sacramento and hearing Mary Falvey for the first time was really important.

R.H.: So was the CAL-TASH [the California chapter of TASH (former-ly known as The Association for Persons with Severe Handicaps)] conference in Fresno in 1989. We began to feel as if we weren't alone.

K.C.: These experiences amplified the message for us along the way. I started to do my own research because when we asked for some inte-gration, we were flatly denied it.

R.H.: The Gartner-Lipsky (1987) article in the *Harvard Educational Review* made perfect sense.

K.C.: It validated the fact that this issue is not just about services for kids with disabilities. The overall system is flawed.

R.H.: We learned about the term *modeling.* We knew that that was exact-ly what Rachel was doing. She learned from the other peers. When we looked at the environment she was in, the special day class, it contained predominantly students with serious emotional disturbance. Rachel started to exhibit behaviors we didn't like. We compared that environment to the kindergarten classroom next door to where Rachel was placed. In that classroom, the kids were having a great time. They didn't have to sit in rigid seating with behavior modification programs. They were encouraged to speak, as compared to being allowed to speak only when spoken to.

K.C.: They didn't have to go into a "box" when they misbehaved. Rotten special day classes are a great motivator for parents seeking inclusion. We were involved in her classrooms along the way. We could see the kindergarten class and compare it with the segregated class. We kept thinking, *Gee, that kindergarten room next door looks great.*

K.C.: Rachel never used the potty in school for almost 3 years. The day we insisted, after a long fight, that a kindergarten buddy accompany her to the bathroom was the first day she ever used the toilet in school. It is little things like that along the way that help you to see the value of inclusion. We knew a fair amount about early childhood development, early intervention, and stimulation.

R.H.: Instead of *stimulation,* which means "more of," we were seeing *restriction*—"less of"—in the special day class.

K.C.: My mother was a preschool teacher. She ran an active class with dancing and music and art. That was in my mind. My daughter was in a class in which every time she did something right, she was given a Goldfish cracker to eat or a penny to put in a bank. She wasn't allowed to talk, but she needed to talk. She wasn't allowed to talk on the special education bus because that could be disturbing. She wasn't often permitted to talk in the special education classroom. She was expected to just follow orders. They told us she would be in a special education class with fewer students. We thought a large class with lots of peers to interact with might be good. If there were 30 kids in the class and each one said one thing to her a day, that would be great for her language development.

R.H.: You have to understand it was right there. This exciting general education classroom was only 3 feet away. We asked if Rachel could be there for 10 minutes a day, and the district said no, it was not appropriate.

K.C.: Rich, it wasn't just knowledge about special education that motivated us. It was knowledge about what is just good education, period. We were looking at two different systems, and we knew which one we wanted for Rachel.

R.A.V.: You fought in court for 5 years. Was there additional knowledge or experience that kept you motivated during that time?

R.H.: As we struggled to set up a program for Rachel and throughout the trial, the folks from the California Research Institute (CRI)—Blair Rodgers, Nam Graham, Wayne Sailor, and Linda Brooks from Davis—were a tremendous help. I remember when Wendy Turnbull, who did the psychological assessment, said to me, "You have come to know your child so well. You cannot refuse Rachel her opportunities." This was a great point of encouragement for me personally. We thought we were doing the right thing. It seemed to be the way that Rachel learned. She seemed to be happy making friends with kids without disabilities, but Wendy's insight gave us validation.

K.C.: Donna Meinder and Paula Gardner from California State University Sacramento were always encouraging and helpful. The Davis parent group remained extremely helpful to us throughout the trial.

R.H.: The district claimed that it would cost more than $109,000 to include Rachel. They had claimed that in order for Rachel to be included, she would need a full-time teacher of the severely handicapped, a full-time resource specialist program teacher, and a full-time teacher's aide. The district referred to the models of inclusion used in Vermont. They claimed that the staff would need to receive in-service training, including sending staff to Vermont to learn about strategies like the Circle of Friends. They stated that all staff, including custodial staff, would have to receive sensitivity training. The custodial staff probably needed it the least. Still, to this day, when I see the custodian at the school where we wanted Rachel to be included, he gives me a thumbs-up sign and a big smile.

R.A.V.: As stated earlier, you won at the due process hearing, in district court, and in the federal appeals court. When it became apparent that the district would continue to fight, you removed Rachel from the public school system and placed her in a private school, Shalom, where she could be with peers without disabilities. When did she finally return to her public school?

K.C.: Rachel spent 4 years in special day classes. Then she went to the Shalom school for 5 years, from kindergarten through Grade 4.

R.H.: Rachel returned and entered a general education public school in fifth grade. She has been in the public school for 4 years—Grades 5–8.

R.A.V.: What have been the positives for Rachel in the public school environment during these past 4 years?

R.H.: One thing that has changed is that, along the way, she has enjoyed many genuine friendships. Students are doing things with Rachel without looking to see if adults are watching or approving. Friendships are key. It is what still motivates Rachel the most to go to school and to work. She also is more academically involved in the curriculum when it is the same curriculum with which the other students are engaged.

K.C.: We are repeatedly amazed at how much academic progress she is making and how much she is getting out of the curriculum. Some of it is abstract.

R.H.: For example, when I asked Rachel what *civil rights* means, she responded, "Fairness, freedom."

K.C.: Having spent so much time modifying the curriculum, I know how doable it is. It is so frustrating for me to know that there are so many teachers who aren't doing this. That results in lost opportunities for students to learn and generalize information. So much of this is good for other students in the class. Because of students like Rachel, teachers are learning things that would have been unthinkable before. *Unthinkable*—that is a fabulous word. They just weren't thinking about what they needed to learn and do until students such as Rachel came to school.

R.H.: Recently, Rachel's math teacher told me, "I think there is a lot more we could be doing. Rachel is really capable." A teacher who was reluctant about Rachel's inclusion in her class told me that Rachel gave a report on poetry in front of the class and used words like *complicated* and *surprised* in her speech. The teacher said that she was really amazed because she didn't know that Rachel knew that kind of language. In our experience, each year, about a month before the school year ends, the reluctant teacher warms up to Rachel. It is usually their comments that I share with the next year's reluctant teacher.

R.A.V.: What have been the greatest challenges that you have faced since Rachel has returned to her neighborhood public school?

R.H.: Uncertainty of trust. We have not always been sure who is monitoring the program. We have a wonderful aide who supports Rachel and does a great job of modifying the curriculum, but things aren't always clearly communicated. Teachers engage in practices that they don't seem to realize are wrong. For example, this year, when Rachel's aide was absent, they sent her to the K–3 special day class for the day. Don't they get it? When Rachel got in the car at the end of the day, I asked, "How was your day? She responded with a "thumbs-down" sign and said, "It's a big bummer." Then we learned from Rachel what they had done. We had to wake them up about that one.

K.C.: Trust is a big piece.

R.H.: It is a huge piece. If you sit around at an IEP meeting and come to an agreement, you assume that the IEP is going to be implemented. Then you learn that it isn't being done. That destroys the trust. You have to watch out for your child. If you don't, who will? Isn't it someone else's responsibility to be sure that the IEP is being implemented? We went to court to win Rachel her rights. If we had not gone to court, Rachel never would have gone to recess and would never have made it out of the special day class. Yet these restrictions still are imposed. What is happening to the other kids whose parents haven't been there to advocate for them?

K.C.: I've been disappointed that they haven't been able to come up with a program to teach Rachel to read. She is teaching herself to read. We also hear things like she shouldn't take family life classes because she might be frightened. Are you kidding? This is a course that she definitely needs. She took it. I remember her coming home the day a panel of teen parents spoke to the class. I said, "Rachel, what did you learn?" She said, "You have to take responsibility. You have to take responsibility. You shouldn't have babies until you are ready to be a mom." The idea here is that students like Rachel need to be in general education classrooms. It is here where she, along with the other students, gets the language and learning of life.

R.A.V.: Rachel is getting ready for another major transition: the transition to the world of high school. It seems to me that, throughout the process, you have been and remain Rachel's strongest advocates and teachers. What are your thoughts as she and you face this transition?

K.C.: Recently, we went to the high school where Rachel will be going. I cried my eyes out through the entire orientation thinking about the transition and the challenges still ahead of us. They showed an orientation film, and the only pictures of students with visible disabilities were those of students doing yardwork. I am getting tired of fighting low expectations, and I am tired of having to make the curricular adaptations. I feel as if we have pulled back some, and I feel terribly guilty about it.

R.H.: You have to realize that we engaged in our strongest, fiercest advocacy when Rachel was our only child. We now have two additional children. When I get angry, I feel like pulling out the court decision and saying, "Look, we went through this, and the district spent $2 million! We don't want to go through it again. We want you to figure it out and tell us what you are going to do to make it work for Rachel."

K.C.: While we were trying to figure out the correct strategy for dealing with this new school, Rachel solved the problem.

R.H.: Rachel, on her own, walked up to the high school principal, stuck out her hand, and said, "Hi, I need friends." And the principal said, "Honey, we have 2,400 friends here for you." Rachel's doing that on her own cut through a lot of political barriers. She got to the heart of that principal.

K.C.: Friendships are paramount for Rachel. They are all she talks about.

R.A.V.: As you prepare for this next step, to which resources or supports do you have access?

R.H.: Well, we are always looking. I went to hear the Vargos present at TASH about what was happening for their daughter in high school. I have seen that wonderful videotape [*High School Inclusion: Equity and Excellence in an Inclusive Community of Learners*, Jorgensen, 1999; distributed by Paul H. Brookes Publishing Co.] from the University of New Hampshire about a New Hampshire high school, Souhegan. We gave the school board a copy of *Petroglyphs: The Writing on the Wall* (Shapiro-Barnard et al., 1996) from the University of New Hampshire, and they gave a copy to the superintendent. And now they have ordered 100 copies for the high school.

K.C.: I have decided that you have to get to the heart first. In the past, I was talking about this reform and that reform. I showed them *Petroglyphs*, and that was it.

R.A.V.: As I sit here and listen to what you have experienced, I am in awe. I am in awe for two reasons. First, it is so unfair for any parent to have to go through what you have had to endure. Second, I am also amazed at the people to whom you have gained access along the way: Tom Neary, Jeff Strully, Nam Graham, Wayne Sailor, Marsha Forest, and Mary Falvey. Many parents don't even have access to one of those folks.

K.C.: And all of those people, when they, and you, come to town to help, it is an extra effort, and you all give so generously.

R.H.: We continue to learn and change our thinking. Recently, I heard Carol Tashie speak at a TASH conference on community-based instruction. Because of that information, Rachel is not leaving the school site. It is new for our district, but she will be working at the school store. Had I not heard Carol, I probably would have gone along with the district's standard plan.

R.A.V.: All of us stand on the shoulders of the parents and educators who came before us, on the shoulders of those who had a greater vision. You are a part of history, part of a major landmark civil rights decision. You, along with other parents of children like Danny Ramirez and Raphael Oberti, have opened general education classroom doors for many other children with disabilities. What advice do you have for parents who are in the same place where you were when you wanted Rachel to be included and were met with resistance?

K.C.: Is what you're saying really true? I guess I didn't really know the impact of the case.

R.H.: At various conferences, I have had many parents come up and say, I went to my IEP meeting and put your decision on the table, and they gave us what we wanted. And yet I wonder who would have heard of us and known of Rachel if we hadn't won the case?

K.C.: Sometimes I feel as if our own school district isn't aware of the decision. Although we have been asked to participate on a task force that is making recommendations on how to restructure special education services in our district, the district is still slow in developing placement options and support for students and staff.

R.H.: As far as advice for parents, know what you want. Build your desire on the knowledge of your child and what are current best practices. You have to have options available. If you have only a special day class available, it is hard to know about or want something else. Families have to figure out what their individual roles are in advocating for their child. The family has to have a game plan.

K.C.: I agree with Rob. Know what you want. Know what your child wants.

R.H.: Last, know your rights. You have to know your child's rights so that you can realize when those rights are being violated and how to do something about it.

R.A.V.: Knowing what you know now, if you had it to do all over, would you do it again? Would you go to court and fight for Rachel's right to be included?

K.C.: No, I wouldn't. It took a huge emotional and financial toll.

R.H.: Financially, it certainly took a huge toll. Financially, it is a crapshoot. You get reimbursed only if you win. Even then, you still don't recover all the costs.

K.C.: Let me amend my answer. I would have moved to Davis or somewhere where they were doing inclusion. I would have gotten to our goal another way. If someone said, "You can move to Davis and enroll your daughter or fight for 5 years, I would have moved. We never thought it would go on for so long.

R.H.: There was a point of no return for me. When we prevailed in Rachel's fair hearing, I wasn't about to move. I wanted Rachel to get what she deserved. I realized that what was at stake was Rachel's childhood as well as her future. Of course, I didn't know that the district was going to stretch it out for another $3\frac{1}{2}$ years.

R.A.V.: Finally, what advice do you have for school personnel?

R.H.: Listen. As Michael Giangreco says, "Put yourself in the shoes of parents."

K.C.: Be flexible. Think about customer service and customer satisfaction. The parents and the students are the customers. Realize that when you have good schools, when you have good teaching practices, it works. Inclusion works for all kids.

Postscript

R.A.V.: At the time this book went to press, Rachel Holland was completing her freshman year in high school. When asked to describe her high school experience thus far, Rachel said, "It's great. The people are great." Robbie, Rachel's dad, adds that, "On the whole, it's been a positive year. We are closer to capturing the opportunities. Rachel has reached new levels of independence. All the training for school personnel and necessary supports, however, have not yet arrived."

REFERENCE

Gartner, A., & Lipsky, D.K. (1987). Beyond special education. *Harvard Educational Review, 57*, 367–395.

Jorgensen, C.M. (1999). *High school inclusion: Equity and excellence in an inclusive community of learners* [Videotape]. Baltimore: Paul H. Brookes Publishing Co.

Sacramento City Unified School District v. Rachel H., 14 F.3d 1398 (9th Cir. 1994).

Shapiro-Barnard, S., Tashie, C., Martin, J., Schuh, M., Malloy, J., Piet, J., Lichtenstein, S., & Nisbet, J. (1996). *Petroglyphs: The writing on the wall.* Durham: University of New Hampshire, Institute on Disability.

V

Future Directions and Reflections

If I Could Dream:
Reflections on the Future of Education

Susan Bray Stainback

"Ding-dong! Ding-dong!" said all the school bells one morning. All the children in the city got ready to go back to school. There were children walking in the streets. There were children in cars. There were children in buses, too. . . .

"Isn't it fun to come back to school?" said Carol. "Now we have many friends to play with again."

"See there is a new boy," said Donald. "And a new girl too!" said Carol. "Let's go over and say hello to them."

Donald and Carol ran over to the two new children.

"Are you coming into our room?" they asked. "Yes," said the new boy and girl. "Our names are Peter and Sally." . . .

> . . . When the children [go] into the room they see other new friends. They saw many old friends, too. There was a boy named Joe who was very, very small. There was Susan in a yellow dress, and Tom who had brought his dog to school. . . . Some of the boys and girls showed the new children where to find books and other things in the room. Then school began. The children had much to tell about the good times they had had all summer. (Marguerite, 1942)

When asked to visualize an ideal or desirable education environment, I knew what was in my mind's eye. However, I realized that it was going to be difficult to write about or to describe what I envisioned. So, being an indoctrinated educator, I looked to the literature to find something that described what I was thinking to be certain that what was included would articulate my vision clearly. I looked at the writings of numerous thinkers, scholars, philosophers, politicians, comedians, and various other visionaries from within and outside formal education circles. While I was spending hours randomly browsing through my bookcase, I found an unusual reference that I had never used before. It had a title that reminded me of my vision of an ideal education environment, so I sat down and read it. The book was called *These Are Our Neighbors*, a second-grade reader published in 1942 by Ginn & Co. The quote that begins this introduction to Section V is an excerpt from that book.

DESIRABLE ELEMENTS FOR EDUCATION ENVIRONMENTS

There are several elements in this and other stories in the book (and the images that they conjure up in my mind) that I believe are desirable in an ideal education environment. Sometimes the most simplistic and most basic concepts in everyday life are the ones that have so much to offer for the improvement of the complex systems that drive our educational and social communities. In this introduction to the "Future Directions and Reflections" section, I share what I perceive some of these elements to be.

Happiness

In my view, an ideal school is a place where students, teachers, and other community members *want* to go. Each day is a *happy, nonthreatening, productive adventure* in learning for everyone involved. It is a place where adults and students go to work together to learn, help one another, and enjoy the experience. As educators, we need to keep every school day— whether it is at the elementary, middle, or secondary level—as exciting, enjoyable, and enticing to students as their first day at school.

In my vision, schools, their staff, and students would be assets and resources to their neighborhoods and a source of support and knowledge for anyone seeking it. They would serve as a small community within the larger community of a town, city, or state and have the attributes of a positively functioning community. A sense of community can transform "a collection of 'I's' to a collective 'we,' thus providing [school members] with a unique sense of identity, belonging, and place" (Sergiovanni, 1994, p. xiii). It is only through such a collective effort that commitment to core social values of justice, tolerance, concern and respect for others and the search for knowledge can be acquired (Dewey, 1970; Solomon, Schaps, Watson, & Battistich, 1992).

With the proper guidance and organization and a commitment to such core social values, school members can make the school a place where students, teachers and other staff, family, and community members *want* to be. (See resources such as O'Brien & Lyle O'Brien [1996], Sapon-Shevin [1990], and Solomon et al. [1992] for suggested activities and considerations for achieving a positive sense of community.)

Egalitarian Policy

In my ideal, school is a place where all members of the school community, both students and adults, are *welcome and belong*. Conditions or exclusionary policies would not be in effect for some members of the student population. School also would not be a place where the status of some students or adults is automatically elevated above or below the status of others because of different learning attributes or other characteristics. Instead, every member of the school would be considered a desirable, worthwhile, important part of the community.

The philosophy of the ideal school would be based on egalitarian principles of inclusion, belonging, and providing a quality education to all students (Schaffner & Buswell, 1996); collaboration (Villa & Thousand, 1996); and caring (Sapon-Shevin, 1990). It also would focus on the philosophy of considering the needs of *all* members of the school community, including students, teachers, staff, administrators, and family members. Mutual respect and understanding among adults and students in decision-making activities and projects selected, procedures designed, and the sharing of individual members' achievements and challenges can increase the probability of everyone's profiting from the school experience in an enjoyable way (Piaget, 1948/1965).

Reciprocal Support

Too often, neither staff nor students feel supported in the school environment. The communication of and attempts to rectify this fact have taken many forms, frequently not positive ones. This is obvious when the figures regarding teacher turnover are examined, particularly in inner-city schools (National Center for Educational Statistics, 1996). Students also feel impotence and despair when they consider themselves on their own. During a local school board meeting at which attempts to disband gangs in the town were being discussed, a high school girl expressed her frustration and that of her friends: "Ask us why we join gangs. It's simple. People want to belong. . . . [T]hey want to have someone they can lean on. In gangs, that's what happens" (Young, 1990, p. A1).

In my ideal school, teachers, students, and staff would feel *secure*. They would always know that, in whichever activity or situation they were engaged, there would be individuals available on whom they could depend to provide any support and assistance they might require. Anxiety, fear of failure, isolation, and ridicule are mitigated by the fact that there is always a fellow student or staff member available to assist with and share a problem or to provide moral support when needed.

It should be noted that the type of support being referred to here is not dependent on monetary resources. In the ideal school, each school member has a responsibility to assist and support fellow school staff or students when others require such help. With such an interdependent and supportive relationship among all school members, it becomes clear to the members not only that all individuals require support but also that everyone has something important to offer to others. The responsibility for support is shared by all members, so there is always assistance available when needed. In addition, all members can feel *worthwhile* and *valued* because, in such an organization, they are valuable, contributing members!

Facilitative Teachers of Lifelong Learning

The teacher as the source and dispenser of knowledge can no longer meet the needs of students in American society. Too much is changing every day to expect that a predetermined set of information or facts will be sufficient to allow students to be successful in the 21st century. Likewise, with the increased recognition of the diverse nature, interests, and learning needs of individual students, one teacher cannot be expected to singlehandedly meet the unique needs of every child in his or her class. For such reasons, if students are going to be provided an education that can see them successfully through their lifetimes, the traditional role of the teacher and the emphasis on standardized procedures and curriculum input needs to change (Fields & Tarlow, 1996).

In an ideal school, teachers are organizers of the setup of the classroom, the students' learning experiences, the resources, and the procedural and practice conditions for learning. Making arrangements for student involvement, interaction, and interdependent learning is a major focus for the teacher. Supplying resources and techniques for locating information and directing the curriculum in a way that students have not only *opportunities* but also *motivation* and *focus* for addressing their learning needs is the teacher's challenge (Moll, 1992). Teachers, like students and other school members, however, require the support of peers, staff, administrators, parents, and students if they are to successfully set up dynamic, enjoyable learning experiences that meet the needs of the students whom they are responsible for teaching.

Meaningful, Critical Knowledge Acquisition

With regard to the curriculum, a focus on learning to learn and the motivation and skills needed for students to become *critical thinkers* and *lifelong learners* is of paramount importance. Although basic skills for learning, such as reading, writing, and communicating, continue to be of profound importance, the focus of these skills must be communicated more clearly as a means to learn rather than ends in and of themselves (Poplin, Wiest, & Thorson, 1996). Likewise, alternatives to these skills for those who need or can benefit from them will become an integral part of the curriculum on an individual basis. Whether these alternative modes of communication involve braille, American Sign Language, computer voice synthesis, or some other form, a teacher needs to be aware of it and provide the student with access to it if it can be of potential benefit to the student's continued learning (Dutton & Dutton, 1990).

In addition, by teaching basic skills within a meaningful context, students can more readily learn the value of the skills they are acquiring; the transfer of their skill use to other learning activities can be facilitated; and their learning can become more personal, interesting, and enjoyable. Students can also use basic skills to learn to evaluate critically and make decisions based on the information available to them (Sleeter & McLaren, 1995). Finally, the skills needed to independently or interdependently gain access to new and needed information will become basic for all students.

As noted previously, critical to the work of the teacher and curricular needs of students is the importance of mutually supportive relationships and a sense of community among all school members (Piaget, 1948/1965; Solomon et al., 1992). No single person or group can be expected to provide students with all that they need to receive an educational experience that can facilitate success in the future. In any school community, people need to work together. "People are interdependent; everyone has a function and everyone has a role to play, and that's what keeps people together and forms a community" (Wilkinson, 1980, p. 452).

Diversity

In an ideal school, diversity is an asset. The view that differences among individuals in education pose difficulties and need to be fixed, improved, or made ready to fit (i.e., homogenized) is replaced by the recognition that *differences are valuable assets* to capitalize on. It is only through recognizing and capitalizing on diversity that great opportunities for learning can occur. Barth stated,

> I would prefer my children be in a school where differences are looked for, attended to, and celebrated as good news, as opportunities for learning. The question with which so many people are preoccupied is "What are the limits of diversity beyond which behavior is unacceptable?" . . . [B]ut the question I would like to see asked more often is "How can we make conscious deliberate use of differences in social class, gender, age, ability, race and interest as resources for learning?" Differences hold great opportunities for learning. Differences offer a free, abundant and renewable resource. I would like to see our compulsion for eliminating differences replaced by an equally compelling force of making use of these differences to improve schools. What is important about people—and about schools—is what is different, not what is the same. (1990, pp. 514–515)

In an ideal school, diversity, in all its many forms, would be celebrated. Opportunities to have students and staff with different backgrounds, characteristics, and experiences would be encouraged, sought out, and valued. Diversity among school members strengthens the school and the classroom and offers everyone greater opportunities for learning (Stainback & Stainback, 1996).

Cooperation

In an ideal school, cooperation is valued above competition. An ideal school involves its members in *working interdependently, sharing,* and *caring* about mutually effective and beneficial goals to further the productivity, happiness, and success of all the members of the school community. Unfortunately, many schools do not share this vision of excellence. Kohn stated,

> Our society's current infatuation with the word "competitiveness" which has leached into discussions about education encourages a confusion between two very different ideas: excellence and the desperate quest to triumph over other people. . . . [A]t a tender age, children learn not to be tender. A dozen years of schooling often do nothing to promote generosity or a commitment to the welfare of others. To the contrary, students are

graduated who think that being smart means looking out for number one. (1991, p. 498)

Teamwork and cooperation with other members of the school community are not only worthwhile as positive learning tools but also are increasingly important as educational goals (Berryman, 1988; Peterson, 1996). As noted previously, Wilkinson (1980) stated that people are interdependent, and each individual has a role to play if goals for education are to be accomplished. Everyone is needed if students are to become lifelong learners who can meet the challenges of the 21st century.

Adhocratic Governance

Bureaucracy, a top-down form of governance, is "marked by diffusion of authority among numerous offices and adherence to inflexible rules of operation" (*American Heritage Dictionary*, 1980, p. 177). Indicative of this type of governance operating in education is the traditional use of basal readers, standardized curricula, and standardized testing.

Many have discussed the problems inherent in using this form of government in an education system whose goal is to meet the ever-changing and challenging educational needs of students to cope effectively in society in the future. Skrtic (see Thousand, 1990) argued that bureaucracy, the predominant paradigm in education, diminishes rather than enhances teachers' abilities to individualize educational services. As Thousand noted, "[B]ureaucratization is intended to insure standardization. To blame the inability to individualize instruction totally on the capacity or will of professionals is misguided in that it blames the teachers for the inadequacies and contradictions of the organizational structure" (1990, p. 31).

Adhocracy is based on the premise that the environment is dynamic and uncertain. In an organization governed by an adhocratic paradigm, innovation and adaptation to the needs of the environment (in this case, a school) are necessary elements for successful operation (Patterson, Purkey, & Parker, 1986).

Key elements in the operation of adhocratic governance in a school are *collaboration, mutual adjustment, shared decision making, empowerment* of all members of the school, *problem solving*, and *critical thinking*. Just as school environments are recognized as being dynamic, so too the curriculum addressed and the decisions made regarding students' education are dynamic. In an adhocratic school, personalized instruction is "continuously invented and reinvented by teachers in actual practice with students who have unique and changing needs"

(Thousand, 1990, p. 32). Through the use of adhocratic governance, all school members can be empowered to gain some control over their lives and the educational situations that they encounter.

FINAL THOUGHTS

After reading this introductory section, some readers may view idealism and an idealistic education system in which all children and adults work together in a happy, productive, and harmonious community as a dream that may never be realized. Educators need not fall prey to such negative thinking, however. Instead, the focus must be on the ideals. By keeping what is desired clearly in focus, there will be less chance of straying from the path to improving not only education but also society in general. A job in education with regard to values involves striving for ideal approaches and conditions rather than simply accepting less desirable ones because they constitute the status quo. If the education system and American society are to move forward, educators need to work to make their ideals the reality, though their ideals may not be achieved easily.

In the late 1800s, Allen (1904/1992), in a treatise that he wrote during the violent changes precipitated by the Industrial Revolution in England, provided a perspective for keeping ideals and visions clearly focused. He stated,

> The greatest achievement was at first and for a time a dream. . . . Dreams are the seedlings of realities. . . .
>
> In all human affairs there are *efforts*, and there are *results*, and the strength of the effort is the measure of the result. Chance is not. "Gifts," powers, material, intellectual, and spiritual possessions are the fruit of effort; they are thoughts completed, objects accomplished, visions realized.
>
> Cherish your visions; cherish your ideals; cherish the music that stirs in your heart, the beauty that forms in your mind, the loveliness that drapes your purest thoughts, for out of them will grow all delightful conditions, all heavenly environments; of these, if you but remain true to them, your world will at last be built. (Allen, 1904/1992, pp. 43–47)

REFERENCES

Allen, J. (1992). *As a man thinketh*. New York: Barnes & Noble. (Original work published 1904)

American Heritage Dictionary. (1980). Boston: Houghton Mifflin.

Barth, R. (1990). A personal vision of a good school. *Phi Delta Kappan, 71*, 512–571.

Berryman, S. (1988, October). *The educational challenge of the American economy*. Paper presented at a forum of the National Education Association, Washington, DC.

Dewey, J. (1970). *Experience and education*. New York: Collier.

Dutton, D.H., & Dutton, D.L. (1990). Technology to support diverse needs in regular classes. In W.C. Stainback & S.B. Stainback (Eds.), *Support networks for inclusive schooling: Interdependent integrated education* (pp. 167–186). Baltimore: Paul H. Brookes Publishing Co.

Fields, M., & Tarlow, M.C. (1996) . Constructivistic approaches to classroom management for students with disabilities. In W.C. Stainback & S.B. Stainback (Eds.), *Controversial issues confronting special education: Divergent perspectives* (pp. 169–183). Needham Heights, MA: Allyn & Bacon.

Kohn, A. (1991). Caring kids: The role of the schools. *Phi Delta Kappan, 72*(7), 496–506.

Marguerite, M. (1942). *These are our neighbors*. Boston: Ginn & Co.

Moll, L. (1992). *Vygotsky and education: Instructional implications and applications of sociohistorical psychology*. Cambridge, England: Cambridge University Press.

National Center for Educational Statistics. (1996). *Digest of educational statistics: 1996*. Washington, DC: U.S. Department of Education.

O'Brien, J., & Lyle O'Brien, C. (1996). Inclusion as a force for school renewal. In S.B. Stainback & W.C. Stainback (Eds.), *Inclusion: A guide for educators* (pp. 29–45). Baltimore: Paul H. Brookes Publishing Co.

Patterson, J.L., Purkey, S.C., & Parker, J.V. (1986). *Productive school systems for a nonrational world*. Alexandria, VA: Association for Supervision and Curriculum Development.

Peterson, M. (1996). Community learning in inclusive schools. In S.B. Stainback & W.C. Stainback (Eds.), *Inclusion: A guide for educators* (pp. 271–293). Baltimore: Paul H. Brookes Publishing Co.

Piaget, J. (1965). *The moral judgement of the child*. New York: Free Press. (Original work published 1948)

Poplin, M., Wiest, D., & Thorson, S. (1996). Alternative instructional strategies to reductionism: Constructive, critical, multicultural, and feminine. In W.C. Stainback & S.B. Stainback (Eds.), *Controversial issues confronting special education: Divergent perspectives* (pp. 153–165). Needham Heights, MA: Allyn & Bacon.

Sapon-Shevin, M. (1990). Initial steps for developing a caring school. In W.C. Stainback & S.B. Stainback (Eds.), *Support networks for inclusive schooling: Interdependent integrated education* (pp. 241–248). Baltimore: Paul H. Brookes Publishing Co.

Schaffner, C.B., & Buswell, B.E. (1996). Ten critical elements for creating inclusive and effective school communities. In S.B. Stainback & W.C.

Stainback (Eds.), *Inclusion: A guide for educators* (pp. 49–65). Baltimore: Paul H. Brookes Publishing Co.

Sergiovanni, T. (1994). *Building community in schools.* San Francisco: Jossey-Bass.

Sleeter, C., & McLaren, P. (1995). *Multicultural education, critical pedagogy, and the politics of difference.* Albany: State University of New York Press.

Solomon, D., Schaps, E., Watson, M., & Battistich, V. (1992). Creating caring school and classroom communities for all students. In R.A. Villa, J.S. Thousand, W.C. Stainback, & S.B. Stainback (Eds.), *Restructuring for caring and effective education: An administrative guide to creating heterogeneous schools* (1st ed., pp. 41–60). Baltimore: Paul H. Brookes Publishing Co.

Stainback, S.B., & Stainback, W.C. (Eds.). (1996). *Inclusion: A guide for educators.* Baltimore: Paul H. Brookes Publishing Co.

Thousand, J.S. (1990). Organizational perspectives on teacher education and renewal: A conversation with Tom Skrtic. *Teacher Education and Special Education, 13,* 30–35.

Villa, R.A., & Thousand, J.S. (1996). Student collaboration: An essential for curriculum delivery in the 21st century. In S.B. Stainback & W.C. Stainback (Eds.), *Inclusion: A guide for educators* (pp. 171–191). Baltimore: Paul H. Brookes Publishing Co.

Wilkinson, J. (1980). On assistance to Indian people. *Social Casework: Journal of Contemporary Social Work, 61,* 451–454.

Young, J. (1990, April 17). Gangs hearing: School board's policy review draws wide range of opinion. *Waterloo Courier,* p. A1.

Chapter 19

Spirituality in Leadership
Implications for Inclusive Schooling

Colleen A. Capper,
Maureen W. Keyes, and George T. Theoharis

We are curious about the role that spirituality plays in the lives of education leaders and in turn to what extent spiritual beliefs influence those leaders who advocate for inclusive schooling. What do we mean by *spirituality*? We believe that spirituality is self-defined, and, rather than offer our own definition in this chapter, we review the literature and research on the ways in which spirituality is expressed in leadership. From our description of these expressions, readers can inform their own view of spirituality. Next, we turn a critical eye toward this literature to probe the connection between spirituality and epistemology. This probing uncovers the shadow side of spiritually based leadership and how this side of leadership might influence leaders' views of inclusion. We conclude the chapter by circling back to the spirituality literature to consider expressions of spiritually centered leadership that can help people avoid the dangers in inclusive school change efforts and in turn support inclusive schooling.

EXPRESSIONS OF
SPIRITUALITY IN LEADERSHIP[1]

In our analysis of the literature related to spiritually centered leadership, four predominant themes emerged: 1) the leader's personal awareness (Dreher, 1996; Hawley, 1993; Inamori, 1995); 2) the significance of relationships both with and among others, recognizing and fostering people's need to connect with each other (Bolman & Deal, 1995; Briskin, 1996; Herman, 1994; Jaworski, 1996; Jones, 1995; Moffett, 1994; Roskind, 1992; Starratt & Guare, 1995); 3) a belief in the presence of a divine being (Briskin, 1996; Dreher, 1996; Hawley, 1993); and 4) a sense of purpose or mission conveyed by the leaders' description of their work as an extension of and intertwined with their spiritual beliefs (Bolman & Deal, 1995; Briskin, 1996; Canfield & Miller, 1996; Hawley, 1993; Inamori, 1995; Jones, 1995; Moffett, 1994; Roskind, 1992; Vaill, 1989; Whitmyer, 1994; Whyte, 1994).

Personal Awareness

Self-awareness plays a critical role in the lives of spiritually centered leaders. Ideas such as self-discovery (Briskin, 1996; Vaill, 1990), self-inquiry (Hawley, 1993), personal mastery (Jones, 1995), self-transformation (Conger, 1994), self-actualization (Sadler, 1996), personal development (Dreher, 1996), personal growth (Moffett, 1994), and self-improvement are evidence of its prominence. The emphasis on awareness of self was coupled with caveats regarding the balance between personal needs and regard for others' search for self and meaning. Larkin (1995) described the leader's ability to empathize, surrender, tolerate, and respect the views of others. In the leader's ongoing spiritual search for discovery and renewal, it becomes essential to "create bonds of caring and compassion" that defy the "tug toward self-interest" (Starratt & Guare, 1995, p. 194).

Gilley (1997) summarized the spiritually centered leader as one who knows that what he or she does is secondary to who he or she is. An essential extension of this aspect of the spiritually centered leader is the critical balance between the inner and outer selves. Although these leaders developed strong relationships with staff and acted in consonance with personal values, they also maintained personal boundaries (Briskin, 1996; Covey, 1991; Dreher, 1996; Gilley, 1997). Although self-awareness and self-discovery played a prominent role in the spiritually centered leader's life, its significance seemed to pale when compared with the leader's other-directedness.

---

[1]In this section, we draw extensively from the work of Nancy Yoder (1997) and acknowledge her for her contribution in this area.

Emphasis on Relationships

Administrators expressing aspects of spirituality in their leadership style describe the significance of relationships in many ways (Jacobson, 1994; McEnroe, 1995; Schmidt, 1995): the importance of caring for others and focusing on their strengths (Dreher, 1996); listening to others intently as foundational to the formation of trusting relationships (Dreher, 1996; Keyes, 1996); building a healthy work environment through opportunities for staff to develop meaningful ties to each other (Roskind, 1992); valuing ethical and moral decision making in all deliberations (Bolman & Deal, 1995; Herman, 1994; Jaworski, 1996; Starratt & Guare, 1995); and developing opportunities for all staff to be involved as an expression of valuing inclusivity highly (Dreher, 1996; Roskind, 1992). Several administrators referred to the centrality that relationships played on their spiritual journey by describing incidents of intentional nurturance (Starratt & Guare, 1995) and a natural commingling of personal and institutional values (Rolls, 1994; Walling, 1994).

Belief in a Divine Power

As opposed to what Palmer termed "'functional atheism' [or] the belief that ultimate responsibility for everything rests with me" (1994, p. 35), spiritually centered leaders acknowledge a divine or cosmic presence in their lives. However, they tended to separate formal religious beliefs from spirituality. In our research, one principal explained her definition of spirituality, "I believe it's something within me, my heart, my mind, my soul. It keeps me focused and doing what's good for children." In defining the ways that her spirituality affects her leadership, another administrator said, "[Spirituality] is so much more than morale. I have had people say how important morale is and how we have to make our workplace somewhere people feel good about, but it is more than that—it is an inner spiritualness—it's a personal experience, a spiritual side without being religious—it keeps me in balance." Another leader explained, "It comes from within, that's what's happened to me. Believing in a greater power than me, it guides me." Vaill (1990) described how leaders need to create a unique definition of spirituality of their own, whether natural, supernatural, secular, or sacred.

Sense of Mission

In several studies (Bolman & Deal, 1995; Briskin, 1996; Hawley, 1993; Inamori, 1995; Jones, 1995; Moffett, 1994; Roskind, 1992; Vaill, 1989), the work of the spiritually centered administrator was described as "one's calling or mission" (see, e.g., Yoder, 1997, p. 65). The definitions for the words *mission, vocation,* and/or *calling* when describing one's work invoked deep connection between one's actions and one's beliefs (Whitmyer, 1994). Spiritually centered leaders referred to the critical role that consonance played between personal belief and outward expression (Briskin, 1996; Gilley, 1997; Hawley, 1993; Jones, 1995), thus underscoring the significance found in the cliché "walk your talk."

Whitmyer (1994) considered his ability to infuse spirituality and leadership by his capacity to develop a seamless expression among his personal values, beliefs, vision, and daily work responsibilities. In other words, spiritually centered leaders believed that their work is an expression of their calling, a demonstration of their commitment to make a difference.

This translation of belief in a calling into an ability to lead was built on a level of personal trust. Vaill (1990) described this sense of trust evident in the behaviors of spiritually centered leaders as essential. He stated that leaders need to develop personal spirituality and encouraged them to create a unique definition of their own of spirituality, whether natural, supernatural, secular, or sacred. Vaill proclaimed that leaders recognize and articulate a deference to intuitive nudgings that point directly to the presence of "something that pervades, energizes, weaves through, infuses, saturates" those moments that make up a day (1990, p. 215).

RESEARCH AND
SPIRITUALLY CENTERED LEADERSHIP

Although evidence of connections between spirituality and leadership practices were found in the literature, empirical data were sparse. Several studies cited issues of spirituality within leadership. Participants described strong connections among themselves, others, and beyond as a basis for personal spirituality.

McGowan (1994) asked participants to discuss spirituality in the workplace. In response, interviewees described spirituality as an important part of their daily responsibilities but cited a sense of frustration when confronted by a leader who denied their need to engage in spiritual exploration and/or connect its aspects with their work. The results of three empirical studies, two sectarian (Amendolara, 1993; McEnroe, 1995) and one nonsectarian (Love, 1991), described spirituality as central in defining one's personal leadership style. Administrators from 24 Roman Catholic churches and 18 Catholic health care organizations, as well as 11 other prominent women, reported their leadership development as deeply connected to their personal journey of faith and spirituality. McEnroe (1995) concluded with five critical attributes of effective leadership: spirituality, personal traits, caring, integrity, and personal expertise.

Several empirical studies focused on spirituality and its role in leadership: the development of a leadership philosophy, style, and leadership behavior. Jacobson (1994) used the Delphi model of research to interview 22 leaders from the fields of politics, education, and business. In his interviews, he explored connections between transformational leadership and spirituality. Results underscored the significance of spirituality for each leader, with recommendations for its integration into all aspects of nonsectarian leadership organizations. Rolls (1994) concluded from a series of in-depth interviews with various leaders that spirituality has a significant impact on the administrators' ability to effect change. In another study, Walling (1994) interviewed 10 leaders from diverse backgrounds to uncover possible intersections between their spiritual journeys and leadership styles. Her results revealed the significance between the administrator's connection to his or her spiritual self and decision making. Thom (1993) conducted a 5-year study of educational administrators to define qualities of successful administrators. These administrators frequently referred to spiritual ideas, evidence of their pivotal role in these individuals' work. Thom concluded that the educational leader is in a "continual state of spiritual development" (1993, p. 169), urging those in administrative roles to both explore and define that "unknown, inner side" of themselves (1993, p. 182).

Two other studies reported serendipitous findings of the ways in which leadership and spirituality influenced organizational reform (Keyes, 1996; Madsen & Hollins, 1997). In a 15-month case study of an administrator implementing inclusive education practices, Keyes found that the principal's spirituality developed the core of her leadership and heavily influenced her views on inclusive education. Madsen and Hollins (1997) conducted a study in several schools in an effort to describe the experiences of African American teachers in majority European American staffed schools. Several teacher leaders underscored the role that their spiritual beliefs played as both a guide for their decision making and a solace during stressful times.

Clearly, whether researchers openly asked leaders to make connections between spirituality and leadership or the theme of spirituality emerged as a by-product of leadership research, leaders' spiritual beliefs influenced their behaviors. Spiritually centered leaders did not attribute their leadership behaviors solely to qualities within themselves or to a known set of skills. Rather, leaders who were influenced by their spiritual beliefs routinely engaged in personal reflection, sought after and cultivated nurturing relationships with others, and viewed their work as a spiritual expression—a connection with the mysteries of humanity.

SPIRITUALITY AND EPISTEMOLOGY: THE SHADOW SIDE OF SPIRITUALITY IN LEADERSHIP

Our review of spirituality-centered leadership suggests that spirituality can be an antidote to traditional norms of leadership governed by hierarchy, control, prediction, and fear. Writers often associate spirit-centered leadership exclusively with positive connotations; however, in this section, we explore some dangers of a leadership style influenced by spirituality.

How we come to believe (i.e., spirituality) and how we come to know (i.e., epistemology) are interrelated and influence one another—perhaps they represent the same idea but are described in different words (P. Palmer, personal communication, April 1997). Capper (1993) examined multiple theoretical perspectives derived from an epistemological continuum (objective to subjective) and an ontological continuum (the nature of our being, from regulation toward radical change) (see Burrell & Morgan, 1979). She analyzed several school reform initiatives from these perspectives that revealed that benevolent school reforms that are not explicitly oriented toward justice perpetuate unequal power relations (Capper, 1994, 1996; Capper & Jamison, 1993; Capper & Reitzug, 1996).

Although many different perspectives exist, we briefly review three of them here.[2] We consider what their implications might mean for how leaders experience their spirituality and in turn influence how school leaders approach issues of inclusive schooling. Although we separate the perspectives from one another, in practice school leaders can shift in and out of varying perspectives, and most religious and spiritual practices draw from across these perspectives. Eck reflected our view of the different perspectives in stating that

> While we speak of [different epistemological or spiritual perspectives] as if they were entirely different [perspectives], let us remember that these ways of thinking . . . may well be part of the ongoing dialogue within ourselves. Since they represent attitudes, ways of thinking, the move from one position to another is often more of a sliding step than a giant leap. (1993, p. 170)

---

[2] Because of space limitations, we do not discuss in this section postmodern ideas and their implications for spirituality.

In the last section of this chapter, we describe expressions of spiritually centered leadership that support inclusive schooling.

Structural Functionalism

A structural functional perspective results from an epistemology that is objective and an ontology oriented toward regulation and control. Although they often seek to make improvements in special education services, principals who adopt structural functional perspectives believe that the difficulty in educating students with disabilities lies in these students' disabilities. These educators believe that it is the responsibility of the school to "fix" the student via special education and are most interested in how the special education bureaucracy might be made more efficient via bureaucratic management and control. They rely on a distant district-level administrator to manage special education services rather than take direct responsibility for the education of all students in their building. These principals advocate for support services without considering change in the instruction environment, encourage a system of referral and labeling, promote short-term relief strategies such as suspensions and alternative schooling, and rely on an expert model of building teams to accomplish these strategies. When making education decisions about a student with special needs, these principals focus on students' disabilities rather than "doing what's right for kids" (E. Fraturra-Kampschoer, personal communication, November 1997). Administrators then slot students with disabilities into existing programs rather than provide services. Leaders who take extreme structural functional views believe that students with disabilities have no place in public schools and that they should sacrifice the needs of these few students in order to accommodate the needs of students without disabilities.

These leaders may not believe in inclusion, or they may believe they are practicing inclusion, but in reality the inclusion efforts of these leaders may be limited because they wish to include students in ways that do not disrupt the flow and function of general education. For example, these educators may limit inclusion to specific times during the school day; that is, they allow students with disabilities to commingle with students enrolled in general education classes during lunch, allied arts classes, and recess. They may argue that only certain groups of students with disabilities may be included (e.g., students with mild disabilities). In so doing, an inordinate amount of time and resources are spent judging who is or is not identified for special education services and then who can and who cannot be included in general education.

Education leaders who take this perspective may try to include students with disabilities in the general education program without considering needed changes in general education for all students to be successful. Then, when students do not succeed or when teachers become frustrated, these educators argue that inclusion does not work and blame students with disabilities. A structural functionalist view does not examine underlying assumptions, resulting in shallow views (e.g., inclusion is just another movement or fad that will go away in time) and contradictory practices (e.g., including students with disabilities in one classroom and then offering a segregated, alternative program for students considered at risk).

Leaders whose spirituality reflects a structural functional perspective advocate one right way to believe. They adhere to strict religious rules about right and wrong behavior and attitudes, and they follow strict interpretations of those rules. A significant amount of time is spent enforcing the rules and judging whether others abide by them. The rules reinforce rigid societal roles to which individuals are expected to conform. From this perspective, education leaders may use religious interpretations to support practices used with children who vary from children who are developing typically. For example, they may use corporal punishment or expel any student who does not comply with the rules. Educators with this perspective may view students with disabilities as resulting from an act of sin or as people who have been cursed by God, causing these students' parents to experience immense shame and anger.

Interpretivism

The interpretivist perspective emanates from a subjective epistemology and an ontology oriented toward control and regulation. Education leaders who take interpretivist perspectives focus on a humanistic goal of meaningful education for all students. Concerned with the welfare of their students and with some concern for the efficiency and effectiveness of their school's programs, these educators hope that special education results in meaningful lives for students with disabilities. From this approach, the education leader serves as a facilitator and a collaborator.

Educators who take interpretivist perspectives do not defer to the experts who deliver student services. They consider the students themselves, the students' families, and teachers to be the experts with regard to the students' gifts and needs. From this perspective, education leaders engage in problem solving and search for positive alternatives based on the unique strengths of each student rather than label students and slot them into existing programs and provide them with only the existing services.

Education leaders who take interpretivist perspectives are open to including students with a wide range of disabilities across the general education program, emphasizing the importance of social relationships for these students. They argue that students with disabilities can benefit greatly from inclusion. They advocate for general education students to support and help the students with labels in the classroom. From an interpretivist perspective, however, the students are viewed narrowly as the sole beneficiaries of such efforts. Students with disabilities from this perspective can easily become objects of sympathy or pity but may not be valued for their gifts. From this perspective, seldom are students with disabilities acknowledged for the ways in which they contribute to the well-being of general education students, and seldom do they have the opportunity to support or help other students.

Although an interpretivist view takes a more humane approach to inclusion, the *general* and *special* education labels remain intact. In order for students to receive special education services, they need to be labeled. Although students with disabilities are included in general education classrooms, education leaders maintain a view that their academic potential is limited. Inclusion from an interpretivist perspective can sometimes become stuck at a particular stage. For example, students with disabilities may be included more often but may not be attending their home school, or students are included in general education but grouped in disproportionate numbers with teachers who are considered more accommodating of students with disabilities.

Moreover, education leaders may emphasize students' and teachers' getting along with one another but may not challenge education practices that limit student potential. These educators may emphasize cooperative learning, multiage classes, team teaching, and collaborative approaches; but the curriculum and instruction in the general education program sometimes may remain unchallenged.

An interpretivist spirituality includes practices that consider multiple approaches or multiple interpretations of doctrines or truths. Leaders whose spirituality embraces interpretivist perspectives emphasize relationships, loving others, caring, and accepting others as they are. These leaders are open to others' views while maintaining their commitment to their own views. An interpretivist spirituality may seem pedantic to the receiver when leaders seek to help others to be more like the leader rather than affirm or accept others. An interpretivism-oriented spirituality may include social justice work such as serving the hungry and the poor, but little effort is devoted to policy changes or antidiscrimination work that could alleviate the causes for these conditions.

Critically Oriented Perspectives

Critically oriented perspectives span the subjective–objective epistemological continuum and ontologically are oriented toward social change. Education leaders who adopt critically oriented perspectives engage in an unyielding quest for social justice. These educators embrace concern for those who experience suffering and oppression, their leadership practices are aimed toward empowerment and transformation, and they emphasize morals and values in decision making. These educators deliberately involve students with disabilities and their families in discussion to identify issues, causes, and solutions based on these students' and families' personal experiences with inequity.

Although not totally eschewing efficiency and effectiveness or dismissing the importance of students' leading meaningful lives, these leaders use services for students with disabilities in a way that is intertwined with the curriculum, instruction, and culture of the school as a way not only to prepare students for meaningful lives but also to give them the knowledge and skills to make a difference in their communities and in society. Students with disabilities are taught to advocate not only for themselves but also for others.

From a critical perspective, inclusion of students with disabilities is not viewed as an add-on or a program. In fact, from this perspective, inclusion may not become an initiative in the district but is grounded in a fundamental restructuring of curriculum and instruction in which all students are considered gifted in varying ways (see Gardner, 1993). Students do not need to bear a label to receive a curriculum and instruction that matches their gifts and learning styles. Students do not need to fail before their learning needs are attended to; creative intense instruction in the early years sustains the students' self-esteem and lays a foundation of high expectations for all the students' years in school. From this perspective, education leaders channel resources into creating and sustaining schools for all students to succeed rather than siphon off huge amounts of funding for special programs to "fix" students and ignore the school itself. Education leaders who take this perspective "take ownership" of all students in their schools.

The critical perspective is not without its own dangers, however. For example, education leaders can become so focused on social transformation that they mount a personal crusade toward inclusion (E. Fraturra-Kampschoer, personal communication, November 1997), which can result in cosmetic rather than deep change (Quinn, 1996) and lead to cynicism and personal burnout.

Spirituality that takes a critically oriented perspective is a spirituality that focuses on equity, justice, and social change. Liberation theology that emanates from the Catholic tradition in South America is one example of a spirituality that can be considered critically oriented (Gutierrez, 1973/1988). Critically oriented spirituality emphasizes relationships with others but maintains a constant consciousness of unequal power relationships and seeks to ensure the participation of all people in decisions. One danger of a critically oriented spirituality is that leaders can become overfocused on social justice and changing others and neglect their own personal and spiritual growth. That is, leaders who adopt this perspective may seek to change others and structures around them but avoid making changes within themselves or dodge family responsibilities and needs in favor of their social justice work.

Many spiritual practices draw from all three perspectives: They follow a standard interpretation of religious readings, they seek community from its members, and part of their work goes toward helping disenfranchised people and alleviating the causes of these people's problems.

Spiritual and Epistemological Perspectives and the Literature

Reexamining the literature on leadership and spirituality through epistemological and spiritual lenses suggests that the three key themes—personal awareness, significance of relationships, and having a sense of purpose or mission—emanate from interpretivist perspectives. Although it appears that these themes move beyond a structural functional perspective, they do not quite capture the critical perspective. We subject these themes to what we term the "Hitler test" to consider whether they are inherently oriented toward justice (see Capper, 1998). Although we realize that comparing these perspectives to Hitler's can be regarded as an extreme comparison, we find this stark contrast to be useful in our work.

We do not know Hitler's level of personal self-awareness; we know only that he was quite aware of his personal need to "cleanse the world" of those whom he believed to be unclean. He highly valued his relationships with others and cultivated relationships with those who were intelligent and highly educated to engender loyalty to him and to his ideas. Hitler also possessed a clear purpose and mission, and he could have perceived his work as a higher calling. As we can see by way of analogy, an education leader may possess the three qualities noted in the spirituality literature; but these qualities may not inherently lead to inclusive practices.

CONCLUSIONS

Our discussion of the shadow side of spirituality suggests that an education leader with a critically oriented spirituality embodies the most hope of working toward inclusion in its truest sense. We return to the three major themes from the leadership and spirituality literature and consider how we might recast them from a critical perspective to support inclusive schooling.

Personal Awareness that Probes Power and Privilege

A spiritually centered leadership that supports inclusive schooling must begin with awareness of leaders' power and privilege in society and the ways in which their daily actions and attitudes reinforce or level power inequities. The research on the role of principals in inclusive schools suggests that principals' experiences influenced their positive views of inclusion. More specifically, we must ask ourselves what our experience with people with disabilities has been during our personal and professional lives and how we feel about these experiences. How have these experiences influenced our views? As adults, do we count among our close friends people with disabilities? What have been our fears? How have we felt discomfort? How have we been willing to learn about people with disabilities, not as a group but as individuals? What myths and stereotypes do we believe about people with disabilities? What messages did our families, communities, schools, and religious institutions give us about people who were different from us? A spirituality that supports inclusive schooling must move beyond general self-reflection, personal growth, and self-improvement to an ongoing personal awareness of the contradictions and possibilities that we experience in relationship to people with varying abilities.

Relationships that Transform Power Inequities

A spirituality that supports inclusive schooling emphasizes the importance of relationships but pushes beyond the goal of nurturing relationships with others and supporting school conditions that provide for positive relationships among staff. Leaders whose spirituality is critically oriented realize that, when working toward leveling power inequities such as those involved with inclusion, resistance and conflict are likely. In fact, they view conflict as an essential component of community and of transformation. Although they believe in the importance of building community as part of their inclusive practices, they realize that community should not become synonymous with the squelching of dissent or concerns. As a community, they expect and welcome questions and see conflict as a way to push forward.

Likewise, they realize that critically oriented work can be difficult and that they cannot do it alone. They develop relationships with like-minded people for ongoing personal support. Although they realize that most people resist change, they seek work environments that support them to strive toward creating and sustaining inclusion.

Sense of Mission Oriented Toward Justice

Leaders who embrace a critically oriented spirituality believe their inclusion work in schools is making the world a better place for all people, which is an extension of their spiritual beliefs. They view themselves and others as bearers of gifts to carry into the world. These leaders believe that they must be good stewards of their own gifts and seek to create the conditions in which the gifts of others can come to fruition. They know that inclusion begins with self-knowledge and personal awareness and seek to create conditions for the people with whom they work to explore their beliefs and take risks.

To avoid the dangers of a critically oriented spirituality, however, they temper their process so as not to mount a personal crusade that can lead to disillusionment and burnout. They see themselves as being involved in the work for the long haul and know that, to sustain themselves, they need to honor the process of others. These leaders remember their own process toward including people with disabilities (indeed, we conjecture that most education leaders working toward inclusion, at some point in their history, have participated in and supported segregated environments for students with disabilities).

Leaders from a critical spirituality strive toward justice that generates within them a passion for inclusion, and they work quite hard to reach this goal. They do so, however, not at the expense of their own families or personal life. Relatedly, though they see themselves as change agents, they ultimately believe that they cannot change anyone except themselves. They endlessly seek to create the conditions in which inclusion can happen but ultimately believe that the outcomes are beyond their control and are spiritually decided.

In sum, this chapter reviews the literature on spiritually centered leadership. It explores the relationship between epistemology and spirituality and their possible shadow sides. In conclusion, we offer possible expressions of spiritually centered leadership that can support inclusive schooling: personal awareness that probes power and privilege, relationships that transform power inequities, and a sense of mission oriented toward justice. Many questions remain, and here we ask one: Do all leaders who support inclusive schooling share a similar set of spiritual beliefs? Future research should empirically examine in which ways spirituality influences the work of education leaders who do and do not support inclusive schooling.

EPILOGUE AND AUTOBIOGRAPHIES

Colleen: I come to this topic not from a distance but from my day-to-day living in a postmodern pastiche of identities and experiences. I cannot separate, nor do I wish to separate, the intertwining braids of my personal spirituality, my beliefs about disability, and my leadership philosophy. After finishing my undergraduate degree, I served as a missionary for the United Methodist Church for 5 years in the Appalachian Mountain area of southeastern Kentucky. I taught and coordinated special education services at Red Bird School. While a missionary, my mom died of leukemia at age 50, I realized I was a lesbian, and I began recovering from multiple addictions. These painful events in the early 1980s shook the roots of my religious foundation, but these experiences have become my greatest spiritual gifts. Although I eventually left the United Methodist Church, I did not abandon my spirituality, and my experiences in Appalachia served to push open my inner doors to lifelong soul work. My partner and I are parents of a 7-year-old son who thrives in school. (He announced at the start of the 1998–1999 school year, "I wish I could go to school for 100 years!") I also lead a seminar on spirituality in leadership in which participants explore the intersections of autobiography, power, and epistemology in their spiritual journeys and in life's work.

Maureen: I too experienced those defining moments—times that, upon glancing backward, have shaped my spiritual beliefs. My Aunt Margaret described one of my first "moments" to me. I was born in 1952 in Milwaukee, Wisconsin. My aunt tells of how, at a young age, I began pushing people to think and act in different ways. Milwaukee was and continues to be a typical midwestern city, segregated in all respects. My aunt would take me places on the bus. She described my ritual of running onto the bus and sitting close to the darkest-skinned African American woman I could find. She told me that, even as a 2-year-old, I was actively pushing my social agenda. I do not mean to sound insensitive or anything less than fully respectful of the times in which I grew up. Nevertheless, this story and others have helped me to understand why I have been so hellbent on figuring out why life is different, so unfair, for some people. I have used the phrase "But it isn't fair" since I was little.

Instead of working directly on issues of racial equality, I found myself drawn into issues of advocacy for and education of children with disabilities and their families. Looking back on my life, as I have begun to piece these stories together (with age 50 being only 4 short years away as I write this), I realize that my role as an advocate has taught me how to advocate for myself. As someone who was abused and often disregarded throughout my life, I have learned to advocate for myself.

As a public school teacher and administrator with nearly 18 years of experience, I have thousands of stories to tell. One recurring theme has been my deep regard for each child's soul. The untrusting glare of teenagers conveys, "Why the hell do you care?" Others' eyes tell me, "Thank God, you care." Through every one of these encounters, I have tried to acknowledge the spirit within each child, so aptly expressed in the Hindi word *namaste* (i.e., the spirit within me honors and respects the spirit within you).

George: I come to this topic from a background that started with a family committed to political activism and social responsibility. I have taken this activism and social responsibility and spent my energies working with and advocating for children. I have developed strong convictions and acted on them with a vision of how the world ought to be and what all children are entitled to have. These convictions have driven my passion in working for and with children.

At an individualized education program (IEP) meeting for a student with significant cognitive disabilities in my first-grade classroom, many professionals carried on about how hard this child was to work with, how lacking in skills he was, and how much he was struggling. I responded, "I don't know what you all do with [the student], but he is reading in my room."

I do not have a special education background. My beliefs about disability and inclusion come from my convictions that all children have unlimited potential and that systematic segregation is not acceptable. As an educator, I worked with children with special needs in inclusive after-school programs, at inclusive summer camps, on inclusive sports teams, and in inclusive classrooms. I did this not because I had to, not because students were forced into my classroom, and not because I had been taught inclusion, but because inclusion makes sense. I have seen, felt, and believed that all of the children with whom I worked had their own needs and that my job as an educator and advocate is to meet them.

REFERENCES

Amendolara, L. (1993). *The charismatic core of lay leaders.* Unpublished dissertation, Fordham University, Bronx, NY.

Bolman, L.G., & Deal, T.E. (1995). *Leading with soul: An uncommon journey of spirit.* San Francisco: Jossey-Bass.

Briskin, A. (1996). *The stirring of soul in the workplace.* San Francisco: Jossey-Bass.

Burrell, G., & Morgan, G. (1979). *Sociological paradigms and organisational analysis: Elements of the sociology of corporate life.* London: Heinemann.

Canfield, J., & Miller, J. (1996). *Heart at work: Stories and strategies for building self-esteem and reawakening the soul at work.* New York: McGraw-Hill.

Capper, C.A. (1993). Educational administration in a pluralistic society: A multiple paradigm approach. In C.A. Capper (Ed.), *Educational administration in a pluralistic society* (pp. 7–35). Albany: State University of New York Press.

Capper, C.A. (1994). ". . . And justice for all": Critical perspectives on outcome-based education in the context of secondary school restructuring. *Journal of School Leadership, 4*(2), 132–155.

Capper, C.A. (1996). "We're not housed in an institution, we're housed in the community": Possibilities and consequences of neighborhood-based interagency collaboration. In J.G. Cibulka & W.J. Kritik (Eds.), *Coordination among schools, families, and communities: Prospects for educational reform* (pp. 299–322). Albany: State University of New York Press.

Capper, C. (1998). Critically oriented and postmodern perspectives: Sorting out the differences and applications for practice. *Educational Administration Quarterly, 34*(3), 354–379.

Capper, C., & Reitzug, U. (1996). Deconstructing site-based management: Possibilities for emancipation and alternative means of control. *Journal of Educational Administration, 5*(1), 56–59.

Capper, C.A., & Jamison, M.T. (1993). Let the buyer beware! Total quality management and educational research and practice. *Educational Researcher, 22*(8), 25–30.

Conger, J.A., & associates. (1994). *Spirit at work: Discovering the spirituality in leadership.* San Francisco: Jossey-Bass.

Covey, S.R. (1991). *Principle-centered leadership.* New York: Summit Books.

Dreher, D. (1996). *The Tao of personal leadership.* New York: Harper Business.

Eck, D.L. (1993). *Encountering God: A spiritual journey from Bozeman to Banaras.* Boston: Beacon Press.

Gardner, H. (1993). *Frames of mind: The theory of multiple intelligences* (10th anniversary ed.). New York: Basic Books.

Gilley, K. (1997). *Leading from the heart: Choosing courage over fear in the workplace.* Boston: Butterworth-Heinemann.

Gutierrez, G. (1988). *A theology of liberation: History, politics, and salvation* (Sr. C. Inda & J. Eagleson, eds. & trans.). Maryknoll, NY: Orbis Books. (Original work published 1973)

Hawley, J.A. (1993). *Reawakening the spirit in work: The power of dharmic management.* San Francisco: Berrett-Koehler.

Herman, S.M. (1994). *The Tao at work: On leading and following.* San Francisco: Jossey-Bass.

Hines, R., Johnson, J.H. (1996). Inclusive classrooms: The principal's role in promoting achievement. *Schools in the Middle, 5*(3), 6–11.

Inamori, K. (1995). *A passion for success: Practical, inspirational, and spiritual insight from Japan's leading entrepreneur.* New York: McGraw-Hill.

Jacobson, S. (1994). *Spirituality and transformational leadership in secular settings: A Delphi study.* Unpublished dissertation, Seattle University, Seattle, WA.

Jaworski, J. (1996). *Synchronicity: The inner path of leadership.* San Francisco: Berrett-Koehler.

Jones, L.B. (1995). *Jesus, CEO: Using ancient wisdom for visionary leadership.* New York: Hyperion.

Keyes, M.W. (1996). *Intersections of vision and practice in an inclusive elementary school: An ethnography of a principal.* Unpublished doctoral dissertation, University of Wisconsin–Madison.

Larkin, D. (1995). *Beyond self to compassionate healer: Transcendent leadership.* Unpublished dissertation, Seattle University, Seattle, WA.

Love, E. (1991). *Woman prophet: The illumination of a journey.* Unpublished dissertation, Seattle University, Seattle, WA.

Madsen, J., & Hollins, E. (1997, April). *Minorities in majority schools.* Paper presented at the annual meeting of the American Educational Research Association, Chicago.

McEnroe, J. (1995, February). Portrait of outstanding leaders. *Trustee,* 6–9.

McGowan, M.L. (1994). *The spiritual thread in experiential education. In Experiential education: A critical resource for the 21st century.* Boulder, CO: Association for Experiential Education.

Moffett, J. (1994). *The universal schoolhouse: Spiritual awakening through education.* San Francisco: Jossey-Bass.

Palmer, P. (1994). Leading from within: Out of the shadow, into the light. In J.A. Conger, *Spirit at work: Discovering the spirituality in leadership* (pp. 19–40). San Francisco: Jossey-Bass.

Quinn, R.E. (1996). *Deep change: Discovering the leader within.* San Francisco: Jossey-Bass.

Rolls, J. (1994). *Leading organizational transformation: The nine characteristics of transformational leaders.* Unpublished doctoral dissertation, The Union Institute.

Roskind, R. (1992). *In the spirit of business: A guide to resolving fears and creating harmony in your worklife.* Berkeley, CA: Celestial Arts.

Sadler, W. (1996). *The I Ching of management: An age old study for new age managers.* Atlanta, GA: Humanics Ltd.

Schmidt, V. (1995). *Awakening intuition: A Delphi study.* Unpublished doctoral dissertation, University of San Diego, CA.

Starratt, R.J., & Guare, R. (1995, Fall/Winter). The spirituality of leadership. *Planning and Changing,* 190–203.

Thom, D.J. (1993). *Educational management and leadership: Word, spirit, and deed for a just society.* Calgary, Alberta, Canada: Detselig Enterprises.

Vaill, P.B. (1989). *Managing as a performing art: New ideas for a world of chaotic change.* San Francisco: Jossey-Bass.

Vaill, P.B. (1990). Executive development as spiritual development. In S. Srivastva, D.L. Cooperrider, & Associates (Eds.), *Appreciative management and leadership: The power of positive thought and action in organizations* (pp. 323–352). San Francisco: Jossey-Bass.

Walling, D. (1994). *Spirituality and leadership.* Unpublished doctoral dissertation, University of San Diego, CA.

Whitmyer, C. (Ed.). (1994). *Mindfulness and meaningful work: Explorations in right livelihood.* Berkeley, CA: Parallax Press.

Whyte, D. (1994). *The heart aroused: Poetry and the preservation of the soul in corporate America.* New York: Doubleday/Currency.

Yoder, N. (1997). *The spirituality centered leader: How personal spirituality influences professional practice.* Unpublished dissertation proposal, University of Wisconsin–Madison.

Chapter 20

Preparing Educators
to Implement Inclusive Practices

Richard A. Villa,
Jacqueline S. Thousand, and James W. Chapple

> Our teachers need to be prepared to teach all America's children.
> (Richard Riley, U.S. Secretary of Education, quoted in Henry, 1997)

> Untrained people do not simply walk into classrooms and automatically
> become successful. (Linda Darling-Hammond, executive director of the
> National Commission on Teaching and America's Future, as quoted in
> Henry, 1997, p. D1)

The National Commission on Teaching and America's Future, a 26-
member, bipartisan, blue-ribbon panel, reviewed 200 studies during a
2-year period and found the following:

- More than 30% of beginning teachers leave the field in the first 5 years.

- In the 1990s, more than 50,000 people who lacked the training
  required for their jobs entered teaching annually on emergency or

substandard licenses, and 27% of new teachers had not completed license requirements in their main teaching areas.

- In schools with the highest minority enrollments, students have less than a 50% chance of getting a science or mathematics teacher who holds a license and a degree in the field in which he or she teaches.
- More than 2 million new teachers will be needed by 2007; stated otherwise, more than half the teachers who will be teaching in 2007 will be trained between 2000 and 2007 (Darling-Hammond, 1997).

In urban areas, recruitment and maintenance of qualified personnel are even more of a challenge. For example, in the second-largest U.S. school district—Los Angeles Unified School District—more than 40% of those employed as special educators in 1997 were working on emergency credentials. In some of New York City's schools, more than 85% of the teachers working in the schools are untrained and inexperienced (A.N. Gartner, personal communication, January 1998). Clearly, the United States is in the middle of a teacher preparation and retention crisis.

The teacher-training crisis is compounded by the fact that the U.S. student population is becoming increasingly diverse. There is no question that the United States is a multicultural society, classrooms are filled with students who are at different academic levels and from many different countries, different cultural and linguistic backgrounds, and different socioeconomic groups. Yet, there is an absence of teaching personnel who mirror the students whom they teach in terms of race, language, and ethnicity. Furthermore, in the 1990s, the movement toward inclusion gained unparalleled momentum. Since 1993, every state has implemented inclusion at some level (Webb, 1994). This means that teachers interact with students whose curriculum and instructional needs cover a wider spectrum than ever before.

Finally, after critically examining the nation's education system, national and state legislators and policy makers have set goals (e.g., Goals 2000: Educate America Act of 1994 [PL 103-227]) and enacted legislation (e.g., the Americans with Disabilities Act [ADA] of 1990 [PL 101-336], the Individuals with Disabilities Education Act [IDEA] of 1990 [PL 101-476], the Individuals with Disabilities Education Act [IDEA] Amendments of 1991 [PL 102-119], the Individuals with Disabilities Education Act [IDEA] Amendments of 1997 [PL 105-17]). This legislation emphasizes in explicit language that educational goals apply to all students, including those traditionally excluded from educational reforms (e.g., students with identified disabilities, students with limited English proficiency, students from minority cultures). The message to the teaching profession is that every teacher is expected to 1) rise to the occasion and be accountable for high expectations, instruction methods, and assessment practices that foster and measure the success of every student; and 2) collaborate with others to instruct all students. The message from policy makers is reinforced by the National Commission on Teaching and America's Future, which articulated what it takes to be an effective teacher (Darling-Hammond, 1997). In addition to subject-matter expertise and knowledge of how children learn and develop, teachers need 1) skills in using a range of instructional strategies and technologies to work effectively with students with diverse characteristics and backgrounds, 2) the ability to collaborate with parents and other teachers, and 3) assessment expertise to be accountable in detecting students' progress and in making data-based decisions.

COMPETENCIES FOR THE 21ST-CENTURY EDUCATOR

Smith and Luckasson (1995) observed that inclusion efforts have not yet affected teacher education programs significantly at either the preservice or the in-service level; fewer than 5% of all general education teachers have been formally prepared for or in inclusive classroom environments. This fact is in stark contrast to the recognized national need for a teacher work force that expects to see and is prepared to educate a diverse student population in inclusive classrooms. For educators to instruct a heterogeneous student body and collaborate with one another in this endeavor, they need to acquire through preservice and in-service experiences a common disposition, conceptual framework, language, and set of technical skills to work with the diverse learners who enter the local schoolhouse door.

This chapter proposes changes in content and format of both preservice teacher preparation and in-service programs and shares examples of programs that exemplify such changes that are based on a presumption that all teachers of the future will work with students with all types of diversity. The specific attitudes, dispositions, knowledge, and skills that need to be addressed in initial teacher preparation and continuing education program agendas are informed by multiple sources, including the voices of teachers who are working, or facing a future of working, in more inclusive and heterogeneous classrooms.

RECOMMENDED CHANGES FOR TEACHER PREPARATION PROGRAMS

School personnel are graduates of our colleges and universities. It is there that they learn there are at least two types of human beings and if you

choose to work with one of them you render yourself legally and conceptually incompetent to work with others. (Sarason, 1982, p. 258)

Sarason (1982) stated that public schools simply mirror-image colleges
and universities. Specifically, the division of teacher preparation programs into separate, distinct, and categorical programs—general education versus special education and its various subcategories of
learning disabilities, emotional and behavior disorders, severe disabilities, English as a second language, gifted and talented—causes educa-
tors-in-preparation neither to expect nor to have the skills to create
successful heterogeneous learning experiences for students of differing
abilities. Is it any wonder that general and special education evolved as
separate systems? Collaborative skills and dispositions are documented to be essential for survival in a profession in which no one person
can possibly meet the needs of all of the students in his or her charge
(Villa, Thousand, Nevin, & Malgeri, 1996). Yet, few educators graduate
from personnel preparation programs having seen adults collaborate
across areas of expertise to model inclusive education practices.

The historically separate general and special education teacher
preparation programs have not provided trainees with intensive training and experience to develop the necessary skills and disposition to be
effective collaborators in planning, teaching, and evaluating instruction (Thousand, Villa, Paolucci-Whitcomb, & Nevin, 1996). To remedy
this situation, preservice general and special education programs also
must place strong emphasis on theory, practice, and experience in collaborative planning, teaching, and problem-solving processes. Special
priority should be given to establishing noncategorical programs that
merge professional training programs so that general, special, and
related-services personnel share common coursework and practicum
experiences. Bassett and colleagues provided the rationale for such collaboration in higher education:

> General education curriculum offers the standards by which the outcomes
> of the educational process are defined; yet arguably, preservice programs
> in special education may not provide adequate content curricula to their
> graduates. Similarly, general education preservice programs may deny
> their graduates meaningful opportunities to learn the rich array of teach-
> ing strategies and support processes that literally define the field of spe-
> cial education. (1996, p. 379)

In 1989, Stainback and Stainback offered steps for facilitating the
merger of personnel preparation programs. First, general and special
education faculty need to collaboratively analyze the existing curricula along with the emerging demands on educators (e.g., proficiency in

the use of technology, collaborative teaming and creative problem solving, linguistic diversity, inclusion of children with disabilities in general education) in order to identify the core values, knowledge, and skills that all teachers should acquire. They most assuredly will discover that there are holes in the traditional curriculum and that new competencies and standards, content, and experiences need to be conceptualized. The authors' examination of several states' new teacher standards, the 1996 Council for Exceptional Children (CEC) core standards for special educators, findings of the National Commission on Teaching and America's Future (Darling-Hammond, 1997), the Joseph P. Kennedy, Jr. Foundation in collaboration with the Office of Special Education Programs (1997), and recent issues of *Teacher Education and Special Education* revealed some common themes recommended for preservice teacher education programs to address:

- Historical, philosophical, social, and legal foundations of education
- Professionalism and ethical practice
- Valuing characteristics of diverse learners
- Multicultural issues in home, school, and community environments
- Child and adolescent development
- Creativity, collaborative teaming processes, and interpersonal communication
- Home, school, and community relations
- Learning theory
- Classroom organization, management, and motivational strategies
- Data-based curriculum design and instructional adaptation for individual differences
- Educational measurement and authentic family-centered and student-focused assessment
- Peer-mediated strategies (e.g., cooperative group learning, peer tutoring, peer mediation)
- Literacy, numeracy, and use of technology
- Contemporary best practices, issues, and trends in education
- Organizational development, leadership, and system change theory

Once competencies have been agreed on, a core set of courses or learning units and field experiences then are developed or reformulated and required of all education majors. In addition to this core, each student would select his or her own specialty areas (e.g., language arts, augmentative and alternative communication systems, bilingual education, employment training) and develop extended competence in his or her selected concentrations through various means (e.g., coursework, institutes, workshops, distance or distributed learning, field experiences, action research). By restructuring professional teacher education preparation programs in this manner, graduates no longer would get the message that there are separate systems of education; instead, they would have the disposition and skill to work collaboratively and creatively with others to merge their unique areas of expertise in order to instruct a diverse student body.

EXEMPLARY TEACHER PREPARATION INITIATIVES

In many institutions of higher education, faculty of the various separate education departments have begun the dialogue with local communities and school personnel to determine how to retool their professional preparation programs to better ready graduates for meeting the challenges of inclusive 21st-century education. In a few places, dialogue has resulted in action and the creation of new and innovative training initiatives that model faculty and community collaboration and depart from traditional ways of inducting educators into their profession. Four such places are Trinity College, Burlington, Vermont; Syracuse University, Syracuse, New York; California State University San Marcos; and the University of Northern Colorado, Greeley. The result of these institutions' initiatives has been the merging of the expertise and knowledge of formerly separated or disjointed higher education and school-based educators.

Trinity College

The certification program at Trinity College is an example of a teacher preparation program that has been restructured in a fashion suggested by Stainback and Stainback (1989). Specifically, all education majors take a common core of courses (i.e., teaching in an integrated environment, foundations of education, educational psychology, child development, senior practicum issues seminar) intended to impart a common core of instruction skills and dispositions to empower them to be teachers of all children. Practicum experiences begin in the second year for most education majors, with 3 hours per week spent in the classroom, and culminate with 16–32 weeks of classroom experience in the final year. An option for all education majors is dual certification in general and special education. To receive dual certification, students take an additional core of courses (i.e., Education of Learners with Special Needs I and II, Classroom Management I and II, and Consultation and Collaboration) typically associated with special education teacher preparation programs. In addition, to gain the perspective of both a general and a special educator, candidates devote half of their final practicum experience to the role of general educator and the other half to the role of special educator, generally within the same classroom.

The Trinity program is continually evolving as faculty examine exemplary educational practices and question the match between the college's offerings and the demands that the inclusive schools in Vermont and across the United States place on new teachers. To ensure that students have multiple opportunities to observe inclusive practices and design, implement, and evaluate inclusive curriculum, instruction, and assessments, the faculty have established site-school partnerships with totally inclusive schools. In addition, when faculty members from Trinity College teach classes of students at the local school site, school-based public school teachers are made available during the day to work with Trinity students who are assigned to that site for their student teaching experiences. Trinity faculty are actively exploring the development of a singular, unified teacher preparation program (M.B. Doyle, personal communication, April 1998). The faculty are studying several colleges that have done just this and have taken particular interest in the Syracuse University model, which is described next.

Syracuse University

The School of Education of Syracuse University has merged its previously separate elementary and special education programs and created a single inclusive elementary and special education teacher preparation program (Meyer & Biklen, 1992) expressly designed to ready all of its candidates to educate an increasingly diverse student population and certify graduates in both elementary and special education. A major program objective is to do more than prepare competent educators but to graduate education professionals who are able to lead communities to a vision of schooling in which equity and excellence are both celebrated. A critical feature of the program is its focus on multicultural education and student acquisition of knowledge and skills needed for the cultural pluralism of U.S. schools at the turn of the 21st century. A series of practicum experiences in inclusive inner-city, urban, and suburban schools affords students opportunities to develop and apply skills to educate students with diverse needs, including students identified as eligible for special education.

Students in the inclusive program benefit from the faculty's modeling of collaboration and cultural pluralism. Specifically, the faculty are drawn from a wide variety of departments within and outside the School of Education (Teaching and Leadership; Cultural Foundations of Education; Instructional Design, Development, and Evaluation; Communication Sciences and Disorders; Reading and Language Arts; College for Human Development; Child and Family Studies).

California State University San Marcos

Collaborative planning and teaming have repeatedly been identified as critical to educating children with and without disabilities successfully in general education. Taking this information to heart, when, in the early 1990s, the founding faculty of the College of Education at California State University San Marcos (CSUSM) sat down to design the structure of the college and its programs, collaboration was the fundamental guiding principle that led to the construction of a college without lines in the sand between faculty.

Recognizing that teachers-in-preparation need to see their professors model the practices that they preach, the elementary, middle-level, secondary, and special education teacher preparation programs of the College of Education at CSUSM chose to structure courses so that general and special education faculty team-teach and model an interdisciplinary, collaborative approach to curriculum and instruction. Within the CSUSM College of Education, there are no divisions or departments that compartmentalize faculty by discipline (e.g., special education, learning and instruction, multicultural/bilingual, mathematics, science, literacy); and monthly governance community meetings include the entire community of faculty and support personnel rather than tenure-track faculty alone. Faculty work closely with local school personnel and are encouraged to conduct research and author scholarly work collaboratively.

A unique collaboration between local communities and the CSUSM College of Education is the establishment of a Distinguished Teachers in Residence program, in which six local educators serve as full-time faculty members for 2-year terms. Their service as university faculty creates release time so that tenure-track faculty may jointly develop and conduct projects identified by local districts to assist schools to improve and innovate (e.g., assist early childhood special education personnel to incorporate technology into their early intervention programs, develop Internet-delivered courses for teachers who cannot or prefer not to come on campus to take courses).

It is noteworthy that, starting in June 2000, all of California's special education teacher preparation programs have a responsibility to collaborate with hiring local school districts in order to provide their newly credentialed graduates continuing education training and support (known as Professional Level II preparation). Within 120 days of employment, new special educators must have a local school mentor assigned to them and be enrolled in a postcredential Level II program (hopefully from their original credentialing institution). Together, the graduate, the local school mentor, and the institution of higher education develop an induction plan, which lays out an individualized 2-year course of study and set of experiences designed to support the new educator's development in the role that he or she was hired to fulfill. The Level II credential requirement is a great prompt for universities and schools to collaborate more closely in all sorts of ways. Furthermore, it is a fabulous example of a state department of education recognizing that 1) every teacher, particularly a new teacher, needs support to thrive in the profession; and 2) the earning of an initial credential, license, or certificate is not the end but the beginning of a lifelong learning process. The new credentialing system is a gift not only to the new teachers but also to the school districts and the universities, because it forces everyone to pause and think about 1) what really is important for new teachers, 2) how to create organized supports for teachers, and 3) how to expand the role of higher education as a co-partner in the continued maintenance of the teaching profession.

University of Northern Colorado

When faculty of general and special teacher education programs teach in isolation from one another, there is the danger that general education graduates will miss opportunities to learn about and develop skills to value, instruct, assess, and develop accommodations and modifications for learners whose learning styles, behaviors, and curricula do not match the content area or grade level of their concentrations. In contrast, special education graduates may not have access to the general education curriculum to the extent that they need it. The University of Northern Colorado in Greeley provides undergraduate teacher preparation in the areas of elementary education, middle school education, secondary school education, and K–12 education in areas such as art, music, physical education, and special education. It has blended formerly separate programs so that faculty share their expertise and curriculum. In addition to university-based courses, students participate in seminars that are co-taught by university faculty and school district teaching personnel on school sites (D.S. Bassett, personal communication, February 2, 1998).

The university's preparation programs have become field based, with students working in partnership schools that for the most part are inclusive. Students stay at each school placement for at least 1 school year. As they work in these environments, they experience the culture of the school, the diversity of the learners, and cope with the day-to-day issues that surface within such in-depth school-based environments. Field experiences begin in the sophomore year, with students observing across the curriculum in areas other than their specific content area. During the second phase, they work with small groups of diverse learners; and field experience is coupled with coursework in educational psychology, assessment, instruction and evaluation techniques, and learning theory. In the third phase, they teach in a school environment within their content area. The fourth phase involves their final advanced student teaching experience.

Because students demonstrate their competence through the construction of portfolios, both faculty and students are able to evaluate the relevance of the experiences and studies that faculty have crafted for students. Portfolios and student verbal reports indicate that this university's restructuring has made coursework and field experience much more relevant to what actually happens in schools.

IN-SERVICE PROGRAMS FOR CREATING INCLUSIVE SCHOOLS

Given that preservice education and the relatively isolated teaching experiences of so many teachers and other school personnel have fallen short of what they report that they need (Lyon, Vaassen, & Toomey, 1989), it lands on the shoulders of local school communities to be primary actors in formulating and delivering a comprehensive in-service training agenda to prepare educators to respond to unique students' needs. A quality in-service program must afford faculty and staff ongoing experiences for continuously upgrading their skills to support increasingly more inclusive learning communities.

Sadly, innovations in teacher preparation such as those just described are not what many educators recall as their preservice preparation experience. Instead, they report being ill prepared to expect and effectively respond to the needs of a widely diverse student body (Lyon et al., 1989). Fortunately, local communities, school districts, and state departments of education need not wait for higher education to "get its act together" (Villa, 1989, p. 175) in order to ready teachers to educate all children in general education environments. Models of local school and joint state department, community, and university collaborative ventures exist in comprehensive in-service training to support inclusive education. In the following subsections, three professional development approaches that have succeeded in creating and/or maintaining systems change for inclusive schooling are described.

Approach #1: Gearing Up for Inclusion in the 1980s

Through a long-range in-service training agenda, a community and its teachers can gear up to create quality inclusive learning environments. Such an agenda was formulated and carried out during a 5-year period in a school district that committed itself to and successfully transformed itself from being an exclusionary district to being one of the first fully inclusive education systems in the United States (Cross & Villa, 1992). The in-service agenda included four tiers of training. The first tier was designed for any member of the community and included content regarding general education research on the characteristics of effective schools (e.g., Block, Efthim, & Burns, 1989), exemplary practices for educating all children in heterogeneous learning environments (e.g., Fox & Williams, 1991), and models for adult collaboration and the development of small-group interpersonal skills (Johnson & Johnson, 1987, 1999; Thousand et al., 1986; Thousand et al., 1996; Thousand & Villa, 1992). The second tier of training was intended to respond to the self-identified needs of parents and community members and addressed issues such as legal rights and procedural safeguards for children with and without disabilities, discipline policies, community-referenced instruction, and transition to adult services and continuing education opportunities.

The third tier of training experiences was designed expressly for people who work with and for children on a day-to-day basis—teachers, paraeducators, volunteers, and administrators. Training introduced concepts and practices in the following areas:

- Outcome-based instruction models (e.g., Block & Anderson, 1975; Guskey, 1997; Spady & Marshall, 1991)

- Alternatives to standardized assessment models (e.g., Deno, 1985; Giangreco, Cloninger, & Iverson, 1998; Idol, Nevin, & Paolucci-Whitcomb, 1999; Perrone, 1991; Ysseldyke & Christenson, 1987)

- Curriculum adaptation approaches (e.g., Campbell, Campbell, Collicott, Perner, & Stone, 1988; Giangreco & Meyer, 1988; Udvari-Solner, 1994; Wood, 1998)

- Strategies for peer-mediated instruction (e.g., cooperative group learning, peer tutoring) and conflict management (e.g., Davidson, 1994; Johnson & Johnson, 1999; Harper, Maheady, & Mallette, 1994, La Plant & Zane, 1994; Schrumpf, 1994)

- Use of technology (Brandt, 1994; Dutton & Dutton, 1990; Heerman, 1988; Thornburg, 1992)

- Responsibility-based classroom and schoolwide behavior management and discipline approaches (e.g., Becker, 1986; Brendtro,

Brokenleg, & Van Bockern, 1990; Curwin & Mendler, 1988; Glasser, 1998; Chapter 6 of this book)

• Methods for teaching and reinforcing students' use of positive social skills (e.g., Elias & Clabby, 1992; Goldstein, 1988; Hazel, Schumaker, Sherman, & Sheldon-Wildgen, 1996; Vernon, 1989)

The fourth tier of training focused on providing supervisors and professional teaching personnel with peer coaching and clinical supervision approaches to assist teachers to be reflective practitioners (Cummings, 1985; Glickman, Gordon, & Ross-Gordon, 1998; Joyce & Showers, 1980, 1995). Interestingly, examining the entire four-tiered agenda as a whole, it is consistent with subsequent findings of qualitative research (see Table 1) in which teachers from a wide variety of schools were interviewed in focus groups (Bradley & West, 1994).

Findings with regard to both exemplary practices (Joyce & Showers, 1995) and teachers (Bradley & West 1994) have emphasized the importance of avoiding one-shot training experiences and making available a variety of training formats (e.g., summer institutes, graduate courses, workshops, required in-service presentations, staff meetings, one-to-one consultation and conversation, mentoring, team teaching, videotaping, coaching). Every effort was made to employ principles of effective teaching by having instructors provide expert models and structure opportunities to develop generalized skill use in actual school and community situations through clinical supervision and peer coaching (Cummings, 1985).

Personnel charged with arranging in-service opportunities also need to consider a menu of intrinsic and extrinsic incentives for encouraging participation of school and community members in training efforts. Every effort was made to highlight for staff *intrinsic* incentives such as 1) opportunity for professional and personal growth; 2) opportunity to advance knowledge and practice in the education fields; 3) increased potential for success in teaching a heterogeneous student body; 4) opportunity to experience collegiality through participation in common training; and 5) meeting expectations of members of the school and the greater community, including district leadership. *Extrinsic* motivators included 1) graduate or recertification credit; 2) salary column movement due to training; 3) remuneration for the cost of training; 4) release time for training; 5) escape to a pleasant, nurturing, nonschool environment; and 6) availability of child care during training. The key, of course, is always to *ask* teachers what it is that they individually and collectively consider rewarding (Villa & Thousand, 1990).

Table 1.   Teacher-identified training components

Program modifications
This area includes an expressed need for information for adapting curriculum and teaching more than one curricula at a time.

Working with others
This area includes collaborative methods for teaching and team building as well as communication, negotiation, and listening skills; creative problem-solving skills such as brainstorming were identified as priority needs.

Impact on students
This area includes gaining information about the effects of inclusion on students with and without disabilities and strategies for preparing students without disabilities to welcome and be meaningful, helping partners to new students with disabilities.

Parent involvement
This area involves communication with parents about the general education program and inclusive practices.

Knowledge of specific disabilities
This area includes an overview of the various types of disabilities of students whom they might encounter as well as specific training, as needed, for working with a student with a particular disability.

Attitudes of educator
This area involves formats to discuss and be listened to about feelings regarding the topic of inclusion. It also includes some direction in establishing a philosophy of inclusion.

Expectations for included students
This area concerns role clarification for adults and peers regarding responsibilities, including methods for becoming knowledgeable about and for accomplishing individualized education program goals through the existing curriculum.

Background of inclusion
This area involves context setting—familiarizing educators with the rationale for and history of the inclusion movement. It also involves the exploration of definitions of *inclusion* and policies and procedures of the school district to promote inclusion.

Approach #2: Promoting Inclusion in a Metropolitan School District

Across the United States, a number of urban school districts have been identified as being out of compliance with the least restrictive environment (LRE) mandates of IDEA (Lipsky & Gartner, 1997). In order to bring these districts into compliance, new collaborative relationships among central office, local school-site personnel, parents, community members, and students must be established (Falvey & Villa, 1997).

Because school personnel are being asked to implement practices that are new to them, they have to be involved as recipients (and designers and evaluators) of a comprehensive and ongoing professional development program that will provide them with the requisite knowledge and skills to educate students with and without identified disabilities and enable them to change their roles in accordance with new expectations (e.g., team planning and teaching of formerly segregated general and special educators).

The tiers of training, the variety of training formats, and the menu of incentives described in the previous gearing-up example served as a blueprint for one metropolitan school district training agenda for helping schools come into compliance with the LRE mandates of federal law (Falvey & Villa, 1997). What follows is not a four-tier model, but a proposed five-tier training model for building community, teacher, and leadership capacity to create and sustain more inclusive education options for a great many more students.

Tier I: Awareness Level Training   In order for personnel to comply with LRE mandates, they must receive training in LRE legal requirements and implementation practices. Content of LRE awareness level training at a minimum includes the following topics:

- Definition of LRE
- LRE legal requirements
- History and evolution of special education service delivery models
- Rationale for LRE
- Recommended practices in LRE implementation
- Roles and responsibilities in implementing LRE
- Models for adult collaboration
- Case studies and examples of educating children with disabilities successfully in the LRE
- Relationship of special education recommended practices to general education school reform initiatives
- System change strategies
- Characteristics of school cultures that welcome, value, and support the learning of students with various abilities
- Strategies for developing a community of learners and peer supports

Avenues for increasing general community and district personnel awareness about LRE mandates and practices include public meetings, television interviews and public service announcements, and periodic newsletters providing district updates regarding IDEA and LRE. All individuals who instruct children and their supervisors (i.e., school board members, administrators, psychologists, teachers, related-services personnel, instruction assistants, other certificated and classified administrative and instruction personnel) would need to participate in more formal workshops or seminars addressing the previous topics.

Tier II: Ongoing Practitioner Training   Clearly, any training agenda that a school community settles on needs to extend across several years to ensure that instruction personnel have the opportunity to progress from acquisition to mastery of the new skills and practices. Modeling and mentoring also are essential to support and reinforce the new skills that have been learned.

After educators have been sensitized to the LRE issues offered through Tier I training, they are better prepared to self-identify what they think they need in order to be prepared to educate students with disabilities within their local school community and classrooms. This is a time when it is appropriate for all certified personnel at each school site to determine future LRE-related training needed for their particular building. Once these needs assessments have been analyzed, a design team composed of not only building principals but also interested staff, parents, university partners, professional development collaboratives in the area, and students themselves can be assembled to develop a local training plan. The training plan sequences and coordinates training within buildings as well as across a reasonable number of partner sites. The plan should provide 1) adequate instruction, models, practice, and reflective dialogue to move educators from acquisition to mastery of the instructional, assessment, discipline, organizational, and other skills that they identify as critical for implementing LRE requirements as well as 2) an authentic evaluation system (e.g., whether the training changes dispositions toward the practice and its actual implementation in the classroom).

Tier III: Training of Leadership Personnel and Support Facilitators   In a study of the LRE policy in six states, Hasazi, Johnston, Liggett, and Schattman found that "how the leadership at each school site chose to look at LRE was critical to how, or even whether, much would be accomplished beyond the status quo" (1994, p. 506). In addition, general education teachers participating in a study conducted in six states and one Canadian province identified administrative support as the most powerful predictor of a positive attitude toward inclusion (Villa, Thousand, Meyers, & Nevin, 1996). Thus, all administrators (e.g., superintendent, curriculum director, personnel director, building principals, other supervisory support personnel) need to have the opportunity to develop an understanding of, support for, and leadership in implementing LRE practices.

Furthermore, any school system that is dramatically out of compliance with IDEA or LRE requirements likely has a shortage of instruction and supervisory personnel who have the skills to serve as consultants, models, and coaches to teachers at the local building level regarding the design of more inclusive educational experiences for children with disabilities. Anyone who is selected to serve in such a support facilitator role clearly needs additional training and regular opportunities to network, problem-solve with, and learn from others with similar responsibilities.

Administrators, critical liaisons, and linchpin support personnel such as those just described have the need for more advanced leadership training in conceptual, technical, and interpersonal skills–related areas such as those suggested in Table 2 (Givner, Haagar, & Falvey, 1999; Villa, Thousand, & Chapple, 1996).

Tier IV: Model Demonstration Lighthouse Sites   There is little argument that people benefit from having examples to observe and imitate and to convince them that new practices can work. Thus, model demonstration or lighthouse sites are needed so that school personnel, parents, and students can be guided by a beacon of recommended practice through visits to and observations in the inclusive classrooms that develop at the sites. Technical assistance and training are necessary to assist selected schools to transform and become lighthouse sites. It is important that model sites be identified at preschool, elementary, middle, and high school levels so that there are demonstrations at each level of the education system. A critical element of the lighthouse training tier is that sites receive ongoing technical assistance and instruction above and beyond the Tiers II and III training that others receive. This assistance should be self-identified based on the recommended practice(s) that the school chooses to develop and model for the district (e.g., cooperative group learning, multiage grouping, a multiple intelligences–based curriculum).

Tier V: A Leadership Academy   Large-scale and complex school systems change is unlikely to be sustained unless there is a forum for schools to 1) wrestle with LRE issues *as they arise* at the building level and 2) renew through introduction to new and emerging practices supportive of inclusive education. Although school-based collaborative teams and teaming processes have proved to be essential for inventing solutions to current challenges and implementing school reform recommendations (Glickman, Gordon, & Ross-Gordon, 1998; Skrtic, 1987; Thousand & Villa, 1990; Chapter 5), another type of team experience can

Table 2.   Potential Tier III training content for administrators and support facilitators

Background and foundation
- Historical and legal aspects of students' and parents' rights, safeguards, and special education practices
- Models, theories, and philosophies that provide the basis for special education programs
- Characteristics of different disabilities and their effect on children's education, development, and quality of life
- Familiarity and experience with working with children with various disabilities

Collaboration
- Collaborative planning, teaming, and teaching
- Creative solution-finding strategies
- Collaborative and consultative skills
- Knowledge of community resources and agencies

Assessment
- Conducting appropriate assessments of students' behavior, including standardized and nonstandardized tests, observation, environmental assessment, functional analysis of behavior, family-friendly assessments, and other techniques
- Identification criteria for various disabilities

Individualization
- Development, implementation, and evaluation of individualized education programs in the least restrictive environment
- Specialized instruction styles and nontraditional teaching practices and procedures
- Implementing lesson plans that are appropriate for diverse learners and that respond to cultural, linguistic, and ability differences
- Selecting, adapting, or modifying the core curriculum to make it accessible to all students
- Instructional adaptations including alternate assignments, supplemental instruction, differential standards, and shortened assignments
- Facilitating the integration of functional skills into the core curriculum
- Transition-planning strategies

Recruiting and supervising others
- Strategies for recruiting, training, and supervising peer tutors
- Strategies for supervising instruction assistants, trainees, student teachers, and volunteers
- Facilitating social interactions and the development of social relationships and networks for students

Instruction
- Cooperative group learning
- Technology as an instruction tool and communicative device
- Strategies for increasing the participation of students with special needs in general education classroom and community environments

Classroom management
- Designing and implementing behavior management programs for individuals and groups of students
- Interpreting the communicative intent of behavior
- Training peers to mediate conflicts

(continued)

Table 2. (*continued*)

Leadership
- Current exemplary practices in special education service delivery
- The relationship between special education service delivery and general education recommended practices

Safety
- Procedures and regulations for reporting child abuse and the legal rights and responsibilities of teachers and students
- Cardiopulmonary resuscitation and first aid

assist a school to *sustain* an innovation. This experience takes the form of an annual leadership academy or institute. At such an academy, experienced teams would 1) serve as a resource to colleagues at the school site who are implementing LRE practices, 2) coordinate and evaluate planning and training initiatives at their school site, and 3) provide some of the actual training through a trainer-of-trainers model. Academy teams, composed of a heterogeneous representation of the school population (i.e., principal, a special educator, general educators, bilingual educators, an instruction assistant, a related services provider, a parent of a student without a disability, a parent of a student with a disability) would meet regularly during the year to plan and evaluate their efforts and then, periodically (at least yearly), unite at an "inclusion leadership academy," where they could jointly address concerns regarding ongoing implementation of inclusive practices as well as receive the latest updates and training.

At the time of publication of this book, this five-tiered training proposal had not been implemented beyond the first tier. The model, however, is a promising one in that it is based on previous successful models, including the one that follows. In the in-service training approach described next, systems change at the building and district levels has been supported for nearly 15 years through a leadership academy approach.

Approach #3: Statewide Summer Leadership Institutes

Since the mid-1980s, Vermont State Department of Education, university, and local school leadership have collaborated to provide summer in-service training to increase schools' capacity to be responsive inclusive communities. The effort grew out of a recognized need for training of school personnel to respond to the transition of children with intensive needs back to their home schools, which already had occurred as a state initiative. The Vermont Department of Education and other human services agencies, the University of Vermont, and local Vermont school districts collaborate to jointly plan and deliver an annual, intensive, weeklong summer leadership institute. The institute's goal is to give family, school, and community members critical knowledge and skills to accommodate the needs of students who present intense challenges. For a school team to attend the institute, it must be heterogeneous, with representation from constituency groups within the school and among community agencies (e.g., administrators, general educators, special educators, other specialists, parents, students, human services providers). Participants learn about and practice communication and small-group skills and the collaborative teaming processes described in Chapter 10 of this book.

The instruction format alternates between teamwork sessions and more formal instruction by parents, students, administrators, teachers, related-services personnel, and instruction assistants from schools with experience in creating inclusion-oriented educational opportunities. Each team has an assigned facilitator who answers technical questions, guides teamwork, and observes and processes the team's effectiveness in collaborating and managing conflict. By the week's end, each team has developed a comprehensive action plan for delivering support to a targeted student and/or meeting a challenge to inclusive education in their school.

An overarching objective of the institute is to create a sense of group cohesion and build a common conceptual framework and language among team members so that they will be better able to support one another in transferring their newly acquired knowledge and skills to colleagues in their home schools when school resumes. This collaborative trainer-of-trainers in-service model has been highly successful in promoting and sustaining systems change in support of inclusive education practices and has been replicated in many states and communities across North America.

Approach #4: Regional Training for School Restructuring in Ohio

Since 1991, the Ohio State Department of Education has afforded local school districts the opportunity to design and implement alternative service delivery models for meeting the needs of children who are eligible for special education. Each district selected for participation had a choice of trying one of four experimental service delivery models that were exceptions to the Ohio standards for educating children with special needs. The outcomes of these model demonstration projects were examined as part of the process of developing new state standards for serving students who are eligible for special education.

In Model I, special and general educators jointly served students with and without disabilities in the general education classroom full time through a team teaching model. In Model I, the primary curriculum used for all children was the general education curriculum. In Model II, special educators worked with children eligible for special education and at-risk students in special classes or learning centers. In Model III, special educators served special education eligible students cross-categorically in special classes or in learning centers. In Model IV, a team determined the most appropriate way to meet individual students' needs, and special educators supported students in a variety of fashions (e.g., team teaching, consultation, providing modified materials to the teacher, small-group instruction). In Model IV, teachers could instruct all students in the same curriculum or use multilevel, overlapping, or alternative curriculum (Giangreco & Meyer, 1988). Models I and IV were the most inclusive models and the ones that were selected by most districts.

In-service education was provided to initial and subsequent Model I and IV personnel and took a variety of forms. First, university and special education regional resource center (SERRC) staff were available to provide technical assistance and training upon request at any time during the school year. In addition, SERRCs provided leadership teams from Models I and IV sites in their region with specific training in collaboration and creative problem solving. Each leadership team was composed of five people: a building administrator, a special educator, a general educator, a parent of a child with disabilities, and a fifth member who could be an additional general or special educator, a speech-language pathologist, a school psychologist, an instruction assistant, or a guidance counselor. Teams participated in intensive training opportunities with ongoing support, during the initial year and in subsequent years if desired. All training formats required each team to develop an action plan for creating a more inclusive school. Incentives for people to participate were continuing education units and a team stipend to be used to purchase materials, pay for substitutes or future workshop participation, throw a team celebration, or whatever the team deemed important.

To determine the viability and success of each model, data were collected at the end of the first and second years of the project's initiation and compared with the same outcomes measured at the end of the preintervention year (Chapple, 1994; Ohio Department of Education, Division of Special Education, 1993). Quantitative student data included the percentage of academic and social individualized education program (IEP) objectives accomplished and reading and mathematics scores. Results showed that students in every disability category served through Models I and IV achieved higher percentages of academic and social IEP objectives at the end of the 2 experimental years as compared with preintervention year-end results. The greatest gains were made by students with multiple disabilities. Qualitative data were collected largely on site through interviews with parents, teachers, and administrators. Analysis of the data revealed increases in positive comments about the benefits of inclusive education on the part of teachers, parents, and administrators. Parents emphasized that their children had learned more, felt better about themselves, and were able to make and keep new friends. In addition to collecting data on student outcomes, a major purpose of the study was to solicit from the innovators their perception of training needed to successfully apply alternative service delivery approaches. Overwhelmingly, teachers recognized staff development as critical to their success in this venture and noted that much of what they needed had not been a part of their preservice training program. The content areas that emerged as the highest priority were collaboration, cooperative learning, team teaching, problem solving, and decision making. Participants believed that they should have received training in these areas before implementation of the program and that they should have been involved in every step of planning from the start of the initiative.

As of mid-1999, the Ohio State Department of Education was using this training structure to promote other school restructuring initiatives for improving education for all students (e.g., prereferral intervention-based assessments, classroom management, SchoolNet Internet access). Further recognizing that all of these initiatives shared a common set of skills, the state department expanded the training content to go beyond issues of inclusive schooling and focus on the core competencies of collaboration, creative problem solving, and teaching and learning for diverse learners. Through this expanded concept of providing integrated training, these opportunities and ongoing support will assist educators in meeting the needs of all children.

CONCLUSIONS: PROFESSIONAL PREPARATION AS A TRIANGLE OF RESPONSIBILITY

In order for inclusive classrooms and schools to become the norm rather than the exception, the barriers to adequate teacher preparation must be addressed. As Villa (1998) noted at the 1997 Annual Conference Inclusion Roundtable of The Association for Persons with Severe Handicaps, responsibility needs to be assumed on at least three levels that may be conceptualized as a triangle of responsibility. First, at the preservice teacher preparation level, institutions of higher education must provide curriculum, instruction, and practicum experiences that empower graduates to have the skills and dispositions to educate an increasingly diverse student population. Second, at the in-service level, school organizations must provide all personnel working in school districts with ongoing, meaningful staff development opportunities that build incumbent staff's capacity in implementing current and emergent recommended practices in inclusive education. Third, at the personal and professional levels, each individual involved in schooling must model the disposition of lifelong learning that we desire our students in public schools to adopt by actually seeking out resources, current information, and support to meet the needs of his or her changing job responsibilities (Villa, 1998).

The creation of inclusive schools and classrooms is dependent on the development of a new collaborative relationship among educators, local education agencies, school districts, and training institutions. Model preservice and in-service programs can be developed. This requires, however, the coordinated actions of local school, higher education, teacher associations, and state department of education personnel. Working together in all aspects of systems change, people concerned with school reform can successfully 1) identify the most meaningful and helpful training content, formats, and incentives; 2) develop successful demonstration sites; 3) provide ongoing training and supervision in school situations; and 4) conduct research that answers questions and, probably more important, helps us discover the questions to ask next (Villa, 1989).

REFERENCES

Americans with Disabilities Act (ADA) of 1990, PL 101-336, 42 U.S.C. §§ 12101 *et seq.*

Bassett, D., Jackson, L., Ferrell, K., Luckner, J., Hagerty, P., Bunsen, T., & MacIssac, D. (1996). Multiple perspectives on inclusive education: Reflections of a university faculty. *Teacher Education and Special Education, 19,* 355–386.

Becker, W.C. (1986). *Applied psychology for teachers: A behavioral cognitive approach.* Chicago: Science Research Associates.

Block, J.H., & Anderson, L.W. (1975). *Mastery learning in classroom instruction.* New York: Macmillan.

Block, J.H., Efthim, H.E., & Burns, R.B. (1989). *Building effective mastery learning schools.* Reading, MA: Addison Wesley Longman.

Bradley, D.F., & West, J.F. (1994). Staff training for the inclusion of students with disabilities: Visions from school-based educators. *Teacher Education and Special Education, 17,* 117–126.

Brandt, R. (Ed.). (1994). *Educational Leadership, 51*(7) [Entire issue].

Brendtro, L., Brokenleg, M., & Van Bockern, S. (1990). *Reclaiming youth at risk: Our hope for the future*. Bloomington, IN: National Education Service.

Campbell, S., Campbell, S., Collicott, J., Perner, D., & Stone, J. (1988). Individualized instruction. *Education New Brunswick: Journal of Education, 3*, 17–20.

Chapple, J.W. (1994, October). *Data demonstrates inclusion works in Ohio.* Paper presented at the Common Goals: Effective Practice and Preparation for the 21st Century Conference. Fourth International Conference on Mental Retardation and Developmental Disabilities, Arlington Heights, IL.

Council for Exceptional Children (CEC). (1996). *Core competencies for special educators.* Reston, VA: Author.

Cross, G., & Villa, R.A. (1992). The Winooski school system: An evolutionary perspective of a school restructuring for diversity. In R.A. Villa, J.S. Thousand, W.C. Stainback, & S.B. Stainback (Eds.), *Restructuring for caring and effective education: An administrative guide to creating heterogeneous schools* (1st ed., pp. 219–237). Baltimore: Paul H. Brookes Publishing Co.

Cummings, C. (1985). *Peering in on peers: Coaching teachers.* Edmonds, WA: Teaching Inc.

Curwin, R., & Mendler, A. (1988). *Discipline with dignity.* Alexandria, VA: Association for Supervision and Curriculum Development.

Darling-Hammond, L. (1997). *What matters most: A competent teacher for every child* [World Wide Web site]. Available at http://www.kiva.net/~pdkintl/darling.html

Davidson, N. (1994). Cooperative and collaborative learning: An integrative perspective. In J.S. Thousand, R.A. Villa, & A.I. Nevin (Eds.), *Creativity and collaborative learning: A practical guide to empowering students and teachers* (pp. 13–30). Baltimore: Paul H. Brookes Publishing Co.

Deno, S.L. (1985). Curriculum-based measurement: The emerging alternative. *Exceptional Children, 52*, 219–232.

Dutton, D.H., & Dutton, D.L. (1990). Technology to support diverse needs in regular classes. In W.C. Stainback & S.B. Stainback (Eds.), *Support networks for inclusive schooling: Interdependent integrated education* (pp. 167–183). Baltimore: Paul H. Brookes Publishing Co.

Elias, M.J., & Clabby, J.F. (1992). *Building social problem-solving skills: Guidelines from a school-based program.* San Francisco: Jossey-Bass.

Falvey, M.A., & Villa, R.A. (1997, December). *Chanda Smith Consent Decree as a Result of a Class Action Lawsuit Against L.A. Schools.* Paper presented at The Association for Persons with Severe Handicaps conference, Boston.

Fox, T.J., & Williams, W. (1991). *Implementing best practices for all students in their local school: Inclusion for all students through family and community involvement, collaboration, and the use of school planning teams and individual student planning teams.* Burlington: Center for Developmental Disabilities, University of Vermont.

Giangreco, M.F., Cloninger, C.J., & Iverson, V.S. (1998). *Choosing outcomes and accommodations for children (COACH): A guide to educational planning for students with disabilities* (2nd ed.). Baltimore: Paul H. Brookes Publishing Co.

Giangreco, M.F., & Meyer, L.H. (1988). Expanding service delivery options in regular schools and classes for students with disabilities. In J.L. Graden, J.E. Zins, & M.J. Curtis (Eds.), *Alternative educational delivery systems: Enhancing instructional options for all students* (pp. 241–267). Washington, DC: National Association of School Psychologists.

Givner, C., Haagar, D., & Falvey, M.A. (1999). *Competencies for inclusion facilitators.* Manuscript in preparation. (Available from Mary A. Falvey, California State University, 5151 State University Drive, Los Angeles, CA 90032.)

Glasser, W. (1998). *Choice theory in the classroom* (Rev. ed.). New York: HarperPerennial.

Glickman, C.D., Gordon, S.P., & Ross-Gordon, J.M. (1998). *Supervision of instruction: A developmental approach* (4th ed.). Needham Heights, MA: Allyn & Bacon.

Goals 2000: Educate America Act of 1994, PL 103-227, 20 U.S.C. §§ 5801 *et seq.*

Goldstein, A.P. (1988). *The Prepare Curriculum: Teaching prosocial competencies.* Champaign, IL: Research Press Co.

Guskey, T.R. (1997). *Implementing mastery learning* (2nd ed.). Belmont, CA: Wadsworth.

Harper, G., Maheady, L., & Mallette, B. (1994). The power of peer-mediated instruction. In J.S. Thousand, R.A. Villa, & A.I. Nevin (Eds.), *Creativity and collaborative learning: A practical guide to empowering students and teachers* (pp. 229–241). Baltimore: Paul H. Brookes Publishing Co.

Hasazi, S., Johnston, P., Liggett, A., & Schattman, R. (1994). A qualitative policy study of the least restrictive environment provision of the Individuals with Disabilities Education Act. *Exceptional Children, 60,* 491–507.

Hazel, J.S., Schumaker, J., Sherman, J., & Sheldon-Wildgen, J. (1996). *ASSET: A social skills program for adolescents* (2nd ed.). Champaign, IL: Research Press Co.

Heerman, B. (1988). *Teaching and learning with computers: A guide for college faculty and administrators.* San Francisco: Jossey-Bass.

Henry, T. (1997, November 21). Many teachers fall short on qualifications. *USA Today*, p. D1.

Idol, L., Nevin, A.I., & Paolucci-Whitcomb, P. (1999). *Collaborative consultation* (3rd ed.). Austin, TX: PRO-ED.

Individuals with Disabilities Education Act [IDEA] Amendments of 1991, PL 102-119, 20 U.S.C. §§ 1400 *et seq.*

Individuals with Disabilities Education Act (IDEA) Amendments of 1997, PL 105-17, 20 U.S.C. §§ 1400 *et seq.*

Individuals with Disabilities Education Act (IDEA) of 1990, PL 101-476, 20 U.S.C. §§ 1400 *et seq.*

Johnson, D.W., & Johnson, R.T. (1987). *A meta-analysis of cooperative, competitive, and individualistic goal structures.* Mahwah, NJ: Lawrence Erlbaum Associates.

Johnson, D.W., & Johnson, R.T. (1999). *Learning together and alone: Cooperative, competitive, and individualistic learning* (5th ed.). Needham Heights, MA: Allyn & Bacon.

Joseph P. Kennedy Jr. Foundation in collaboration with the Office of Special Education Programs, U.S. Department of Education. (1997, January). *Building partnerships: Preparing special education teachers for the 21st century.* Washington, DC: Author.

Joyce, B., & Showers, B. (1980). Improving inservice training: The message of research. *Educational Leadership, 37,* 379–385.

Joyce, B.R., & Showers, B. (1995). *Student achievement through staff development: Fundamentals of school renewal* (2nd ed.). New York: Addison Wesley Longman.

LaPlant, L., & Zane, N. (1994). Partner learning systems. In J.S. Thousand, R.A. Villa, & A.I. Nevin (Eds.), *Creativity and collaborative learning: A practical guide to empowering students and teachers* (pp. 261–273). Baltimore: Paul H. Brookes Publishing Co.

Lipsky, D.K., & Gartner, A.N. (1997). Court decisions regarding inclusive education. In D.K. Lipsky & A.N. Gartner (Eds.), *Inclusion and school reform: Transforming America's classrooms* (pp. 85–98). Baltimore: Paul H. Brookes Publishing Co.

Lyon, G.R., Vaassen, M., & Toomey, F. (1989). Teachers' perceptions of their undergraduate and graduate preparation. *Teacher Education and Special Education, 12,* 164–169.

Meyer, L.H., & Biklen, D. (1992). *Inclusive elementary and special education teacher preparation program.* Syracuse, NY: Syracuse University, Division for the Study of Teaching and Division of Special Education and Rehabilitation.

Ohio Department of Education, Division of Special Education. (1993). *Highlights in Special Education, 14,* 2–3.

Perrone, V. (1991). *Expanding student assessment.* Alexandria, VA: Association for Supervision and Curriculum Development.

Sarason, S.B. (1982). *The culture of the school and the problem of change* (2nd ed.). Needham Heights, MA: Allyn & Bacon.

Schrumpf, F. (1994). The role of students in resolving conflicts. In J.S. Thousand, R.A. Villa, & A.I. Nevin (Eds.), *Creativity and collaborative learning: A practical guide to empowering students and teachers* (pp. 275–291). Baltimore: Paul H. Brookes Publishing Co.

Skrtic, T.M. (1987). An organizational analysis of special education reform. *Counterpoint, 8*(2), 15–19.

Smith, D.D., & Luckasson, R.L. (1995). *Introduction to special education: Teaching in an age of challenge* (2nd ed.). Needham Heights, MA: Allyn & Bacon.

Spady, W., & Marshall, K. (1991). Beyond traditional outcome-based education. *Educational Leadership, 49*(2), 67–72.

Stainback, S.B., & Stainback, W.C. (1989). Facilitating merger through personnel preparation. In S.B. Stainback, W.C. Stainback, & M. Forest (Eds.), *Educating all students in the mainstream of regular education* (pp. 139–150). Baltimore: Paul H. Brookes Publishing Co.

Thornburg, D.D. (1992). *Edutrends 2010: Restructuring, technology, and the future of education.* San Carlos, CA: Starsong Publications.

Thousand, J.S., Fox, T., Reid, R., Godek, J., Williams, W., & Fox, W. (1986). *The homecoming model: Educating students who present intensive educational challenges within regular education environments* (Monograph no. 7-1). Burlington: University of Vermont, Center for Developmental Disabilities.

Thousand, J.S., & Villa, R.A. (1990). Sharing expertise and responsibilities through teaching teams. In W.C. Stainback & S.B. Stainback (Eds.), *Support networks for inclusive schooling: Integrated interdependent education* (pp. 151–166). Baltimore: Paul H. Brookes Publishing Co.

Thousand, J.S., Villa, R.A. (1992). Sharing expertise and responsibilities through teaching teams. In W.C. Stainback & S.B. Stainback (Eds.), *Support networks for inclusive schooling: Interdependent integrated education* (pp. 151–166). Baltiimore: Paul H. Brookes Publishing Co.

Thousand, J.S., Villa, R.A., Paolucci-Whitcomb, P., & Nevin, A.I. (1996). A rationale for collaborative consultation. In S.B. Stainback & W.C. Stainback (Eds.), *Controversial issues confronting special education: Divergent perspectives* (2nd ed., pp. 223–232). Needham Heights, MA: Allyn & Bacon.

Udvari-Solner, A. (1994). A decision-making model for curricular adaptations in cooperative groups. In J.S. Thousand, R.A. Villa, & A.I. Nevin (Eds.), *Creativity and collaborative learning: A practical guide to empowering students and teachers* (pp. 59–77). Baltimore: Paul H. Brookes Publishing Co.

Vernon, A. (1989). *Thinking, feeling, behaving: An emotional education curriculum for children: Grades 1–6; Grades 7–12* (2 vols.). Champaign, IL: Research Press Co.

Villa, R.A. (1989). Model public school inservice programs: Do they exist? *Teacher Education and Special Education, 12,* 173–176.

Villa, R.A. (1998, March). 1997 TASH annual conference: Inclusion roundtable. *TASH Newsletter, 24*(3), 15–17.

Villa, R.A., & Thousand, J.S. (1990). Administrative supports to promote inclusive schooling. In W. Stainback & S. Stainback (Eds.), *Support networks for inclusive schooling: Integrated interdependent education* (pp. 201–218). Baltimore: Paul H. Brookes Publishing Co.

Villa, R.A., Thousand, J.S., & Chapple, J.W. (1996). Preparing teachers to support inclusion: Preservice and inservice programs. *Theory into Practice, 35*(1), 42–50.

Villa, R.A., Thousand, J.S., Meyers, H., & Nevin, A.I. (1996). Teacher and administrator perceptions of heterogeneous education. *Exceptional Children, 63*(1), 29–45.

Villa, R.A., Thousand, J.S., Nevin, A.I., & Malgeri, C. (1996). Instilling collaboration for inclusive schooling as a way of doing business in public education. *Remedial and Special Education, 17*(3), 169–181.

Webb, N. (1994). Special education: With new court decisions backing them, advocates see inclusion as a question of values. *Harvard Education Letter, 10*(4), 1–3.

Wood, J.W. (1998). *Adapting instruction to accommodate students in inclusive* settings (3rd ed.). Upper Saddle River, NJ: Merrill.

Ysseldyke, J.E., & Christenson, S.L. (1987). *The Instructional Environment Scale: A comprehensive methodology for assessing an individual student's instruction.* Austin, TX: PRO-ED.

Chapter 21

From Normalization to Enrichment

A Retrospective Analysis of the
Transformation of Special Education Principles

Edvard Befring,
Jacqueline S. Thousand, and Ann I. Nevin

A critical challenge for the special education field involves society's responses to diversity. Originally proposed by Van der Klift and Kunc (1994) and further elaborated in Chapter 6 of this book, these responses can be categorized as *marginalization, reform, tolerance,* and *valuing.* These four responses to diversity may be useful in understanding the transformation of the principles that undergird special education practices.

Principles of segregation of students with special needs into separate institutions related to the first response, marginalization, can be traced back to antiquity. *Marginalization* refers to those responses that help a society avoid, segregate, or put an end to people who are different from the majority of its members. *Reform* responses can be found in the remedial, therapeutic, and life-skills programs that were intended to help students with special needs become "rehabilitated." Principles related to the reform response include notions such as special classes within a general school. Principles related to *tolerance* responses include training-based models of special education, wherein general educators are taught to be more tolerant of children with disabilities as well as to become more skilled in meeting these students' instruction needs. These responses contributed to the temporal integration of students with and without disabilities but did not necessarily advance the social acceptance of people who vary from the majority in the dominant culture of a society. Principles related to *valuing* responses include the enrichment perspective (Befring, 1997a), a strengths-based alternative to an impairment-based medical diagnostic approach of assessing, designing, implementing, and evaluating supports and services for students with disabilities that are described and illustrated in the section of this chapter entitled "Enrichment Perspective: A New Perspective for Moving Beyond Integration to Inclusion."

What follows is an international historical overview that is intended to set the context for understanding the principles that guide contemporary special education practices. The chapter traces history of the first special schools, established in the late 17th century, which reflected egalitarian democratic and social justice ideals, through the reform efforts of the 1950s and 1960s, which brought to light the essentially segregated and marginalized nature of these efforts. The reform efforts themselves, based on notions of rehabilitation, though enlightened for their times, came to be perceived as attempts to change the essential nature of people with disabilities. The more enlightened views of tolerance that brought students into general education classes, without necessarily changing the nature of the environment or the supports available for educators, resulted in many injustices to children with disabilities. Within a climate of social justice and worldwide appreciation of the education of students with disabilities as represented by the United Nations' Salamanca Statement (UNESCO [United Nations Educational, Scientific, and Cultural Orgainization], 1994), the notions of valuing children with disabilities become possible.

FIRST SPECIAL SCHOOLS

In a European context, the first practical teaching initiatives for students with disabilities were instituted during the late 1700s. Prior to that era, the prevailing view was that a person's disability was the result of the power of fate and that consequently remedial measures were superfluous. Inspired by the Age of Enlightenment and by the philosophy of equality that triggered the French Revolution, people with disabilities came to be seen in a new light. The first education institutions were established in France, Switzerland, and Germany to provide children with sensory impairments (deafness and/or blindness) and dual sensory impairments with instruction to improve their chances of joining society.

The first academic initiative for deaf children took place in 1770 in Paris. Until that time, deafness had been associated with intellectual disabilities because deaf individuals did not speak (and thus were described as being "dumb"). During the Renaissance, however, the learned class recognized that speech difficulties often were associated with hearing problems and that neither intellectual nor emotional shortcomings were related to deafness. Nearly 40 years passed before another country replicated the French educational approach. Scandinavian countries were the first to follow France's lead. In 1807, Sweden established an institute for the deaf. Denmark introduced compulsory school attendance for the deaf in 1817. In Norway, the first public institution for the "deaf and dumb" was established in 1825. Across the Atlantic, in the new nation of the United States of America, Benjamin Rush first introduced the idea of teaching people with sensory disabilities in the late 1700s, and in 1817, in Connecticut, Thomas Gallaudet established the American Asylum for the Education and Instruction of the Deaf and Dumb.

The first teaching initiative for children who were socially disadvantaged was established in Norway in 1841. This was a so-called welfare home for children of school age who were socially neglected. The Norwegian welfare home arose out of the social and criminal prevention wave that swept over Europe during the second half of the 1700s. One of the common slogans of the time that welfare home proponents in Norway used was: "Rescue poor, forsaken children; rescue souls; cheat the gallows and the penitentiary out of as many potential inmates as possible" (*Asyl-og Skoletidende [Kindergarten and School Journal]*, 1841, p. 71). The welfare homes often were located on farms in rural areas, based on the assumption that living and working in harmony with the forces of nature, with plants and animals, is best for maintaining the equilibrium of the body and soul. This educational or learning perspective provided inspiration for the Scandinavian development of schools for students with emotional and social problems.

In 1779, in the United States, future President Thomas Jefferson proposed state-supported schools to help educate the children of Virginia who were poor and socially disadvantaged. Unfortunately, this did not become a reality until the late 1880s, when Horace Mann helped persuade the rich to back state-supported schools to Americanize the masses of European immigrants.

Even though individuals with visual impairments had the power of speech, they, too, were marginalized. The first school for children who were blind opened its doors in Paris in 1784, basing its approach on the prevailing educational philosophy of the time that these children needed to develop dexterity and sensitive fingertips to compensate for their lack of vision. In Scandinavia, the first schools for children who were blind were established in the early 1800s (1806 in Sweden, 1811 in Denmark, and 1861 in Norway). In the United States, the New England Asylum for the Education of the Blind was opened in 1829 in Watertown, Massachusetts.

For children with developmental delays or mental retardation, the past casts long shadows. Notions that the disabilities of these children were a result of defective parentage led to compulsory sterilization, and the concept of uneducability emerged and unfortunately survives in some places today. In Paris, the ground-breaking efforts of Eduard Seguin led to his establishment in 1838 of the first school for the weak performers and outcasts. Seguin was strongly influenced by the *democratic ideals* of the French Revolution. He stressed that children should develop their emotional life, their practical skills, and their reasoning skills. Moreover, their educational experiences should be interesting, functionally relevant, and adapted to each child's distinctiveness. When a political reaction to his views became uncomfortable, Seguin emigrated to the United States, where he carried on his work as an early leader in special education, both in theory and in practice.

Other efforts in Scandinavia and the United States on behalf of children who were labeled as having mental retardation laid the foundations for special education as it is known at the turn of the 21st century. In Norway, Johan Anton Lippestad established the first remedial class in 1874 and subsequently, in 1875, a school for students with mental retardation. Similarly, in the United States, the Experiential School for Teaching and Training Idiotic Children was established in 1846 in Barre, Massachusetts. In the 1850s, also in the United States, Samuel Howe advocated for the education of all children, an idea that took literally another 125 years to emerge as a mandate in the form of the Education for All Handicapped Children Act of 1975 (PL 94-142).

This brief historical overview of European and American practices shows how Western societies have treated people in the classical categories related to sensory, socioeconomic, and cognitive challenges. It is interesting to note that the pioneering efforts just described were initiated by individuals who represented disparate religious, secular, and socialistic and social-democratic ideals and whose collective actions shaped a number of fundamental concepts about caring for and educating children that led to a philosophy and practice of inclusive education and community. A pedagogical environment that excluded those who were the most needy was no longer acceptable.

TOWARD PRINCIPLES AND PRACTICES OF INCLUSIVE EDUCATION

This section describes historical efforts through the late 20th century to implement principles and practices of inclusive education in Norway, the United States, and other Western countries.

Norwegian Experience

In 1881, the Norwegian Parliament passed the first Norwegian law concerned with special education. The Act Concerning the Education of Abnormal Children (cited in Befring, 1994, pp. 257–258) first addressed education for deaf children who were blind and experienced cognitive challenges. In 1896, the Child Welfare Act (as cited in Befring, 1994, p. 258) was passed, which instituted the municipal Child Welfare Council, the world's first child protection system. The Act further paved the way for the establishment of special "school homes" for children and young people who presented behavioral challenges. The establishment of school homes transferred to the school system responsibility for juvenile delinquency, a responsibility that previously had been that of the criminal justice system.

The 1951 Special Schools Act formally established state-run schools for children with hearing, vision, and speech impairments; children with mental retardation; and children with adjustment problems. Although there had long existed various kinds of remedial classes in the Norwegian public schools, it was the 1955 amendment to the Public School Act that mandated that municipal governments provide remedial instruction for all students who needed such support. This stimulated the development of special education services within public schools and the urgent need for trained professionals, which led to the establishment in 1961 of the Norwegian Postgraduate College of Special Education (since renamed the Institute for Special Education) at the University of Oslo.

During the 1960s, the universal elementary and lower secondary educational system for all children took precedence. This interrupted the planned expansion of the separate special education system, which would have increased the number of children served by special schools from 2,500 to 8,000 children. An examination of special education practices precipitated a debate about inclusion and set the stage for the 1975 legislation that emphasized the inclusion of all children in education.

Notably, in the same year, similar legislation, PL 94-142 was enacted in the United States.

In the 1970s, school policy regarding special education took new directions. The principles of inclusion and normalization led to the abolition of special legislation and special administrative systems for special education. Children with and without disabilities were to be governed by the same laws and the same school administration. Further development of special schools (which was on the rise in the 1800s) was halted. All children were viewed as having an unalienable right to belong to the social network of their local school. This meant that socially separating some pupils into special institutions was to be the exception rather than the rule and that educators were responsible for accommodating children's learning differences. With the 1975 legislation, it was the responsibility of educators to safeguard pupils' rights "to be taught in accordance with their abilities and their capacity for learning" (¶ 7.1). The abolition of the notion that there were those who were not educable or teachable was a milestone not just for special education but for education in general.

U.S. Experience

In the United States, a parallel history to Norway's can be traced with regard to special education and inclusion. Even with the passage of compulsory attendance laws in the early 1890s, many American children with disabilities continued to be excluded from public schools. Special classes and special day schools (as distinguished from residential schools) gained momentum. When, in the 1950s, special classes in public schools gained popularity as a preferred education delivery system for most students with mild disabilities, there remained an expectation that certain children with moderate and severe disabilities would continue to be educated in residential environments. An unexpected motivational source for change came from the Civil Rights movement. When in 1954 the U.S. Supreme Court ruled that "separate is not equal" in the landmark *Brown v. Board of Education* decision, questions about the exclusionary policies towards African Americans and other racial and ethnic minorities were generalized to children with disabilities. Major challenges to the practice of segregating students with disabilities were advanced by advocacy groups such as the national Association for Retarded Citizens (since renamed The Arc of the United States: A National Organization on Mental Retardation) as well as by special educational researchers like Blatt (1970) and Dunn (1968), who questioned not only the moral principles of segregation but also the efficacy in terms of humane treatment and human learning outcomes. In this context, new principles emerged, such as Lilly's

(1970) notion of special education as a training-based model whereby special educators trained and supported classroom teachers rather than being the sole teachers of children identified as having special needs. The cascade of services theoretically suggested by Reynolds (1962) and empirically validated for Minneapolis schoolchildren by Deno (1970) replaced the separate schooling model of special education. The cascade described a continuum of placements and supports ranging from consultative support within general education classrooms to more separate options such as separate class or institutional placements. The normalization principle, the principle that all individuals have a right to normalized life experiences (including schooling) suggested by Wolfensberger and Nirje (1972) and Wolfensberger (1998), took hold. These principles, along with the Civil Rights movement, provided an impetus for a critical examination of past principles and the development of new principles and practices.

The concept of providing instruction in the least restrictive environment (LRE) is anchored in the continuum or cascade of services model, which historically has been viewed as a series of places for delivering special education (e.g., institution, special school, special class) rather than as a set of supports or educational interventions. PL 94-142 and its subsequent amendments and reauthorizations (the Individuals with Disabilities Education Act [IDEA] of 1990 [PL 101-476], the Individuals with Disabilities Education Act [IDEA] Amendments of 1991 [PL 102-119], and the Individuals with Disabilities Education Act [IDEA] Amendments of 1997 [PL 105-17]) legalized the LRE requirement to protect the civil rights of children with disabilities to receive their education in the same environment as their peers without disabilities. Unfortunately, the LRE human rights concept was transformed into a kind of instructional "decision tree" similar to the cascade of services and was used to sort children. Some people in fact invoked the cascade of services to justify the continued segregation of students with certain disabilities (e.g., emotional and behavioral challenges, severe disabilities). The instructional cascade that Reynolds (1977) suggested did much to advance the idea that specialists can modify and adapt the more normalized general classroom environments to ensure that the civil rights of the child were not violated; that is, to ensure that the child could remain with his or her classmates.

International Experience

From the mid-1960s, the movement toward inclusive educational opportunity received a substantial ideological and political boost from international organizations. For example, in 1966, Article 13 of the

United Nations (UN) Convention on Economic, Social and Cultural Rights established everyone's right to an education as a fundamental precondition to human development and as a basis for human dignity. Notably, the convention's articles are binding international law, which all countries must observe. The convention promoted the idea that everyone, regardless of perceived learning potentials, has the right to an education (UN Convention, 1966, Article 13, ¶ 2a). The UN further recognized the rights of individuals with disabilities by declaring 1981 as the International Year of Disabled Persons and promoting full participation and equality.

International law and resolutions alone do not create local change. Social reform on the local level also needs to occur. The European Center for Education Research and Innovation acknowledged that "high quality education for all involves more than developing policies for the educational system alone. . . . It includes also a concern with the wider social environment" (Evans, 1995, p. 4). This observation is echoed by UNESCO's Salamanca Statement and Framework for Action on Special Needs Education:

> While inclusive schools provide a favorable setting for achieving equal opportunity and full participation, their success requires a concerted effort, not only by teachers and school staff, but also by peers, parents, families, and volunteers. The reform of social institutions is not only a technical task; it depends, above all,, upon the conviction, commitment and good will of the individuals who constitute society. (1994, p. 11)

Both of the preceding statements recognize the importance of building public awareness of the benefits of education for individuals with disabilities and the importance of forwarding an educational perspective that simultaneously appeals to the public, clarifies the benefits in the education of children with and without disabilities, and supports the education of children with disabilities within their own community's schools.

GAPS BETWEEN PRINCIPLES AND PRACTICE

Special education is concerned primarily with crafting individual adaptations and providing individualized support and compensatory aids for individual children. Special education, however, also operates within a context that goes beyond individual students' needs; it operates within the sociopolitical context of a school and the greater community and in conjunction with different professions, agencies, and administrative bodies (Saether, 1996). Thus, the practice of special education is influenced by other forces that can create a gap between recommended and actual practices. Two common gaps between principles and practices are in the areas of service delivery and the genuine inclusion versus the mere physical inclusion of a child in a classroom.

Service Delivery Challenges

A major societal problem that special education has uncovered is the worldwide problems related to internal coordination and interaction (i.e., collaboration) among different professions, institutions, and public human services agencies. Children with disabilities and their families often are the first to experience these problems in a tangible way. Individuals in need of services describe their experiences as follows: "We are consigned to wandering from one person to the other, telling our story of suffering, again and again, and nothing happens" (Befring, 1994, p. 281). The result is that children with disabilities and their legal guardians often are left to their own devices. It must be emphasized that this is professionally and administratively unacceptable. The principles of an instructional cascade of services (Reynolds, 1977) and a constellation of services (Nevin, Villa, & Thousand, 1992; Villa, Udis, & Thousand, 1994) suggest alternative delivery systems that bring the services to the child rather than leaving families the responsibility of seeking and coordinating services.

Genuine Inclusion versus Physical Integration

The history of special education in Norway and the United States traced earlier in this chapter point out that the 1960s and 1970s marked a new era in special education. Specifically, it became public policy (e.g., U.S. federal public law with the promulgation of PL 94-142, similar legislation in Norway) and practice for public schools to have an educational responsibility to all children and young people. Legislated rights, however, in no way ensures individualized instruction. In Norway, such individualization was achieved by a kind of "tempo differentiation," which involved adjusting the pace of a student's progress through a curriculum with little adjustment of the curriculum content or processes of instruction (Nilsen, 1993). It is noteworthy that this approach to adapting instruction so that students with special needs gain access to the core curriculum is exactly what PL 105-17, the 1997 IDEA Amendments, in the United States require.

Physical inclusion of a student on a school campus is not the same as inclusion in the social community of the classroom and the school. Befring's (1997b) analysis of student and parent personal reports and letters revealed the feelings of isolation, humiliation, and fear experienced by students who are merely physically integrated. These children and young people are at risk of experiencing indifference from educators or from professional inability to design effective individualized environments. In either case, the students' experiences can be safeguarded when professionals establish a priority to develop the will and the skill to design and redesign individualized education programs (IEPs) that attend not only to academics but also social relationships and students' emotional well-being. To fail to do so guarantees that it will be only a matter of time before a new system emerges, perhaps one with a thrust toward a return to more segregated environments.

ENRICHMENT PERSPECTIVE: A NEW PERSPECTIVE FOR MOVING BEYOND INTEGRATION TO INCLUSION

Three major principles underpin the Scandinavian welfare state. First, the community is responsible for providing a safety net for all people to use when needed (e.g., when illness or accidents occur, when one reaches old age). Second, the community is responsible for enabling each of its members to develop a rich personality and achieve his or her full potential. To achieve these ends, everyone must be afforded free access to education, recreation, and cultural events. Third, all social and health policies are based on the principle of positive discrimination—that is, the notion of giving most to those who need the most. Taken together, these three principles provide a foundation for a new perspective for guiding special education practice in the future, known in Norway as the Enrichment Perspective (Befring, 1990, 1994, 1997a).

From an Enrichment Perspective, an education system, community, or society that adapts and is responsive to the unique learning and other characteristics (e.g., language, cultural) of its members enriches everyone, students and teachers alike. In other words, the learning community (i.e., school, classroom, neighborhood) that is good for children with special education needs is a learning community that is ideal for nurturing the well-being and education of all of the other children in that community. The Enrichment Perspective directs educators to craft genuine academic, social, emotional, recreational, community, and cultural inclusion and provide whatever support is needed for each child to have schooling experiences that represent and promote quality of life.

The Enrichment Perspective departs from the prevailing impairment or medical approach of special education, in which attention is directed at assessing and identifying a student's impairments to "fix" them through appropriate applications of remediations (i.e., a remediation response to difference). It offers an alternative strengths or mastery approach based on the notions that 1) every human being has learned something that can be the foundation for learning something more, 2) future learning is based on past learning, 3) everyone has an interest or interests (e.g., music, sports, art) on which to focus their attention as a motivation for mastery, and 4) mastery and motivation go hand in hand in expanding individuals' personal competence. From this "strengths perspective" (Saleebey, 1997), the purpose of schooling and the function of special education is to recognize and build on students' strengths rather than focus on their weaknesses.

The Norwegian Enrichment Perspective is similar to the most enabling environment concept, forwarded in the United States by Witkin and Fox (1992) as a replacement for the least restrictive environment concept and language in the IDEA legislation. The most enabling environment is one that maximizes an individual's freedoms and provides the necessary support resources to achieve an individual's well-being. It is the environment—the school and the individual's school experiences—that must be analyzed and (re)designed so that each individual may achieve maximum outcomes. The Enrichment Perspective also is an expression of a constructivist and development-oriented education approach (i.e., meeting each student wherever he or she enters the learning endeavor) that is regaining international recognition and support (Udvari-Solner, 1996).

The Enrichment Perspective, including all students—with their various distinctive attributes—simultaneously creates the requisite unified social context for learning and offers the opportunity and challenge to enhance the learning context. Diversity among learners establishes a context for more diverse social interactions. Diversity forms the basis for valuing versus tolerating or remediating students' differences. The Enrichment Perspective brings into question the principles and practice of homogeneous grouping and sorting, which 1) accelerates special education diagnostic activity, 2) intensifies tendencies to establish two groups of students—the diagnosed and the yet to be examined, and 3) results in an artificially and unnaturally segregated community. Such conditions are not ones in which students can experience dignity or be prepared for adult life in a richly diverse and heterogeneous society.

Forces Countering the Enrichment Perspective

As with the vision and practice of inclusive education, resistance or countering forces to embracing the Enrichment Perspective are likely to arise (Villa & Thousand, 1995). One countering force is the predominance of competition in schooling and the notion that it is needed in the process of schooling. Competition legitimizes comparative evaluation methods and all types of tracking, stratification, and exclusive arrangements (e.g., programs for students labeled as gifted and talented). It thrives despite empirical evidence and experience that indicate the relative advantage of employing cooperative learning methods in collaborative environments (Kohn, 1992). Kohn emphasized that personal integrity and high ethical standards develop mainly through positive, collaborative social interactions and shared responsibility for one another. Integrity and ethical standards actually can be impaired if people learn to consider fellow humans primarily as rivals by constantly being encouraged to perform better than others. Competitive ethics and practices represent tremendous barriers to schools' attempting to promote an inclusive, unified schooling concept in which the Enrichment Principle can be applied.

Resistance to the Enrichment Principle might also arise out of prevailing beliefs about the ability of individuals with disabilities to learn. Recall that it once was believed that deaf individuals lacked speech because of intellectual and behavioral limitations. This belief justified their exclusion from social activity. Cardano (1501–1575), cited in Befring (1994), challenged this notion and postulated that the senses can substitute for one another; that is, when hearing fails, other senses take its place. Cardano suggested that deaf individuals need to learn to "hear by reading and to speak by writing" (quoted in Befring, 1994, p. 299), and the first schools for the deaf were based on this theory. Throughout history, negative, often superstitious notions about various disabilities justified abuses, social exclusion, and educational neglect. Such beliefs take more subtle forms but are evident in comments such as, "I don't understand why Bob is in this general education class. After all, he has multiple disabilities and can't learn anything by being here."

Educational Promise of Adopting the Enrichment Perspective

Metacognitive competence is a curriculum domain. Early in the 20th century, Maria Montessori (1870–1952) left the medical profession and made her mark in both educational theory and educational practice. She showed that children with mental retardation (who at that time were considered to be uneducable) could use their learning processes to learn how to read and write, do arithmetic, and acquire many other academic and functional life skills. Montessori became known especially for her pioneering efforts in education on behalf of children who experienced great hardship and for her creative development of self-instruction materials. She posited that all children have a built-in capacity for self-development and that such self-development requires opportunity.

The "all children as learners" perspective that characterizes the Enrichment Perspective also suggests that individuals can be the architects or facilitators of their own learning. Befring (1997a) described the construct of metacognitive competence—that is, knowing how one learns and using methods and strategies to control and promote one's own learning and knowledge. Insight into one's own learning process (the metacognitive skill) is exhibited, for example, when competent readers slow their reading rate when they encounter a difficult passage in order to give themselves extra mental processing time. They summarize what they have read, pose questions to clarify the content, interpret and consider possible connections with other subject matter, and exhibit a questioning attitude with subsequent text. Many students with learning difficulties do not seem to have acquired such metacognitive strategies through their daily early childhood experiences. So, when encouraged to keep trying, they continue to fail and eventually come to perceive themselves as unable to learn or as being less-than-able learners.

There appears to be a relationship between metacognitive competence and achievement that intensifies as students progress through the grades, suggesting that personal insight into one's own most useful learning strategies is an important factor in school success (see, e.g., Brown, 1994). It becomes the educator's responsibility, then, to assist children to develop this metacognitive self-awareness so that they may become promoters of their own learning. This can be accomplished by teachers creating opportunities for students to experience mastery of some task or concept and guiding them to identify and practice the process by which they mastered that task or concept. All educators need to develop expertise in guiding students to metacognitive awareness because students' insight and skill regarding the dimensions of their own meta-learning appears to be key to their academic success and the related psychological learning dimensions of self-confidence, self-respect, and motivation.

Role Redefinition for Students and Educators

If a school community values the differences between and within students, it follows that the educators in that school understand the need to employ a broad range of new instruction approaches, including capitalizing on students as mediators of instruction as tutors, partner learners, cooperative group members, and co-teachers with the faculty. (See Villa & Thousand, 1996, for examples of students engaged in instruction as well as advocacy and decision-making roles.) In supportive instruction roles, students with and without disabilities have the opportunity to break away from the competitive peer relationships fostered in traditional stratified schools and discover their own strengths and learning or teaching potential as they assist others to learn and be part of the school and classroom community. A research promise of adopting the Enrichment Perspective is that, through their peer teaching and support, children and youth will do as Nordic scholar Logstrup proposed: "learn to use our power in such a way that it serves our fellow humans" (1989, p. 73). The research promise is that the unified, inclusive school driven by the Enrichment Perspective will create a context in which children can learn to care about and take care of one another and that this caring will carry into adulthood, when, as citizens, these graduates of an inclusive school community will work to create more democratic conditions in which the welfare of all is the central concern.

To illustrate the potential changing role of students when the Enrichment Principle is applied, Villa (1995) described how teachers proactively involved teenagers in the design and implementation of supports and resources for Bob, a teen with multiple disabilities. In anticipation of Bob's joining their school community, classmates identified areas that they thought would make Bob feel welcome in junior high school. They agreed to take on new roles such as volunteer tutors for Bob, peer supports to travel with Bob between classes, and Bob's peer buddies in after-school co-curricular activities. When Bob moved to another town and another school, his peer support circle begged to speak with Bob's new teachers and classmates so that his transition would be facilitated. As one of Bob's teachers noted, "The attitudes and behaviors they modeled were lessons for us all about friendship and mutual respect. What they taught made the way easier for many handicapped students here" (Lewis, as quoted in Villa, 1995, p. 132). Both Bob and the members of his peer support circle benefited.

CONCLUSIONS

A major challenge for contemporary societies and their institutions (i.e., schools) is to develop ethics and practical means for valuing and including members of society who, for whatever reason, could be marginalized (e.g., segregated), reformed (e.g., rehabilitated), or tolerated (e.g., allowed to gain access) rather than valued for who they are. A fundamental challenge of special education, then, is to ensure that children with disabilities are not isolated, stigmatized, or merely tolerated. To achieve this kind of acceptance and inclusion, it is necessary to help educators, students, and community members to understand an enrichment versus impairment perspective regarding human differences. The Enrichment Perspective suggests that if the right conditions are provided for people who are vulnerable, ideal conditions are created for everybody else as well. Furthermore, the environments, experiences, and opportunities that are provided for the most vulnerable and least advantaged serve as a good indication of the overall quality of a given society or a given school.

When a school community adopts an Enrichment Perspective, there is an increased likelihood for all children and youth to experience respect for their cultural and learning differences and receive appropriate educational experiences to prepare them for adulthood and for every member of the community to live in a more dignified manner. The Enrichment Perspective holds promise for status to be given to differences and for diversity to be celebrated rather than lamented; it holds promise for the elimination of isolation and disenfranchisement of children with disabilities and other differentiating characteristics (e.g., learners of English as a second language).

Clearly, to actualize new perspectives such as the Enrichment Perspective requires self-examination and a renewal of basic professional and ethical attitudes. It requires professionals to shorten their professional distance from those they serve and put their expertise on the line for the purposes of enlightening others to the benefits of embracing an alternative to the impairment view of diversity that the Enrichment Perspective represents.

REFERENCES

Asyl-og Skoletidende [Kindergarten and School Journal]. (1841). *1*(9–10), 71.

Befring, E. (1990). Special education in Norway. *International Journal of Disability, Development, and Education, 37,* 125–136.

Befring, E. (1994). *Loering og skole [Learning and school].* Oslo: Det Norske Samlaget.

Befring, E. (1997a). The enrichment perspective: A special educational approach to an inclusive school. *Remedial and Special Education, 18*(3), 182–187.

Befring, E. (1997b). *Oppvekst og loering [Growing up and learning].* Oslo: Det Norske Samlaget.

Blatt, B. (1970). *Exodus from pandemonium: Human abuse and a reformation of public policy.* Needham Heights, MA: Allyn & Bacon.

Brown, A.L. (1994). The advancement of learning. *Educational Researcher, 8,* 4–12.

Brown v. Board of Education, 347 U.S. 483 (1954).

Deno, E. (1970). Special education as developmental capital. *Exceptional Children, 37,* 229–237.

Deno, E. (1978). *Educating children with emotional, learning, and behavior problems.* Minneapolis: University of Minnesota, Department of Psychoeducational Studies, National Support Systems Project.

Dunn, L. (1968). Special education for the mildly handicapped: Is much of it justifiable? *Exceptional Children, 35,* 5–22.

Education for All Handicapped Children Act of 1975, PL 94-142, 20 U.S.C. §§ 1400 *et seq.*

Evans, P. (1995). Conclusions and policy implications. In P. Evans (Ed.), *Our children at risk* (pp. 137–145). Paris: Organization for Economic Cooperation and Development, Centre for Educational Research and Innovation.

Individuals with Disabilities Education Act (IDEA) Amendments of 1991, PL 102-119, 20 U.S.C. §§ 1400 *et seq.*

Individuals with Disabilities Education Act (IDEA) Amendments of 1997, PL 105-17, 20 U.S.C. §§ 1400 *et seq.*

Individuals with Disabilities Education Act (IDEA) of 1990, PL 101-476, 20 U.S.C. §§ 1400 *et seq.*

Kohn, A. (1992). *No contest: The case against competition* (Rev. ed.). Boston: Houghton Mifflin.

Lilly, M.S. (1970). Special education: A teapot in a tempest. *Exceptional Children, 37,* 745–749.

Lilly, M.S. (1971). A training based model for special education. *Exceptional Children, 37,* 745–749.

Logstrup, K.E. (1989). *Den etiske forankring [The ethical foundation].* Copenhagen: Gyldendahl.

Nevin, A.I., Villa, R.A., & Thousand, J.S. (1992). An invitation to invent the extraordinary: Response to Morsink. *Remedial and Special Education, 13*(6), 44–46.

Nilsen, S. (1993). *Undervisningsttilpassing i grunnskolen [Educational adaptation in primary school].* Oslo: University of Oslo.

Reynolds, M. (1962). A framework for considering some issues in special education. *Exceptional Children, 28,* 267–270.

Reynolds, M. (1977). The instructional cascade. In A. Rehman & T. Riggen (Eds.), *Leadership series in special education: Vol. 4. The least restrictive alternative* (pp. 37–48). Minneapolis: University of Minnesota Audio-Visual Library.

Saleebey, D. (Ed.). (1997). *The strengths perspective in social work practice* (2nd ed.). Reading, MA: Addison Wesley Longman.

Saether, I.L. (1996). *Behandlingtilbudet for mennesker foedt med leppe-kjeve-ganespalte i Norge [Treatment and education for people born with lip-jaw-palate split in Norway].* Oslo: University of Oslo.

Udvari-Solner, A. (1996). Theoretical influences on the establishment of inclusive practices. *Cambridge Journal of Education, 26*(1), 101–119.

United Nations. (1966). *UN convention.* New York: Author.

United Nations Educational, Scientific, and Cultural Organization (UNESCO). (1994). *The Salamanca statement and framework for action on special needs education* (Document no. 94/WS/18). Geneva: Author.

Van der Klift, E., & Kunc, N. (1994). Beyond benevolence. In J.S. Thousand, R.A. Villa, & A.I. Nevin (Eds.), *Creativity and collaborative learning: A practical guide to empowering students and teachers* (pp. 391–401). Baltimore: Paul H. Brookes Publishing Co.

Villa, R.A. (1995). Voices of inclusion: Everything about Bob was cool, including the cookies. In R.A. Villa & J.S. Thousand (Eds.), *Creating an inclusive school* (pp. 125–135). Alexandria, VA: Association for Supervision and Curriculum Development.

Villa, R.A., & Thousand, J.S. (1995). *Creating an inclusive school.* Alexandria, VA: Association for Supervision and Curriculum Development.

Villa, R.A., & Thousand, J.S. (1996). Student collaboration: An essential for curriculum delivery in the 21st century. In S. Stainback & W. Stainback (Eds.), *Inclusion: A guide for educators* (pp. 171–191). Baltimore: Paul H. Brookes Publishing Co.

Villa, R.A., Udis, J., & Thousand, J.S. (1994). Responses for children experiencing behavioral and emotional challenges. In J.S. Thousand, R.A. Villa, & A.I. Nevin (Eds.), *Creativity and collaborative learning: A practical guide to empowering students and teachers* (pp. 369–390). Baltimore: Paul H. Brookes Publishing Co.

Witkin, S., & Fox, L. (1992). Beyond the least restrictive environment. In R.A. Villa, J.S. Thousand, W. Stainback, & S. Stainback (Eds.). *Restructuring for caring and effective education: An administrative guide to creating heterogeneous schools* (1st ed., pp. 325–334). Baltimore: Paul H. Brookes Publishing Co.

Wolfensberger, W. (1998). *A brief introduction to social role valorization: A high-order concept for addressing the plight of societally devalued people, and for structuring human services* (3rd rev. ed.). Syracuse, NY: Syracuse University, Training Institute for Human Service Planning, Leadership and Change Agentry.

Wolfensberger, W., & Nirje, B. (1972). *Normalization: The principle of normalization in human services.* Toronto: National Institute on Mental Retardation.

Chapter 22

The Universal Design for Promoting Self-Determination

Mary-Ellen Fortini and Mary FitzPatrick

Self-determination became one of the buzz words of the 1990s. It is used in the fields of special education and service delivery for people with developmental disabilities as well as in community efforts of Native Americans. As a result of its multiple uses, the term has created confusion.

WHAT IS SELF-DETERMINATION?

What is self-determination, and why is it important? Part of the confusion results from the term's different meanings at different levels. According to the *American Heritage Dictionary, self-determination* is "determination of one's own fate or course of action without compulsion; free will (1985, p. 1112). Wehmeyer (1996) stated that self-determination is the process by which an individual with or without disabilities becomes the primary causal agent for the decisions made in his or her life. Self-determination also refers to the development of skills and opportunities for people to make decisions, experience control, and have choices in their lives (Nerney & Crowley, 1995). It would seem that the development of these skills is an expected outcome for all students completing a public education. In fact, there are those who argue that the primary goal of education is to give students the skills and tools necessary for self-determination (Halloran, 1993; Wehmeyer, 1996; Wehmeyer, Agran, & Hughes, 1998).

Self-determination refers to an individual's attitudes toward and ability to make choices about his or her life. Self-determination is best thought of as a continuum. An individual may have more self-determination in some aspects of life than in others. For example, one may have control over where he or she lives but little control in the workplace. Many people assume that they have control of the decisions and choices that affect their lives. Historically, however, people with developmental disabilities have not had the experiences or the opportunities to have such control over the decisions made about their lives. The passage of the Individuals with Disabilities Education Act (IDEA) of 1990 (PL 101-476) and its amendments (IDEA Amendments of 1991 [PL 102-119], IDEA Amendments of 1997 [PL 105-17]), which require that, whenever possible, students with disabilities participate in their individualized education program (IEP), represented one step toward promoting self-determination in the school system.

Wehmeyer and colleagues (1998) discussed self-determination as an educational outcome and stated that promoting self-determination skills is a critical part of transition services. They identified four essential characteristics of self-determined behavior:

1. The person acts autonomously.
2. The person's behaviors are self-regulated.
3. The person initiates and responds to events in a psychologically empowered manner.
4. The person acts in a self-realizing manner.

Wehmeyer and colleagues also offered 10 strategies for supporting students' successful transitions to adult life in a manner that promotes self-determination. They suggested that, during students' school years, educators should focus on

1. Teaching social skills
2. Teaching self-management and independence
3. Identifying independence objectives
4. Assessing social acceptance

5. Identifying peer, family, and co-worker support

6. Identifying students' preferences and choices

7. Monitoring social acceptance over time

8. Identifying environmental support

9. Matching support to students' needs

10. Teaching choice making and decision making

Self-determined behavior leads individuals to become the causal agents in their own lives, and the education system plays a critical role in developing students' self-determined behavior.

Self-Determination and Systems Change

Quite frequently, one of the barriers to self-determination for someone with a disability is that the systems that provide support and services historically have not allowed much choice. In schools, this means that students with disabilities, particularly those with developmental disabilities, may not have the same range of choices that other students have. Adults with developmental disabilities may have limited options in the areas of housing, employment, or community services.

In addition to its definition at the individual level, the term *self-determination* is used to describe the systems changes that are occurring in the adult services delivery system to support individuals to make decisions that affect their lives (Nerney & Shumway, 1996). In this sense, the term *self-determination* refers to a process of systems change in which agencies and providers that support people with developmental disabilities become responsive to the desires and goals of the individuals whom they support. A service delivery system that supports self-determination emphasizes the role of the individual in making decisions about supports and promotes home- and community-based supports. It offers individuals and their families the maximum amount of choice, control, and flexibility in how those supports are organized and delivered. The Robert Wood Johnson Foundation has funded 19 states to promote self-determination by changing the service delivery system to become more consumer directed and to offer individuals and families more control and choices in services and supports. Largely as a result of this initiative, the term *self-determination* has become synonymous with the systems change necessary to promote individuals' self-determination skills.

Principles Underlying Systems Change

In order to support and promote self-determination, a service delivery system must be responsive to individuals' desires and needs. Beyond being responsive, systems that support self-determination are designed and function in a way that the person and the person's family and friends lead the creation of outcomes and learning. According to Nerney and Shumway (1996), the philosophical foundation for systems change is based on four principles: freedom, authority, support, and responsibility. Freedom is the ability of people with disabilities, along with freely chosen family members and friends, to plan their own lives with necessary support rather than purchase a program, which defines the services and how they are delivered. A system that supports freedom gives one the opportunity to have the option of using public dollars to build a life rather than purchase a predetermined program. In such a system, one is able to control resources through an individual budget and make decisions about the kinds of support received and who provides that support. When life situations change or as more experience and confidence in making choices are gained, people change their supports. Individuals are encouraged to dream, and, with selected people, creativity in designing the best possible arrangement of supports is inspired. Thus, the individual has a sense of freedom to succeed as well as freedom to take risks.

In a school system, freedom means that students have opportunities to dream and be active participants in the direction of their education. Students create an educational opportunity that is flexible and enhances progress toward realizing their dreams. A school system that supports freedom embraces diversity, identifies and builds on the strengths of individual students, and provides teachers with the skills necessary to respond to the needs of each child. By encouraging instruction that enhances each student's own style of learning, the school system would, in fact, make "special education the norm rather than the exception" (Goldman & Gardner, 1997, p. 371). Referral to special education is unnecessary because all students have an individualized education program that uses the experts needed. Through a promotion of freedom, every student benefits from schooling that is more personalized.

Authority refers to the ability of a person with a disability to control how funding for supports is spent. There is meaningful control over some limited amount of the money that makes supports possible. When the person with a disability needs help to control this money and plan his or her life, the individual decides who gives that help. The role of support people, who are selected by the individual, is to assist an individual to state what is really wanted and who the individual wants to provide assistance.

In education systems that have integrated the principles of self-determination into their practices, *authority* refers to the ability of students and parents to decide a course of action for each student (perhaps through IEPs) that leads the student closer to his or her vision. Students and their families have the authority to decide which classes and which teachers would benefit them most in their quest. The notion that the professional has to be in charge is changed to a shared authority in which family members and the student are the experts on the team.

Support refers to the systematic arrangement of resources and personnel—both formal and informal—that assist a person with a disability to live a life in the community that is rich in social associations and sets up conditions for the person to make meaningful contributions. This means having the help needed to plan and live a life. Such help comes from people whom the person with a disability chooses, including family and friends. As for all people, developing relationships with others in the community and becoming more involved in different aspects of the community such as work, recreation, church events, or other activities become of highest importance.

In schools, *support* refers to the ability of students and their families to use administrators; teachers; other students; and, when needed, specialists to create the optimal education experience. Education personnel focus on and enhance the strengths of each student. Support includes team-building skills, collaborative and cooperative learning opportunities, and strong relationships between the schools and the community. When behavior problems or conflicts are encountered, the process of resolution begins with the use of a problem-solving approach with the student and his or her family. For example, if John is having difficulty with completing homework assignments, the first intervention occurs when the teacher asks John why he is having difficulty with completing his homework. It may be that the work is too difficult for John or that his home situation is not conducive to completing his homework tasks. Rather than discipline John or call in his parents to discipline him, a problem-solving approach provides him with work that he can do independently or creates an environment (perhaps even during the school day) in which John has some quiet time to complete his homework, with a tutor if necessary. If that does not work, the next step in problem solving might be to work with the family to determine whether there are any problems that might affect John's ability to complete his homework. The problem-solving approach starts with the student and brings in other experts only as needed.

Responsibility includes the person holding valued roles in the community through engaging in meaningful work, belonging to organizations, developing spirituality, and being involved in genuine relationships with others. Responsibility implies accountability for spending public dollars in ways that improve the quality of life of people with disabilities. Ultimately, when individuals with disabilities have the ability to give back to the community, assume meaningful work, develop their talents and skills, and take the risks associated with the choices that they have made, the whole community's quality of life improves. Support people help individuals with disabilities make decisions that are reasonable and lead to further growth.

Students and families have similar responsibilities within the education system. There is an expectation of belonging and reciprocity. The development of choice- and decision-making skills is of utmost importance. Members of the education system create an environment in which the information, knowledge, and resources are made available to students and their families to decide what is to be learned. Following through on commitments that have been made is guaranteed.

Although the term *self-determination* is used with regard to various systems changes, what is really meant is that the system is changing in order to support and promote individuals' self-determination. Wehmeyer stated,

> The movement to support and promote self-determination is about treating people with dignity and respect. It is about enabling people with disabilities to achieve independence, integration, and inclusion to the greatest extent possible by providing them the opportunities to learn the skills they need and the chance to put those skills into action. It is about empowerment, choice, and control. (1996, p. 33)

PURPOSE OF EDUCATION

One role of the public education system is to prepare youth for their adult roles in American society. The structure of the education system is both "a reflection of society's priorities and a battleground for competing visions" (Lipsky & Gartner, 1997, p. 249). A compliant classroom environment may lead to the preparation of a compliant workforce. The significant ways in which industry and business have changed to enter the global marketplace fixes the focus on innovation, cooperation, and continuous quality improvement (Gabor, 1990; Walton, 1986). Creating new markets and new market share is vital in a world in which even the processes of manufacturing and production occur in stages, often with several countries involved in the assembly process.

To prepare all students to enter into such a diverse work environment requires a dramatically different set of skills and concepts, and an adjusted world view. A major responsibility of educators is to create an environment in which students are prepared, through cooperative educational goal structures and other strategies, to enter the worlds of work and adulthood. The design of this environment must promote the best outcomes for all students by incorporating the principles of universal design.

Principles of Universal Design

Universal design is a concept that refers to the creation and design of products and environments in such a way that they can be used without the need for modifications or specialized designs for particular circumstances. Buildings that are accessible and telecommunications devices that can be used by anyone are examples of the employment of universal designs. Designers of buildings and telecommunications devices have found that by incorporating the concepts of universal design, the market for their products is larger and thus more people use their devices. In addition, such devices cost less to produce than do the adaptations and accommodations that might otherwise need to be added to the device later.

A simple example of universal design is curb cuts. Curb cuts were designed to allow wheelchair users to gain access to sidewalks and walkways. They are relatively expensive to add to a sidewalk after the sidewalk has been laid (which was how most curb cuts were incorporated in the 20th century), yet cost almost nothing to include if sidewalks are designed that way originally. Once curb cuts are incorporated into sidewalk design, however, it is not only wheelchair users who use them: Strollers are easier to push across the curb, joggers find the strides they take from sidewalk to street less jarring to their joints, and almost everyone with and without disabilities uses the curb cut. It is thus a universal design.

Another example is the incorporation of voice recognition into computer technology. When China opened its market to computers, designers were faced with the difficult problem of the design of a keyboard that had Chinese characters. Through the use of voice technology, however, this problem was ameliorated. Voice recognition, designed as an expensive add-on for people with disabilities, is used to recognize any language. This universal design led to the opening of a previously untapped global market.

The Center for Universal Design at North Carolina State University (1995) identified seven principles of universal design, which are depicted in Table 1. These seven principles can be used to evaluate existing designs and guide the design process, although not all principles may be relevant to all designs. The authors of this chapter believe that the principles of universal design can be applied to edu-

Table 1. Guidelines for elements needed to adhere to the principles of universal design in education

Principles of universal design	Elements necessary in education
Equitable use: The design is useful and marketable to any group of users.	Provide the same access to information for all students; identical whenever possible, equivalent when not Avoid segregating or stigmatizing any students
Flexibility in use: The design accommodates a wide range of individual preferences and abilities.	Provide choice in methods of learning Accommodate multiple intelligences in presentation Provide adaptability to the student's pace
Simple and intuitive use: Use of the design is easy to understand, regardless of the user's experience, knowledge, language skills, or current concentration level.	Eliminate unnecessary complexity Be consistent with student expectations Accommodate a wide range of literacy and language skills Arrange information consistent with its importance Provide effective prompting for sequential actions Provide timely feedback during and after task completion
Perceptible information: The design communicates necessary information effectively to the user, regardless of ambient conditions or the user's sensory abilities.	Use different modes (pictorial, verbal, tactile) for redundant presentation of essential information Provide adequate contrast between essential information and other information Maximize "legibility" of essential information in all sensory modalities Differentiate elements in ways that can be described (i.e., make it easy to give instructions or directions) Provide compatibility with a variety of techniques or devises used by people with sensory limitations
Tolerance for error: The design minimizes the hazards and the adverse consequences of accidental or unintended actions.	Use errors as a means for teaching students additional skills and information Provide fail-safe features Promote risk taking in safe environments

(continued)

Table I.   (continued)

Principles of universal design	Elements necessary in education
Low physical effort: The design can be used efficiently and comfortably and with a minimum of fatigue	Create a physical environment that allows students to interact with each other and environment
	Use of ergonomic design in seating and placement of tools
	Minimize unnecessary sustained physical effort
Size and space for approach and use: Appropriate size and space are provided for approach, reach, manipulation, and use regardless of the user's body size, posture, or mobility.	Provide a clear line of sight to important elements for all students
	Make reach to all components comfortable for all students
	Accommodate variations in hand and grip size
	Provide adequate space for the use of assistive devices or personal assistance

cation systems, particularly when self-determination is included as an educational outcome for all students. Inclusive education in the broadest sense defines success as the success of all the individuals in the classroom. This concept is echoed more and more in the worlds of industry and business. Preparing children to realize success as individuals in the global village requires the inclusion of all stakeholders. At the heart of these sweeping changes is a shift to consumer-driven services in which the customer's wants or needs are of primary consideration. All efforts toward quality improvement are focused on finding out how products and changes have moved in the direction of what the customer needs and wants. Ultimately, this requires a customer who knows what he or she needs and wants.

When self-determination is a desired educational outcome, the first step is to consider the cultural and organizational changes that are necessary to truly support such a paradigm change. Many areas of life are undergoing significant changes in focus and direction. In business, government, health care, and education, there is a trend toward consumer-directed services. The application of this approach to education requires the principles of self-determination to be central in order for students to develop the skills necessary to become informed consumers.

Importance of Vision

The key building block is vision, regardless of whether one is talking about individuals' self-determination, an educational outcome, or the systems change needed to promote individuals' self-determination. Vision is emphasized in the literature on school restructuring (Thousand, Rosenberg, Bishop, & Villa, 1997), self-determination (Nerney & Shumway, 1996), leadership, and business success (Covey, Merrill, & Merrill, 1994; Gabor, 1990; Gardner, 1995; Senge, 1990). Vision means not simply how the outcome is envisioned but also what is understood about the tools needed to reach the desired outcome and the changing roles of all stakeholders to create the new structure.

In addressing the needs of students with the most severe challenges, schools have found themselves in the position of retrofitting the education process. In many other applications of retrofitting, doing so unnecessarily increases costs and wastes enormous amounts of time. The cost of special education certainly attests to this fact (Lipsky & Gartner, 1997). Inclusive education (Jorgensen, 1998; Lipsky & Gartner, 1997) and self-determination projects with adults (Conroy & Yuskauskas, 1996; Yuskauskas, Conroy, & Elks, 1997) have demonstrated that individuals are more prepared to face life's challenges when they are included in schools and communities and prepared to be the causal agents of the decisions that are made about their lives. The required changes in structure and culture of the schools and the implied changes needed for inclusion and self-determination are in fact the universal design needed to truly prepare all students to take their places in a rapidly changing work force. Part of the reason why inclusion and self-determination feel right and are so effective may be due to the universality of these concepts, and educators would do well to bring the rest of their student citizens into the goodness that has been discovered. Systems change for inclusion is needed not only to promote students' self-determination but also to truly prepare them for life.

Changing Roles

In the service delivery system, direct support staff (also known as *service providers*) have been the interface between the principles of change and the outcomes for the individuals being supported. To the extent that support people value these principles and provide opportunities for individuals to gain experiences and skills, the individuals who are supported become more self-determined. The role of service providers has changed from being the person who takes care of an individual with disabilities to one who works for the individual by providing support and connecting the individual with people and opportunities in the community. A comparable shift in roles occurs for teachers in schools that are implementing these principles. The roles of teachers change from "the sage on the stage" to "the guide on the side." Rather than being the experts who have all of the answers, teachers guide students to be their own problem solvers and the decision makers in their own lives.

Similarly, the role of service coordinators (sometimes called *case managers*) is shifting from that of directing and recommending the services that the individual needs to that of working for the individual to facilitate planning and future direction. Rather than provide individuals and families with a limited number of choices and recommendations, the service coordinator works for individuals to identify desired outcomes and works with friends and family members whom the individuals select to facilitate the implementation of that dream. A parallel shift in roles takes place for special education specialists and guidance counselors. Rather than direct IEPs and identify goals for students, the student and family are in charge of creating their vision and the guidance counselors and special educators facilitate discussions of how to make that dream come true.

Relationship of Principles to Outcomes and Implementation

Foundations for change relate to both the Circle of Courage described in Chapter 3 and the Vermont Common Core of Learning that Thousand and colleagues (1997) described. The four dimensions of the Native American paradigm, Circle of Courage, represent the four areas of development necessary to produce courageous youth: belonging, mastery, independence, and generosity. The Vermont Common Core Curriculum outcomes are personal development, communication, problem solving, and social responsibility. Figure 1 shows the relationships among the principles of self-determination, the Circle of Courage, and the goals of the Vermont Core Curriculum. The Circle of Courage presents the outcomes for development, the Vermont Core Curriculum presents one way of creating an education system that promotes these outcomes, and the principles of self-determination present an underlying set of values and beliefs that can direct such a systems change.

The principles, outcomes, and implementation are related in several specific ways. First, all are consumer centered and consumer directed. The desired outcomes cannot be achieved if the consumer (i.e., the student) is not the driving force behind the decision making. Second, to be successful, all stakeholders must be empowered by the

Figure 1.   The relationships among the principles of self-determination, the Circle of Courage, and the Vermont Core Curriculum goals. (Adapted from Thousand, Rosenberg, Bishop, & Villa [1997].)

system in which they operate to have input into and get results from the process. In schools, this means that the students, faculty, family members, administrators, and others who are affected by the change are included in what that change looks like. In the adult delivery system, those who are affected by change in the system include consumers, family members, support providers, and provider agencies. Third, all require a paradigm shift in how the goals of existing systems are defined and implemented. This is a necessary ingredient for achieving true consumer direction and empowerment.

A number of curricula and instruction strategies promote self-determination (Field & Hoffman, 1996; Martin, Marshall, Maxson, & Jerman, 1996; Powers, Wilson, Turner, & Rein, 1995; Ward & Kohler, 1996). It is not enough, however, just to teach the skills or to change students' and families' attitudes. It is important that the education system change in order to support self-determination among its staff and consumers. Much as the adult delivery system is reexamining the way in which services and supports are organized and delivered (Nerney & Crowley, 1995; Nerney & Shumway, 1996), the education system is reexamining the way in which its services and supports are organized and delivered through many innovative school reform efforts (Jorgensen, 1998; Lipsky & Gartner, 1997).

> Schools of the future should strive to be communities of learners where intellectual development and adaptability to change become the driving forces for everyone—students and staff alike—but where the climate is humane and caring, promoting respect for diversity. (Poster of Essential Schools Project, Souhegan High School, Amherst, New Hampshire)

If schooling prepares each child to become a contributing member of the community, all activities of learning need to be integrated into creating that outcome. The learning process itself is a way of creating and developing children's place in the community of which they are a part (i.e., in school, the classroom). The system modeling (even from the earliest years), the sense of place and belonging, the sense of responsibility to contribute, and the appreciation for the gift of each person are essential parts of the role of education.

If the ultimate outcome and purpose of education is preparation for work, living as a contributing member of society, and developing an attitude that values lifelong learning, then self-determination as a desirable educational outcome is obvious. With the four principles of freedom, authority, responsibility, and support, preparing students to direct the course of their lives and their education becomes a necessary foundational skill for living a responsible, productive life.

CONCLUSIONS

Successful systems change that promotes inclusion and self-determination creates schools that welcome, value, and support all students so that they can be active participants in a community and in the world. Self-determination is the desired educational outcome for all students. Creating environments that provide students with the abilities and skills that they need to make the decisions that affect their lives becomes an important goal. This is the desired outcome for all students, including those with and without disabilities. The systems change required to support this shift creates an education system that is consumer driven. Self-determination and inclusive education provide the universal design necessary for individuals to be active contributing members of the community rather than fostering dependence in these individuals and thus having to develop adaptations and accommodations for them after their public education is completed.

Skills development alone for students with disabilities is insufficient for promoting their self-determination. The focus on skills development suggests that the problems inherent in making the transition from school to work and adulthood are due to the students' impairments. Rather, the focus should be on changing the ways in which instruction is provided and the education system is configured. If self-determination comprises the abilities and opportunities to become the causal agent in one's life, then the role of educators is to develop individuals' abilities, and the purpose of transition services is to provide opportunities. Field, Hoffman, and Posch stated, "Acceptance of a focus on self-determination requires a fundamental shift in the way educational planning and implementation are conducted. It also holds the potential for increasing both the effectiveness and relevance of education for youth with and without disabilities" (1997, p. 292).

The structure of the organization, the values and beliefs of the culture that are modeled in school, and the practices and action patterns that express these must be examined to ensure that there is a coherent and consistent alignment of thought and action. In the design of schools, the principles of vision and self-determination act as a universal design feature for all people. Ultimately, the goal is provision of a quality education that meets students' educational needs in the context of political and social justice.

REFERENCES

American Heritage Dictionary (2nd college ed.). (1985). Boston: Houghton Mifflin.

Center for Universal Design. (1995). *The principles of universal design* [World wide web site: http://www2.ncsu.edu/ncsu/design/cud]. Raleigh: North Carolina State University.

Conroy, J.W., & Yuskauskas, A. (1996). *Independent evaluation of the Monadnock Self-Determination Project.* Ardmore, PA: Center for Outcome Analysis.

Covey, S.R., Merrill, A.R., & Merrill, R.R. (1994). *First things first: To live, to love, to learn, to leave a legacy.* New York: Simon & Schuster.

Field, S., & Hoffman, A. (1996). *Steps to self-determination: A curriculum to help adolescents learn to achieve their goals.* Austin, TX: PRO-ED.

Field, S., Hoffman, A. & Posch, M. (1997). Self-determination during adolescence: A developmental perspective. *Remedial and Special Education, 18*(5), 285–293.

Gabor, A. (1990). *The man who discovered quality: How W. Edwards Deming brought the quality revolution to America: The stories of Ford, Xerox, and GM.* New York: Times Books.

Gardner, H. (1995). *Leading minds: An anatomy of leadership.* New York: BasicBooks.

Goldman, J. & Gardner, H. (1997). Multiple paths to educational effectiveness. In D.K. Lipsky & A. Gartner (Eds.), *Inclusion and school reform: Transforming America's classrooms* (pp. 353–374). Baltimore: Paul H. Brookes Publishing Co.

Individuals with Disabilities Education Act (IDEA) Amendments of 1991, PL 102-119, 20 U.S.C. §§ 1400 *et seq.*

Individuals with Disabilities Education Act (IDEA) Amendments of

1997, PL 105-117, 20 U.S.C. §§ 1400 *et seq.*

Individuals with Disabilities Education Act (IDEA) Amendments of 1990, PL 101-476, 20 U.S.C. §§ 1400 *et seq.*

Jorgensen, C.M. (1998). *Restructuring high schools for all students: Taking inclusion to the next level.* Baltimore: Paul H. Brookes Publishing Co.

Halloran, W.D. (1993). Transition services requirement: Issues, implications, challenge. In R.C. Eaves & P.J. McLaughlin (Eds.), *Recent advances in special education and rehabilitation* (pp. 210–224). Boston: Andover Medical Publishers.

Lipsky, D.K., & Gartner, A.N. (Eds.). (1997). *Inclusion and school reform: Transforming America's classrooms.* Baltimore: Paul H. Brookes Publishing Co.

Martin, J.E., Marshall, L.H., Maxson, L., & Jerman, P. (1996). *ChoiceMaker Self-Determination Curriculum: Self-directed IEP.* Longmont, CO: Sopris West.

Nerney, T., & Crowley, R.F. (1995). *An affirmation of community: A revolution of vision and goals.* New Brunswick, NJ: Robert Wood Johnson Foundation.

Nerney, T., & Shumway, D. (1996). *Beyond managed care: Self-determination for people with disabilities.* New Brunswick, NJ: Robert Wood Johnson Foundation.

Powers, L.E., Wilson, R., Turner, A., & Rein, C. (1995). *TAKE CHARGE: Facilitator's guide.* Lebanon, NH: Dartmouth Medical School.

Senge, P.M. (1990). *The fifth discipline: The art and practice of the learning organization.* New York: Doubleday/Currency.

Thousand, J., Rosenberg, R.L., Bishop, K.D., & Villa, R.A. (1997). The evolution of secondary inclusion. *Remedial and Special Education, 18,* 270–284.

Walton, M. (1986). *The Deming management method.* New York: Dodd, Mead.

Ward, M.J., & Kohler, P.D. (1996). Teaching self-determination: Content and process. In L.E. Powers, G.H.S. Singer, & J.A. Sowers (Eds.), *On the road to autonomy: Promoting self-competence in children and youth with disabilities* (pp. 275–322). Baltimore: Paul H. Brookes Publishing Co.

Wehmeyer, M.L. (1996). Self-determination as an educational outcome: Why is it important to children, youth, and adults with disabilities? In D.J. Sands & M.L. Wehmeyer (Eds.), *Self-determination across the life span: Independence and choice for people with disabilities* (pp. 17–36). Baltimore: Paul H. Brookes Publishing Co.

Wehmeyer, M.L., Agran, M., & Hughes, C. (Eds.). (1998). *Teaching self-determination to students with disabilities: Basic skills for successful transition.* Baltimore: Paul H. Brookes Publishing Co.

Yuskauskas, A., Conroy, J., & Elks, M. (1997). *Live free or die: A qualitative analysis of systems change in the Monadnock Self-Determination Project.* Ardmore, PA: Center for Outcome Analysis.

Chapter 23

Passing the Torch

Cecelia Ann, Joseph F., and Judith Ann Pauley

CHRISTMAS 1997

Dear Friends,

It hardly seems possible, but another year has passed and here we are again. What a great year it has been. This year's letter is from Cecelia.[1]

Joe and Judy Pauley

Hi Everyone!

I loved Trinity College in Burlington, Vermont; but it was too far from home, and I got homesick. So I am home from Trinity this year. My dad

---

[1]Unlike many students with Down syndrome in the United States, Cecelia was fully included in general education classes during her high school years. She also sang in the chorus, was a member of the Spanish Club, and served as a cheerleader for the varsity football team. Because she did and continues to want to communicate her experiences about the importance of including all students in school and community life, Cecelia has worked closely with her father to prepare and deliver speeches across the country on the topic of inclusive education. This chapter traces the history of how Cecelia came to be a valued and valuable member of her high school and post–high school community and a bearer of the inclusive education torch.

and mom helped Montgomery College to start a program here, so I can go to Montgomery College instead. I go to college classes every morning and work at three jobs in the afternoon. My dad says it is important for me to have many different job experiences. I work at Flaps Restaurant on Tuesdays and at the library 3 afternoons a week. I also have my own radio show on the Montgomery College radio station on Wednesday afternoons.

I bet you want to know how I got my own radio show. Well, I saw an ad for a disc jockey on the bulletin board at Montgomery College right before Christmas. I didn't tell anyone; but I filled out the application, got an interview, and was hired! They showed me how to run the equipment in the control room. Then I worked the show by myself from 2:00 to 3:00 in the afternoon. I get to pick the records I want to play, write my scripts for the shows, and do the whole show. My dad came to the studio to watch my first show, and it was great! After I played two songs, I thought Dad would like, I got on the air and said, "Hey, Dad, how did you like that?"

I got a big honor this year. I was invited to sit on the stage with President Clinton when he signed the Individuals with Disabilities Education Act (IDEA) Amendments of 1997 (PL 105-17). Three students were nominated to introduce the president at the ceremony. I wasn't picked, but it was cool to be nominated. Anyhow, my mom and dad got to go to the ceremony and a reception at the White House. When the President came into the room, I was closest to the door, so I got to talk to him first. I told him I was in a rebel phase, and he said, "Oh, I do rebel!"

One thing more. This April I will be a published author. I wrote a chapter, "The View from the Student's Side of the Table."[2] My family helped me, and we think it rates a "wow!" The people I wrote it for must have liked it, too, because they left it just the way I wrote it.

This year we have an exchange student from Croatia. She got all A's in her first term. We are all going to Disney World and Pompano Beach at Christmas.

Grandma is 99 and still loves to go for rides, to shop, and get ice cream.

I hope your year was as great as mine. Happy New Year!

Cecelia

In her Christmas letter, Cecelia was able to celebrate what she has done because of a journey begun in the spring of 1991, when we, Cecelia's parents—Joe and Judy Pauley—telephoned Dr. Lou Brown of the University of Wisconsin–Madison to ask for an appointment to see what the city of Madison was doing with regard to inclusive education. Dr. Brown suggested that we contact Richard Villa and Jacqueline Thousand at the University of Vermont because Vermont was closer to our home state of Maryland and because "great things" were happen-

---

[2]Pauley, C.A. (1998). The view from the student's side of the table. M.L. Wehmeyer & D. Sands (Eds.), *Making it happen: Student involvement in education planning, decision making, and instruction* (pp. 123–128). Baltimore: Paul H. Brookes Publishing Co.

ing regarding inclusion in Vermont. We contacted and met Jacque and Rich in June 1991, maintained contact with them throughout the year, and arranged for our family and two teachers from Montgomery County, Maryland, where we reside, to attend an annual, weeklong Summer Institute sponsored by the University of Vermont in July 1992. This set the stage for the passing of the "inclusion torch" in Montgomery County.

The whole Vermont institute experience was an eye opener. We learned about the concept of inclusive education and instructional and systems change strategies for promoting it. We learned more than ever not to judge people by their external appearance and that it was possible for everyone to belong in society, including in schools. We even found 70 institute participants who volunteered to appear as expert witnesses at a hearing in our federal lawsuit against our school system. (The school system had refused to allow Cecelia to be included in her home high school, thereby forcing us to file a civil rights complaint with the U.S. Department of Justice.) Perhaps the most important occurrence, however, was that our family met Christine Durovich and her mother, Lorraine.

It was an institute tradition to invite students to attend sessions and to present their experiences. So, near the end of the week, a panel of teenagers with and without identified disabilities spoke to the adults at the institute. The panel was composed of three high school students from Winooski, Vermont, including Christine Durovich,[3] who, like Cecelia, had Down syndrome. Cecelia was the fourth panel member. All four were given the chance to stay overnight that evening at the resort at which the institute was held. Because it was the evening of the institute's annual Motown dance party, they were able to dance and party together into the night. Cecelia quickly was taken in as one of the gang. In fact, the teens obviously were having so much fun together that an observer, the guide for a traveling motorcycle club, gave them $100 to have even more fun! Without telling Cecelia, the other three girls voted to give the money to Cecelia to help defray the legal expenses in her effort to be included in her home school.

The students' panel was inspirational, too. Christine's classmates talked about how they had benefited from being peer tutors and peer buddies. They talked about their hopes for their own and one another's futures. Christine talked about what it meant to her to be included. She

---

[3]Harris, T. (1994). Christine's inclusion: An example of peers supporting one another. In J.S. Thousand, R.A. Villa, & A.I. Nevin (Eds.), *Creativity and collaborative learning: A practical guide to empowering students and teachers* (pp. 293–301). Baltimore: Paul H. Brookes Publishing Co.

told everyone that she had just graduated from high school in Winooski and was going to enter Trinity College in Burlington, Vermont, with the support of what is known as the ENHANCE Program. Although Cecelia was not yet included in her local high school, after hearing Christine, she declared, "After high school, I want to go to college, too."

As Cecelia's parents, we had been informed by her teachers that Cecelia was not even reading or writing at a functional level. Our first response was to think going to college was outside Cecelia's capabilities. Yet, hearing Christine talk about college opened our eyes to possible new dimensions for her, not only during her high school years but afterward. We filed the information away in our brains and decided to watch Cecelia's development and to see whether college might be in the cards for her.

At the end of July 1991, we returned home from Vermont and began making plans for Cecelia to enter her home high school, Winston Churchill High School, that fall. The school system seemed to disagree that Churchill was an appropriate placement for Cecelia. Actually, without communicating this to us, they were delaying their decision until the new high school principal was approved by the board of education and could give his input before they admitted Cecelia to the school.

FRESHMAN YEAR

Cecelia entered Churchill High School under the worst possible conditions. The teachers had no advance notice that she was coming. There was no advance planning for her arrival. None of the teachers had received training or consultation in how to support a student such as Cecelia, and there were no clear, organized support mechanisms at the school to assist teachers to support Cecelia. Things worked that first year for Cecelia because of the dedication of the teachers and the determination of the principal, but initially it was not easy.

As might be expected, the first 60 days of school were a near-disaster. Cecelia had never been in a general education classroom before, and some of her behaviors were inappropriate. This was particularly true in one class, from which the teacher eventually asked that Cecelia be removed. Fortunately, another teacher asked to have Cecelia in her class, stating that she wanted to see what Cecelia could do. At the 60-day review, reports tended to focus solely on what Cecelia could not do—she could not read, write, add, and so forth. Fortunately, one exceptional teacher commented, "Yes, but she is happy, happy, happy." This was the beginning of the turnaround at Churchill.

After the review, teachers seemed to begin to see and focus on Cecelia's strengths rather than on her disability. One of Cecelia's teachers wrote, "Cecelia has a pleasant disposition. She likes everyone. She makes friends quickly. She is completely genuine. She likes attention and quickly responds positively to praise. She has a mind of her own and can be persistent rather than stubborn." To help Cecelia succeed in her classes, teachers began to capitalize on what she could do and was good at.

What were the results? In her freshman year, Cecelia read *To Kill a Mockingbird*, *The Odyssey*, and several other classics with the support of videotapes and simplified versions of the texts. She began to write short stories, and she wrote a term paper about Williamsburg, Virginia. We had a hard time believing that Cecelia had gone from no reading or writing skills to this—surely, we thought, she previously had some of these basic skills, but no one had observed them. In math, she learned to add and subtract, and the teacher made the material come alive for her by tying it to practical, meaningful life skills such as making change when shopping.

A quantum leap in Cecelia's progress came at the beginning of the second semester. Many of her problem behaviors had disappeared, but one remained—Cecelia wanted attention and tended to interrupt classes to get it. In response to this situation, one of Cecelia's teachers suggested setting up an academic peer buddy system to support her in her classes. A group of students volunteered to spend one of their study periods in one of Cecelia's classes to help her in that class. This worked and snowballed, opening up for Cecelia her first real entree to teen social life. For instance, several of Cecelia's buddies were cheerleaders, and they made sure that she attended the school's basketball games with them.

By the end of the school year, Cecelia had made so much academic, social, and emotional progress that everyone was delighted. Her buddies described how much they had learned from Cecelia, and her teachers were unanimous in their praise of her. She had become an accepted member of her class and of the school community. One of her teachers wrote, "We see growth in all of our students, but in Cecelia the growth is exponential, and that is fun for a teacher." The captain of the soccer team wrote an essay about Cecelia as the person whom he admired most. He ended the essay by writing, "Cecelia is inspirational to me because she maintains a positive attitude despite her obstacles. . . . She demonstrates that within each of us, there is potential waiting to be tapped to enable one to succeed beyond expectations." Cecelia ended her freshman year by testifying before the board of education. Board members, who had been skeptical of including Cecelia in general education classes, commented on how impressed they were with her self-confidence and poise.

SOPHOMORE YEAR

Cecelia's buddies all chose to continue to be her natural supports in her sophomore year, so her year got off to a great start. Her academic progress continued, as did her social skills development. Capitalizing on her desire for attention, she was assigned acting parts in scenes in each of the books that she and her classmates read in English class. When the class read *Romeo and Juliet,* she acted it out with classmates. She wrote a term paper comparing *Romeo and Juliet* with her favorite musical, *West Side Story.* In history class, she was given papers to write every few weeks on topics that the class was studying. Her reward for completing them successfully was an opportunity to deliver her report to the class, complete with sketches and models that she had made or with photographs she had taken. In math class, she was doing pre-algebra work. Erin, her buddy in math class, had difficulty in math herself, so Erin's parents had hired a tutor for her the year before. In studying with Cecelia, Erin used many of the same games and techniques that her tutor had used with her. Math suddenly became one of Cecelia's favorite subjects.

In her second semester English class, Cecelia learned to write speeches and present them to her classmates. This opened up an entirely new career prospect for her. By the end of the year, she was the luncheon speaker at the Kennedy Krieger Institute at The Johns Hopkins University. She wrote her speech, illustrated it with pictures, and delivered it with great confidence and skill. Many of those present asked Cecelia to speak to various groups in their hometowns. She agreed and subsequently spoke at an international conference at the College of William and Mary and to many other groups, including, once again, our local board of education. Her presentation to the board earned her a standing ovation from those attending the meeting and the board members.

Self-Esteem and Social Acceptance

Cecelia's self-esteem was sky high by this point. She loved her classes. She was learning a lot, she had a social life, and she was maturing. She went to football and basketball games and cheered with the cheerleaders. She got her cheerleader's sweater, which she wore with great pride as she joined them on the basketball court. Perhaps the most exciting development of the year for Cecelia, however, was a trip to Orlando, Florida, with the school's chorus and not her parents. The chorus rode all night on a bus, swam the afternoon they arrived, partied that night, won first place in a national competition on Saturday morning, visited International Studios that afternoon, were awarded their prizes that night, and visited Disney World on Sunday, only to reboard the bus that evening and drive all night back to Maryland.

At the end of Cecelia's sophomore year, two of her buddies decided to write their term papers on the topic of inclusive education. They interviewed Cecelia's father, Joe, for information for the paper and, in response to one of Joe's statements, they both said in unison, "Everyone at Churchill thinks of Cecelia as Cecelia, a member of the sophomore class. No one thinks of her as a person with a disability."

Thinking Ahead to College

Throughout the first 2 years of Cecelia's high school experience, we maintained contact with Lorraine Durovich, who kept us informed of her daughter Christine's progress at Trinity. We also established contact with the director of Trinity's ENHANCE Program. Meanwhile, Cecelia's academic progress and emotional growth in high school convinced us that attending college in a modified program was indeed a viable option for her. So, as Cecelia progressed in general classes in her home high school, we gathered more information about the ENHANCE Program. We also approached our local Montgomery College about beginning a similar program in Montgomery County, Maryland. Initially, the college was resistant, but it eventually agreed to look into the feasibility of running a program for youth with "developmental challenges" between the ages of 18 and 21 in cooperation with the Montgomery County public school system.

JUNIOR YEAR

In the summer between Cecelia's sophomore and junior years, Cecelia continued to make presentations at conferences on inclusion, to the Kiwanis Club, and to the county council as it considered the county's special education budget. Cecelia enrolled in English, history, math, computer technology, child development, and chorus classes. In English, she studied *Macbeth, Oedipus the King, A Man for All Seasons,* and *Catcher in the Rye.* In history, she wrote term papers, complete with endnotes, and presented them orally to her classmates. In math, she continued to work on making change and budgeting. In child development, she wrote a paper on her scoliosis and her two spinal operations and worked in the child care center located at Churchill to prepare for her possible later employment in the child care field. In computer class, she learned keyboarding and practical computer applications. In chorus, she sang in three school concerts. In the fall concert, she performed a solo. Dressed up as Little Orphan Annie, complete with a red wig, she sang "Tomorrow" from the musical *Annie*. Cecelia also continued with 2 hours of speech-language therapy a week.

Cecelia's social life continued to grow. She continued cheerleading at football and basketball games. Whenever our family went to the mall or out to eat, we invariably met Cecelia's friends from Churchill who greeted her with high-fives and stopped to chat as teens do. A special day for Cecelia was her 17th birthday, when one of the football squad's leaders gave Cecelia a birthday card on which he and 58 other students wrote messages. This young man wrote, "Cecelia, thanks for being such a terrific friend. You always know how to cheer everyone up. Keep on smiling."

Because Cecelia enjoyed her work in the high school child care center so much, she decided that she would like to work in a nearby community child care center. She went there for a job interview and apparently impressed the staff so much that they hired her immediately. She was thrilled, but in the end choosing this place of employment proved to be a mistake. Cecelia had attended the child care center as a child, and some of the staff continued to treat her as they had when she was a child rather than treating her as a colleague. As a result, some of her old "inappropriate" behaviors resurfaced, and everyone involved agreed that it was best for Cecelia to stop working there while new employment opportunities were explored for her.

The end of the school year culminated with Cecelia's being selected as the keynote speaker at an international conference on inclusion that was co-sponsored by the Office of Economic Cooperation and Development and the U.S. Department of Education. After Cecelia gave her speech, Carlos Oberti, the father of Raphael Oberti, said he wanted to change Cecelia's name to Hope because she had given him hope for the future of Raphael. Raphael's family won a landmark court case concerned with inclusion. That night at the conference dinner, Cecelia moved confidently from table to table, speaking with conference participants. Many of the Europeans gave Cecelia their business cards and asked Cecelia to write to them. The Korean delegates told Cecelia that they wished they could take her home with them to show everyone what was possible.

SENIOR YEAR

For Cecelia, each year at Churchill seemed better than the previous one. That remained true for her senior year. Cecelia worked as a volunteer in a local nursing facility with a job coach from a nonprofit organization. The nonprofit organization was sponsored by the Marriott

Corporation, which supports individuals with mental or physical challenges to make the transition into the workplace. In this volunteer job, she played games with residents, set the tables, transported residents in wheelchairs to various activities, and visited residents in their rooms. Her natural friendliness and enthusiasm were considered infectious. She also interviewed for a paying job preparing food in the kitchen at Flaps of Potomac, a local restaurant.

Academically, Cecelia again enrolled in English, math, art, computer science, and chorus. She also worked 1 hour a day in the health room and 1 hour a day in the cafeteria. In the health room, she sorted mail, prepared ice packs, made beds, answered the telephone, and took messages. In the cafeteria, she washed dishes. In English, she read *The Crucible, Richard the Third,* and three other books. In math, she continued to work on budgeting. In chorus, she sang in three concerts and went on another trip to Disney World to sing in a national competition, where she and four of her best friends went everywhere together and had a great time. She had 2 hours of speech-language therapy each week, with the speech-langage therapist helping her to work on her vocabulary and on budgeting.

Socially, Cecelia had another great year. She continued to be invited to speak to various schools, service clubs, and advocacy groups,[4] further boosting her self-confidence, poise, and self-esteem. Her chorus teacher asked her to audition for a part in the school's rock-and-roll revue entitled "Blast from the Past." She badly wanted to audition, but her jobs conflicted with rehearsals. She explained this to the director, who told her that since she had worked hard for 4 years, she had earned a chance to be in "Blast." He added that he would arrange the rehearsals so that the cast rehearsed Cecelia's numbers on the days on which she did not have to work. Cecelia auditioned, got the part she wanted, and sang in several chorus numbers. At the cast party, she received an award for being the "Most Enthusiastic Cast Member." She stayed out until 3:00 A.M. She attended the senior prom and the after-prom party, coming home the next day at 7:00 A.M. At the after-prom party, she won the door prize of a television and videocassette recorder, which was celebrated by her classmates as if they had won the prize themselves.

---

[4]She spoke to the staff at the Kennedy Institute in Washington, D.C.; at the Arc National Convention in Indianapolis; to regional Arc groups in Indiana, Florida, Maryland, and Washington, D.C.; and to education classes at Johns Hopkins University, the University of Maryland, the University of Virginia, George Washington University, McGill University in Canada, and several smaller colleges. In addition, Montgomery County public schools asked her to speak to their newly hired special education teachers and to speak monthly to elementary school children as part of the Maryland Exceptional Leaders program.

It was in the second semester of Cecelia's last year of high school that she began to express some real concerns about what she wanted to do after graduation. She had been accepted into the ENHANCE Program at Trinity College in Burlington, Vermont. She wanted to attend Trinity and experience college life by living in the dormitory, but she was nervous because the college was a 10-hour drive away from her home. We had already had success with Montgomery College, the local community college, to begin a program in cooperation with the Montgomery County public school system. Cecelia liked the idea of going to college near her home; but because there were no dorms at Montgomery College, she realized that she would have to live at home and thus would miss out on campus life. Also, it would be a brand-new program, so she would not be able to see beforehand what it would be like. These uncertainties resulted in a return of some of Cecelia's "inappropriate" behaviors and some time spent in detention. In the end, Cecelia opted to attend Trinity, and the behaviors disappeared.

At graduation, Cecelia walked across the stage with all of her classmates to receive her diploma from Governor Glendening. In his commencement address, Maryland's governor congratulated the students in the senior class for all of their many academic and athletic achievements and then added, "I especially want to congratulate you on having said to Cecelia Pauley, 'Come join us.'"

BEYOND HIGH SCHOOL: COLLEGE

Cecelia enrolled in Trinity College in late August 1996, with supports being provided by the ENHANCE Program. About 1 week before she enrolled, she visited the campus and applied for a job in the cafeteria. She filled out the application form, listing her work references in Maryland, and when she arrived on campus to begin classes, she was able to begin working immediately. She worked in the kitchen and helped set tables, fill salt shakers, and so forth. She also had a job coach from the Department of Vocational Rehabilitation, who interviewed her to determine her interests and began to prepare her to work in an office.

Cecelia lived in the dormitory with her suitemate, Lisa, who helped Cecelia organize her day and adjust to college life. The two got along well, and Cecelia quickly made many more acquaintances in the dorm, with whom she partied, went to restaurants, and went shopping at the mall. Cecelia also participated in several extracurricular activities. She was in an original play performed by the drama club and sang in the church choir. She also was a Eucharistic minister and helped distribute Communion during Mass.

Academically, she audited three freshman courses: Freshman English, Freshman Orientation, and Basic Computer Applications. In addition, she audited two life skills courses: 1) Jobs—Finding Them and Keeping Them and 2) Adult Problem Solving. In English class, she wrote the book chapter that she described in the Christmas 1997 letter that appears at the beginning of this chapter. Growth in her independence and decision-making ability was obvious. Cecelia enjoyed her classes and was doing well in them until her sister had a baby in October. After the baby was born, all Cecelia seemed to be interested in was seeing and holding the baby. When, by November, she had not yet seen the baby, she expressed being homesick. When she came home at Thanksgiving, she decided, with obvious mixed feelings, to withdraw from Trinity College.

Fortunately for Cecelia, we, her parents, had been advocating for the replication of the ENHANCE Program with officials at Montgomery College for the previous 2 years. The Provost of Continuing Education at the college was supportive of the idea. So, in a partnership with the staff of the Transition Office in the Montgomery County public school system, a pilot program for people ages 18–21 years had begun in September 1996 with four students. This pilot program expanded to 18 students on two campuses, so that when Cecelia was back in Montgomery County, she was able to enroll in the program in January 1997.

Initially, Cecelia attended life skills classes in the mornings at Montgomery College and worked four afternoons a week at two different jobs. She regained her position at Flaps Restaurant, working in food preparation in the kitchen, and she worked at a nursing facility in Potomac, playing games with the residents, helping them with their meals, and just talking with them. Although she was much adored at the nursing facility, the Transition Office helped arrange an interview for a job at which she began collating packets, stuffing envelopes, and delivering mail.

It took a few months of being home for Cecelia to confess to her dad that she realized what she was missing by not going away to college and living in the dormitory. She added that after she finished at Montgomery College, she wanted to go away to a college that was near enough to home so that she could come home on weekends if she wanted and near enough so that her nephews and nieces could visit her. So, the advocacy began once again, and we approached several colleges in Maryland and Washington, D.C., with some expressing quick and genuine interest in starting a program similar to the Montgomery College and Trinity ENHANCE programs. We were not alone this time because other parents in Montgomery County are equally enthusiastic about post–high school opportunities, including enabling community and dormitory residence experiences for young adults who are older than age 21 and thus are no longer eligible for special education under IDEA because they have aged out of the public education system.

In September 1997, Cecelia returned to Montgomery College, where she continued to take life skills and computer classes in the morning and to work at two jobs in the afternoon. As her Christmas letter indicated, she continued to work in food preparation at Flaps Restaurant and to work as a disc jockey at Montgomery College. On Saturday mornings, she attended a drama class at the college. She was active in a tennis clinic run by Potomac Community Resources, sang in the church choir, was a Eucharistic minister at her church, and acted in original plays put on by the Bethesda Academy of the Performing Arts. Cecelia's "best buddy," who supports her at Montgomery College, and another support person who was paired with Cecelia through Potomac Community Resources frequently socialize with her. As Cecelia's parents, we made every effort to let go and empower Cecelia to make her own decisions, and generally she made good ones.

CONCLUSIONS

What about today? What's up with Cecelia? Well, she continues to go to school and to work; enjoys her ever-expanding social life and family; and speaks whenever she can to parent, advocacy, teacher, and other groups concerned with social justice. She believes, as we do, that her advocacy work is as important as the other dimensions of her life because it enables the torch of inclusion that Christine Durovich handed to her to be passed to others. The light can only grow brighter with each handing over.

REFERENCES

Harris, T. (1994). Christine's inclusion: An example of peers supporting one another. In J.S. Thousand, R.A. Villa, & A.I. Nevin (Eds.), *Creativity and collaborative learning: A practical guide to empowering students and teachers* (pp. 293–301). Baltimore: Paul H. Brookes Publishing Co.

Individuals with Disabilities Education Act (IDEA) Amendments of 1997, PL 105-17, 20 U.S.C. §§ 1400 *et seq.*

Pauley, C.A. (1998). The view from the student's side of the table. In M.L. Wehmeyer & D.J. Sands (Eds.), *Making it happen: Student involvement in education planning, decision making, and instruction* (pp. 123–128). Baltimore: Paul H. Brookes Publishing Co.

Chapter 24

Epilogue

From the Inside Out and the Outside In

Aaron Muravchik

It is my first day working as a substitute teacher. The last time I was inside a public school was at my son's high school graduation 12 years earlier and, before that, to sign his individualized education program (IEP). The secretary says I'll be teaching a "class of SLDs" in Grades K–4. The classrooms for students with SLD are not in the main school building but in a small building across the street. There are 22 kids in my room. To me, they look like typical kids. Almost all of them have been instructed to start with work on their cursive writing, trying to replicate exactly a teacher-generated model of individual letters on the left side of the line. The models themselves seem arbitrary and more flowery than necessary. As I circulate around the classroom, making suggestions for improvements, every student responds by laboriously erasing what they've done until that point, even when I tell them that there's no need to. They are all expert erasers.

At lunch, I don't have the courage to face the lunchroom, so I go to the teachers' lounge and get a soda. I tell myself it's to network with the other teachers. I begin a conversation with the young woman next to me. I tell her it's my first day, and . . .

"You get the learning disabled. Boy, they threw you right into the pool," she says.

"They've actually been lovely. They said this was the SLD class, but they seem like just plain kids to me. What's SLD mean, anyway?" I reply.

"It's . . . something . . . learning disabled."

"Thanks. That's what I thought. But they just seem like a class of regular kids to me."

"Yeah. Those are just the kids who can't keep up. The really retarded ones are MH. Just stay away from the EHs and the SEDs, and you'll be all right. They're the behavior problems."

"Thanks. There sure are a lot of acronyms to learn."

"Then, some of them are VEs. They are varying exceptionalities."

"Aren't we all?" I mutter, looking down at my soda.

The following section is an autobiographical narrative consisting of recollections and reflections of my experience as a student in public schools between 1955 and 1965. I was a student who received a few special labels and some special services as a result of one label, but seemingly none at all as a result of another. A couple of decades later (between 1980 and 1986), I was the single parent of a child who faced a similar situation. These recollections are bolstered by recent interviews with my son and my parents regarding their recollections of the same events in two different eras of special education. Of course, recollections, especially those going back 40 years, are not the same as empirical evidence. Rather, they are the subjective interpretations of the moment, edited by the merciful gushing stream of time and the mind. Yet, what we retain, like the morning residue of last night's fleeting dream, isn't arbitrary, but rather that which somehow carried profound symbolism or meaning for us.

THERE AND BACK AGAIN: A PERSONAL HISTORY

I grew up in a family culture of progressive activism, for which I'm eternally grateful, although I seemed to learn more about how to change the world than how to live in it. Apparently, my cognitive development occurred in spurts. My mother told me I didn't speak until I was "2 or 3 [years old], but then [you] spoke in paragraphs."

From my earliest recollections, I was afraid of going to school—afraid of physical violence outside the building and of ridicule and humiliation inside the classroom. Sadly, those feelings changed only in degree at various times and in how I expressed them. I didn't really learn to read until the third grade, when I read a children's biography of Abraham Lincoln, which I loved and much of which I still recall. After that, my reading took a leap. A few months later, in a group IQ test, I tested in the "normal" range; but as my older brother (who I saw as my protector) had been selected to go to a different school because he was labeled as "gifted," I wanted to go to that school, too. My mother, convinced that I too was exceptionally bright, took me to be tested individually at New York University, where my IQ score was determined to be in the 99th percentile. Based on that score, I was allowed to compete (28 students were selected from a group of 125) for a slot in the "gifted" class (at a different school), and I was selected. Apparently, once I was chosen, my reading ability soared. By the fourth grade, I was writing lengthy stories and plays.

Going to the new school meant using public transportation to commute to Harlem and attending, as a Caucasian, a school in which 95% of the students were of other ethnicities. Yet, the 3 years that I attended that school were the most comfortable and secure of my entire public school experience. I think there was an exceptional principal there who seemed to have a deep respect for and caring about learning and learners, and the tone she set permeated the school's atmosphere.

To say I was also labeled with emotional disturbance isn't entirely accurate. One day, early in the fourth grade, my teacher had me deliver a group of files to the main office. Once I was alone in the stairway, I took a peek at what it was I was carrying. To my shock, I realized that I had the class' individual student records! These were our permanent records so often referred to when a student was misbehaving by way of the threat of the student's receiving some kind of permanent black mark that would dog him or her forever! I quickly opened mine and glanced at it. On the left side of an orange sheet of oak tag was a list of dozens of ailments and abnormalities with boxes to the right. Three of the boxes had checks beside them: "Asthma," which I had; "Speech Defects," which I was removed from my class periodically to work on; and "Emotionally Disturbed"! Emotionally disturbed! I struggled to control my horror. Traumatized, I quickly closed the file, delivered the whole package to the office, and never told a soul about what I'd seen. It seems my secret remained well kept, because, in all the years of public school that followed, including some spectacular successes and failures, to the best of my knowledge, I was never once given or offered any special relevant program or service. (On rechecking that in the 1990s, I found that my sixth-grade teacher had once sent my parents a lengthy letter saying that she thought that I might have some problems and could benefit from talking to someone, which my parents found baffling and chose to ignore.)

In the fifth and sixth grades, I had the same wonderful teacher with whom I felt comparatively comfortable and whom I felt cared about me. To this day, I think of her often and how important she was to my life. It was with her that I discovered my love for visual art and began writing poetry. I believe that those years were the peak of my public education experience. That sounds flip, but it's substantiated by some test scores that I recall from my junior high school years, which were the most miserable years of my childhood. On entering the seventh grade, I was given an achievement test that was divided into math and English sections. A perfect score was 12, which, I'd been told, represented the grade level of a high school senior. I scored 11.4 and 11.6 on the math and English sections, respectively. On the same test about 1 year later, my scores had gone down by about one point in each category. By the time I reached the ninth grade (the year I was removed from the accelerated class that I'd been in previously), my scores had slipped by another point, so that I was deemed to be functioning at my typical grade level. I guess I'd "mainstreamed" myself.

In the decade that I spent in public education, the only time I recall ever even talking to a guidance counselor was in my sophomore (i.e., final) year of high school in May 1965. I'd been offered a chance to join the final day of the now historic Selma–Montgomery march, which would have meant missing a day of school. When I asked to officially be excused, I was told to ask my guidance counselor. The guidance counselor saw me for 5 minutes and rejected the request. I went to the march anyway and dropped out of school for good—probably for my own good—at the end of that term.

Thus, in the case of my own exceptional student education in the mid-20th century, it was more a question of whether I received any special services rather than how they were manifested and structured. Although I can't say what would have happened if I hadn't gotten into the "gifted" program at the better school, I feel I got a great deal from it and without it wouldn't have fared nearly as well.

It's curious how apparently flawed the assessment instruments (i.e., tests) of the time must have been, and I wonder how much that's changed. What does the fact that I was in the "normal" range on the group IQ test but in the 99th percentile on the individual test suggest? On the achievement tests in junior high school, was I really losing academic skills at the rate of a grade level per year? I don't have answers to these questions. My guess is that the explanation is a combination of the tests' being flawed, my general emotional state at the time, my comfort level in the test environment, and my degree of motivation to do well on the tests. I think there's also an element of my responding to the level of external expectation, going from being typical to being brilliant and back again to typical over the course of a decade.

To this day, the mysterious label of emotional disturbance and its unknown origin remain a bit haunting. What's troubling is that there was something to it. I was not a happy kid, and maybe I could have gotten some help early on to adjust better or to manage my emotions more effectively. Although most of my classmates who had been labeled as gifted later went on to the best high schools and colleges, I dropped out of school, spent much of the next decade with addictions to drugs and/or alcohol, got into trouble with the law, and became a teen father. Two decades later, I suffered a couple years (1987–1989) of acute depression.

My involvement with public schools resumed in 1982, as the single parent of a child who was especially challenged and challenging. During most of his early childhood, my son, Eben, lived with his mother during the school year and spent his summers with me in Vermont. He appeared to be a happy, "typical" kid. But in the fifth grade, when his mother moved from the New York City suburbs into the city, he began to experience emotional and behavior problems. By the time he completed the sixth grade, he was clearly a child who was troubled. I decided he should try coming to live with me in Vermont, and, with much relief at the proposal, his mother agreed. (He was then at the same age at which my public education had peaked and I had begun to crash so dramatically.)

Anticipating possible problems, I met with the principal of the rural K–8 school that he would be attending before the term began. On the first day of school, I walked him to the place where the bus would pick him up and went home with my fingers crossed, just praying that the telephone wouldn't ring. But it did. It was the principal asking me to come in because Eben had gotten into a fight with another student and then left the school building without permission to "walk it off." By the end of that week, he'd been expelled, and I was trying to figure out what to do next. I enrolled him in a small alternative school in Burlington, Vermont, about which I had many doubts. After a few months there, he was put on an indefinite suspension until he could make a case to the school meeting for being allowed to return, which he could never quite do. Days turned into weeks and months. The best thing I did was to buy him a couple of punching bags—a speed bag and a heavy bag, which he used daily to exhaust his energy and anger. By the end of the school year, I was banging on them pretty regularly, too.

In the spring, I was contacted by the local school district, which was doing some monitoring. I was told that Eben must be in school and was invited for a consultation. The administrator with whom I met wanted to send Eben for a psychiatric evaluation, which was done. I remember vividly—and gratefully—being called by the evaluating psychiatrist and asked if I'd like to see Eben's report before he submitted it to the school district. I said I did; but when I received a copy, I was shocked and upset. It contained neither a single redeeming sentence nor a shred of hope. If there were such a thing as a "throwaway kid," this was his profile. I lobbied, with some small degree of success, to get the scathing tone of the report diminished before it was submitted to the district. Based on this evaluation, the district labeled him Severely Emotionally Disturbed ("SED") and assigned him to an out-of-district rural school for problem kids. The school had 25 students ages 14–19 and 8 staff members. When Eben was first assigned to that school, he resisted going, for his own reasons. He desperately wanted us to move 28 miles from our rural home to Burlington, where he could have a bit more independence with regard to mobility and the opportunity to socialize more freely. Desperate myself, I decided I'd use the strength of his desire as a lever or bribe. I proposed a contract whereby if he could put together a successful school year at the school to which he'd been assigned, we would take an apartment in Burlington for the following year if he still wanted to move there. The terms of my proposal were not open to negotiation.

What the school district wouldn't do in terms of this placement was transport him to the new school and back home again (although they had allocated about $14 per day for this purpose). Essentially, that task fell to me. Adding to my frustration with this arrangement, the school used a policy called *rock pile,* which was basically a traditional detention program to address discipline problems, but without any attempt to coordinate it with me. Thus, when he broke the rules and was kept after school, I was kept after school too—waiting in the parking area. That year became the only time in my life that I was ever on welfare.

Despite all of these problems, Eben made significant progress that year. He became a little easier to live with. His grades were okay. He studied a little and did his homework. When I interviewed Eben at the end of the 1990s about what had worked for him, he offered two explanations: One was our pact to move to Burlington. In addition, he told me, "I just remember that school was the last stop. If you didn't make it there, you were put in Woodside [the juvenile detention center], and I was too young to go there."

As per our contract, the next year we moved into the city. In general, this was an easier arrangement for both of us. Eben attended general education classes at Burlington High School, except for one period per day of special education. As a parent, I tried to advocate for what I thought he needed and tried to maximize my input about how much and which kinds of special support he would get. Generally, though not entirely, these efforts were met with a kind of passive resistance, much like what Lisa and Alan Houghtelin report in the "Reflection" at the end of Section III. Once each term, I was called in to the school to sign Eben's IEP. I eventually came to realize that my signature was really needed, so I learned to use that as a lever to maximize my input at those meetings. To me, it seemed like Eben and the school had developed a symbiotic, unspoken contract whereby each side would do as little as necessary for Eben to eke by. His one special class each day, rather than focusing on emotional or behavioral goals, was largely academic remediation, and Eben used it in large part to get his homework done. There was one moment of near-triumph when I had painstakingly orchestrated a meeting with a few of Eben's teachers, the guidance counselor, and Eben himself prior to the final formulation of the term's IEP; but Eben found the meeting so threatening that he ran from the room 5 minutes into it and never returned.

The 3 years that Eben spent at Burlington High School were neither a spectacular success nor a glaring failure but rather a measure of both. He did graduate in 1986, although he was hardly prepared for life after school, and he has suffered at lot since then. To the extent that it was a success, I questioned him about what had worked. Eben described his relationship with one man, a school guidance counselor who always had been available to him, although sometimes Eben would go for months without seeing this counselor. In Eben's words, the man was "critical in getting me through high school. He took a special interest in me. He routed me around trouble. I felt like he cared about me. That was very unusual."

Hearing him say "cared about me" really rang a bell for me, and I immediately thought of my fifth- and sixth-grade teacher, who I had believed cared about me and who had made such a difference in my life. When I ask myself if it's really very unusual to find a teacher who cares about his or her students, my instinctive answer is "no." Many teachers, or perhaps most, do care. So, how is it that if this caring carries such weight with learners, it is so rare that this caring is conveyed to them successfully? I don't have an exact answer to that question, but I think it's important to try to find out why. I imagine that there are a combination of factors—institutional and/or cultural—that create barriers to this simple, critical interpersonal connection. These are the kinds of issues that I discuss in the section that follows.

FEARS, CARES, WORRIES, AND DARES

This book contains many eloquent accounts of bold and exciting ideas that are being advocated and even applied in thoughtful and courageous ways by dedicated people. The account of the restructuring taking place at Whittier High School is exciting and hope inspiring. Lisa and Alan Houghtelin's brief personal story is so moving that I feel changed by it. The other writers are of a common mind-set and more expert than I in this field. In this section, I'll try to turn this sense of being a little on the outside into an asset. I'll bring the perspective of one who is less sure of where we should be going or whether it's possible to get there. I'll speak as a concerned citizen who's spent much of his life apart from educational institutions, a public education consumer and parent, and a substitute teacher and would-be full-time public school teacher looking in from the outside. I'll ask hard questions, express my concerns or doubts, and point to possible conflicts. I do this not to tear down these ideas but in the spirit of the broad and open dialogue embraced throughout this book and with the understanding that, before these dreams can ever become common practice, they must undergo a testing more rigorous than any I can ever offer.

Fears: Shoot for the Stars, but Keep an Ear to the Ground: Concerns About Mandates

Last fall I interviewed for an elementary school position teaching English for Speakers of Other Languages (ESOL) in one of Florida's richest and most successful (at least in terms of students' achievement scores) districts. During the interview, the principal explained a teaching arrangement whereby I would teach in a portable classroom—a trailer, basically—with another ESOL teacher who'd have a different set of students.

"How will you manage this?" the principal asked.

"Okay," I responded. "We can teach as a team and use a lot of small-group work."

"No, you're teaching separate groups."

"Well, we can share certain activities, themes, learning stations."

"No, these are separate classes."

"You mean they're physically divided? There's a wall or something dividing the space?"

"No, there's no wall. It's the same portable, but you teach on your side while she teaches on her side. With both of you teaching different classes in the same portable at the same time, it's easy for your students to get distracted. What I'm asking is, How you'll manage this?"

"The best I can," I replied lamely.

I walked out of there talking to myself silently. Clearly, not everybody had taken the first step regarding even the least radical of new practices—even when it was much easier to do so than not.

Stainback (see Introduction to Section V) states, "It is our job as educators to strive for an ideal rather than simply accept less desirable approaches and conditions because they constitute the status quo." That's true. As educational visionaries, idealists, and pioneers, we should expect and accept nothing less from ourselves than the pursuit of greatness in our education programs and institutions. If we're convinced that we have many of the right answers—as the contributors to this book clearly are—we should spread the word; share, promote, and advocate for these ideas; show the way; and help others to lay the foundation for change. It's gratifying for me, coming back into the public schools as a "sub," to see some of the changes that have occurred since I was a student. Seating arrangements facilitate cooperative learning, themes combining specializations are being employed in curricula, more hands-on student projects are being assigned, and learning stations are being assembled, to name but a few innovations. But even as we keep our eyes on the stars in terms of what education could be, let's also keep a finger on the pulse of what actually can—and all too often does—happen "on the ground."

Udvari-Solner and Keyes (Chapter 15) beautifully and tellingly quote an exemplary principal: "You're always in the process. You're always trying to get to the place [that] you will never get to." I place tremendous importance on the *process* by which the pioneers—the contributors to this book—have honed and actualized their visions: challenging conventional practices; envisioning new and better alternatives; advocating for these visions; collaborating on the nuts and bolts of realizing change; and eagerly and openly experimenting, assessing, reformulating, and reassessing. I feel some nervousness, however, about handing out the result of this process as a packaged formula to those who haven't arrived at it by finding their own way to it.

Consider an analogy. When a woman first conceives and then carries the fetus within her body for 9 months, feels it growing, and then endures the pain and magic of childbirth, she loves the child to whom she's given life and, almost without exception, is wholly ready to nurture it. Even couples who want to be parents and undergo the long and arduous process of adoption usually become loving, nurturing parents. Is it realistic, however, to expect the same of the couple who open their door one morning to find that, during the night, an unwanted child has been left on their doorstep?

Knoster, Villa, and Thousand (Chapter 5) paraphrase Wheatley's view that "schools cannot be changed by imposing a model developed elsewhere," and I agree with them. Mandating changes to those who haven't willingly gone through the wrenching process and don't feel compelled to find better ways, or don't even possess an openness to them once others have presented them, worries me. My fear is that kids will get less of what they need rather than more. I don't consider human beings to be inherent risk takers. They're more likely to be grumbling followers than visionaries, and their working within mammoth bureaucracies with undemocratic hierarchical cultures (e.g., public school systems) tends to intensify their shortcomings. Programs that are funded or underfunded (or suddenly defunded) by politicians driven by the political winds of the moment, codified from a distance by lawyers, administered by self-serving nonbelievers, and delivered by the unprepared, overburdened, and resentful may not provide a positive result. When programs are presented as legal mandates, however, non–risk takers can't ignore them either. Thus, the money and manpower for these changes first go toward accountability, which all too often means just the opposite: Precious resources are wasted on creating the appearance of compliance, a paper trail of "documentation [that] . . . yields little . . . to assist . . . in . . . instruction. Instead, it enables professionals to comply with legal requirements" (Chapter 1). Villa and Thousand, in Chapter 1, estimate that more than half of special education funding goes toward noninstruction services.

Last week, I was substitute teaching in a sixth-grade science class. The students were watching a videotape about local marine life, on which, I informed them, according to the teachers' instructions, they would be given a quiz. I circulated around the room, trying to monitor students' comprehension, notetaking styles, and so forth. Most of the students were sitting in pairs taking notes; but in the back of the class, a girl sat by herself at a bare desk. She smiled at me shyly as I approached. When I asked her if she wanted to take notes, she responded in Spanish, telling me that she spoke no English at all ("*No hablo Inglés*") and that she had been in the United

States for 2 weeks (*"Llegó hace dos semanas"*). There was no aide, no peer tutor, and no other support. I wondered whether this was the school's idea of inclusion. Later that day, I eavesdropped on a conversation in the teachers' lounge about teaching positions being slashed—the school's one ESOL slot was being eliminated.

The preceding anecdote illustrates a fear that I have about inclusion. How do we prevent inadequate supports or no supports from being dressed up and called *inclusion*? A number of well-intentioned and just social and human rights programs have accomplished great things on limited scales but became counterproductive in terms of those whom they were intended to serve when they became over-politicized mandates that were incompetently mass-produced. Tragically, what tends to happen is the elimination of the suspect institution or practice is realized, but the improved substitute program isn't. How can we keep mandated full inclusion in public schools from being like the move to deinstitutionalize people with mental illness and move them into community-based group homes? In that case, the all-too-often horrid institutions were shut down; but the system dropped the ball in terms of providing adequate alternatives, leaving those people literally on the streets, where, tragically, many still remain decades later. The same thing is happening in New York City's admittedly less sincere welfare-to-work program. In 1998, *The New York Times* ran a front-page series (see Swarns, 1998) on the plight of families who were being threatened with cuts in benefits despite the fact that the city had failed miserably in fulfilling its end of the bargain by not providing essential supports that it had promised (e.g., child care, job training).

Care Models: The Good News and the Bad News

A large number of the inclusive education recommended practices models for legislation, programs, policies, and practices in this book are based on the work that has been done and continues in rural states such as Vermont—the state where I've lived most of my adult life. To my thinking, in terms of justice and humanism, Vermont is one of the few places in the United States that is still moving forward while the majority of the country is racing backward. Vermont's population of well under 1 million is one of the most ethnically homogeneous in the nation. The state has a long cultural tradition of progressive politics and taking care of its citizens. It was the first to abolish slavery and played a key role in the Underground Railroad. Its lone Congressional representative, Bernie Sanders, is a former socialist and registered independent who is by far the most progressive member of the U.S. House. State legislators are paid between $12,000 and $18,000 per year.

I'm mentioning these facts because you probably couldn't find another area of the United States that is more receptive to embracing progressive, new ideas or equally able to translate them into practice. Education pioneers in places with less-progressive climates, huge and diverse populations, big-league political power struggles, and monstrous bureaucracies (e.g., Los Angeles) should be prepared for a rockier road. However, it's hopeful to keep in mind that we already have examples of many of these practices being realized in communities—big and small, rich and poor—all around the United States as well as in less-developed countries such as Honduras and Vietnam.

CARES: THE CHALLENGE OF CHANGING THE CULTURE OF OUR SCHOOLS

When I was working on my master's degree in English as a second language (ESL), I took a course called "Teaching Speaking and Listening." Besides several highly structured required assignments, we were asked to write a short paper on any relevant topic that we chose. I wrote one the premise of which was that it's difficult to learn to speak in school because school cultures teach us not to speak but rather to be silent. I cited numerous examples from our own class. The work was not well received. In fact, it earned a worse grade than anything else I wrote during my entire graduate program.

Many of the chapters in this book refer to changing a school's "culture," which is exactly what's necessary in U.S. public schools. The very nature of culture, however, offers much of the explanation for why schools seem so intractable. Culture runs deep—to the gut, in fact, to the very bone marrow. One's culture is learned unconsciously and intertwined with one's language. It is just as deep-rooted in our being as our language, and, much like our own language, it seems like it must be universal until we encounter a different one. Culture prescribes attitudes and behaviors that become subconscious and ever-present, even for activities as basic as how we walk or how we sit. It dictates how to interpret events and how to do things that we assume all human beings naturally interpret and do in the same way. In our interactions, it tells us how or if we take turns in a conversation, how close we should stand to each other, how and whom we should touch and when and where to do so, how much eye contact to maintain, and even how often and when to blink! In my experience, many of the best ethical themes in this book—equality, tolerance of diversity—aren't universal but largely cultural.

Culture, like language, is dynamic, not static. Instead, it's constantly evolving; but this evolution is by nature gradual. New jargon and slang that catches on takes a generation or two to find its way into the dictionaries and be accepted by all speakers. Likewise, even the most successful of policies and programs that radically alter the school's climate will require at least a few decades of continuous practice before they're internalized at the cultural level.

Mammoth and longstanding institutions in a society reflect the society's culture but also have strong subcultures of their own: the military, the criminal justice system, and the public schools, for example. The cultural ethics of public school at are learned when we first arrive at school at the age of 5, impressionable and dependent. These include a strict hierarchical pyramid of power and strong ethics of silence, obedience, and sameness. Returning to school years later as teachers or administrators doesn't change what we've internalized. Most of what's changed is our place on the pyramid.

> I always get a little jealous when someone tells me about their high school reunion because I'll never have one. The closest I ever came was a spontaneous meeting one day in the dead of winter 1973. I was working by myself on a scaffold, finishing the cathedral ceiling in a ski resort condominium. At midmorning, a carpenter came in to begin laying the hardwood floor. It was John—a classmate and friend from my Grades 4–6 "gifted" class of 15 years earlier! We were in our mid-20s then, about the time we had been expected to blossom into successful professional careers. Over a bag lunch, we got caught up, recollecting and reminiscing about old chums and feelings of the past. It turned out to be a wonderful and unusually open chat. What I remember most clearly and still find remarkable was that we managed to confess having had an experience that, at the time, we each believed was uniquely ours and ours alone: We recalled always needing to pee more often than was permitted and being afraid to ask, so we didn't.

> "I trained myself to go in my pants, let one drop out and wait for it to absorb in my underpants—just enough not to show—and a little later, peeing another drop," John confided.
>
> "Yeah! Me too!" I admitted.

> I guess this learning wasn't exactly what you'd consider at the top of Maslow's pyramid . . . , and those were my *good* years in school!
>
> Twenty-five years later, driving to school on my first day as a substitute teacher, my belly's all in a knot. I won't know the kids'

names, the most basic school routines, simple procedures that all of the second graders know. By far, my biggest fear is needing to pee.

A few days later, I call one of the school districts' job vacancy hotlines. Of course, I get a recording that goes on and on without getting to any vacancies: "Prior to being recommended by the superintendent, all persons will be required to take a board-approved drug test." "That's not so bad," I tell myself. "At least I'll be allowed to pee."

Worries: Obstacles to Belonging, Community, and Inclusion

It's too difficult to separate the concepts of the need and the right to belong, the goal of establishing a sense of community in a school, and the concept of full inclusion in such a community. To me, they are inextricably interwoven, with equality as an underlying theme. These are perhaps the most important of the many valuable goals put forth in these chapters. In my eyes, they are made even more critical and also more difficult to achieve by the fact that American society appears to be moving away from these much-needed ideals. As part of American society, of course, our schools tend to reflect what's going on in it. Perhaps we can find a way of actualizing these humanistic principles in our public schools in spite of this so that, as our youth emerge from these nurturing environments into adulthood, they will have internalized some of these values. They could then become the change agents who begin to reverse this alarming cultural trend and move American society back toward valuing a sense of community and maintaining the naturally accompanying concept of well-being that embraces a sense of "ours" and not just "mine." I pray that that's possible.

THREE AREAS OF CONCERN

In this section, I discuss my thoughts about some of the obstacles to realizing these critical ideals in American society. This discussion is not limited to including exceptional students in general education classes. It takes a broader view of inclusiveness, belonging, and community. The first two subsections are rooted in contemporary conditions, and the third subsection takes a look inward at our own psyche regarding these issues.

Political and Cultural Obstacles in American Society

"I'm okay. You don't matter." If I had to coin a phrase to describe the way American cultural trends at the turn of the 21st century feel to me, that would be it. Van Bockern, Brendtro, and Brokenleg (Chapter 3) states, "Young people have never been more self-centered, and consumed with money, power, and status"; but this isn't a matter of a passing teen fad. It's evident at every level of American society, from the global currency raiders to pop culture's adoration of styles that both flaunt affluence and disregard consideration of others (e.g., expensive cigars, gas-guzzling sports utility vehicles, aggressive and exploitative rap tunes). I think part of the explanation is the unforeseen by-product of the end of the Cold War, when communism imploded so dramatically. The void it left has somehow been filled by a new in-your-face hypercapitalism—a no-holds-barred, lean-and-mean, free-market, winner-take-all giddiness.

Although communism as it manifested in the 20th century was an abomination and got exactly what it deserved, an unmitigated free-market ethic (i.e., a society based almost solely on competition) is also inherently flawed. In terms of education, the chapters in this book contain many references to the need to move from competitive models toward more cooperative ones. In fact, the premise of Chapter 6, that education must be based on students' needs and the supposition that social justice in education is everyone getting what they need, is reminiscent of Marxism's famous premise of "from each according to his ability, to each according to his need" (Marx & Engels, 1848/1999).

Economically, in the 1990s, the United States has been in the longest peacetime boom in its history, which all agree won't last forever. Despite the rosy economic numbers, in my opinion, rather than seizing this opportunity to push the envelope of how great a nation the United States can become, at the end of the 20th century, we've been racing toward becoming a Third World society. Although all would agree that the U.S. economy is booming, my question is, A boom for whom? There's no nation on earth that is so poor that it doesn't have a single citizen who is rich. The key to the greatness of a nation isn't in big numbers, but in how justly its assets are distributed—that is, a nation's greatness should not be measured by how the well-off are doing but by how its least-advantaged citizens are faring. Economic statistics show that America's most wealthy have been doing fabulously in the 1990s while the least privileged have struggled to tread water. From a demographic point of view, an increasingly larger percentage of the disadvantaged are our kids.

In a National Public Radio broadcast commentary, Schorr (1998) criticized the greed popularized by the upper class and the stratification of the upper and working classes in the United States. According to Schorr, when the smoke of the current economic boom clears, what we'll have is a shrunken middle class and a society more clearly stratified into the haves and the have-nots than any of us have seen in our lives.

In terms of the goals that this book expresses, these are disturbing facts. Even as we race forward toward bold visions of how great U.S. public schools can be, we should stay on our toes and be prepared to dig in our heels, if necessary, in terms of protecting the ground we've traditionally held. In the late 1980s, America's health care system was based on a balance of various ethics; but at the turn of the 21st century, it's clearly driven by the bottom line. One hopeful factor is that public schools are just that: public, not-for-profit, and something to which every child is entitled. But even this shouldn't be taken for granted. That word *entitled*, as in *entitlements*, has become the "E" word. Even in the current U.S. era of national wealth, the list of Americans' entitlements is being shortened by leaps and bounds.

In this cultural mentality in which well-being is viewed in terms of "mine," not "ours," the bottom line is the dominant ethic, and social safety nets are eroding rather than being reinforced. We should expect the worst from our institutions and assume that nothing is sacred. Consider what's been happening to the criminal justice system. In the sink-or-swim spirit, the failure to meet society's expectations is viewed entirely as the failure of the individual and not of the society. The prevailing sentiment can be boiled down to "Lock them up and throw away the key." Thus, at the end of the 20th century, the United States had incarcerated more than 1.7 million—close to 1%—of its adult citizens, far more than at any time in its history and far more than any other industrialized country except Russia. In fact, the United States had more inmates than graduate students (Belenko, 1998). We're also executing prisoners—the ultimate denial of belonging—at an unprecedented rate. In addition, though the criminal justice system has a long tradition of being exclusively part of the public domain, we've failed to fund it adequately and have begun to see experimentation with privatization.

So far, the only challenges to the public school system as a whole have been the push for school vouchers and the suggestion that the U.S. Department of Education be dismantled. We should expect our schools, school systems, and teachers to come under more fire from, for example, the press and politicians. My guess is that public schooling will survive; but in doing so, it will continue to move further out of the mainstream of American society.

In particular, we can expect programs for the most needy and the least powerful, such as special education and limited English proficiency programs, to be increasingly targeted. Even as I write this chapter, state and federal programs for language-minority students are under wholesale attack (e.g., the passage of California's Proposition 227, which slashed special services for nonnative speakers of English).

It's a little harder politically to vote directly against wheelchairs for children who can't walk. However, in the case of children with less-endearing challenges—children who exhibit challenging behaviors, for example—the prevailing wind is not to invest in finding better ways of working with them but rather to arrest them, try them as adults, and lock them up for a long, long time. For those who believe in the importance of a caring and inclusive community and a definition of well-being based on "ours" (not just "mine")—keep your eyes open and your powder dry.

Technological Obstacles

> If you want to come over with a can of gas and burn us to the ground, press "one." (Billingsley, 1998; reprinted by special permission from King Features Syndicate)

There's no question that part of the reason why American society has witnessed a diminishing of the importance of its communities—and the accompanying sense of community—is technological, in particular progress in the areas that expand our mobility and enlarge our sphere of communications. Americans typically move every 4 years. We no longer pass our neighbors on the street, because we're in our cars. In the evenings, we no longer congregate in front of our houses to chat or visit the family next door, because we prefer our own cable television stations, and we can call our friends in the next state cheaply.

In Chapter 3, Van Bockern, Brendtro, and Brokenleg discuss "technologically rich but spiritually impoverished schools and communities," and I don't believe this is a coincidental connection. Advances in technology not only militate against community but also militate against equality (and the sense of belonging, which I think is predicated on the other two). Although there's no stopping progress, we can become aware of how these innovations promote inequity and alienation—the opposite of belonging—and incorporate that knowledge into whether and how we use them. Besides the seductive and dependency-producing nature of these innovations, there are several problems, not the least of which is simply gaining access to them, which further polarizes the powerful and the powerless. A report broadcast on National Public Radio in May 1998 mentioned that 60% of American homes don't have a computer and that 70% of African American and Latino homes don't. Yet, as these modern conveniences become more and more commonplace, it becomes harder for those without them—those already less advantaged—to compete with those who have them.

Furthermore, these systems are generally designed and put into place by technologists who represent special interests, not by humanists, and are ruled by social Darwinism rather than the spirit of cooperation in terms of how they are used. Too often, the thinking is, if letting go a customer service representative and using an automated telephone-answering system can save our organization 1 minute of paid employee time by getting a caller to invest 5 minutes of his or her time (and telephone bill) to wait on hold or leave a voice-mail message, then it is an efficiency improvement. This may explain why, in spite of the proliferation of all of the alleged time-saving devices, surveys show that Americans generally report that they are working longer hours and have less free time rather than more.

> I call a professor to see whether she's received a job application package on which I've spent many hours. Instead of a "live person" at the other end of the line, I get a friendly, sincere-sounding recorded message: "I am sorry I can't be here to take your call. Leave your number. I'll get right back to you." I leave a message, but I don't receive a call back. I repeat the call 2 days later, and 2 days after that, and so forth; but I never receive a call from the professor or even from her secretary. This is far worse than if I'd spoken to somebody and received a rejection or even a quick brush-off—"I have no time for you. Bye."—which at least would include a human equation I could be sure of and an opportunity for closure. Instead, I am left with the feeling that the apology and promise to return the call are as genuine as they sound . . . for everybody but me. I'm somehow voiceless and invisible—essentially, a nonperson.

Human Obstacles

My beliefs about human nature and the questions of belonging, inclusion, community, and equality have many seemingly contradictory facets. The very concept of community has both an inclusive and an exclusive nature: Those inside our community are "us," and those outside are "them." I envision a network of concentric circles representing loyalty, like ripples from a stone thrown in a lake—with community being somewhere in the middle—neither the innermost circle (which would be myself and probably my immediate family) nor the outermost circle (which would be other citizens of my country, other human beings, other living things, and so forth). Ideally, each circle would offer another level of belonging that the individual could experience. Interestingly, the latter half of the 20th century saw a weakening of the importance of many of these metaphorical circles—not just geographic communities but also family ties, religious communities, and so forth. This may account for the sense I have that American society is suffering from a lack of belonging and instead experiencing alienation (i.e., the opposite of belonging). Apparently, I'm not alone in this perception. Van Bockern, Brendtro, and Brokenleg (Chapter 3) discuss their view that "contemporary civilization is threatened by a loss of . . . [a] sense of community."

Within each circle, even the most principled and idealistic individuals tend to have different rules for balancing loyalty with principles. So, for example, one would never expect to hear a caring parent—even the most idealistic parent—tell a teacher, "I really want to help my child with his homework, and I have the time; but it wouldn't be fair to the other kids in the class whose parents aren't able to." (Although as teachers, it's good to keep this disparity in mind.) The reality is that most of us would spend a buck on a treat for our family dog before we would spend that buck on food for the needy kid across town.

A grander and more directly relevant example of this seeming multiplicity of ethical standards can be found in the Vermont Act 60 (Vermont Board of Education, "General Powers and Duties," 16 Vt. Stat. Ann. ch. 3, § 164), touted as the most progressive legislation currently in the education field. Although it's far too enlightened to promote a mission of students being prepared to compete with each other, its stated goal, to "prepare students to . . . compete in the global marketplace," has less sting because it frames this competition as not being among *us* (Vermont's citizens), but rather, with *them* (outside the circle—that is, all the world's citizens).

It also seems to me that within almost every human society, community, or family unit as well as in other animal species, the capacity for complex systems of cooperation co-exists simultaneously with highly competitive systems. I think the same is true of each of us individually—that we have both the natural capacity for a great degree of sharing, cooperation, inclusiveness, and acceptance as well as the capacity for the opposite, and our conduct won't be one or the other but a mish-mash of both simultaneously. Thus, my thoughts on this topic are to encourage us all to be introspective, to consider the "ways in which [our] daily attitudes reinforce or level power inequities" (Chapter 19, page 524), to look inward with the expectation that we'll find a complex duality of opposite forces at work, and to strive to be aware of them. Let's hold the light up to even our seemingly meaningless and unrelated daily rituals and consider inclusion or exclusion in the broadest possible terms—that is, the ability of all to gain access. Thus, when you wake up in the morning and dress for success, be aware that part of what's going on is establishing your belonging in an exclusive "club" from which most other citizens of the world—because they have no access to such garb—are excluded. Alternatively, if I write a book chapter and *employ jargon that most lay people would find incomprehensible* instead of *using words that are easy to understand*, I'm actualizing a decision about the "club" or community I want to be part of and who I want to have access to my chapter and who I don't.

Dares: What We Teach, How We Teach It: The Importance of "Walking the Talk"

> The explicit teaching and modeling of patterns of behavior and habits that represent "responsible" behavior often never occur. (Chapter 6, page 144)

I question the theme repeated in many of these chapters that "all people can learn." Not that I doubt it. I would stress a different focus: All people *do* learn, albeit at many different paces and using different learning styles. They naturally acquire knowledge that they deem meaningful, useful, and relevant. The quandary is that what students learn is often a far cry from what we as educators may want them to learn.

Much of what's learned by schoolchildren is not planned or overt. Rather, it's deduced spontaneously or even unconsciously through experiences and observations. Many of these experiences and observations are interpersonal—interactions with and observations of others in their daily lives, not the least of whom are their teachers and other adult school personnel. Thus, not only must teachers try to connect the lessons that we want to impart to that which will seem useful and meaningful to the learners, but we must all also accept that what we convey to learners goes far beyond the content of our lesson plans to include our every utterance and action. This is especially critical for those of us who view our role as teaching human and social values: caring, responsibility, citizenship, social justice, honesty, and so forth.

Nor is this dynamic applicable only to the teacher–student relationship. Principals and administrators must accept this responsibility as well. In their case, they must go beyond an awareness of their personal interactions and consider the messages they're conveying via the policies and systems that they put in place on a school- or systemwide level. They must understand that, for better or for worse, the school system itself serves as a role model! If administrators want to teach students to be respectful, they must model that by being respectful of students. If they want teachers to be humanistic, sensitive, and value the individual, they can't facilitate this by doing the opposite or creating systems that beat these traits out of teachers before they ever arrive in the classroom.

I travel 50 miles out of the city in which I'm living to a small, more rural district to sign on as a substitute teacher because I believe it will be a less dehumanizing place to work. My fantasy is to establish a more personal relationship with the district that is based on mutual trust and respect. I fill out reams of paperwork. I'm required to provide sealed transcripts of my college education. I'm required to send the district's reference forms to three former supervisors who must return them directly to the district. I'm told to divulge my petty and now-ancient criminal history, "including any sealed or expunged records" (a Florida statute that I believe is unconstitutional). When I do, I'm required to obtain official documents from the courts regarding these offenses, which is no small feat and takes more than a month. I'm required (as are all applicants) to be fingerprinted and pay $45 to have the Federal Bureau of Investigation investigate me. So much for trust. As a last step, I'm required to sign and have notarized a "loyalty oath" swearing to uphold the constitutions of the United States and the state of Florida. I consider telling them that I believe that that would be a contradiction in that I've already cooperated with requirements that I thought were unconstitutional, but I'm already feeling too battered, and I just want a chance to teach. However, a few days later, when I'm feeling a bit more chipper, I call the personnel office and have a chat with the secretary:

"I took an oath to uphold the constitution of the state of Florida, but I should tell you, I've never even seen the document," I report.

"Most of us never have," the secretary replies sympathetically.

"Do you have a copy of it I could read?"

"Here? No."

"But you've taken the oath?"

"You have to to work here," she says.

This is typical bureaucratic behavior and is not unrelated to my earlier discussion of a paper trail of compliance, which "often means just the opposite." Dressed up to look like attention to responsibilities, it's actually an abdication of responsibility. Systems tend to evolve a "bring me the witch's broomstick" approach to every conceivable situation and remote liability, by which the institution covers its back at the expense of the basic dignity of the individual. Such a system not only destroys trust and runs roughshod over self-esteem but also all too often produces the opposite result from that which it was meant to ensure: in this case, creating a staff of perjurers in the name of guaranteeing ethics and morality.

The day after my conversation with the school secretary about the loyalty oath, there is yet another story broadcast on the radio about Florida's inability to find enough qualified teachers.

The Bright Side:
The Good News Is, You Can Make a Difference

We're all heroes if you catch us at the right moment. (Frears, 1992)

I've spent much of this chapter pointing out difficulties and raising doubts, expressing pessimism—almost cynicism—about realizing major systemwide reform, but I'd like to speak to the flip side of that and end on a more positive and hopeful note. I'm not saying that we shouldn't advocate for radical, systemwide reform; of course, we should. However, we should also consider incorporating a bottom-up approach to changing which we can use daily. History tells us that, under even the most horrid of circumstances, the actions of a single individual—even a relatively powerless individual—can have a profound effect on the lives of others. Just as the obstacles to creating a caring and effective education shouldn't be underestimated, neither should the value of each and every effort to do so, even the incremental little daily differences each of us can make. As Van Bockern, Brendtro, and Brokenleg point out in Chapter 3, even as they are fragile and vulnerable, our children have the potential for great strength and resiliency. Thus, a few strands of goodness in a tangle of mediocrity and troubles may offer enough support for a child to pull him- or herself through.

Of course, changing requires courage, and many of the chapters in this book discuss the theme of courage—finding the courage to change or to facilitate change. I think that most of us are capable of great courage or great cowardice. A critical determiner of which one of our selves shows up—the hero or the coward—has much to do with our convictions, how strong our vision is, and how much we've internalized our convictions and our vision. When the vision is clear enough, fear has little room to fester; the road you must walk becomes apparent, and the courage to walk that road comes naturally. Often other people sense your assuredness and begin to look to you for leadership. In that sense, courageous is contagious! This isn't the high profile and momentary courage of the popular icon: the one glorious celebrated moment when the dragon is slain, the maiden is rescued, and the crowd stands applauding. It's more like the patient, quiet courage that made the sit-ins of the Civil Rights movement so dramatic and effective: the ability to remain peaceful and dignified on the path where you know you belong amid a tempest of abuse and injustice.

I think the greatest courage belongs to those who walk that path even when they know that the ideal outcome—or even something close to the ideal—is unattainable. This is the courage you must find every day, even though it's often invisible to the casual observer. This courage is best exemplified by people with disabilities and their parents. From one such party to all others, what I want to tell you is this: YOU ARE ALL HEROES! Your courage is far greater than that of the dragon-slaying knight. It's the courage to get out of bed each morning, make breakfast, go to work, and have a normal day even when nothing about your life feels "normal." Yours is the courage to never stop hoping and striving for the best. It's the courage to translate your reality into the tiny daily battles that can be fought and, at times, even won.

The easiest and perhaps also the hardest place to create change is in ourselves. Interestingly, the authors of Chapter 19 say that the most effective leaders ultimately believe they cannot change anybody but themselves. They point out three general themes of spirituality that exemplary leaders embrace: personal awareness, significance of relationship, and sense of purpose or mission. My thoughts about maximizing our own ability to make a difference parallel these.

In terms of personal awareness, I believe that it's critical to nurture your own love of learning and embrace it as a lifelong process. Question set formulas and pat answers. Hold sacred and advocate for the process(es) of learning (remembering that they're inherently messy): curiosity, questioning, openness, experimentation, inquiry, imitation, success, failure, collaboration, argument, critical thought, evaluation, reflection, and so forth.

In terms of a sense of purpose or mission, take time to think about what you believe about yourself, people, children, learning, and what's important to learn. Use these thoughts to guide your vision. Embrace this vision, and let it guide your actions daily—steadfastly, but not blindly—with enough openness and flexibility to allow your convictions to evolve, and incorporate what you learn as you pursue them. Become clear about the internal and external obstacles. Validate your successes—even the tiny ones.

Finally, with regard to significance of relationship, remember that, as an educator, you are a role model, and much of what you impart is by way of example. Be aware that you are a model of humanness—maybe the best one your learners have. Accept that human interpersonal relationships are critical—perhaps most critical—to the learning process. (As both my son's and my personal recollections bear out, it was a single relationship with an educator that was the key to whatever measure of success we each feel we had in school.) Treasure every interpersonal connection you can make with learners. Look them in the eyes. Cherish their humanity. Stretch your caring and respect. Arrive at work each day ready to learn as well as to teach, with your mind and your heart open, and with the conviction that on that very day you can and will make a difference in somebody's life.

REFERENCES

Belenko, S. (1998, January 8). *Behind bars: Substance abuse and America's prison population* [Report]. New York: Columbia University, National Center on Addiction and Substance Abuse (CASA).

Billingsley, R. (1998, March 15). *Curtis* [Syndicated comic strip]. New York: King Features Syndicate.

Frears, S. (Director). (1992). *Hero* [Film]. Los Angeles: Columbia TriStar Home Video.

Marx, K., & Engels, F. (1999). *The communist manifesto* (J.E. Toews, ed. & trans.). Boston: Bedford/St. Martin's Press. (Original work published 1848)

Schorr, D. (1998, April 7). Commentary. *All things considered* [Radio broadcast]. Washington, DC: National Public Radio.

Swarns, R.L. (1998, April 14). Mothers poised for workfare face acute lack of day care. *New York Times*, p. A1.

REFLECTION

Closing the Circle

Richard A. Villa and Jacqueline S. Thousand

We invite you to reflect on what you have read and learned about in this book and then to identify and commit to at least one action for promoting the four Circle of Courage outcomes (belonging, mastery, independence, and generosity) for at least one student (and/or one adult) in your immediate education community. We further invite you to share your learnings, actions, and continuing concerns with us and with others who are concerned about restructuring for caring and effective education by visiting the following World Wide Web site: http://www.brookespublishing.com/e-catalog/books/villa-3866/index.htm. We issue both of these invitations because the remaining piece of the inclusion puzzle is you. It is, after all, the collective actions of individuals that create change. *You* are the change.

Index

Page references followed by *f* or *t* indicate figures or tables, respectively.